Computational Discrete Mathematics

Combinatorica, an extension to the popular computer algebra system *Mathematica*®, is the most comprehensive software available for educational and research applications of discrete mathematics, particularly combinatorics and graph theory. This book is the definitive reference/user's guide to *Combinatorica*, with examples of all 450 *Combinatorica* functions in action, along with the associated mathematical and algorithmic theory. The authors cover classical and advanced topics on the most important combinatorial objects: permutations, subsets, partitions, and Young tableaux, as well as all important areas of graph theory: graph construction operations, invariants, embeddings, and algorithmic graph theory.

In addition to being a research tool, *Combinatorica* makes discrete mathematics accessible in new and exciting ways, by encouraging computational experimentation and visualization. The book is suitable for self-study and as a primary or supplementary textbook for discrete mathematics courses.

Sriram Pemmaraju is Professor of Computer Science at The University of Iowa. His research interests are in discrete mathematics, graph algorithms, and distributed computing.

Steven Skiena is Professor of Computer Science at SUNY Stony Brook. He is also the author of *The Algorithm Design Manual*; *Calculated Bets: Computers, Gambling, and Mathematical Modeling to Win*; and *Programming Challenges: The Programming Contest Training Manual*.

Computational Discrete Mathematics
Combinatorics and Graph Theory with *Mathematica*

SRIRAM PEMMARAJU
The University of Iowa

STEVEN SKIENA
SUNY at Stony Brook

CAMBRIDGE
UNIVERSITY PRESS

PUBLISHED BY THE PRESS SYNDICATE OF THE UNIVERSITY OF CAMBRIDGE
The Pitt Building, Trumpington Street, Cambridge, United Kingdom

CAMBRIDGE UNIVERSITY PRESS
The Edinburgh Building, Cambridge CB2 2RU, UK
40 West 20th Street, New York, NY 10011-4211, USA
477 Williamstown Road, Port Melbourne, VIC 3207, Australia
Ruiz de Alarcón 13, 28014 Madrid, Spain
Dock House, The Waterfront, Cape Town 8001, South Africa

http://www.cambridge.org

First published 2003

Printed in the United States of America

Typeface Palatino   *System* LATEX 2$_\varepsilon$ [AU]

A catalog record for this book is available from the British Library.

Library of Congress Cataloging in Publication Data

Pemmaraju, Sriram V., 1966–
Computational discrete mathematics : combinatorics and graph theory with Mathematica / Sriram Pemmaraju, Steven S. Skiena.
  p. cm.
Includes bibliographical references and index.
ISBN 0-521-80686-0
1. Combinatorica (Computer file) 2. Combinatorial analysis – Data processing. 3. Graph theory – Data processing.
I. Skiena, Steven S. II. Title.
QA164.P45 2003
511′.6–dc21   2002041688

ISBN 0 521 80686 0 hardback

Table of Contents

Preface

The excitement of discrete mathematics comes from discovery, the act of uncovering beautiful and important properties of graphs, partitions, permutations, and other combinatorial objects. The appeal of discrete mathematics is its concreteness, that you can draw these objects on a blackboard and get a feel for them in a way quite different from more abstract areas of mathematics.

Unfortunately, only very small structures can be built on a blackboard; computers are needed to experiment with larger ones. The goal of *Combinatorica* is to advance the study of combinatorics and graph theory by making a wide variety of functions available for active experimentation. Together, this book and *Combinatorica* provide a unique resource for discovering discrete mathematics.

■ About *Combinatorica*

Combinatorica has been perhaps the most widely used software for teaching and research in discrete mathematics since its initial release in 1990. *Combinatorica* is an extension to *Mathematica*, which has been used by researchers in mathematics, physics, computer science, economics, and anthropology. *Combinatorica* received a 1991 EDUCOM Higher Education Software Award for Distinguished Mathematics Software and has been employed in teaching from grade school to graduate school.

But times change, in this case for the good. Desktop computers (and *Mathematica*) are now more than 100 times faster than when *Combinatorica* was originally developed. Computational problems unimaginable on research machines then can now be done at home by high school students. *Mathematica* itself has gone through several versions, resulting in a significantly improved user interface, more functionality, better performance, and improved typesetting facilities.

This book presents the second-generation version of *Combinatorica*, which is a dramatic improvement over the original. Enhancements since the previous version include:

- *Improved Performance* – We have made incredible strides in efficiency since the original *Combinatorica*. All examples in the original edition of *Implementing Discrete Mathematics* involved graphs of fewer than 100 vertices, because larger examples were either impossible or hopelessly slow. Now we can work on interesting graphs with tens of thousands of vertices and hundreds of thousands of edges. Indeed, all the examples in this book run comfortably on a two-year-old laptop computer that has seen better days!

- *Improved Graph Representation and Visualization* – The *Combinatorica* graph structure has been completely revamped, enabling us to efficiently represent very large graphs, with edge/vertex weights, labels, and graphics. These improvements make *Combinatorica* a viable platform for developing significant graph applications in *Mathematica*.
  Color graphics displays and printers are now ubiquitous, although they were prohibitively expensive back in 1990. In response, we have brought a new degree of color and style to *Combinatorica* graphics. Graphs can now be drawn with a variety of edge and vertex presentations and give

complete freedom to highlight and position graph elements. We provide the power to animate interesting structures and algorithms on graphs, and to transform these videos to animated GIF files for Web pages.

- *New Functionality – Combinatorica* now adds more than 450 functions for combinatorics and graph theory to *Mathematica* – twice as many as the previous version. Existing functions have been made more sophisticated, with new options and better algorithms. The new *Combinatorica* provides extensive support for Pólya's theory of counting and algebraic combinatorics, as well as new combinatorial objects such as set partitions and restricted growth functions. These changes reflect demands from our users, recent developments in combinatorics and graph theory, and the additional functionality of new releases of *Mathematica*.

Combinatorica is included with every copy of *Mathematica* as `DiscreteMath`Combinatorica``. The *Combinatorica* described in this book appears in *Mathematica* Version 4.2 and beyond, but our package is backwards compatible with earlier versions of *Mathematica*. The latest release of *Combinatorica* is available from our Web site `http://www.combinatorica.com`, where we maintain software, data, and other materials of interest to the *Combinatorica* community. Register at `www.combinatorica.com` to hear about updates to the package.

■ What's Between the Covers

This book is a successor to *Implementing Discrete Mathematics* [Ski90], the original description of *Combinatorica*. This book, like the program itself, is a complete rewrite. Here, we present a general computational approach to discrete mathematics that will serve as the definitive user's guide/manual to *Combinatorica*. What's new?

- *Introductory User's Guide – Combinatorica* has been widely used by groups of people who know relatively little graph theory, in interesting ways that we had never envisioned. We now begin with a substantial user's guide containing numerous examples of how to use the package and surveying the range of what *Combinatorica* can do.

- *Conversion Guide* – We have tried our best to provide backwards compatibility, but in a small number of cases providing backwards compatibility conflicted with other goals such as increasing efficiency or providing better functionality. Thus a small number of *Combinatorica* functions will not work they way they used to in the old package. We include a section that enumerates functions that have changed and give new *Combinatorica* code that replicates the old behavior.

- *Selected Function Implementations* – The previous version of this book contained literally every line of *Mathematica* code that made up *Combinatorica*. With the new package three times larger than the old one, maintaining this policy is neither feasible nor desirable. Instead, we present the implementations of only the most enlightening and important algorithms. These have been kept away from the preliminary chapter to aid and comfort new *Combinatorica* users.

- *Expanded Tutorial Component* – We have significantly improved and expanded the tutorial component of this book. Now, in addition to being a reference, supplement, or guide to self-study, it can serve as a textbook for *Mathematica*-based undergraduate discrete mathematics courses. In particular, the first author has taught such courses at both IIT Bombay and the University of Iowa. This is the only combinatorics/graph theory textbook we are aware of that is built around significant software.

There is more than enough material here to teach full-semester, experimentally enhanced courses in combinatorics and graph theory. *Mathematica* is now quite well established at many colleges and universities around the world. It is highly likely that your school already has a site license for *Mathematica*. Contact your campus computing center if you need more information on this. Students in such schools/departments will particularly benefit from our approach.

- *New Exercises* – Finally, we have included three interesting classes of exercises at the end of each chapter. Some are thought problems, typically requesting proofs of well-known or interesting theorems in combinatorics or graph theory that we illustrate as examples of *Combinatorica* in action. Some are programming exercises, where the reader is encouraged to extend or improve existing *Combinatorica* functions. The remainder suggest interesting discrete mathematics experiments to conduct using *Combinatorica*.

This book concentrates on two distinct areas in discrete mathematics. The first section deals with combinatorics, loosely defined as the study of counting. We provide functions for generating combinatorial objects such as permutations, partitions, and Young tableaux, as well as for studying various aspects of these structures.

The second section considers graph theory, which can be defined equally loosely as the study of binary relations. We consider a wide variety of graphs and provide functions to generate them. Although graphs are combinatorial structures, understanding them requires pictures or embeddings. Thus we provide functions to create a variety of graph embeddings, enabling a given structure to be viewed in several different ways. Algorithmic graph theory is an important interface between mathematics and computer science, and in this text we present a variety of polynomial- and exponential-time algorithms to solve computational problems in graph theory.

These two sections are relatively independent of each other, so feel free to jump in the middle if you are primarily interested in graph theory.

This book is designed as a guide to manipulating discrete structures. You will find no formal proofs in this book, but enough discussion to understand and appreciate the literally hundreds of algorithms and theorems contained within. Further, we provide extensive references as pointers to the appropriate results. Since the body of the text contains the most interesting of more than 450 *Combinatorica* functions, it is also an excellent guide for writing your own *Mathematica* programs. We include a brief guide to *Mathematica* for the uninitiated to help in this regard.

This book is also a complete reference manual for using *Combinatorica* to explore discrete mathematics. As you read the book we urge you to play with the package. Documentation for all *Combinatorica* functions appears in the *Glossary of Functions* at the end of the book, and cross-references to examples using a particular function in an interesting way appear in the index.

■ Why *Mathematica*?

At its initial release in 1990, *Combinatorica* was the largest package ever written for the then-recently released *Mathematica*. Today *Mathematica* has established itself as the mathematical tool of choice, with more than one million users.

Building a discrete mathematics package in *Mathematica* has several advantages. Arbitrary precision arithmetic means we are free of the burdens of computer word length. Where appropriate, we have access to portable PostScript graphics, bringing life to graphs and their embeddings. Working with symbolic formulas makes convenient such techniques as generating functions and chromatic polynomials. The freedom of a high-level language with so much mathematics already under the hood liberates us to explore a much larger fraction of what is known about discrete mathematics.

The chief drawback to using such a high-level language as *Mathematica* is that we lose tight control over the time complexity of our algorithms. The model of computation that it presents (the Wolf-RAM?) is dramatically and mysteriously different from the traditional random access machine. In this new version, we have tamed the Wolf-RAM – achieving efficiencies that allow interaction with large and interesting structures in real time.

■ Acknowledgments

We would like to thank all the people who helped make this book and the new *Combinatorica* a reality.

First, we thank the people at Wolfram Research Inc. (WRI). John Novak provided an amazing amount of support throughout the development of the package, guiding us through some of the more obscure aspects of *Mathematica* and providing the interface between us and various *Mathematica* gurus at WRI. Eric Weisstein played with several versions of *Combinatorica*, reported lots of bugs, and contributed code for some of the graph constructors. Arnoud Buzing, Darren Glosemeyer, Shiral Devmal, Anna Pakin, and Andy Shiekh of the "bug testing department" bugged us regularly with bug reports. Daniel Lichtblau and Robby Villegas made suggestions that improved the package. Bill White patiently answered questions about WRI's version of LaTeX. Stephen Wolfram's interest in *Combinatorica* since its beginning has had much to do with its becoming a reality.

The insights of Joan Trias into graph drawings and representation significantly shaped the graph data structure we employ in the new *Combinatorica*. Lenny Heath commented extensively on initial drafts of the first two chapters. Kaushal Kurapati helped with perl scripts for integrating *Combinatorica* code and *Combinatorica* examples into the text. Eugene Curtin's package on Pólya theory helped crystallize some of our initial ideas on functionality needed for Pólya-theoretic computations. Levon Lloyd built a nice Java-based editor for *Combinatorica* graphs and King Mak developed interesting algorithm animations – check these out. We especially thank Marty Golumbic for his efforts to bring us together to finish this book and Alberto Apostolico for providing a home where part of it was written.

Lauren Cowles, Alan Harvey, and Elise Oranges of Cambridge University Press helped us throughout the publication process.

Two batches of students at IIT Bombay and one at Iowa survived the first author's teaching experiments with *Combinatorica*. We thank all the people who have downloaded preliminary versions of the new *Combinatorica* and have sent us encouragement and bug reports.

We cannot neglect those who helped with the previous version of *Combinatorica* or the book. Anil Bhansali made a significant contribution to the original *Combinatorica* by writing many of the functions, managing the testing of the code, and performing sundry tasks. The original work on *Combinatorica* was done at Apple Computer in the summer of 1988. Allan Wylde, then of Addison-Wesley, provided encouragement and a means to communicate this to the world. Fred Buckley, Nora Hartsfield, Matthew Markert, Marko Petkovšek, Ilan Vardi, Jürgen Koslowski, and Rick Wilson all provided helpful pre-publication feedback on *Combinatorica* and/or *Implementing Discrete Mathematics*. A variety of other Stony Brook (Philip Hsu, Phil Lewis, Yaw-Ling Lin, Gene Stark, Brian Tria, Alan Tucker, Shipei Zhang), Addison-Wesley (Jan Benes, Laura Likely, Karl Matsumoto), and WRI (Dave Ballman, John Bonadies, Martin Buchholz, Joe Grohens, Igor Rivin, Monte Sayer, Lisa Shipley, Cameron Smith) people all helped out in one way or another.

On a personal level, we thank Amma, Nanna, Sachi, Geeta, and Rama Rao, who provided encouragement and support for the first author. Mom, Dad, Len, and Rob provided moral and emotional support for the second author.

■ Caveat

It is traditional for the author to magnanimously accept the blame for whatever deficiencies remain. We don't. Any errors, deficiencies, or problems in this book are somebody else's fault, but report them to bugs@combinatorica.com so we can determine who to blame.

Sriram Pemmaraju
Dept. of Computer Science
University of Iowa
Iowa City, IA 52240-1419
sriram@combinatorica.com

Steven S. Skiena
Dept. of Computer Science
State University of New York
Stony Brook, NY 11794-4400
skiena@combinatorica.com

■ Dedication

Combinatorialists know how to count their blessings. As a proof of correctness, both of us got the same answer of $2 + \epsilon$ when we did the counting.

We dedicate this book to our respective wives, Santhi and Renee. The writing of this book was a long and complicated process involving cross-country travel, hours at the keyboard, lengthy phone calls, and even fears of terrorist actions and thermonuclear war! We thank them for their love and patience during this period, before, and beyond.

We also dedicate this book to our daughters, Ela and Bonnie. We look forward to the day, not so long from now, when the pretty pictures in this book will help us explain to you the joy of doing and understanding discrete mathematics.

Finally, we dedicate this book to our respective future children, both well on the way to joining us. We will be meeting you both about the time this book is published. We don't know you yet, but certainly know that we love you.

1. *Combinatorica*: An Explorer's Guide

Discrete mathematics is a subject for explorers. *Combinatorica* has been designed to make it easy to generate and visualize graphs and experiment with other combinatorial structures such as permutations, partitions, and Young tableaux. Manipulating these objects with *Combinatorica* helps the curious mind to recognize patterns, make conjectures, and then conduct systematic searches to confirm or refute them. The sole prerequisite for this book is a curiosity about discrete structures.

This brief introductory chapter demonstrates the power of *Combinatorica* for exploring discrete mathematics. With over 450 functions, *Combinatorica* can be somewhat overwhelming for beginners. Here we give brief examples of some of its most popular functions in action. This overview serves as a user's guide to *Combinatorica*, showing the proper mindset to get started with the package.

This chapter contains tables with the names of all *Combinatorica* functions broken down by category. Skimming through these tables now will give you an idea of what the package can do. Referring to these tables later can help you to recall or identify the name of the function you need. Don't forget the glossary and index, as well as the online help available in *Mathematica*. These tools will help you to navigate the *Combinatorica* jungle and get on with your explorations.

The rest of this book provides a deeper look at how *Combinatorica* works, illustrating the theory and algorithms behind each function, as well as its implementation in the *Mathematica* programming language. We hope the sampling of *Combinatorica* examples in this chapter inspires you to dive into the rest of the book.

Despite our attempts to maintain backwards compatibility, a small number of *Combinatorica* functions no longer behave as they used to in the old package. In Section 1.3 we provide a guide for porting code from old *Combinatorica* into the new package. The examples in this chapter require only minimal knowledge of *Mathematica* to understand. We provide a brief introduction to *Mathematica* programming in Section 1.4 to help the uninitiated.

About the illustration overleaf:

Combinatorica provides many functions for constructing graphs. A few of the built-in graph construction functions do not have parameters and construct a single interesting graph. The function FiniteGraphs collects them together in one list for convenient reference. ShowGraphArray permits the display of multiple graphs in one window.

```
ShowGraphArray[Partition[FiniteGraphs, 5]]
```

1.1 Combinatorial Objects: Permutations, Subsets, Partitions

Basic combinatorial objects such as permutations, subsets, and partitions are the raw materials from which discrete mathematics is built. The ability to construct, count, and manipulate them has a surprising variety of applications, as well as its own inherent beauty.

This loads the *Combinatorica* package included with *Mathematica*, a necessary step before using any *Combinatorica* functions.

```
In[1]:= <<DiscreteMath`Combinatorica`
```

■ 1.1.1 Permutations and Subsets

Permutations and subsets are the most basic combinatorial objects, dealing with the arrangement and selection of elements, respectively. *Combinatorica* provides functions for constructing these objects both randomly and deterministically, to rank and unrank them, and to compute invariants on them. Here we provide examples of some of these functions in action.

Permutations are arrangements or orderings of the numbers 1 to n.

```
In[2]:= Permutations[3]
Out[2]= {{1, 2, 3}, {1, 3, 2}, {2, 1, 3}, {2, 3, 1},
    {3, 1, 2}, {3, 2, 1}}
```

The Permute operator enables us to apply a permutation to rearrange arbitrary items.

```
In[3]:= Permute[{A,B,C,D}, Permutations[3]]
Out[3]= {{A, B, C}, {A, C, B}, {B, A, C}, {B, C, A},
    {C, A, B}, {C, B, A}}
```

Each permutation has an *inverse*, a distinct permutation that rearranges it to the *identity* permutation.

```
In[4]:= Permute[{5,2,4,3,1}, InversePermutation[{5,2,4,3,1}] ]
Out[4]= {1, 2, 3, 4, 5}
```

These permutations are generated in minimum change order, where successive permutations differ by exactly one transposition. The function Permutations constructs permutations in lexicographic order.

```
In[5]:= MinimumChangePermutations[{a,b,c}]
Out[5]= {{a, b, c}, {b, a, c}, {c, a, b}, {a, c, b},
    {b, c, a}, {c, b, a}}
```

The ranking function takes a permutation of 1 through n and associates a unique integer in the range 0 through $n! - 1$ to it.

```
In[6]:= RankPermutation[{8, 9, 7, 1, 6, 4, 5, 3, 2}]
Out[6]= 321953
```

The unranking function is the inverse of the ranking function; here we take a rank and get the original permutation back.

```
In[7]:= UnrankPermutation[%, 9]
Out[7]= {8, 9, 7, 1, 6, 4, 5, 3, 2}
```

With $(3!) = 6$ distinct permutations of three elements, we are likely to see all of them in a sample of 20 random permutations. But it is unlikely that the first 6 permutations in the sample will all be distinct.

```
In[8]:= Table[RandomPermutation[3], {20}]
Out[8]= {{3, 1, 2}, {1, 3, 2}, {1, 2, 3}, {3, 1, 2},
    {1, 3, 2}, {1, 3, 2}, {2, 3, 1}, {3, 2, 1}, {3, 1, 2},
    {1, 2, 3}, {3, 1, 2}, {1, 2, 3}, {2, 1, 3}, {1, 3, 2},
    {1, 3, 2}, {2, 3, 1}, {2, 1, 3}, {2, 1, 3}, {2, 3, 1},
    {3, 1, 2}}
```

Any permutation can be decomposed into disjoint cycles, providing an alternate and useful way of viewing permutations. A cycle of length 1 is a *fixed point*, and it corresponds to an element being mapped onto itself by the permutation. Cycles of length 2 correspond to swaps.

```
In[9]:= p = RandomPermutation[10]; {p, ToCycles[p]}
Out[9]= {{1, 5, 2, 10, 4, 9, 6, 7, 8, 3},
    {{1}, {5, 4, 10, 3, 2}, {9, 8, 7, 6}}}
```

A classic combinatorial problem is counting how many different ways necklaces can be made out of k beads using a given set of colors. The beauty of Pólya's approach to this problem is that it yields a polynomial, the coefficients of whose terms provide answers to a more general problem. From the polynomial computed in this example, we see that there are 10 6-bead necklaces with 3 beads colored *a*, 2 beads colored *b*, and 1 bead colored *c*. *Combinatorica* provides extensive support for Pólya theory.

```
In[10]:= NecklacePolynomial[6, {a, b, c}, Cyclic]

        6    5      4 2      3 3      2 4      5
Out[10]= a + a b + 3 a b + 4 a b + 3 a b + a b +

        6    5      4       3 2       2 3
        b + a c + 5 a b c + 10 a b c + 10 a b c +

          4       5      4 2       3 2       2 2 2
        5 a b c + b c + 3 a c + 10 a b c + 16 a b c +

           3 2       4 2      3 3       2 3
        10 a b c + 3 b c + 4 a c + 10 a b c +

           2 3      3 3      2 4         4       2 4
        10 a b c + 4 b c + 3 a c + 5 a b c + 3 b c +

          5    5    6
        a c + b c + c
```

Substituting 1 for each of the variables *a*, *b*, and *c* in the above polynomial gives us the total number of 6-bead necklaces that can be constructed using an infinite supply of beads of each of 3 colors.

```
In[11]:= % /. {a -> 1, b -> 1, c -> 1}
Out[11]= 130
```

The number of inversions (pairs of out-of-order elements) in a permutation is equal to that in its inverse.

```
In[12]:= (p=RandomPermutation[50]; {Inversions[p],
        Inversions[InversePermutation[p]]})
Out[12]= {606, 606}
```

This constructs all 4-element subsets. They are listed in Gray code or minimum change order, where each subset differs in exactly one element from its neighbors.

In[13]:= **Subsets[{1,2,3,4}]**

Out[13]= {{}, {4}, {3, 4}, {3}, {2, 3}, {2, 3, 4}, {2, 4},
    {2}, {1, 2}, {1, 2, 4}, {1, 2, 3, 4}, {1, 2, 3},
    {1, 3}, {1, 3, 4}, {1, 4}, {1}}

A *k*-subset is a subset with exactly *k* elements in it. Since the lead element is placed in first, the *k*-subsets of a given set are generated in lexicographic order.

In[14]:= **KSubsets[{1,2,3,4,5},3]**

Out[14]= {{1, 2, 3}, {1, 2, 4}, {1, 2, 5}, {1, 3, 4},
    {1, 3, 5}, {1, 4, 5}, {2, 3, 4}, {2, 3, 5}, {2, 4, 5},
    {3, 4, 5}}

BinarySearch	LexicographicPermutations
DerangementQ	LongestIncreasingSubsequence
Derangements	MinimumChangePermutations
DistinctPermutations	NextPermutation
EncroachingListSet	PermutationQ
FromCycles	PermutationType
FromInversionVector	PermutationWithCycle
HeapSort	Permute
Heapify	RandomHeap
HideCycles	RandomPermutation
IdentityPermutation	RankPermutation
Index	RevealCycles
InversePermutation	Runs
InversionPoset	SelectionSort
Inversions	SignaturePermutation
InvolutionQ	ToCycles
Involutions	ToInversionVector
Josephus	UnrankPermutation

Combinatorica functions for permutations.

BinarySubsets	RandomKSubset
DeBruijnSequence	RandomSubset
GrayCodeKSubsets	RankBinarySubset
GrayCodeSubsets	RankGrayCodeSubset
KSubsets	RankKSubset
LexicographicSubsets	RankSubset
NextBinarySubset	Strings
NextGrayCodeSubset	Subsets
NextKSubset	UnrankBinarySubset
NextLexicographicSubset	UnrankGrayCodeSubset
NextSubset	UnrankKSubset
NthSubset	UnrankSubset

Combinatorica functions for subsets.

AlternatingGroup	ListGraphs
AlternatingGroupIndex	ListNecklaces
CycleIndex	MultiplicationTable
CycleStructure	NecklacePolynomial
Cycles	OrbitInventory
Cyclic	OrbitRepresentatives
CyclicGroup	Orbits
CyclicGroupIndex	Ordered
Dihedral	PairGroup
DihedralGroup	PairGroupIndex
DihedralGroupIndex	PermutationGroupQ
EquivalenceClasses	SamenessRelation
KSubsetGroup	SymmetricGroup
KSubsetGroupIndex	SymmetricGroupIndex

Combinatorica functions for Pólya-theoretic computations.

■ 1.1.2 Partitions, Compositions, and Young Tableaux

A *partition* of a positive integer n is a set of k strictly positive integers whose sum is n. A *composition* of a positive integer n is a particular arrangement of nonnegative integers that adds up to n. A composition differs from a partition in that 0's can be part of a composition and different arrangements of the same set of numbers correspond to different compositions. A *set partition* of n elements is a grouping of all the elements into nonempty, nonintersecting subsets. Finally, a *Young tableau* is a two-dimensional structure of integers $1, \ldots, n$, where the number of elements in each row is defined by an integer partition of n, the elements of each row and column are in increasing order, and the rows are left-justified. These four related combinatorial objects have a host of interesting applications and properties.

Here are the 11 integer partitions of 6. Observe that they are given in reverse lexicographic order.

```
In[15]:= Partitions[6]
Out[15]= {{6}, {5, 1}, {4, 2}, {4, 1, 1}, {3, 3},
    {3, 2, 1}, {3, 1, 1, 1}, {2, 2, 2}, {2, 2, 1, 1},
    {2, 1, 1, 1, 1}, {1, 1, 1, 1, 1, 1}}
```

Relative to the number of permutations or the number of subsets of n elements, the number of partitions of n grows slowly. Therefore, complete tables can be generated for larger values of n.

```
In[16]:= Table[ Length[Partitions[i]], {i,1,20}]
Out[16]= {1, 2, 3, 5, 7, 11, 15, 22, 30, 42, 56, 77, 101,
    135, 176, 231, 297, 385, 490, 627}
```

Ferrers diagrams represent partitions as patterns of dots. They provide a useful tool for visualizing partitions, because moving the dots around provides a mechanism for proving bijections between classes of partitions. Here we construct the Ferrers diagram of a random partition of 100.

```
In[17]:= FerrersDiagram[RandomPartition[100]]
```

A *composition* of n is a particular arrangement of nonnegative integers whose sum is n. Here, every composition of 5 into 3 parts is generated exactly once.

```
In[18]:= Compositions[5,3]
Out[18]= {{0, 0, 5}, {0, 1, 4}, {0, 2, 3}, {0, 3, 2},
    {0, 4, 1}, {0, 5, 0}, {1, 0, 4}, {1, 1, 3}, {1, 2, 2},
    {1, 3, 1}, {1, 4, 0}, {2, 0, 3}, {2, 1, 2}, {2, 2, 1},
    {2, 3, 0}, {3, 0, 2}, {3, 1, 1}, {3, 2, 0}, {4, 0, 1},
    {4, 1, 0}, {5, 0, 0}}
```

Set partitions represent the ways we can partition distinct elements into subsets. Among other things, they are useful for representing colorings and clusterings.

```
In[19]:= SetPartitions[3]
Out[19]= {{{1, 2, 3}}, {{1}, {2, 3}}, {{1, 2}, {3}},
    {{1, 3}, {2}}, {{1}, {2}, {3}}}
```

This list of tableaux of shape {2, 2, 1} illustrates the amount of freedom available for arranging numbers in tableau structures. The smallest element always sits in the upper left-hand corner, but the largest element has considerable freedom. For the shape {2, 2, 1}, the largest element can be the last element in the second row or in the third row.

```
In[20]:= Tableaux[{2,2,1}]
Out[20]= {{{1, 4}, {2, 5}, {3}}, {{1, 3}, {2, 5}, {4}},
   {{1, 2}, {3, 5}, {4}}, {{1, 3}, {2, 4}, {5}},
   {{1, 2}, {3, 4}, {5}}}
```

By iterating through the different integer partitions as shapes, all tableaux of a particular size can be constructed.

```
In[21]:= Tableaux[3]
Out[21]= {{{1, 2, 3}}, {{1, 3}, {2}}, {{1, 2}, {3}},
   {{1}, {2}, {3}}}
```

The *hook length formula* can be used to count the number of tableaux for any shape. Using the hook length formula over all partitions of n computes the number of tableaux on n elements.

```
In[22]:= NumberOfTableaux[10]
Out[22]= 9496
```

The function RandomTableau selects each one of the 117,123,756,750 tableaux of this shape with equal likelihood.

```
In[23]:= TableForm[ RandomTableau[{6,5,5,4,3,2}] ]
Out[23]//TableForm= 1    2    4    10   11   21
                    3    5    12   15   19
                    6    7    13   16   25
                    8    14   20   23
                    9    18   24
                    17   22
```

Any sequence of $n^2 + 1$ distinct integers must contain either an increasing or a decreasing subsequence of length $n + 1$. This result has an elegant proof using tableaux. So in this example, at least one of the two numbers is at least 8.

```
In[24]:= p = RandomPermutation[7^2 + 1];
         Map[Length[LongestIncreasingSubsequence[#]]&,
         {p, Reverse[p]}]
Out[25]= {13, 11}
```

Compositions	NextPartition
DominatingIntegerPartitionQ	PartitionQ
DominationLattice	Partitions
DurfeeSquare	RandomComposition
FerrersDiagram	RandomPartition
NextComposition	TransposePartition

Combinatorica functions for integer partitions and compositions.

CoarserSetPartitionQ	RankRGF
FindSet	RankSetPartition
InitializeUnionFind	SetPartitionListViaRGF
KSetPartitions	SetPartitionQ
PartitionLattice	SetPartitionToRGF
RGFQ	SetPartitions
RGFToSetPartition	ToCanonicalSetPartition
RGFs	UnionSet
RandomKSetPartition	UnrankKSetPartition
RandomRGF	UnrankRGF
RandomSetPartition	UnrankSetPartition
RankKSetPartition	

Combinatorica functions for set partitions.

ConstructTableau	RandomTableau
DeleteFromTableau	TableauClasses
FirstLexicographicTableau	TableauQ
InsertIntoTableau	Tableaux
LastLexicographicTableau	TableauxToPermutation
NextTableau	TransposeTableau

Combinatorica functions for Young tableaux.

BellB	NumberOfKPaths
Cofactor	NumberOfNecklaces
Distribution	NumberOfPartitions
Eulerian	NumberOfPermutationsByCycles
NumberOf2Paths	NumberOfPermutationsByInversions
NumberOfCompositions	NumberOfPermutationsByType
NumberOfDerangements	NumberOfSpanningTrees
NumberOfDirectedGraphs	NumberOfTableaux
NumberOfGraphs	StirlingFirst
NumberOfInvolutions	StirlingSecond

Combinatorica functions for counting.

1.2 Graph Theory and Algorithms

Graph theory is the study of the properties of graphs, where a *graph* is a set of vertices with a set of edges, where each edge is defined by a pair of vertices. Graphs appear everywhere and can model almost anything, including road networks, electronic circuits, social interactions, and even the World Wide Web.

The largest and most interesting parts of *Combinatorica* deal with constructing and visualizing graphs, computing their properties, and implementing graph algorithms. A brief overview of *Combinatorica* graphs is given in the following sections.

■ 1.2.1 Representing Graphs

The representation of graphs takes on different requirements depending on whether the intended consumer is a person or a machine. Computers digest graphs best as data structures such as adjacency matrices or lists. People prefer a visualization of the structure as a collection of points connected by lines, which implies adding geometric information to the graph.

This constructs the *three-dimensional butterfly graph* and displays it using the ShowGraph function. *Combinatorica* contains a large number of functions for constructing graphs and a variety of functions to display them.

In[26]:= **ShowGraph[ButterflyGraph[3]];**

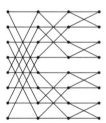

Here, an array of complete graphs on *n* vertices, for $n = 5, 6, 7$, is constructed and displayed using the function ShowGraphArray.

In[27]:= **ShowGraphArray[Table[CompleteGraph[n], {n, 5, 7}]];**

The internals of the graph representation are not shown to the user – only a notation with the number of edges and vertices, followed by whether the graph is directed or undirected. A tree with n vertices has $n - 1$ edges, and this is confirmed here.

```
In[28]:= RandomTree[20]
Out[28]= -Graph:<19, 20, Undirected>-
```

The standard embedding of an n-dimensional butterfly graph consists of $2^n \cdot (n + 1)$ vertices placed, in groups of 2^n, equally spaced, on $(n + 1)$ vertical lines. A graph object in *Combinatorica* carries its embedding information with it, and this is extracted in this example by the function `Vertices`.

```
In[29]:= Vertices[ButterflyGraph[2]]
Out[29]= {{1., -1.5}, {2., -1.5}, {3., -1.5}, {1., -0.5},
    {2., -0.5}, {3., -0.5}, {1., 0.5}, {2., 0.5},
    {3., 0.5}, {1., 1.5}, {2., 1.5}, {3., 1.5}}
```

The number of vertices in a graph is termed the *order* of the graph. The number of vertices in an *n-dimensional hypercube* is 2^n. We can use the *Combinatorica* function `V` to extract this information.

```
In[30]:= V[Hypercube[4]]
Out[30]= 16
```

`M` returns the number of edges in a graph. The number of edges in a complete graph of n vertices is $n(n - 1)/2$; this is confirmed here.

```
In[31]:= M[CompleteGraph[5]]
Out[31]= 10
```

A variety of options that control the appearance of a graph can be associated with each graph object. Here we use the function `SetGraphOptions` to set the colors of vertices and edges of the graph.

```
In[32]:= g = SetGraphOptions[CompleteGraph[4], VertexColor -> Red,
            EdgeColor -> Blue]
Out[32]= -Graph:<6, 4, Undirected>-
```

Options associated with a graph can be global, that is, they affect the entire graph, or they can be local, that is, they affect specific vertices and edges of the graph. In the previous example, the options were global, whereas in this example we set local as well as global options. Thus vertices 1 and 2 are colored green and shown as large disks; vertex 3 is colored blue, and it continues to be represented by the default disk size; vertex 4 is unaffected by all of this. The final option setting colors all edges red.

```
In[33]:= ShowGraph[g = SetGraphOptions[ CompleteGraph[4],
            {{1, 2, VertexColor -> Green, VertexStyle -> Disk[Large]},
            {3, VertexColor -> Blue}}, EdgeColor -> Red ] ];
```

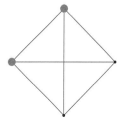

Providing the `All` tag to `Vertices` shows any nondefault options associated with specific vertices. The `All` option can be similarly provided as a tag to the `Edges` function, to extract all edge information.

```
In[34]:= Vertices[g, All]
Out[34]= {{{0, 1.}, VertexColor -> RGBColor[0., 1., 0.],
    VertexStyle -> Disk[Large]},
   {{-1., 0}, VertexColor -> RGBColor[0., 1., 0.],
    VertexStyle -> Disk[Large]},
   {{0, -1.}, VertexColor -> RGBColor[0., 0., 1.]},
   {{1., 0}}}
```

The function `GraphOptions` can be used to extract any nondefault global options associated with a graph.

```
In[35]:= GraphOptions[g]
Out[35]= {EdgeColor -> RGBColor[1., 0., 0.]}
```

Edges	SetEdgeWeights
GetEdgeWeights	SetGraphOptions
GetVertexWeights	SetVertexLabels
GraphOptions	SetVertexWeights
M	V
SetEdgeLabels	Vertices

Combinatorica functions for setting and extracting basic graph information.

A *star* is a tree with one vertex of degree $n - 1$. Adding any new edge to a star produces a cycle of length 3. `AddEdges` is one of many functions that can be used to modify graphs.

```
In[36]:= ShowGraph[ AddEdges[Star[10], {{1,2}, {4,5}}] ];
```

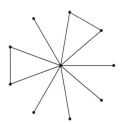

Here we delete the central vertex of a $3 \times 3 \times 3$ grid graph. This results in a renumbering of the vertices 1 through 26, as shown here.

```
In[37]:= ShowGraph[DeleteVertices[GridGraph[3, 3, 3], {14}],
           VertexNumber -> True];
```

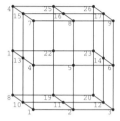

An *induced subgraph* of a graph G is a subset of the vertices of G together with any edges whose endpoints are both in this subset. Here is an induced subgraph of a 20×20 grid graph, induced by a randomly chosen subset of the vertices.

```
In[38]:= ShowGraph[ InduceSubgraph[GridGraph[20, 20],
           RandomSubset[Range[400]]] ];
```

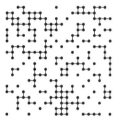

The *contract* operation replaces a pair $\{u, v\}$ of vertices by one vertex uv and modifies the edge set by replacing any edge $\{x, u\}$ or $\{x, v\}$ by an edge $\{x, uv\}$. The edge $\{u, v\}$, if it exists, is deleted. As this example shows, the contract operation can result in multiple edges between a pair of vertices.

```
In[39]:= ShowGraph[g = Contract[GridGraph[3, 3], {1, 5}]];
```

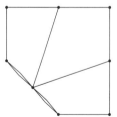

A graph is called *simple* if it does not have self-loops or multiple edges between pairs of vertices. The *Combinatorica* function MakeSimple converts an arbitrary graph into the underlying simple graph.

In[40]:= **ShowGraph[MakeSimple[g]];**

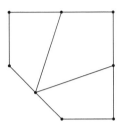

AddEdge	DeleteVertex
AddEdges	DeleteVertices
AddVertex	InduceSubgraph
AddVertices	MakeDirected
ChangeEdges	MakeSimple
ChangeVertices	MakeUndirected
Contract	PermuteSubgraph
DeleteCycle	RemoveMultipleEdges
DeleteEdge	RemoveSelfLoops
DeleteEdges	ReverseEdges

Combinatorica functions for modifying graphs.

In old *Combinatorica*, adjacency matrices were used to represent a graph. In the new package, an edge list is used. This change has made many of the functions on graphs significantly faster and flexible.

It easy to go between different graph representations. Here we construct an adjacency matrix for the random tree constructed in the above example. Since every tree with more than one vertex has at least two leaves, we should see at least two rows with a single nonzero.

In[41]:= **Edges[g=RandomTree[6]]**

Out[41]= {{1, 5}, {3, 5}, {3, 4}, {2, 4}, {2, 6}}

In[42]:= **(m = ToAdjacencyMatrix[g]) // TableForm**

Out[42]//TableForm=

0	0	0	0	1	0
0	0	0	1	0	1
0	0	0	1	1	0
0	1	1	0	0	0
1	0	1	0	0	0
0	1	0	0	0	0

FromAdjacencyMatrix takes us back from an adjacency matrix representation to a *Combinatorica* graph object. In going from a graph to an adjacency matrix and back we loose embedding information. Here, the vertices of the graph are in default embedding – evenly spaced on the circumference of a circle.

In[43]:= **ShowGraph[FromAdjacencyMatrix[m]];**

The adjacency list representation of a graph consists of n lists, one list for each vertex v_i, $1 \le i \le n$, which records the vertices to which v_i is adjacent. Typically, adjacency lists for different vertices differ in size, and the adjacency list representation is a much more compact representation of a graph than an adjacency matrix representation.

In[44]:= **ToAdjacencyLists[g] // TableForm**

Out[44]//TableForm=

5	
4	6
4	5
2	3
1	3
2	

FromAdjacencyLists	ToAdjacencyLists
FromAdjacencyMatrix	ToAdjacencyMatrix
FromOrderedPairs	ToOrderedPairs
FromUnorderedPairs	ToUnorderedPairs
IncidenceMatrix	

Combinatorica functions for graph format translation.

■ 1.2.2 Drawing Graphs

One of the highlights of the new *Combinatorica* is the dramatic improvement in the ShowGraph function. When combined with other graph drawing functions provided in *Combinatorica*, we get a flexible, easy-to-use, graph-drawing tool to draw graphs in a variety of interesting ways.

Every graph has a default vertex number, and this can be turned on in ShowGraph. In addition, arbitrary vertex labels can be assigned to vertices. Options of *Mathematica*'s Plot function have all been inherited by ShowGraph. To illustrate this, we set the background color for the graph.

In[45]:= **ShowGraph[Cycle[5], VertexNumber -> True,**
          VertexLabel -> {"B", "C", "A", "D", "E"}, Background -> LightBlue];

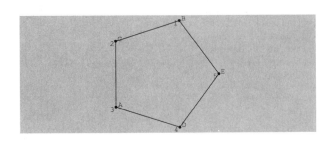

This shows off more of the large variety of options that can be used in ShowGraph. The options VertexStyle, VertexColor, and EdgeStyle are particular to ShowGraph, while the options PlotLabel and TextStyle are inherited from Plot.

In[46]:= **ShowGraph[GridGraph[3, 3], VertexStyle -> Box[Large],**
          EdgeStyle -> ThickDashed, VertexColor -> Red,
          PlotLabel -> "A Grid Graph", TextStyle -> {FontSize -> 12}];

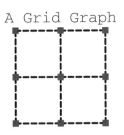

Some of the inherited options have been extended so that they can be used in new ways. For example, PlotRange can be used to "zoom" into a subset of vertices. This can be quite useful in revealing the structure of large or dense graphs.

In[47]:= **ShowGraph[Hypercube[5], PlotRange->Zoom[{1, 2, 3, 4}],**
          VertexNumber->True,
          TextStyle->{FontSize->14}];

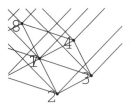

Different drawings or embeddings of a graph can reveal different aspects of its structure. Here we show the default embedding of the *dodecahedral graph* on the left and its *ranked embedding* on the right. In the ranked embedding, vertices are placed on distinct vertical lines based on their distances from vertex 3.

In[48]:= **ShowGraphArray[{g = DodecahedralGraph, RankedEmbedding[g, {3}]}];**

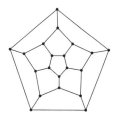 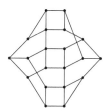

Box	NormalDashed
Center	PlotRange
Directed	Small
Disk	Thick
EdgeColor	ThickDashed
EdgeDirection	Thin
EdgeLabel	ThinDashed
EdgeLabelColor	Undirected
EdgeLabelPosition	UpperLeft
EdgeStyle	UpperRight
EdgeWeight	VertexColor
HighlightedEdgeColors	VertexLabel
HighlightedEdgeStyle	VertexLabelColor
HighlightedVertexColors	VertexLabelPosition
HighlightedVertexStyle	VertexNumber
Large	VertexNumberColor
LoopPosition	VertexNumberPosition
LowerLeft	VertexStyle
LowerRight	VertexWeight
Normal	Zoom

Combinatorica options for ShowGraph and related graph-drawing functions.

In a *radial embedding* a vertex is placed
at the center of a circle with the rest of
the vertices placed on concentric circles
around the center. Here we show the
dodecahedral graph along with its
radial embedding.

In[49]:= **ShowGraphArray[{g, RadialEmbedding[g, 1]}];**

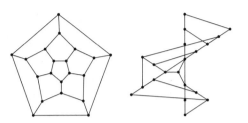

A random tree geis a radial embedding
by default. The radial embedding of a
tree is guaranteed to be
non-self-intersecting.

In[50]:= **ShowGraph[RandomTree[30]];**

By arbitrarily selecting a root, any tree
can be represented as a rooted tree.

In[51]:= **ShowGraph[RootedEmbedding[RandomTree[50],1]];**

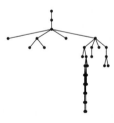

An interesting general heuristic for drawing graphs models the graph as a system of springs and lets *Hooke's law* space the vertices. Here it does a good job of showing that the graph consists of four connected components. This is because nonadjacent vertices repel each other and this forces the connected components to drift apart.

In[52]:= **ShowGraphArray[NestList[SpringEmbedding,**
          CirculantGraph[20, 4], 3]];

AnimateGraph	RootedEmbedding
CircularVertices	RotateVertices
DilateVertices	ShakeGraph
Highlight	ShowGraph
RadialEmbedding	ShowGraphArray
RandomVertices	ShowLabeledGraph
RankGraph	SpringEmbedding
RankedEmbedding	TranslateVertices

Combinatorica functions for drawing graphs.

■ 1.2.3 Generating Graphs

Many graphs consistently prove to be interesting, in the sense that they are models of important binary relations or have unique graph-theoretic properties. Often, these graphs can be parametrized, such as the hypercube of n dimensions, giving a concise notation for expressing an infinite class of graphs. We start off with several operations that act on graphs to give different graphs and which, together with parametrized graphs, give the means to construct essentially any interesting graph.

Graph products can be very interesting. This embedding of a product has been designed to show off its structure; it is formed by shrinking the first graph and translating it to the position of each vertex in the second graph.

In[53]:= **ShowGraph[GraphProduct[Cycle[4], CompleteGraph[5]]];**

The *line graph* L(G) of a graph G has a vertex of L(G) associated with each edge of G and an edge of L(G) if, and only if, the two edges of G share a common vertex. Here we construct the line graph of a dodecahedral graph.

In[54]:= **ShowGraph[LineGraph[DodecahedralGraph]];**

Circulant graphs are graphs whose adjacency matrix can be constructed by rotating a vector *n* times and include complete graphs and cycles as special cases. Even random circulant graphs have an interesting, regular structure.

In[55]:= **ShowGraph[CirculantGraph[21,**
     RandomKSubset[Range[10],3]]];

Some graph generators create directed graphs with self-loops, such as this *de Bruijn* or *shift register* graph encoding all length-5 substrings of a binary alphabet.

In[56]:= **ShowGraph[DeBruijnGraph[2,5]];**

Hypercubes of dimension d are the graph product of cubes of dimension $d-1$ and the complete graph K_2. Here, a Hamiltonian cycle of the hypercube is highlighted. Colored highlighting and graph animations are also provided in the package.

In[57]:= **ShowGraph[Highlight[Hypercube[4],**
        {Partition[HamiltonianCycle[Hypercube[4]], 2, 1]}]];

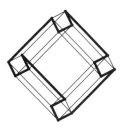

Two- and three-dimensional *grid graphs* can be easily constructed. `ShowGraphArray` permits the display of multiple graphs in one window.

In[58]:= **ShowGraphArray[{GridGraph[5,5], GridGraph[5,5,5]}];**

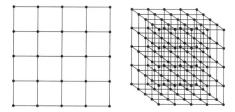

The *girth* of a graph is the length of a smallest cycle in the graph. A *k-regular graph* is a graph in which every vertex has degree k. Here we show the *g-cage graph*, for $g = 3, 4, ..., 8$, which is a smallest 3-regular graph with girth g.

In[59]:= **ShowGraphArray[Partition[Table[CageGraph[g], {g, 3, 8}], 3]];**

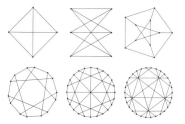

Here we show 3-regular graphs with 12 vertices. RegularGraph takes *k* and *n* and produces a random *n*-vertex *k*-regular graph; however, it is not guaranteed that each *n*-vertex *k*-regular graph is equally likely to be selected.

In[60]:= **ShowGraphArray[gt = Table[RegularGraph[3, 12], {4}]];**

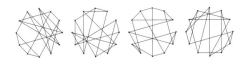

MakeGraph is one of the most useful *Combinatorica* functions for constructing graphs. It takes a set *S* and a predicate *P* on ordered pairs from *S* and returns a directed graph with vertex set *S* and edges (i, j) if $P(i, j)$ is true. In this example, *S* is the set of all binary strings of length 4, and the predicate connects binary strings that differ in exactly 1 bit. The default embedding of a graph produced by MakeGraph is a circular embedding.

In[61]:= **ShowGraph[g = MakeGraph[Strings[{0, 1}, 4], Apply[Plus, Map[Abs, (#1 - #2)]] == 1&, Type -> Undirected]];**

But filtering the above embedding through SpringEmbedding reveals a nice structure. This is no surprise, because this graph is just the four-dimensional hypercube!

In[62]:= **ShowGraph[SpringEmbedding[g, 50]];**

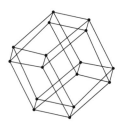

BooleanAlgebra
ButterflyGraph
CageGraph
CartesianProduct
ChvatalGraph
CirculantGraph
CodeToLabeledTree
CompleteBinaryTree
CompleteGraph
CompleteKPartiteGraph
CompleteKaryTree
CoxeterGraph
CubeConnectedCycle
CubicalGraph
Cycle
DeBruijnGraph
DodecahedralGraph
EmptyGraph
ExactRandomGraph
ExpandGraph
FiniteGraphs
FolkmanGraph
FranklinGraph
FruchtGraph
FunctionalGraph
GeneralizedPetersenGraph
GraphComplement
GraphDifference
GraphIntersection
GraphJoin
GraphPower
GraphProduct
GraphSum
GraphUnion
GrayGraph
GridGraph
GrotztschGraph
Harary
HasseDiagram
HeawoodGraph

HerschelGraph
Hypercube
IcosahedralGraph
IntervalGraph
KnightsTourGraph
LabeledTreeToCode
LeviGraph
LineGraph
MakeGraph
McGeeGraph
MeredithGraph
MycielskiGraph
NoPerfectMatchingGraph
NonLineGraphs
OctahedralGraph
OddGraph
OrientGraph
Path
PermutationGraph
PetersenGraph
RandomGraph
RandomTree
RealizeDegreeSequence
RegularGraph
RobertsonGraph
ShuffleExchangeGraph
SmallestCyclicGroupGraph
Star
TetrahedralGraph
ThomassenGraph
TransitiveClosure
TransitiveReduction
Turan
TutteGraph
Uniquely3ColorableGraph
UnitransitiveGraph
VertexConnectivityGraph
WaltherGraph
Wheel

Combinatorica graph-constructor functions.

■ 1.2.4 Properties of Graphs

Graph theory is the study of properties of graphs. Among the properties of interest are such things as connectivity, cycle structure, maximum clique size, and chromatic number. Here we demonstrate how to compute several different graph properties.

The *breadth-first traversal* is one of the most basic and useful graph traversal algorithms. Various graph properties can be evaluated by first doing a breadth-first traversal on the graph. For example, questions like, "Is the graph bipartite?" or "What is the diameter of the graph?" can be answered via breadth-first search. Here we show the breadth-first tree, produced by doing a breadth-first traversal of a $4 \times 4 \times 4$ grid graph. Alongside, we also show a spring embedding of the breadth-first tree, to better reveal its structure.

```
In[63]:= h = BreadthFirstTraversal[g = GridGraph[4, 4, 4], 1, Tree];
         ShowGraphArray[{h, SpringEmbedding[h, 100]}];
```

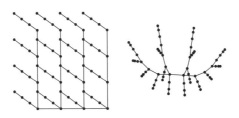

The *depth-first traversal* is a graph traversal that is complementary to a breadth first traversal. Depth-first traversal is useful in evaluating properties such as the biconnectivity of a graph. Here we show the depth-first tree, obtained by doing a depth-first traversal of a $4 \times 4 \times 4$ grid graph. The depth-first tree and the breadth first tree of a graph typically differ dramatically, as revealed by their spring embeddings.

```
In[65]:= h = DepthFirstTraversal[g, 1, Tree];
         ShowGraphArray[{h, SpringEmbedding[h, 100]}];
```

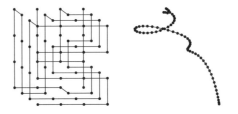

An undirected graph is *connected* if a path exists between every pair of vertices. Deleting an edge from a connected graph can disconnect it. Such an edge is called a *bridge*.

```
In[67]:= ConnectedQ[ DeleteEdge[ Star[10], {1,10} ] ]

Out[67]= False
```

It is quite likely that the subgraph induced by a random vertex subset of a 20×20 grid graph is disconnected.

```
In[68]:= Length[ConnectedComponents[
             InduceSubgraph[GridGraph[20, 20], RandomSubset[400]]]]

Out[68]= 41
```

An *orientation* of an undirected graph
G is an assignment of exactly one
direction to each of the edges of G.
Note that arrows denoting the direction
of each edge are automatically drawn
in displaying directed graphs.

In[69]:= **ShowGraph[OrientGraph[Wheel[10]]];**

An *articulation vertex* of a graph G is a
vertex whose deletion disconnects G.
Any graph with no articulation vertices
is said to be *biconnected*. A graph with
a vertex of degree 1 cannot be
biconnected, since deleting the other
vertex that defines its only edge
disconnects the graph.

In[70]:= **BiconnectedComponents[**
            RealizeDegreeSequence[{4,4,3,3,3,2,1}]]
Out[70]= {{5, 7}, {1, 2, 3, 4, 5, 6}}

The only articulation vertex of a star is
its center, even though its deletion
leaves $n - 1$ connected components.
Deleting a leaf leaves a connected tree.

In[71]:= **ArticulationVertices[Star[10]]**
Out[71]= {10}

A graph is said to be k-connected if
there does not exist a set of $k - 1$
vertices whose removal disconnects the
graph. The wheel is the basic
triconnected graph.

In[72]:= **VertexConnectivity[Wheel[10]]**
Out[72]= 3

A graph is k-edge-connected if there
does not exist a set of $k - 1$ edges
whose removal disconnects the graph.
The edge connectivity of a graph is at
most the minimum degree δ, since
deleting those edges disconnects the
graph. Complete bipartite graphs
realize this bound.

In[73]:= **EdgeConnectivity[CompleteGraph[3,4]]**
Out[73]= 3

A directed graph in which half the
possible edges exist is almost certain to
contain a cycle. Directed acyclic graphs
are often called DAGs.

In[74]:= **AcyclicQ[RandomGraph[100, 0.5, Type -> Directed]]**
Out[74]= False

An Eulerian cycle is a complete tour of
all of the edges of a graph. An
Eulerian cycle of a bipartite graph
bounces back and forth between the
stages.

In[75]:= **EulerianCycle[CompleteGraph[4,4]]**
Out[75]= {7, 2, 8, 1, 5, 4, 6, 3, 7, 4, 8, 3, 5, 2, 6, 1, 7}

AcyclicQ	PartialOrderQ
AntiSymmetricQ	PerfectQ
BiconnectedQ	PlanarQ
BipartiteQ	PseudographQ
CliqueQ	ReflexiveQ
CompleteQ	RegularQ
ConnectedQ	SelfComplementaryQ
EmptyQ	SelfLoopsQ
EquivalenceRelationQ	SimpleQ
EulerianQ	TransitiveQ
GraphicQ	TreeIsomorphismQ
HamiltonianQ	TreeQ
IdenticalQ	TriangleInequalityQ
IndependentSetQ	UndirectedQ
IsomorphicQ	UnweightedQ
IsomorphismQ	VertexCoverQ
MultipleEdgesQ	

Combinatorica functions for graph predicates.

Any labeled graph G can be colored in a certain number of ways with exactly k colors. This number is determined by the chromatic polynomial of the graph.

```
In[76]:= ChromaticPolynomial[
                GraphUnion[CompleteGraph[2,2], Cycle[3]], z ]
              2       3       4       5       6    7
Out[76]= -6 z  + 21 z  - 29 z  + 20 z  - 7 z  + z
```

Substituting for z, we see that this graph cannot be 2-colored, but it does have lots of distinct 3-colorings.

```
In[77]:= {% /. z -> 2, % /. z -> 3}
Out[77]= {0, 108}
```

A *Hamiltonian cycle* of a graph G is a cycle that visits every *vertex* in G exactly once, as opposed to an Eulerian cycle, which visits each *edge* exactly once. Here we demonstrate that the icosahedral graph contains a Hamiltonian cycle by computing it and then highlighting it.

```
In[78]:= c = Partition[HamiltonianCycle[g = IcosahedralGraph], 2, 1];
            ShowGraph[ Highlight[g, {c}]];
```

Here we highlight a *maximum clique* in
a random graph. A maximum clique is
a complete subgraph with maximum
number of vertices. Computing a
maximum clique is not just NP-hard; it
is hard even to approximate to any
reasonable factor [ALM+92].

```
In[80]:= g = RandomGraph[10, .7];
         ShowGraph[Highlight[g, {MaximumClique[g]}]];
```

ArticulationVertices	HamiltonianPath
Automorphisms	InDegree
Backtrack	Isomorphism
BiconnectedComponents	M
Bridges	MaximalMatching
ChromaticNumber	MaximumAntichain
ChromaticPolynomial	MaximumClique
ConnectedComponents	MaximumIndependentSet
DegreeSequence	MaximumSpanningTree
Degrees	MinimumChainPartition
DegreesOf2Neighborhood	MinimumSpanningTree
Diameter	MinimumVertexColoring
Distances	MinimumVertexCover
Eccentricity	OutDegree
EdgeChromaticNumber	Radius
EdgeColoring	Spectrum
EdgeConnectivity	StronglyConnectedComponents
Equivalences	TreeToCertificate
EulerianCycle	V
Girth	VertexColoring
GraphCenter	VertexConnectivity
GraphPolynomial	VertexCover
HamiltonianCycle	WeaklyConnectedComponents

Combinatorica functions for graph invariants.

■ 1.2.5 Algorithmic Graph Theory

Finally, there are several graph-theoretic problems that are of particular interest because of the algorithms that solve them. These problems include computing shortest paths, minimum spanning trees, matchings, and network flows. These are some of the most intensely studied graph-theoretic problems because a typical real-world application will almost certainly contain an instance of one of these problems.

We start by assigning edge weights, randomly chosen in the range 0 through 1, to the edges of a 5 × 5 grid graph and compute a shortest-path spanning tree. If the edge weights are all one unit, then the shortest-path spanning tree of a grid graph is defined in terms of *Manhattan distance*, where the distance between points with coordinates (x, y) and (u, v) is $|x - u| + |y - v|$. However, with edge weights assigned randomly, the shortest-path spanning tree could contain some convoluted paths.

In[82]:= **g = SetEdgeWeights[GridGraph[5, 5]];**
         ShowGraph[ShortestPathSpanningTree[g, 1]];

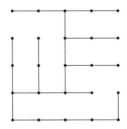

A *minimum spanning tree* of a weighted graph is a set of $n - 1$ edges of minimum total weight that form a spanning tree of the graph. Any spanning tree is a minimum spanning tree when the graphs are unweighted.

In[84]:= **ShowGraph[MinimumSpanningTree[CompleteGraph[6,6,6]]];**

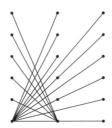

We start with a complete graph with 50 vertices, embed the vertices randomly on the plane, and then assign Euclidean distances to the edges. A minimum spanning tree of the resulting graph is shown. Notice that this graph contains no edge intersections. This can be easily shown to be true in general whenever edge weights satisfy the triangle inequality.

In[85]:= **g = SetEdgeWeights[RandomVertices[CompleteGraph[50]],**
         WeightingFunction -> Euclidean];
         ShowGraph[MinimumSpanningTree[g]];

Cayley proved that the number of spanning trees of a complete graph is n^{n-2}.

```
In[87]:= NumberOfSpanningTrees[CompleteGraph[10]]
Out[87]= 100000000
```

Assuming unit capacities, $n-1$ units of flow can be pushed from one vertex to another in a complete graph with n vertices.

```
In[88]:= NetworkFlow[CompleteGraph[7], 1, 7]
Out[88]= 6
```

More information can be obtained by providing the tag Edge to the function. It shows edges along which positive flow is being sent (along with the flows).

```
In[89]:= NetworkFlow[CompleteGraph[7], 1, 7, Edge]
Out[89]= {{{1, 2}, 1}, {{1, 3}, 1}, {{1, 4}, 1},
    {{1, 5}, 1}, {{1, 6}, 1}, {{1, 7}, 1}, {{2, 7}, 1},
    {{3, 7}, 1}, {{4, 7}, 1}, {{5, 7}, 1}, {{6, 7}, 1}}
```

A *matching*, in a graph G, is a set of edges of G such that no two of them share a common vertex. A *maximal matching* is a matching to which no edge can be added without violating the matching property. A *perfect matching* is a matching in which there is an edge incident on every vertex. The matching shown here is maximal, but not perfect. It is not hard to see that this graph has no perfect matching.

```
In[90]:= ShowGraph[Highlight[g = NoPerfectMatchingGraph,
    {MaximalMatching[g]}]];
```

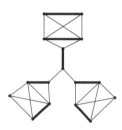

The function BipartiteMatching produces a matching of largest size in a bipartite graph. Typically, a maximal matching does not have the largest possible size.

```
In[91]:= g = InduceSubgraph[GridGraph[20, 20], RandomSubset[400]];
    {Length[BipartiteMatching[g]], Length[MaximalMatching[g]]}
Out[92]= {83, 75}
```

The divisibility relation between integers is reflexive, since each integer divides itself, and antisymmetric, since x cannot divide y if $x > y$. Finally, it is transitive, as $x \backslash y$ implies $y = c\,x$ for some integer c, so $y \backslash z$ implies $x \backslash z$.

```
In[93]:= ShowGraph[ g = MakeGraph[Range[8],(Mod[#1,#2]==0)&],
    VertexNumber -> True ];
```

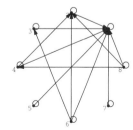

Since the divisibility relation is reflexive, transitive, and antisymmetric, it is a *partial order*.

In[94]:= **PartialOrderQ[g]**

Out[94]= True

A graph *G* is *transitive* if, for any three vertices *x, y, z*, edges {*x, y*}, {*y, z*} ∈ *G* imply {*x, z*} ∈ *G*. The transitive reduction of a graph *G* is the smallest graph *R(G)* such that *C(G) = C(R(G))*. The *transitive reduction* eliminates all implied edges in the divisibility relation, such as 4 \ 8, 1 \ 4, 1 \ 6, and 1 \ 8.

In[95]:= **ShowGraph[TransitiveReduction[g], VertexNumber -> True];**

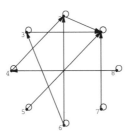

The *Hasse diagram* clearly shows the lattice structure of the Boolean algebra, the partial order defined by inclusion on the set of subsets.

In[96]:= **ShowGraph[HasseDiagram[MakeGraph[Subsets[4],**
((Intersection[#2,#1]===#1)&&(#1 != #2))&]]];

The Hasse diagrams of certain important partial orders can be produced by functions that are now built into *Combinatorica*. An example is the *domination lattice*, which shows a partial order on integer partitions. As we go up this poset, we go from many parts to few parts.

In[97]:= **ShowGraph[DominationLattice[8, VertexLabel -> True],**
PlotRange->0.25];

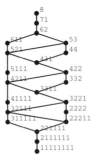

This shows that the graphs
corresponding to the Platonic solids are
all planar.

```
In[98]:= Map[PlanarQ, {CubicalGraph, DodecahedralGraph,
            OctahedralGraph, TetrahedralGraph, IcosahedralGraph}]
Out[98]= {True, True, True, True, True}
```

AllPairsShortestPath	Neighborhood
ApproximateVertexCover	NetworkFlow
BellmanFord	ParentsToPaths
BipartiteMatching	ResidualFlowGraph
BreadthFirstTraversal	ShortestPath
BrelazColoring	ShortestPathSpanningTree
CostOfPath	StableMarriage
DepthFirstTraversal	TopologicalSort
Dijkstra	TravelingSalesman
ExtractCycles	TravelingSalesmanBounds
FindCycle	TwoColoring
GreedyVertexCover	

Combinatorica functions for graph algorithms.

Algorithm	Optimum
Brelaz	Parent
Euclidean	RandomInteger
Greedy	Simple
Invariants	Strong
LNorm	Type
NoMultipleEdges	Weak
NoSelfLoops	WeightRange
One	WeightingFunction

Combinatorica options for miscellaneous graph functions.

1.3 *Combinatorica* Conversion Guide

This section is meant specifically for users of the old *Combinatorica* package, as a quick reference for porting code into the new *Combinatorica*. This section is essentially an enumeration of all functions whose usage has changed from the old version to the new.

■ 1.3.1 The Main Differences

The new *Combinatorica* has about twice as many functions as the old *Combinatorica*. All the functions of the old *Combinatorica* appear in the new *Combinatorica* as well, but most of them have changed (at least internally) in significant ways. This is a good thing. First, many of them have become orders of magnitude faster. Second, many of them provide much more sophisticated functionality. In essentially rewriting the package and making it much better, we have tried our best to provide backwards compatibility. However, there are a small number of functions in the old *Combinatorica* that don't quite behave the same in the new *Combinatorica*. A list of these functions is provided in the following subsection.

The main reasons these functions behave differently are

(A) The basic data structure is now an edge list instead of an adjacency matrix.

(B) Each graph is explicitly (and internally) defined to be either directed or undirected.

In this sequence of examples, we construct a random tree in the new *Combinatorica* and examine its structure.

```
In[99]:= g = RandomTree[10]
Out[99]= -Graph:<9, 10, Undirected>-
```

The graph object in the new *Combinatorica* contains three items, an edge list, a vertex list, and a sequence of options wrapped around by the header Graph. In this example, the sequence of options is empty, and so this graph object contains only two items...

```
In[100]:= Length[g]
Out[100]= 2
```

...around which the header Graph is wrapped.

```
In[101]:= g[[0]]
Out[101]= Graph
```

The first item is a sequence of edges. In contrast, the first item in an old-style *Combinatorica* graph object is an adjacency matrix. Note the extra brackets around the edges to accommodate options we might want to associate with individual edges.

```
In[102]:= g[[1]]
Out[102]= {{{2, 4}}, {{4, 7}}, {{6, 7}}, {{5, 6}}, {{5, 8}},
          {{1, 8}}, {{1, 9}}, {{1, 3}}, {{3, 10}}}
```

The second item is a sequence of planar coordinates for vertices. Again, the extra brackets around the coordinates are for options that we might want to associate with individual vertices.

```
In[103]:= g[[2]]
Out[103]= {{{0, 0}}, {{-6., 0.}}, {{0.5, 0.866025}},
           {{-5., 0.}}, {{-2., 0.}}, {{-3., 0.}}, {{-4., 0.}},
           {{-1., 0.}}, {{0.5, -0.866025}}, {{1., 1.73205}}}
```

More details on the structure of a new *Combinatorica* graph object can be obtained by running ?Graph. If a user is explicitly inputting a graph, care has to be taken to make sure that it has the correct structure. Code that depends on old-style *Combinatorica* graphs can be easily modified to work with the new by using FromAdjacencyMatrix to convert matrices to graphs.

Here is how an old-style graph object looks, without the header Graph wrapped around it.

```
In[104]:= oldG = {{{0, 1, 1, 0}, {0, 0, 0, 1}, {1, 0, 0, 0},
           {1, 1, 0,  0}}, {{0, 0}, {1, 1}, {0.3, 0.8}, {0.8, 0.3}}}
Out[104]= {{{0, 1, 1, 0}, {0, 0, 0, 1}, {1, 0, 0, 0},
           {1, 1, 0, 0}}, {{0, 0}, {1, 1}, {0.3, 0.8},
           {0.8, 0.3}}}
```

Filtering this through FromAdjacencyMatrix is sufficient to construct a graph object in the new *Combinatorica*. The second argument of FromAdjacencyMatrix is the embedding of the vertices, which the function uses as the embedding of the constructed graph. If no embedding was supplied, then the function would use the default embedding on the circumference of a circle.

```
In[105]:= ShowGraph[FromAdjacencyMatrix[oldG[[1]], oldG[[2]]]];
```

A graph object can constructed by hand and explicitly typed out and provided to functions. Here is an example. However, we discourage this because the user has to make sure that the syntax for the various pieces in the graph is carefully observed. For example, edges and vertices have an extra set of parentheses around them. Also, edges in an undirected graph must be listed as $\{i, j\}$, where $i \leq j$.

```
In[106]:= g = Graph[{{{1, 3}}, {{2, 3}}, {{1, 4}}, {{2, 5}}, {{1, 5}}},
           {{{0, 0}}, {{0,1}}, {{1, 1}}, {{1, 1.5}}, {{2, 1}}}]
Out[106]= -Graph:<5, 5, Undirected>-
```

Instead, we recommend using a function such as FromUnorderedPairs to construct a graph. The function will perform some syntax checking and allows the user some flexibility in specifying the graph.

```
In[107]:= g = FromUnorderedPairs[{{1, 3}, {2, 3}, {4, 1}, {2, 5}, {5, 1}},
           {{0, 0}, {0,1}, {1, 1}, {1, 1.5}, {2, 1}}]
Out[107]= -Graph:<5, 5, Undirected>-
```

For example, when provided as input to FromUnorderedPairs, edges in an undirected graph can be listed without worrying about the relative order of the endpoints.

```
In[108]:= IsomorphicQ[FromUnorderedPairs[{{1, 2}, {3, 2}, {3, 1}}],
             FromUnorderedPairs[{{1, 2}, {2, 3}, {1, 3}}]]
Out[108]= True
```

Another advantage of using FromUnorderedPairs and similar functions is that the embedding information is optional and the function will provide a default (circular) embedding, if necessary.

```
In[109]:= ShowGraph[FromUnorderedPairs[Flatten[Table[{{i, i + 1},
             {i, i + 2}}, {i, 10}], 1]]];
```

Every new *Combinatorica* graph is explicitly tagged as either directed or undirected. This information is stored within the graph data structure as an option. This implies that, unlike in the old *Combinatorica*, the same graph object cannot be sometimes interpreted as an undirected graph and sometimes as a directed graph. This makes some function usages from the old *Combinatorica* redundant.

In this example, we construct a random directed graph. The option Type informs RandomGraph whether the graph to be constructed should be directed. On examining the graph object, the function ShowGraph realizes that the graph is directed and therefore draws edges with arrows.

```
In[110]:= ShowGraph[g = RandomGraph[6, .5, Type -> Directed],
             VertexNumber -> True];
```

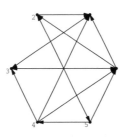

The graph object now consists of three items, with the third item indicating that the graph is directed.

```
In[111]:= {Length[g], g[[3]]}
Out[111]= {3, EdgeDirection -> True}
```

Any edge that is added to graph *g* is automatically interpreted as a directed edge. Therefore the tag Directed is redundant here. This usage causes an error message and the tag is ignored, but a directed edge from 1 to 2 is added to the graph.

```
In[112]:= AddEdge[g, {1, 2}, Directed]
AddEdge::obsolete:
   Usage of Directed as a second argument to AddEdge is
   obsolete.
Out[112]= -Graph:<15, 6, Directed>-
```

■ 1.3.2 Functions Whose Usage Has Changed

AddEdge

The `Directed` tag in functions such as `AddEdge` no longer makes sense because the added edge is considered to be undirected or directed depending on the graph, not on the edge. The usage of the `Directed` tag here causes an error message to be emitted. In this example, edge {1, 3} is interpreted to be an undirected edge because *g* is undirected. Were *g* directed, the directed edge (1, 3) would have been added to *g*.

```
In[113]:= g = Cycle[5];
          ShowGraph[AddEdge[g, {1, 3}, Directed]];
```

```
AddEdge::obsolete:
   Usage of Directed as a second argument to AddEdge is
   obsolete.
```

ChangeEdges

The second argument of `ChangeEdges` is no longer an adjacency matrix, but a list of edges.

Going from an adjacency matrix to a list of edges is easy. If, we start with an adjacency matrix...

...this is how we convert it into an edge list.

```
In[115]:= h = ChangeEdges[g, {{1, 2}, {2, 3}}]
```

```
Out[115]= -Graph:<2, 5, Undirected>-
```

```
In[116]:= m = ToAdjacencyMatrix[g]
```

```
Out[116]= {{0, 1, 0, 0, 1}, {1, 0, 1, 0, 0},
          {0, 1, 0, 1, 0}, {0, 0, 1, 0, 1}, {1, 0, 0, 1, 0}}
```

```
In[117]:= Edges[FromAdjacencyMatrix[m]]
```

```
Out[117]= {{1, 2}, {1, 5}, {2, 3}, {3, 4}, {4, 5}}
```

CircularVertices

`CircularVertices` is now obsolete, having been replaced by `CircularEmbedding`. This was done to make function names more consistent. `CircularVertices` currently remains available but will be removed in future versions of the package.

```
In[118]:= ?CircularVertices
```

```
CircularVertices[n] constructs a list of n points equally
   spaced on a circle. CircularVertices[g] embeds the
   vertices of g equally spaced on a circle. This function
   is obsolete; use CircularEmbedding instead.
```

Here are five points equally spaced on a circle.

```
In[119]:= CircularEmbedding[5]
```

```
Out[119]= {{{0.309017, 0.951057}}, {{-0.809017, 0.587785}},
           {{-0.809017, -0.587785}}, {{0.309017, -0.951057}},
           {{1., 0}}}
```

Contract

Contract may produce graphs with multiple parallel edges. Such graphs were not possible in the old *Combinatorica* but are possible in the new *Combinatorica*.

```
In[120]:= ShowGraphArray[{g = Cycle[5], Contract[g, {1, 3}]},
          VertexNumber -> True];
```

The function MakeSimple can be used to get rid of multiple parallel edges and self-loops, in case the user wants to replicate the behavior of Contract in the old *Combinatorica*. Here we make the above graph simple and in the process get rid of the multiple parallel edges between 1 and 4.

```
In[121]:= ShowGraph[MakeSimple[Contract[g, {1, 3}]]];
```

DeleteCycle

The Directed tag in DeleteCycle no longer makes sense because the cycle type depends on whether the input graph is directed or undirected. The tag is ignored and an error message is emitted.

```
In[122]:= DeleteCycle[Cycle[5], {1, 2, 3, 4, 5, 1}, Directed]
```

```
DeleteCycle::obsolete:
   Usage of Directed as a second argument to DeleteCycle
   is obsolete.
```

```
Out[122]= -Graph:<0, 5, Undirected>-
```

DeleteEdge

The `Directed` tag in `DeleteEdge` no longer makes sense because the edge type depends on whether the input graph is directed or undirected. The tag is ignored and an error message is emitted.

In[123]:= **DeleteEdge[Cycle[5], {1, 2}, Directed]**

DeleteEdge::obsolete:
   Usage of Directed as a second argument to DeleteEdge is
   obsolete.

Out[123]= -Graph:<4, 5, Undirected>-

Edges

Edges returns a list of edges rather than the adjacency matrix.

To replicate the behavior of the old *Combinatorica*'s `Edges` function, use `ToAdjacencyMatrix`.

In[124]:= **Edges[g]**

Out[124]= {{1, 2}, {2, 3}, {3, 4}, {4, 5}, {1, 5}}

In[125]:= **ToAdjacencyMatrix[g]**

Out[125]= {{0, 1, 0, 0, 1}, {1, 0, 1, 0, 0},
      {0, 1, 0, 1, 0}, {0, 0, 1, 0, 1}, {1, 0, 0, 1, 0}}

EulerianCycle

The `Directed` tag in `EulerianCycle` no longer makes sense because the cycle type depends on whether the input graph is directed or undirected. The tag is ignored and an error message is emitted.

In[126]:= **EulerianCycle[CompleteGraph[5], Directed]**

EulerianCycle::obsolete:
   Usage of Directed as a second argument to EulerianCycle
   is obsolete.

Out[126]= {2, 3, 1, 4, 5, 3, 4, 2, 5, 1, 2}

EulerianQ

The `Directed` tag in `EulerianQ` no longer makes sense because the cycle type depends on whether the input graph is directed or undirected. The tag is ignored and an error message is emitted.

In[127]:= **EulerianQ[CompleteGraph[5], Directed]**

EulerianQ::obsolete:
   Usage of Directed as a second argument to EulerianQ is
   obsolete.

Out[127]= True

ExpandGraph

ExpandGraph currently works but is obsolete and will be phased out. Use AddVertices instead. This shows how equivalent behavior can be obtained via AddVertices.

In[128]:= **ShowGraph[AddVertices[Cycle[4], 5]];**

FindCycle

FindCycle does not support the Directed tag. Whether the function finds a directed or an undirected cycle depends on the graph.

In[129]:= **FindCycle[Cycle[5], Directed]**

FindCycle::obsolete:
    Usage of Directed as a second argument to FindCycle is
      obsolete.

Out[129]= {5, 1, 2, 3, 4, 5}

GrayCode

Gray codes refer to an arrangement of combinatorial objects such that there is minimum change between consecutive objects. The new *Combinatorica* provides support for Gray code orderings of several additional combinatorial objects beyond just subsets. For this reason, we decided to change the name of GrayCode to GrayCodeSubsets, so that the fact that we are talking about subsets becomes explicit.

In[130]:= **{GrayCode[{1, 2, 3}],**
         GrayCodeSubsets[{1, 2, 3}]} // ColumnForm

Out[130]=

{{}, {3}, {2, 3}, {2}, {1, 2}, {1, 2, 3}, {1, 3}, {1}}
{{}, {3}, {2, 3}, {2}, {1, 2}, {1, 2, 3}, {1, 3}, {1}}

NetworkFlowEdges

Combinatorica now provides significantly expanded functionality for network flows. By using different tags, the user can seek a variety of information from the function NetworkFlow. For example, the user can get just the value of a maximum flow or the set of edges through which positive flow is being transported or the set of edges that form a minimum cut. This function renders the function NetworkFlowEdges from the old *Combinatorica* obsolete.

To illustrate the usage of NetworkFlow we construct an edge-weighted graph.

```
In[131]:= g = SetEdgeWeights[GridGraph[3, 2], WeightingFunction ->
              RandomInteger, WeightRange -> {1, 100}]
Out[131]= -Graph:<7, 6, Undirected>-
```

This is the set of edges through which positive flow is being sent, listed along with the amount of flow being sent through each edge.

```
In[132]:= f = NetworkFlow[g, 1, 6, Edge]
Out[132]= {{{1, 2}, 31}, {{2, 3}, 5}, {{2, 5}, 26},
            {{3, 6}, 5}, {{5, 6}, 26}}
```

This produces an adjacency matrix with flows, as it used to in the old *Combinatorica*. However, we consider this function obsolete and recommend that users use NetworkFlow instead.

```
In[133]:= NetworkFlowEdges[g, 1, 6] // TableForm
Out[133]//TableForm= 0    31    0    0    0    0
                     31   0     5    0    26   0
                     0    5     0    0    0    5
                     0    0     0    0    0    0
                     0    26    0    0    0    26
                     0    0     5    0    26   0
```

The output of NetworkFlow can be easily massaged into an adjacency matrix form in case it is important to mimic the behavior of NetworkFlowEdges.

```
In[134]:= {e, v} = {Map[First, f], Map[Last, f]};
          ToAdjacencyMatrix[SetEdgeWeights[FromUnorderedPairs[e], v],
          EdgeWeight] /. Infinity -> 0 // TableForm
Out[135]//TableForm= 0    31    0    0    0    0
                     31   0     5    0    26   0
                     0    5     0    0    0    5
                     0    0     0    0    0    0
                     0    26    0    0    0    26
                     0    0     5    0    26   0
```

NthPermutation

To make the names more consistent, we defined UnrankPermutation. This renders NthPermutation obsolete.

```
In[136]:= ?NthPermutation

NthPermutation[n, l] gives the nth lexicographic
   permutation of list l. This function is obsolete; use
   UnrankPermutation instead.
```

This illustrates the usage of UnrankPermutation.

```
In[137]:= Clear[a, b, c, d, e]; UnrankPermutation[10, {a, b, c, d, e}]
Out[137]= {a, c, e, b, d}
```

Polya

One of the highlights of the new *Combinatorica* is the large number of functions for Pólya-theoretic computations. These render Polya obsolete.

For example, here we use
`OrbitInventory` to produce the
polynomial that `Polya[g, m]`
produced, assuming that *g* is the cyclic
group of order 8.

In[138]:= `Clear[m, x];`
        `OrbitInventory[CycleIndex[CyclicGroup[8], x], x, m]`

Out[139]= $\dfrac{m}{2} + \dfrac{m^2}{4} + \dfrac{m^4}{8} + \dfrac{m^8}{8}$

In the old *Combinatorica* the cyclic
group would have to be explicitly
generated, while now we have
functions such as `SymmetricGroup`,
`CyclicGroup`, `DihedralGroup`,
`AlternatingGroup`, etc., that generate
groups commonly used in
Pólya-theoretic calculations.

In[140]:= `DihedralGroup[4]`

Out[140]= {{1, 2, 3, 4}, {4, 1, 2, 3}, {3, 4, 1, 2},
        {2, 3, 4, 1}, {4, 3, 2, 1}, {3, 2, 1, 4}, {2, 1, 4, 3},
        {1, 4, 3, 2}}

ShowGraph

`ShowGraph` has changed dramatically,
and its abilities are one highlight of the
new *Combinatorica*. This example
reveals some of the new functionality
of `ShowGraph`, but the only real way to
understand the improvement in
`ShowGraph` is by experimenting with it.
The new *Combinatorica* also contains
the functions `Highlight` and
`ShowGraphArray`, which enhance the
graph drawing capabilities of the
package significantly.

In[141]:= `ShowGraph[GridGraph[3, 3], {{{1, 2}, EdgeStyle -> Thick},`
        `{5, 6, VertexStyle -> Box[Large]}},`
        `EdgeColor -> Red, Background -> Yellow]`

Using `Directed` as a tag for `ShowGraph`
makes no sense. *Combinatorica* responds
with an obsolete error message while
ignoring the provided tag.

In[142]:= `ShowGraph[CompleteGraph[5], Directed];`

`ShowGraph::obsolete:`
    `Usage of Directed as a second argument to ShowGraph is`
    `obsolete.`

1.4 An Overview of *Mathematica*

In this section, we give an overview of the *Mathematica* programming language, which *Combinatorica* is implemented in and runs on top of. Familiarity with the *Mathematica* language is important for understanding the implementation of our algorithms but *not* to experiment with *Combinatorica*. So do not worry too much about this section during your initial exposure to the package. Just remember that it is here in case you want help understanding our code or some of the constructs used in our more complicated examples.

The most complete reference on *Mathematica* is [Wol99], which includes a full language description as well as a cogent explanation of the philosophy of *Mathematica* and how it compares to other programming languages. You need to have a copy of the language description in front of you for serious work with *Mathematica*. Fortunately, it is included as on-line help in modern versions of *Mathematica*.

With a programming language as rich as *Mathematica*, the novice is likely to be overwhelmed with the number of different ways to do things. In fact, it takes a good deal of experience to find the *correct* way to write a particular program. The functions in this book provide good examples of real *Mathematica* programs, since many of them have been rewritten several times for clarity and efficiency.

The self-help facility in *Mathematica* provides a brief description of each function available on-line. Typing ?Append gives you a description of the Append function, while ??Append provides additional information that may or may not be useful. Included with the distribution of our combinatorial and graph-theoretic functions are documentation strings for all of the major functions, so these can be accessed in an identical manner.

Packages such as *Combinatorica* must be loaded into *Mathematica*, after which the new functions are indistinguishable from built-in *Mathematica* functions.

```
In[143]:= <<DiscreteMath`Combinatorica`
```

The help string for each of the functions that we develop is identical to the description in the glossary of procedures in the back of this book.

```
In[144]:= ?Permute
Permute[l, p] permutes list l according to permutation p.
```

For these new functions, the implementation is given when ?? is used. These implementations are not formatted as nicely as in the text or in the Combinatorica.m source file. We recommend that you read the source file if you really want to study our code.

```
In[145]:= ??PermutationQ
PermutationQ[p] yields True if p is a list representing a
    permutation and False otherwise.
Attributes[PermutationQ] = {Protected}
PermutationQ[
    DiscreteMath`Combinatorica`Private`e_List] :=
    Sort[DiscreteMath`Combinatorica`Private`e] ===
    Range[Length[DiscreteMath`Combinatorica`Private`e]]
```

The * character is a wildcard, matching everything. With wildcards, the names of all matched functions are returned.

```
In[146]:= ?Add*

AddEdge        AddOnHelpPath AddVertex      AddVertices

AddEdges       AddTo
```

It is beyond the scope of this book to provide a complete introduction to the *Mathematica* language. However, in the interest of making our treatment self-contained, we give a terse guide to the major constructs of *Mathematica*. Since the discussion is limited to the facilities we use frequently, graphics and symbolic computation will not be included.

■ 1.4.1 The Structure of Functions

Mathematica is best thought of as a *functional* programming language. All functions in *Mathematica* are call-by-value, meaning that it is impossible to write a function that changes the value of its arguments. Although it is possible to change the value of a global variable within a *Mathematica* function, it is usually not a great idea. The correct way to get a result from a function is to return it as a value.

Since the text of this book contains many syntactically correct *Mathematica* functions, we limit the discussion here to a single example, which illustrates several features but does not compute anything meaningful:

```
FunctionName[arg1_Integer?OddQ, Graph, argn_List] :=
     Module[{v1, vk},
            v1 = vk = arg1;
            vk
     ] /; MemberQ[argn,arg1]
```

Example *Mathematica* Function

This function could be invoked using FunctionName[3,Graph,{1,3}], with the arguments bound to the names arg1 and argn. The underscore _ signifies that a pattern is to be matched, with _Integer?OddQ to match an object with *head* Integer such that the predicate OddQ returns True. Further, the entire function matches only if the membership condition is satisfied, where such conditions are defined with /;. Module is an optional structure used to create local variables, in this case the names v1 and vk.

This loads the above function.   `In[147]:= <<extraCode/example.m`

When invoked as above, this function   `In[148]:= FunctionName[3,Graph,{1,3}]`
should return 3.
                                          `Out[148]= 3`

The function returns unevaluated unless all of its preconditions are satisfied.

```
In[149]:= FunctionName[5,Graph,{1,3}] || FunctionName[3,List,{1,3}] ||
          FunctionName[2,Graph,{1,2}]
Out[149]= FunctionName[5, Graph, {1, 3}] ||

      FunctionName[3, List, {1, 3}] ||

      FunctionName[2, Graph, {1, 2}]
```

The value that a function returns is either the value of the last statement executed within the function, or the value of x if `Return[x]` is invoked. Statements within the body of a function are separated by `;`, which returns a `Null` value.

Mathematica uses dynamic scoping to associate names with variables, meaning that the name is bound to the most recently created, active instance of the variable. Thus, if a variable is not declared in the `Module` of the current function, the one that called it is checked, and so on up the calling chain until the global name space is reached. Variables become dereferenced when a `Module` is exited or when cleared with `Clear[x]`.

A nice property of *Mathematica* is that it is an *extensible* language, meaning that new functions are invoked in the same way as built-in functions. Thus *Combinatorica* can be thought of as an extension to *Mathematica* for discrete mathematics. There is no reason why you need be aware that *Combinatorica* functions are *not* part of *Mathematica* after they are loaded.

We shall observe the standard *Mathematica* conventions for naming functions. Every name is completely spelled out, with no abbreviations used. The first letter of each word is capitalized and multiword titles are concatenated. These rules serve to ensure logical consistency, at the expense of a little typing. For example, the name of the function to find the inverse of a permutation is `InversePermutation`, not `Inversepermutation`, not `InversePerm`, and definitely not `InPerm`. Predicates, functions that return `True` or `False`, all have names that end with `Q`. Thus, the name of the function that tests whether a list is a permutation is `PermutationQ`.

■ 1.4.2 Mathematical Operations

Mathematica has a large number of mathematical operations available, most of which are self-explanatory, since they follow the naming convention discussed above.

The basic binary arithmetic operations are `+`, `-`, `*`, `/`, and `^` for exponentiation. The functional equivalences of these are `Plus`, `Subtract`, `Times`, `Divide`, and `Power`. The assignment operator is `=` or `Set`. There is a full range of trigonometric functions, including the basic `Sin`, `Cos`, and `Tan`. `Ceiling` and `Floor` round real numbers up or down, while `Abs` finds the absolute value of its argument. Pseudorandom integers and reals over a specified interval can be generated with `Random`. Most of the 1000-plus functions built in to *Mathematica* are of this flavor, and we avoid giving a complete list here.

There are assignment operators for the basic arithmetic operations: `+=`, `-=`, `*=`, and `/=`.

```
In[150]:= (x=10; x*=10)
Out[150]= 100
```

As in the C language, there are pre- and post-increment and decrement operators, which return the value after or before it changes.

```
In[151]:= {++x,x++}
Out[151]= {101, 101}
```

This is the first middle binomial coefficient $\binom{2n}{n}$ with residue $(-1)^n$ when $2n + 1$ is composite, thus answering an open problem in [GKP89].

```
In[152]:= Mod[ Binomial[5906,2953], 5907]
Out[152]= 5906
```

Mathematica has two main data types for representing numbers. By default, exact rational arithmetic is used for all computations. This means that arbitrary precision integers are used, with fractions reduced to their lowest terms. If this level of precision is unnecessary, Real numbers are much faster and more convenient, with N[x] being the way to convert x to Real with the default precision.

Observe that Pi remains unexpanded without N, since any expansion results in a loss of precision. The number of digits in the expansion of π can be specified with N.

```
In[153]:= {N[Pi,100], Pi}
Out[153]= {3.141592653589793238462643383279502884197169399371
          5105820974944592307816406286208998628034825342117068,
          Pi}
```

Working with arbitrary precision arithmetic takes some getting used to, for irrational quantities are not evaluated as numbers until treated with N. Fortunately, this is a book about *discrete* mathematics, and so these problems do not arise often.

```
In[154]:= Sqrt[28]
Out[154]= 2 Sqrt[7]
```

Zeno's paradox states that someone repeatedly moving halfway to the goal line never scores a touchdown. The Sum command implements the $\sum$ notation of mathematics. Observe that the result is given as a rational number, since it was not specified otherwise.

```
In[155]:= Sum[ 1/(2^i), {i,1,100}]
         1267650600228229401496703205375
Out[155]= ───────────────────────────────
         1267650600228229401496703205376
```

N is used to convert a rational number to a real. Computations on reals are much faster since there is no reduction to lowest terms.

```
In[156]:= Sum[ N[ 1/(2^i) ], {i,1,100}]
Out[156]= 1.
```

The Product command is analogous to the $\prod$ notation, here computing 100!. Observe that the iterator notation starts with $i = 1$ by default, incrementing by 1 each time.

```
In[157]:= Product[i, {i,100}]
Out[157]= 9332621544394415268169923885626670049071596826438\
          6214685929638952175999932299156089414639761565182862536\
          97920827223758251185210916864000000000000000000000000
```

All major matrix operations are available in *Mathematica*.

```
In[158]:= {Eigenvalues[IdentityMatrix[4]], Det[IdentityMatrix[4]]}
Out[158]= {{1, 1, 1, 1}, 1}
```

Dot products are used for matrix multiplication.

```
In[159]:= TableForm[{{1},{2},{3}} . {{1,2,3}}]
Out[159]//TableForm= 1   2   3
                     2   4   6
                     3   6   9
```

A wide variety of number-theoretic functions also prove useful.

```
In[160]:= Divisors[16] && FactorInteger[4332749032784732342]
Out[160]= {1, 2, 4, 8, 16} &&
          {{2, 1}, {1459, 1}, {1484835172304569, 1}}
```

■ 1.4.3 List Manipulation

The basic data structure in *Mathematica* is the *list,* which has a tremendous amount of versatility. Permutations are represented as lists, as are partitions and subsets. Matrices and Young tableaux are lists of lists, while `Graph` structures are basically a collection of two lists of lists.

Mathematica provides several ways to access a particular element or set of elements from a list, by presenting the illusion that a list is an array. The *i*th element of a list *l* is given by `l[[i]]` or `Part[l,i]`, and so by letting a counter *i* run from 1 to `Length[l]` each element of the list can be accessed in a sequential fashion. A list of the first *n* elements of *l* is given by `Take[l,n]`, while the last *n* elements are extracted by `Take[l,-n]`. A list *without* the first *n* elements of *l* is obtained by `Drop[l,n]`. Various special cases of these operations are available, such as `First`, `Last`, and `Rest`.

Lists can be enlarged with `Join`, `Append`, and `Prepend`. Nested lists can be restructured by `Partition` or `Flatten`, which adds or removes the innermost levels of parentheses from a list. The nesting associated with regular, two-dimensional lists such as matrices can be rearranged with `Transpose`. A circular shift of the elements of a list is achieved by `RotateLeft` or `RotateRight`. The elements of a list can be placed in the appropriate canonical order with `Sort` and then reversed with `Reverse`. `Replace` and `ReplaceAll` can be used to edit arbitrary structures according to transformation rules.

It is important to realize that all of these operations leave the original list unchanged. Besides =, very few operations in *Mathematica* have side effects. `AppendTo` and `PrependTo` are exceptions; they have the same syntax as `Append` and `Prepend` but change the value of the first argument. Using the array notation, the *i*th element of a list can be changed, as in `l[[i]] = 5;`, but *Mathematica* rewrites the entire list *l* when doing this, so modifying an element of a list is in fact a linear-time operation.

First and Rest are equivalent to CAR and CDR in old versions of Lisp. Range[n] is a very useful function that returns a list of the first *n* positive integers.

```
In[161]:= {First[Range[10]], Rest[Range[10]]}
Out[161]= {1, {2, 3, 4, 5, 6, 7, 8, 9, 10}}
```

These two restructuring operations give the same results on these lists, since the first-level list contains only two elements. Most operations by default work only on first-level structures. The % is shorthand for the result of the previous input.

```
In[162]:= {Reverse[%], RotateLeft[%,1]}
Out[162]= {{{2, 3, 4, 5, 6, 7, 8, 9, 10}, 1},
          {{2, 3, 4, 5, 6, 7, 8, 9, 10}, 1}}
```

Join merges two lists on equal terms, while Append makes the second argument the last element of the first argument, which must be a list.

```
In[163]:= MatrixForm[ {Join[{1,2,3},{4,5,6}], Append[{1,2,3},{4,5,6}],
          Prepend[{1,2,3},{4,5,6}]}]
Out[163]//MatrixForm= {1, 2, 3, 4, 5, 6}
                      {1, 2, 3, {4, 5, 6}}
                      {{4, 5, 6}, 1, 2, 3}
```

Regular two-dimensional list structures, such as matrices, can be transposed.

```
In[164]:= Transpose[{{1,2},{3,4},{5,6}}]
Out[164]= {{1, 3, 5}, {2, 4, 6}}
```

Partition is a very useful function for partitioning the elements of a list into regular-sized structures. Here the list is partitioned into two element lists, where successive lists have an overlap of one element.

```
In[165]:= Partition[{a,b,c,d,e,f},2,1]
Out[165]= {{a, b}, {b, c}, {c, d}, {d, e},
          {e, {{{1, 2}, 31}, {{2, 3}, 5}, {{2, 5}, 26},
          {{3, 6}, 5}, {{5, 6}, 26}}}}
```

All major set operations are supported as operations on lists. Lists that represent sets are sorted, with the multiplicities removed.

```
In[166]:= Union[ Intersection[{5,2,3,2},{1,2,3}],
          Complement[{1,2,3,4,5},{1,2}] ]
Out[166]= {2, 3, 4, 5}
```

Mathematica has a notion of Infinity that can be used to simplify computations with Min and Max operations.

```
In[167]:= Max[{3, 5, 5.6, Infinity, 2}]
Out[167]= Infinity
```

■ 1.4.4 Iteration

To exploit the fact that computers execute programs faster than people can write them, a language must have some facility for looping, or executing a block of code more than once. In a structured language, this is usually done through *iteration*. *Mathematica* has statements similar to While and For from C and Do as in Fortran. Unique to *Mathematica* is Table, which constructs a list where the *i*th element is some prescribed function of *i*.

Since data structures in *Mathematica* are lists, it is often necessary to perform some function on each element of a list, or to compute some function of the entire list. The right way to do this is with Map and Apply. Map[f,l], where f is some function and l is a list, returns a list where the *i*th element is f[l[[i]]]. Apply[f,l] invokes f exactly once, where the *i*th argument of f is taken as l[[i]]. Map can be emulated in a clumsy way using Table, but Apply[f,l] is *not* the same as f[l], since there will be an extra set of brackets around l that we do not want.

EvenQ is a function that returns True if the argument is even, so mapping it over the integers alternates False and True.

In[168]:= **Map[EvenQ, Range[10]]**

Out[168]= {False, True, False, True, False, True, False, True, False, True}

Here Map and Apply work together to test whether Range[10] consists of all even numbers.

In[169]:= **Apply[And, Map[EvenQ, Range[10]]]**

Out[169]= False

Without the Apply, And does not do its thing.

In[170]:= **And[Map[EvenQ,Range[10]]]**

Out[170]= {False, True, False, True, False, True, False, True, False, True}

Both Map-Apply and Apply-Map can be useful paradigms for working with lists. This computes the sums of each sublist.

In[171]:= **Map[(Apply[Plus,#])&,{{1,2},{3,4},{5,6}}]**

Out[171]= {3, 7, 11}

Scan is identical to Map, except that a list is not constructed. Any useful computation with Scan is done via side effects.

Because Map, Scan, and Apply take functions as arguments, making full use of them requires a convenient mechanism for declaring short functions. Such short functions are called *pure* functions because no name is associated with them. An example of a pure function in *Mathematica* is (Apply[Plus,#])&, as declared above. The argument to this nameless function is #, which is treated in the same way as any other parameter. An alternative way to define this pure function is Function[n,Apply[Plus,n]], which can be used to prevent # from being confused with nested pure functions.

Here is the previous example with an alternative representation of the pure function.

In[172]:= **Map[Function[n,Apply[Plus,n]], {{1,2},{3,4},{5,6},{7,8}}]**

Out[172]= {3, 7, 11, 15}

The most natural way to implement many of the algorithms in this book is through *recursion*, breaking the problem into smaller problems of the same type. If the subproblems are truly of the same type, they can be solved by calling the same function that solved the bigger one. For this reason, recursive implementations of programs follow almost directly from an inductive definition of a problem [Man89]. *Mathematica* supports recursion, and we use it often as a fast and elegant alternative to iteration. As a consequence of how *Mathematica* is implemented, a recursive program is often faster than an equivalent iterative one.

■ 1.4.5 Ten Little *n*-Sums

To illustrate the range of different control structures available in *Mathematica*, and the effect that the right choice can have on efficiency, in the following we give ten different ways to sum up the first million positive integers. You might be surprised at the timing results, although of course this is one particular version of *Mathematica* running on one particular machine. The timings are given as ratios with respect to the best time. Your mileage may vary.

The fastest way to compute this sum directly is to construct the list of integers and use `Apply`. The reason is that no explicit iteration is being performed, with the moral being that using built-in functions like `Range` coupled with functional operators like `Map` and `Apply` is usually the right way to go.

```
In[173]:= t = Timing[Apply[Plus,Range[1000000]]]
Out[173]= {4.59 Second, 500000500000}
```

The `Do` loop is the most straightforward iteration structure. There is no exit from the loop until the prescribed number of iterations takes place, even with a `Return`.

```
In[174]:= Timing[s=0; Do[s+=i,{i,1000000}]; s] / t
Out[174]= {4.3159, 1}
```

The `For` loop has initialization, test, increment, and body sections, all of which are separated by commas. The price for this extra flexibility over the `Do` is efficiency.

```
In[175]:= Timing[ For[s=0; i=1, i<=1000000, i++, s += i]; s] / t
Out[175]= {9.05011, 1}
```

The `While` loop is not as natural for this problem, since the counter must be maintained explicitly, but in fact `For` is simply a disguised `While`.

```
In[176]:= Timing[ s=0; i=1; While[i<=1000000, s+=(i++)]; s] / t
Out[176]= {8.98911, 1}
```

`Scan` is even less natural for this problem. A list of the numbers from 1 to 1,000,000 is constructed and then traversed, maintaining a running sum.

```
In[177]:= Timing[ s=0; Scan[(s+=#)&, Range[1000000]]; s] / t
Out[177]= {6.56645, 1}
```

`Sum` is the cleanest way to compute this sum, since it is an implementation of the $\sum$ operator. It is faster than most other implementations, but it is *not* the fastest way to solve the problem. `Clear[i]` removes the previous value of `i`. The iteration operations are sometimes fussy about this.

```
In[178]:= Clear[i]; Timing[ Sum[i,{i,1,1000000}] ] / t
Out[178]= {1.16776, 1}
```

Our second class of implementations is based on list construction operations. With respect to summations, this means building a list of all partial sums before extracting the one that is desired. Although this is a roundabout way to perform the computation, it is instructive because list construction operations will be used throughout the book more often than iteration.

`Table` is the simplest way to construct a list.

```
In[179]:= Timing[s=0; Last[ Table[s+=i,{i,1000000}] ] ] / t
Out[179]= {4.5817, 1}
```

FoldList applies a function to each of the prefixes of the list, returning a list of the results, and Fold returns the last element of the list constructed by FoldList. For sufficiently short lists, this function is surprisingly competitive with Apply, considering you get all of the other sums for free.

```
In[180]:= Timing[ Fold[Plus, 0, Range[1000000]]]/t
Out[180]= {1.55991, 1}
```

Although Map is being used inappropriately in this example, it is the best way to apply a function to each element of the list. The increment function is being applied to 1,000,000 elements in this list, making a new list of which the first 999,999 elements are ignored, and *still* Map is competitive with the iteration structures.

```
In[181]:= Timing[ s=0; Last[ Map[(s+=#)&, Range[1000000]] ] ] / t
Out[181]= {9.30719, 1}
```

As Gauss noticed while still a child, the sum of the first n integers is $n(n + 1)/2$. This illustrates that improving the algorithm is always more important than improving the implementation.

```
In[182]:= Timing[ Binomial[100001,2] ]
Out[182]= {0. Second, 5000050000}
```

■ 1.4.6 Conditionals

Conditional statements change the flow of control during the execution of a program and are the basis of any interesting computation. In the imperative style of *Mathematica* programming, the If statement is used to select between alternatives. No explicit "then" or "else" is specified, as the appropriate clause is identified by its position in If[condition, then, else]. The "else" clause is optional. Switch generalizes If to more than two-way branches.

A variety of unary predicates (OddQ, EvenQ, MatrixQ) and binary predicates (MemberQ, OrderedQ) are included with *Mathematica*, most but not all of which obey the convention that the names of predicates end with Q. Exceptions include Positive and Negative. Particularly important are the relational operations >, <, <=, >=, and == and the Boolean connectives And, Or, and Not, with shorthand forms of &&, ||, and !, respectively.

One subtlety is the distinction between SameQ and Equal. When two variables x and y have not been bound to specific quantities, in a strict sense the question of whether they are "equal" has no answer. SameQ or === tests whether its two arguments are identical and always returns True or False.

Since X is not bound, no Boolean value results.

```
In[183]:= X == 5
Out[183]= X == 5
```

Leaving out one equal sign makes this an assignment instead of a comparison and can lead to hard-to-find bugs.

```
In[184]:= X = 5
Out[184]= 5
```

Now either SameQ or Equal will return True.

```
In[185]:= X === 5 && X == 5
Out[185]= True
```

Several higher-order constructs permit us to get conditional behavior without the explicit use of If. Position identifies which elements in a list satisfy a given condition, in a format that can be used by the conditional mapping function MapAt. Select returns a list of which elements in a given list satisfy a particular criterion. Count computes how often a particular element occurs in a list.

The odd positions in this 11-element list contain the even values. The positions are given within brackets because Position traverses nested structures. The pattern match is necessary when using Position.

```
In[186]:= Position[Range[10,20], _?EvenQ]
Out[186]= {{1}, {3}, {5}, {7}, {9}, {11}}
```

Select returns the (possibly empty) set of elements satisfying the condition.

```
In[187]:= Select[Range[10,20],EvenQ]
Out[187]= {10, 12, 14, 16, 18, 20}
```

■ 1.4.7 Compiling *Mathematica* Code

An important source of speedup in *Combinatorica* is due to compiling selected pieces of *Mathematica* code. Functions such as SpringEmbedding and AllPairsShortestPath are faster than in the old *Combinatorica* by several orders of magnitude because of code compilation. *Mathematica* provides great flexibility by not requiring users to specify the types of function arguments up-front. For example, a user may send an integer, a real, a list, an algebraic expression, or a symbol into a function for an argument. This flexibility imposes considerable space and time overhead. If a user knows the types of function arguments beforehand, and if these are simple – either integers or reals or Booleans or regularly structured lists of these types, then such a function can be compiled. *Mathematica* will store this function as a CompiledObject consisting of efficient internal code.

Here is an iteration that goes through a half-million times with an initial value of $t = 0.37$.

```
In[188]:= Timing[t = 0.37; Do[t = 4t(1 - t), {500000}]; t]
Out[188]= {13.31 Second, 0.844712}
```

Here the expression is compiled into a two-argument function called fc. The first argument x has a default machine real type, while the second argument has an explicitly specified Integer type. The result is a CompiledFunction object.

```
In[189]:= fc = Compile[{x, {n, _Integer}},
              Module[{t}, t = x; Do[t = 4t(1 - t), {n}]; t]]
Out[189]= CompiledFunction[{x, n},
     Module[{t}, t = x; Do[t = 4 t (1 - t), {n}]; t],
     -CompiledCode-]
```

Note the difference in running times between the compiled and the uncompiled versions.

```
In[190]:= Timing[fc[0.37, 500000]]
Out[190]= {1.1 Second, 0.844712}
```

This tension between flexibility and speed has led to many interesting design choices in *Combinatorica*. We wanted a flexible graph data structure with the ability to store drawing information that took advantage of any sparsity that the input graph might have. These considerations implied a somewhat "irregular" graph data structure, one that could not be sent in as an argument to compiled functions. Therefore, to be able to Compile a *Combinatorica* graph function, we must first construct a "regular" graph representation, for example, an adjacency matrix. For fast graph functions such as BreadthFirstTraversal, the overhead of converting the graph data structure into a more regular representation is too much, so compiling code makes no sense. For certain slower graph functions such as AllPairsShortestPath, converting the graph into an adjacency matrix and compiling the function leads to a substantial savings in time.

```
AllPairsShortestPath[g_Graph] := {} /; (V[g] == 0)
AllPairsShortestPath[g_Graph] :=
        Module[{p = ToAdjacencyMatrix[g, EdgeWeight, Type->Simple], m},
            m = V[g]*Ceiling[Max[Cases[Flatten[p], _Real | _Integer]]]+1;
            Zap[DP1[p /. {0 -> 0.0, x_Integer -> 1.0 x, Infinity -> m*1.0}, m]] /. m -> Infinity
        ]

DP1 = Compile[{{p, _Real, 2}, {m, _Integer}},
        Module[{np = p, k, n = Length[p]},
            Do[np = Table[If[(np[[i, k]] == 1.0*m) || (np[[k, j]] == 1.0*m),
                        np[[i,j]], Min[np[[i,k]]+ np[[k,j]], np[[i,j]]]
                    ], {i,n},{j,n}
                ], {k, n}];
            np
        ]
    ]
```

Compiling Code in AllPairsShortestPath

In the function AllPairShortestPath shown above, the graph *g* is first converted into a matrix *p* via the ToAdjacencyMatrix function. This matrix may contain integers, reals, and possibly ∞. To prepare this matrix further, integers in *p* are replaced by equivalent reals and ∞ is replaced by a large enough real. Then this matrix of reals is sent in as an argument to the compiled function DP1.

Here we time AllPairsShortestPath on a six-dimensional hypercube with random edge weights.

```
In[191]:= g = SetEdgeWeights[Hypercube[6]];
          Timing[AllPairsShortestPath[g];]
Out[192]= {4.08 Second, Null}
```

And here we time an uncompiled version of the function on the same graph.

```
In[193]:= << extraCode/UnCompiledAPSP;
          Timing[APSP[ToAdjacencyMatrix[g, EdgeWeight]];]
Out[194]= {15.52 Second, Null}
```

2. Permutations and Combinations

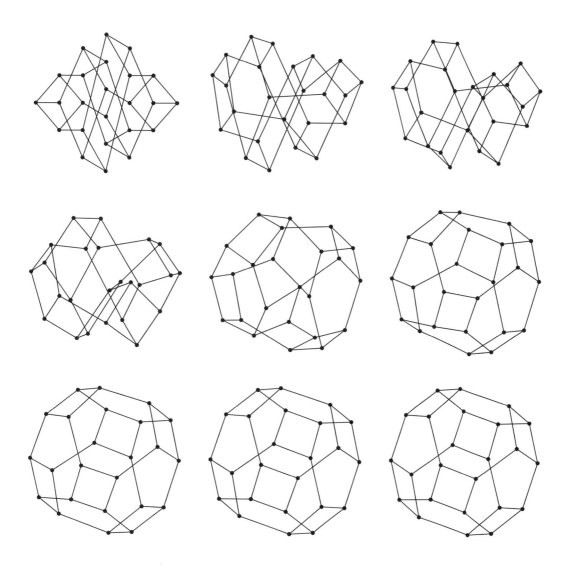

Combinatorics is the study of counting, and over the years mathematicians have counted a variety of different things. More recently, mathematicians have become interested in enumeration and random selection from sets of objects. Tools from computer science are crucial in ensuring that these tasks are done efficiently.

Perhaps the most fundamental combinatorial object is the *permutation*, which we define as an ordering of the integers 1 to n without repetition. Closely related to permutations are *combinations*, that is, distinct subsets of a set whose order does not matter. In this chapter, we provide algorithms for enumerating and selecting permutations and combinations in a variety of ways, each of which has distinct useful properties.

Even though permutations and combinations are simple structures, studying them closely leads to many important concepts in mathematics and computer science. We will encounter recurrence relations, generating functions, dynamic programming, randomized algorithms, and Hamiltonian cycles in this chapter. The programming examples included here provide a proper introduction to the *Mathematica* programming style. We will see that writing efficient functions in *Mathematica* is a different game than in conventional programming languages.

About the illustration overleaf:

An exchange of any two adjacent elements of a permutation yields a different permutation, and by applying adjacent transpositions in a certain order all $n!$ distinct permutations can be constructed. The illustration shows the *adjacent transposition graph* of the set of permutations on four elements, where each vertex represents a permutation and there is an edge whenever two permutations differ by exactly one adjacent transposition. All nine pictures show the same graph; on the top left is a *ranked embedding*, which is then transformed, using a *spring embedding* algorithm, into the *truncated octahedron* shown on the bottom left. By using tools that we will develop, we can construct and display this adjacent transposition graph as follows:

```
atr = MemberQ[Table[p = #1; {p[[i]], p[[i + 1]]} = {p[[i + 1]], p[[i]]}; p, {i, Length[#1]-1}], #2]&;
g = RankedEmbedding[MakeGraph[Permutations[4], atr, Type->Undirected], {1}];
ShowGraphArray[Partition[Table[SpringEmbedding[g, i], {i, 0, 40, 5}], 3]]
```

2.1 Generating Permutations

A permutation can be viewed as a linear arrangement of objects or as a rearrangement operation. When thought of as an operation, a permutation specifies distinct new positions for each of n objects arranged linearly. We define a *size-n permutation* (an *n-permutation*, in short) to be an ordering of the integers 1 to n without repetition. We will use π to denote permutations and use $\pi(i)$ to denote the ith element in π. Our first *Mathematica* function determines if a given object is a permutation.

```
PermutationQ[e_List] := (Sort[e] === Range[Length[e]])
```

Testing a Permutation

Mathematica array notation provides a slick way to permute a set of objects according to a particular permutation, since elements of one list can be used as indices to select elements of another. The same technique can be used to swap two values without an explicit intermediate variable or to select an arbitrary subset of a set.

```
Permute[l_List,p_?PermutationQ] := l [[ p ]]
Permute[l_List,p_List] := Map[ (Permute[l,#])&, p] /; (Apply[And, Map[PermutationQ, p]])
```

Permuting a List

This loads the *Combinatorica* package.

In[1]:= **<<DiscreteMath`Combinatorica`**

Our restriction of permutations to the integers from 1 to n is not limiting, since we can easily permute a list of whatever we are interested in.

In[2]:= **Permute[{a,b,c,d,e},{5,3,2,1,4}]**

Out[2]= {e, c, b, a, d}

Multiplying permutations should be understood as composing the rearrangement operations. More precisely, if π_1 and π_2 are n-permutations, then $\pi_1 \times \pi_2$ is the rearrangement operation that corresponds to applying π_2 followed by π_1. Thus Permute provides an implementation of permutation multiplication.

(a,b,c,d,e) is rearranged by (1,5,4,2,3) followed by (4,5,1,3,2).

In[3]:= **Permute[Permute[{a,b,c,d,e}, {1,5,4,2,3}], {4,5,1,3,2}]**

Out[3]= {b, c, a, d, e}

This is equivalent to rearranging (a,b,c,d,e) by the product (1,5,4,2,3) × (4,5,1,3,2).

In[4]:= **p=Permute[{1,5,4,2,3}, {4,5,1,3,2}]; Permute[{a,b,c,d,e}, p]**

Out[4]= {b, c, a, d, e}

The multiplication of permutations is not commutative.

In[5]:= **p == Permute[{4,5,1,3,2},{1,5,4,2,3}]**

Out[5]= False

But it is associative. Here we see that $(a \times b) \times c = a \times (b \times c)$.

```
In[6]:= Permute[Permute[a = RandomPermutation[20],
                    b = RandomPermutation[20]
               ], c = RandomPermutation[20]
          ] === Permute[a, Permute[b, c]]
Out[6]= True
```

The *identity* is the permutation $(1, 2, ..., n)$ that maps every element to itself. For every permutation π there is a unique permutation, denoted π^{-1}, such that $\pi \times \pi^{-1} = \pi^{-1} \times \pi$ equals the identity. π^{-1} is the *multiplicative inverse* or, more simply, the *inverse* of π. Clearly, $\pi^{-1}[j] = k$ if and only if $\pi[k] = j$.

```
InversePermutation[p_?PermutationQ] :=
     Module[{inverse=p},
          Do[ inverse[[ p[[i]] ]] = i, {i,Length[p]} ];
          inverse
     ]
IdentityPermutation[n_Integer] := Range[n]
```

The Inverse of a Permutation and the Identity Permutation

The product of a permutation and its inverse is the identity.

```
In[7]:= Permute[p = RandomPermutation[20], InversePermutation[p]] ==
               IdentityPermutation[20]
Out[7]= True
```

The rest of this section will be devoted to the problems of generating, ranking, and unranking permutations. Their solutions include interesting algorithms that provide an introduction to building combinatorial objects with *Mathematica*.

■ 2.1.1 Lexicographically Ordered Permutations

Constructing all permutations is such an important operation that *Mathematica* includes the function Permutations to do it. Algorithms for constructing permutations are surveyed in [Sed77].

The most straightforward way to construct all permutations of the n items of a list l is to successively pull each element out of l and prepend it to each permutation of the $n - 1$ other items. This procedure tells us right away that $n!$ is the number of permutations of n items.

A faster way to do this in *Mathematica* is by iteratively generating the next permutation in lexicographic order. The lexicographic successor of a size-n permutation π is obtained as follows. First find the largest decreasing suffix of π, say $\pi[i + 1, ..., n]$. Since this suffix is largest, $\pi[i] < \pi[i + 1]$. Therefore, $\pi[i + 1, ..., n]$ contains an element $\pi[j]$ that is the smallest element greater than $\pi[i]$. Exchange $\pi[i]$ and $\pi[j]$ and then reverse $\pi[i + 1, ..., n]$. For example, let $\pi = (4, 3, 1, 5, 2)$. The largest decreasing suffix is $(5, 2)$ and $\pi[i] = 1$. The smallest element in this suffix larger than 1 is 2. The subsequent exchanging and reversing gives $(4, 3, 2, 1, 5)$. NextPermutation, shown below, implements this algorithm.

```
NextPermutation[l_List] := Sort[l] /; (l === Reverse[Sort[l]])

NextPermutation[l_List] :=
     Module[{n = Length[l], i, j, t, nl = l},
          i = n-1; While[ Order[nl[[i]], nl[[i+1]]] == -1, i--];
          j = n; While[ Order[nl[[j]], nl[[i]]] == 1, j--];
          {nl[[i]], nl[[j]]} = {nl[[j]], nl[[i]]};
          Join[ Take[nl,i], Reverse[Drop[nl,i]] ]
     ]
```

Constructing the Next Permutation

A size-12 random permutation and its lexicographic successor.

```
In[8]:= {p = RandomPermutation[12], NextPermutation[p]} //ColumnForm
Out[8]= {7, 12, 4, 1, 3, 10, 5, 6, 8, 11, 2, 9}
        {7, 12, 4, 1, 3, 10, 5, 6, 8, 11, 9, 2}
```

The lexicographic successor of the last permutation is the first.

```
In[9]:= NextPermutation[ Reverse[Range[8]] ]
Out[9]= {1, 2, 3, 4, 5, 6, 7, 8}
```

Enumerating lexicographically ordered permutations is now simply a matter of repeatedly calling NextPermutation. The cost of calling a function $n! - 1$ times adds up quickly, so for the sake of speed we use the code from NextPermutation explicitly in LexicographicPermutations. We also use the *Mathematica* function NestList that, given as inputs a function f, an expression x, and an integer n, returns the sequence $(f^0(x), f^1(x), f^2(x), \ldots, f^n(x))$. Here $f^0(x) = x$ and in general, $f^i(x)$ is obtained by starting with x and applying f repeatedly i times. Using such a function not only leads to compact code, but it is also faster than explicitly constructing the list.

However, the most substantial speedup over the earlier version of this function is due to the use of the *Mathematica* function Compile. *Mathematica*'s programming language does not force us to specify the types of inputs upfront. However, this imposes a substantial time and space overhead that can be avoided when we know a priori that all input has a specific, simple type. *Mathematica* can compile functions whose arguments are integers, reals, Boolean, or regularly structured lists of these types. This internal code is stored as a CompiledFunction object that is executed when the function is called. The compiled LexicographicPermutations is roughly ten times faster than the uncompiled version.

```
LP = Compile[{{n, _Integer}},
        Module[{l = Range[n], i, j, t},
             NestList[(i = n-1; While[ #[[i]] > #[[i+1]], i--];
                  j = n; While[ #[[j]] < #[[i]], j--];
                  t = #[[i]]; #[[i]] = #[[j]]; #[[j]] = t;
                  Join[ Take[#,i], Reverse[Drop[#,i]] ])&,
                  l, n!-1
             ]
        ]
     ]
```

```
LexicographicPermutations[0] := {{}}
LexicographicPermutations[1] := {{1}}

LexicographicPermutations[n_Integer?Positive] := LP[n]
LexicographicPermutations[l_List] := Permute[l, LexicographicPermutations[Length[l]] ]
```

Constructing Lexicographically Ordered Permutations

As you can see, the permutations are generated in lexicographic order. The built-in generator Permutations also constructs them in lexicographic order.

```
In[10]:= LexicographicPermutations[3]
Out[10]= {{1, 2, 3}, {1, 3, 2}, {2, 1, 3}, {2, 3, 1},
    {3, 1, 2}, {3, 2, 1}}
```

UnCompiledLexPerms is identical to LexicographicPermutations, except that it is not compiled. The execution time ratios reveal how many times faster the compiled version is than the uncompiled version.

```
In[11]:= <<extraCode/UnCompiledLexPerms;
    Table[Timing[UnCompiledLexPerms[n];][[1, 1]]/
        Timing[LexicographicPermutations[n];][[1, 1]],
        {n, 6, 9}
    ]
Out[12]= {8.5, 11.1818, 11., 8.08787}
```

Using compiled code does not prevent LexicographicPermutations from being able to generate permutations of arbitrary objects. It does this in a slightly indirect manner by first generating all size-*n* permutations for the right *n* and then applying these one at a time onto the given sequence of objects. Despite this, it is faster to use the compiled version of the function even for sequences of objects that are technically not permutations.

```
In[13]:= Clear[P, Q, R, S];
    LexicographicPermutations[{P, Q, R, S}]
Out[14]= {{P, Q, R, S}, {P, Q, S, R}, {P, R, Q, S},
    {P, R, S, Q}, {P, S, Q, R}, {P, S, R, Q}, {Q, P, R, S},
    {Q, P, S, R}, {Q, R, P, S}, {Q, R, S, P}, {Q, S, P, R},
    {Q, S, R, P}, {R, P, Q, S}, {R, P, S, Q}, {R, Q, P, S},
    {R, Q, S, P}, {R, S, P, Q}, {R, S, Q, P}, {S, P, Q, R},
    {S, P, R, Q}, {S, Q, P, R}, {S, Q, R, P}, {S, R, P, Q},
    {S, R, Q, P}}
```

Here we compare our implementation of permutation enumeration to *Mathematica*'s. Despite being a compiled object, LexicographicPermutations is slower than the built-in Permutations.

```
In[15]:= Table[Timing[ LexicographicPermutations[i]; ][[1,1]]
    /Timing[ Permutations[Range[i]]; ][[1,1]], {i,7,9}]
Out[15]= {3., 3.5, 2.60479}
```

This results of this timing experiment should not be too surprising. Even if both functions used the same underlying algorithm, one would expect Permutations to be faster because it is part of the *Mathematica* kernel and exists in machine code. In contrast, LexicographicPermutations exists in internal *Mathematica* code that is supposedly "close" to machine code of a typical computer. In addition to being faster, Permutations can also handle multisets correctly, which is something that LexicographicPermutations cannot do.

Permutations deals with multisets correctly...

```
In[16]:= Permutations[{1, 1, 2}]
Out[16]= {{1, 1, 2}, {1, 2, 1}, {2, 1, 1}}
```

...while LexicographicPermutations does not.

```
In[17]:= LexicographicPermutations[{1, 1, 2}]
Out[17]= {{1, 1, 2}, {1, 2, 1}, {1, 1, 2}, {1, 2, 1},
          {2, 1, 1}, {2, 1, 1}}
```

A natural measure of the amount of work that LexicographicPermutations does is the total number of element exchanges or *transpositions* performed. Let π be a permutation and let $\pi[i+1,...,n]$ denote its longest decreasing suffix. One transposition is needed to introduce $\pi[i]$ into this suffix and $\lfloor(n-i)/2\rfloor$ transpositions are needed to reverse the suffix. Thus NextPermutation performs $1 + \lfloor(n-i)/2\rfloor$ transpositions when acting on a permutation π whose longest decreasing suffix starts at position $(i+1)$. How many transpositions does LexicographicPermutations perform in generating all n-permutations?

The average number of transpositions per permutation appears to approach a limit as n increases. But we can only exhaustively test small values of n. Mean is not built-in, but it is defined in the *Mathematica* add-on package Statistics`DescriptiveStatistics`, which is loaded when *Combinatorica* is.

```
In[18]:= Table[ Mean[
          Map[(i=n-1; While[#[[i]] > #[[i+1]],i--]; 1+Floor[(n-i)/2])&,
          Permutations[n]]]]//N, {n,1,6}]
Out[18]= {1., 1.5, 1.5, 1.54167, 1.54167, 1.54306}
```

For size-100 permutations, we must rely on random sampling, evaluating 1000 random permutations. The number of transpositions required by NextPermutation is calculated for each, and the average of these is reported. This result approaches the same limit.

```
In[19]:= Mean[
          Map[(i=99; While[#[[i]] > #[[i+1]], i--]; 1+Floor[50-i/2])&,
          Table[RandomPermutation[100], {1000}]] ]//N
Out[19]= 1.55
```

The magic limit turns out to be $Cosh(1)$, where $Cosh(z) \equiv (e^z + e^{-z})/2$ is the hyperbolic cosine function.

```
In[20]:= N[ Cosh[1] ]
Out[20]= 1.54308
```

This result motivates the problem of generating permutations in an order that minimizes the total number of transpositions used. This problem will be solved in Section 2.1.4.

■ 2.1.2 Ranking and Unranking Permutations

Since there are $n!$ distinct permutations of size n, any ordering of permutations defines a bijection with the integers from 0 to $n! - 1$. Such a bijection can be used to give several useful operations. For example, if we seek a permutation with a certain property, it can be more efficient to repeatedly construct and test the ith permutation than to build all $n!$ permutations in advance and search.

A *ranking* function for an object determines its position in the underlying total order. For permutations in lexicographic order, the rank of a permutation may be computed by observing that all permutations sharing the same first element k are ranked $(k-1)(n-1)!$ to $k(n-1)! - 1$. After deleting the first element and adjusting the rest of the elements so that we have an $(n-1)$-permutation, we can recurse on the smaller permutation to determine the exact rank. For example, the permutation $(2, 3, 1, 5, 4)$ has rank between 24 and 47 by virtue of its first element. Once 2 is deleted, the rest of the permutation is adjusted from $(3, 1, 5, 4)$ to $(2, 1, 4, 3)$, and the rank of $(2, 1, 4, 3)$ is obtained. Once the contribution of the first element is noted, the element is stripped and the rest of the permutation is adjusted.

```
RankPermutation[{1}] := 0
RankPermutation[{}] := 0

RankPermutation[p_?PermutationQ] :=
    Block[{$RecursionLimit = Infinity},
        (p[[1]]-1) (Length[Rest[p]]!) +
        RankPermutation[ Map[(If[#>p[[1]], #-1, #])&, Rest[p]]]
    ]
```

Ranking Permutations

An *unranking* algorithm constructs the ith object in the underlying total order for a given rank i. The previous analysis shows that the quotient obtained by dividing i by $(n-1)!$ gives the index of the first element of the permutation. The remainder is used to determine the rest of the permutation.

Applying the unranking algorithm $n!$ times gives an alternate method for constructing all permutations in lexicographic order.

```
In[21]:= Table[UnrankPermutation[n, Range[3]], {n, 0, 5}]

Out[21]= {{1, 2, 3}, {1, 3, 2}, {2, 1, 3}, {2, 3, 1},
          {3, 1, 2}, {3, 2, 1}}
```

The ranking function proves that Permutations uses lexicographic sequencing.

```
In[22]:= Map[RankPermutation, Permutations[{1,2,3}]]

Out[22]= {0, 1, 2, 3, 4, 5}
```

■ 2.1.3 Random Permutations

With $n!$ distinct permutations of n items, it is impractical to test a conjecture on all permutations for any substantial value of n. However, experiments on several large, *random* permutations can give confidence that any results we get are not an artifact of how the examples were selected. We have already seen how permutations of size 100 can be randomly sampled to determine the average number of transpositions to take a permutation to its lexicographic successor. We will see many more examples of random sampling of combinatorial objects in this book. Functions for generating random instances of most interesting combinatorial structures are included. Many start by constructing a random permutation.

The fastest algorithm for random permutations starts with an arbitrary permutation and exchanges the ith element with a randomly selected one from the first i elements, for each i from n to 1. The nth element is therefore equally likely to be anything from 1 to n, and it follows by induction that any permutation is equally likely and is produced with probability 1/*n*!. RandomPermutation is compiled to make it faster, which is possible because it only manipulates a list of integers.

```
RP = Compile[{{n, _Integer}},
        Module[{p = Range[n],i,x,t},
            Do [x = Random[Integer,{1,i}];
                t = p[[i]]; p[[i]] = p[[x]]; p[[x]] = t,
                {i,n,2,-1}
            ];
            p
        ]
    ]

RandomPermutation[n_Integer] := RP[n]
RandomPermutation[l_List] := Permute[l, RP[Length[l]]]
```

Constructing a Random Permutation

If the random permutation is indeed random, then all six permutations of three elements must be generated roughly the same number of times, provided we generate enough of them.

```
In[23]:= Distribution[Table[RandomPermutation[3],{300}]]

Out[23]= {52, 45, 62, 45, 56, 40}
```

UnCompiledRandPerm is the uncompiled version of RandomPermutation. The execution time ratios clearly show that compilation gives a significant speedup.

```
In[24]:= <<extraCode/UnCompiledRandPerm;
         Table[Timing[UnCompiledRandPerm[n];][[1, 1]]/
         Timing[RandomPermutation[n];][[1, 1]], {n, 1000, 2000, 100}]

Out[25]= {11., 11., 13., 14., 15., 16., 8.5, 9., 9.5, 10.,
         10.5}
```

If the random permutation is indeed random, then the average first element in a size-100 permutation should hover around 50.

```
In[26]:= Mean[Table[First[RandomPermutation[100]], {1000}]] // N

Out[26]= 49.272
```

Care must be taken that random objects are indeed selected with equal probability from the set of possibilities. Nijenhuis and Wilf [NW78, Wil89] considered this problem in depth, and their books are the source of many of the algorithms that we implement. *Markov chain Monte Carlo* methods have been recently applied to generate combinatorial objects such as regular graphs and spanning trees uniformly at random [Bro89, Wil96, JS90].

The plot below, which displays the running times of RandomPermutation for permutation sizes from 100 to 10,000, indicates a linear running time. The same function, running on pre-version 4.0 *Mathematica*, exhibits a quadratic running time. This improvement is due to an important new *Mathematica* feature called *packed arrays*. When appropriate, large linear lists or large, regularly structured nested lists of numbers are *automatically* stored as packed arrays of machine-sized integers or real numbers. The implication of this is that writing into such an array becomes an $O(1)$ time operation, in contrast with the linear time that it takes to write into a typical *Mathematica* data structure.

For RandomPermutation, this means that exchanging elements in the list p takes $O(1)$ time. Thus the overall running time of the function is linear. These two new features – packed arrays and compilation – have been used throughout *Combinatorica*. Along with improved algorithms, they have led to a substantial overall speedup in the package.

This timing plot indicates a linear running time for RandomPermutation. The function is extremely fast and here it takes only a small fraction of a second to generate a 10,000-element random permutation!

```
In[27]:= ListPlot[Table[{i, Mean[Table[Timing[RandomPermutation[i];]
            [[1, 1]], {10}]]},{i, 100, 10000, 100}], PlotJoined -> True]
```

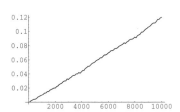

■ 2.1.4 Minimum Change Permutations

LexicographicPermutations gives just one way of generating permutations. Sedgewick's survey paper [Sed77] describes over 30 permutation generation algorithms published as of 1977! These other permutation generation algorithms typically produce permutations in nonlexicographic orders with special properties. In this section, we study an algorithm that uses a total of $(n! - 1)$ transpositions in generating all permutations. In other words, the permutations are arranged such that every two adjacent permutations differ from each other by exactly one transposition.

Sedgewick's study [Sed77] revealed an algorithm by Heap [Hea63] to be generally the fastest permutation generation algorithm. We implement this algorithm as MinimumChangePermutation. Heap's idea is best described using the following recursive framework that can be used to describe many permutation generation algorithms:

> Set $\pi[i] = i$ for all $i = 1, 2, ..., n$
> for $c = 1$ to n do
> > 1. generate all permutations of $\pi[1, ..., n - 1]$, keeping $\pi[n]$ in place;
> > (at the end of Step 1, π contains the last generation permutation)
> > 2. exchange $\pi[n]$ with an element in $\pi[1, ..., n - 1]$ whose position is $f(n, c)$.

$f(n,c) \in \{1,\dots,n-1\}$ is simply a function of n and c, the number of times permutations of $\pi[1,\dots,n-1]$ have been generated. Different permutation generation algorithms differ in values for $f(n,c)$. Heap's algorithm uses the somewhat mysterious function:

$$f(n,c) = \begin{cases} 1 & \text{if } n \text{ is odd} \\ c & \text{otherwise.} \end{cases}$$

For example, let $n = 4$ and start with $\pi = (1,2,3,4)$. During the first execution of the for-loop, $c = 1$ and the first step is to generate all permutations of $\pi[1,2,3]$. Heap's algorithm generates permutations in the order $123, 213, 312, 132, 231, 321$.

Generating all size-3 permutations by Heap's algorithm.	*In[28]:=* `MinimumChangePermutations[3]`
	Out[28]= {{1, 2, 3}, {2, 1, 3}, {3, 1, 2}, {1, 3, 2},
	{2, 3, 1}, {3, 2, 1}}
The first six size-4 permutations as generated by Step 1 of Heap's algorithm.	*In[29]:=* `MinimumChangePermutations[4][[ Range[6] ]]`
	Out[29]= {{1, 2, 3, 4}, {2, 1, 3, 4}, {3, 1, 2, 4},
	{1, 3, 2, 4}, {2, 3, 1, 4}, {3, 2, 1, 4}}

After Step 1 is complete, π has value $(3,2,1,4)$ and then $\pi[4]$ and $\pi[1]$ are exchanged because $f(4,1) = 1$. Thus the second execution of the loop starts with $\pi = (4,2,1,3)$. In Step 1 of the second execution of the for-loop, 3 remains fixed as the last element of π while the first three get permuted as before.

This example shows the remaining sequence of size-4 permutations generated by Heap's algorithm. All consecutive permutations differ by exactly one transposition.	*In[30]:=* `MinimumChangePermutations[4][[ Range[7,24] ]]`
	Out[30]= {{4, 2, 1, 3}, {2, 4, 1, 3}, {1, 4, 2, 3},
	{4, 1, 2, 3}, {2, 1, 4, 3}, {1, 2, 4, 3}, {1, 3, 4, 2},
	{3, 1, 4, 2}, {4, 1, 3, 2}, {1, 4, 3, 2}, {3, 4, 1, 2},
	{4, 3, 1, 2}, {4, 3, 2, 1}, {3, 4, 2, 1}, {2, 4, 3, 1},
	{4, 2, 3, 1}, {3, 2, 4, 1}, {2, 3, 4, 1}}

To see that exactly one transposition suffices to take a permutation to its successor in Heap's algorithm, partition the sequence of permutations into blocks, with each block containing permutations with an identical last element. Each such block is produced by a recursive call to generate permutations of size $(n-1)$. In going from the last permutation of a block to the first permutation of the successor, exactly one transposition is used. Within each block, the last element remains fixed and only the first $(n-1)$ elements of the list are moved. By induction we know that each permutation (except the last) in each block can be transformed into its successor by a single transposition.

The 5-permutations as enumerated by Heap's algorithm and partitioned into blocks containing the same last element. The first and last elements of each block are reported. A single transposition suffices to move from the last permutation in a block to the first permutation of the next.

```
In[31]:= Map[{First[#], Last[#]} &,
         Split[MinimumChangePermutations[Range[5]],
         (Last[#1] === Last[#2]) &]]
Out[31]= {{{1, 2, 3, 4, 5}, {2, 3, 4, 1, 5}},
          {{5, 3, 4, 1, 2}, {3, 4, 1, 5, 2}},
          {{2, 4, 1, 5, 3}, {4, 1, 5, 2, 3}},
          {{3, 1, 5, 2, 4}, {1, 5, 2, 3, 4}},
          {{4, 5, 2, 3, 1}, {5, 2, 3, 4, 1}}}
```

Our implementation of Heap's algorithm is iterative. Instead of a single loop control variable c, we have an array of loop control variables that keep track of the n for-loops. The array c essentially keeps track of each of the n for-loop control variables.

```
MinimumChangePermutations[l_List] := LexicographicPermutations[l] /; (Length[l] < 2)
MinimumChangePermutations[l_List] :=
    Module[{i=1,c,p=l,n=Length[l],k},
          c = Table[1,{n}];
          Join[{l},
             Table[While [ c[[i]] >= i, c[[i]] = 1; i++];
                    If[OddQ[i], k=1, k=c[[i]] ];
                    {p[[i]],p[[k]]} = {p[[k]],p[[i]]};
                    c[[i]]++; i = 2; p,
                    {n!-1}
             ]
          ]
    ]
MinimumChangePermutations[n_Integer] := MinimumChangePermutations[Range[n]]
```

Sequencing Permutations in Minimum Change Order

To better illustrate the transposition structure of permutations, we introduce some of the graph-theoretic tools we will develop in the latter part of this book. A *graph* is a collection of pairs of elements, called *edges*, drawn from a finite, nonempty set of elements, called *vertices*. When the edges are ordered pairs, the resulting graphs are called *directed graphs*. If we represent the vertices by points and the edges by curves connecting pairs of points, we get a visual representation of the underlying structure. In a *transposition graph*, the vertices correspond to permutations, with edges connecting pairs of permutations that differ by exactly one transposition.

A *binary relation* on a set S is a subset of ordered pairs of elements in S. Here we define a binary relation on n-permutations.

```
In[32]:= tr=MemberQ[Flatten[Table[p = #1;
          {p[[i]], p[[j]]} = {p[[j]], p[[i]]};
          p, {i, Length[#1] - 1}, {j, i + 1, Length[#1]}], 1], #2]&;
```

Two n-permutations are related if and only if one can be obtained from the other by a transposition.

```
In[33]:= {tr[{4,3,1,2},{4,3,2,1}], tr[{4,3,1,2},{1,2,3,4}]}
Out[33]= {True, False}
```

Here, using the relation defined above, we construct the transposition graph for 4-permutations.

In[34]:= **g = MakeGraph[Permutations[4], tr, Type -> Undirected];**

The *degree* of a vertex is the number of edges connecting it to other vertices. Each 4-permutation is one transposition away from six other 4-permutations and so each vertex has degree 6. In general, vertices in the transposition graph of *n*-permutations have degree $\binom{n}{2}$.

In[35]:= **DegreeSequence[g]**

Out[35]= {6, 6, 6, 6, 6, 6, 6, 6, 6, 6, 6, 6, 6, 6, 6, 6, 6, 6, 6, 6, 6, 6, 6, 6}

This graph is drawn using RankedEmbedding, so that the vertices are arranged in columns according to the fewest number of transpositions needed to get to the leftmost vertex.

In[36]:= **ShowGraph[tg4 = RankedEmbedding[g, {1}]];**

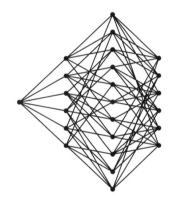

There are 6 permutations that are one transposition away from the permutation on the left, 11 permutations two away, and 6 permutations three away.

In[37]:= **Distribution[RankGraph[g, {1}]]**

Out[37]= {1, 6, 11, 6}

This distribution of permutations by transposition "distance" is counted by the *Stirling numbers of the first kind.*

In[38]:= **Table[StirlingFirst[4,i],{i,4,1,-1}]**

Out[38]= {1, 6, 11, 6}

The function MakeGraph used above is one of several graph construction functions that *Combinatorica* provides. MakeGraph takes as input a set of objects (permutations, in the above example) and a relation defined on these objects and produces a graph that represents the relation. Section 6.5.1 provides details of this and other graph construction functions. The graph construction functions in *Combinatorica* are complemented by a variety of graph drawing functions. RankedEmbedding has been used above to arrange the vertices by distance from a specific vertex.

We next show the sequence of permutations produced by `MinimumChangePermutation` as a path in a transposition graph. We show this on a transposition graph of size-3 permutations because this graph is less crowded than the transposition graph of size-4 permutations.

The transposition graph on size-3 permutations. `SpringEmbedding` *tries* (not always successfully) to reveal the symmetry and structure of the graph. Here it does a good job. Spring embeddings and other types of graph drawings are discussed in Section 5.5.

```
In[39]:= ShowGraph[tg3 = SpringEmbedding[MakeGraph[Permutations[3],
         tr, Type -> Undirected, VertexLabel -> True]],
         PlotRange -> 0.15];
```

The sequence of permutations from `MinimumChangePermutations` is shown as a path in this graph. This path is a *Hamiltonian path*, that is, a path that visits every vertex of the graph without repetition. Since the first and the last vertices of the path are adjacent, the path can be extended to a *Hamiltonian cycle*.

```
In[40]:= m = Partition[ Map[RankPermutation[#] + 1 &,
         MinimumChangePermutations[{1, 2, 3}]], 2, 1];
         ShowGraph[Highlight[tg3, {m},
         HighlightedEdgeColors->{Blue}], PlotRange -> 0.15];
```

However, this is not true in general; the first and the last size-4 permutations produced by `MinimumChangePermutations` are not adjacent in the transposition graph.

```
In[42]:= {First[MinimumChangePermutations[4]],
         Last[MinimumChangePermutations[4]]}
```

`Out[42]= {{1, 2, 3, 4}, {2, 3, 4, 1}}`

Permutations can always be sequenced in *maximum change order*, where neighboring permutations differ in all positions unless $n = 3$. Such a sequence can be constructed by finding a Hamiltonian path on the appropriate adjacency graph [Wil89]. This graph is disconnected for $n = 3$, but [EW85, RS87] show how to enumerate n-permutations in maximum change order for all $n \geq 4$. See Section 3.2.2 for more details.

```
In[43]:= Permutations[{1,2,3,4}] [[ HamiltonianPath[
           MakeGraph[Permutations[{1,2,3,4}], (Count[#1-#2,0] == 0)&]
         ]]]
Out[43]= {{1, 2, 3, 4}, {2, 1, 4, 3}, {1, 3, 2, 4},
          {2, 4, 1, 3}, {1, 3, 4, 2}, {2, 1, 3, 4}, {1, 2, 4, 3},
          {2, 3, 1, 4}, {1, 4, 2, 3}, {2, 3, 4, 1}, {1, 4, 3, 2},
          {3, 1, 2, 4}, {2, 4, 3, 1}, {4, 1, 2, 3}, {3, 2, 1, 4},
          {4, 1, 3, 2}, {3, 2, 4, 1}, {4, 3, 1, 2}, {3, 4, 2, 1},
          {4, 2, 1, 3}, {3, 1, 4, 2}, {4, 2, 3, 1}, {3, 4, 1, 2},
          {4, 3, 2, 1}}
```

We could get even more ambitious and ask if permutations can be generated in an order in which each permutation is obtained from the previous by a transposition of *adjacent* elements. The *adjacent transposition graph* contains an edge for each pair of permutations that differ by exactly one *adjacent* transposition. The adjacent transposition graph is a *spanning subgraph* of the transposition graph because it contains *all* of the vertices of the transposition graph and some of the edges.

This function relates pairs of permutations that can be obtained from a transposition of adjacent elements.

```
In[44]:= atr = MemberQ[Table[p = #1; {p[[i]], p[[i+1]]} =
           {p[[i+1]], p[[i]]}; p, {i, Length[#1] - 1}], #2]&;
```

This is the *adjacent transposition graph* for 4-permutations. In this drawing, the graph displays a nice symmetry, but the graph can also be drawn in other pleasing ways.

```
In[45]:= ShowGraph[RankedEmbedding[g = MakeGraph[
           Permutations[4], atr, Type -> Undirected,
           VertexLabel -> True], {1}], PlotRange->0.1];
```

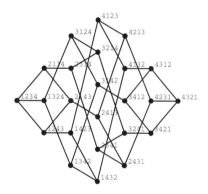

Knuth [Knu73b] shows this graph drawn as a *truncated octahedron*, a 14-faced polyhedron that can be obtained by lopping off each of the 6 corners of a regular octahedron. SpringEmbedding constructs this embedding for us.

In[46]:= `ShowGraph[ats4 = SpringEmbedding[g], PlotRange->0.15];`

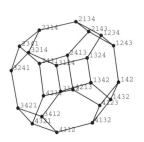

A Hamiltonian path of an adjacent transposition graph corresponds to an ordering of permutations in which successive permutations differ by exactly one adjacent transposition. The Johnson-Trotter permutation generation algorithm [Joh63, Tro62] is a proof that every adjacent transposition graph contains a Hamiltonian path. In fact, Chase [Cha73] shows that the transposition graph of a multiset always contains a Hamiltonian path.

This Hamiltonian cycle starts with 1234, 1243, 1423, 1432, ... After 1432 the Johnson-Trotter algorithm would have produced 4132. This is proof that this graph contains more than one Hamiltonian path starting at 1234.

In[47]:= `ShowGraph[Highlight[ats4,`
           `{Partition[HamiltonianCycle[ats4], 2, 1]},`
           `HighlightedEdgeColors->{Blue}]];`

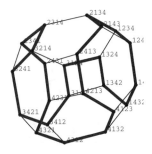

In fact, it contains many Hamiltonian cycles, 88 to be exact! This inspires the question: As a function of n, how many distinct Hamiltonian cycles does the adjacent transposition graph on n-permutations have?

In[48]:= `Length[HamiltonianCycle[ats4, All]]`

Out[48]= 88

In the past two decades, researchers have focused on problems of enumerating combinatorial objects in an order in which successive objects differ in some prespecified small way. The term *combinatorial Gray code* was introduced in 1980 to refer to any method that enumerates combinatorial objects in this manner. Gray codes are known for a large number of combinatorial objects [Sav97].

2.2 Inversions and Inversion Vectors

A pair of elements $(\pi(i), \pi(j))$ in a permutation π represents an *inversion* if $i > j$ and $\pi(i) < \pi(j)$. An inversion is a pair of elements that are out of order, and so they play a prominent role in the analysis of sorting algorithms.

■ 2.2.1 Inversion Vectors

For any n-permutation π, we can define an *inversion vector* v as follows. For each integer i, $1 \le i \le n-1$, the ith element of v is the number of elements in π greater than i to the left of i. The function `ToInversionVector`, shown below, computes the inversion vector of a given permutation. As implemented, it runs in $\Theta(n^2)$ time; however, more sophisticated algorithms exist that can compute this in $O(n \lg n)$ time.

```
ToInversionVector[p_?PermutationQ] :=
    Module[{i,inverse=InversePermutation[p]},
        Table[ Length[ Select[Take[p,inverse[[i]]], (# > i)&] ], {i,Length[p]-1}]
    ] /; (Length[p] > 0)
```

Obtaining the Inversion Vector

The inversion vector contains only $n-1$ elements since the number of inversions of n is always 0. The ith element can range from 0 to $n-i$, so there are indeed $n!$ distinct inversion vectors, one for each permutation.

```
In[49]:= ToInversionVector[{5,9,1,8,2,6,4,7,3}]

Out[49]= {2, 3, 6, 4, 0, 2, 2, 1}
```

Marshall Hall [Tho56] demonstrated that no two permutations have the same inversion vector and also showed how to obtain the corresponding permutation from an inversion vector. Let π be an n-permutation and let v be its inversion vector. Suppose we have the sequence S obtained by ordering elements in $\{i+1, i+2, ..., n\}$ according to their order in π. The value v_i tells us the number of elements larger than i that occur to the left of i in π, so we can insert i into S v_i positions from the left. This gives us a correct ordering of the elements in $\{i, i+1, ..., n\}$. We start with the list $\{n\}$ and iteratively insert each i from $n-1$ down to 1 in the list, obtaining π. The function `FromInversionVector` is shown below.

```
FromInversionVector[vec_List] :=
    Module[{n=Length[vec]+1,i,p}, p={n}; Do [p = Insert[p, i, vec[[i]]+1], {i,n-1,1,-1}]; p]
```

Inverting the Inversion Vector

A permutation and its inversion vector provide different representations of the same structure.

```
In[50]:= {p=RandomPermutation[10], ToInversionVector[p]}
Out[50]= {{2, 3, 9, 10, 4, 6, 1, 5, 7, 8},
          {6, 0, 0, 2, 3, 2, 2, 2, 0}}
```

Composing these two functions gives an identity operation.

```
In[51]:= FromInversionVector[ToInversionVector[{5,9,1,8,2,6,4,7,3}] ]
Out[51]= {5, 9, 1, 8, 2, 6, 4, 7, 3}
```

Random inversion vectors are easy to construct because each individual element is generated independently. Here we generate random inversion vectors of size 4, convert them into permutations, and demonstrate that all 24 permutations occur with roughly equal frequency.

```
In[52]:= Distribution[Map[FromInversionVector, Table[Table[
            Random[Integer, {0, 4-i}], {i, 3}], {10000}]]]
Out[52]= {418, 414, 412, 410, 390, 411, 436, 403, 418, 399,
          437, 445, 446, 405, 397, 378, 404, 397, 419, 412, 464,
          424, 442, 419}
```

This generates five random inversion vectors for different sizes up to 2000 to serve as test data for timings.

```
In[53]:= Map[Length, pt = Table[Table[Random[Integer, {0, n - i}],
            {i, n - 1}], {n, 0, 2000, 100}, {5}] ]
Out[53]= {5, 5, 5, 5, 5, 5, 5, 5, 5, 5, 5, 5, 5, 5, 5, 5,
          5, 5, 5, 5, 5}
```

We timed FromInversionVector on each of these random inversion vectors. The quadratic behavior of FromInversionVector shows up fairly clearly in this plot.

```
In[54]:= ListPlot[Map[ ({Length[First[#]], Mean[ Table[
            Timing[FromInversionVector[ #[[j]] ];][[1,1]] , {j, 5} ] ]})&,
            pt] ]
```

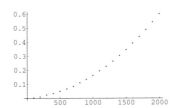

Another method of highlighting the inversions in a permutation uses permutation graphs. The *permutation graph* G_π of a permutation π is a graph whose vertex set is $\{1, 2, ..., n\}$ and whose edges $\{i, j\}$ correspond exactly to (i, j) being an inversion in permutation π. The structure of permutation graphs permits fast algorithms for certain problems that are intractable for general graphs [AMU88, BK87].

Here is a 15-element permutation h whose structure we will explore.

```
In[55]:= h=RandomPermutation[15]
Out[55]= {11, 10, 13, 3, 5, 15, 2, 4, 1, 8, 9, 7, 12, 14, 6}
```

Here we compute the degrees of vertices in the permutation graph of h. Elements responsible for many inversions have high degree, while vertices of zero degree are in the correct position with smaller elements appearing earlier and larger elements appearing later.

```
In[56]:= Degrees[g=PermutationGraph[h]]
Out[56]= {8, 7, 5, 6, 6, 9, 7, 6, 6, 10, 10, 3, 10, 2, 9}
```

The total number of inversions in a permutation is equal to the number of edges in its permutation graph.

```
In[57]:= {Inversions[h], M[g]}
Out[57]= {52, 52}
```

Here we highlight a maximum-size *clique* in the permutation graph. A clique is a subset of the vertices, such that every pair of vertices in the subset is connected by an edge. Although finding a maximum-size clique is difficult even to approximate [GJ79, Hoc97], the problem is easy for permutation graphs. Every clique in a permutation graph corresponds to a decreasing sequence in the corresponding permutation.

```
In[58]:= ShowGraph[Highlight[g, {MaximumClique[g]},
         HighlightedVertexColors -> {Blue}], VertexNumber -> True,
         TextStyle -> {FontSize -> 12}];
```

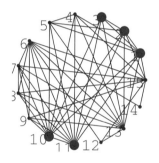

There is a longest decreasing subsequence in the permutation whose size is the same as the size of a maximum clique in its permutation graph.

```
In[59]:= LongestIncreasingSubsequence[Reverse[h]]
Out[59]= {1, 2, 3, 10, 11}
```

■ 2.2.2 Counting Inversions

The total number of inversions in a permutation is a classic measure of order (or disorder) [Knu73b, Man85a, Ski88] and can be obtained by summing up the inversion vector.

```
Inversions[{}] := 0
Inversions[p_?PermutationQ] := Apply[Plus,ToInversionVector[p]]
```

Counting Inversions

The number of inversions in a permutation is equal to that of its inverse [Knu73b]. The claim follows immediately from the fact that $(\pi(i), \pi(j))$ is an inversion in π if and only if (i, j) is an inversion in π^{-1}.

```
In[60]:= p = RandomPermutation[30];
         {Inversions[p], Inversions[InversePermutation[p]]}
Out[61]= {230, 230}
```

The number of inversions in a permutation ranges from 0 to $\binom{n}{2}$, where the largest number of inversions comes from the reverse of the identity permutation.

```
In[62]:= {Inversions[Reverse[Range[100]]], Binomial[100, 2]}
Out[62]= {4950, 4950}
```

Every number from 0 to $\binom{n}{2}$ is realizable as an inversion total for some permutation.

```
In[63]:= Union[Map[Inversions, Permutations[5]]]
Out[63]= {0, 1, 2, 3, 4, 5, 6, 7, 8, 9, 10}
```

A neat proof that there are an average of $n(n-1)/4$ inversions per permutation is that the number of inversions in a permutation and its reverse permutation always total to $\binom{n}{2}$.

```
In[64]:= ( p = RandomPermutation[100];
         Inversions[p] + Inversions[Reverse[p]] )
Out[64]= 4950
```

Thus it is easy to find the number of inversions in a permutation. But the "inverse" question of how many n-permutations have exactly k inversions is harder. The easiest solution uses *generating functions*. Generating functions [Wil90] provide some of the most powerful tools for dealing with combinatorial problems. The *ordinary generating function* of a sequence $(g_0, g_1, g_2, ...)$ is a function $G(z)$ defined as

$$G(z) = g_0 + g_1 \cdot z + g_2 \cdot z^2 + g_3 \cdot z^3 + \cdots .$$

Thus $G(z)$ is just a representation of the sequence $(g_0, g_1, g_2, ...)$. However, it is also an algebraic object that can be subjected to a variety of algebraic operations that often yield a great deal of information about the sequence.

Let $I_n(k)$ denote the number of n-permutations with k inversions. A more useful way to think about $I_n(k)$ is that it is the number of inversion vectors of n-permutations that sum up to k. So the relevant objects are inversion vectors $(v_1, v_2, ..., v_{n-1})$ that sum to k. Note that v_1 can contribute any integer in the range $[0, n-1]$ to the sum k, v_2 can contribute any integer in the range $[0, n-2]$ to the sum k, and so on. Now consider the product

$$(1) \cdot (1 + z) \cdot (1 + z + z^2) \cdots (1 + z + z^2 + \cdots + z^{n-1}).$$

The possible contributions of v_1 are represented by the powers of the terms in the last bracket, the contributions of v_2 are represented by the powers of the terms in the second to last bracket, and so on. Thus the coefficient of z^k in the product is exactly $I_n(k)$. This implies that

$$I(z) = \sum_{k=0}^{n-1} I_n(k) z^k = \prod_{i=1}^{n-1} (1 + z + z^2 + \cdots + z^i) = \frac{1}{(1-z)^n} \prod_{i=1}^{n-1} (1 - z^i).$$

Expanding this polynomial and picking the right coefficient provides an approach to computing $I_n(k)$.

The coefficients of this polynomial are $I_7(k)$ for each k between 0 and 21. Observe that $I_n(k) = I_n(\binom{n}{2} - k)$ for all k. This follows from the fact that any pair of elements that is an inversion in a permutation p is not so in the reverse of p.

```
In[65]:= p = Expand[Product[Cancel[(z^i - 1)/(z - 1)], {i, 7}]]

           2       3       4        5
Out[65]= 1 + 6 z + 20 z + 49 z + 98 z + 169 z +

         6        7        8        9        10         11
    259 z + 359 z + 455 z + 531 z + 573 z  + 573 z  +

         12        13        14        15        16
    531 z  + 455 z  + 359 z  + 259 z  + 169 z  +

        17       18       19       20    21
    98 z  + 49 z  + 20 z  + 6 z  + z
```

The *Mathematica* function Coefficient can be used to pick out coefficients of specific terms of a polynomial.

```
In[66]:= p = Coefficient[p, z, 16]

Out[66]= 169
```

This coefficient gives the number of 7-element permutations with 16 inversions.

```
In[67]:= NumberOfPermutationsByInversions[7,16]

Out[67]= 169
```

The function below implements the above approach of using generating functions to compute the number of *n*-permutations with *k* inversions.

```
NumberOfPermutationsByInversions[n_Integer?Positive] :=
    Module[{p = Expand[Product[Cancel[ (z^i -1)/(z-1)], {i, 1, n}]]}, CoefficientList[p, z]]
NumberOfPermutationsByInversions[n_Integer, k_Integer] := 0 /; (k > Binomial[n,2])
NumberOfPermutationsByInversions[n_Integer, 0] := 1
NumberOfPermutationsByInversions[n_Integer, k_Integer?Positive] := NumberOfPermutationsByInversions[n][[k+1]]
```

Computing the Number of Permutations with *k* Inversions

■ 2.2.3 The Index of a Permutation

The *index* of a permutation π is the sum of all subscripts j such that $\pi(j) > \pi(j+1)$, $1 \le j < n$. MacMahon [Mac60] proved that the number of permutations of size n having index k is the same as the number having exactly k inversions.

```
Index[p_?PermutationQ]:= Module[{i}, Sum[ If [p[[i]] > p[[i+1]], i, 0], {i,Length[p]-1} ]]
```

Computing the Index of a Permutation

These are the six permutations of length 4 with index 3.

```
In[68]:= Select[Permutations[{1,2,3,4}], (Index[#]==3)&]

Out[68]= {{1, 2, 4, 3}, {1, 3, 4, 2}, {2, 3, 4, 1},

    {3, 2, 1, 4}, {4, 2, 1, 3}, {4, 3, 1, 2}}
```

As MacMahon proved, there is an equal number of permutations of length 4 with three inversions. A bijection between the two sets of permutations is not obvious [Knu73b].

```
In[69]:= Select[Permutations[{1,2,3,4}], (Inversions[#]==3)&]

Out[69]= {{1, 4, 3, 2}, {2, 3, 4, 1}, {2, 4, 1, 3},
          {3, 1, 4, 2}, {3, 2, 1, 4}, {4, 1, 2, 3}}
```

Sixty-five years after MacMahon's result was published, Foata and Schützenberger discovered a remarkable extension: The number of permutations with k inversions and index ℓ is equal to the number of permutations with ℓ inversions and index k. This result immediately implies MacMahon's result.

Evidence for the Foata-Schützenberger bijection. For $n = 7$, the number of permutations with four inversions and index 10 equals number of permutations with ten inversions and index 4.

```
In[70]:= p = Permutations[Range[7]];
         {Length[Select[p, ((Index[#]==10) && (Inversions[#]==4)&]],
          Length[Select[p, ((Index[#]==4 ) && (Inversions[#]==10))&]]}

Out[71]= {9, 9}
```

■ 2.2.4 Runs and Eulerian Numbers

Read from left to right, any permutation can be partitioned into a set of ascending sequences or *runs*. A sorted permutation consists of one run, while a reverse permutation consists of n runs, each of one element. For this reason, the number of runs is also used as a measure of the presortedness of a permutation [Man85a]. *Combinatorica* contains a function Runs to partition a permutation into runs.

A random 20-permutation...

```
In[72]:= p = RandomPermutation[20]

Out[72]= {7, 11, 17, 20, 3, 8, 16, 12, 10, 13, 18, 9, 14,
          1, 4, 2, 19, 5, 15, 6}
```

...and its runs.

```
In[73]:= Runs[p]

Out[73]= {{7, 11, 17, 20}, {3, 8, 16}, {12}, {10, 13, 18},
          {9, 14}, {1, 4}, {2, 19}, {5, 15}, {6}}
```

The number of runs in an n-permutation plus the number of runs in its reverse equals $(n + 1)$.

```
In[74]:= Length[Runs[p = RandomPermutation[1000]]] +
         Length[ Runs[ Reverse[p]]]

Out[74]= 1001
```

Interestingly, the average length of the first run is shorter than the average length of the second run [Gas67, Knu73b].

```
In[75]:= Map[N[Mean[#]] &, Transpose[Table[Map[Length,
         Runs[RandomPermutation[100]]][[{1,2}]], {500}]]]

Out[75]= {1.792, 1.844}
```

Why? The first element of the first run is an average element of the permutation, while the first element of the second run must be less than the previous element in the permutation.

```
In[76]:= Map[N[Mean[#]] &, Transpose[Table[Map[First,
         Runs[RandomPermutation[100]]][[{1,2}]], {500}]]]

Out[76]= {50.368, 34.608}
```

The *Eulerian* numbers $\left\langle {n \atop k} \right\rangle$ count the number of permutations π of length n with exactly k "descents," $\pi(j) > \pi(j+1)$. This is the same as the number of permutations with $(k+1)$ runs. A recurrence for the Eulerian numbers follows by noting that a size-n permutation π with $(k+1)$ runs can be built only in the following ways:

(i) by taking an $(n-1)$-permutation with $(k+1)$ runs and appending n to one of the runs;

(ii) by taking a $(n-1)$-permutation with k runs and inserting n into a run, thereby splitting it into two runs.

It is easy to see that every size-n permutation with $(k+1)$ runs can be obtained by (i) or (ii) and no size-n permutation can be obtained via both (i) and (ii). This implies the recurrence

$$\left\langle {n \atop k} \right\rangle = (k+1)\left\langle {n-1 \atop k} \right\rangle + (n-k)\left\langle {n-1 \atop k-1} \right\rangle, \quad n \geq 1,\; k \geq 1,$$

where $\left\langle {n \atop 0} \right\rangle$ counts the number of permutations with a single run and is therefore 1, for all $n \geq 1$.

The function `Eulerian`, shown below, uses this recurrence relation to compute Eulerian numbers. The function provides an example of *dynamic programming* in *Mathematica*. Whenever the value of $\left\langle {n \atop k} \right\rangle$ is computed, it is stored in the symbol `Eulerian1[n, k]`. This means that, whenever this value is needed in the future, a constant-time table lookup is performed instead of an expensive recomputation.

```
Eulerian[n_Integer,k_Integer] := Block[{$RecursionLimit = Infinity}, Eulerian1[n, k]]
Eulerian1[0,k_Integer] := If [k==0, 1, 0]
Eulerian1[n_Integer, k_Integer] := 0 /; (k >= n)
Eulerian1[n_Integer, 0] := 1
Eulerian1[n_Integer,k_Integer] := Eulerian1[n,k] = (k+1) Eulerian1[n-1,k] + (n-k) Eulerian1[n-1,k-1]
```

Counting the Number of Permutations with k Runs

A list of the number of size-10 permutations with i runs, $0 \leq i \leq 9$. The symmetry of this list indicates that $\left\langle {n \atop k} \right\rangle = \left\langle {n \atop n-1-k} \right\rangle.$

```
In[77]:= Table[ Eulerian[10, i], {i, 0, 9}]
Out[77]= {1, 1013, 47840, 455192, 1310354, 1310354, 455192,
          47840, 1013, 1}
```

This follows from the fact that if π has $(k+1)$ runs, then the reverse of π has $(n-k)$ runs.

```
In[78]:= {Length[Runs[p=RandomPermutation[100]]], Length[Runs[Reverse[p]]]}
Out[78]= {44, 57}
```

The symmetry $\left\langle {n \atop k} \right\rangle = \left\langle {n \atop n-1-k} \right\rangle$ implies that the average number of descents in a size-n permutation is $(n-1)/2$.

```
In[79]:= Sum[r = Length[Runs[RandomPermutation[100]]]-1, {200}]/200 //N
Out[79]= 49.655
```

2.3 Combinations

Subsets rank with permutations as the most ubiquitous combinatorial objects. As with permutations, subsets can be generated in a variety of interesting orders. In this section we will examine three such orders.

An important subset of the subsets is those containing the same number of elements. In elementary combinatorics, permutations are always mentioned in the same breath as *combinations*, which are collections of elements of a given size where order does not matter. Thus a combination is exactly a set with k elements or a *k-subset* for some k, and we will use the terms interchangeably.

■ 2.3.1 Subsets via Binary Representation

An element of a set is either in a particular subset or not in it. Thus a sequence of n bits, with one bit for each of the n set elements, can represent any subset. This binary representation provides a method for generating all subsets, for we can iterate through the 2^n distinct binary strings of length n and use each as a descriptor of a subset. This can be done by simply calling the function Strings (see Section 2.3.5) to generate all binary strings of length n. The bijection between length-n binary strings and the set of integers $\{0, 1, \ldots, 2^n - 1\}$ given by

$$b_{n-1}b_{n-2}\ldots b_2 b_1 b_0 \iff \sum_{i=0}^{n-1} 2^i b_i$$

is in fact the standard way of representing integers in computers. When interpreted as integers, the length-n binary strings produced by the function Strings occur in the order $0, 1, \ldots, 2^n - 1$. This is rather convenient for ranking, unranking, and finding the next subset. For example, the function Unrank simply needs to compute the binary representation of the given integer. *Mathematica* has a built-in function called Digits to do precisely this.

```
BinarySubsets[l_List] := Map[(l[[Flatten[Position[#, 1], 1]]])&, Strings[{0, 1}, Length[l]]]

BinarySubsets[0] := {{}}
BinarySubsets[n_Integer?Positive] := BinarySubsets[Range[n]]

NextBinarySubset[set_List,subset_List] := UnrankBinarySubset[RankBinarySubset[set,subset]+1, set]

RankBinarySubset[set_List,subset_List] :=
     Module[{i,n=Length[set]},
          Sum[ 2^(n-i) * If[ MemberQ[subset,set[[i]]], 1, 0], {i,n}]
     ]

UnrankBinarySubset[n_Integer, 0] := {}
```

```
UnrankBinarySubset[n_Integer, m_Integer?Positive] := UnrankBinarySubset[Mod[n, 2^m], Range[m]]
UnrankBinarySubset[n_Integer, l_List] :=
    l[[Flatten[Position[IntegerDigits[Mod[n, 2^Length[l]], 2, Length[l]], 1], 1]]]
```

Subsets from Bit Strings

The representation of each subset is obtained by incrementing the binary representation of the previous subset. This corresponds to inserting the last missing element into a subset and then removing all subsequent elements.

Here we start with the empty set and generate all subsets by repeatedly calling NextBinarySubset. Generating subsets incrementally is efficient if we seek the first subset with a given property, since not every subset need be constructed.

Because n is taken modulo the number of subsets, any positive or negative integer can be used to specify the rank of a subset.

```
In[80]:= Clear[a, b, c, d]; BinarySubsets[{a,b,c,d}]
Out[80]= {{}, {d}, {c}, {c, d}, {b}, {b, d}, {b, c},
    {b, c, d}, {a}, {a, d}, {a, c}, {a, c, d}, {a, b},
    {a, b, d}, {a, b, c}, {a, b, c, d}}
```

```
In[81]:= NestList[NextBinarySubset[{a, b, c, d}, #] &, {}, 15]
Out[81]= {{}, {d}, {c}, {c, d}, {b}, {b, d}, {b, c},
    {b, c, d}, {a}, {a, d}, {a, c}, {a, c, d}, {a, b},
    {a, b, d}, {a, b, c}, {a, b, c, d}}
```

```
In[82]:= UnrankBinarySubset[-10,{a,b,c,d}]
Out[82]= {b, c}
```

The amount of work done in transforming one subset to another can be measured by the number of insertion and deletion operations needed for this task. For example, the subsets $\{b, c, d\}$ and $\{a\}$ occur consecutively in the output of BinarySubsets[{a, b, c, d}]. Four operations – three deletions and one insertion – are needed to transform $\{b, c, d\}$ into $\{a\}$. How many insertion-deletion operations are performed by BinarySubsets in generating all 2^n subsets? This is examined in the examples below.

Here we calculate the average number of insertion-deletion operations it takes to generate all subsets of an n-element set, for n varying from 1 to 10. To compute the number of operations needed to go from a set s to its successor, we calculate the largest element i missing from a subset s, noting that $(n - i + 1)$ is the number of operations needed.

In fact, the total number of insertion-deletion operations performed by BinarySubsets in generating all 2^n subsets of an n-element set is $2^{n+1} - (n + 2)$.

```
In[83]:= Table[s = BinarySubsets[Range[n]];
    Mean[Table[n - Max[Complement[Range[n], s[[i]]]] + 1,
    {i, 2^n - 1}]], {n, 10}] // N
Out[83]= {1., 1.33333, 1.57143, 1.73333, 1.83871, 1.90476,
    1.94488, 1.96863, 1.98239, 1.99022}
```

```
In[84]:= Table[ N[ (2^(n+1)-(n+2)) / (2^n-1)], {n,10}]
Out[84]= {1., 1.33333, 1.57143, 1.73333, 1.83871, 1.90476,
    1.94488, 1.96863, 1.98239, 1.99022}
```

Ranking combinatorial structures makes it easy to generate random instances of them, for we can pick a random integer between 0 and $M - 1$, where M is the number of structures, and perform an unranking operation. Picking a random integer between 0 and $2^n - 1$ is equivalent to flipping n coins, each determining whether an element of the set appears in the subset.

```
RandomSubset[set_List] := UnrankSubset[Random[Integer,2^(Length[set])-1],set]

RandomSubset[0] := {}
RandomSubset[n_Integer] := UnrankSubset[Random[Integer,2^(n)-1], Range[n]]
```

Generating Random Subsets

Since the sizes of random subsets obey a binomial distribution, very large or very small subsets are rare compared to subsets with approximately half the elements.

```
In[85]:= Distribution[ Table[ Length[RandomSubset[Range[10]]], {1024}],
           Range[0,10] ]
Out[85]= {1, 14, 34, 124, 217, 230, 226, 122, 44, 11, 1}
```

Here is the actual binomial distribution, for comparison.

```
In[86]:= Table[Binomial[10, i], {i, 0, 10}]
Out[86]= {1, 10, 45, 120, 210, 252, 210, 120, 45, 10, 1}
```

However, each distinct subset occurs with roughly equal frequency since RandomSubset picks subsets uniformly at random.

```
In[87]:= Distribution[ Table[ RandomSubset[{1,2,3,4}], {1024}],
           Subsets[{1,2,3,4}] ]
Out[87]= {72, 59, 44, 69, 71, 66, 59, 64, 70, 75, 79, 57,
         62, 54, 57, 66}
```

■ 2.3.2 Gray Codes

We have seen that permutations can be generated to limit the difference between adjacent permutations to one transposition. Combinations can also be generated in "minimum change order." The study of combinatorial Gray codes traces it origins to an elegant enumeration devised by Frank Gray and patented in 1953.

Gray's scheme [Gra53], subsequently referred to as the *standard reflected Gray code*, is an ordering of subsets so that adjacent subsets differ by the insertion or deletion of exactly one element. It can be described as follows. Say our goal is to construct a reflected Gray code G_n of subsets of a size-n set. Suppose that we have a Gray code G_{n-1} of subsets of the last $(n-1)$ elements of the set. Concatenate G_{n-1} with a reversed copy of G_{n-1}. Clearly, all subsets differ by one from their neighbors, except in the center, where they are identical. Adding the first element to the subsets in the bottom half maintains the Gray code property while distinguishing the center two subsets by exactly one element. This gives us G_n.

Many different Gray codes are possible. This technique of taking an enumeration of substructures, concatenating it with a reflection of the enumeration, and then extending it to an enumeration of the entire set of structures pervades most Gray code constructions.

When subsets are viewed as bit strings, a Gray code of a size-*n* set corresponds to a sequence of *n*-bit strings in which each bit string differs from its neighbors by exactly one bit. This sequence is exactly a Hamiltonian path in a well-known graph, the *n-dimensional hypercube*. The vertex set of an *n*-dimensional hypercube is the set of all *n*-bit strings, and its edges connect all pairs of strings that differ by exactly one bit. The existence of a Gray code is proof that an *n*-dimensional hypercube has a Hamiltonian path.

In the reflected Gray code, the last subset differs from the first by exactly one element, implying the existence of a Hamiltonian cycle in the *n*-dimensional hypercube. Here a four-dimensional hypercube is constructed using the *Combinatorica* function `Hypercube`. A Hamiltonian cycle in this graph is constructed, giving us a Gray code for subsets of a size-4 set.

```
In[88]:= ShowGraph[Highlight[g=Hypercube[4], {Partition[
             HamiltonianCycle[g], 2, 1]}, HighlightedEdgeColors->{Blue}]]
```

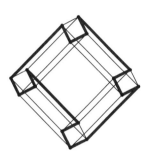

There is nothing unique about a Gray code, since each Hamiltonian cycle in the hypercube corresponds to a distinct Gray code. The exact number of Hamiltonian cycles in an *n*-dimensional hypercube is not known, not even asymptotically [Wil89].

```
In[89]:= Length[HamiltonianCycle[Hypercube[4], All]]

Out[89]= 2688
```

```
GrayCodeSubsets[n_Integer?Positive] := GrayCodeSubsets[Range[n]]

GrayCodeSubsets[ { } ] := { {} }

GrayCodeSubsets[l_List] :=
    Block[{s, $RecursionLimit = Infinity},
        s = GrayCodeSubsets[Take[l, 1-Length[l]]];
        Join[s, Map[Prepend[#, First[l]] &, Reverse[s]]]
    ]
```

Constructing Reflected Gray Codes

Each subset differs in exactly one element from its neighbors. Observe that the last eight subsets all contain 1, while none of the first eight do.

```
In[90]:= GrayCodeSubsets[{1,2,3,4}]

Out[90]= {{}, {4}, {3, 4}, {3}, {2, 3}, {2, 3, 4}, {2, 4},
          {2}, {1, 2}, {1, 2, 4}, {1, 2, 3, 4}, {1, 2, 3},
          {1, 3}, {1, 3, 4}, {1, 4}, {1}}
```

GrayCodeSubsets is much faster than
BinarySubsets.

```
In[91]:= Table[Timing[ Length[BinarySubsets[ Range[i]]];][[1, 1]]/
             Timing[ Length[GrayCodeSubsets[ Range[i]]];][[1, 1]],
         {i, 10, 15}]
Out[91]= {4.66667, 7.25, 5.45455, 7.94118, 7.22222, 7.4}
```

Reflected Gray codes have many beautiful properties. One of these leads to elegant algorithms for ranking and unranking subsets listed in this order. Let integer $m < 2^n$ have binary representation $b_{n-1}b_{n-2}...b_1b_0$, that is, $m = \sum_{i=0}^{n-1} b_i 2^i$. If $c_{n-1}c_{n-2}...c_1c_0$ is the binary representation of the subset with rank m in the reflected Gray code, then it can be shown that [Wil89]

$$c_i = (b_i + b_{i+1}) \pmod 2 \text{ for all } i, 0 \le i \le n - 1.$$

Here we suppose that $b_n = 0$. This immediately leads to an unranking algorithm that computes the binary representation of rank $m = b_{n-1},...,b_2b_1b_0$; uses the above result to compute $C = c_0, c_1, ..., c_{n-1}$, the binary representation of the subset; and finally computes the subset itself from C.

The above equation connecting the c_i's and the b_i's can be easily reversed to obtain $b_i = (c_i + c_{i+1} + \cdots + c_{n-1}) \pmod 2$ for all i, $0 \le i \le n - 1$. This immediately leads to a ranking algorithm. Other properties of Gray codes are discussed in [Gil58].

```
UnrankGrayCodeSubset[0, {}] := {}

UnrankGrayCodeSubset[m_Integer, s_List] :=
    Module[{c = Table[0, {Length[s]}], n = Length[s], b, nm},
        nm = Mod[m, 2^n];
        b = IntegerDigits[nm, 2, Length[s]];
        c[[ 1 ]] = b[[1]];
        Do[c[[i]] = Mod[b[[i]] + b[[i-1]], 2], {i, 2, n}];
        s[[ Flatten[Position[c, 1], 1] ]]
    ]
RankGrayCodeSubset[l_List, s_List] :=
    Module[{c = Table[If[MemberQ[s, l[[i]]], 1, 0], {i, Length[l]}], b = Table[0, {Length[l]}], n = Length[l]},
        b[[ 1 ]] = c[[ 1 ]];
        Do[b[[i]] = Mod[b[[i - 1]] + c[[i]], 2], {i, 2, n}];
        FromDigits[b, 2]
    ]
```

Ranking and Unranking Binary Reflected Gray Codes

Unranking the sequence 0 through 15 produces subsets in Gray code order.

```
In[92]:= Table[ UnrankGrayCodeSubset[i, {a, b, c, d}], {i, 0, 15}]
Out[92]= {{}, {d}, {c, d}, {c}, {b, c}, {b, c, d}, {b, d},
         {b}, {a, b}, {a, b, d}, {a, b, c, d}, {a, b, c},
         {a, c}, {a, c, d}, {a, d}, {a}}
```

Ranking these inverts the process to get back to the sequence 0 through 15.

```
In[93]:= Map[ RankGrayCodeSubset[{a, b, c, d}, #] &, %]
Out[93]= {0, 1, 2, 3, 4, 5, 6, 7, 8, 9, 10, 11, 12, 13, 14,
         15}
```

The algorithms for ranking and unranking subsets in Gray code order immediately give us an algorithm for getting the next subset of a given subset in Gray code order: rank, increment, and unrank. A more interesting and efficient algorithm is hinted at by the following example.

Here we list the subsets of $\{a,b,c,d\}$ in Gray code order along with the element that was inserted or deleted to get the next subset. The output reveals an interesting pattern. For a k-subset, where k is even, the element inserted or deleted is d, the last element. Otherwise, the element operated on occurs immediately before the last element in the subset. For example, the last element in the subset $\{a,b,c\}$ is c, and so b is deleted from it to get the next subset.

```
In[94]:= s = GrayCodeSubsets[{a, b, c, d}];
         Table[{s[[i]], Join[Complement[s[[i]], s[[i + 1]] ],
            Complement[s[[i + 1]], s[[i]] ]]}, {i, 15}] // ColumnForm

Out[95]= {{}, {d}}
         {{d}, {c}}
         {{c, d}, {d}}
         {{c}, {b}}
         {{b, c}, {d}}
         {{b, c, d}, {c}}
         {{b, d}, {d}}
         {{b}, {a}}
         {{a, b}, {d}}
         {{a, b, d}, {c}}
         {{a, b, c, d}, {d}}
         {{a, b, c}, {b}}
         {{a, c}, {d}}
         {{a, c, d}, {c}}
         {{a, d}, {d}}
```

This observation can be proved easily by induction and leads to the following code for `NextGrayCodeSubset`.

```
NextGrayCodeSubset[l_List, s_List] :=
      If[ MemberQ[s,l[[1]]], Rest[s], Prepend[s,l[[1]]] ] ] /; EvenQ[Length[s]]

NextGrayCodeSubset[l_List, s_List] :=
      Module[{i = 1},
            While[ ! MemberQ[s, l[[i]] ], i++];
            If[MemberQ[s, l[[i+1]] ], Rest[s], Insert[s, l[[i+1]], 2 ] ]]
```

Computing the Next Subset in Gray Code Order

`NextGrayCodeSubset` provides a compact way of enumerating subsets in reflected Gray code order when used along with the *Mathematica* function `NestList`.

```
In[96]:= NestList[NextGrayCodeSubset[{a, b, c, d}, #] &, {}, 15]

Out[96]= {{}, {a}, {a, b}, {b}, {b, c}, {a, b, c}, {b, c},

          {a, b, c}, {b, c}, {a, b, c}, {b, c}, {a, b, c},

          {b, c}, {a, b, c}, {b, c}, {a, b, c}}
```

∎ 2.3.3 Lexicographically Ordered Subsets

We can lexicographically order subsets by viewing them as sequences written in increasing "alphabetical order." Lexicographically ordered subsets can be constructed using a recurrence with a similar flavor to Gray codes. In lexicographic order, all of the subsets containing the first element appear before any of the subsets that do not. Thus we can recursively construct all subsets of the rest of the elements lexicographically and make two copies. The leading copy gets the first element inserted in each subset, while the second one does not.

```
LexicographicSubsets[{}] := {{ }}
LexicographicSubsets[l_List] :=
    Block[{$RecursionLimit = Infinity, s = LexicographicSubsets[Rest[l]]},
        Join[{{}}, Map[Prepend[#, l[[1]]] &, s], Rest[s]]
    ]

LexicographicSubsets[0] := {{ }}
LexicographicSubsets[n_Integer] := LexicographicSubsets[Range[n]]
```

Generating Subsets in Lexicographic Order

In lexicographic order, two subsets are ordered by their smallest elements. Thus the 2^{n-1} subsets containing 1 appear together in the list.

```
In[97]:= LexicographicSubsets[{1,2,3,4}]
Out[97]= {{}, {1}, {1, 2}, {1, 2, 3}, {1, 2, 3, 4},
    {1, 2, 4}, {1, 3}, {1, 3, 4}, {1, 4}, {2}, {2, 3},
    {2, 3, 4}, {2, 4}, {3}, {3, 4}, {4}}
```

The code for LexicographicSubsets and GrayCodeSubsets is so similar that there is only a slight difference in running time between them.

```
In[98]:= Table[Timing[ LexicographicSubsets[Range[i]];][[1, 1]]/
            Timing[GrayCodeSubsets[Range[i]];][[1, 1]], {i, 10, 15}]
Out[98]= {1.5, 1.25, 1.375, 1.23529, 1.22222, 1.17333}
```

Here we generate 15 lexicographically consecutive subsets of $\{a, b, c, d, e, f\}$ starting with $\{a, b, d, f\}$. This function provides an alternate way of scanning subsets. Suppose we are looking for a superset of a given subset *s* with a property *P*. Then it is better to scan subsets in lexicographic order starting from *s* rather than either of the other orders we have studied.

```
In[99]:= Clear[a,b,c,d,e,f];
        NestList[ NextLexicographicSubset[{a, b, c, d, e, f}, #]&,
        {a, b, d, f}, 15]
Out[100]= {{a, b, d, f}, {a, b, e}, {a, b, e, f}, {a, b, f},
    {a, c}, {a, c, d}, {a, c, d, e}, {a, c, d, e, f},
    {a, c, d, f}, {a, c, e}, {a, c, e, f}, {a, c, f},
    {a, d}, {a, d, e}, {a, d, e, f}, {a, d, f}}
```

Of the three subset generation methods we have seen, generating in Gray code order seems to be the most efficient. So we alias our generic subset generating, ranking, and unranking functions to the corresponding ones for Gray codes.

■ 2.3.4 Generating *k*-Subsets

A *k-subset* is a subset with exactly *k* elements in it. The simplest way to construct all *k*-subsets of a set uses an algorithm to construct all of the subsets and then filters out those of the wrong length. However, since there are 2^n subsets and only $\binom{n}{k}$ *k*-subsets, this is very wasteful when *k* is small or large relative to *n*. A simple recursive construction starts from the observation that each *k*-subset on *n* elements either contains the first element of the set or it does not. Prepending the first element to each $(k-1)$-subset of the other $n-1$ elements gives the former, and building all of the *k*-subsets of the other $n-1$ elements gives the latter. This can also be thought of as a combinatorial proof of the well-known binomial identity

$$\binom{n}{k} = \binom{n-1}{k-1} + \binom{n-1}{k}.$$

While the running time of this algorithm is proportional to the size of the output, $O(k\binom{n}{k})$, it proves even more efficient to write a function to compute the next k-subset in lexicographical order and then use that repeatedly.

Given a k-subset X of $\{1, 2, ..., n\}$, the next k-subset of X in lexicographical order can be constructed as follows. Suppose the elements of X are listed in increasing order. Let $i, i + 1, ..., n$ be the longest suffix of X with consecutive elements. If i is the first element in X, then X is the last k-subset in lexicographic order and its successor is $\{1, 2, ..., k\}$. Otherwise, the element in X immediately before i is some $j, j < i$. Note that $(j + 1)$ is not in X. The lexicographic successor of X is obtained by changing j to $j + 1$ and resetting the suffix $i, i + 1, ..., n$ to $j + 2, j + 3, ...$ This is the algorithm implemented below, taking advantage of *Mathematica*'s Compile function.

```
NKS = Compile[{{n, _Integer}, {ss, _Integer, 1}},
        Module[{h = Length[ss], x = n},
            While[x === ss[[h]], h--; x--];
            Join[Take[ss, h - 1], Range[ss[[h]]+1, ss[[h]]+Length[ss]-h+1]]
        ]
    ]

NextKSubset[s_List,ss_List] := Take[s,Length[ss]] /; (Take[s,-Length[ss]] === ss)
NextKSubset[s_List,ss_List] :=
    Map[s[[#]] &, NKS[Length[s], Table[Position[s, ss[[i]]][[1, 1]], {i, Length[ss]}]]]
```

Generating the Next Lexicographically Ordered k-Subset

Here are the ten 3-subsets of $\{a, b, c, d, e, f\}$ that immediately follow $\{a, b, e\}$ in lexicographic order.

```
In[101]:= NestList[NextKSubset[{a, b, c, d, e, f}, #] &, {a, b, e}, 10]
Out[101]= {{a, b, e}, {a, b, f}, {a, c, d}, {a, c, e},
    {a, c, f}, {a, d, e}, {a, d, f}, {a, e, f}, {b, c, d},
    {b, c, e}, {b, c, f}}
```

Now enumerating all k-subsets in simply a matter of calling NextKSubset repeatedly.

Since the lead element is always positioned first, the k-subsets are generated in lexicographic order.

```
In[102]:= KSubsets[{1,2,3,4,5},3]
Out[102]= {{1, 2, 3}, {1, 2, 4}, {1, 2, 5}, {1, 3, 4},
    {1, 3, 5}, {1, 4, 5}, {2, 3, 4}, {2, 3, 5}, {2, 4, 5},
    {3, 4, 5}}
```

Rewriting KSubsets as an iterative function and using compiled code leads to considerable speedup over the corresponding recursive function. The function was implemented recursively in the old package.

```
In[103]:= <<extraCode/RecursiveKSubsets;
        Table[ Timing[ RecursiveKSubsets[Range[20], i];][[1, 1]]/
        Timing[KSubsets[Range[15], i];][[1, 1]], {i, 5, 7}]
Out[104]= {33., 57.0714, 99.5263}
```

To solve the problem of ranking a k-subset in lexicographic order, consider a subset X written in canonical order, that is, $x_1 < x_2 < \cdots < x_k$. The subsets that appear before X in lexicographic order are of two kinds: (i) those that contain an element smaller than x_1 and (ii) those whose smallest element is x_1, but the remaining elements form a set that is lexicographically smaller than $\{x_2, x_3, \dots, x_k\}$. To count the number of subsets of the first kind, we note that the number of k-subsets of $\{1, 2, \dots, n\}$ whose smallest element is i is $\binom{n-i}{k-1}$. So the number of subsets of the first kind is $\sum_{i=1}^{x_1-1} \binom{n-i}{k-1}$. The number of subsets of the second kind is calculated by observing that this is simply a smaller ranking problem in which we want to find the rank of $\{x_2, \dots, x_k\}$ in the lexicographically ordered list of subsets of $\{x_1 + 1, x_1 + 2, \dots, n\}$. Below we give an implementation of this recurrence.

```
RankKSubset[ss_List, s_List] := 0 /; (Length[ss] === Length[s])
RankKSubset[ss_List, s_List] := Position[s, ss[[1]]][[1, 1]] - 1 /; (Length[ss] === 1)
RankKSubset[ss_List, s_List] :=
    Block[{n = Length[s], k = Length[ss],
        x = Position[s, ss[[1]]][[1, 1]], $RecursionLimit = Infinity},
        Binomial[n, k] - Binomial[n-x+1, k] + RankKSubset[Rest[ss], Drop[s, x]]
    ]
```

Ranking a k-Subset

The 20 3-subsets of $\{a, b, c, d, e, f\}$ are listed in lexicographic order and ranked. Naturally, the output is the integers 0 through 19, in that order.

```
In[105]:= Map[RankKSubset[#, {a, b, c, d, e, f}] &,
            KSubsets[{a, b, c, d, e, f}, 3] ]
Out[105]= {0, 1, 2, 3, 4, 5, 6, 7, 8, 9, 10, 11, 12, 13, 14,
    15, 16, 17, 18, 19}
```

We also use these ideas to unrank a k-subset. Suppose a subset $X = \{x_1, x_2, \dots, x_k\} \subseteq \{1, 2, \dots, n\}$, $x_1 < x_2 < \cdots < x_n$, has rank m. Then the total number of k-subsets of $\{1, 2, \dots, n\}$ that contain an element smaller than x_1 is at most m. This translates into the inequality

$$\sum_{i=1}^{x_1-1} \binom{n-i}{k-1} = \binom{n}{k} - \binom{n-x_1+1}{k} \le m.$$

Also, the total number of k-subsets of $\{1, 2, \dots, n\}$ that contain an element smaller than *or equal* to x_1 is greater than m. This translates into the inequality

$$\sum_{i=1}^{x_1} \binom{n-i}{k-1} = \binom{n}{k} - \binom{n-x_1}{k} > m.$$

These inequalities give us a way of finding x_1, leading to the code below for UnrankKSubset.

```
UnrankKSubset[m_Integer, 1, s_List] := {s[[m + 1]]}
UnrankKSubset[0, k_Integer, s_List] := Take[s, k]
UnrankKSubset[m_Integer, k_Integer, s_List] :=
    Block[{i = 1, n = Length[s], x1, u, $RecursionLimit = Infinity},
```

```
u = Binomial[n, k]; While[Binomial[i, k] < u - m, i++]; x1 = n - (i - 1);
Prepend[UnrankKSubset[m-u+Binomial[n-x1+1, k], k-1, Drop[s, x1]], s[[x1]]]
]
```

Unranking a *k*-Subset

The numbers in the sequence 0 through 19 are unranked to give 3-subsets of {*a*, *b*, *c*, *d*, *e*, *f*}. As expected, we get all 3-subsets in lexicographic order.

In[106]:= **Map[UnrankKSubset[#, 3, {a, b, c, d, e, f}] &, Range[0, 19]]**

Out[106]= {{a, b, c}, {a, b, d}, {a, b, e}, {a, b, f},

{a, c, d}, {a, c, e}, {a, c, f}, {a, d, e}, {a, d, f},

{a, e, f}, {b, c, d}, {b, c, e}, {b, c, f}, {b, d, e},

{b, d, f}, {b, e, f}, {c, d, e}, {c, d, f}, {c, e, f},

{d, e, f}}

Here is the 100,000th 10-subset in the lexicographic list of 10-subsets of the set 1 through 20.

In[107]:= **UnrankKSubset[99999, 10, Range[20]]**

Out[107]= {2, 3, 4, 6, 10, 11, 13, 15, 17, 18}

And here we compute its rank and see that UnrankKSubset and RankKSubset act as inverses, as they should.

In[108]:= **RankKSubset[%, Range[20]]**

Out[108]= 99999

Can *k*-subsets be ordered in a Gray code order, yielding minimum change from one *k*-subset to the next? It takes at least two insertion-deletion operations to transform one *k*-subset into another. So a Gray code order should obtain each *k*-subset from the previous one with an insertion plus a deletion. We gain confidence that such an order exists from the following examples.

Here is the relation connecting pairs of subsets that are two operations (one deletion and one insertion) apart.

In[109]:= **sr = ((Length[Complement[#1, #2]] === 1) &&**
(Length[Complement[#2, #1]] === 1))&;

This shows a graph whose vertices are 3-subsets of {1, 2, 3, 4, 5}, and each edge in the graph connects a pair of subsets that are two operations apart. The PlotRange option has been used here to ensure that the labels are not cut off in the picture. SpringEmbedding does a good job revealing the structure in this graph.

In[110]:= **ShowGraph[g = SpringEmbedding[MakeGraph[KSubsets[Range[5],**
3], sr, Type->Undirected, VertexLabel->True]], PlotRange->0.1]

A Hamiltonian cycle in the graph tells us that 3-subsets of $\{1,2,3,4,5\}$ can be listed in a Gray code order. The structure of the graph revealed by SpringEmbedding naturally suggests other Hamiltonian cycles.

```
In[111]:= ShowGraph[Highlight[g, {Partition[HamiltonianCycle[g],2,1]},
              HighlightedEdgeColors -> {Blue}], PlotRange -> 0.1]
```

Indeed, the graph contains many different Hamiltonian cycles/Gray codes.

```
In[112]:= Length[HamiltonianCycle[g, All]]

Out[112]= 6432
```

Wilf [Wil89] suggests the following algorithm for generating k-subsets in Gray code order. Let $A(n,k)$ denote the list of k-subsets of $[n]$ in Gray code order, with the first set in the list being $\{1,2,...,n\}$ and the last one being $\{1,2,...,k-1,n\}$. $A(n,k)$ can be constructed recursively by concatenating $A(n-1,k)$ to the list obtained by reversing $A(n-1,k-1)$ and appending n to each subset in $A(n-1,k-1)$. The correctness of this recurrence can be proved easily by induction. GrayCodeKSubsets implements this algorithm.

```
GrayCodeKSubsets[n_Integer?Positive, k_Integer] := GrayCodeKSubsets[Range[n], k]

GrayCodeKSubsets[l_List, 0] := {{}}
GrayCodeKSubsets[l_List, 1] := Partition[l, 1]
GrayCodeKSubsets[l_List, k_Integer?Positive] := {l} /; (k == Length[l])
GrayCodeKSubsets[l_List, k_Integer?Positive] := {} /; (k > Length[l])

GrayCodeKSubsets[l_List, k_Integer] :=
    Block[{$RecursionLimit = Infinity},
        Join[GrayCodeKSubsets[Drop[l, -1], k],
            Map[Append[#, Last[l]]&,
                Reverse[GrayCodeKSubsets[Drop[l,-1], k-1]]
            ]
        ]
    ]
```

Generating k-Subsets in Gray Code Order

Here are 4-subsets of {*a,b,c,d,e,f*} listed in Gray code order. Each subset is obtained from its neighbors by an insertion and a deletion.

In[113]:= **GrayCodeKSubsets[{a, b, c, d, e, f}, 4]**

Out[113]= {{a, b, c, d}, {a, b, d, e}, {b, c, d, e},

{a, c, d, e}, {a, b, c, e}, {a, b, e, f}, {b, c, e, f},

{a, c, e, f}, {c, d, e, f}, {b, d, e, f}, {a, d, e, f},

{a, b, d, f}, {b, c, d, f}, {a, c, d, f}, {a, b, c, f}}

To construct a random *k*-subset, it is sufficient to select the first *k* elements in a random permutation of the set and then sort them to restore the canonical order. An alternate algorithm is obtained by using UnrankKSubset: Generate a random integer between 0 and $\binom{n}{k} - 1$ and unrank it to get a random *k*-subset of {1, 2, ..., *n*}. However, UnrankKSubset is quite slow, so this is not competitive with the random permutation algorithm.

We can get a random 50,000-subset of a set of 100,000 elements in far less time than it takes to unrank a 250-element subset of a set of 500 elements! Thus it is wasteful to use UnrankKSubset to pick a random *k*-subset.

In[114]:= **{Timing[UnrankKSubset[Random[Integer, Binomial[500, 250]-1],**
       250, Range[500]];],
       Timing[RandomKSubset[100000, 50000];]}

Out[114]= {{11.62 Second, Null}, {1.55 Second, Null}}

A more subtle, but no more efficient algorithm appears in [NW78].

```
RandomKSubset[n_Integer,k_Integer] := RandomKSubset[Range[n],k]
RandomKSubset[s_List, k_Integer] := s[[Sort[RandomPermutation[Length[s]][[Range[k] ]]]]]
```

Generating Random *k*-Subsets

Here we generate random subsets of increasing size.

In[115]:= **TableForm[Table[RandomKSubset[10,i], {i,10}]]**

Out[115]//TableForm= 5

1	7								
4	5	7							
1	4	5	8						
1	3	8	9	10					
1	2	4	7	8	10				
1	2	3	5	6	7	8			
1	2	3	4	6	7	9	10		
1	2	3	4	5	6	8	9	10	
1	2	3	4	5	6	7	8	9	10

The distribution of 3-subsets appears to be uniform.

In[116]:= **Distribution[Table[RandomKSubset[5,3], {200}]]**

Out[116]= {15, 25, 30, 20, 19, 21, 14, 22, 16, 18}

■ 2.3.5 Strings

There is a another simple combinatorial object that will prove useful in several different contexts. Indeed, we have already seen it used in constructing subsets by binary representation. A *string* of length k on an alphabet M is an arrangement of k not necessarily distinct symbols from M. Such strings should not be confused with the character string, which is a data type for text in *Mathematica*. The m^k distinct strings for an alphabet of size m can be constructed using a simple recursive algorithm that generates all length-$(k-1)$ strings on M and then prepends each of the m symbols to each string.

```
Strings[l_List,0] := { {} }

Strings[l_List, k_Integer] := Strings[Union[l], k] /; (Length[l] =!= Length[Union[l]])
Strings[l_List,k_Integer] := Distribute[Table[l, {k}], List]
```

Constructing all Strings on an Alphabet

All length-2 strings from the alphabet $\{P, Q, R\}$ are constructed. This recursive construction prepends each symbol successively to all strings of length $(k-1)$, thus yielding the strings in lexicographic order.

In[117]:= **Strings[{P, Q, R}, 2]**

Out[117]= {{P, P}, {P, Q}, {P, R}, {Q, P}, {Q, Q}, {Q, R},
      {R, P}, {R, Q}, {R, R}}

2.4 Exercises

■ 2.4.1 Thought Exercises

1. Prove that the expected value of the first element of a random n-permutation is $(n + 1)/2$.

2. Prove there exists an n-permutation p with exactly k inversions for every integer k, where $0 \le k \le \binom{n}{2}$.

3. Prove that the number of runs in an n-permutation plus the number of runs in its reverse equals $(n + 1)$.

4. Show that the average number of descents (one less than the number of runs) in a size-n permutation is $(n - 1)/2$.

5. Use NumberOfPermutationsByInversions to generate a table of $I_n(k)$ values for integers n and k, $1 \le n \le 10$ and $1 \le k \le 10$. Examine this table to determine a simple recurrence relation for $I_n(k)$, $k < n$. Prove the correctness of the recurrence.

6. How many permutations on n elements have inversion vectors that consist of $n - 1$ distinct integers? Can you characterize the permutations with this property?

7. Let O_n denote the number of insertion-deletion operations performed by BinarySubsets in generating all 2^n subsets of an n-element set. Prove that for all positive integers n, $O_n = 2O_{n-1} + n$. Solve this recurrence.

8. Show that the number of n-bit strings with exactly k 0's and with no two consecutive 0's is $\binom{n - k + 1}{k}$.

9. An undirected graph is *transitively orientable* if each of its edges can be directed so that (a, c) is a (directed) edge whenever (a, b) and (b, c) are, for any vertex b.
   (a) Show that if G is a permutation graph, then both G and its complement are transitively orientable. The *complement* of a graph $G = (V, E)$ is a graph $G^c = (V, E^c)$ in which each pair of distinct vertices a, b is connected by an edge if $\{a, b\}$ is not an edge in G.

   (b) Show that the converse of the above is also true. Based on this proof, derive an algorithm that determines if a given undirected graph G is a permutation graph. If G is a permutation graph, then your algorithm should return a permutation π for which the graph is a permutation graph.

10. Let n be a positive integer and let m be an integer such that $0 \le m < 2^n$. Suppose that m has binary representation $b_{n-1}b_{n-2}\ldots b_1 b_0$, that is, $m = \sum_{i=0}^{n-1} b_i 2^i$. If $c_{n-1}c_{n-2}\ldots c_1 c_0$ is the binary representation of the subset with rank m in the reflected Gray code, then show that $c_i = (b_i + b_{i+1}) \pmod 2$ for all $i, 0 \le i \le n - 1$. Here we suppose that $b_n = 0$.

■ 2.4.2 Programming Exercises

1. As implemented, RankPermutation takes $\Theta(n^2)$ time. An alternate algorithm for RankPermutation uses inversion vectors.

   (a) Show how to compute the rank of an n-permutation in $\Theta(n)$ time, given its inversion vector.

   (b) Implement a NewRankPermutation function using the algorithm implied in (a) and compare its running time with the running time of the current implementation.

2. Heap's algorithm defines a certain total order on permutations. Study this carefully and devise and implement ranking and unranking algorithms for this total order.

3. The recurrence for the Eulerian numbers $\left\langle {n \atop k} \right\rangle$ provides a way of generating permutations with k runs. Write functions to rank, unrank, and generate random size-n permutations with exactly k runs.

4. Write functions RankString, UnrankString, RandomString, and NextString.

5. Experiment with the function GrayCodeKSubsets to find a pattern in the insertions and deletions in going from one k-subset to the next. Use this observation to write an iterative version of the function. Compile this code and compare its running time with the current recursive function.

6. Write rank and unrank functions for k-subsets listed in Gray code order.

7. Enhance LexicographicPermutations so that it deals with multiset permutations correctly. Specifically, given a permutation of a multiset, devise an algorithm to generate the next multiset in lexicographic order. Use this to enhance NextPermutation so that it correctly deals with multisets and use the new NextPermutation to obtain a new LexicographicPermutations.

8. Enhance RankPermutation, UnrankPermutation, and RandomPermutation to deal with multisets correctly.

■ 2.4.3 Experimental Exercises

1. Change RandomPermutation so that the random index to swap is drawn from $[1, n]$ intead of $[1, i]$. Are these permutations still random? If not, which permutations are selected most/least often?

2. How much longer, on average, is the first run of a random permutation than the second? What does the expected length of the ith run converge to for large i?

3. Use the *Combinatorica* function Strings to generate all n-bit strings and from these select those that do not have two consecutive 0's. Count the number of such strings for various n. Is this number familiar to you?

3. Algebraic Combinatorics

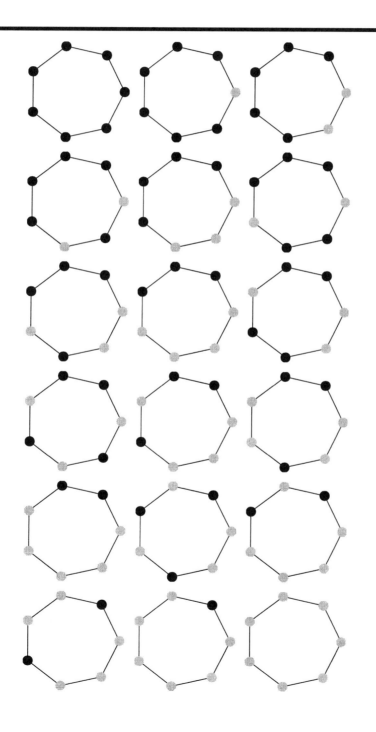

Often we want to count combinatorial objects that posses inherent symmetries. For example, how many different ten-bead necklaces can we make, given a large supply of red and blue beads? To answer this question correctly, we must properly account for necklaces that can be obtained from each other by rotations or reflections. Problems like these are considered in *Pólya theory*. Using group-theoretic tools and the cycle structure of permutations, Pólya theory provides a way of counting and enumerating combinatorial objects whose symmetries render some of them equivalent.

In this chapter, we first discuss the cycle structure of permutations and the various properties of permutations that depend on cycle structure. We then introduce some elementary group-theoretic notions and finally present Pólya theory along with various applications.

About the illustration overleaf:

The *necklace problem* asks for the number of distinct necklaces that can be made from beads of different colors. There are 128 seven-bit strings, each defining a two-coloring of the beads in a seven-bead necklace. However, this greatly overcounts the number of necklaces, because two necklaces are the same if one can be rotated or flipped to match the other. Pólya theory is the study of counting and enumerating objects that have been partitioned into groups of equivalent objects due to certain "symmetries." The illustration shows the 18 distinct seven-bead necklaces using beads of two colors. The command used to produce this illustration is

```
ln = Map[{Flatten[Position[#, 0]], Flatten[Position[#, 1]]} &,
OrbitRepresentatives[DihedralGroup[7], Strings[{0, 1}, 7]]];
ShowGraphArray[Partition[Map[Highlight[Cycle[7], #, HighlightedVertexColors -> {Black, Gray},
HighlightedVertexStyle -> Disk[0.10]] &, ln], 3]];
```

3.1 The Cycle Structure of Permutations

Permutations can be thought of as rearrangement operations, where the permutation $(4, 2, 1, 3)$ is interpreted as taking the first element to the fourth position, the fourth element to the third position, and the third element back to the first position. Since no permutation maps two distinct elements to the same element, we can always continue in this manner, sequencing through distinct elements until we get back to the first element i, thus forming a cycle.

Every permutation can thus be equivalently described by a set of disjoint cycles, where each cycle specifies a circular shift of the elements to be permuted. For example, the permutation $\pi = (5, 3, 4, 2, 6, 1)$ can be written as $\{(5, 6, 1), (3, 4, 2)\}$. Observe that π takes 1 to 5, 5 to 6, and 6 back to 1, closing the first cycle. This representation of a permutation as a set of disjoint cycles is called the *cycle structure* of a permutation. As we shall see in this section, the cycle structure of a permutation reveals much about the permutation.

There is a certain freedom associated with representing permutations by their cycle structure. Since the cycles are disjoint, they can be specified in any order. Further, since each cycle specifies a circular shift of the given elements, there is no distinguished starting point, and any rotation of a cycle describes the same cycle. Thus the cycle structure $\{(2, 3, 4), (6, 1, 5)\}$ also defines π.

This loads the *Combinatorica* package.

```
In[1]:= <<DiscreteMath`Combinatorica`
```

The identity n-permutation consists of n singleton cycles or fixed points.

```
In[2]:= ToCycles[{1,2,3,4,5,6,7,8,9,10}]
Out[2]= {{1}, {2}, {3}, {4}, {5}, {6}, {7}, {8}, {9}, {10}}
```

The reverse of the identity permutation contains only cycles of length 2, with one singleton cycle if n is odd. Cycles of length 2 correspond to transpositions.

```
In[3]:= ToCycles[Reverse[Range[10]]]
Out[3]= {{10, 1}, {9, 2}, {8, 3}, {7, 4}, {6, 5}}
```

Any permutation π with a maximum cycle length of 2 is an *involution*, meaning that multiplying π by itself gives the identity. We will study involutions in greater detail in Section 3.2.1.

```
In[4]:= Permute[ Reverse[Range[10]], Reverse[Range[10]] ]
Out[4]= {1, 2, 3, 4, 5, 6, 7, 8, 9, 10}
```

Since each cycle structure defines a unique permutation, converting to and from the cycle structure is an identity operation.

```
In[5]:= p=RandomPermutation[100]; p===FromCycles[ToCycles[p]]
Out[5]= True
```

However, going from a cycle structure to a permutation and then back may not yield the same cycle structure.

```
In[6]:= ToCycles[FromCycles[{{1}, {3, 5, 4}, {2}}]]
Out[6]= {{1}, {2}, {5, 4, 3}}
```

ToCycles produces the cycle structure in canonical order: Elements within each cycle are reordered so that the smallest element appears last.

```
In[7]:= Map[(Last[#]==Min[#])&, ToCycles[RandomPermutation[30]]]

Out[7]= {True, True, True, True}
```

Further, the cycles themselves are sorted in increasing order of the smallest element.

```
In[8]:= Map[(Last[#])&, ToCycles[RandomPermutation[1000]]]

Out[8]= {1, 2, 4, 5, 6, 10, 24, 39, 101, 137, 439, 507}
```

The cycle structure of a permutation $\pi = (\pi_1, \pi_2, \ldots, \pi_n)$ can be constructed by starting with π_1 and following the chain of successors until it gets back to p_1, finishing the cycle. We can then trace the cycle associated with the smallest element that is not in this first cycle and repeat until all elements are covered. While this is clearly a linear-time algorithm, it is a little tricky to so implement it in *Mathematica* because of the need to avoid writing into large irregular data structures.

```
ToCycles[p_?PermutationQ] :=
     Module[{k, j, first, np = p, q = Table[0, {Length[p]}]},
          DeleteCases[
            Table[If[np[[i]] == 0,
                 {},
                 j = 1; first = np[[i]]; np[[i]] = 0;
                 k = q[[j++]] = first;
                 While[np[[k]] != 0, q[[j++]] = np[[k]]; np[[k]] = 0; k = q[[j-1]]];
                 Take[q, j-1]
                 ],
                 {i, Length[p]}
            ],
            _?(#==={}&)
          ]
     ]
```

Extracting the Cycle Structure of a Permutation

Care has been taken to ensure that our *Mathematica* implementation of ToCycles runs in linear time. The difficulty is that each time we discover a new cycle, we must add it to the collection of cycles we are maintaining. However, this write operation might take time proportional to the size of the current collection, leading to a worst-case $\Theta(n^2)$ running time. We have overcome this difficulty and implemented ToCycles in linear time.

```
In[9]:= rpt = Table[RandomPermutation[i], {i, 0, 1000, 100}, {j, 10}];
        ListPlot[Table[{100 i, Mean[Table[Timing[ToCycles[rpt[[i+1, j]]];]
        [[1, 1]], {j,10}]]}, {i,0,10}], PlotJoined -> True]
```

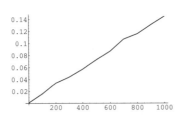

From the cycle structure, we can recover the original permutation by stepping through each element of each cycle. The code for `FromCycles` below makes slick use of several *Mathematica* functions: `RotateRight`, `Flatten`, `Transpose`, and `Sort`.

```
FromCycles[cyc_List] := Map[Last, Sort[Transpose[Map[Flatten, {Map[RotateRight, cyc], cyc}]]]]
```

Reconstructing a Permutation from Its Cycle Structure

This series of examples explains the algorithm. We start with a 6-permutation with two cycles.	*In[11]:=* **cyc = {{2, 3, 4}, {6, 1, 5}}** *Out[11]=* {{2, 3, 4}, {6, 1, 5}}
Each cycle is rotated right one step to get a new cycle structure.	*In[12]:=* **newCyc = Map[RotateRight, cyc]** *Out[12]=* {{4, 2, 3}, {5, 6, 1}}
Then the old and the new cycle structures are put together and flattened. This gives a two-line description of the permutation, which maps each element in the top row to the corresponding element in the bottom row.	*In[13]:=* (**twoLine = Map[Flatten, {newCyc, cyc}]**) // ColumnForm *Out[13]=* {4, 2, 3, 5, 6, 1} {2, 3, 4, 6, 1, 5}
This mapping is made explicit here...	*In[14]:=* **pairs = Transpose[twoLine]** *Out[14]=* {{4, 2}, {2, 3}, {3, 4}, {5, 6}, {6, 1}, {1, 5}}
...and sorted.	*In[15]:=* **orderedPairs = Sort[pairs]** *Out[15]=* {{1, 5}, {2, 3}, {3, 4}, {4, 2}, {5, 6}, {6, 1}}
The sequence of second elements gives the permutation we seek.	*In[16]:=* **Map[Last, orderedPairs]** *Out[16]=* {5, 3, 4, 2, 6, 1}

So many built-in *Mathematica* functions have been used to implement this function that its asymptotic running time is somewhat murky. Specifically, it is easy to implement this code in a high-level language such as C/C++ or Java with running time $\Theta(n)$, but whether this is true in the "Wolf-RAM" model of computation is unclear. However, a good rule of thumb is to use *Mathematica* built-in functions whenever possible, even if we lose control of the precise running time. The gain in speed from using *Mathematica* kernel code usually justifies the risk.

■ 3.1.1 Odd and Even Permutations

The cycle structure contains a wealth of information about a permutation. The number of cycles in a permutation is a measure of how hard it is to sort the permutation by transpositions. This is because a transposition increases or decreases the number of cycles in a permutation by exactly 1. In particular, transposing a pair of elements belonging to the same cycle splits the cycle, while transposing a pair of elements belonging to different cycles joins the cycles.

t is a transposition of 1 and 4; when applied to p, it splits the first cycle into two.

```
In[17]:= p = {{3, 1, 4}, {2, 5, 6}}; t = {4, 2, 3, 1, 5, 6};
         ToCycles[ Permute[ FromCycles[p], t] ]
Out[18]= {{3, 1}, {5, 6, 2}, {4}}
```

t is a transposition of 1 and 5; when applied to p, it joins the two cycles into one.

```
In[19]:= p = {{3, 1, 4}, {2, 5, 6}}; t = {5, 2, 3, 4, 1, 6};
         ToCycles[ Permute[ FromCycles[p], t] ]
Out[20]= {{6, 2, 5, 4, 3, 1}}
```

Starting from a random 100-permutation, a sequence of 30 permutations is generated, each obtained from the previous permutation by a random transposition. Observe that the numbers of cycles in successive permutations differ by 1.

```
In[21]:= p = RandomPermutation[100]; Map[Length[ToCycles[#]] &,
         FoldList[Permute, p, Table[PermutationWithCycle[100,
         RandomKSubset[100,2]],
         {30}]]]
Out[21]= {2, 3, 2, 3, 2, 1, 2, 1, 2, 3, 4, 5, 4, 5, 6, 7,
         6, 7, 6, 5, 4, 5, 6, 7, 6, 5, 6, 5, 6, 5, 6}
```

Let π be an n-permutation with c cycles. Sorting π is equivalent to transforming it into a permutation with n cycles. Since a transposition can increase the number of cycles by at most 1, at least $(n - c)$ transpositions are needed to sort π. That this suffices follows because there always exists a transposition that, when applied to any any nonidentity permutation, increases the number of cycles by 1.

Consider the transposition graph of n-permutations that we constructed in Section 2.1.4, where the vertices are permutations and edges link permutations separated by exactly one transposition. We can partition the vertex set of this graph into a set X of permutations with an even number of cycles and a set Y of permutations with an odd number of cycles.

Here is the relation that relates pairs of n-permutations that are one transposition away from each other.

```
In[22]:= tr = MemberQ[Flatten[Table[p = #1;
                      {p[[i]], p[[j]]} = {p[[j]], p[[i]]};
             p, {i, Length[#1] - 1},
             {j, i + 1, Length[#1]}], 1], #2]&;
```

This graph is *bipartite*, meaning that the vertex set can be partitioned into sets X and Y such that all edges in the graph go between X and Y.

```
In[23]:= BipartiteQ[tg5 = MakeGraph[Permutations[5], tr,
         Type -> Undirected]]
Out[23]= True
```

Any sequence of transpositions that sorts π corresponds to a path from π to the identity permutation in the transposition graph. Since the graph is bipartite with parts X and Y, every such path alternately visits X and Y. This implies that the length of *any* sequence of transpositions that sorts π has the same parity. This allows us to characterize a permutation as even or odd by the parity of sequences of transpositions that sort the permutation. The *signature* or *sign* of a permutation π is +1 if the number of transpositions in the sequence is even and −1 if it is odd. From this discussion, it follows that the parity of $(n - c)$ determines the sign of π. This is implemented in the code below, where we define a function SignaturePermutation that computes the sign of a permutation.

```
SignaturePermutation[p_?PermutationQ] := (-1) ^ (Length[p]-Length[ToCycles[p]])
```

Finding the Signature of a Permutation

Exactly half of the 120 size-5 permutations are even. This can be seen by noting that any single transposition can be viewed as a bijection between the set of even permutations and the set of odd permutations.

```
In[24]:= Length[Select[Permutations[Range[5]],
            (SignaturePermutation[#]===1)&]]
Out[24]= 60
```

All permutations have the same sign as their inverse. This follows from the fact that a permutation and its inverse have the same number of cycles. More fundamentally, one gets the inverse by reversing each cycle.

```
In[25]:= p = RandomPermutation[1000];
          {SignaturePermutation[p],
           SignaturePermutation[InversePermutation[p]]}
Out[26]= {-1, -1}
```

This calculates the fewest number of transpositions needed to sort the random 5-permutation p. This is also the length of a shortest path in the transposition graph of 5-permutations from p to the identity permutation.

```
In[27]:= {p=RandomPermutation[5], 5 - Length[ToCycles[p]]}
Out[27]= {{2, 5, 3, 4, 1}, 2}
```

We confirm the above by explicitly calculating a shortest path from p to the identity permutation by calling the *Combinatorica* function `ShortestPath`. The shortest path is expressed here as a sequence of ranks of permutations, where vertices start from 1 and permutations from 0.

```
In[28]:= ShortestPath[tg5, RankPermutation[p]+1, 1]
Out[28]= {46, 106, 1}
```

This is a minimum-length sequence of transpositions needed to transform the random 5-permutation to the identity.

```
In[29]:= Map[(UnrankPermutation[#-1,5])&, %]
Out[29]= {{2, 5, 3, 4, 1}, {5, 2, 3, 4, 1}, {1, 2, 3, 4, 5}}
```

Suppose we are interested in the minimum number of transpositions needed to go from an n-permutation π to an n-permutation π'.

```
In[30]:= {p=RandomPermutation[5],  q=RandomPermutation[5]}
Out[30]= {{5, 4, 1, 2, 3}, {2, 4, 3, 1, 5}}
```

This is the same as the number needed to go between $\alpha\pi$ and $\alpha\pi'$ for any n-permutation α. Thus we can calculate the distance between π and π' by calculating the distance between $\pi^{-1}\pi'$ and the identity.

```
In[31]:= Map[UnrankPermutation[#-1, 5]&,
          ShortestPath[tg5, RankPermutation[p]+1, RankPermutation[q]+1]]
Out[31]= {{5, 4, 1, 2, 3}, {5, 4, 1, 3, 2},
          {5, 4, 3, 1, 2}, {2, 4, 3, 1, 5}}
```

This experiment confirms the above claim. The length of a shortest path from $p^{-1} \times q$ to the identity is the same as the length of a shortest path from p to q.

```
In[32]:= Map[UnrankPermutation[#-1, 5]&,
            ShortestPath[tg5, RankPermutation[ Permute[InversePermutation[p],q]
            ]+1, 1]]
Out[32]= {{4, 2, 5, 3, 1}, {5, 2, 4, 3, 1},
            {5, 2, 3, 4, 1}, {1, 2, 3, 4, 5}}
```

Calculating the signature of a permutation happens to be one of the few combinatorial functions built into *Mathematica*. One expects that the built-in version will be faster, but starting around permutations of size 400 our implementation overtakes it.

```
In[33]:= Table[p = Table[RandomPermutation[i], {j, 10}];
            Mean[Table[Timing[SignaturePermutation[p[[j]]]];][[1, 1]],
            {j, 10}]]/ Mean[Table[Timing[Signature[p[[j]]]];][[1, 1]],
            {j, 10}]], {i, 200, 500, 50}]
Out[33]= {2.33333, 1.54167, 1.29412, 1.08511, 0.967213,
            0.857143, 0.768421}
```

And as the permutations become much larger, the built-in version continues to become relatively slower. This performance almost certainly comes from our fast implementation of ToCycles.

```
In[34]:= p = RandomPermutation[5000];
            {Timing[Signature[p];], Timing[SignaturePermutation[p];]}
Out[35]= {{9.67 Second, Null}, {0.73 Second, Null}}
```

■ 3.1.2 Types of Permutations

Let π be an n-permutation. For each integer i, $1 \le i \le n$, let λ_i be the number of length-i cycles in π. The sequence $\lambda = (\lambda_1, \lambda_2, \dots, \lambda_n)$ is called the *type* of permutation π. Note that $\sum_{i=1}^{n} \lambda_i$ gives the number of cycles in π and that $\sum_{i=1}^{n} i \cdot \lambda_i = n$. Types will prove very useful when we get to Pólya theory.

```
PermutationType[p_?PermutationQ] :=
     Module[{m = Map[Length, ToCycles[p]], c = Table[0, {Length[p]}]},
          Do[c[[ m[[i]] ]]++, {i, Length[m]}];
          c
     ]
```

Finding the Type of a Permutation

The type of the identity.

```
In[36]:= PermutationType[Range[11]]
Out[36]= {11, 0, 0, 0, 0, 0, 0, 0, 0, 0, 0}
```

The type of its reverse.

```
In[37]:= PermutationType[Reverse[Range[11]] ]
Out[37]= {1, 5, 0, 0, 0, 0, 0, 0, 0, 0, 0}
```

The types of a permutation and its inverse are identical.

```
In[38]:= p = RandomPermutation[11]; q = InversePermutation[p];
            PermutationType[p] === PermutationType[q]
Out[39]= True
```

How many permutations are there of a particular type $\lambda = (\lambda_1, \lambda_2, \dots, \lambda_n)$? To count them, write down all $n!$ n-permutations and insert parentheses so as to construct $n!$ cycle structures, each of type

λ. There are many duplicates in this list. In particular, consider for any i, $1 \le i \le n$, the λ_i length-i cycles. Taking the i elements in each length-i cycle as a block and permuting the λ_i blocks gives us a different cycle structure for the same permutation. This implies that each permutation appears $\lambda_1! \cdot \lambda_2! \cdots \lambda_n!$ times in the list. Similarly, any of the i cyclic rotations of a length-i cycle gives a different cycle structure representation for the same permutation. This implies that each permutation appears $1^{\lambda_1} \cdot 2^{\lambda_2} \cdots n^{\lambda_n}$ times in the list, so the number of permutations of type λ are

$$\frac{n!}{\lambda_1! \cdot \lambda_2! \cdots \lambda_n! \cdot 1^{\lambda_1} \cdot 2^{\lambda_2} \cdots n^{\lambda_n}}.$$

```
NumberOfPermutationsByType[l_List] := (Length[l]!)/Apply[Times, Table[l[[i]]!i^(l[[i]]), {i, Length[l]}]]
```

Finding the Number of Permutations of a Given Type

There are 120 6-permutations with one cycle. In general, there are $(n-1)!$ n-permutations with one cycle.	`In[40]:= NumberOfPermutationsByType[{0,0,0,0,0,1}]`
	
	`Out[40]= 120`

There are 144 6-permutations with one singleton cycle and one length-5 cycle. In general, there are $n(n-2)!$ n-permutations with one singleton cycle and one length-$(n-1)$ cycle.	`In[41]:= NumberOfPermutationsByType[{1,0,0,0,1,0}]`
	
	`Out[41]= 144`

An *integer partition* of a positive integer n is a set of positive integers whose sum is n. Note that an integer partition is a set and so order is irrelevant. The connection between types and integer partitions provides a quick preview of these important combinatorial objects. We will study integer partitions in detail in Chapter 4. There are exactly as many types of n-permutations as there are integer partitions of n because a type simply specifies the sizes of disjoint cycles that a permutation is partitioned into. Thus functions for generating integer partitions become useful in the context of types as well.

Here we generate all partitions of 5. The canonical way of writing partitions is in nonincreasing order of the elements.	`In[42]:= pl = Partitions[5]`
	
	`Out[42]= {{5}, {4, 1}, {3, 2}, {3, 1, 1}, {2, 2, 1},`
	`{2, 1, 1, 1}, {1, 1, 1, 1, 1}}`

We then convert each integer partition into a type to build a list of all types of 5-permutations.	`In[43]:= tl = Table[t = {0, 0, 0, 0, 0};`
	`Scan[t[[#]]++ &, pl[[i]]]; t, {i, Length[pl]}]`
	
	`Out[43]= {{0, 0, 0, 0, 1}, {1, 0, 0, 1, 0},`
	`{0, 1, 1, 0, 0}, {2, 0, 1, 0, 0}, {1, 2, 0, 0, 0},`
	`{3, 1, 0, 0, 0}, {5, 0, 0, 0, 0}}`

Here we generate the number of permutations of each type. The reader can verify that the sum of the number of permutations of all types is 5! = 120.

```
In[44]:= Map[{#, NumberOfPermutationsByType[#]} &, tl] // ColumnForm

Out[44]= {{0, 0, 0, 0, 1}, 24}
         {{1, 0, 0, 1, 0}, 30}
         {{0, 1, 1, 0, 0}, 20}
         {{2, 0, 1, 0, 0}, 20}
         {{1, 2, 0, 0, 0}, 15}
         {{3, 1, 0, 0, 0}, 10}
         {{5, 0, 0, 0, 0}, 1}
```

■ 3.1.3 Hiding Cycles

The parentheses in the cyclic representation of a permutation turn out to be unnecessary, since the cycles can be unambiguously represented without them. To drop the parentheses, rotate each cycle so the minimum element is first and then sort the cycles in decreasing order of the minimum element. This gives us a canonical cycle structure representation of permutations. We can easily and unambiguously go back and forth between a canonical cycle structure and the permutation obtained by simply dropping parentheses. This choice of a canonical cycle structure is not unique [SW86], but it is interesting. HideCycles takes the cycle structure of a permutation, converts it into canonical form, and drops parentheses, thereby converting it into a permutation.

```
HideCycles[c_List] :=
     Flatten[Sort[Map[(RotateLeft[#,Position[#,Min[#]] [[1,1]] - 1])&, c], (#1[[1]] > #2[[1]])& ]]
```

Hiding the Cycle Structure

The cycle structure can be revealed again by scanning the permutation from left to right and starting a new cycle before each left-to-right minimum. Care has been taken to ensure that the following implementation of RevealCycles runs in $\Theta(n)$ time. Two passes are made over the given permutation p, the first to note the positions of the left-to-right minima and the second to partition p according to these positions.

```
RevealCycles[p_?PermutationQ] :=
     Module[{m = Infinity},
         Map[Take[p, {#[[1]], #[[2]] - 1}]&,
             Partition[
                Join[DeleteCases[Table[If[ p[[i]] < m, m = p[[i]]; i, 0], {i, Length[p]}], 0],
                     {Length[p] + 1}
                ], 2, 1
             ]
         ]
     ]
```

Revealing the Hidden Cycle Structure

This permutation contains three cycles, one of each size.

```
In[45]:= ToCycles[{6,2,1,5,4,3}]

Out[45]= {{6, 3, 1}, {2}, {5, 4}}
```

Ordering these cycles by their last elements makes the parentheses unnecessary. Observe that the permutation that we get is *not* the one we started with.

```
In[46]:= HideCycles[%]

Out[46]= {4, 5, 2, 1, 6, 3}
```

Although HideCycles permuted the order of the cycles, the permutation is correctly defined.

```
In[47]:= RevealCycles[ HideCycles[ ToCycles[{6,2,1,5,4,3}] ] ]

Out[47]= {{4, 5}, {2}, {1, 6, 3}}
```

Let π be an arbitrary n-permutation and let π' be a permutation obtained by constructing the cycle structure of π and then hiding cycles. This correspondence between π and π' defines a function, say f, from the set of n-permutations to itself. This $f(\pi)$ is the permutation obtained by applying ToCycles to π followed by HideCycles. It is easy to see that f is a bijection and f^{-1} corresponds to applying RevealCycles first followed by FromCycles.

Here is the bijection enumerated for size-3 permutations.

```
In[48]:= Map[{#, HideCycles[ToCycles[#]]} &,
             Permutations[Range[3]]] // ColumnForm

Out[48]= {{1, 2, 3}, {3, 2, 1}}
         {{1, 3, 2}, {2, 3, 1}}
         {{2, 1, 3}, {3, 1, 2}}
         {{2, 3, 1}, {1, 2, 3}}
         {{3, 1, 2}, {1, 3, 2}}
         {{3, 2, 1}, {2, 1, 3}}
```

And here is its inverse.

```
In[49]:= Map[{#, FromCycles[RevealCycles[#]]} &,
             Permutations[Range[3]]] // ColumnForm

Out[49]= {{1, 2, 3}, {2, 3, 1}}
         {{1, 3, 2}, {3, 1, 2}}
         {{2, 1, 3}, {3, 2, 1}}
         {{2, 3, 1}, {1, 3, 2}}
         {{3, 1, 2}, {2, 1, 3}}
         {{3, 2, 1}, {1, 2, 3}}
```

Any bijection from a set onto itself defines a permutation on the set. Therefore, applying ToCycles followed by HideCycles defines an $n!$-permutation on the set of n-permutations. Here is the resulting 24-permutation defined on the set of lexicographically ordered 4-permutations.

```
In[50]:= Map[ RankPermutation[HideCycles[ToCycles[#]]] + 1 &,
             Permutations[4]]

Out[50]= {24, 18, 22, 10, 12, 16, 23, 17, 19, 1, 2, 13, 20,
          4, 21, 7, 11, 3, 6, 14, 8, 15, 5, 9}
```

Here we compute the 720-permutation on the set of 6-permutations and examine the sizes of its cycles. There is one giant cycle and a few small cycles. Is this a characteristic of this permutation? It is easy to see that this permutation cannot have any singleton cycles.

```
In[51]:= Map[Length, ToCycles[Map[ RankPermutation[ HideCycles[
             ToCycles[#] ] ] + 1&, Permutations[6]]]]

Out[51]= {694, 17, 4, 5}
```

■ 3.1.4 Counting Cycles

The correspondence between cycles and permutations from the previous section has many applications. For example, it tells us how many cycles a permutation has on average. Because of the `HideCycles` correspondence between cycle structures and permutations, this problem is equivalent to finding the average number of left-to-right minima in a permutation.

To answer this question, let π be a randomly chosen n-permutation. For each i, $1 \le i \le n$, let a random variable $X_i = 1$ if $\pi(i)$ is a left-to-right minimum and $X_i = 0$ otherwise. If we let p_i denote the probability that $\pi(i)$ is a left-to-right minimum, then $E[X_i] = p_i$. $X = \sum_{i=1}^{n} X_i$ is the total number of left-to-right minima in π and the expectation of X, $E[X]$, is what we seek:

$$E[X] = E[\sum_{i=1}^{n} X_i] = \sum_{i=1}^{n} E[X_i] = \sum_{i=1}^{n} p_i.$$

The second equality follows from the linearity of expectation. The key step now is in noting that p_i equals the probability that $\pi(i)$ is minimum in $\{\pi(1), \pi(2), \cdots, \pi(i)\}$. This happens with probability $1/i$. Therefore

$$E[X] = 1 + \frac{1}{2} + \frac{1}{3} + \cdots + \frac{1}{n} = H_n,$$

where H_n denotes the nth *harmonic number*. Since $H_n = \Theta(\lg n)$, on average, the number of cycles in an n-permutation is $\Theta(\log n)$.

For $n = 5$ the average cycle length can be calculated exactly.

```
In[52]:= Mean[Map[Length[ToCycles[#]] &, Permutations[Range[5]]]] // N
Out[52]= 2.28333
```

And this turns out to be identical to the fifth harmonic number.

```
In[53]:= HarmonicNumber[5] //N
Out[53]= 2.28333
```

For $n = 100$ we can only randomly sample the set of size-100 permutations. We use a sample of size 200 and get an approximate answer.

```
In[54]:= Mean[Map[Length[ToCycles[#]] &, Table[RandomPermutation[100],
         {200}]]] // N
Out[54]= 5.25
```

Here is H_{100} for comparison.

```
In[55]:= HarmonicNumber[100] //N
Out[55]= 5.18738
```

The number of n-permutations with exactly k cycles is an important combinatorial number, denoted $\left[{n \atop k} \right]$. To determine $\left[{n \atop k} \right]$, we can formulate a recurrence based on the cycle structures of all permutations on $(n-1)$ elements. Either the nth element forms a singleton cycle or it does not. If it does, there are $\left[{n-1 \atop k-1} \right]$ ways to arrange the rest of the elements to form $(k-1)$ cycles. If not, the nth element can be inserted in every possible position of every cycle of the $\left[{n-1 \atop k} \right]$ ways to make k cycles out of $(n-1)$ elements. This recurrence defines the *Stirling numbers of the first kind*, named after the Scottish mathematician James Stirling (1692–1772):

$$\left[{n \atop k} \right] = \left[{n-1 \atop k-1} \right] + (n-1)\left[{n-1 \atop k} \right], \text{ for } n, k \ge 1.$$

We designate $\begin{bmatrix} 0 \\ 0 \end{bmatrix}$ to be 1. It is easy to see that $\begin{bmatrix} n \\ k \end{bmatrix}$ is 0 if either n or k is 0, but not both. The following code implements this recurrence to compute the Stirling numbers of the first kind. We use the algorithmic technique of *dynamic programming* to speed up this implementation, as we did with `Eulerian` in Section 2.2.4.

```
NumberOfPermutationsByCycles[n_Integer,m_Integer] := Abs[StirlingS1[n,m]]
StirlingFirst[n_Integer,m_Integer] := StirlingFirst1[n,m] /; ((n>=0)&&(m>=0))
StirlingFirst1[n_Integer,0] := If [n == 0, 1, 0]
StirlingFirst1[0,m_Integer] := If [m == 0, 1, 0]

StirlingFirst1[n_Integer,m_Integer] :=
     Block[{$RecursionLimit = Infinity},
          StirlingFirst1[n,m] = (n-1) StirlingFirst1[n-1,m] + StirlingFirst1[n-1, m-1]
     ]
```

Counting Permutations by Cycles

These are the 11 permutations of four elements with exactly two cycles. This is consistent with formula's prediction.

```
In[56]:= {Length[Select[ Map[ToCycles,Permutations[4]], (Length[#]==2)&]],
          NumberOfPermutationsByCycles[4,2]}
Out[56]= {11, 11}
```

Here we revisit the transposition graph on 5-permutations and report the distribution of distances of all vertices from the identity permutation. There is the identity permutation at distance 0, 10 vertices at distance 1, 35 at distance 2, and so on.

```
In[57]:= Distribution[BreadthFirstTraversal[tg5, 1, Level]]
Out[57]= {1, 10, 35, 50, 24}
```

These correspond to the Stirling numbers of the first kind, because of the connection between the number of cycles in permutations and the transposition distance to the identity.

```
In[58]:= Table[StirlingFirst[5, i], {i, 5, 1, -1}]
Out[58]= {1, 10, 35, 50, 24}
```

Our definition of the Stirling numbers of the first kind follows Knuth [GKP89, Knu73a] and differs from the built-in *Mathematica* function `StirlingS1`. The latter alternates positive and negative, depending on the parity of the sum of the arguments.

```
In[59]:= {StirlingFirst[6,3], StirlingS1[6,3]}
Out[59]= {225, -225}
```

However, *Mathematica*'s implementation is much faster than ours, so we define `NumberOfPermutationsByCycles` in terms of the built-in function.

```
In[60]:= {Timing[StirlingS1[400, 200];], Timing[StirlingFirst[400, 200];]}
Out[60]= {{0.53 Second, Null}, {32.49 Second, Null}}
```

3.2 Special Classes of Permutations

In this section, we discuss two interesting classes of permutations that can be identified on the basis of their cycle structure. The first class, *involutions*, are permutations that contain cycles of size at most 2, and the second class, *derangements*, are permutations that contain no cycles of length 1.

■ 3.2.1 Involutions

Involutions are permutations that are their own multiplicative inverses. Equivalently, involutions are permutations whose cycle structure consists exclusively of fixed points and transpositions.

```
InvolutionQ[p_?PermutationQ] := p[[p]] == Range[Length[p]]
```

Testing for Involutions

There are ten involutions on four elements.

```
In[61]:= in4 = Select[ Permutations[4], InvolutionQ ]
Out[61]= {{1, 2, 3, 4}, {1, 2, 4, 3}, {1, 3, 2, 4},
          {1, 4, 3, 2}, {2, 1, 3, 4}, {2, 1, 4, 3}, {3, 2, 1, 4},
          {3, 4, 1, 2}, {4, 2, 3, 1}, {4, 3, 2, 1}}
```

This can be verified by selecting permutations whose maximum cycle length is 2, since involutions are exactly the permutations with a maximum cycle length of 2.

```
In[62]:= Select[Map[ToCycles, Permutations[4]], (Max[Map[Length,#]]
           <= 2)&]
Out[62]= {{{1}, {2}, {3}, {4}}, {{1}, {2}, {4, 3}},
          {{1}, {3, 2}, {4}}, {{1}, {4, 2}, {3}},
          {{2, 1}, {3}, {4}}, {{2, 1}, {4, 3}},
          {{3, 1}, {2}, {4}}, {{3, 1}, {4, 2}},
          {{4, 1}, {2}, {3}}, {{4, 1}, {3, 2}}}
```

Since these are involutions, squaring them gives the identity permutation.

```
In[63]:= Map[(Permute[#,#])&, in4]
Out[63]= {{1, 2, 3, 4}, {1, 2, 3, 4}, {1, 2, 3, 4},
          {1, 2, 3, 4}, {1, 2, 3, 4}, {1, 2, 3, 4}, {1, 2, 3, 4},
          {1, 2, 3, 4}, {1, 2, 3, 4}, {1, 2, 3, 4}}
```

The number of involutions t_n of size n is given by the recurrence

$$t_n = t_{n-1} + (n-1)t_{n-2}$$

for all integers $n \geq 2$, with $t_1 = t_0 = 1$. This recurrence can be understood by observing that, in any size-n involution, the element n appears either as a singleton cycle appended to a size-$(n-1)$ involution or as part of a 2-cycle appended to a size-$(n-2)$ involution. The partner of n in the 2-cycle can be any one of the other $(n-1)$ elements. We obtain an alternate way of computing t_n by noting that an involution with exactly k 2-cycles has type $(n - 2k, k, 0, 0, ..., 0)$. Using the formula for the number of permutations of a given type and summing over all possible values of k we get

$$t_n = \sum_{k=0}^{\lfloor n/2 \rfloor} \frac{n!}{(n - 2k)! 2^k k!}.$$

No simple closed form for this is known [Knu73b], so evaluating this sum turns out to be the most efficient way of calculating t_n.

```
NumberOfInvolutions[n_Integer] := Module[{k}, n! Sum[1/((n - 2k)! 2^k k!), {k, 0, Quotient[n, 2]}]]
```

The Number of Involutions on n Elements

Counting involutions for $n \leq 10$.

```
In[64]:= Table[NumberOfInvolutions[i], {i, 10}]
Out[64]= {1, 2, 4, 10, 26, 76, 232, 764, 2620, 9496}
```

Yet another way of computing the number of involutions is by noting that the number of involutions on n elements is exactly the number of distinct Young tableaux. This bijection will be established in Section 4.4.2.

```
In[65]:= Table[NumberOfTableaux[i], {i, 10}]
Out[65]= {1, 2, 4, 10, 26, 76, 232, 764, 2620, 9496}
```

Involutions recursively enumerates all involutions of a certain size. Here are all the size-4 involutions.

```
In[66]:= Involutions[4]
Out[66]= {{2, 1, 4, 3}, {2, 1, 3, 4}, {3, 4, 1, 2},
         {3, 2, 1, 4}, {4, 3, 2, 1}, {4, 2, 3, 1}, {1, 3, 2, 4},
         {1, 4, 3, 2}, {1, 2, 4, 3}, {1, 2, 3, 4}}
```

The number of involutions produced is consistent with the prediction.

```
In[67]:= {Length[Involutions[4]], NumberOfInvolutions[4]}
Out[67]= {10, 10}
```

No specific attention was paid to the generation order of Involutions. An intriguing question is whether involutions can also be generated in some "minimum change" or Gray code order. The following examples explore this issue by constructing transposition graphs on involutions.

The transposition graph on size-4 involutions is *connected*, that is, for each pair of vertices there is a path connecting them. This means that we can go from one involution to another by transpositions that take us through involutions only.

```
In[68]:= ConnectedQ[ g4 = MakeGraph[Involutions[4],
             (Count[#1 - #2, 0] == (Length[#1] - 2))&,
             Type -> Undirected, VertexLabel->True] ]
Out[68]= True
```

That this is true in general is easy to see by constructing a path starting from a source involution p. Break up each of the 2-cycles in p by applying transpositions to get to the identity permutation I. Finally, construct each of the 2-cycles in the destination involution q from I by applying transpositions. The graph in this example has no Hamiltonian path, implying that there is no listing of size-4 involutions in which a single transposition takes us from one involution to the next.

In[69]:= `ShowGraph[g = SpringEmbedding[g4,100], PlotRange->0.25]`

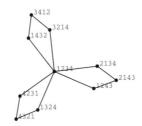

■ 3.2.2 Derangements

A *derangement* is a permutation π with no element in its proper position, meaning that there exists no i satisfying $\pi(i) = i$. Thus each derangement is a permutation without a fixed point, having no cycle of length 1. The recurrence

$$d_n = (n-1)(d_{n-1} + d_{n-2})$$

gives the number of derangements of size $n \geq 2$, with $d_1 = 0$ and $d_0 = 1$. This can be established by the following argument. For $n \geq 2$, the set of size-n derangements can be partitioned into two subsets: those in which n is part of a 2-cycle and those in which n is part of a larger cycle. Derangements in which n is part of a 2-cycle can be constructed as follows. Take one of the $(n-1)d_{n-2}$ permutations of $(n-1)$ elements with exactly one fixed point, append n, and exchange the fixed point with n. Derangements in which n is part of a larger cycle can be constructed as follows. Take one of the d_{n-1} derangements of $(n-1)$ elements and insert the element n into any one of the cycles. We get $(n-1)d_{n-1}$ permutations, depending on where n is inserted.

Simple algebraic manipulation of the above recurrence yields the following:

$$d_n = n \cdot d_{n-1} + (-1)^n \text{ for } n \geq 1.$$

Implementing this recurrence leads to slightly faster code because here d_n depends only on d_{n-1}, not on both d_{n-1} and d_{n-2}. This is the route that we take in implementing `NumberOfDerangements`, which is shown below.

```
DerangementQ[p_?PermutationQ] := !(Apply[ Or, Map[( # === p[[#]] )&, Range[Length[p]]] ])

NumberOfDerangements[0] := 1
NumberOfDerangements[n_Integer?Positive] :=
     Block[{$RecursionLimit = Infinity}, n * NumberOfDerangements[n-1] + (-1)^n]
```

```
Derangements[0] := { {} }
Derangements[n_Integer] := Derangements[Range[n]]
Derangements[p_?PermutationQ] := Select[ Permutations[p], DerangementQ ]
```

Obtaining and Counting Derangements

This shows the first ten values of d_n.

In[70]:= **Table[NumberOfDerangements[i], {i,1,10}]**

Out[70]= {0, 1, 2, 9, 44, 265, 1854, 14833, 133496, 1334961}

Here are all the size-4 derangements. They are shown in their cycle form to emphasize the absence of fixed points.

In[71]:= **Map[ToCycles, Derangements[4]]**

Out[71]= {{{2, 1}, {4, 3}}, {{2, 3, 4, 1}}, {{2, 4, 3, 1}},
   {{3, 4, 2, 1}}, {{3, 1}, {4, 2}}, {{3, 2, 4, 1}},
   {{4, 3, 2, 1}}, {{4, 2, 3, 1}}, {{4, 1}, {3, 2}}}

Our code for generating derangements simply selects the permutations without fixed points from all the permutations. We are justified in this seemingly sloppy approach because at least one-third of all permutations are derangements!

The ratio of the number of size-n derangements to the number of n-permutations is always greater than one-third, except for the trivial case $n = 1$.

In[72]:= **Table[N[NumberOfDerangements[i]/(i!)], {i,1,10}]**

Out[72]= {0., 0.5, 0.333333, 0.375, 0.366667, 0.368056,
   0.367857, 0.367882, 0.367879, 0.367879}

In fact, this ratio quickly converges to the magic number $1/e$.

In[73]:= **1/N[E]**

Out[73]= 0.367879

Rounding $n!/e$ gives a nicer way to compute the number of derangements.

In[74]:= **Table[Round[n!/N[E]], {n,1,10}]**

Out[74]= {0, 1, 2, 9, 44, 265, 1854, 14833, 133496, 1334961}

All of this implies that if a confused secretary randomly stuffs n different letters into n pre-addressed envelopes, the probability that none of them ends up where they are supposed to is close to $1/e$. Figuring out this probability is sometimes called the *secretary problem*.

In Section 2.1.4, we briefly discussed the problem of enumerating permutations in "maximum change" order, that is, in an order in which consecutive permutations differ in all positions. Given a pair of permutations π and π' that differ in all positions, it is easy to see that the permutation $\alpha = \pi^{-1} \times \pi'$ is a derangement. In other words, to get from a permutation π to a permutation π' that differs from π in all positions, we apply the derangement α on π.

This motivates the definition of a *derangement graph*, whose vertices are n-permutations and two vertices π and π' are connected by an edge if there is some derangement α such that $\alpha = \pi^{-1} \times \pi'$.

In[75]:= **dr = DerangementQ[Permute[InversePermutation[#1], #2]]&;**
   dg4 = MakeGraph[Permutations[4], dr, Type -> Undirected]

Out[76]= -Graph:<108, 24, Undirected>-

A Hamiltonian path in this graph corresponds to an enumeration of permutations in maximum change order. Is the derangement graph on n-permutations always Hamiltonian for arbitrary n?

```
In[77]:= Permutations[4] [[ HamiltonianCycle[dg4] ]]
Out[77]= {{1, 2, 3, 4}, {2, 1, 4, 3}, {1, 3, 2, 4},
    {2, 4, 1, 3}, {1, 3, 4, 2}, {2, 1, 3, 4}, {1, 2, 4, 3},
    {2, 3, 1, 4}, {1, 4, 2, 3}, {2, 3, 4, 1}, {1, 4, 3, 2},
    {3, 1, 2, 4}, {2, 4, 3, 1}, {4, 1, 2, 3}, {3, 2, 1, 4},
    {4, 1, 3, 2}, {3, 2, 4, 1}, {4, 3, 1, 2}, {3, 4, 2, 1},
    {4, 2, 1, 3}, {3, 1, 4, 2}, {4, 2, 3, 1}, {3, 4, 1, 2},
    {4, 3, 2, 1}, {1, 2, 3, 4}}
```

Jackson [Jac80] proved that any k-regular, biconnected graph with at most $3k$ vertices is Hamiltonian. A *biconnected* graph is one from which at least two vertices need to be deleted to cause the graph to break up into more than one connected piece. This notion will be explored in Section 7.2.4. The derangement graph on n-permutations is k-regular with k equal to $\approx n!/e$. It is not difficult to show that, for all $n > 3$, the derangement graph on n-permutations is indeed biconnected and hence Hamiltonian.

This is an illustration of Jackson's theorem. This call to `RegularGraph` constructs a "semirandom" instance of a 30-vertex 10-regular graph. If this graph is biconnected, it is also Hamiltonian.

```
In[78]:= {BiconnectedQ[g = RegularGraph[10, 30]], HamiltonianQ[g]}
Out[78]= {True, True}
```

Such graphs do not have to be connected, let alone biconnected.

```
In[79]:= {BiconnectedQ[g = GraphUnion[2,RegularGraph[10, 15]]],
            HamiltonianQ[g]}
Out[79]= {False, False}
```

Jackson's theorem tells us that derangement graphs contain Hamiltonian cycles, but no more. In particular, it does not tell us how to construct a Hamiltonian cycle in such a graph efficiently and therefore does not yield an enumeration algorithm for permutations in maximum change order. However, constructive solutions to this problem appear in [EW85, RS87].

3.3 Pólya Theory

How many distinct dice can a dice maker make? There are 6! = 720 ways of numbering the faces of a cube with six distinct numbers, but many of these numberings turn out to be identical because of the "symmetries" of the cube.

Here are two dice with their faces opened up. Numbers 3 and 1 are written on the top and bottom faces, respectively, of both dice. Numbers 5, 2, 6, and 4 are written on the back, left, front, and right faces, respectively, of the dice on the left. Take the die on the left and rotate it 90° counterclockwise about the axis that passes through the centers of the top and bottom faces (numbered 1 and 3). The result is the die on the right. Thus these two labelings yield the same die.

```
In[80]:= << extraCode/ShowOpenCube;
         Show[GraphicsArray[{ShowOpenCube[{1, 2, 3, 4, 5, 6}],
         ShowOpenCube[{1, 5, 3, 6, 4, 2}]}]]
```

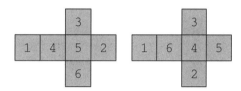

As in the example above, the symmetry of the cube renders many labelings of cubes equivalent. In fact, there are only 30 distinct dice out of 720 labelings. What is remarkable is that, since antiquity, only one of these 30 dice has been the "standard" die used throughout the world [Kri85]. More generally, Gardner [Gar78] mentions that, for a Platonic solid with f faces and e edges, the number of distinct ways of numbering the faces of the solid with f distinct numbers is exactly $f!/2e$.

Dice counting is an instance of a more general problem in which a *group* (the group of symmetries of the cube) acts on a set (the set of 720 labelings of the faces of the cube), thereby inducing equivalence classes or *orbits*. Pólya was the first to systematically study the combinatorial aspects of group actions on sets, and the resulting theory bears his name. *Pólya theory* is used to count and construct combinatorial objects such as isomers of chemical compounds, codes, graphs, necklaces, and colorings of Platonic solids.

■ 3.3.1 Permutation Groups

A *group* is a nonempty set S together with a binary operation $*$ satisfying the axioms

1. **Closure:** For all $a, b \in S$, $a * b \in S$.

2. **Associativity:** For all $a, b, c \in S$, $(a * b) * c = a * (b * c)$.

3. **Existence of Identity:** There is an element $e \in S$, called the *identity*, such that for all $a \in S$, $a * e = a$.

4. **Existence of Inverse:** For each $a \in S$, there is an element in S denoted a^{-1}, called the *inverse* of a, such that $a * a^{-1} = e$.

Groups are fundamental algebraic objects that show up in unexpected places: Here they arise in the enumeration of combinatorial objects. The number of elements in a group is called its *order*; a *finite group* has finite order. We will be interested, almost exclusively, in *permutation groups*, that is, groups in which S is a set of permutations and $*$ is the permutation multiplication operation. This permits us to abuse notation in the following sense: When we say G is a permutation group, we will take G to be a set of permutations, with the assumption that the accompanying binary operation is understood. Permutation groups have been used in the past two centuries as a tool for exploring geometrical, algebraic, and combinatorial symmetries [DM91].

Symmetric, Cyclic, Dihedral, and Alternating Groups

We now define the most common permutation groups. The set of all n-permutations is the *symmetric group*, denoted S_n. The *cyclic group* C_n contains the n permutations obtained by performing circular shifts on $(1, 2, ..., n)$. The *dihedral group* D_{2n} contains the n permutations in C_n and an additional n permutations obtained by reversing these. The *alternating group* A_n is the set of all even n-permutations. The cyclic and the dihedral groups play a crucial role in the *necklace problem*, a classic application of Pólya theory. Functions to generate these groups are as follows.

```
SymmetricGroup[n_Integer] := Permutations[n] /; (n >= 0)

CyclicGroup[0] := {{}}
CyclicGroup[n_Integer] := Table[RotateRight[Range[n], i], {i, 0, n-1}]

DihedralGroup[0] := {{}}
DihedralGroup[1] := {{1}}
DihedralGroup[2] := {{1, 2}, {2, 1}}
DihedralGroup[n_Integer?Positive] := Module[{c = CyclicGroup[n]}, Join[c, Map[Reverse, c]]]

AlternatingGroup[l_List] := Select[Permutations[l], (SignaturePermutation[#]===1)&] /; (Length[l] > 0)
AlternatingGroup[n_Integer?Positive] := Select[Permutations[n], (SignaturePermutation[#]===1)&]
```

Generating Common Permutation Groups

The cyclic group of order 5.

```
In[82]:= CyclicGroup[5]
Out[82]= {{1, 2, 3, 4, 5}, {5, 1, 2, 3, 4},
          {4, 5, 1, 2, 3}, {3, 4, 5, 1, 2}, {2, 3, 4, 5, 1}}
```

D_{14} can be partitioned into three sets, based on the types of the permutations. The identity permutation has seven fixed points, the permutations inherited from C_7 consist of a single cycle of length 7, and the remaining seven permutations have three 2-cycles and a fixed point.

```
In[83]:= Union[Map[PermutationType, DihedralGroup[7]]]
Out[83]= {{0, 0, 0, 0, 0, 0, 1}, {1, 3, 0, 0, 0, 0, 0},
          {7, 0, 0, 0, 0, 0, 0}}
```

The signature of the product of permutations equals the product of the signatures of the permutations. This implies that the product of even permutations is even, thereby implying that A_n satisfies the closure axiom.

```
In[84]:= p = RandomPermutation[100]; q = RandomPermutation[100];
         SignaturePermutation[p] SignaturePermutation[q] ===
         SignaturePermutation[ Permute[p, q] ]
Out[85]= True
```

Automorphism Groups

Another group that will be important in the enumeration of graph colorings is the *automorphism group* of a graph. An *automorphism* of a graph G is a renaming of the vertices of G that results in an identical graph. More precisely, a automorphism of a graph $G = (V, E)$ is a bijection $f : V \to V$ satisfying $\{u, v\} \in E$ if and only if $\{f(u), f(v)\} \in V$. The set of automorphisms of a graph is called the *automorphism group* of the graph. This group provides a tool for understanding symmetries in a graph and has been used as a foundation for graph drawing algorithms that seek to display these symmetries [LNS85].

Wheel is one of many *Combinatorica* graph construction functions described in Chapter 6. The problem of computing the automorphism group of a graph will be discussed in Section 8.6 in the larger context of graph isomorphisms.

```
In[86]:= ShowGraph[c = Wheel[6], VertexNumber -> True,
         TextStyle -> {FontSize -> 13}, PlotRange -> 0.05];
```

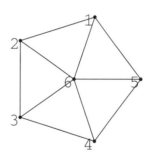

The automorphism group of Wheel[6] contains ten permutations. In each, vertex 6 is a fixed point. Five of the permutations are obtained by the five rotations on vertices 1 through 5. The other five are obtained by reflecting the graph about an axis passing through vertices i and 6 for each i, $1 \le i \le 5$.

```
In[87]:= Automorphisms[ Wheel[6] ]
Out[87]= {{1, 2, 3, 4, 5, 6}, {1, 5, 4, 3, 2, 6},
         {2, 1, 5, 4, 3, 6}, {2, 3, 4, 5, 1, 6},
         {3, 2, 1, 5, 4, 6}, {3, 4, 5, 1, 2, 6},
         {4, 3, 2, 1, 5, 6}, {4, 5, 1, 2, 3, 6},
         {5, 1, 2, 3, 4, 6}, {5, 4, 3, 2, 1, 6}}
```

This physical interpretation of the automorphism group of a 6-vertex wheel makes it clear that this group is *isomorphic* to the dihedral group D_{10}. A group G with binary operator $*$ is isomorphic to a group H with binary operator $+$ if there is a bijection $f : G \to H$ such that $f(a * b) = f(a) + f(b)$. The bijection f is called an *isomorphism*. In other words, two isomorphic groups are identical, except that their elements have different names.

Every graph has at least one automorphism, the identity element.

```
In[88]:= Automorphisms[f = FruchtGraph]
Out[88]= {{1, 2, 3, 4, 5, 6, 7, 8, 9, 10, 11, 12}}
```

For every group *G*, there exists a graph whose automorphism group is isomorphic to *G* [Fru39]. The *Frucht graph* is the smallest 3-regular graph whose group consists only of the identity element.

```
In[89]:= ShowGraph[f];
```

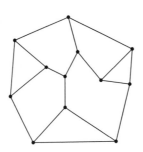

The automorphism group of the complement of a graph is the same as that of the original graph.

```
In[90]:= g=RandomGraph[10, 0.2];
         Automorphisms[g] == Automorphisms[GraphComplement[g]]
Out[91]= True
```

Our aim in introducing permutation groups into *Combinatorica* is primarily for solving combinatorial enumeration problems. We make no attempt to efficiently represent permutation groups or to solve many of the standard computational problems in group theory. A user looking for a computational discrete algebra system should try *GAP* [GAP99] or *Magma* [BC02].

Multiplication Table

A convenient way of checking whether a set *S* of objects along with a binary operation $*$ is a group is to generate the *multiplication table* of *S* with respect to $*$. This is the $|S| \times |S|$ two-dimensional table whose (i, j)th entry is *k* if and only if (iff) the *i*th element multiplied by the *j*th element in *S* equals the *k*th element in *S*. The following function computes the multiplication table of a group.

```
MultiplicationTable[elems_List, op_] :=
    With[{rules = Append[Thread[elems -> Range[Length[elems]]], _ -> 0]},
        Outer[Replace[op[##], rules] &, elems, elems, 1]]
```

Generating the Multiplication Table of a Set of Objects

The multiplication table of any permutation group is a *Latin square*. In an $n \times n$ Latin square, each row is an n-permutation and so is each column. Furthermore, one of the rows is the identity permutation and so is one of the columns.

```
In[92]:= MultiplicationTable[DihedralGroup[3], Permute] // TableForm
Out[92]//TableForm= 1   2   3   4   5   6
                    2   3   1   5   6   4
                    3   1   2   6   4   5
                    4   6   5   1   3   2
                    5   4   6   2   1   3
                    6   5   4   3   2   1
```

■ 3.3.2 Group Action

At the core of Pólya theory is the notion of a group acting on a set. We introduce this through an example. Let S be the set of all 2-subsets of $\{1, 2, 3, 4\}$, and let π be an arbitrary 4-permutation. For any 2-subset $s = \{x_1, x_k\}$, π can be thought of as mapping this set to $\{\pi(x_1), \pi(x_2)\}$, denoted $\pi(s)$. Note that $\pi(s)$ is also a 2-subset and is therefore an element of S. Thus π can be thought of as a mapping from S to itself, and, more specifically, it is easy to see that $\pi : S \to S$ is a bijection. Assuming that the elements of S are labeled 1 through 6 in some order, π can be thought of as inducing a 6-permutation rearranging the elements of S. We denote this by $\pi(S)$.

Here the elements of S are transformed by the permutation $\pi = (4, 1, 2, 3)$. The top row shows S and the bottom row shows $\pi(S)$. The objects being permuted are sets, not tuples, and so $\{1, 4\}$ and $\{4, 1\}$ are identical. Thus $\pi(S)$ must be a permutation of S.

```
In[93]:= pi = {4, 1, 2, 3};
         {S=KSubsets[Range[4],2], p=Map[pi[[#]]&,S]} //ColumnForm
Out[94]= {{1, 2}, {1, 3}, {1, 4}, {2, 3}, {2, 4}, {3, 4}}
         {{4, 1}, {4, 2}, {4, 3}, {1, 2}, {1, 3}, {2, 3}}
```

Now let G be a group of 4-permutations. It can be verified that the set of 6-permutations $H = \{\pi(S) \mid \pi \in G\}$ is also a group. Furthermore, for any $\pi, \pi' \in G$, $\pi(S) \times \pi'(S) = (\pi \times \pi')(S)$. The two groups G and H in this example are said to be homomorphic. In general, a group G with a binary operator $*$ is *homomorphic* to a group H with a binary operator $+$ if there exists a mapping $f : G \to H$ such that $f(a * b) = f(a) + f(b)$ for all $a, b \in G$. In this case, the mapping f is called a *homomorphism*. It is easy to verify that h preserves the identity and inverses. In other words, h maps the identity in G to the identity in H, and h maps π^{-1} to the inverse of $h(\pi)$.

Group isomorphism is group homomorphism with an extra condition: The mapping h has to be a bijection. A group G is said to *act* on a set S if there is a homomorphism from G to a group H of permutations of S. Most problems that can be solved using Pólya-theoretic techniques involve a group acting on a set S of subsets or ordered subsets. We define KSubsetGroup to take as input a group G of n-permutations and a set S of k-subsets of $\{1, 2, ..., n\}$; it returns the group $H = \{\pi(S) \mid \pi \in G\}$, where $\pi(S)$ is defined as in the above example.

This shows the permutation group induced on the set of all 2-subsets of $\{1, 2, 3, 4\}$ by C_4. Since there are six 2-subsets, this is a permutation group of 6-permutations.

```
In[95]:= q = KSubsetGroup[CyclicGroup[4], S]
Out[95]= {{1, 2, 3, 4, 5, 6}, {3, 5, 6, 1, 2, 4},
          {6, 2, 4, 3, 5, 1}, {4, 5, 1, 6, 2, 3}}
```

This multiplication table shows that the induced set of permutations indeed is a group.

```
In[96]:= MultiplicationTable[q, Permute] // TableForm

Out[96]//TableForm= 1   2   3   4
                    2   3   4   1
                    3   4   1   2
                    4   1   2   3
```

Here S is the set of all ordered 2-subsets of $\{1, 2, 3, 4\}$.

```
In[97]:= ToOrderedPairs[CompleteGraph[4]]
         S = Select[Flatten[Table[{i, j}, {i, 4}, {j, 4}], 1],
         #[[1]] != #[[2]] &]

Out[98]= {{1, 2}, {1, 3}, {1, 4}, {2, 1}, {2, 3}, {2, 4},
          {3, 1}, {3, 2}, {3, 4}, {4, 1}, {4, 2}, {4, 3}}
```

This is the permutation group induced on the set of all ordered 2-subsets of $\{1, 2, 3, 4\}$ by C_4. Since there are 12 2-subsets, this is a permutation group of 12-permutations. This example shows the use of the tag `Ordered` that can be used as a third argument to `KSubsetGroup`.

```
In[99]:= q = KSubsetGroup[CyclicGroup[4], S, Ordered]

Out[99]= {{1, 2, 3, 4, 5, 6, 7, 8, 9, 10, 11, 12},
          {10, 11, 12, 3, 1, 2, 6, 4, 5, 9, 7, 8},
          {9, 7, 8, 12, 10, 11, 2, 3, 1, 5, 6, 4},
          {5, 6, 4, 8, 9, 7, 11, 12, 10, 1, 2, 3}}
```

Here we first compute the automorphism group of a 5-vertex wheel and then pass these automorphisms into `KSubsetGroup` to compute a permutation group on the edges of the graph.

```
In[100]:= g = Wheel[5]; ag = Automorphisms[g];
          KSubsetGroup[ag, Edges[g]]

Out[101]= {{1, 2, 3, 4, 5, 6, 7, 8},
           {1, 4, 3, 2, 8, 7, 6, 5}, {2, 1, 4, 3, 5, 8, 7, 6},
           {2, 3, 4, 1, 6, 7, 8, 5}, {3, 2, 1, 4, 6, 5, 8, 7},
           {3, 4, 1, 2, 7, 8, 5, 6}, {4, 1, 2, 3, 8, 5, 6, 7},
           {4, 3, 2, 1, 7, 6, 5, 8}}
```

■ 3.3.3 Equivalence Classes and Orbits

A *binary relation* R on a set S is a subset of the Cartesian product $S \times S$. In other words, R is some subset of ordered pairs of elements from S. R is said to be

- *reflexive* if it contains (i, i) for every $i \in S$;
- *transitive* if for every $i, j, k \in S$, $(i, j) \in S$ and $(j, k) \in S$ imply that $(i, k) \in S$;
- *symmetric* if for every $i, j \in S$, $(i, j) \in S$ implies that $(j, i) \in S$.

R is an *equivalence relation* if it is reflexive, symmetric, and transitive. Equivalence relations have several nice properties, particularly that the elements can be partitioned into *equivalence classes* such that every pair of elements within the same equivalence classes are related and no pair of elements from different classes are related. In *Combinatorica*, we define Boolean functions `ReflexiveQ`, `SymmetricQ`, and `TransitiveQ` that respectively test if a given relation is reflexive, symmetric, or transitive. Based on these, we also define a function `EquivalenceRelationQ` to test if a relation is an equivalence relation. These functions accept a relation specified in one of two ways, either (i) as a square matrix whose nonzero entries denote related pairs of elements or (ii) as a graph whose edges represent related pairs of elements. These functions interpret the edges of an undirected graph as pairs of directed edges headed in opposite directions.

The divisibility relation between integers is reflexive since each integer divides itself.

```
In[102]:= ReflexiveQ[ g=MakeGraph[Range[8],(Mod[#1,#2]==0)&] ]
Out[102]= True
```

It is not symmetric because, if x divides y, then y does not divide x unless they are equal. The relation defines a directed graph.

```
In[103]:= SymmetricQ[ g ]
Out[103]= False
```

The relation is transitive, as $x \setminus y$ implies $y = cx$ for some integer c, so $y \setminus z$ implies $x \setminus z$.

```
In[104]:= TransitiveQ[ g ]
Out[104]= True
```

We start with the automorphism group of a 6-vertex wheel graph and define the following binary relation on the vertices: i is related to j if there is some automorphism π such that $\pi(i) = j$. This is an equivalence relation with two equivalence classes, one of size 5 and the other a singleton. The singleton equivalence class corresponds to the central vertex in the wheel, which is mapped to itself by every automorphism.

```
In[105]:= ag = Automorphisms[g = Wheel[6]];
          r = MemberQ[Table[ag[[i, #1]], {i, Length[ag]}], #2]&;
          ShowGraph[MakeGraph[Range[6], r, Type -> Undirected]];
```

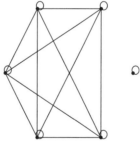

We compute the same relation as above, but this time on *edges*: Edge i is related to edge j if there is permutation that takes i to j. This is still an equivalence relation, however; the equivalence classes are of size 5 each. The edges incident on the central vertex form one group, and the rest of the edges form the other group. That this relation is an equivalence relation is not a coincidence.

```
In[108]:= ag = KSubsetGroup[ag, Edges[g]];
          ShowGraph[MakeGraph[Range[10], r, Type -> Undirected]];
```

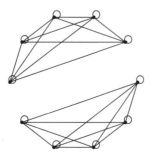

A graph is *vertex-transitive* if for any pair of vertices (i, j) there is an automorphism π satisfying $\pi(i) = j$. Similarly, a graph is *edge-transitive* if for any pair of edges (e, e') there is a permutation π of the edges, induced by an automorphism, such that $\pi(e) = e'$. The above examples show that the wheel graph is neither vertex-transitive nor edge-transitive. The *Folkman graph* shown here is the smallest nontrivial edge-transitive but not vertex-transitive graph.

```
In[110]:= ShowGraph[FolkmanGraph];
```

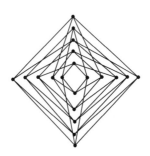

Let G be a group that acts on a set S. By definition of a group action, there is a homomorphism f from G to a group H of permutations of S. For any $\pi \in G$, let π_f be a short form for the element $f(\pi)$. Define a binary relation $\sim$ on S as $i \sim j$ if and only if $\pi_f(i) = j$ for some $\pi \in G$. That $\sim$ is an equivalence relation is left as an exercise for the reader. The *orbits* of a group G acting on a set S are the equivalence classes of $\sim$. Counting, enumerating, and producing an "inventory" of orbits is at the heart of Pólya theory. In an earlier example, we demonstrated the action of the automorphism group of the 6-vertex wheel graph on the set of edges of the graph. This group action induced two orbits, each with five edges.

The *Cauchy-Frobenius lemma* is a beautiful result, often called "Burnside's lemma," that states that the number of orbits of the group G acting on a set S is

$$\frac{1}{|G|}\left(\sum_{\pi \in G} \psi(\pi)\right),$$

where $\psi(\pi)$ is the number of fixed points in π_f. This result has a wide range of applications, one of them being in the proof of Pólya's theorem.

The automorphism group of the 6-vertex wheel graph acts on the edges of the graph to induce a group of 10-permutations. Here we sum up the fixed points of the permutations in this group...

```
In[111]:= Apply[Plus, Map[First[PermutationType[#]] &, ag]]
Out[111]= 20
```

...and divide by the order of the group to get the number of orbits.

```
In[112]:= % / Length[ag]
Out[112]= 2
```

The function `OrbitRepresentatives` returns a representative from each orbit of a group acting on a set. It turns out to be quite useful in enumeration problems involving group actions on sets.

```
Orbits[g_List, x_List, f_:Permute] :=
     Module[{y = x, n = Length[g], orbit, out = {}},
          While[y != {},
               orbit = Table[Apply[f, {y[[1]], g[[i]]}], {i, 1, n}];
               y = Complement[y, orbit];
               AppendTo[out, orbit];
               Length[y]
          ];
          out
     ]
OrbitRepresentatives[g_List, x_List, f_:Permute] :=
     Module[{y = Orbits[g, x, f]},
          Table[y[[i]][[1]], {i, Length[y]}]
     ] /; ((Length[g] > 0) && (Length[x] > 0)) && (Length[ g[[1]] ] == Length[ x[[1]] ])
```

Computing Orbits and Their Representatives

OrbitRepresentatives takes a permutation group G, a set S, and a function $f : S \times G \to S$. The function f is essentially a homomorphism from G into a set of permutations of S. For each $s \in S$, the set $\{f(s,\pi) : \pi \in G\}$ is the orbit of G acting on S that contains the element s. If the function f is not supplied, the default Permute is used. This works provided each $s \in S$ is a length-n sequence and G is a group of size-n permutations, as in all our examples.

We now present three classic examples of enumeration involving a group acting on a set: (i) necklace enumeration; (ii) dice enumeration; and (iii) graph enumeration.

Necklace Enumeration

The *necklace problem* is to enumerate (or count) the total number of *distinct* necklaces that can be made with n beads, assuming that we have an infinite supply of beads available in each of c colors. A pair of necklaces is distinct if one cannot be obtained from the other by a rotation, reflection, or any combination of these operations.

The set of necklaces is given by the set of functions $\phi : \{1, 2, ..., n\} \to C$, where C is a set of c colors. The group acting on this set of necklaces, rendering some of them equivalent, is the dihedral group D_{2n}. OrbitRepresentatives can be used to enumerate representatives of the orbits of D_{2n} acting on the set of necklaces. These representatives are simply the set of distinct necklaces.

This shows all distinct 5-bead necklaces made with red and blue beads. The 32 red-blue strings that we can write down reduce to eight distinct necklaces.

```
In[113]:= OrbitRepresentatives[ DihedralGroup[5], Strings[{R, B}, 5]]

Out[113]= {{R, R, R, R, R}, {B, B, B, B, B},
           {B, B, B, B, R}, {B, B, B, R, R}, {B, B, R, B, R},
           {B, B, R, R, R}, {B, R, B, R, R}, {B, R, R, R, R}}
```

This is the number of length-7 strings
that one can make using the alphabet
$\{R, B, G\}$. For our purposes, these are
7-bead necklaces.

In[114]:= **Length[Strings[{R, B, G}, 7]]**

Out[114]= 2187

This is the number of *distinct* 7-bead
necklaces using at most three colors. It
turns out that the list of 2187 necklaces
contains only 198 distinct necklaces.

In[115]:= **Length[OrbitRepresentatives[DihedralGroup[7],**
        Strings[{R, B, G}, 7]]]

Out[115]= 198

Dice Enumeration

The next example we present is dice enumeration. We started this section by noting that there are 30
distinct dice. We now show how to enumerate these using *Combinatorica*. If we ignore the symmetries
of the cube, there are 720 ways of labeling the faces 1 through 6. The symmetries of a cube can be
expressed as a permutation group of the vertices of the cube. As explained in an example below, there
are 24 operations that one can perform to rotate and reflect the cube. These operations constitute a
permutation group of *vertex symmetries* with 24 8-permutations, since the cube has eight vertices. This
group acts on the set of faces of the cube to induce the permutation group of *face symmetries* of the
cube. This group of face symmetries of the cube acts on the set of 720 face numberings of the cube,
and the orbits of this action correspond to distinct dice.

We load the standard add-on package
Graphics`Polyhedra` containing the
definitions of various polyhedra,
including the five Platonic solids.

In[116]:= **<<Graphics`Polyhedra`;**

Here we display the Cube object
defined in the Graphics`Polyhedra`
package. The labeling of the vertices
shown here is what we use in the
following examples.

In[117]:= **Show[Graphics3D[{Cube[], v = Vertices[Cube];**
        Table[Text[i, v[[i]] - 0.05], {i, 7}]}],
        TextStyle -> {FontWeight -> "Bold", FontSize -> 16}]

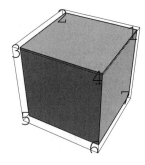

This is the group of symmetries of a cube expressed as permutations of the vertices. The first nine permutations in this list are obtained by rotating the cube about the three axes that pass through the centers of opposite faces. The next six permutations are obtained by rotating the cube about six axes that pass through the centers of opposite edges. The next eight are obtained by rotating the cube about the four body diagonals of the cube. The last permutation is the identity, obtained by doing nothing to the cube!

```
In[118]:= c=<<extraCode/CubeVertexSymmetries
Out[118]= {{2, 3, 4, 1, 6, 7, 8, 5},
    {3, 4, 1, 2, 7, 8, 5, 6}, {4, 1, 2, 3, 8, 5, 6, 7},
    {2, 8, 5, 3, 6, 4, 1, 7}, {8, 7, 6, 5, 4, 3, 2, 1},
    {7, 1, 4, 6, 3, 5, 8, 2}, {4, 3, 5, 6, 8, 7, 1, 2},
    {6, 5, 8, 7, 2, 1, 4, 3}, {7, 8, 2, 1, 3, 4, 6, 5},
    {2, 1, 7, 8, 6, 5, 3, 4}, {5, 6, 4, 3, 1, 2, 8, 7},
    {7, 6, 5, 8, 3, 2, 1, 4}, {5, 8, 7, 6, 1, 4, 3, 2},
    {4, 6, 7, 1, 8, 2, 3, 5}, {5, 3, 2, 8, 1, 7, 6, 4},
    {1, 7, 8, 2, 5, 3, 4, 6}, {1, 4, 6, 7, 5, 8, 2, 3},
    {8, 2, 1, 7, 4, 6, 5, 3}, {3, 2, 8, 5, 7, 6, 4, 1},
    {8, 5, 3, 2, 4, 1, 7, 6}, {6, 4, 3, 5, 2, 8, 7, 1},
    {6, 7, 1, 4, 2, 3, 5, 8}, {3, 5, 6, 4, 7, 1, 2, 8},
    {1, 2, 3, 4, 5, 6, 7, 8}}
```

The permutation group of vertex symmetries shown above acts on the faces of the cube and induces a permutation group of the faces. To construct this group, we start with the set of faces of the cube by using the function Faces in the Polyhedra package.

```
In[119]:= s = Map[Sort, Faces[Cube]]
Out[119]= {{1, 2, 3, 4}, {1, 4, 6, 7}, {1, 2, 7, 8},
    {2, 3, 5, 8}, {5, 6, 7, 8}, {3, 4, 5, 6}}
```

We then generate the group of face symmetries induced by the group of vertex symmetries. Note that each permutation here is a 6-permutation because the cube has six faces. The function Faces produces the faces of the cube in the order top, right, back, left, bottom, and front with respect to the picture of the cube shown earlier. The faces are numbered 1 through 6 in this order.

```
In[120]:= g = KSubsetGroup[c, s]
Out[120]= {{1, 3, 4, 6, 5, 2}, {1, 4, 6, 2, 5, 3},
    {1, 6, 2, 3, 5, 4}, {4, 1, 3, 5, 2, 6},
    {5, 4, 3, 2, 1, 6}, {2, 5, 3, 1, 4, 6},
    {6, 2, 1, 4, 3, 5}, {5, 2, 6, 4, 1, 3},
    {3, 2, 5, 4, 6, 1}, {3, 4, 1, 2, 6, 5},
    {6, 4, 5, 2, 3, 1}, {5, 3, 2, 6, 1, 4},
    {5, 6, 4, 3, 1, 2}, {2, 1, 6, 5, 4, 3},
    {4, 5, 6, 1, 2, 3}, {3, 1, 2, 5, 6, 4},
    {2, 3, 1, 6, 4, 5}, {3, 5, 4, 1, 6, 2},
    {4, 6, 1, 3, 2, 5}, {4, 3, 5, 6, 2, 1},
    {6, 5, 2, 1, 3, 4}, {2, 6, 5, 3, 4, 1},
    {6, 1, 4, 5, 3, 2}, {1, 2, 3, 4, 5, 6}}
```

Using OrbitRepresentatives we generate the distinct dice. There are 30 of these.

```
In[121]:= Length[o = OrbitRepresentatives[g, Permutations[6]]]
Out[121]= 30
```

We then display the 30 distinct dice as "opened up" cubes with their faces labeled.

```
In[122]:= <<extraCode/ShowOpenCube;
          Show[GraphicsArray[Partition[Map[ShowOpenCube, o], 5]]]
```

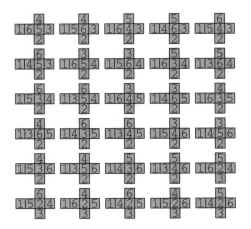

Graph Enumeration

Our final example is graph enumeration. If we assume that the vertices of the graph are labeled with distinct labels, then there are

$$\left(\binom{n}{2} \atop m \right)$$

possible graphs with n vertices and m edges. This corresponds to the number of ways of picking m 2-subsets out of a total possible $\binom{n}{2}$ 2-subsets. Enumerating these graphs is also straightforward because it is simply the k-subset enumeration problem.

The problem of enumerating *unlabeled* graphs is much harder, because symmetries in the structure of the graph will render indistinguishable many graphs that were counted separately in the labeled version of the problem.

The two graphs shown here are distinct if the vertices are assumed to be labeled, but they are identical in the unlabeled version of the problem. There are 15 labeled 4-vertex graphs with four edges, but there are only two unlabeled graphs with four vertices and four edges.

In[124]:= **g = Cycle[4]; h = PermuteSubgraph[Cycle[4],{1,3,2,4}];**
 ShowGraphArray[{g, h}, VertexNumber -> True];

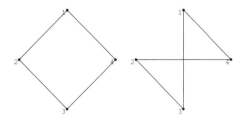

Using the function `OrbitRepresentatives`, we construct a function called `ListGraphs` that enumerates unlabeled graphs.

Here are the nine undirected graphs with six vertices and four edges.

In[126]:= **ShowGraphArray[Partition[ListGraphs[6, 4], 3]];**

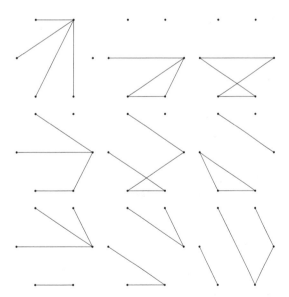

Here are the four directed graphs with three vertices and three directed edges.

`In[127]:= ShowGraphArray[1 = ListGraphs[3, 3, Directed], HeadScaling -> Relative];`

OrbitRepresentatives is a general-purpose function whose power lies in its generality. However, OrbitRepresentatives is too slow for most enumeration problems, including the problem of enumerating graphs. The problem of enumerating orbit representatives of a group acting on a set is very hard, even though for specific problems such as necklace enumeration algorithms that run in time proportional to the size of the output are known [CRS⁺00, RS00]. For tables of enumerated graphs visit `www.combinatorica.com`.

■ 3.3.4 Cycle Index of Permutation Groups

We need to develop one last tool before presenting Pólya's theorem, the notion of the cycle index of a permutation. The *cycle index* of a permutation group G of n-permutations is a polynomial $Z(G; x_1, x_2, ..., x_n)$ defined as:

$$Z(G; x_1, x_2, ..., x_n) = \frac{1}{|G|} \sum_{\pi \in G} x_1^{\lambda_1(\pi)} x_2^{\lambda_2(\pi)} \cdots x_n^{\lambda_n(\pi)},$$

where $\lambda = (\lambda_1(\pi), \lambda_2(\pi), ..., \lambda_n(\pi))$ is the permutation type of $\pi \in G$. Here $x_1, x_2, ..., x_n$ are arbitrary formal variables and $Z(G; x_1, x_2, ..., x_n)$ is a polynomial in these. The function CycleIndex, shown below, takes a group G of n-permutations and a symbol x and computes $Z(G; x[1], x[2], ..., x[n])$.

```
CycleStructure[p_?PermutationQ, x_Symbol] := Apply[Times, Map[x[Length[#]]&, ToCycles[p]]]
CycleIndex[g_List, x_Symbol] :=
    Expand[Apply[Plus, Map[CycleStructure[#, x]&, g]]/Length[g]] /; (Length[g] > 0)
```

Computing the Cycle Index of a Permutation Group

This is the cycle index of the group of vertex symmetries of the cube. This polynomial is a compact representation of the structure of the group. *Mathematica* contains various useful functions to manipulate such polynomials.

`In[128]:= CycleIndex[<< extraCode/CubeVertexSymmetries, x]`

$$Out[128]= \frac{x[1]^8}{24} + \frac{3\,x[2]^4}{8} + \frac{x[1]^2\,x[3]^2}{3} + \frac{x[4]^2}{4}$$

`CycleIndex` is a general-purpose function that requires that the elements of the input permutation group be enumerated entirely. This is computationally infeasible for many groups. However, the cycle index of certain specific groups can be computed without enumerating the group elements. We know how to count the number of n-permutations of a given type $\lambda = (\lambda_1, \lambda_2, \cdots, \lambda_n)$ from Section 3.1.2, so permutations of type λ contribute

$$\frac{1}{|G|}\left(\frac{n!}{\lambda_1! \cdot \lambda_2! \cdots \lambda_n! \cdot 1^{\lambda_1} \cdot 2^{\lambda_2} \cdots n^{\lambda_n}}\right) \cdot x_1^{\lambda_1} \cdot x_2^{\lambda_2} \cdots x_n^{\lambda_n}$$

to the cycle index of the symmetric group S_n. The cycle index of S_n is therefore obtained by summing the above contribution over all permutation types. Possible types of n-permutations correspond to the number of partitions of n. Since these are far fewer than n-permutations, it is much more efficient to compute a sum over the partitions.

This example dramatizes the difference in the rates of growth of the number of n-permutations and the number of partitions of n. The number of terms in the cycle index of S_{15} is only 176, but it will be impossible to compute this by first enumerating S_{15}.

```
In[129]:= Table[{PartitionsP[n], n!}, {n, 15}]

Out[129]= {{1, 1}, {2, 2}, {3, 6}, {5, 24}, {7, 120},
    {11, 720}, {15, 5040}, {22, 40320}, {30, 362880},
    {42, 3628800}, {56, 39916800}, {77, 479001600},
    {101, 6227020800}, {135, 87178291200},
    {176, 1307674368000}}
```

```
SymmetricCoefficient[y_[i_], y_]    := i;
SymmetricCoefficient[y_[i_]^k_, y_] := i^k k!;
SymmetricCoefficient[u_ v_, y_] :=
     Block[{$RecursionLimit = Infinity}, SymmetricCoefficient[u, y]*SymmetricCoefficient[v, y]]

SymmetricGroupIndex[n_Integer?Positive, x_Symbol] :=
     Apply[Plus,
         Map[#/SymmetricCoefficient[#, x]&,
             Map[Apply[Times, #]&, Map[x, Partitions[n], {2}]]
         ]
     ]
```

Computing the Cycle Index of the Symmetric Group

This is the cycle index of S_6. There are 11 terms in this polynomial, exactly as many as there are partitions of 6.

```
In[130]:= SymmetricGroupIndex[6, x]
```

$$Out[130]= \frac{x[1]^6}{720} + \frac{x[1]^4 \, x[2]}{48} + \frac{x[1]^2 \, x[2]^2}{16} + \frac{x[2]^3}{48} +$$

$$\frac{x[1]^3 \, x[3]}{18} + \frac{x[1] \, x[2] \, x[3]}{6} + \frac{x[3]^2}{18} + \frac{x[1]^2 \, x[4]}{8} +$$

$$\frac{x[2] \, x[4]}{8} + \frac{x[1] \, x[5]}{5} + \frac{x[6]}{6}$$

The cyclic group has a beautiful property that makes it rather easy to compute its cycle index. Every permutation in C_n has n/d cycles, each of length d for some divisor d of n. Such a permutation contributes $x_d^{n/d}$ to the cycle index of C_n. To obtain the cycle index of C_n, we need to know for each divisor d of n how many permutations of C_n have n/d d-cycles. This number turns out to be familiar.

For any positive integer n, the *Euler function* $\phi(n)$ denotes the number of natural numbers x, $1 \le x < n$, such that x is relatively prime to n. For prime n, $\phi(n) = n - 1$.

```
In[131]:= EulerPhi[23]

Out[131]= 22
```

Each ordered pair (d,s) in this list has form (d,s), where d is a divisor of 100 and s is the number of permutations in C_{100} that have cycles of length d. For example, there are 20 permutations in C_{100} that have cycles of length 25.

```
In[132]:= d = Divisors[100]; c = Map[ToCycles, CyclicGroup[100]];
          Transpose[{d, Table[Length[Select[c, (Length[#] ===
          100/d[[i]]) &]], {i, Length[d]}]}]

Out[133]= {{1, 1}, {2, 1}, {4, 2}, {5, 4}, {10, 4}, {20, 8},
          {25, 20}, {50, 20}, {100, 40}}
```

This list shows the pairs $(d, \phi(d))$ for each divisor d of 100. This list is identical to the one above since $\phi(d)$ is the number of permutations in C_n with cycles of length d.

```
In[134]:= Transpose[{d = Divisors[100], Map[EulerPhi[#] &, d]}]

Out[134]= {{1, 1}, {2, 1}, {4, 2}, {5, 4}, {10, 4}, {20, 8},
          {25, 20}, {50, 20}, {100, 40}}
```

Using `EulerPhi` makes it easy to implement `CycleGroupIndex` to compute the cycle index of a cyclic group.

```
CyclicGroupIndex[n_Integer?Positive, x_Symbol] :=
    Expand[Apply[Plus, Map[x[#]^(n/#) EulerPhi[#]&, Divisors[n]] ]/n ]
```
Computing the Cycle Index of the Cyclic Group

The cycle index of C_{100}.

```
In[135]:= CyclicGroupIndex[100, x]
```

$$Out[135]= \frac{x[1]^{100}}{100} + \frac{x[2]^{50}}{100} + \frac{x[4]^{25}}{50} + \frac{x[5]^{20}}{25} + \frac{x[10]^{10}}{25} +$$

$$\frac{2\,x[20]^5}{25} + \frac{x[25]^4}{5} + \frac{x[50]^2}{5} + \frac{2\,x[100]}{5}$$

The cycle index of the dihedral group D_{2n} is obtained by observing that D_{2n} contains permutations in C_n plus n "reflections." As mentioned earlier, when n is even, half of the reflections have type $(2, (n/2 - 1), 0, \ldots, 0)$ and the other half have type $(n/2, 0, \ldots, 0)$. When n is odd, the n reflections have type $(1, (n-1)/2, 0, \ldots, 0)$. Therefore,

$$Z(D_{2n}; x_1, x_2, \ldots, x_n) = \frac{1}{2}Z(C_n; x_1, x_2, \ldots, x_n) + \begin{cases} \frac{1}{4}(x_2^{n/2} + x_1^2 x_2^{n/2-1}) & \text{if } n \text{ is even} \\ \frac{1}{2}x_1 x_2^{(n-1)/2} & \text{if } n \text{ is odd.} \end{cases}$$

Combinatorica contains a function `DihedralGroupIndex` that implements the above equation.

The cycle index of the dihedral group D_{200}.

$In[136]:=$ **DihedralGroupIndex[100, x]**

$$Out[136]= \frac{x[1]^{100}}{200} + \frac{x[1]^2 x[2]^{49}}{4} + \frac{51 x[2]^{50}}{200} + \frac{x[4]^{25}}{100} +$$

$$\frac{x[5]^{20}}{50} + \frac{x[10]^{10}}{50} + \frac{x[20]^5}{25} + \frac{x[25]^4}{10} + \frac{x[50]^2}{10} + \frac{x[100]}{5}$$

The cycle index of the alternating group can be easily calculated by noting that

$$Z(A_n; x_1, x_2, \ldots, x_n) = Z(S_n; x_1, x_2, \ldots, x_n) + Z(S_n; x_1, -x_2, \ldots, (-1)^{n+1} x_n).$$

To see this, observe that the effect of permuting elements by a cycle $(x_1, x_2, \ldots, x_k)$ can be achieved by applying $(k-1)$ transpositions $(x_k, x_{k-1}), (x_k, x_{k-2}), \ldots, (x_k, x_1)$ in that order. Thus an even (odd) cycle is the product of an odd (even) number of transpositions. This, along with the fact that an even permutation is one that can be expressed as the product of an even number of transpositions, implies that a permutation π is even if and only if the number of even cycles in π is odd. Hence, we get the cycle index of A_n from the cycle index of S_n by removing terms corresponding to permutations that have an odd number of even cycles. *Combinatorica* contains a function `AlternatingGroupIndex`, which implements the above equation.

The cycle index of the alternating group A_5.

$In[137]:=$ **AlternatingGroupIndex[5, x]**

$$Out[137]= \frac{x[1]^5}{60} + \frac{x[1] x[2]^2}{4} + \frac{x[1]^2 x[3]}{3} + \frac{2 x[5]}{5}$$

Combinatorica also contains a function `PairGroupIndex` to compute the cycle index of the pair groups $G^{\{2\}}$ and $G^{(2)}$. The interesting thing about these functions is that it is sufficient to give the cycle index of G as input instead of the G itself. This is a big advantage, since the cycle index of a group is typically a much smaller object than the group itself. Rather than work with the groups G and $G^{\{2\}}$ or $G^{(2)}$, the functions accept only their cycle indices.

Here we calculate the cycle index of $S_7^{\{2\}}$ in two ways. First we calculate $S_7^{\{2\}}$ explicitly and then calculate its cycle index.

$In[138]:=$ **g = SymmetricGroup[7]; Timing[CycleIndex[PairGroup[g], x];]**

$Out[138]=$ {38.09 Second, Null}

Next we calculate the cycle index of S_7 and use that in `PairGroupIndex` to calculate the cycle index of $S_7^{\{2\}}$. As expected, the latter approach is much faster.

$In[139]:=$ **Timing[PairGroupIndex[CycleIndex[g, x], x];]**

$Out[139]=$ {8.77 Second, Null}

■ 3.3.5 Applying Pólya's Theorem

We are now ready to present Pólya's theorem. Pólya's theorem is an elegant combination of the theory of groups and powerful tools involving generating functions. It tells us that by substituting appropriate values for variables in the cycle index of a group, we get a generating function that tells us a lot about the orbits of the group's action on a set. This approach turns out to be extremely efficient for a variety of counting problems.

As a warm-up, consider the necklace problem with seven beads and three colors.

Here we substitute the value $(p^i + q^i + r^i)$ for each $x[i]$ in the cycle index of the dihedral group D_{14}. The result is a polynomial in p, q, and r for which the exponents of each term sum to 7. The coefficient of term $p^a q^b r^c$ is the number of necklaces with seven beads in which a beads are colored p, b beads are colored q, and c beads are colored r. This particular polynomial tells us that there are 18 seven-bead necklaces with three p-beads, two q-beads, and two r-beads. The coefficients of p^7, q^7, and r^7 are all 1, since there is only one monochromatic necklace of each color.

```
In[140]:= poly = Expand[DihedralGroupIndex[7, x] /. Table[x[i] ->
              (p^i + q^i + r^i), {i, 7}]]

                7    6        5  2      4  3      3  4
Out[140]= p  + p  q + 3 p  q  + 4 p  q  + 4 p  q  +

            2  5      6      7      6          5          4  2
         3 p  q  + p q  + q  + p  r + 3 p  q r + 9 p  q  r +

             3  3        2  4          5       6        5  2
         10 p  q  r + 9 p  q  r + 3 p q  r + q  r + 3 p  r  +

            4  2         3  2  2          2  3  2         4  2
         9 p  q r  + 18 p  q  r  + 18 p  q  r  + 9 p q  r  +

            5  2      4  3         3  3         2  2  3
         3 q  r  + 4 p  r  + 10 p  q  r  + 18 p  q  r  +

             3  3        4  3        3  4        2  4
         10 p q  r  + 4 q  r  + 4 p  r  + 9 p  q  r  +

            2  4      3  4        2  5          5        2  5
         9 p q  r  + 4 q  r  + 3 p  r  + 3 p q r  + 3 q  r  +

           6      6    7
         p r  + q r  + r
```

Substituting 1 for each of p, q, and r gives us the sum of all the coefficients in the polynomial. This is the total number of seven-bead necklaces with at most three colors. This can also be obtained by substituting 3 for every $x[i]$ in the cycle index of D_{14}.

```
In[141]:= poly /. {p -> 1, q -> 1, r -> 1}

Out[141]= 198
```

Let G be a group of n-permutations and let Φ be the set of all functions $\phi : \{1, 2, \ldots, n\} \to R$, where R is some finite set of size r. Note that the number of functions in Φ is r^n. We want information about the orbits of the action of the group G on the set Φ. To each $r \in R$ we associate a *weight* denoted $w(r)$. The weight $w(r)$ can be either a number or a symbol. From the weights of elements in R we can obtain weights for functions in Φ as follows. To each function $\phi \in \Phi$ we associate the weight

$$w(\phi) = \prod_i w(\phi(i)),$$

where the product is taken over all $i \in \{1, 2, \ldots, n\}$. The key observation now is that if ϕ and ϕ' belong to the same orbit, then $w(\phi) = w(\phi')$. In other words, all functions in an orbit have the same weight. This allows us to define the weight of the orbit C, $w(C)$, as $w(\phi)$ for any $\phi \in C$. The *inventory* of the set of orbits is $\sum_C w(C)$, where the sum is over all orbits. Pólya's theorem tells us that inventory of the orbits can be computed by simply substituting for $x[i]$ in the cycle index of G the term $\sum_{r \in R} w(r)^i$. As the examples below show, if we assign appropriate weights to the elements in R, the inventory of the orbits becomes a compact representation of a lot of information about the orbits.

The function below uses Pólya's theorem to compute the inventory of a set of orbits. It takes a cycle index in variables $x[1], x[2], \ldots$ and a list of weights $w_1, w_2, \ldots$ and computes the polynomial obtained by substituting in the cycle index $x[i]$ by $(w_1^i + w_2^i + \cdots)$. In an alternate version, if it is given an integer r instead of a list of weights, it replaces in the cycle index each $x[i]$ by r, thereby calculating the number of orbits.

```
OrbitInventory[ci_?PolynomialQ, x_Symbol, weights_List] :=
     Expand[ci /. Table[x[i] -> Apply[Plus, Map[#^i&, weights]],
                    {i, Exponent[ci, x[1]]}
          ]
     ]

OrbitInventory[ci_?PolynomialQ, x_Symbol, r_] :=
     Expand[ci /. Table[x[i] -> r, {i, Exponent[ci, x[1]]} ]]
```

Computing the Inventory Using Pólya's Theorem

Here we show examples of the use of `OrbitInventory`.

In the necklace example at the beginning of the section, we saw D_{14} acting on Φ, the set of functions $\phi : \{1, 2, \ldots, 7\} \to \{p, q, r\}$. Here p, q, and r represent the colors of the beads, and each ϕ represents a necklace. Suppose that $w(p) = p$, $w(q) = q$, and $w(r) = r$. In this example, the inventory of the orbits of the action of D_{14} on Φ is calculated. First we compute the orbits of D_{14} acting on Φ, by calling the function `Orbits`. We then compute the weights of the orbits and finally sum these all up. As predicted by Pólya's theorem, this turns out to be identical to the polynomial obtained by substituting $(p^i + q^i + r^i)$ for $x[i]$ in the cycle index of D_{14} (see the example at the beginning of this subsection).

```
In[142]:= Apply[Plus, Map[ Apply[Times, #[[1]] ] &,
               Orbits[DihedralGroup[7], Strings[{p, q, r}, 7]]]]
```

$$Out[142]= p^7 + p^6 q + 3 p^5 q^2 + 4 p^4 q^3 + 4 p^3 q^4 +$$

$$3 p^2 q^5 + p q^6 + q^7 + p^6 r + 3 p^5 q r + 9 p^4 q^2 r +$$

$$10 p^3 q^3 r + 9 p^2 q^4 r + 3 p q^5 r + q^6 r + 3 p^5 r^2 +$$

$$9 p^4 q r^2 + 18 p^3 q^2 r^2 + 18 p^2 q^3 r^2 + 9 p q^4 r^2 +$$

$$3 q^5 r^2 + 4 p^4 r^3 + 10 p^3 q r^3 + 18 p^2 q^2 r^3 +$$

$$10 p q^3 r^3 + 4 q^4 r^3 + 4 p^3 r^4 + 9 p^2 q r^4 +$$

$$9 p q^2 r^4 + 4 q^3 r^4 + 3 p^2 r^5 + 3 p q r^5 + 3 q^2 r^5 +$$

$$p r^6 + q r^6 + r^7$$

If we assign a unit weight to each element in R, then each function gets assigned a unit weight. This means each orbit also has a unit weight, and therefore the sum of the weights of the orbits is simply the number of orbits. This also means that $\sum_{r \in R} w(r)^i = r$. Therefore, by Pólya's theorem, substituting r into the cycle index of a group gives us the number of orbits of the action of the group on the set Φ.

The number of necklaces with n beads using no more than m colors can be obtained by making the substitution $x[i] \to m$ for all i in the cycle index of D_{2n}. Here we show there are a lot of 20-bead necklaces with at most ten colors.

```
In[143]:= OrbitInventory[DihedralGroupIndex[20, x], x, 10]
Out[143]= 2500000027750006012
```

In the dice problem, the group G of face symmetries of the cube acts on the set Φ of functions $\phi : \{1, 2, \ldots, 6\} \to \{p, q, r, s, t, u\}$. Let the assignment of weights be $w(p) = p, w(q) = q, \ldots, w(u) = u$. Then the inventory of the orbits of G acting on Φ is obtained by substituting $(p^i + q^i + r^i + s^i + t^i + u^i)$ for $x[i]$ in the cycle index of G. The resulting polynomial in $p, q, r, s, t,$ and u has 462 terms, the first ten of which are shown.

```
In[144]:= 1 = OrbitInventory[CycleIndex[KSubsetGroup[
             c = <<extraCode/CubeVertexSymmetries,
             Map[Sort, Faces[Cube]]], x], x, {p,q,r,s,t,u}];
          {Length[1], 1[[Range[10]]]}
                         6    5        4  2        3  3        2  4
Out[145]= {462,  p  + p  q + 2 p  q  + 2 p  q  + 2 p  q  +

            5      6      5        4          3  2
           p q  + q  + p  r + 2 p  q r + 3 p  q  r}
```

This shows two things. First, it tells us that each term in the above inventory has the form $p^a q^b r^c s^d t^e u^f$, where $a + b + \cdots + f = 6$. Second, the coefficient of this term tells us that there 2226 distinct ways of coloring the faces of the cube with no more than six colors.

```
In[146]:= 1 /. {p -> x, q -> x, r -> x, s -> x, t -> x, u -> x}
                  6
Out[146]= 2226 x
```

The coefficient of $pqrstu$ in this polynomial is 30, telling us the number of ways of coloring the faces of the cube with six distinct colors.

```
In[147]:= Coefficient[1, p q r s t u]
Out[147]= 30
```

There are only two ways of coloring the cube with three faces having one color and the other three having a second color.

```
In[148]:= Coefficient[1, p^3 q^3]
Out[148]= 2
```

The set of labeled graphs with n vertices can be represented by the set of functions $\phi : \{1, 2, \ldots, \binom{n}{2}\} \to \{0, 1\}$, where the possible edges are labeled 1 through $\binom{n}{2}$ and the assignment of 0 or 1 indicates the absence or presence of an edge. The pair group $S_n^{(2)}$ acts on this set of functions, and the orbits of this action are the distinct unlabeled graphs.

If we assign weights $w(0) = 1$ and $w(1) = x$ and compute the inventory of the orbits of $S_n^{\{2\}}$ acting on the set of functions, we get a polynomial in x in which each term Cx^i tells us that there are C unlabeled graphs with n vertices and i edges. Note that with the above mentioned assignment of weights we need to make the substitution $x[i] \to (1 + x^i)$ in the cycle index of $S_n^{\{2\}}$ in order to compute the inventory.

```
In[149]:= OrbitInventory[ PairGroupIndex[
              SymmetricGroupIndex[10, y], y], y, {1, x}]

Out[149]= 1 + x + 2 x  + 5 x  + 11 x  + 26 x  + 66 x  +
                     2      3       4       5       6

           165 x  + 428 x  + 1103 x  + 2769 x  + 6759 x  +
                7        8         9          10          11

           15772 x  + 34663 x  + 71318 x  + 136433 x  +
                  12         13          14           15

           241577 x  + 395166 x  + 596191 x  + 828728 x  +
                   16          17          18           19

           1061159 x  + 1251389 x  + 1358852 x  + 1358852 x  +
                    20           21            22            23

           1251389 x  + 1061159 x  + 828728 x  + 596191 x  +
                    24           25           26          27

           395166 x  + 241577 x  + 136433 x  + 71318 x  +
                   28          29           30          31

           34663 x  + 15772 x  + 6759 x  + 2769 x  +
                  32         33         34         35

           1103 x  + 428 x  + 165 x  + 66 x  + 26 x  +
                 36        37        38       39       40

           11 x  + 5 x  + 2 x  + x  + x
               41     42     43    44   45
```

Computing the number of unlabeled graphs is an important problem. Pólya's theorem lets us compute a "graph polynomial" that encodes the number of unlabeled n-vertex graphs.

```
GraphPolynomial[0, _] := 1
GraphPolynomial[n_Integer?Positive, x_] :=
     OrbitInventory[PairGroupIndex[SymmetricGroupIndex[n, x], x], x, {1, x}]

GraphPolynomial[0, _, Directed] := 1
GraphPolynomial[n_Integer?Positive, x_, Directed] :=
     OrbitInventory[PairGroupIndex[SymmetricGroupIndex[n, x], x, Ordered],
               x,
               {1, x}
     ]
NumberOfGraphs[0] := 1
NumberOfGraphs[n_Integer?Positive] := OrbitInventory[PairGroupIndex[SymmetricGroupIndex[n, x], x], x, 2 ]
NumberOfGraphs[n_Integer, 0] := 1 /; (n >= 0)
NumberOfGraphs[n_Integer?Positive, m_Integer] := Coefficient[GraphPolynomial[n, x], x^m]
```

Computing the Number of Unlabeled Graphs

The number of unlabeled graphs starts out innocently enough...

```
In[150]:= Table[NumberOfGraphs[i], {i, 1, 9}]

Out[150]= {1, 2, 4, 11, 34, 156, 1044, 12346, 274668}
```

...but grows rapidly. There are over 10^{39} unlabeled graphs with 20 vertices, so no attempt to enumerate unlabeled graphs is going to get very far!

```
In[151]:= Table[NumberOfGraphs[i], {i, 10, 20}] // ColumnForm

Out[151]= 12005168
          1018997864
          165091172592
          50502031367952
          29054155657235488
          31426485969804308768
          64001015704527557894928
          245935864153532932683719776
          1787577725145611700547878190848
          24637809253125004524383007491432768
          645490122795799841856164638490742749440
```

A directed graph with six vertices has at most 30 edges. Here is the polynomial whose term $C \cdot x^i$ denotes that C is the number of directed graphs with six vertices and i (directed) edges.

```
In[152]:= GraphPolynomial[6, x, Directed]
```

$$Out[152]= 1 + x + 5 x^2 + 17 x^3 + 76 x^4 + 288 x^5 + 1043 x^6 +$$
$$3242 x^7 + 8951 x^8 + 21209 x^9 + 43863 x^{10} + 78814 x^{11} +$$
$$124115 x^{12} + 171024 x^{13} + 207362 x^{14} + 220922 x^{15} +$$
$$207362 x^{16} + 171024 x^{17} + 124115 x^{18} + 78814 x^{19} +$$
$$43863 x^{20} + 21209 x^{21} + 8951 x^{22} + 3242 x^{23} +$$
$$1043 x^{24} + 288 x^{25} + 76 x^{26} + 17 x^{27} + 5 x^{28} + x^{29} + x^{30}$$

3.4 Exercises

■ 3.4.1 Thought Exercises

1. Show that the reverse of the identity permutation contains only cycles of length 2, with one singleton cycle if n is odd.

2. The *order* of a permutation π is the smallest k such that π^k equals the identity. Prove that there always exists such a k, and show how to compute it from the cycle structure of π.

3. Show that there always exists a transposition that, when applied to any nonidentity permutation, increases the number of cycles by 1.

4. Prove that every permutation has the same sign as its inverse.

5. Prove that half of all size-n permutations are even and half are odd for all $n > 1$.

6. Show that the minimum number of transpositions needed to go between a size-n permutation π and π' equals the number needed to go between $\alpha\pi$ and $\alpha\pi'$ for any n-permutation α.

7. Prove that a permutation and its inverse have identical types.

8. Show there are $(n-1)!$ n-permutations with one cycle, and $n(n-2)!$ n-permutations with one singleton cycle and one length-$(n-1)$ cycle.

9. Show that the automorphism group of the complement of a graph is the same as that of the original graph.

10. What are the two colorings of the cube with three faces having one color and the other three having a second color?

11. Prove the correctness of the entries in columns (3) and (4) of the following table. The first column lists the five Platonic solids and the second column lists the number of vertices in each of these. Columns (3) and (4) refer to the group of vertex symmetries of these solids. Specifically, column (3) lists the number of permutations in each of the groups and column (4) lists the cycle index of each group.

Polyhedron	$|V|$	$|G|$	Cycle index
Tetrahedron	4	12	$(x_1^4 + 8x_1x_3 + 3x_2^2)/12$
Octahedron	6	24	$(x_1^6 + 6x_1^2x_4 + 3x_1^2x_2^2 + 6x_2^3 + 8x_3^2)/24$
Cube	8	24	$(x_1^8 + 8x_1^2x_3^2 + 9x_2^4 + 6x_4^2)/24$
Icosahedron	12	60	$(x_1^{12} + 24x_1^2x_5^2 + 15x_2^6 + 20x_3^4)/60$
Dodecahedron	20	60	$(x_1^{20} + 20x_1^2x_3^6 + 15x_2^{10} + 20x_5^4)/60$

12. Using the table of cycle indices given above, compute the number of distinct dice that one can make using (i) tetrahedra, (ii) octahedra, (iii) icosahedra, and (iv) dodecahedra.

13. Chemists consider molecules that can be made from one C (carbon) atom linked to four radicals, each of which may be $HOCH_2$ (hydroxymethyl), C_2H_5 (ethyl), Cl (chlorine), or H (hydrogen). There are good reasons for using a picture of this situation in which the C atom is located at the center of a regular tetrahedron and the radicals occupy the corners. Show that there are 36 molecules and of these 15 contain one H radical.

■ 3.4.2 Programming Exercises

1. Implement a linear-time algorithm for extracting a permutation from its cycle structure. Compare the running time of this implementation with that of our implementation of `FromCycles`.

2. Write a function to generate all permutations of a given type $\lambda = (\lambda_1, \lambda_2, ..., \lambda_n)$.

3. The recurrence for t_n, the number of size-n involutions, provides a way of generating involutions. Write functions to (i) generate all size-n involutions, (ii) generate random involutions, and (iii) rank/unrank involutions.

4. Write a function that takes the name S of a Platonic solid as the first augment; a tag `Edge`, `Vertex`, or `Face` as the second argument; and a list L of colors as the third argument and returns the number of distinct colorings of the vertices, faces, or edges of S using colors from L.

5. Implement functions `VertexTransitiveQ` and `EdgeTransitiveQ` that respectively test if a given graph is vertex-transitive and edge-transitive. Using these functions, demonstrate that the Folkman graph is indeed edge-transitive but not vertex-transitive.

■ 3.4.3 Experimental Exercises

1. Section 3.2.1 contains an example that shows that size-4 involutions cannot be listed in a minimum change order in which we go from one involution to the next by a single transposition. Experiment by constructing transposition graphs of size-n involutions for $n > 4$. Is it true in general that such a minimum change order does not exist for involutions? What if we allowed two transpositions to go from one involution to the next?

2. Estimate the average length of a cycle in a size-n permutation. Here the average is taken over all cycles in the cycle structure of the permutation. Come up with your estimate by generating random permutations. Can you prove your estimate?

3. Estimate the average size of an automorphism group of a tree. Use the function `RandomTree` in your experiments to generate random trees.

4. Partitions, Compositions, and Young Tableaux

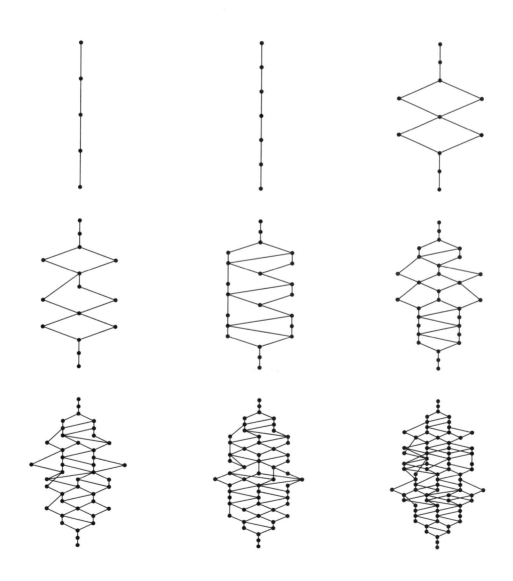

Permutations and subsets are one-dimensional structures, comprising the simple arrangement and selection of objects. This chapter considers more complicated combinatorial objects, some of which are inherently two-dimensional: partitions, compositions, Young tableaux, and set partitions.

A *set partition* is a partition of a set into subsets. A *partition* of an integer n is a set of positive integers that sum up to n. A *composition* of n represents n as the sum of nonnegative integers where order matters. Thus there are only three partitions of six into three parts but 28 compositions of six into three parts. *Young tableaux* are arrangements of n integers whose shape can be described by a partition of n, such that each row and column is sorted.

About the illustration overleaf:

Many interesting structures can be defined on the set of integer partitions of n. Here we display structures called *domination lattices* on integer partitions of n, for $n = 5, 6, \ldots, 13$. Intuitively, we have fine partitions at the bottom of a domination lattice, and these partitions become coarser as we travel upwards. Thus the bottom element in each of the pictures is $(1, 1, \ldots, 1)$ and the topmost element is (n). The command for producing this illustration is

```
ShowGraphArray[Partition[Table[DominationLattice[i], {i, 4, 12}], 3]]
```

4.1 Integer Partitions

Not content with having founded graph theory, Euler also initiated the study of integer partitions. An *integer partition* (in short, *partition*) of a positive integer n is a set of strictly positive integers that sum up to n. The following function PartitionQ tests if a given list is an integer partition.

```
PartitionQ[p_List] := (Min[p]>0) && Apply[And, Map[IntegerQ,p]]
PartitionQ[n_Integer, p_List] := (Apply[Plus, p] === n) && (Min[p]>0) && Apply[And, Map[IntegerQ,p]]
```

Identifying an Integer Partition

This loads the *Combinatorica* package.

$In[1]:=$ **<<DiscreteMath`Combinatorica`**

$(2, 3, 4, 1)$ is a partition of 10, even if it is not written in the conventional nonincreasing form.

$In[2]:=$ **PartitionQ[10, {2, 3, 4, 1}]**

$Out[2]=$ True

In the early twentieth century, the celebrated collaboration between Hardy and Ramanujan led to a remarkable formula for the number of partitions of n. Despite their apparent simplicity, the study of partitions has led to deep connections among many central areas in number theory [AO01]. We have already visited partitions in the context of the types of permutations (Section 3.1.2). We will revisit them in the study of Young tableaux in Section 4.4.

■ 4.1.1 Generating Partitions

The partitions of n can be efficiently constructed using a recursive definition, just like permutations and subsets. This computation is best done by solving a more general problem, that of constructing all partitions of n with largest part at most k. Below we define a function Partitions that takes arguments n and k and returns an enumeration of the partitions of n with a maximum element no greater than k. Since the elements of a partition are strictly positive, the largest element can be at most n, so Partitions[n,n] gives all the partitions of n.

Any partition of n with largest part at most k either contains a part of size k or it does not. The partitions that do can be constructed by prepending k to all partitions of $n - k$ with largest part at most k. The partitions that do not are all the partitions of n with largest part at most $k - 1$. This recursive procedure is implemented in the function below.

```
Partitions[n_Integer] := Partitions[n,n]

Partitions[n_Integer,_] := {} /; (n<0)
Partitions[0,_] := { {} }
Partitions[n_Integer,1] := { Table[1,{n}] }
```

```
Partitions[_,0] := {}

Partitions[n_Integer, maxpart_Integer] :=
    Block[{$RecursionLimit = Infinity},
        Join[Map[(Prepend[#,maxpart])&, Partitions[n-maxpart,maxpart]],
            Partitions[n,maxpart-1]
        ]
    ]
```

Generating all Partitions of n

Here are the 11 partitions of 6. Observe that they are given in reverse lexicographic order.

```
In[3]:= Partitions[6]
Out[3]= {{6}, {5, 1}, {4, 2}, {4, 1, 1}, {3, 3},
    {3, 2, 1}, {3, 1, 1, 1}, {2, 2, 2}, {2, 2, 1, 1},
    {2, 1, 1, 1, 1}, {1, 1, 1, 1, 1, 1}}
```

Most of these partitions do not contain a part bigger than 3.

```
In[4]:= Partitions[6,3]
Out[4]= {{3, 3}, {3, 2, 1}, {3, 1, 1, 1}, {2, 2, 2},
    {2, 2, 1, 1}, {2, 1, 1, 1, 1}, {1, 1, 1, 1, 1, 1}}
```

This recursive procedure for enumerating partitions is a proof for the following identity on $p_{n,k}$, the number of partitions of n with maximum element at most k:

$$p_{n,k} = p_{n-k,k} + p_{n,k-1}, \text{ for } n \geq k > 0.$$

Letting $p_{n,0} = 0$ for all $n > 0$ and $p_{0,k} = 1$ for all $k \geq 0$ gives us a recurrence relation for $p_{n,k}$. The total number of partitions of n, p_n, is equal to $p_{n,n}$, and so this recurrence can be used to compute p_n as well. We will later see how to compute p_n more efficiently using a beautiful formula due to Euler.

```
NumberOfPartitions[n_Integer, k_Integer] := NumberOfPartitions2[n, k] /; ((n >= 0) && (k >= 0))

NumberOfPartitions2[n_Integer?Positive, 0] := 0
NumberOfPartitions2[0, k_Integer] := 1
NumberOfPartitions2[n_Integer?Positive, 1] := 1
NumberOfPartitions2[n_Integer?Positive, k_Integer?Positive] := NumberOfPartitions[n] /; (k >= n)

NumberOfPartitions2[n_Integer, k_Integer] :=
    Block[{$RecursionLimit = Infinity},
        NumberOfPartitions2[n, k] = NumberOfPartitions2[n, k-1] + NumberOfPartitions2[n-k, k]
    ]
```

Calculating the Number of Partitions

This is the table of values for $p_{n,k}$ for $n = 1, 2, \ldots, 8$ and $k \leq n$. The entries along the diagonal give the total number of partitions of n. The second column shows that $p_{n,2} = \lfloor n/2 \rfloor + 1$.

```
In[5]:= Table[NumberOfPartitions[i, j], {i, 8}, {j, i}] // TableForm
Out[5]//TableForm= 1
                   1    2
                   1    2    3
                   1    3    4    5
                   1    3    5    6    7
                   1    4    7    9    10   11
                   1    4    8    11   13   14   15
                   1    5    10   15   18   20   21   22
```

The rules for generating the successor to a partition in reverse lexicographic order are fairly straightforward. Let $p = (p_1, p_2, \ldots, p_k)$ be a partition with $p_1 \geq p_2 \geq \cdots \geq p_k$. If the smallest part $p_k > 1$, then peel off one from it, thus increasing the number of parts by one. If not, find the largest j such that part $p_j > 1$ and replace parts $p_j, p_{j+1}, \ldots, p_k$ by

$$\left\lfloor \frac{\sum_{i=j}^{k} p_i}{p_j - 1} \right\rfloor = \left\lfloor \frac{p_j + (k - j)}{(p_j - 1)} \right\rfloor$$

copies of $p_j - 1$, with a last element containing any remainder. The wraparound condition occurs when the partition is all 1's.

```
NextPartition[p_List] := Join[Drop[p,-1],{Last[p]-1,1}]  /; (Last[p] > 1)

NextPartition[p_List] := {Apply[Plus,p]}  /; (Max[p] == 1)

NextPartition[p_List] := NPT[p];

NPT = Compile[{{p, _Integer, 1}},
        Module[{k = Length[p], q = Table[0, {Length[p] + 2}], j, m, r},
            j = Position[p, 1][[1, 1]] - 1;
            Do[q[[i]] = p[[i]], {i, j - 1}];
            m = Quotient[p[[j]] + (k - j), p[[j]] - 1];
            Do[q[[i]] = p[[j]] - 1, {i, j, j + m - 1}];
            r = Mod[p[[j]] + (k - j), p[[j]] - 1];
            q[[j + m]] = r;
            DeleteCases[q, 0]
        ]
    ]
```

Constructing the Next Partition

Calling NextPartition repeatedly
generates the complete set of partitions
in reverse lexicographic order.

```
In[6]:= ( p=Table[1,{6}];
              Table[p=NextPartition[p],{NumberOfPartitions[6]}] )
Out[6]= {{6}, {5, 1}, {4, 2}, {4, 1, 1}, {3, 3},
    {3, 2, 1}, {3, 1, 1, 1}, {2, 2, 2}, {2, 2, 1, 1},
    {2, 1, 1, 1, 1}, {1, 1, 1, 1, 1, 1}}
```

Wilf defined "minimum change" for partitions as decreasing one part by 1 and increasing another
part by 1. Here, a "part" of size 0 may increase to 1 and a part of size 1 may decrease to 0. He then
posed the question: Is it possible to enumerate partitions in this Gray code order?

This is the binary relation that connects
pairs of partitions that can be obtained
from each other by incrementing one
part and decrementing another.

```
In[7]:= pr = Module[{t = #1 - #2}, Count[t, 1] == 1 &&
              Count[t, -1] == 1 && Count[t, 0] == Length[t]-2]&;
```

This relation assumes that the
partitions contain the same number of
elements, so we pad them with 0's.

```
In[8]:= p = Map[Join[#, Table[0, {7 - Length[#]}]] &, Partitions[7, 5]]
Out[8]= {{5, 2, 0, 0, 0, 0, 0}, {5, 1, 1, 0, 0, 0, 0},
    {4, 3, 0, 0, 0, 0, 0}, {4, 2, 1, 0, 0, 0, 0},
    {4, 1, 1, 1, 0, 0, 0}, {3, 3, 1, 0, 0, 0, 0},
    {3, 2, 2, 0, 0, 0, 0}, {3, 2, 1, 1, 0, 0, 0},
    {3, 1, 1, 1, 1, 0, 0}, {2, 2, 2, 1, 0, 0, 0},
    {2, 2, 1, 1, 1, 0, 0}, {2, 1, 1, 1, 1, 1, 0},
    {1, 1, 1, 1, 1, 1, 1}}
```

Here is the minimum change graph on
partitions of 7 with maximum part at
most 5. SpringEmbedding draws it
with exactly one crossing. The graph is
not regular at all, with vertex degrees
varying from 1 to 7. The presence of a
degree-1 vertex implies that the graph
is not Hamiltonian. But does it have a
Hamiltonian path?

```
In[9]:= ShowGraph[g75 = SpringEmbedding[MakeGraph[p, pr, Type->Undirected,
              VertexLabel -> True]], PlotRange->0.3];
```

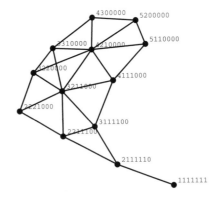

The answer is affirmative, as this computation shows.

```
In[10]:= HamiltonianPath[g75]

Out[10]= {1, 2, 4, 3, 6, 7, 10, 8, 5, 9, 11, 12, 13}
```

These are the minimum change graphs on partitions of n with maximum part at most k, for varying n and k.

```
In[11]:= ShowGraphArray[gs = Table[RankedEmbedding[MakeGraph[
             pnk = Map[Join[#, Table[0, {n - Length[#]}]] &, Partitions[n, k]],
             pr, Type -> Undirected], {1}], {n, 4, 6}, {k, 2, n}]];
```

All of these graphs except the graph for $n = 6$ and $k = 4$ contain a Hamiltonian path from the lexicographically smallest partition to the lexicographically largest partition.

```
In[12]:= Map[(HamiltonianQ[AddEdge[#, {{1, V[#]}}]])&, Flatten[gs,1] ]

Out[12]= {True, True, True, True, True, True, True, True,
           True, False, True, True}
```

This shows that the graph for $n = 6$ and $k = 4$ also has a Hamiltonian path, though not one that starts at the lexicographically smallest and ends at the lexicographically largest partition.

```
In[13]:= HamiltonianPath[gs[[3, 3]]]

Out[13]= {9, 8, 5, 7, 6, 4, 3, 1, 2}
```

Savage [Sav89] showed that for all $n, k \geq 1$, except $(n, k) = (6, 4)$, the partitions of n with maximum part no greater than k can be enumerated in minimum change order starting at the lexicographically smallest partition and ending at the lexicographically largest. Partitions of 6 with maximum part at most 4 can also be enumerated in minimum change order, starting with the partition with all 1's and ending with the partition $(4, 1, 1)$.

■ 4.1.2 Generating Functions and Partitions

Some of the most elegant applications of generating functions in combinatorics appear in the context of partitions. Let $P(z) = \sum_{n=0}^{\infty} p(n)z^n$ be the generating function for the number of partitions of n. Euler noticed that $P(z)$ is equal to the product

$$(1 + z + z^2 + \cdots)(1 + z^2 + z^4 + \cdots)(1 + z^3 + z^6 + \cdots)\cdots,$$

where the ith bracket in the above product has the form $(1 + z^i + z^{2i} + z^{3i} + \cdots)$. As an example, let us calculate the coefficient of z^4 in the expansion. The z^4 term can be obtained in exactly five ways:

1. Pick z^4 from bracket 4 and 1 from every other bracket.

2. Pick z^3 from bracket 3, z from bracket 1, and 1 from every other bracket.

3. Pick z^4 from bracket 2 and 1 from every other bracket.

4. Pick z^2 from bracket 2, z^2 from bracket 1, and 1 from every other bracket.

5. Pick z^4 from bracket 1 and 1 from every other bracket.

Thus the coefficient of z^4 in the expansion of the above product is 5.

In general, the number of ways of obtaining z^n is equal to the number of ways of choosing $z^{1 \cdot c_1}$ from bracket 1, $z^{2 \cdot c_2}$ from bracket 2, $z^{3 \cdot c_3}$ from bracket 3, and so on, such that $1 \cdot c_1 + 2 \cdot c_2 + 3 \cdot c_3 + \cdots = n$. In other words, the coefficient of z^n in the expansion of the above product is the number of ways of picking nonnegative integers $c_1, c_2, c_3, \ldots$ such that $1 \cdot c_1 + 2 \cdot c_2 + 3 \cdot c_3 + \cdots = n$. Interpreting c_i as the number of copies of i that are chosen, we see this as $p(n)$, the number of ways of partitioning n. Rewriting the geometric series $(1 + z^i + z^{2i} + z^{3i} + \cdots)$ as $1/(1 - z^i)$, we get that

$$P(z) = \prod_{i=1}^{\infty} \frac{1}{(1 - z^i)}.$$

Mathematica contains considerable machinery for dealing with generating functions. This example uses the function `Series` to compute the first ten terms of the power series expansion of a function.

```
In[14]:= Product[Series[1/(1 - z^i), {z, 0, 10}], {i, 10}]
                     2      3      4      5       6
Out[14]= 1 + z + 2 z  + 3 z  + 5 z  + 7 z  + 11 z  +

              7       8       9        10       11
         15 z  + 22 z  + 30 z  + 42 z   + O[z]
```

The coefficients of the terms of this polynomial are indeed the number of partitions of n.

```
In[15]:= Table[NumberOfPartitions[n], {n, 0, 10}]
Out[15]= {1, 1, 2, 3, 5, 7, 11, 15, 22, 30, 42}
```

How is this generating function for the number of partitions useful? It can be mined for a series of beautiful identities involving partitions. Here we give a slick generating function-based proof that, for any positive integer n, the number of partitions of n with distinct parts equals the number of partitions of n with all odd parts.

The product $(1 + z)(1 + z^2)(1 + z^3) \cdots$ is the generating function for the number of partitions with distinct parts. The product

$$\frac{1}{(1 - z)} \frac{1}{(1 - z^3)} \frac{1}{(1 - z^5)} \cdots$$

is the generating function for the number of partitions with all odd parts. These two expressions are identical because

$$(1 + z)(1 + z^2)(1 + z^3) \cdots = \frac{(1 - z^2)}{(1 - z)} \frac{(1 - z^4)}{(1 - z^2)} \frac{(1 - z^6)}{(1 - z^3)} \cdots = \frac{1}{(1 - z)} \frac{1}{(1 - z^3)} \frac{1}{(1 - z^5)} \cdots.$$

Thus the coefficients of the terms are identical, establishing the equality. Here is an example.

This returns the partitions of 11 with distinct parts. There are 12 of these...

```
In[16]:= Select[Partitions[11], (Length[Union[#]] == Length[#] &)]

Out[16]= {{11}, {10, 1}, {9, 2}, {8, 3}, {8, 2, 1}, {7, 4},
         {7, 3, 1}, {6, 5}, {6, 4, 1}, {6, 3, 2}, {5, 4, 2},
         {5, 3, 2, 1}}
```

...and these are the partitions of 11 in which all parts are odd. There are 12 of these as well.

```
In[17]:= Select[Partitions[11], Apply[And,Map[Function[x,OddQ[x]],#]]&]

Out[17]= {{11}, {9, 1, 1}, {7, 3, 1}, {7, 1, 1, 1, 1},
         {5, 5, 1}, {5, 3, 3}, {5, 3, 1, 1, 1},
         {5, 1, 1, 1, 1, 1, 1}, {3, 3, 3, 1, 1},
         {3, 3, 1, 1, 1, 1, 1}, {3, 1, 1, 1, 1, 1, 1, 1, 1},
         {1, 1, 1, 1, 1, 1, 1, 1, 1, 1, 1}}
```

Another important use of $P(z)$ is in deriving the remarkable identity

$$p(n) = p(n-1) + p(n-2) - p(n-5) - p(n-7) + \cdots.$$

Euler noticed that the reciprocal of the partition generating function satisfies the following beautiful identity:

$$\prod_{i=1}^{\infty}(1 - z^i) = 1 - z - z^2 + z^5 + z^7 - z^{12} - \cdots.$$

This is known as *Euler's Pentagonal Theorem*. The integers of the form $k(3k+1)/2$, that is, $0, 1, 2, 5, 7, 12, 15, \ldots$, are called *pentagonal numbers*. Thus Euler's Pentagonal Theorem can be written as

$$\prod_{i=1}^{\infty}(1 - z^i) = \sum_{k=-\infty}^{\infty}(-1)^k z^{(3k^2+k)/2}.$$

Here we expand the product of the first ten terms in Euler's Pentagonal Theorem. The resulting polynomial is correct in the coefficients of z^n for any n, $0 \le n \le 10$, because these terms will not be affected by any of the subsequent multiplications. Some of the remaining terms have coefficients that are not in the set $\{-1, 0, +1\}$, but these will eventually cancel out.

```
In[18]:= Expand[Product[(1 - z^i), {i, 10}]]
                   2    5    7     11     12     13     14
Out[18]= 1 - z - z  + z  + z  + z   - z   - z   - z   -
          15     18     19     20     21       22     25     26
        2 z   + z   + z   + z   + z   + 3 z   - z   - z   -
          27       28       29     30       33     34     35     36
        2 z   - 2 z   - z   - z   + 3 z   + z   + z   + z   +
          37       40     41     42     43     44     48     50     53
        z   - 2 z   - z   - z   - z   + z   + z   + z   - z   -
          54     55
        z   + z
```

Now we start with

$$\left(\prod_{i=1}^{\infty}\frac{1}{(1-z^i)}\right) \times \left(\prod_{i=1}^{\infty}(1-z^i)\right) = 1.$$

Using the fact that the first product is the generating function of the number of partitions and using Euler's Pentagonal Theorem for the second product, we get

$$\left(\sum_{n=0}^{\infty} p(n)z^n\right) \times (1 - z - z^2 + z^5 + z^7 - z^{12} - \cdots) = 1.$$

The coefficient of z^n on the left of the equation is

$$p(n) - p(n-1) - p(n-2) + p(n-5) + p(n-7) - \cdots,$$

while it is zero on the right. Equating coefficients on the two sides, we get

$$p(n) = p(n-1) + p(n-2) - p(n-5) - p(n-7) + \cdots.$$

In other words,

$$p(n) = \sum_{k=1}^{\infty} (-1)^{(k+1)} \left(p(n - k(3k+1)/2) + p(n + k(3k+1)/2)\right).$$

This is an infinite series, but it has only $O(n^{1/2})$ nonzero terms. Using this to compute $p(n)$ is much more efficient than using the recurrence for $p(n,n)$, so we use this identity to compute $p(n)$ in *Combinatorica*.

```
NumberOfPartitions[n_Integer] := NumberOfPartitions1[n]
NumberOfPartitions1[n_Integer] := 0  /; (n < 0)
NumberOfPartitions1[n_Integer] := 1  /; (n == 0)

NumberOfPartitions1[n_Integer] :=
      Block[{$RecursionLimit = Infinity, k},
          NumberOfPartitions1[n] =
          Sum[(-1)^(k+1) NumberOfPartitions1[n - k (3k-1)/2] +
              (-1)^(k+1) NumberOfPartitions1[n - k (3k+1)/2],
              {k, Ceiling[ (1+Sqrt[1.0 + 24n])/6 ], 1, -1}
          ]
      ]
```

Computing the Number of Integer Partitions

Over 80 years ago, Percy MacMahon computed the values of $p(n)$ for all n up to 200 using this identity. This table of values for $p(n)$ proved immensely useful for Hardy and Ramanujan, who were trying to check the accuracy of their formula for $p(n)$. Since then, much larger tables of $p(n)$ have appeared [GGM58].

In[19]:= **NumberOfPartitions[200]**

Out[19]= 3972999029388

We do not know how much time it took MacMahon to calculate $p(200)$, but with *Combinatorica* it takes just a few seconds to calculate $p(1000)$.

In[20]:= `Timing[NumberOfPartitions[1000]]`

Out[20]= {3.27 Second, 24061467864032622473692149727991}

■ 4.1.3 Ferrers Diagrams

Ferrers (or Ferrars [And76]) diagrams represent partitions as patterns of dots. They provide a useful tool for visualizing partitions, because moving the dots around provides a mechanism for proving bijections between classes of partitions. For example, the increment/decrement operation of the minimum change ordering on partitions is equivalent to moving a dot from one row to another. *Combinatorica* contains a function `FerrersDiagram` that produces a Ferrers' diagram.

Here is the Ferrers diagram for the partition $(8, 6, 4, 4, 3, 1)$. The Ferrers diagram provides an easy way to prove that the number of partitions of n with largest part k is equal to the number of partitions of n with k parts, since transposing one gives an example of the other.

In[21]:= `FerrersDiagram[{8,6,4,4,3,1}]`

```
• • • • • • • •
• • • • • •
• • • •
• • • •
• • •
•
```

`TransposePartition` exchanges rows for columns in a partition, thus *transposing* it.

```
TransposePartition[{}] := {}

TransposePartition[p_List] :=
     Module[{s=Select[p,(#>0)&], i, row, r},
          row = Length[s];
          Table [r = row; While [s[[row]]<=i, row--]; r, {i,First[s]}]
     ]
```

Transposing a Partition

This Ferrers diagram is a transpose of the previous one. The first row has six dots corresponding to the six dots in the first column of the previous Ferrers diagram. Rex Dwyer observed [Sav89] that if a pair of partitions can be obtained from each other by minimum change (i.e., increment one part and decrement another), then their transposes can also be obtained from each other by minimum change. Since partitions of n with maximum element at most k can be listed in Gray code order, this means that partitions of n with at most k parts can also be listed in Gray code order.

```
In[22]:= FerrersDiagram[TransposePartition[{8,6,4,4,3,1}]];
```

The Ferrers diagram can be generalized by replacing the underlying square grid by other regular patterns in the plane, with interesting results [Pro89].

■ 4.1.4 Random Partitions

A formula for counting the number of different structures of a given type usually leads to an algorithm for constructing random instances of the structure. For each of the possible ways to create the first element of a structure, the enumeration formula can be used to give the number of ways to complete it. Using these counts, we can randomly select the first part in such a way that the complete structures are uniformly distributed.

As we have seen, the number of partitions $p_{n,k}$ of n with largest part at most k is given by the recurrence

$$p_{n,k} = p_{n-k,k} + p_{n,k-1}.$$

The largest part l in a random partition can be found by selecting a random number x such that $1 \le x \le p_{n,n}$, with l determined by $p_{n,l-1} < x \le p_{n,l}$.

Unfortunately, this function requires tabulating values of a two-dimensional function, which can be expensive for large values of n. Nijenhuis and Wilf [NW78] provide the following more efficient algorithm, which randomly selects the magnitude of a part d and its multiplicity j from n, recursing to find a random partition of $n - dj$.

```
RandomPartition[n_Integer?Positive] :=
  Module[{mult = Table[0, {n}], j, d, r=n, z},
    While[ (r > 0),
      d = 1;  j = 0;
      z = Random[] r PartitionsP[r];
      While [z >= 0, j++; If [r-j*d < 0, {j=1; d++;}]; z -= j*PartitionsP[r-j*d]];
      r -= j d; mult[[j]] += d;
    ];
```

```
   Reverse[Flatten[Table[Table[j, {mult[[j]]}], {j, Length[mult]}]]]
 ]
```

Constructing Random Partitions

The rectangle defined by the Ferrers diagram of a random partition for any value of $n > 3$ can be expected to contain more empty space than dots, even though exchanging the roles of dots and the empty positions defines another Ferrers diagram.

In[23]:= **FerrersDiagram[RandomPartition[1000]];**

Repeating an experiment from [NW78] illustrates that each partition is equally likely to occur with this implementation.

In[24]:= **Distribution[Table[RandomPartition[6], {880}]]**

Out[24]= {82, 69, 69, 82, 91, 81, 78, 97, 76, 64, 91}

4.2 Compositions

A *composition* of n is a particular arrangement of nonnegative integers that sum up to n. Compositions are perhaps a little less pleasing than partitions, since order matters and zero elements can be included. There is an infinite number of compositions of an integer, unless the number of parts is bounded. Compositions are easier to generate and count than partitions, however.

■ 4.2.1 Random Compositions

The number of compositions of n into k parts equals $\binom{n+k-1}{n}$. This follows from the observation that a composition of n can be represented by inserting $(k-1)$ dividers into a row of n dots such that the numbers of dots between consecutive dividers equals the parts in the composition.

```
NumberOfCompositions[n_,k_] := Binomial[ n+k-1, n ]
```
Counting Compositions

This observation can be used to generate a random composition by using a random $(k-1)$-subset to select the dividers.

```
RandomComposition[n_Integer,k_Integer] :=
    Map[
        (#[[2]] - #[[1]] - 1)&,
        Partition[Join[{0},RandomKSubset[Range[n+k-1],k-1],{n+k}], 2, 1]
    ]
```
Generating Random Compositions

There are 28 compositions of six into three parts.

```
In[25]:= NumberOfCompositions[6,3]
Out[25]= 28
```

The quality of the random compositions reflects the quality of the random k-subsets generator.

```
In[26]:= Distribution[ Table[RandomComposition[6,3], {1000}] ]
Out[26]= {33, 34, 26, 44, 29, 38, 30, 34, 29, 36, 32, 37,
    31, 40, 41, 38, 38, 34, 38, 52, 39, 34, 30, 38, 30, 33,
    46, 36}
```

■ 4.2.2 Generating Compositions

This bijection between compositions and *k*-subsets also provides a method for listing all the compositions of an integer. By using *k*-subsets generated in lexicographic order, the resulting compositions will also be lexicographically ordered.

```
Compositions[n_Integer,k_Integer] :=
    Map[
        (Map[(#[[2]]-#[[1]]-1)&, Partition[Join[{0},#,{n+k}],2,1] ])&,
        KSubsets[Range[n+k-1],k-1]
    ]
```

Constructing All Compositions

Compositions of six into three parts are generated in lexicographic order. Going from one composition to the next typically involves incrementing one part and decrementing another. This is not always true, however, as in the transition from $(0,6,0)$ to $(1,0,5)$. Is it possible to enumerate compositions in Gray code order?

```
In[27]:= Compositions[6,3]

Out[27]= {{0, 0, 6}, {0, 1, 5}, {0, 2, 4}, {0, 3, 3},
    {0, 4, 2}, {0, 5, 1}, {0, 6, 0}, {1, 0, 5}, {1, 1, 4},
    {1, 2, 3}, {1, 3, 2}, {1, 4, 1}, {1, 5, 0}, {2, 0, 4},
    {2, 1, 3}, {2, 2, 2}, {2, 3, 1}, {2, 4, 0}, {3, 0, 3},
    {3, 1, 2}, {3, 2, 1}, {3, 3, 0}, {4, 0, 2}, {4, 1, 1},
    {4, 2, 0}, {5, 0, 1}, {5, 1, 0}, {6, 0, 0}}
```

We define the binary relation that connects pairs of compositions that can be obtained from each other using one increment and one decrement operation.

```
In[28]:= cr = Module[{diff = #1 - #2}, Count[diff, 1] == 1 &&
    Count[diff, -1] == 1 && Count[diff, 0] == Length[diff]-2]&;
```

Remarkably enough, the minimum change graph on compositions is a grid of triangles. This is a good example of how *Combinatorica*'s tools for visualizing graphs can lead to insights about the underlying combinatorial objects. It is easy to trace many distinct Hamiltonian paths in this grid, each of which correspond to a Gray code enumeration of compositions. Klingsberg [Kli82] has shown that, like permutations and combinations, compositions also can be sequenced in a minimum change order.

```
In[29]:= ShowGraph[g = RankedEmbedding[MakeGraph[Compositions[6, 3],
    cr, Type -> Undirected], {1}]];
```

Here is a Hamiltonian cycle that is found fairly quickly.

```
In[30]:= Timing[ HamiltonianCycle[g] ]

Out[30]= {1.33 Second, {1, 2, 3, 4, 5, 6, 7, 13, 12, 11,
    10, 9, 15, 16, 17, 18, 22, 21, 20, 24, 25, 27, 28, 26,
    23, 19, 14, 8, 1}}
```

The next composition can be constructed directly, instead of converting a composition to a *k*-subset using NextKSubset and then back to a composition.

```
NextComposition[l_List] :=
      Append[Table[0,{Length[l]-1}], Apply[Plus, l]] /; First[l]==Apply[Plus,l]

NextComposition[l_List] := NC[l]
NC = Compile[{{l, _Integer, 1}},
        Module[{n = Apply[Plus, l], nl = l, t = Length[l]},
              While[l[[t]] == 0, t--];
              nl[[t-1]]++;
              Do[nl[[i]] = 0, {i, t, Length[l]}];
              nl[[Length[l]]] = Apply[Plus, Take[l, -(Length[l] - t + 1)]] - 1; nl
        ]
    ]
```

Constructing the Next Composition

Here are the same compositions constructed earlier, although in a different order. Specifically, they are the reversals of the lexicographically sequenced compositions.

In[31]:= **NestList[NextComposition, {0,0,6}, 28]**

Out[31]= {{0, 0, 6}, {0, 1, 5}, {0, 2, 4}, {0, 3, 3},
　　{0, 4, 2}, {0, 5, 1}, {0, 6, 0}, {1, 0, 5}, {1, 1, 4},
　　{1, 2, 3}, {1, 3, 2}, {1, 4, 1}, {1, 5, 0}, {2, 0, 4},
　　{2, 1, 3}, {2, 2, 2}, {2, 3, 1}, {2, 4, 0}, {3, 0, 3},
　　{3, 1, 2}, {3, 2, 1}, {3, 3, 0}, {4, 0, 2}, {4, 1, 1},
　　{4, 2, 0}, {5, 0, 1}, {5, 1, 0}, {6, 0, 0}, {0, 0, 6}}

4.3 Set Partitions

A *set partition* is just that, a partition of the elements of a set into subsets. In this section, we study algorithms for enumerating, ranking, unranking, and generating random instances of set partitions. Set partitions and the combinatorial numbers that count them show up in a variety of unexpected places and have been the focus of much research.

Here are the set partitions of $\{a, b, c, d\}$. The order in which subsets are listed in each set partition does not matter. The order in which elements are listed in each subset also does not matter. A set partition with k subsets can be thought of as a distribution of distinguishable objects into k indistinguishable boxes.

```
In[32]:= SetPartitions[{a, b, c, d}]

Out[32]= {{{a, b, c, d}}, {{a}, {b, c, d}},
    {{a, b}, {c, d}}, {{a, c, d}, {b}}, {{a, b, c}, {d}},
    {{a, d}, {b, c}}, {{a, b, d}, {c}}, {{a, c}, {b, d}},
    {{a}, {b}, {c, d}}, {{a}, {b, c}, {d}},
    {{a, b, d}, {c}}, {{a, b}, {c}, {d}},
    {{a, c}, {b}, {d}}, {{a, d}, {b}, {c}},
    {{a}, {b}, {c}, {d}}}
```

We define the following canonical way of listing a set partition. Assuming a total order on the input set X, write each subset in increasing order with the subsets themselves arranged in increasing order of their minimum elements.

Here the input is assumed to be a set partition of $\{a, b, c, d, e\}$. The default order on these symbols is used to transform the given set partition into canonical form.

```
In[33]:= ToCanonicalSetPartition[{{b}, {c, e}, {d, a}}]

Out[33]= {{a, d}, {b}, {c, e}}
```

Here the underlying order on the set is explicitly given as $e < d < c < b < a$. This is used to produce a canonical ordering of the set partition that is different from the one constructed above.

```
In[34]:= ToCanonicalSetPartition[{{b}, {c, e}, {d, a}}, {e, d, c, b, a}]

Out[34]= {{e, c}, {d, a}, {b}}
```

Testing whether a given list is a set partition is a fundamental operation.

```
SetPartitionQ[sp_] := (ListQ[sp]) && (Depth[sp] > 2) && SetPartitionQ[sp, Apply[Union, sp]]

SetPartitionQ[sp_, s_List] := (ListQ[sp]) && (Depth[sp] > 2) &&
                    (Apply[And, Map[ListQ, sp]]) && (Sort[Flatten[sp, 1]] === Sort[s])
```

Testing if a List Is a Set Partition

Yes, this is a set partition of $\{a, b, c, d, e, f\}$,...

```
In[35]:= SetPartitionQ[{{a, c}, {d, e}, {f}, {b}}, {a, b, c, d, e, f}]

Out[35]= True
```

...but it is not a set partition of $\{a,b,c,d\}$.

```
In[36]:= SetPartitionQ[{{a, c}, {d, e}, {f}, {b}}, {a, b, c, d}]
Out[36]= False
```

This is not a set partition since c appears in two subsets.

```
In[37]:= SetPartitionQ[{{a, c}, {d, c}, {f}, {b}}, {a, b, c, d, e, f}]
Out[37]= False
```

Since no second argument is given here, the function simply tests to see if the subsets are disjoint.

```
In[38]:= SetPartitionQ[{{a, c}, {1, 3}}]
Out[38]= True
```

■ 4.3.1 Generating Set Partitions

A subset in a set partition is usually called a *part* or a *block*. Set partitions of $\{1, 2, ..., n\}$ with exactly k blocks can be generated recursively by noting that every set partition either contains the element 1 by itself as a singleton set or 1 as a block with some other elements. Set partitions of the first type can be generated by constructing all set partitions with $(k-1)$ blocks of $\{2, 3, ..., n\}$ and then inserting the set $\{1\}$ into each set partition. Set partitions of the second type can be constructed by generating all set partitions with k blocks of $\{2, 3, ..., n\}$ and then inserting the element 1 into each subset in each partition. The function KSetPartitions implements this idea.

```
KSetPartitions[{}, 0] := {{}}
KSetPartitions[s_List, 0] := {}
KSetPartitions[s_List, k_Integer] := {} /; (k > Length[s])
KSetPartitions[s_List, k_Integer] := {Map[{#} &, s]} /; (k === Length[s])
KSetPartitions[s_List, k_Integer] :=
    Block[{$RecursionLimit = Infinity},
        Join[Map[Prepend[#, {First[s]}] &, KSetPartitions[Rest[s], k - 1]],
            Flatten[
              Map[Table[Prepend[Delete[#, j], Prepend[#[[j]], s[[1]]]],
                    {j, Length[#]}]
                ]&,
                KSetPartitions[Rest[s], k]
              ], 1
            ]
        ]
    ] /; (k > 0) && (k < Length[s])

KSetPartitions[0, 0] := {{}}
KSetPartitions[0, k_Integer?Positive] := {}
KSetPartitions[n_Integer?Positive, 0] := {}
KSetPartitions[n_Integer?Positive, k_Integer?Positive] := KSetPartitions[Range[n], k]
```

Constructing Set Partitions with k Blocks

Here are the seven set partitions of $\{a, b, c, d\}$ with two blocks. Only one has a as a singleton set.

```
In[39]:= KSetPartitions[{a, b, c, d}, 2]
Out[39]= {{{a}, {b, c, d}}, {{a, b}, {c, d}},
     {{a, c, d}, {b}}, {{a, b, c}, {d}}, {{a, d}, {b, c}},
     {{a, b, d}, {c}}, {{a, c}, {b, d}}}
```

The number of set partitions of n elements into two blocks is $2^{n-1} - 1$. Why? Because the block with element 1 can contain any *proper* (noncomplete) subset of the other $n - 1$ elements.

```
In[40]:= Map[Length, Table[ KSetPartitions[i,2], {i,1,10}] ]
Out[40]= {0, 1, 3, 7, 15, 31, 63, 127, 255, 511}
```

This is the set of vertex labels for a graph whose vertices are 2-block set partitions of $\{1, 2, 3, 4, 5\}$. Since there are only two blocks, specifying one block completely specifies the entire set partition. This is the shortcut we take here.

```
In[41]:= l52 = Map[StringJoin[Map[ToString, #[[1]]]] &, sp52 =
     KSetPartitions[5, 2]]
Out[41]= {1, 12, 1345, 123, 145, 1245, 13, 1234, 15, 125,
     134, 1235, 14, 124, 135}
```

Here we build the relation that connects pairs of 2-block set partitions of $\{1, 2, 3, 4, 5\}$ that can be obtained by moving an element from one block to another.

```
In[42]:= spr = (MemberQ[{1, 4}, Sum[Abs[Position[#1, i][[1, 1]] -
     Position[#2, i][[1, 1]]], {i, 5}]]) &;
```

The vertices of this graph are 2-block set partitions of $\{1, 2, 3, 4, 5\}$. The vertices are labeled with the block containing 1. A pair of set partitions (x, y) is connected by an edge if y can be obtained from x by moving an element to a different block. For example, the four neighbors of $\{\{1\}, \{2, 3, 4, 5\}\}$ are obtained by deleting an element from the second subset and inserting it into the first. This operation corresponds to a "minimum change" in going from one 2-block set partition to another.

```
In[43]:= ShowGraph[g=SetVertexLabels[MakeGraph[KSetPartitions[5, 2], spr,
     Type->Undirected], l52], PlotRange->0.09];
```

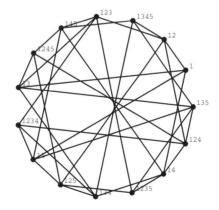

This Hamiltonian cycle tells us that 2-block set partitions of $\{1,2,3,4,5\}$ can be listed in Gray code order. However, KSetPartitions does not do so, instead listing set partitions in the order in which they appear on the circle above. So each "missing" edge between a pair of consecutive vertices on the circle corresponds to a set partition from which the next set partition was not obtained minimally. In Section 4.3.4, we explore further the problem of enumerating set partitions in Gray code order.

```
In[44]:= ShowGraph[Highlight[g, {Partition[HamiltonianCycle[g],2,1]},
          HighlightedEdgeColors -> {Gray}], PlotRange -> 0.1];
```

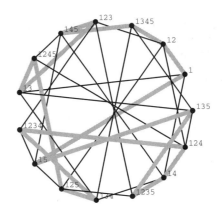

The set of all set partitions is generated by constructing those with k blocks, for every $1 \le k \le n$.

```
SetPartitions[{}] := {{}}
SetPartitions[s_List] := Flatten[Table[KSetPartitions[s, i], {i, Length[s]}], 1]

SetPartitions[0] := {{}}
SetPartitions[n_Integer?Positive] := SetPartitions[Range[n]]
```

Constructing All Set Partitions

This is the set of all set partitions of the set $\{a,b,c,d\}$. Each set partition is in canonical order.

```
In[45]:= SetPartitions[{a, b, c, d}]

Out[45]= {{{a, b, c, d}}, {{a}, {b, c, d}},

    {{a, b}, {c, d}}, {{a, c, d}, {b}}, {{a, b, c}, {d}},

    {{a, d}, {b, c}}, {{a, b, d}, {c}}, {{a, c}, {b, d}},

    {{a}, {b}, {c, d}}, {{a}, {b, c}, {d}},

    {{a, d}, {b}, {c}}, {{a, b}, {c}, {d}},

    {{a, c}, {b}, {d}}, {{a, d}, {b}, {c}},

    {{a}, {b}, {c}, {d}}}
```

■ 4.3.2 Stirling and Bell Numbers

The number of set partitions of $\{1, 2, \ldots, n\}$ having k blocks is a fundamental combinatorial number called the *Stirling number of the second kind*. In Section 3.1.4, we encountered the other kind of combinatorial numbers that James Stirling lent his name to. We use $\left\{ {n \atop k} \right\}$ to denote the number of set partitions of $\{1, 2, \ldots, n\}$ having k blocks. Our notation of $\binom{n}{k}$, $\left[{n \atop k} \right]$, and $\left\{ {n \atop k} \right\}$ for binomial numbers, Stirling numbers of the first kind, and Stirling numbers of the second kind, respectively, follows Knuth's plea in favor of this notation [Knu92].

The recursive procedure mentioned in the previous section for generating set partitions of n elements with k blocks gives a proof of the following "Pascal triangle"–like identity:

$$\left\{ {n \atop k} \right\} = \left\{ {n-1 \atop k-1} \right\} + k \left\{ {n-1 \atop k} \right\},$$

for all integers $k, n > 0$, where $\left\{ {n \atop 0} \right\} = \left\{ {0 \atop k} \right\} = 0$ for integers $n > 0$ and $k > 0$ and $\left\{ {0 \atop 0} \right\} = 1$.

This recurrence can be verified for the entries in this table showing $\left\{ {n \atop k} \right\}$ for all $n = 1, 2, \ldots, 10$ and relevant k. Several patterns are evident from this table. For example, the sequence of next-to-last elements by row, $1, 3, 6, 10, 15, \ldots$, is the familiar "n choose 2" sequence, suggesting that $\left\{ {n \atop n-1} \right\} = \binom{n}{2}$.

```
In[46]:= Table[StirlingSecond[n, k], {n, 10}, {k, 1, n}] // ColumnForm
Out[46]=
    {1}
    {1, 1}
    {1, 3, 1}
    {1, 7, 6, 1}
    {1, 15, 25, 10, 1}
    {1, 31, 90, 65, 15, 1}
    {1, 63, 301, 350, 140, 21, 1}
    {1, 127, 966, 1701, 1050, 266, 28, 1}
    {1, 255, 3025, 7770, 6951, 2646, 462, 36, 1}
    {1, 511, 9330, 34105, 42525, 22827, 5880, 750, 45, 1}
```

Rather than compute Stirling numbers of the second kind using the above recurrence, we use the following beautiful identity that relates these Stirling numbers to binomial coefficients:

$$\left\{ {n \atop k} \right\} = \frac{1}{k!} \sum_{i=1}^{k} (-1)^{(k-i)} \binom{k}{i} i^n.$$

```
StirlingSecond[n_Integer,0] := If [n == 0, 1, 0]
StirlingSecond[0,k_Integer] := If [k == 0, 1, 0]

StirlingSecond[n_Integer?Positive, k_Integer?Positive] :=
    Sum [ (-1)^(k-i)*Binomial [k, i]*(i^n), {i, 1, k}]/k!
```

Computing Stirling Numbers of the Second Kind

There are many ways of partitioning a 100-element set into blocks of 50, in fact, more than 10^{100} of them!

```
In[47]:= StirlingSecond[100, 50]
Out[47]= 430983237009366340421514301547258695943520289614340\
         613912441741131280319058853783145598261659992013900
```

Here is a timing comparison of the two ways of computing Stirling numbers of the second kind. Using the recurrence to compute $\left\{ {200 \atop 100} \right\}$ is much slower than the sum involving binomial numbers.

```
In[48]:= <<extraCode/RecursiveStirling2;
         {Timing[RecursiveStirling2[200, 100];], Timing[ Stirling2[200,
         100];]}
Out[49]= {{6.51 Second, Null}, {0. Second, Null}}
```

Mathematica has a built-in function StirlingS2 to compute the Stirling numbers of the second kind. Surprisingly, the built-in function seems slower than our implementation.

```
In[50]:= Table[ Timing[StirlingS2[100 i, 50 i];]/
         Timing[StirlingSecond[100 i, 50 i];], {i, 2, 5}]
Out[50]= {{2.66667, 1}, {2.8, 1}, {2.88889, 1},
         {2.92857, 1}}
```

The same test, run again, tells a different story! This time the *Mathematica* built-in function is consistently faster. The cause of this unreliable behavior is the dynamic programming *Mathematica* uses to implement the recurrence for Stirling numbers of the second kind. Results from the earlier timing example are still around in memory and available for quick lookup.

```
In[51]:= Table[ Timing[StirlingS2[100 i, 50 i];]/
         Timing[StirlingSecond[100 i, 50 i];], {i, 2, 5}]
Out[51]= {{0., 1}, {0.4, 1}, {0.555556, 1}, {0.714286, 1}}
```

The total number of set partitions of $\{1, 2, ..., n\}$ is the nth *Bell number*, denoted B_n, another fundamental combinatorial number. Bell numbers are named after E. T. Bell, who is better known for his riveting accounts of the lives of famous mathematicians in *Men of Mathematics* [Bel86] than for his contributions to combinatorics. Clearly, $B_n = \sum_{k=1}^{n} \left\{ {n \atop k} \right\}$, and hence this formula can be used to compute them. However, an alternative recurrence provides a faster way of computing the Bell numbers. A simple bijection establishes the identity. A set partition of $\{1, 2, ..., n\}$ can be constructed by choosing the subset containing 1 first and then prepending the chosen subset to set partitions of the rest of the elements. $\binom{n-1}{k}$ is the number of ways of choosing a $(k+1)$-subset containing 1, and B_{n-k-1} is the number of set partitions of the rest of the elements. Summed over all possible k and simplified using the symmetry of binomial numbers, we get:

$$B_n = \sum_{k=0}^{n-1} \binom{n-1}{k} B_{n-(k+1)} = \sum_{k=0}^{n-1} \binom{n-1}{k} B_k.$$

```
BellB[n_Integer] := BellB1[n]
BellB1[0] := 1
BellB1[n_]:= Block[{$RecursionLimit = Infinity}, BellB1[n] = Sum [Binomial[n-1, k]*BellB1[k], {k, 0, n-1}]]
```

Computing the Bell Number

B_{300} can be computed about twice as fast by using the recurrence relation instead of the sum of Stirling numbers.

```
In[52]:= {Timing[ N[BellB[300]] ],
          Timing[N[ Sum[StirlingSecond[300, k], {k, 300}] ]]}
                                              453
Out[52]= {{10.67 Second, 9.59371716083927 10    },

                                           453
          {17.49 Second, 9.59371716083927 10    }}
```

Dynamic programming has been used to speed up the computation of the Bell numbers. The biggest payoff comes when Bell numbers from old computations are still around in memory. This is why B_{310} takes virtually no time after B_{300} has been computed.

```
In[53]:= Timing[N[ BellB[310] ]]

                                           472
Out[53]= {0.96 Second, 3.315493362145864 10    }
```

■ 4.3.3 Ranking, Unranking, and Random Set Partitions

We now turn to the problems of ranking and unranking set partitions. The function `SetPartitions` lists set partitions with one block first, followed by set partitions with two blocks, and so on, ending with the set partition in which every block is a singleton. Thus the problem of ranking and unranking set partitions (as enumerated by the function `SetPartitions`) reduces to the problem of ranking and unranking set partitions with a fixed number of blocks.

Suppose we want to compute the rank of a set partition S of a set X whose first element is x. Let S_x denote the block in S containing x. The function `KSetPartitions` first enumerates all set partitions of X in which x appears in a singleton set. These set partitions are enumerated according to the order in which the $(k-1)$-block set partitions of $X - \{x\}$ are enumerated. This means that if $S_x = \{x\}$, then the rank of S equals the rank of $S - \{x\}$ in the enumeration of set partitions of $X - \{x\}$. Following the set partitions in which x appears by itself, `KSetPartitions` enumerates set partitions in which x appears in blocks of size 2 or more. To construct these set partitions, the function `KSetPartitions` first enumerates the k-block set partitions of $X - \{x\}$. Let this sequence be $S_1, S_2, S_3, \ldots$. The desired sequence is constructed by inserting x into each of the k blocks of S_1 in turn – this gives rise to k set partitions – followed by inserting x into each of the k blocks of S_2, and so on. From this recursive construction of set partitions, the following recurrence for the rank of set partitions follows. In the following we use X' for $X - \{x\}$; S' for the set partition of X', in canonical form, obtained by removing x from S; and j for the position in S' of the subset $S_x - \{x\}$:

$$\text{Rank }(S, X) = \begin{cases} \text{Rank }(S', X') & \text{if } S_x = \{x\} \\ \left\{{n-1 \atop k-1}\right\} + k \text{ Rank }(S', X') + (j-1) & \text{otherwise.} \end{cases}$$

Since `SetPartitions` lists partitions in increasing order of number of blocks, the rank of S in the list of all set partitions of X (not just the ones with k blocks) is $\sum_{i=1}^{k-1} \left\{{n \atop i}\right\}$ plus the rank of S in the list of k-block set partitions. In the following we present code for `RankKSetPartition` and `RankSetPartition`, functions for ranking set partitions within k-block set partitions and within all set partitions, respectively.

```
RankSetPartition [sp_?SetPartitionQ] :=
    Module[{n = Length[s = Sort[Flatten[sp, 1]]], k = Length[sp]},
        Sum[StirlingSecond[n, i], {i, 1, k-1}] + RankKSetPartition [sp, s]
    ]

RankSetPartition [sp_List, s_List] :=
    Module[{n = Length[s], k = Length[sp]},
        Sum[StirlingSecond[n, i], {i, 1, k-1}] + RankKSetPartition [sp, s]
    ] /; SetPartitionQ[sp, s]

RankKSetPartition[sp_?SetPartitionQ] :=
    Module[{s = Sort[Flatten[sp, 1]]},
        RankKSetPartition1[ToCanonicalSetPartition[sp, s], s]
    ]

RankKSetPartition[sp_List, s_List] :=
    RankKSetPartition1[ToCanonicalSetPartition[sp, s], s] /; SetPartitionQ[sp, s]
```

Ranking a Set Partition

The set partitions produced by SetPartitions are ranked. As expected, this produces the natural numbers.

In[54]:= **Map[RankSetPartition, SetPartitions[{a, b, c, d}]]**

Out[54]= {0, 1, 2, 3, 4, 5, 6, 7, 8, 9, 10, 11, 12, 13, 14}

The rank of sp in the list of all eight-element set partitions is larger than its rank in the list of such set partitions with exactly four blocks.

In[55]:= **sp = {{a, f}, {b}, {g, c, d}, {e, h}};**
        {RankKSetPartition[sp], RankSetPartition[sp]}

Out[56]= {616, 1710}

The difference between the two ranks in the above example is exactly the number of set partitions of $\{a, b, c, d, e, f, g, h\}$ with one, two, or three blocks.

In[57]:= **{%[[2]]-%[[1]], Sum[StirlingSecond[8,i], {i,1,3}]}**

Out[57]= {1094, 1094}

We also provide the inverse functions UnrankKSetPartition and UnrankSetPartition. Since UnrankSetPartition can be easily derived from UnrankKSetPartition, we focus on the latter first. This can be constructed from the recurrence relation for the rank of a k-block set partition. Suppose we are given a set X with n elements; an integer k, $1 \leq k \leq n$; and an integer r, $0 \leq r < \left\{{n \atop k}\right\}$ and are asked to find the k-block set partition of X with rank r in the list of k-block set partitions of X generated by KSetPartitions. The recurrence for set partition rank tells us there are two cases. If $r < \left\{{n-1 \atop k-1}\right\}$, then the given set partition contains the first element of X as a singleton, so we can recursively unrank r to get a $(k-1)$-block set partition of the rest of X. If $r \geq \left\{{n-1 \atop k-1}\right\}$, then we know that the first element of X occurs in a set of size 2 or more. The position j of this set is the remainder when $r - \left\{{n-1 \atop k-1}\right\}$ is divided by k, and the quotient from this division is the rank of the rest of the set partition. The algorithm continues recursively. We find the "position" j of this set, recursively find the rest of set partition, and insert the first element of X into the jth set.

```
UnrankKSetPartition[r_Integer, {}, 0] := {}

UnrankKSetPartition[0, set_List, k_Integer?Positive] :=
    Append[Table[{set[[i]]}, {i, 1, k-1}],
        Take[set, -(Length[set]-k+1)]
    ] /; (k <= Length[set])

UnrankKSetPartition[r_Integer?Positive, set_List, k_Integer?Positive] :=
    Block[{n = Length[set], t, j, $RecursionLimit = Infinity},
        If[r < StirlingSecond[n-1, k-1],
            Prepend[UnrankKSetPartition[r, Rest[set], k-1],
                {First[set]}
            ],
            t = r - StirlingSecond[n-1, k-1];
            j = 1 + Mod[t, k];
            tempSP = UnrankKSetPartition[Quotient[t, k], Rest[set], k];
            Prepend[Delete[tempSP, j], Prepend[tempSP[[j]], First[set]]]
        ]
    ] /; (k <= Length[set])

UnrankKSetPartition[r_Integer, n_Integer, k_Integer] :=
    UnrankKSetPartition[r, Range[n], k] /; (k <= n) && (k >= 0)
```

Unranking a Set Partition with k Blocks

This gives the ten-block set partition of $\{1, 2, \ldots, 20\}$ that has 100,076 set partitions before it in the list of ten-block set partitions generated by KSetPartitions.

```
In[58]:= UnrankKSetPartition[100076, Range[20], 10]
Out[58]= {{1}, {2}, {3}, {4}, {5}, {6}, {7},
    {8, 11, 14, 15, 17}, {9, 10, 18, 19, 20}, {12, 13, 16}}
```

As required, the rank and unrank functions are inverses of each other.

```
In[59]:= RankKSetPartition[%, Range[20]]
Out[59]= 100076
```

The rank of a set partition with k blocks in the list of all set partitions is $\sum_{i=1}^{k-1} \left\{ {n \atop i} \right\}$ plus the rank of the set partition in the list of all set partitions with k blocks. Given just the rank r in the list of all set partitions, we first need to find k, the number of blocks in the set partition. This is simply the largest k such that $\sum_{i=1}^{k-1} \left\{ {n \atop i} \right\} \leq r$. Once k is found, then $r - \sum_{i=1}^{k-1} \left\{ {n \atop i} \right\}$ is unranked using UnrankKSetPartition.

```
UnrankSetPartition[0, set_List] := {set}

UnrankSetPartition[r_Integer?Positive, set_List] :=
    Block[{n = Length[set], k = 0, sum = 0, $RecursionLimit = Infinity},
        While[sum <= r, k++; sum = sum + StirlingSecond[n, k]];
```

```
        UnrankKSetPartition[r - (sum - StirlingSecond[n, k]), set, k]
    ] /; (r < BellB[ Length[set] ])

UnrankSetPartition[0, 0] = {{}}
UnrankSetPartition[r_Integer, n_Integer?Positive] := UnrankSetPartition[r, Range[n]] /; (r >= 0)
```

Unranking a Set Partition

This gives the set partition of {1, 2, ..., 20} that has 100,076 set partitions before it in the list of all set partitions generated by the function SetPartitions.

In[60]:= **UnrankSetPartition[100076, Range[20]]**

Out[60]= {{1, 2, 3, 5, 6, 8, 11, 17},

        {4, 7, 9, 10, 12, 13, 14, 15, 16, 18, 19, 20}}

Generating a random set partition is easy using UnrankKSetPartition, so we provide functions RandomKSetPartitions and RandomSetPartitions to do this.

```
RandomKSetPartition [{}, 0] := {}
RandomKSetPartition [set_List, k_Integer?Positive] :=
    UnrankKSetPartition [
      Random[Integer, {0, StirlingSecond[Length[set], k]-1}], set, k
    ] /; ((Length[set] > 0) && (k <= Length[set]))

RandomKSetPartition [0, 0] := {}
RandomKSetPartition [n_Integer?Positive, k_Integer?Positive] := RandomKSetPartition [Range[n], k] /; (k <= n)
RandomSetPartition[{}] := {}
RandomSetPartition [set_List] :=
    UnrankSetPartition [Random[Integer, {0, BellB[Length[set]]-1}], set] /; (Length[set] > 0)

RandomSetPartition [n_Integer] := RandomSetPartition [ Range[n] ]
```

Generating a Random Set Partition

A randomly chosen set partition of {1, 2, ..., 10} and a randomly chosen set partition of {1, 2, ..., 10} having four blocks.

In[61]:= **{RandomSetPartition[10],**
        RandomKSetPartition[10, 4]} // ColumnForm

Out[61]= {{1, 3, 6, 8, 10}, {2, 4, 7}, {5}, {9}}
        {{1, 2, 6}, {3, 5, 8, 9}, {4}, {7, 10}}

This shows the distribution of the number of blocks in 5000 randomly chosen set partitions of {1, 2, ..., 10}. The distribution increases first and then decreases.

In[62]:= **Distribution[Map[Length, Table[RandomSetPartition[10], {5000}]]]**

Out[62]= {25, 427, 1466, 1823, 958, 265, 35, 1}

This, modulo the rare terms, reflects the actual distribution of $\left\{{n \atop k}\right\}$.

In[63]:= **Table[StirlingSecond[10,i], {i,1,10}]**

Out[63]= {1, 511, 9330, 34105, 42525, 22827, 5880, 750, 45,

    1}

■ 4.3.4 Set Partitions and Restricted Growth Functions

There is a neat bijection between set partitions and certain structures called restricted growth functions. A *restricted growth function* (in short, RGF) is a function f with domain and range equal to $\{1, 2, \dots, n\}$ satisfying the conditions

$$f(1) = 1 \qquad \text{and} \qquad f(i) \le \max_{1 \le j < i}\{f(j)\} + 1 \text{ for } 1 < i \le n.$$

The latter condition "restricts" the growth of the function by requiring that $f(i)$ be at most one more than the maximum of the previous function values. We will usually write an RGF f as the sequence $(f(1), f(2), \dots, f(n))$.

These are the RGFs on $\{1, 2, 3, 4\}$ listed in lexicographic order. The lexicographic successor of $(1, 1, 1, 2)$ is not $(1, 1, 1, 3)$ because the latter sequence is not an RGF. For the last element to have value 3, at least one of the first three elements has to have value 2.

```
In[64]:= RGFs[4]

Out[64]= {{1, 1, 1, 1}, {1, 1, 1, 2}, {1, 1, 2, 1},
          {1, 1, 2, 2}, {1, 1, 2, 3}, {1, 2, 1, 1}, {1, 2, 1, 2},
          {1, 2, 1, 3}, {1, 2, 2, 1}, {1, 2, 2, 2}, {1, 2, 2, 3},
          {1, 2, 3, 1}, {1, 2, 3, 2}, {1, 2, 3, 3}, {1, 2, 3, 4}}
```

To see the bijection, take a set partition S of $\{1, 2, \dots, n\}$ in canonical form. We construct a function f on $\{1, 2, \dots, n\}$ by setting $f(i) = j$ if element i is in block j in S. This implies that $f(1) = 1$ because element 1 appears in block 1 in a set partition written in canonical form. Furthermore, if elements 1 through $(i - 1)$ occur in blocks 1 through $(j - 1)$, then element i can occur only in blocks 1 through j. This corresponds to the constraint that restricts the growth of the function. One can start with an RGF f on $\{1, 2, \dots, n\}$ and construct a set partition of $\{1, 2, \dots, n\}$ by throwing element i in block j, if $f(i) = j$. It is easy to check that the set partition thus generated is in canonical form.

It is sometimes easier to think about the RGFs than the corresponding set partitions because RGFs have a linear structure. `SetPartitionToRGF` and `RGFToSetPartition` implement the bijection described above.

Generate the set partition corresponding to the RGF $(1, 2, 1, 1, 3)$ in canonical form.

```
In[65]:= RGFToSetPartition[{1, 2, 1, 1, 3}]

Out[65]= {{1, 3, 4}, {2}, {5}}
```

Inverting the above transformation gets us the original RGF back.

```
In[66]:= SetPartitionToRGF[%]

Out[66]= {1, 2, 1, 1, 3}
```

The number of blocks in the set partition equals the maximum value that the corresponding function takes.

```
In[67]:= {Length[p=RandomSetPartition[100]], Max[SetPartitionToRGF[p]]}

Out[67]= {26, 26}
```

This is the set of all 4-element RGFs constructed by generating the set partitions of $\{1, 2, 3, 4\}$ and transforming these into RGFs. The resulting list is not in lexicographic order.

```
In[68]:= Map[SetPartitionToRGF, SetPartitions[4]]

Out[68]= {{1, 1, 1, 1}, {1, 2, 2, 2}, {1, 1, 2, 2},
          {1, 2, 1, 1}, {1, 1, 1, 2}, {1, 2, 2, 1}, {1, 1, 2, 1},
          {1, 2, 1, 2}, {1, 2, 3, 3}, {1, 2, 2, 3}, {1, 2, 3, 2},
          {1, 1, 2, 3}, {1, 2, 1, 3}, {1, 2, 3, 1}, {1, 2, 3, 4}}
```

Now we turn to the problem of generating RGFs. It turns out to be fairly easy to generate RGFs in lexicographic order. For an RGF f not equal to $(1, 2, 3, \ldots, n)$, let i be the largest value such that $f(i) < \max_{1 \le j < i}\{f(j)\} + 1$. In other words, i is the largest value such that $f(i)$ can be incremented without violating the RGF property. The lexicographic successor of f is the function obtained by incrementing $f(i)$ and setting $f(j) = 1$ for all larger j.

This is the list of RGFs on $\{1, 2, 3, 4\}$ in lexicographic order.

```
In[69]:= RGFs[4]
Out[69]= {{1, 1, 1, 1}, {1, 1, 1, 2}, {1, 1, 2, 1},
    {1, 1, 2, 2}, {1, 1, 2, 3}, {1, 2, 1, 1}, {1, 2, 1, 2},
    {1, 2, 1, 3}, {1, 2, 2, 1}, {1, 2, 2, 2}, {1, 2, 2, 3},
    {1, 2, 3, 1}, {1, 2, 3, 2}, {1, 2, 3, 3}, {1, 2, 3, 4}}
```

These RGFs are now turned into set partitions. Going from an RGF to its lexicographic successor is equivalent to the following operation on set partitions. Let x be the maximum element in a nonsingleton block in the set partition. Move all elements larger than x into the first block and bump up x into the next block. Viewed in terms of insertions and deletions on set partitions, this is hardly a minimum change operation.

```
In[70]:= Map[RGFToSetPartition, %]
Out[70]= {{{1, 2, 3, 4}}, {{1, 2, 3}, {4}},
    {{1, 2, 4}, {3}}, {{1, 2}, {3, 4}}, {{1, 2}, {3}, {4}},
    {{1, 3, 4}, {2}}, {{1, 3}, {2, 4}}, {{1, 3}, {2}, {4}},
    {{1, 4}, {2, 3}}, {{1}, {2, 3, 4}}, {{1}, {2, 3}, {4}},
    {{1, 4}, {2}, {3}}, {{1}, {2, 4}, {3}},
    {{1}, {2}, {3, 4}}, {{1}, {2}, {3}, {4}}}
```

Generating RGFs is faster than generating set partitions.

```
In[71]:= Table[Timing[SetPartitions[i];]/Timing[RGFs[i];], {i, 7, 9}]
Out[71]= {{4., 1}, {3., 1}, {2.61458, 1}}
```

However, using RGFs to generate set partitions is slower than generating them directly because of the conversion cost.

```
In[72]:= Table[ Timing[Map[RGFToSetPartition, RGFs[i]];]/
        Timing[SetPartitions[i];], {i, 7, 9}]
Out[72]= {{13.3529, 1}, {19.5833, 1}, {24.5698, 1}}
```

RGFs provide an encoding for set partitions that makes it easy to ask Gray code enumeration questions. For example, is there an enumeration of RGFs such that each RGF differs from the previous in exactly one position and in that position by only 1? This "minimum change" corresponds to deleting one element from a block and inserting it into an adjacent block. We now pose this as a question of determining whether an appropriate graph has a Hamiltonian cycle.

This is a binary relation on RGFs that connects pairs of RGFs that differ in exactly one position and in that position by exactly 1.

```
In[73]:= rgfr = (Count[#1-#2, 0] == Length[#1]-1) &&
                (Count[Abs[#1 - #2], 1] == 1)&;
```

This is the "minimum change" graph on RGFs constructed using the binary relation defined above. The graph contains a degree-1 vertex, implying that it has no Hamiltonian cycle; however, it may still have a Hamiltonian path, one of whose endpoints is necessarily the degree-1 vertex $(1, 2, 3, 4)$.

```
In[74]:= g = MakeGraph[RGFs[4], rgfr, Type->Undirected, VertexLabel->True];
         ShowGraph[g, PlotRange -> 0.15];
```

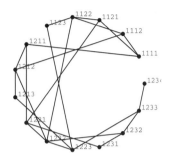

Here we see that this graph on the RGFs has no Hamiltonian path.

```
In[76]:= HamiltonianPath[g]
Out[76]= {}
```

In fact, Ehrlich [Ehr73] shows that for infinitely many values of n, RGFs on $\{1, 2, \ldots, n\}$ do not have a Gray code of this sort. The notion of minimum change can be relaxed a little, allowing for pairs of RGFs that differ in exactly one position, by at most 2, to be connected.

This relaxes the definition of "minimum change" a little.

```
In[77]:= rgfr = (Count[#1-#2, 0] == Length[#1] - 1) &&
               (Count[Abs[#1 - #2], 1] <= 2)&;
```

The resulting graph is a *supergraph* of the one constructed above. The added edges are revealed in the *difference* of the two graphs. The old graph did not have a Hamiltonian path, but the new graph...

```
In[78]:= g1 = MakeGraph[RGFs[4], rgfr, Type -> Undirected];
         ShowGraphArray[{g1, GraphDifference[g1,g]}];
```

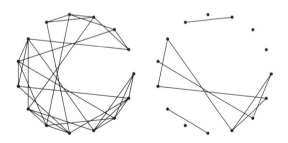

...has more than 700 Hamiltonian cycles.

```
In[80]:= Length[HamiltonianCycle[g1, All]]
Out[80]= 748
```

Savage [Sav97] mentions that it is indeed possible to list RGFs in this relaxed Gray code order, even with some additional restrictions.

4.4 Young Tableaux

Many combinatorial problems are properly interpreted as two-dimensional structures. For example, suppose we are interested in counting the number of ways to arrange n left parentheses and n right parentheses so that they make balanced formulas. For $n = 3$, there are five distinct formulas: $((()))$, $()(())$, $(())()$, $(()())$, and $()()()$. Now consider a $2 \times n$ matrix containing the numbers $1, ..., 2n$, such that each row and column is in increasing order. There is a bijection between the balanced formulas and these matrices, by interpreting the $(1, i)$th entry in the matrix to be the position of the ith left parenthesis, and the $(2, j)$th entry to be the position of the jth right parenthesis. Since the columns are ordered, the left parenthesis always comes before the corresponding right parenthesis. This example illustrates the importance of ordered structures of ordered lists.

A *Young tableau of shape* $(n_1, n_2, ..., n_m)$, where $n_1 \geq n_2 \geq \cdots \geq n_m > 0$, is an arrangement of $n_1 + n_2 + \cdots + n_m$ distinct integers in an array of m rows with n_i elements in row i such that entries in each row and in each column are in increasing order. Below we provide a function `TableauQ` that tests if a given two-dimensional structure is a tableau. Even though our definition says that a tableau should contain distinct integers, `TableauQ` allows repetitions. Even though all the tableaux we will consider here will contain distinct integers, in other contexts it is useful to allow repetition [Knu70].

```
TableauQ[{}] = True
TableauQ[t_List] :=
        And [
                Apply[And, Map[(Apply[LessEqual,#])&, t] ],
                Apply[And, Map[(Apply[LessEqual,#])&, TransposeTableau[t]] ],
                Apply[GreaterEqual, ShapeOfTableau[t] ],
                Apply[GreaterEqual, Map[Length,TransposeTableau[t]] ]
        ]
TransposeTableau[tb_List] :=
        Module[{t=Select[tb,(Length[#]>=1)&],row},
                Table[
                        row = Map[First,t];
                        t = Map[ Rest, Select[t,(Length[#]>1)&] ];
                        row,
                        {Length[First[tb]]}
                ]
        ]
ShapeOfTableau[t_List] := Map[Length,t]
```

Identifying Young Tableaux

This is a tableau of shape $(3, 3, 1)$.
Other same-shape tableaux containing
1 through 7 are also possible.

```
In[81]:= (t = {{1, 2, 5},{3, 4, 7}, {6}}) // TableForm

Out[81]//TableForm= 1    2    5

                    3    4    7

                    6
```

This test confirms that this is a tableau.	*In[82]:=* **TableauQ[t]**
	Out[82]= True

Exchanging 6 and 7 gives a tableau of the same shape and with the same seven elements.	*In[83]:=* **{t[[2, 3]], t[[3, 1]]} = {t[[3, 1]], t[[2, 3]]};** **TableauQ[t]**
	Out[84]= True

But this is not a tableau; note the first two elements of the second row.	*In[85]:=* **TableauQ[{{1,2,5,9,10},{5,4,7,13},{4,8,12},{11}}]**
	Out[85]= False

Our interest in Young tableaux is combinatorial and follows Knuth [Knu73b], although their original application was algebraic. Young tableaux are also known as *plane partitions*. Another detailed treatment is [Sta71], which includes open problems.

■ 4.4.1 Insertion and Deletion

There is a remarkable bijection between permutations and ordered pairs of Young tableaux of the same shape. One of the implications of this is a bijection between involutions and Young tableaux. This bijection depends on two operations that are inverses of each other: an insertion operation and a deletion operation. These prove useful in several different contexts.

Here are the ten involutions of length 4.	*In[86]:=* **Involutions[4]**
	Out[86]= {{2, 1, 4, 3}, {2, 1, 3, 4}, {3, 4, 1, 2}, {3, 2, 1, 4}, {4, 3, 2, 1}, {4, 2, 3, 1}, {1, 3, 2, 4}, {1, 4, 3, 2}, {1, 2, 4, 3}, {1, 2, 3, 4}}

Here are the ten tableaux that can be made with four distinct elements. These tableaux have different shapes, and the shapes are simply the partitions of 4. The function Tableaux, which we will discuss in Section 4.4.3, generates all tableaux of a given shape.	*In[87]:=* **Map[Tableaux, Partitions[4]] // ColumnForm**
	Out[87]= {{{1, 2, 3, 4}}} {{{1, 3, 4}, {2}}, {{1, 2, 4}, {3}}, {{1, 2, 3}, {4}}} {{{1, 3}, {2, 4}}, {{1, 2}, {3, 4}}} {{{1, 4}, {2}, {3}}, {{1, 3}, {2}, {4}}, {{1, 2}, {3}, {4}}} {{{1}, {2}, {3}, {4}}}

Suppose we have a Young tableau T and an element x not in T. The insertion operation, on input T and x, returns a tableau T' that contains all the elements of T plus the extra element x. The shape of T' is identical to the shape of T except for one row, in which T' contains one more element than T. The insertion operation is implemented via the following algorithm. We start by attempting to insert x into the first row of T. If the element x is greater than the last element of the row, it can be placed at the end, resulting in the new tableau T'. If not, then we look for the least element y in the row that is larger than x. The element x takes y's place in the first row and "bumps" y down into the next row, where the insertion procedure starts anew with y. Eventually, either an element ends up on the end of a row or we run out of rows and the item must reside on a new row.

```
InsertIntoTableau[e_Integer, t_?TableauQ] := First[InsertIntoTableau[e, t, All]]

InsertIntoTableau[e_Integer,{}, All] := {{{e}}, 1}
InsertIntoTableau[e_Integer, t1_?TableauQ, All] :=
      Module[{item=e,row=0,col,t=t1},
            While [row < Length[t],
                  row++;
                  If [Last[t[[row]]] <= item,
                        AppendTo[t[[row]],item];
                        Return[{t, row}]
                  ];
                  col = Ceiling[ BinarySearch[t[[row]],item] ];
                  {item, t[[row,col]]} = {t[[row,col]], item};
            ];
            {Append[t, {item}], row+1}
      ]
```

Inserting a New Element into a Young Tableau

The new element 3 bumps the element 7 down to the next row. Element 7 finds a place at the end of the second row. The insertion changes the shape of the tableau from $(3, 2, 1)$ to $(3, 3, 1)$.

In[88]:= **InsertIntoTableau[3, {{1, 2, 7}, {3, 4}, {6}}]**

Out[88]= {{1, 2, 3}, {3, 4, 7}, {6}}

We can use the insertion algorithm to construct a Young tableau associated with a permutation π, by starting with an empty tableau and inserting each element of the permutation into the tableau in the order $\pi(1), \pi(2), \dots, \pi(n)$.

```
ConstructTableau[p_List] := Module[{T}, T[a_, b_] := InsertIntoTableau[b, a]; Fold[T, {}, p]]
```

Constructing Young Tableaux

Each permutation generates a tableau, which is not necessarily unique.

In[89]:= **ConstructTableau[{6,4,9,5,7,1,2,8}]**

Out[89]= {{1, 2, 7, 8}, {4, 5}, {6, 9}}

In particular, this permutation generates the same tableau as the previous one.

In[90]:= **ConstructTableau[{6,4,9,5,7,8,1,2}]**

Out[90]= {{1, 2, 7, 8}, {4, 5}, {6, 9}}

Deletion is the inverse of insertion, in the following sense. Suppose that x was inserted into a tableau T, resulting in a new tableau T'. Further suppose that in row r, T' contains one more element than T. Then the deletion operation with inputs T' and r returns the tableau T. The algorithm for the deletion operation is essentially the opposite of the insertion algorithm. The last element in row r, say a, gets kicked up to row $(r-1)$, replacing the largest element smaller than a in the row. The replaced element, say b, gets kicked up to row $(r-2)$, and so on, until an element gets kicked out of the first row.

```
DeleteFromTableau[t1_?TableauQ,r_Integer]:=
     Module [{t=t1, col, row, item=Last[t1[[r]]]},
            col = Length[t[[r]]];
            If[col == 1, t = Drop[t,-1], t[[r]] = Drop[t[[r]],-1]];
            Do [
                  While [t[[row,col]]<=item && Length[t[[row]]]>col, col++];
                  If [item < t[[row,col]], col--];
                  {item,t[[row,col]]} = {t[[row,col]],item},
                  {row,r-1,1,-1}
            ];
            t
     ]
```

Deleting an Element From a Young Tableau

Observe that this tableau is missing 3.	*In[91]:=* **TableForm[ConstructTableau[{6,4,9,5,7,1,2,8}]]**

Out[91]//TableForm=

1	2	7	8
4	5		
6	9		

Inserting a 3 into the tableau bumps 7 from the first row and thus adds an element to the second row.	*In[92]:=* **TableForm[InsertIntoTableau[3,%]]**

Out[92]//TableForm=

1	2	3	8
4	5	7	
6	9		

Deleting the last element from the second row restores the tableau to its initial state.	*In[93]:=* **TableForm[DeleteFromTableau[%,2]]**

Out[93]//TableForm=

1	2	7	8
4	5		
6	9		

■ 4.4.2 Permutations and Pairs of Tableaux

From any given n-permutation π, we can build a pair of tableaux (P, Q) of identical shape, containing elements 1 through n. Start with a pair (P_0, Q_0) of empty tableaux. In the generic ith step of the algorithm, we have the tableaux pair (P_{i-1}, Q_{i-1}). Insert element $\pi(i)$ into tableau P_{i-1} and call the resulting tableau P_i. Let r be the row in P_i that has one extra element as a result of the insertion. Construct Q_i from Q_{i-1} by adding element i at the end of row r. Note that i is larger than any other element in Q_i, and hence it is the largest element in its row. Furthermore, there are no elements immediately below i. This implies that Q_i continues to be a tableau after the insertion of i. In general, it can be easily verified that P_i and Q_i are tableaux of identical shapes with P_i containing elements $\pi(1), \pi(2), ..., \pi(i)$ and Q_i containing elements $1, 2, ..., i$. Denote by (P, Q) the tableaux pair (P_n, Q_n) that we end up with after all the insertions.

We saw in an earlier example that two different permutations π and π' can lead to the same tableau P. However, the order in which P is constructed in one case is different from the order in which it is constructed in the other case. So "annotating" P with the tableau Q that is a record of how P was created is enough to disambiguate between the two situations. More precisely, we can construct a unique n-permutation π, given a tableaux pair (P, Q) of identical shape and each containing the elements 1 through n. This construction essentially reverses the construction of (P, Q) from π. We start looking for the element n in Q and if we find it in a row r, then that means that the last insertion into P caused row r to expand. We then delete element n from Q and perform the deletion operation on P at row r. In a generic step of this algorithm, we look for the largest element in Q. If i is the largest element in Q and it appears in row r_i, we then delete i from Q and perform the deletion operation on P at row r_i.

These algorithms give a bijection between ordered pairs of Young tableaux (P, Q) of the same shapes and permutations [Knu70, Sch61]. This is the celebrated *Robinson-Schensted-Knuth correspondence*.

```
PermutationToTableaux[{}] := {{}, {}}

PermutationToTableaux[p_?PermutationQ] :=
     Module[{pt = {{p[[1]]}}, qt = {{1}}, r},
          Do[{pt, r} = InsertIntoTableau[p[[i]], pt, All];
             If[r <= Length[qt], AppendTo[qt[[r]], i], AppendTo[qt, {i}]],
             {i, 2, Length[p]}
          ];
          {pt, qt}
     ]

TableauxToPermutation[p1_?TableauQ,q1_?TableauQ] :=
     Module[{p=p1, q=q1, row, firstrow},
          Reverse[
             Table[
                    firstrow = First[p];
                    row = Position[q, Max[q]] [[1,1]];
                    p = DeleteFromTableau[p,row];
                    q[[row]] = Drop[ q[[row]], -1];
                    If[ p == {},
                          First[firstrow],
                          First[Complement[firstrow,First[p]]]
                    ],
                    {Apply[Plus,ShapeOfTableau[p1]]}
                 ]
             ]
     ] /; ShapeOfTableau[p1] === ShapeOfTableau[q1]
```

The Robinson-Schensted-Knuth Correspondence

To illustrate this bijection, we start with a random 10-permutation...

In[94]:= **p = RandomPermutation[10]**

Out[94]= {1, 3, 6, 4, 7, 10, 8, 5, 9, 2}

...and construct the corresponding tableaux pair. Note that these two tableaux have the same shapes and contain the elements 1 through 10.

```
In[95]:= {P, Q} = PermutationToTableaux[p]
Out[95]= {{{1, 2, 4, 5, 8, 9}, {3, 7}, {6}, {10}},
          {{1, 2, 3, 5, 6, 9}, {4, 7}, {8}, {10}}}
```

This takes us from the tableaux pair back to the original permutation.

```
In[96]:= TableauxToPermutation[P, Q]
Out[96]= {1, 3, 6, 4, 7, 10, 8, 5, 9, 2}
```

An important feature of this bijection is that the permutation π corresponds to the tableaux pair (P, Q) if and only if π^{-1} corresponds to the tableaux pair (Q, P).

The two tableaux corresponding to p reappear, but they are flipped in order.

```
In[97]:= q = InversePermutation[p];
         PermutationToTableaux[q]
Out[98]= {{{1, 2, 3, 5, 6, 9}, {4, 7}, {8}, {10}},
          {{1, 2, 4, 5, 8, 9}, {3, 7}, {6}, {10}}}
```

Since cycles have length at most 2, this is an involution. See Section 3.2.1 for more details on involutions.

```
In[99]:= p = FromCycles[{ {1, 4}, {3}, {2, 5}, {6, 7}}]
Out[99]= {4, 5, 3, 1, 2, 7, 6}
```

The tableaux pair corresponding to an involution contains identical permutations. This follows from the fact that if $\pi = \pi^{-1}$, then the corresponding tableaux pairs (P, Q) and (Q, P) are identical, implying that $P = Q$.

```
In[100]:= PermutationToTableaux[p]
Out[100]= {{{1, 2, 6}, {3, 5, 7}, {4}},
           {{1, 2, 6}, {3, 5, 7}, {4}}}
```

■ 4.4.3 Generating Young Tableaux

Systematically constructing all the Young tableaux of a given shape is a more complex problem than building the other combinatorial objects we have seen. Part of the problem is defining a logical sequence for the two-dimensional structures. We follow the construction of [NW78] and start by defining functions `LastLexicographicTableau` and `FirstLexicographicTableau`.

We define the first lexicographic tableau to consist of *columns* of contiguous integers.

```
In[101]:= TableForm[FirstLexicographicTableau[{4,3,3,2}]]
Out[101]//TableForm= 1   5   9    12
                     2   6   10
                     3   7   11
                     4   8
```

The last lexicographic tableau consists of *rows* of contiguous integers.

```
In[102]:= TableForm[ LastLexicographicTableau[{4,3,3,2}] ]
Out[102]//TableForm= 1    2    3    4
                     5    6    7
                     8    9    10
                     11   12
```

In the lexicographically last tableau, all rows consist of a contiguous range of integers. Thus for each integer k, the subtableau defined by the elements $1, ..., k$ has k in the last row of the subtableau t. In general, to construct the lexicographically next tableau, we identify the smallest k such that k is *not* in the last row of its subtableau. Say this subtableau of k elements has shape $\{s_1, ..., s_m\}$. The next tableaux will be the lexicographically first tableau with k in the next rightmost corner of the subtableaux, with the elements of t that are greater than k appended to the corresponding rows of the new subtableau.

The list of tableaux of shape $\{2, 2, 1\}$ illustrates the amount of freedom available to tableau structures. The smallest element is always in the upper left-hand corner, but the largest element is free to be the rightmost position of the last row defined by all the *distinct* parts of the partition.

```
In[103]:= Tableaux[{2,2,1}]
Out[103]= {{{1, 4}, {2, 5}, {3}}, {{1, 3}, {2, 5}, {4}},
           {{1, 2}, {3, 5}, {4}}, {{1, 3}, {2, 4}, {5}},
           {{1, 2}, {3, 4}, {5}}}
```

By iterating through the different integer partitions as shapes, all tableaux of a particular size can be constructed.

```
In[104]:= Tableaux[3]
Out[104]= {{{1, 2, 3}}, {{1, 3}, {2}}, {{1, 2}, {3}},
           {{1}, {2}, {3}}}
```

■ 4.4.4 Counting Tableaux by Shape

Each position p within a Young tableau defines an L-shaped *hook*, consisting of p, all the elements below p, and all the elements to the right of p. The *hook length formula* gives the number of tableaux of a given shape as $n!$ divided by the product of the hook length of each position, where n is the number of positions in the tableau. A convincing argument that the formula works is as follows: Of the $n!$ ways to label a tableau of a given shape, only those where the minimum element in each hook is in the corner can be tableaux, so for each hook the probability that the tableau condition is satisfied is one over the hook length. Unfortunately, this argument is bogus because these probabilities are not independent, but correct proofs that the formula works appear in [FZ82, Knu73b, NW78].

```
NumberOfTableaux[{}] := 1
NumberOfTableaux[s_List] :=
      Module[{row,col,transpose=TransposePartition[s]},
             (Apply[Plus,s])! /
             Product [
                    (transpose[[col]]-row+s[[row]]-col+1),
                    {row,Length[s]}, {col,s[[row]]}
             ]
      ]

NumberOfTableaux[n_Integer] := Apply[Plus, Map[NumberOfTableaux, Partitions[n]]]
```

The Hook Length Formula

The hook length formula can be used to count the number of tableaux for any shape, which for small sizes can be confirmed by constructing and counting them.

```
In[105]:= {NumberOfTableaux[{3,2,1}], Length[Tableaux[{3,2,1}]]}
Out[105]= {16, 16}
```

Using the hook length formula over all partitions of n computes the number of tableaux on n elements.

```
In[106]:= NumberOfTableaux[10]
Out[106]= 9496
```

A *biparential heap* [MS80] is a triangular data structure where each element is greater than both its parents (shown to the left and above each element). Pascal's triangle is an example of a biparential heap.

```
In[107]:= RandomTableau[ Reverse[Range[8]] ] // TableForm
Out[107]//TableForm= 1    2    3    4    10   16   17   18
                     5    6    11   12   23   30   31
                     7    8    15   22   32   34
                     9    19   21   26   33
                     13   20   25   27
                     14   24   28
                     29   36
                     35
```

The structure of a biparential heap is determined by a Young tableau of the given shape. Here we compute the number of biparential heaps on 55 distinct elements.

```
In[108]:= NumberOfTableaux[ Reverse[Range[10]] ]
Out[108]= 44261486084874072183645699204710400
```

Our study of Young tableaux was motivated by the number of well-formed formulas that can be made from n sets of parentheses, which we showed is the number of distinct tableaux of shape $\{n, n\}$. Since any balanced set of parentheses has a leftmost point $k + 1$ at which the number of left and right parentheses are equal, peeling off the first left parenthesis and the $(k + 1)$st right parenthesis leaves two balanced sets k and $n - 1 - k$ parentheses, which leads to the following recurrence:

$$C_n = \sum_{k=0}^{n-1} C_k C_{n-1-k} = \binom{2n}{n}/(n + 1).$$

This recurrence defines the *Catalan numbers*, which occur in a surprising number of problems in combinatorics, from the number of triangulations of a convex polygon to the number of paths across a lattice that do not rise above the main diagonal. This recurrence can be solved using generating functions to reveal the nice closed form

$$C_n = \frac{1}{(n + 1)} \binom{2n}{n}.$$

The *Mathematica* add-on package `DiscreteMath`CombinatorialFunctions`` contains this definition of the function `CatalanNumber`.

This function is named `CatalanNumber` to avoid conflict with the built-in *Mathematica* function `Catalan`, which returns Catalan's constant.

```
In[109]:= Table[CatalanNumber[i], {i,2,20}]
Out[109]= {2, 5, 14, 42, 132, 429, 1430, 4862, 16796, 58786,
           208012, 742900, 2674440, 9694845, 35357670, 129644790,
           477638700, 1767263190, 6564120420}
```

As we have seen, the Catalan numbers are a special case of the hook length formula.

```
In[110]:= Table[ NumberOfTableaux[{i,i}], {i,2,20}]
Out[110]= {2, 5, 14, 42, 132, 429, 1430, 4862, 16796, 58786,
           208012, 742900, 2674440, 9694845, 35357670, 129644790,
           477638700, 1767263190, 6564120420}
```

■ 4.4.5 Random Tableaux

Constructing tableaux of a given shape randomly with a uniform distribution is another sticky problem solved in [NW78]. The key observation is that the largest element in the tableau must go in a rightmost corner of the shape, and that once the appropriate corner is selected the construction can proceed to position all smaller elements. Selecting a corner at random from the list of candidates will not give a uniform construction, since there are different numbers of ways to complete the tableau, depending on the shape left after the insertion. Using `NumberOfTableaux`, this can be computed for each of the possible shapes, and so a truly random corner selection can be made. `RandomTableau` implements this procedure.

Each of the 117,123,756,750 tableaux of this shape will be selected with equal likelihood.

```
In[111]:= TableForm[ RandomTableau[{6,5,5,4,3,2}] ]
Out[111]//TableForm= 1    2    3    6    9    15
                     4    8    10   18   21
                     5    12   17   22   23
                     7    13   19   25
                     11   16   24
                     14   20
```

Repeating the experiment in [NW78] illustrates that each of the 16 tableaux occurs with roughly equal frequency.

```
In[112]:= Distribution[ Table[RandomTableau[{3,2,1}], {1000}] ]
Out[112]= {75, 72, 63, 53, 66, 66, 58, 56, 54, 55, 64, 61,
           57, 56, 82, 62}
```

■ 4.4.6 Longest Increasing Subsequences

When we construct a tableau with the insertion algorithm, every element begins its life in some position in the first row, from which it may later be bumped. The elements that originally entered in the *i*th column are said to belong to the *i*th *class* of the tableau, and this class distinction leads to an interesting algorithm to find the longest increasing scattered subsequence of a permutation [Sch61]. `TableauClasses` partitions the elements of a permutation into classes.

```
TableauClasses[p_?PermutationQ] :=
    Module[{classes=Table[{},{Length[p]}],t={}},
        Scan [(t = InsertIntoTableau[#,t];
            PrependTo[classes[[Position[First[t],#] [[1,1]] ]], #])&,
            p
        ];
        Select[classes, (# != {})&]
    ]
```

Partitioning a Permutation into Classes

Note that $4, 5, 7, 8$ form a longest increasing (scattered) subsequence of the following tableau, which contains the same number of columns.

In[113]:= **TableauClasses[{6,4,9,5,7,1,2,8,3}]**

Out[113]= {{1, 4, 6}, {2, 5, 9}, {3, 7}, {8}}

The reverse permutation has $3, 5, 9$ as a longest increasing subsequence, making it the longest decreasing subsequence of the original permutation.

In[114]:= **TableauClasses[{3,8,2,1,7,5,9,4,6}]**

Out[114]= {{1, 2, 3}, {4, 5, 7, 8}, {6, 9}}

This connection between the number of classes and the length of the longest scattered subsequence is not a coincidence. For an element of the permutation to enter the tableau in the kth column, there had to be elements creating $k-1$ columns before it. A column is created whenever the inserted element is greater than the last element of the first row, so clearly the elements that start new columns form an increasing subsequence. The fact that it is the *longest* increasing subsequence is a consequence of the first class corresponding to the left-to-right minima of the permutation and the kth class being the left-to-right minima of the permutation minus the elements of the first $k-1$ classes.

```
LongestIncreasingSubsequence[{}] := {}
LongestIncreasingSubsequence[p_?PermutationQ] :=
    Module[{c,x,xlast},
        c = TableauClasses[p];
        xlast = x = First[ Last[c] ];
        Append[Reverse[Map[(x = First[Intersection[#, Take[p, Position[p,x][[1,1]]]]])&,
                    Reverse[Drop[c,-1]]
                ]
            ],
            xlast
        ]
    ]
```

Identifying the Longest Increasing Subsequence in a Permutation

The longest increasing *contiguous* subsequence can be found by selecting the largest of the runs in the permutation. Finding the largest scattered subsequence is a much harder problem.

A pigeonhole result [ES35] states that any sequence of $n^2 + 1$ distinct integers must contain either an increasing or a decreasing scattered subsequence of length $n + 1$. Thus at least one of these sequences must be at least eight integers long.

```
In[115]:= First[ Sort[ Runs[p=RandomPermutation[50]], (Length[#1] >
             Length[#2])&] ]
Out[115]= {9, 26, 32, 39}
```

```
In[116]:= {LongestIncreasingSubsequence[p],
             LongestIncreasingSubsequence[Reverse[p]]}
Out[116]= {{4, 6, 9, 11, 13, 15, 24, 31, 36, 38, 40, 44},
             {2, 3, 7, 14, 16, 27, 30, 32, 35, 45}}
```

4.5 Exercises

■ 4.5.1 Thought Exercises

1. Write down the generating function for the number of partitions of n in which each part is at most 6.

2. Write down the generating function for the number of partitions of n in which each part is a multiple of 3.

3. Devise a *bijective* proof for the fact that for any positive integer n, the number of partitions of n with distinct parts equals the number of partitions of n with all odd parts. A bijective proof of an identity involves establishing a one-one correspondence between the set represented by the left-hand side and the set represented by the right-hand side.

4. Prove that the number of integer partitions with two parts $p_{n,2} = \lfloor n/2 \rfloor + 1$.

5. Prove that the size of the Durfee square remains unchanged in transposing an integer partition.

6. Explain why the minimum change graph on compositions is a grid of triangles.

7. Prove that the tableaux pair corresponding to an involution contains identical permutations.

8. Prove that $\left\{ {n \atop n-1} \right\} = \binom{n}{2}$.

9. Why is k not an argument for `UnrankKSetPartition`?

10. Consider the following attempt to generate a random RGF f on $\{1, 2, \ldots, n\}$: Set $f(1) = 1$; after generating $f(1), f(2), \ldots, f(i-1)$, we generate $f(i+1)$ by picking an integer in the set $\{f(i), f(i)+1, \ldots, n\}$, uniformly at random. Does this generate RGFs uniformly at random? If yes, prove it; if no, show two RGFs and prove that they are generated with distinct probabilities.

■ 4.5.2 Programming Exercises

1. A recursive algorithm to generate a list of all set partitions of $\{1, 2, \ldots, n\}$ in minimum change order is as follows [Lay76]. Let π be any partition of $\{2, 3, \ldots, n\}$. The *children* of π are obtained by inserting 1 into one of the blocks of π or adjoining 1 to π as a singleton block. Suppose inductively we have a list L_{n-1} of set partitions of $\{2, 3, \ldots, n\}$ in minimum change order. Take the first set partition in L_{n-1} and list its children in natural order, that is, 1 into the first block, 1 into the second block, and so on. Then take the children on the second set partition in L_{n-1} and list them in reverse order, and repeat this alternation with each group of siblings.
Implement this algorithm. Also, use the idea to devise an algorithm to list the set partitions of $\{1, 2, \ldots, n\}$ with k blocks, for a given k, in minimum change order.

2. Let us suppose that the identities

$$\left\{{n \atop k}\right\} = \left\{{n-1 \atop k-1}\right\} + k\left\{{n-1 \atop k}\right\} \qquad \text{and} \qquad \left[{n \atop k}\right] = \left[{n-1 \atop k-1}\right] + (n-1)\left[{n-1 \atop k}\right]$$

are valid for *all* integers, not just nonnegative integers. Assume the standard boundary conditions: If $n = k = 0$, both numbers are 1; otherwise, if $n = 0$ or $k = 0$, both numbers are 0. This leads to unique solutions to the two recurrences, thereby giving us values for Stirling numbers with negative arguments. Extend the functions `StirlingFirst` and `StirlingSecond` so that they work for negative arguments as well.

Using this function, produce a table of $\left\{{n \atop k}\right\}$ values for $k \in [-5...5]$ and $n \in [-5...5]$. Examine the table carefully and conclude a neat "duality" between Stirling numbers of the two kinds.

3. An alternate recurrence [NW78] for the number of integer partitions of n is

$$p_n = \frac{1}{n}\sum_{m=0}^{n-1}\sigma(n-m)p_m,$$

where $p_0 = 1$ and $\sigma(k)$ is the sum of the divisors of k. Does this recurrence give a better way to calculate p_n than `NumberOfPartitions`? You may use the built-in *Mathematica* function `DivisorSigma[1,k]` to compute $\sigma(k)$.

4. Design and implement an efficient algorithm for constructing all partitions of n with distinct parts. Compare it to using `Select` and `Partitions`.

5. Repeat the previous exercise, constructing all partitions of n into odd parts, even parts, distinct odd parts, and finally all *self-conjugate* partitions, meaning they are equal to their transpose.

6. Implement a function [Sav89] to generate the partitions of n in Gray code order, as defined in the chapter.

■ 4.5.3 Experimental Exercises

1. Experiment with `NumberOfTableaux` to determine the shape that, for a given number of elements, maximizes the number of Young tableaux over all partitions of n.

2. A partition p *contains* partition q if the Ferrers diagram of p contains the Ferrers diagram of q. For example, $\{3,3,2\}$ contains both $\{3,3,1\}$ and $\{3,2,2\}$ as well as many smaller partitions. *Young's lattice* Y_p [SW86] is the partial order of the partitions contained within p ordered by containment. Use `MakeGraph` to construct Young's lattice for an arbitrary partition p.

3. `ConstructTableau` takes a permutation to a Young tableau that is not necessarily unique. For the permutations of length n, which tableaux are the most frequently generated?

4. Experiment to determine the expected amount of vacant dots in the rectangle defined by the Ferrers diagram of a random partition of size n.

5. It is easy to observe from various examples in this chapter that $p(n)$ grows quite slowly as compared to $n!$. How does $p(n)$ compare to 2^n? Experiment by comparing $p(n)$ with a variety of functions. Do you think $p(n)$ grows exponentially?

6. Examining the sequence

$$\left\{{n \atop 1}\right\}, \left\{{n \atop 2}\right\}, \dots, \left\{{n \atop n}\right\}$$

for a few values of n should convince the reader that elements in this sequence increase strictly starting at 1, reach a maximum value, and then decrease strictly down to 1. Strangely enough, this property is an unproven conjecture! Aigner [Aig79] proves that this sequence strictly increases until it reaches a plateau of at most 2 maxima and then strictly decreases. Write a function that takes a positive integer n and tests the uniqueness of the maximum value in $\{\left\{{n \atop k}\right\} \mid k \in [n]\}$. What is the largest value of n that you can reasonably test using this technique?

7. A result of Canfield [Can78b] provides a faster way of testing the conjecture described above. Let K_n be a positive integer such that

$$\left\{{n \atop K_n}\right\} \geq \left\{{n \atop k}\right\} \text{ for all } k \in \{1, 2, \dots, n\}.$$

Then, for sufficiently large n, $K_n = \lfloor t \rfloor$ or $K_n = \lfloor t \rfloor + 1$, where t is the solution to the equation

$$\frac{(t + 2)t \log(t + 2)}{t + 1} = n.$$

Write a function that takes a positive integer n and uses this technique to test the uniqueness of maxima conjecture for Stirling numbers of the second kind. What is the largest value of n for which this test can be performed in a reasonable amount of time?

5. Graph Representation

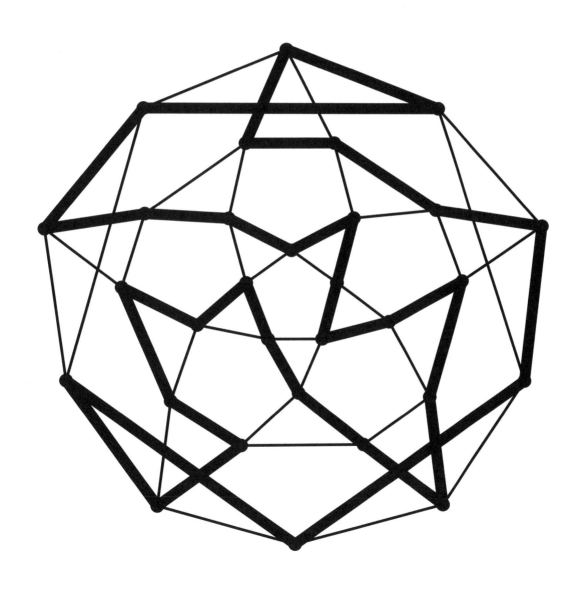

We define a *graph* to be a set of *vertices* with a set of pairs of these vertices called *edges*. This terminology is readily understood if not quite universal, since *point*, *node*, *junction*, and *0-simplex* have been used as synonyms for vertex and *line*, *arc*, *branch*, and *1-simplex* as synonyms for edge [Har69].

The representation of graphs takes on different requirements depending on whether the intended consumer is a person or a machine. Computers digest graphs best as data structures such as adjacency matrices or lists. People prefer a visualization of the structure as a collection of points connected by lines, which implies adding geometric information to the graph. In this chapter, we discuss a variety of graph data structures. We also develop graph drawing algorithms to exploit *Mathematica* graphics. Finally, we provide tools for storing graphs and thus interfacing with other systems.

This chapter is mostly devoted to nut and bolt routines that we will use throughout the text, but which have relatively little mathematical content. The impatient reader might want to give this chapter a quick skim, but be warned that *Combinatorica*'s graph representation has become much more sophisticated relative to the old package. Any user interested in implementing their own graph functions will find this chapter indispensable.

About the illustration overleaf:

This shows a Hamiltonian cycle in the line graph of a dodecahedral graph. The line graph of any Hamiltonian graph is itself Hamiltonian. The command to compute the cycle and highlight it in the graph drawing is

```
c = Partition[ HamiltonianCycle[g=LineGraph[DodecahedralGraph]], 2, 1];
ShowGraph[Highlight[g,{c}]];
```

5.1 Data Structures for Graphs

In this section, we will study how graphs are represented in *Combinatorica*, which supports a variety of graph data structures for efficiency and ease of programming. We start with a detailed description of the canonical `Graph` structure, before going on to other representations used in our algorithms.

■ 5.1.1 The Internal Representation

A *Combinatorica* graph structure consists of two or more pieces of information wrapped around by the header `Graph`. In its simplest form, the representation uses only two pieces, the first for edges and the second for vertices.

We use an *edge list* representation as our internal data structure for the topology of *Combinatorica* graphs. This proves especially convenient when programming in *Mathematica* and provides us with a flexible way to store embedding and drawing information associated with a graph.

Load the *Combinatorica* package.

```
In[1]:= <<DiscreteMath`Combinatorica`
```

This displays a star graph with six vertices. In general, a *star graph* with *n* vertices is a tree with one vertex of degree $n - 1$. This example uses the option `VertexNumber->True` to turn on the display of numbers associated with vertices.

```
In[2]:= ShowGraph[Star[6], VertexNumber->True];
```

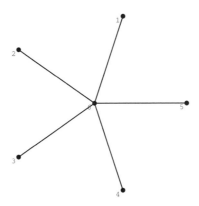

The internals of the graph representation are, by design, hidden from the user. Instead, we provide a brief description of the graph, giving the number of edges, number of vertices, and whether the graph is directed.

```
In[3]:= g = Star[6]

Out[3]= -Graph:<5, 6, Undirected>-
```

The header of g is Graph. Wrapping this header around the data structure is useful for error checking and to avoid confusion with other objects in the system.

```
In[4]:= Head[g]
Out[4]= Graph
```

The first element of g is a list of edges. More precisely, associated with each edge in g is a list whose first element is an ordered pair representing the edge.

```
In[5]:= g[[1]]
Out[5]= {{{1, 6}}, {{2, 6}}, {{3, 6}}, {{4, 6}}, {{5, 6}}}
```

The *correct* way for the user to get this information is by using the function Edges.

```
In[6]:= Edges[g]
Out[6]= {{1, 6}, {2, 6}, {3, 6}, {4, 6}, {5, 6}}
```

The second element of g is a list of vertices. Associated with each vertex in g is a list whose first element is the position of the point representing the vertex.

```
In[7]:= g[[2]]
Out[7]= {{{0.309017, 0.951057}}, {{-0.809017, 0.587785}},
    {{-0.809017, -0.587785}}, {{0.309017, -0.951057}},
    {{1., 0}}, {{0, 0}}}
```

The *correct* way for the user to get this information is by using the function Vertices.

```
In[8]:= Vertices[g]
Out[8]= {{0.309017, 0.951057}, {-0.809017, 0.587785},
    {-0.809017, -0.587785}, {0.309017, -0.951057}, {1., 0},
    {0, 0}}
```

SetGraphOptions is used to change the way in which vertices and edges of the graph are drawn. Since these options affect *all* the vertices and edges, we view them as "global" options. Later we will show how to set options so as to affect only a subset of vertices and edges.

```
In[9]:= ShowGraph[h = SetGraphOptions[Star[6],
        VertexStyle -> Box[Large], EdgeStyle -> NormalDashed] ];
```

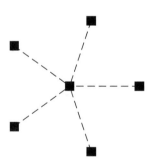

Global information about how we want the graph drawn is stored as options in the graph data structure following the list of vertices. The third and fourth pieces of h are options that specify styles for drawing vertices and edges, respectively.

```
In[10]:= {h[[3]], h[[4]]}
Out[10]= {VertexStyle -> Box[Large],
    EdgeStyle -> NormalDashed}
```

The *correct* way to get this information is by using the function `GraphOptions`.

```
In[11]:= GraphOptions[h]
Out[11]= {VertexStyle -> Box[Large],
          EdgeStyle -> NormalDashed}
```

Here we define and display a 6-vertex star graph with vertices 1 and 5 drawn as large discs. This example shows how drawing styles are set "locally" to affect only a specified subset of edges or vertices.

```
In[12]:= ShowGraph[t = SetGraphOptions[Star[6],
           {{1, 5, VertexStyle -> Disk[Large]}}]];
```

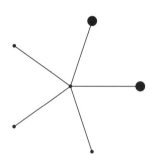

The fact that we want vertices 1 and 5 to be drawn as large discs is stored in the first and fifth vertex lists. Information stored locally, in a list corresponding to a vertex or to an edge, supersedes global information.

```
In[13]:= Vertices[t,All]
Out[13]= {{{0.309017, 0.951057},
           VertexStyle -> Disk[Large]}, {{-0.809017, 0.587785}},
           {{-0.809017, -0.587785}}, {{0.309017, -0.951057}},
           {{1., 0}, VertexStyle -> Disk[Large]}, {{0, 0}}}
```

In summary, graphs consist of a sequence of objects wrapped around with the `Graph` header. The first element in the sequence is a list of edges, the second is a list of vertices, and any elements that follow are global options. All local options that affect a specific vertex or edge are stored in the list corresponding to that particular edge or vertex.

One advantage to making the drawing information a part of the graph's representation is that it is usually difficult to determine what the "right" drawing should be. This varies according to the structure and application of the graph in question. Thus, once we have a desired embedding, we view it as part of the graph. Throughout this book, we will see many operations that construct graphs from other graphs in which a reasonable embedding of the resulting graph can be built using the embeddings of the component graphs.

■ 5.1.2 Edge Lists

The biggest change in *Combinatorica* has been replacing adjacency matrices by edge lists as the internal graph data structure. Now the memory used by a graph is proportional to the number of vertices plus the number of edges in the graph. This change has had a dramatic effect on the ability of *Combinatorica* to process large graphs.

This generates a three-dimensional $40 \times 40 \times 40$ grid graph, which is orders of magnitude larger than what the previous version of *Combinatorica* could have handled.

```
In[14]:= g = GridGraph[40, 40, 40]

Out[14]= -Graph:<187200, 64000, Undirected>-
```

Edge lists represent graphs as a list of edges, where each edge is represented by an ordered or unordered pair of vertices. This representation makes it easy to implement primitives that extract basic information about a graph, such as M returns the number of edges M and vertices V. The functions Edges and Vertices return the list of edges and vertices of the given graph, respectively.

```
M::obsolete = "Usage of Directed as a second argument to M is obsolete."
M[Graph[e_List, _List, ___?OptionQ]] := Length[e]
M[g_Graph, Directed] := (Message[M::obsolete]; M[g])

V[Graph[_List, v_List, ___?OptionQ]] := Length[v]

Edges[Graph[e_List, _List, ___?OptionQ]] := Map[First[#]&, e]
Edges[Graph[e_List, _List, ___?OptionQ], All] := e

Edges[g_Graph, EdgeWeight] :=
        Map[{First[#], EdgeWeight} /.
            Flatten[{Rest[#], GraphOptions[g], Options[Graph]}]&,
            Edges[g, All]
        ]

Vertices[Graph[_List, v_List, ___?OptionQ]] := Map[First[#]&, v]
Vertices[Graph[_List, v_List, ___?OptionQ], All] := v
```

Definition of Graph Extraction Primitives

In K_n, the *complete graph* on n vertices, every vertex is adjacent to every other vertex. Here, K_5 is assigned to g and is displayed with the vertex numbers turned on. The numbers 1 through n are automatically assigned to the vertices of an n-vertex graph by the graph constructor function, in this case CompleteGraph.

```
In[15]:= ShowGraph[g = CompleteGraph[5], VertexNumber -> True,
            TextStyle -> {FontSize -> 13}, PlotRange -> 0.1];
```

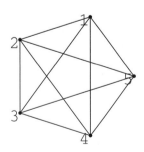

K_5 has ten edges and five vertices.

```
In[16]:= {M[g], V[g]}

Out[16]= {10, 5}
```

The number of edges in a complete graph with n vertices is $\binom{n}{2}$, here demonstrated for $n = 20$.

```
In[17]:= {M[CompleteGraph[20]], Binomial[20, 2]}
Out[17]= {190, 190}
```

The edges of K_5 are all 2-subsets of the numbers 1 through 5.

```
In[18]:= Edges[g]
Out[18]= {{1, 2}, {1, 3}, {1, 4}, {1, 5}, {2, 3}, {2, 4},
          {2, 5}, {3, 4}, {3, 5}, {4, 5}}
```

Here the complete graph on 5 vertices is defined with edges $(1, 2)$ and $(2, 5)$ thickened. This additional drawing information is stored in the lists corresponding to these edges.

```
In[19]:= ShowGraph[g = SetGraphOptions[CompleteGraph[5], {{{1, 2}, {2, 5},
         EdgeStyle -> Thick}}]];
```

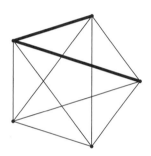

Using the tag `All` makes `Edges` return the drawing information associated with edges as well. The tag `All` can be used with the same effect as an argument to the function `Vertices`.

```
In[20]:= Edges[g, All]
Out[20]= {{{1, 2}, EdgeStyle -> Thick}, {{1, 3}}, {{1, 4}},
          {{1, 5}}, {{2, 3}}, {{2, 4}},
          {{2, 5}, EdgeStyle -> Thick}, {{3, 4}}, {{3, 5}},
          {{4, 5}}}
```

Many graph algorithms deal with edge-weighted graphs. The `EdgeWeight` tag returns edge-weight information with the topology. Unweighted edges are assigned a weight of 1 by default. In Section 5.2.2 we show how to assign weights to vertices and edges of graphs.

```
In[21]:= Edges[g, EdgeWeight]
Out[21]= {{{1, 2}, 1}, {{1, 3}, 1}, {{1, 4}, 1},
          {{1, 5}, 1}, {{2, 3}, 1}, {{2, 4}, 1}, {{2, 5}, 1},
          {{3, 4}, 1}, {{3, 5}, 1}, {{4, 5}, 1}}
```

The functions `ToOrderedPairs` and `ToUnorderedPairs` and their inverses, `FromOrderedPairs` and `FromUnorderedPairs`, enable us to move back and forth between graphs and lists of integer pairs that represent edges.

```
Options[ToOrderedPairs] = {Type -> All}

ToOrderedPairs[g_Graph, opts___?OptionQ] :=
    Module[{type, op},
```

```
        type = Type /. Flatten[{opts, Options[ToOrderedPairs]}];
        op = If[UndirectedQ[g], Double[Edges[g]], Edges[g]];
        If[type === Simple, Union[Select[op, (#[[1]] != #[[2]])&]], op]
  ]
Options[ToUnorderedPairs] = {Type -> All};

ToUnorderedPairs[g_Graph, opts___?OptionQ] :=
    Module[{type, el},
        type = Type /. Flatten[{opts, Options[ToUnorderedPairs]}];
        el = If[UndirectedQ[g], Edges[g], Map[Sort, Edges[g]]];
        If[type === All, el, Union[Select[el, (#[[1]] != #[[2]])&]]]
    ]
```

Going From a Graph to Pairs

Whether such a list is interpreted as ordered or unordered pairs depends on whether the graph is *directed* or *undirected*

```
In[22]:= ShowGraphArray[{Cycle[5], Cycle[5, Type->Directed]},
             VertexNumber->True]
```

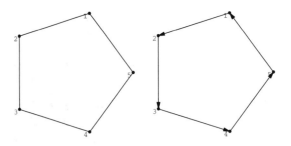

Here we list the undirected edges of an undirected graph.

```
In[23]:= ToUnorderedPairs[ Cycle[5] ]
Out[23]= {{1, 2}, {2, 3}, {3, 4}, {4, 5}, {1, 5}}
```

Creating ordered pairs from undirected edges doubles the number of pairs.

```
In[24]:= ToOrderedPairs[ Cycle[5] ]
Out[24]= {{2, 1}, {3, 2}, {4, 3}, {5, 4}, {5, 1}, {1, 2},
          {2, 3}, {3, 4}, {4, 5}, {1, 5}}
```

Directed graphs already have ordered pairs, so we are back to one pair per cycle edge.

```
In[25]:= ToOrderedPairs[ Cycle[5, Type->Directed] ]
Out[25]= {{1, 2}, {2, 3}, {3, 4}, {4, 5}, {5, 1}}
```

The functions ToOrderedPairs and ToUnorderedPairs can also deal with graphs that are not simple. An option Type is provided that tells these functions whether to consider the entire graph or the underlying simple graph.

`In[26]:= ShowGraph[h = AddEdges[Cycle[5], {{1, 1}, {1, 2}}]];`

This function call produces seven edge pairs, one for every edge you can see in the above picture.

`In[27]:= ToUnorderedPairs[h]`

`Out[27]= {{1, 2}, {2, 3}, {3, 4}, {4, 5}, {1, 5}, {1, 1},`
`        {1, 2}}`

With this setting of the option Type we get only pairs corresponding to the underlying simple graph.

`In[28]:= ToUnorderedPairs[h, Type->Simple]`

`Out[28]= {{1, 2}, {1, 5}, {2, 3}, {3, 4}, {4, 5}}`

Combinatorica provides functions FromUnorderedPairs and FromOrderedPairs that transform unordered and ordered pairs, respectively, into graphs. These functions are essentially the inverses of ToUnorderedPairs and ToOrderedPairs.

The number of vertices in the reconstructed graph is defined by the maximum integer appearing in a pair. The circular embedding is used by default for the reconstructed graph, although an alternate embedding can be specified.

`In[29]:= ShowGraphArray[{FromUnorderedPairs[p = {{1, 2}, {7, 1}, {2, 4},`
`        {4, 5}}], FromOrderedPairs[p]}, VertexNumber->True];`

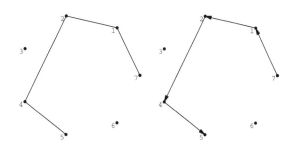

The embedding, edge direction, and weight information may be lost in the conversion between representations, unless explicitly maintained and restored.

In[30]:= **ShowGraphArray[{Star[5],**
FromOrderedPairs[ToOrderedPairs[Star[5]]]}];

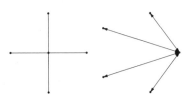

■ 5.1.3 Adjacency Lists

The adjacency list representation of an n-vertex graph consists of n lists, one list for each vertex i, $1 \leq i \leq n$, which records the vertices that i is adjacent to. Although slower than adjacency matrices for edge existence queries, adjacency lists are faster for almost everything else. Most important, like edge lists, they use space proportional to the size of the graph and so are more efficient for algorithms on sparse graphs.

One of the most important functions in *Combinatorica* is ToAdjacencyLists, which takes the internal edge list representation of a graph and returns the equivalent adjacency list representation. This function is used as the first step in most graph-related functions, and hence it is crucial that it be fast. Converting an edge list to an adjacency list is quite fast, especially as compared to functions that involve adjacency matrices. As a result, many graph-related functions in the new *Combinatorica* exhibit a dramatic speedup, especially when dealing with sparse graphs.

Each vertex in K_4 is adjacent to all other vertices. Hence each list of neighbors is of size 3.

In[31]:= **ToAdjacencyLists[CompleteGraph[4]]**

Out[31]= {{2, 3, 4}, {1, 3, 4}, {1, 2, 4}, {1, 2, 3}}

Here is a graph with multiple edges connecting vertices 2 and 3 and a self-loop at 4. The new *Combinatorica* correctly displays and processes multiple edges and self-loops.

In[32]:= **ShowGraph[g = AddEdges[Wheel[5], {{2, 3}, {4, 4}}],**
VertexNumber->True,
TextStyle -> {FontSize -> 12}, PlotRange -> 0.1];

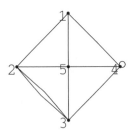

Multiedge and self-loop adjacencies in graphs are all faithfully reported. 2 appears twice in 3's list of neighbors and 3 appears twice in 2's list of neighbors representing the two edges $(2, 3)$. 4 appears in its own list of neighbors representing the self-loop $(4, 4)$.

```
In[33]:= ToAdjacencyLists[g] // ColumnForm

Out[33]= {2, 4, 5}
         {1, 3, 3, 5}
         {2, 2, 4, 5}
         {1, 3, 4, 5}
         {1, 2, 3, 4}
```

ToAdjacencyLists allows an option called Type that takes on values All or Simple. Type -> Simple ignores self-loops and multiple edges.

```
In[34]:= ToAdjacencyLists[g, Type -> Simple] // ColumnForm

Out[34]= {2, 4, 5}
         {1, 3, 5}
         {2, 4, 5}
         {1, 3, 5}
         {1, 2, 3, 4}
```

The tag EdgeWeight can be used in ToAdjacencyLists to get edge weights in addition to adjacencies. Each neighbor is represented by an ordered pair containing the neighbor followed by the weight of the edge connecting to the neighbor. SetEdgeWeights defaults to assign random weights in the range $[0, 1]$ to the edges of the graph.

```
In[35]:= ToAdjacencyLists[SetEdgeWeights[Star[4]],
         EdgeWeight] // ColumnForm

Out[35]= {{4, 0.0560708}}
         {{4, 0.6303}}
         {{4, 0.359894}}
         {{1, 0.0560708}, {2, 0.6303}, {3, 0.359894}}
```

A more interesting set of edge weights is the set of Euclidean distances of the graph's vertex positions. These are all the same for a star, since all vertices are equidistant from the center.

```
In[36]:= ToAdjacencyLists[SetEdgeWeights[Star[4],
         WeightingFunction->Euclidean], EdgeWeight] // ColumnForm

Out[36]= {{4, 1.}}
         {{4, 1.}}
         {{4, 1.}}
         {{1, 1.}, {2, 1.}, {3, 1.}}
```

ToAdjacencyLists is fast enough that it can process fairly quickly graphs with 78,300 edges and 27,000 vertices. Old *Combinatorica* worked with the adjacency matrix representations of graphs and this made computations on such large graphs impossible.

```
In[37]:= Timing[ Length[ ToAdjacencyLists[ g = GridGraph[30, 30, 30] ] ] ]

Out[37]= {21.13 Second, 27000}
```

The function FromAdjacencyLists is the inverse of ToAdjacencyLists, in that it takes an adjacency list representation of a graph and constructs the equivalent graph.

Taking a graph to adjacency lists and then back using FromAdjacencyLists is an identity operation. However, the original embedding information is lost and replaced by the default circular embedding. A *complete k-ary tree* is a rooted tree in which all internal vertices have exactly *k* children and all leaves are at the same level.

```
In[38]:= g = CompleteKaryTree[20, 4];
        h = FromAdjacencyLists[ToAdjacencyLists[g]];
        ShowGraphArray[{g, h}];
```

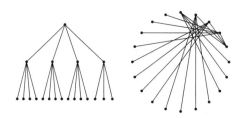

FromAdjacencyLists allows an option Type to specify whether to construct a directed or an undirected graph. The default setting is Undirected. Reconstructing an undirected graph as directed gives a digraph in which for every pair there are edges in both directions.

```
In[41]:= ShowGraphArray[{
        FromAdjacencyLists[ToAdjacencyLists[Cycle[10]], Type->Directed],
        FromAdjacencyLists[ToAdjacencyLists[Cycle[10]] ]
        }];
```

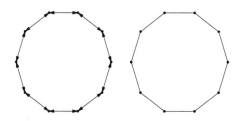

We can correctly reconstruct a directed graph from its adjacency lists by using the Type -> Directed option in FromAdjacencyLists.

```
In[42]:= IdenticalQ[ g = RandomGraph[10, .3, Type->Directed],
        FromAdjacencyLists[ToAdjacencyLists[g], Type->Directed] ]
Out[42]= True
```

FromAdjacencyLists has a running time of $\Theta(m)$, where *m* is the number of edges in the graph.

```
In[43]:= g = GridGraph[15, 15, 15];
        {Timing[al = ToAdjacencyLists[g];],
        Timing[FromAdjacencyLists[al];]}
Out[44]= {{1.33 Second, Null}, {1.34 Second, Null}}
```

■ 5.1.4 Adjacency Matrices

The adjacency matrix representation of a graph will prove useful for certain functions, such as in computing all pairs' shortest paths and testing graph isomorphism. The adjacency matrix of an *n*-vertex graph always contains n^2 entries, so adjacency lists are better than matrices in dealing with large sparse graphs. The code for ToAdjacencyMatrix is given below. The adjacency matrix is produced row by row, and the *i*th row is produced by starting with a list of 0's and incrementing positions specified by the neighbors of *i*.

```
Options[ToAdjacencyMatrix] = {Type -> All};

ToAdjacencyMatrix[g_Graph, opts___?OptionQ] :=
    Module[{e = ToAdjacencyLists[g], blanks = Table[0, {V[g]}], type, am},
        type = Type /. Flatten[{opts, Options[ToAdjacencyMatrix]}];
        am = Table[nb = blanks; Scan[nb[[#]]++ &, e[[i]]]; nb,
            {i, Length[e]}
          ];
        If[type === Simple,
          Do[am[[i, i]] = 0, {i, V[g]}]; am /. _Integer?Positive -> 1,
          am
        ]
    ]
```

Converting to Adjacency Matrices

In the adjacency matrix of a complete graph, all entries off the main diagonal are 1.

```
In[45]:= ToAdjacencyMatrix[CompleteGraph[4]] // TableForm

Out[45]//TableForm= 0   1   1   1
                    1   0   1   1
                    1   1   0   1
                    1   1   1   0
```

Adding edge $(1, 2)$ to K_4 creates two edges between 1 and 2. This is correctly reported in the adjacency matrix.

```
In[46]:= ToAdjacencyMatrix[AddEdges[CompleteGraph[4],
            {1, 2}]] // TableForm

Out[46]//TableForm= 0   2   1   1
                    2   0   1   1
                    1   1   0   1
                    1   1   1   0
```

Using the EdgeWeight tag in ToAdjacencyMatrix produces a matrix with edge weights. In this example, the infinity in slot $[1, 3]$ says there is no edge between 1 and 3, while the number in slot $[1, 2]$ says there is an edge $(1, 2)$ of given weight.

```
In[47]:= g = SetEdgeWeights[Path[4], WeightingFunction -> RandomInteger,
            WeightRange -> {10, 20}]; ToAdjacencyMatrix[g, EdgeWeight] //
            TableForm

Out[47]//TableForm= Infinity   17         Infinity   Infinity
                    17         Infinity   19         Infinity
                    Infinity   19         Infinity   19
                    Infinity   Infinity   19         Infinity
```

FromAdjacencyMatrix is the inverse of ToAdjacencyMatrix. It takes a matrix with non-negative integers, interprets it as an adjacency matrix of a graph, and reconstructs the corresponding graph.

The *Petersen graph* is a graph whose vertices represent 2-subsets of a size-5 set and whose edges connect pairs of disjoint subsets [HS93]. Here the adjacency matrix of the Petersen graph is reconstructed using `FromAdjacencyMatrix`. The result is still the Petersen graph, but it is embedded in an unfamiliar manner.

```
In[48]:= g = PetersenGraph; ShowGraphArray[{g,
         h = FromAdjacencyMatrix[ ToAdjacencyMatrix[g]]}];
```

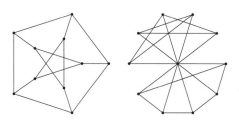

Are you suspicious about the degree-10 "vertex" at the center of the new embedding? Don't be – it isn't really there. A second look at the new embedding will tell you that the "vertex" at the center is just an illusion caused by the intersection of several edges in the graph.

```
In[49]:= DegreeSequence[ h ]
Out[49]= {3, 3, 3, 3, 3, 3, 3, 3, 3, 3}
```

To resolve the issue, we test if the two graphs shown above are isomorphic. A pair of graphs are *isomorphic* if they are identical except for vertices having different names.

```
In[50]:= IsomorphicQ[g, h]
Out[50]= True
```

Here we add edges to K_3 causing multiple parallel edges and self-loops. Taking this graph to its adjacency matrix and back preserves self-loops and multiple edges correctly.

```
In[51]:= g = AddEdges[CompleteGraph[3], {{1, 2}, {1, 1}}];
         h = FromAdjacencyMatrix[ ToAdjacencyMatrix[g]];
         IsomorphicQ[g, h]
Out[53]= True
```

Here we construct a list of three-dimensional grid graphs to use in the following timing experiments.

```
In[54]:= gt = Table[GridGraph[10, 10, i], {i, 20}];
```

Load the *Mathematica* standard package `Graphics`MultipleListPlot``, which defines functions to put multiple plots in the same picture.

```
In[55]:= <<Graphics`MultipleListPlot`
```

Here is a comparison of the performance of adjacency matrices and lists on three-dimensional grid graphs. For large sparse graphs, ToAdjacencyLists is faster than ToAdjacencyMatrix. The more important advantage of adjacency lists is that they are the more compact representation. Adjacency matrices of large, sparse graphs may not fit in memory, making a list representation the only feasible option.

```
In[56]:= lm = Table[Timing[ToAdjacencyMatrix[gt[[i]]];][[1,1]], {i,20}];
         ll = Table[Timing[ToAdjacencyLists[gt[[i]]];][[1,1]], {i,20}];
         MultipleListPlot[lm, ll, PlotJoined -> True, AxesOrigin -> {1,
         lm[[1]]}];
```

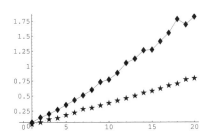

■ 5.1.5 Incidence Matrices

The *incidence matrix* of a graph with n vertices and m edges is an $n \times m$ 0-1 matrix with entry $[v, e] = 1$ if and only if vertex v is incident on edge e. Incidence matrices were first defined by Kirchhoff [Kir47] in the context of a problem on spanning trees. Incidentally, Kirchhoff was a resident of Königsberg, the most important city in the history of graph theory.

```
IncidenceMatrix[g_Graph] :=
    Module[{e = Edges[g]},
        If[UndirectedQ[g],
           Table[If[MemberQ[e[[j]], i], 1, 0], {i, V[g]}, {j, M[g]}],
           Table[If[i === First[e[[j]]], 1, 0], {i, V[g]}, {j, M[g]}]
        ]
    ]
```

Constructing the Incidence Matrix of a Graph

Every column in an incidence matrix contains two 1's. In the incidence matrix of a tree there are at least two rows that contain exactly one 1.

```
In[59]:= IncidenceMatrix[RandomTree[5]] // TableForm

Out[59]//TableForm= 1   0   0   0
                    0   1   0   0
                    0   0   1   0
                    1   0   1   1
                    0   1   0   1
```

5.2 Modifying Graphs

In this section, we provide primitives for editing graphs. The first set of primitives modify the topology of the graph, while the second set modify associated information such as drawing styles, weights, and labels.

■ 5.2.1 Additions, Deletions, and Changes

ChangeVertices and ChangeEdges are useful primitives that allow the user to replace the vertex set or the edge set of a graph. The first argument to ChangeVertices is a graph, and the second is a vertex list. Each vertex can be specified by its coordinates as $\{x, y\}$ or by its coordinates plus drawing information as $\{\{x, y\}, options\}$. ChangeEdges provides similar functionality.

Here is the 4 × 4 grid graph in its usual embedding followed by the embedding of evenly spaced vertices on the circumference of a circle.
ChangeVertices is a way to replace one embedding by another.

In[60]:= **ShowGraphArray[{g = GridGraph[4, 4], ChangeVertices[g,**
            CircularVertices[16]]}];

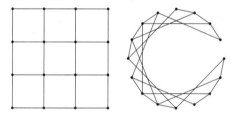

Edges of the 4 × 4 grid graph are replaced by the edges of the complete graph on 16 vertices. This gives a grid embedding of a complete graph. Collinearity of vertices renders several edges in the graph invisible, showing the advantage of using a circular embedding.

In[61]:= **ShowGraphArray[{ CompleteGraph[16], ChangeEdges[g,**
            Edges[CompleteGraph[16]]]}];

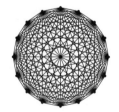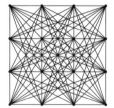

ChangeVertices and ChangeEdges perform some rudimentary error checking to make sure that we do not end up constructing nonsensical graphs. We check to make sure that the new set of vertices is at least as large as the old set. If not, we might end up with edges connecting nonexistent vertices. ChangeEdges checks to ensure that all edges in the new set are between existing vertices.

Since graphs are built from vertices and edges, we need primitives to add and delete them. We first present the AddEdges function, which allows the user to add a single edge, several edges, or several edges along with associated drawing information.

```
AddEdges[g_Graph, edgeList:{{{_Integer, _Integer},___?OptionQ}...}] :=
     Module[{ne = If[UndirectedQ[g],
                   Map[Prepend[Rest[#], Sort[First[#]]]&, edgeList],
                   edgeList
                 ]
          },
          ChangeEdges[g, Join[Edges[g, All], ne]]
     ]

AddEdges[g_Graph, edgeList:{{_Integer,_Integer}...}] :=
     AddEdges[g, Map[{#}&, edgeList] ]

AddEdges[g_Graph, edge:{_Integer,_Integer}] := AddEdges[g, {edge}]
```

Adding Edges

Here several edges are added in one shot to a star graph. Loops and multiple edges are all par for the course. The undirected edge (1, 10) can be specified either as {1, 10} or {10, 1}.

In[62]:= **ShowGraph[AddEdges[Star[10], {{2, 1}, {10, 1}, {3, 4}, {3, 3},
          {6, 5}, {7, 8}}]];**

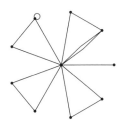

Drawing information can be provided when new edges are added. Here we specify that the new edge $(1,2)$ be drawn thick and the new edge $(3,4)$ be drawn dashed.

In[63]:= **ShowGraph[AddEdges[Star[10], {{{2, 1}, EdgeStyle -> Thick},**
{{3, 4}, EdgeStyle -> NormalDashed}}]];

The function `DeleteEdges` can be used to delete either a single edge or multiple edges from the graph. The function is complicated by the presence of multiedges. What happens if there are multiple edges connecting vertices 1 and 2 and we delete edge $(1,2)$? We address this issue by providing a tag `All` that forces `DeleteEdges` to delete *all* edges that match. Otherwise, exactly one matching edge is deleted for each given pair.

K_5 is constructed and displayed, and then all its edges are deleted. The resulting empty graph is shown alongside.

In[64]:= **ShowGraphArray[{g = CompleteGraph[5], DeleteEdges[g,**
KSubsets[Range[5], 2]]}];

We start with a graph g that contains three edges $(1,2)$. Using `DeleteEdges` without the tag `All` deletes just one of the three edges, while using the tag would delete all three edges.

In[65]:= **g = AddEdges[CompleteGraph[3], {{1, 2}, {1, 2}}];**
ShowGraphArray[NestList[(DeleteEdges[#,{{1,2}}])&, g, 3]];

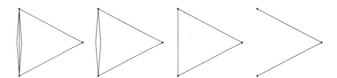

Here we start with a directed cycle. The graph contains the directed edge $(1,2)$, and so deleting $(1,2)$ deletes an edge. But deleting $(2,1)$ deletes nothing.

```
In[67]:= g = Cycle[4, Type->Directed];
         h1 = DeleteEdges[g, {1, 2}];
         h2 = DeleteEdges[g, {2, 1}];
         ShowGraphArray[{g, h1, h2}, VertexNumber -> True];
```

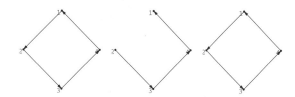

The function `AddVertices` allows the user to add one or more vertices to a graph with or without explicitly specifying the locations of the vertices. If the user specifies that *n* vertices are to be added, an empty graph with *n* vertices is created and its union with the input graph is returned. By an *empty graph* we mean a graph with no edges. *Combinatorica* contains a function `EmptyGraph` to construct an empty graph with a specified number of vertices. If the user chooses to specify the actual embedding of the vertices to be added, we join the new vertex list to the vertex list of the graph. `DeleteVertices` can be used to delete one or more vertices from a graph by specifying the vertex numbers that the user wants deleted.

This adds ten isolated vertices to a 10-cycle. The new vertices are placed on the boundary of an ellipse to the right of the original graph.

```
In[71]:= ShowGraph[ AddVertices[Cycle[10], 10]];
```

Here we add ten vertices to a 10-cycle, by providing the locations of the new vertices. These locations are obtained by taking the coordinates of the vertices of the cycle and shrinking them toward the origin.

```
In[72]:= g = Cycle[10];
         ShowGraph[ AddVertices[g, 0.5*Vertices[g]]];
```

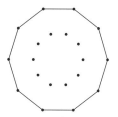

Deleting a vertex deletes all edges incident on it, and so deleting the center of a star leaves an empty graph.

```
In[74]:= ShowGraphArray[{Star[10], DeleteVertices[Star[10], {10}]}];
```

Deleting a set of vertices v is equivalent to returning the graph induced by the complement of v. This is how DeleteVertices works.

```
In[75]:= g = RandomGraph[10, 0.5]; s = RandomSubset[10];
         IsomorphicQ[ DeleteVertices[g,s],
         InduceSubgraph[g,Complement[Range[10],s]]]
Out[76]= True
```

■ 5.2.2 Setting Graph Options

In Section 5.2.1, we discussed primitives for modifying the topology of the graph. Here we show how to modify associated information such as drawing styles, and edge and vertex labels and weights. The most important function is SetGraphOptions, which can be used *globally* to affect the whole graph or *locally* to affect only a subset of edges or vertices. Edge weights, vertex weights, edge labels, and vertex labels are also specified by options, and so these can also be set using SetGraphOptions. However, for the sake of convenience, we provide specific functions for setting edge and vertex weights and labels.

SetGraphOptions can be used to set several options simultaneously. Here EdgeStyle is globally set to NormalDashed. Thus all edges are to be drawn dashed unless superseded by local options, as is the case for Thick edges $(1, 2)$ and $(2, 3)$. The nonexistent edge $(3, 5)$ is simply ignored. VertexStyle is set for 1 and 2, so only these vertices are shown as large boxes. The rest use the default disk drawing.

```
In[77]:= ShowGraph[h = SetGraphOptions[Cycle[5],
         {{1, 2, VertexStyle -> Box[Large]},
         {{1,2},{2,3},{3,5}, EdgeStyle->Thick, EdgeColor->Gray}},
         EdgeStyle -> NormalDashed]];
```

Here the weights of the edges of a graph are set to the Euclidean distances between the endpoints.

```
In[78]:= g = SetEdgeWeights[AddEdge[Cycle[6], {1, 4}],
         WeightingFunction -> Euclidean]
Out[78]= -Graph:<7, 6, Undirected>-
```

The edge weights are now displayed as labels of the edges of the graphs. These edge weights tell us that *n* vertices of a cycle are placed evenly spaced on the circumference of a unit circle.

In[79]:= **ShowGraph[SetEdgeLabels[g, GetEdgeWeights[g]], TextStyle->{FontSize->12}];**

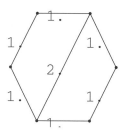

This sets the edge weights of the wheel to binary values. The option WeightingFunction can be Random, RandomInteger, Euclidean, or LNorm[n]. The default values for WeightingFunction and WeightRange are Random and {0,1}, respectively.

In[80]:= **GetEdgeWeights[SetEdgeWeights[Wheel[5], WeightingFunction-> RandomInteger, WeightRange->{0,1}]]**

Out[80]= {1, 0, 1, 1, 0, 0, 0, 0}

Weights can be assigned to edges explicitly by providing a list of weights, one weight per edge.

In[81]:= **g = SetEdgeWeights[Star[5], {10, 21, 32, 49}];**
GetEdgeWeights[g]

Out[82]= {10, 21, 32, 49}

The weights are assigned to the edges in the order in which they are listed. The function Edges can be used to find this order.

In[83]:= **Edges[g, All]**

Out[83]= {{{1, 5}, EdgeWeight -> 10},

{{2, 5}, EdgeWeight -> 21}, {{3, 5}, EdgeWeight -> 32},

{{4, 5}, EdgeWeight -> 49}}

SetVertexWeights assigns weights to vertices and provides functionality that is very similar to that of SetEdgeWeights. We also provide functions SetVertexLabels, SetEdgeLabels, GetVertexLabels, and GetVertexWeights.

Here the vertices of the star get cyclically assigned the labels A and B. That is, A is assigned to vertex 1, B is assigned to vertex 2, A is assigned to vertex 3, and so on. Extra labels are ignored when the list is longer than the number of vertices in the graph.

In[84]:= **ShowGraph[SetVertexLabels[Star[10], {"A", "B"}]];**

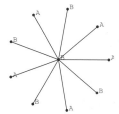

5.3 Classifying Graphs

The graph theory literature is rich with algorithms for determining whether a given graph satisfies a certain property. In this book, we will provide functions testing whether a graph is *bipartite*, *Eulerian*, *Hamiltonian*, or *perfect*, as well as other interesting properties. However, first we need predicates to solve more basic classification problems. Is the given graph directed? Does it have a self-loop? Such tests are essential, because many algorithms work correctly only when the graph has satisfied such conditions.

A graph with self-loops is called a *pseudograph*, while a *multigraph* is a graph that contains multiple edges connecting pairs of vertices. These can be tested using PseudographQ and MultipleEdgesQ, respectively. A *simple graph* contains no self-loops or multiple edges and is tested via function SimpleQ. Most of classical graph theory applies only to simple graphs.

An *empty graph* contains no edges, while a *complete graph* is a simple graph with all possible edges. EmptyQ and CompleteQ test these properties. We also provide predicates UndirectedQ and UnweightedQ to test whether a graph is undirected or has nonunit edge weights, respectively. The code for all these functions is simple and self-explanatory.

```
PseudographQ[g_Graph] := MemberQ[Edges[g], _?(Function[l, l[[1]] == l[[2]]])]
MultipleEdgesQ[g_Graph] := Module[{e = Edges[g]}, Length[e] != Length[Union[e]]]
SimpleQ[g_Graph] := (!PseudographQ[g]) && (!MultipleEdgesQ[g])
EmptyQ[g_Graph] := (Length[Edges[g]]==0)
CompleteQ[g_Graph] :=
        Block[{n = V[g], m = M[g]},
            (SimpleQ[g] && ((UndirectedQ[g] && (m == n(n-1)/2)) || (!UndirectedQ[g] && (m == n(n-1)))))
        ]
UndirectedQ[g_Graph] := (!MemberQ[GraphOptions[g], EdgeDirection->On]) &&
                        (!MemberQ[GraphOptions[g], EdgeDirection->True])
UnweightedQ[g_Graph] := (Count[GetEdgeWeights[g],1] === M[g])
```

Elementary Graph Predicates

All cycles with three or more vertices are simple. They have no self-loops and no multiple edges. A 2-cycle is two edges connecting a single pair of vertices and is therefore not simple.

```
In[85]:= Map[SimpleQ, Table[Cycle[i], {i, 2, 10}]]
Out[85]= {False, True, True, True, True, True, True, True,
    True}
```

The addition of a second copy of edge (1, 2) to a cycle makes it nonsimple.

```
In[86]:= SimpleQ[h = AddEdges[Cycle[5], {1, 2}]]
Out[86]= False
```

This graph is not a pseudograph. The lack of simplicity is not caused by self-loops, but by multiple edges between pairs of vertices.

```
In[87]:= {PseudographQ[h], MultipleEdgesQ[h]}
Out[87]= {False, True}
```

The addition of the self-loop $(1, 1)$ makes the graph a pseudograph.

In[88]:= **PseudographQ[AddEdges[h, {1, 1}]]**

Out[88]= True

This graph is undirected and only has default unit edge weights...

In[89]:= **{UnweightedQ[h], UndirectedQ[h]}**

Out[89]= {True, True}

...unlike this edge-weighted, directed cycle.

In[90]:= **h = SetEdgeWeights[Cycle[4, Type->Directed]];**
　　　　　　{UnweightedQ[h], UndirectedQ[h]}

Out[91]= {False, False}

Often we encounter algorithms that require the input graph to be simple. In dealing with such algorithms, we test whether the given graph is simple. If not, we use MakeSimple before passing it on as input. Related functions include RemoveSelfLoops and RemoveMultipleEdges.

This example illustrates the behavior of the functions RemoveSelfLoops, RemoveMultipleEdges, and MakeSimple, respectively.

In[92]:= **g = AddEdges[CompleteGraph[3], {{1, 2}, {3, 3}}];**
　　　　　　ShowGraphArray[{{g, RemoveSelfLoops[g],
　　　　　　RemoveMultipleEdges[g], MakeSimple[g]}}];

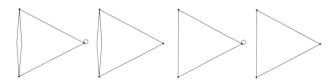

Combinatorica provides a function MakeUndirected that takes a directed graph and returns the underlying undirected graph.

A random directed graph is shown here along with its underlying undirected graph.

In[94]:= **g = RandomGraph[10, .3, Type -> Directed]; h = MakeUndirected[g];**
　　　　　　ShowGraphArray[{g, h}];

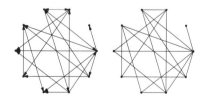

5.4 Displaying Graphs

Mathematica graphics are represented by primitives such as Line and Point. Graphics objects are rendered by *Mathematica* in PostScript, a portable graphics language, that makes it easy to print and export drawings of graphs. It is even possible within *Mathematica* to produce a sequence of graph drawings, "animate" the sequence, and then produce an animated gif file to slap on your Web page. This provides a convenient way for producing animations of algorithms.

ShowGraph is the function that displays graphs. It is dramatically improved in the new *Combinatorica* and is one of the highlights of the package. Features include:

- Vertices can be shown in different shapes, styles, and colors.

- Edges can be shown in different styles and colors.

- Vertex numbers, vertex labels, and edge labels can be displayed in a variety of ways, with easy control of their sizes and positions.

- Multiple edges and self-loops are shown correctly.

- Different styles and corresponding options for drawing arrows are inherited from the Graphics`Arrow` package.

- All the options that can be used in the *Mathematica* function Plot are inherited by ShowGraph. These options can be used to change the background color of a picture, display a caption, zoom in on a certain area, and so on.

The ShowGraph function takes one or more arguments. The first argument is a graph object, while the remaining arguments are options.

Display a randomly selected 7-vertex tree. The vertex numbers are shown because of the option VertexNumber -> True. By default they are displayed below and to the left of the vertices, but this can be changed. The Background option, which is set to Gray in this example, is inherited from Plot.

In[96]:= **ShowGraph[RandomTree[7], VertexNumber->True, Background->Gray];**

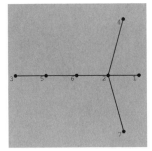

■ 5.4.1 The Vertex and Edge Options

This shows 17 options that can be used with ShowGraph, along with their default values. For example, VertexNumberPosition, the position of vertex numbers relative to the vertices, defaults to LowerLeft. VertexLabelPosition defaults to UpperRight, so that they do not run into each other when both vertex numbers and labels are displayed. PlotRange and AspectRatio are inherited from the *Mathematica* function Plot. These appear here because the default values for ShowGraph are different from their settings in Plot.

```
In[97]:= Options[ShowGraph]

Out[97]= {VertexColor -> RGBColor[0., 0., 0.],
    VertexStyle -> Disk[Normal], VertexNumber -> False,
    VertexNumberColor -> RGBColor[0., 0., 0.],
    VertexNumberPosition -> LowerLeft,
    VertexLabel -> False,
    VertexLabelColor -> RGBColor[0., 0., 0.],
    VertexLabelPosition -> UpperRight, PlotRange -> Normal,
    AspectRatio -> 1, EdgeColor -> RGBColor[0., 0., 0.],
    EdgeStyle -> Normal, EdgeLabel -> False,
    EdgeLabelColor -> RGBColor[0., 0., 0.],
    EdgeLabelPosition -> LowerLeft,
    LoopPosition -> UpperRight, EdgeDirection -> False}
```

The following table describes options allowed in ShowGraph that pertain to displaying vertices and attributes related to vertices.

option name	default value	explanation
VertexColor	Black	sets color of objects representing vertices
VertexStyle	Disk[Normal]	sets vertex shape and size
VertexNumber	False	hides or displays vertex numbers
VertexNumberColor	Black	sets vertex number color
VertexNumberPosition	LowerLeft	sets position of vertex number
VertexLabel	False	hides or displays vertex labels
VertexLabelColor	Black	sets vertex label color
VertexLabelPosition	UpperRight	sets position of vertex label

Vertex options in ShowGraph.

The following table gives possible values for each vertex option in ShowGraph.

option name	possible values
VertexColor	any color defined in the package Graphics`Colors`
VertexStyle	X[Y], where X can be Disk or Box, while Y can be Small, Normal, Large, or a non-negative real number
VertexNumber	True or False
VertexNumberColor	any color defined in the package Graphics`Colors`
VertexNumberPosition	Center, LowerLeft, UpperRight, LowerRight, UpperLeft, or an offset given by an ordered pair of reals $\{x, y\}$
VertexLabel	False or a list of labels, where the labels are assigned to vertices in order.
VertexLabelColor	any color defined in the package Graphics`Colors`
VertexLabelPosition	Center, LowerLeft, UpperRight, LowerRight, UpperLeft, or an ordered pair of reals $\{x, y\}$

Possible settings for vertex options in ShowGraph.

The variable AllColors in add-on package Graphics`Colors` contains the names of all 192 supported colors in *Mathematica*. However, many of these do not stand out on a typical screen. *Combinatorica* uses the following subset of colors whenever it is required to color objects such as vertices or edges:

Black, Red, Blue, Green, Yellow, Purple, Brown, Orange, Olive, Pink, DeepPink, DarkGreen, Maroon, Navy

The ordering of these colors is arbitrary but relevant because some *Combinatorica* functions cycle through the list of colors one color at a time.

Using large vertices runs the risk of obscuring vertex labels and numbers. Setting `VertexNumberPosition` to an appropriate offset moves the vertex numbers. But shifting the vertex numbers may move them out of the range of the plot. Here `PlotRange` is increased by 10% to accommodate the vertex numbers.

In[98]:= `ShowGraph[Cycle[5], VertexNumber -> True,`
`    VertexNumberPosition -> {-0.04, -0.04},`
`    VertexStyle -> Box[Large],`
`    VertexColor -> Gray, PlotRange -> .1];`

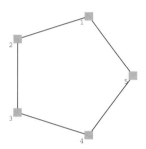

The option `VertexLabel` is used to set and display vertex labels. If there are more vertices than labels, as in this example, the labels are used cyclically. The default position of the labels is "upper right," but here the `VertexLabelPosition` option has been used to position them below and to the right of the vertices.

In[99]:= `ShowGraph[Cycle[5], VertexNumber -> True,`
`    VertexNumberPosition->{-0.04,-0.04}, VertexStyle->Box[Large],`
`    VertexColor -> Gray, VertexLabel -> {"A", "B", "C"},`
`    VertexLabelPosition -> LowerRight, PlotRange -> .1,`
`    TextStyle->{FontSize->12}];`

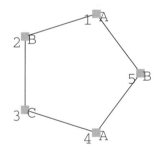

The following table describes options allowed in `ShowGraph` that pertain to displaying edges and attributes related to edges.

option name	*default value*	*explanation*
EdgeColor	Black	sets edge color
EdgeStyle	Normal	sets edge style
EdgeLabel	False	hides or displays edge labels
EdgeLabelPosition	LowerRight	sets position of edge label
LoopPosition	UpperRight	sets position of self-loops
EdgeDirection	False	displays edges as undirected or directed

Edge options in ShowGraph.

option name	*possible values*
EdgeColor	any color defined in the package Graphics`Colors`
EdgeStyle	Thick, Normal, Thin, ThickDashed, NormalDashed, or ThinDashed
EdgeLabel	False or a list of labels, where the labels are assigned to the edges in order
EdgeLabelColor	any color defined in the package Graphics`Colors`
EdgeLabelPosition	Center, LowerLeft, UpperRight, LowerRight, UpperLeft, or an offset given by an ordered pair of reals $\{x, y\}$
LoopPosition	UpperRight, UpperLeft, LowerLeft, LowerRight
EdgeDirection	True or False

Possible settings for edge options in ShowGraph.

The Petersen graph is shown with edges thick and dashed and the size of the vertices increased so that they are not obscured by the thicker edges. The thickness, style (dashed versus plain), and color of edges can all be controlled using various options.

In[100]:= **ShowGraph[PetersenGraph, VertexStyle->Disk[Large],
        EdgeColor->Red, EdgeStyle->ThickDashed,
        Background->LightBlue];**

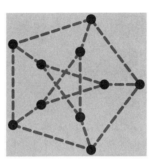

Edge labels are set using the option EdgeLabels. Here they are positioned at the center of the corresponding edges using EdgeLabelPosition. The positioning of the edge labels is relative to the midpoints of the edges. Edges are colored Gray to make the edge labels stand out. As in the case of vertex labels, edge labels are assigned cyclically, in the edge order of the graph.

In[101]:= **ShowGraph[PetersenGraph, VertexNumber -> True,
        EdgeLabel->{"A","B","C","D","E","F"}, EdgeColor->Gray,
        EdgeLabelPosition -> Center, PlotRange -> .1];**

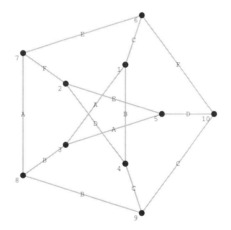

Self-loops and multiple edges connecting the same pairs of vertices are all displayed correctly. The position of the loops relative to the vertex can be controlled by the LoopPosition option.

In[102]:= **g = AddEdges[Cycle[5], {{1, 1}, {1, 1}, {3, 3}, {4, 5}, {4, 5}}];**
ShowGraph[g, LoopPosition->LowerLeft];

This shows the 5-vertex wheel drawn as a directed graph. Each edge (i, j) is treated as a directed edge from i to j. The wheel graph is undirected, but since edges of an undirected graph are stored as pairs with the first vertex number smaller than the second, we obtain a drawing in which all edges are directed from smaller to larger vertex numbers.

In[104]:= **ShowGraph[Wheel[5], EdgeDirection -> True,**
VertexNumber -> True];

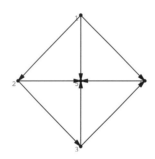

■ 5.4.2 Inherited Options

Any option that is allowed by the *Mathematica* function Plot is allowed in ShowGraph as well.

Here the complete *k*-ary tree is shown, demonstrating a few of the options that ShowGraph inherits from Plot. The plot label is set via the option PlotLabel, and the option TextStyle is used to make it stand out.

```
In[105]:= ShowGraph[CompleteKaryTree[20, 4], Background -> Yellow,
            PlotLabel -> "The Complete 4-ary tree",
            TextStyle -> {FontFamily -> Times, FontSize -> 10}];
```

The Complete 4-ary tree

One of the options that ShowGraph inherits from Plot is PlotRange. However, PlotRange can be used in ShowGraph in a couple of new ways. Specifically, setting PlotRange to a real α increases the plot range to $(1 + \alpha)$ times its original size. This can be used to expand or shrink the plot range. Another feature in ShowGraph is the ability to "zoom" in to a subset of vertices by setting PlotRange appropriately.

This shows the five-dimensional hypercube. This rather small and crowded picture is the result of expanding the plot range to 1.5 times its original size.

```
In[106]:= ShowGraph[Hypercube[5], PlotRange->.5];
```

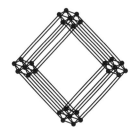

To see the edges between vertices more clearly, we can zoom in to a portion of the graph. Here we focus on the neighborhood of the vertices 1, 2, 3, and 4. From this picture, it is clear that every vertex has degree 5, as expected.

```
In[107]:= ShowGraph[Hypercube[5], PlotRange ->
            Zoom[{1, 2, 3, 4}], VertexNumber -> True,
            TextStyle->{FontSize->14}];
```

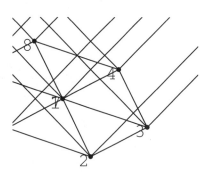

ShowGraph also inherits options from the Graphics`Arrow` package that allow control of the shape or size of the arrows that represent directed edges.

These options provide ways of controlling the shape of arrows. For example, HeadCenter describes the location of the center of the base of the arrowhead along the length of the arrow, as a factor of the length of the arrowhead. Changing this can affect the shape of the arrowhead.

```
In[108]:= Options[Arrow]

Out[108]= {HeadScaling -> Automatic,
    HeadLength -> Automatic, HeadCenter -> 1,
    HeadWidth -> 0.5, HeadShape -> Automatic,
    ZeroShape -> Automatic}
```

Here we change the arrowhead shape on a directed cycle. The center of the base of the arrowhead is moved close to the tip of the arrow. Here HeadCenter is changed from its default value of 1 to 0.4, making the arrows look more like two line segments rather than a filled triangle.

```
In[109]:= ShowGraph[Cycle[3, Type -> Directed],
            HeadCenter -> 0.4];
```

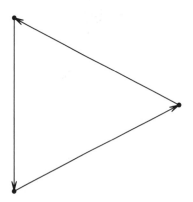

■ 5.4.3 A Hierarchy of Options

Drawing information and other attributes are stored in the body of a graph. What happens when there is a conflict between the options set within a graph and the options provided to the ShowGraph function?

Here VertexStyle is set to Box[Large] within a graph. Then VertexStyle is set to Disk[Normal] in the call to ShowGraph. The options set within the graph have greater precedence. As a result, vertices are shown as large boxes rather than normal-sized disks.

```
In[110]:= g = SetGraphOptions[RandomGraph[10, .4],
            VertexStyle -> Box[Large]];
          ShowGraph[g, VertexStyle -> Disk[Normal]];
```

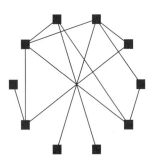

In general, the following precedence rules disambiguate the use of options. Options that are set within a graph for individual vertices or edges – the "local" options – have the highest precedence. Options set within a graph that pertain to all vertices or to all edges – the "global" options – have lower precedence. Options outside a graph, such as in ShowGraph, have the lowest precedence.

Edges $(1, 2)$ and $(2, 3)$ have their EdgeStyle option set to ThickDashed. This takes precedence over any other setting of this option that affects these edges. The EdgeStyle option is globally set to Thick within the graph and affects all edges except $(1, 2)$ and $(2, 3)$. The attempt in ShowGraph to display all the edges of the graph "normally" has no effect, since this setting has the lowest precedence.

```
In[112]:= g = SetGraphOptions[Cycle[5], {{{1, 2}, {2, 3},
            EdgeStyle -> ThickDashed}}, EdgeStyle -> Thick];
          ShowGraph[g, VertexStyle -> Box[Large], EdgeStyle -> Normal];
```

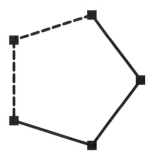

A directed graph contains the setting `EdgeDirection -> True` internally. Thus the attempt to turn edge direction off in `ShowGraph` is useless. Instead, pass it through `MakeUndirected` if you do not want to see the arrows.

```
In[114]:= ShowGraph[RandomGraph[10, .3, Type->Directed],
              EdgeDirection->False];
```

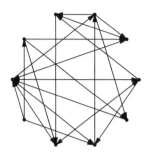

■ 5.4.4 Highlighting and Animation

Combinatorica provides three functions that enhance and complement `ShowGraph` in different ways. The first, `ShowGraphArray`, is a function for displaying tables of graphs. This is useful in showing a graph evolve through a graph algorithm and can be thought of as a "static" animation function.

This is a 2 × 2 table of grid graphs. The option `VertexStyle -> Disk[Large]` affects all four graphs. The option `GraphicsSpacing` is inherited from the *Mathematica* function `GraphicsArray`. The default spacing between the pictures corresponds to a setting of .1 for `GraphicsSpacing`. Here we see a greater separation than usual because we have increased `GraphicsSpacing` to 0.4.

```
In[115]:= ShowGraphArray[gt={{GridGraph[10, 10], GridGraph[3, 3]},
              {GridGraph[2, 2, 2], GridGraph[4, 4]}},
              VertexStyle -> Disk[Large], GraphicsSpacing -> .4];
```

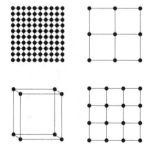

Here we see the same set of four graphs, but displayed as a 1 × 4 table. The dimensions of the table are given by the list structure of the first argument to ShowGraphArray. In the previous example, the list had the structure {{*g*1, *g*2}, {*g*3, *g*4}}; here the list structure is {{*g*1, *g*2, *g*3, *g*4}}.

In[116]:= **ShowGraphArray[Flatten[gt, 1], VertexStyle -> Disk[Large]];**

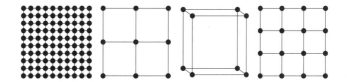

Highlight can be used along with ShowGraph to "highlight" features of the graph, such as the subgraphs produced by *Combinatorica* functions such as DepthFirstTraversal, MinimumSpanningTree, HamiltonianCycle, and VertexColoring.

Here we construct a Hamiltonian cycle of a four-dimensional hypercube. The output of HamiltonianCycle is a list of vertices whose first and last elements are identical.

In[117]:= **c = HamiltonianCycle[h = Hypercube[4]]**

Out[117]= {1, 2, 3, 4, 8, 5, 6, 7, 11, 10, 9, 12, 16, 15, 14, 13, 1}

Using the *Mathematica* function Partition to turn the list of vertices into a list of edges.

In[118]:= **el = Partition[c, 2, 1]**

Out[118]= {{1, 2}, {2, 3}, {3, 4}, {4, 8}, {8, 5}, {5, 6}, {6, 7}, {7, 11}, {11, 10}, {10, 9}, {9, 12}, {12, 16}, {16, 15}, {15, 14}, {14, 13}, {13, 1}}

A Hamiltonian cycle in the four-dimensional hypercube is highlighted. The second argument to Highlight is a set of subsets of edges or vertices of the graph. The function uses different colors to highlight each subset of objects. In this example, the set contains only one subset of edges. The option HighlightedEdgeColors specifies what colors to use for highlighting edges.

In[119]:= **ShowGraph[Highlight[h, {el}, HighlightedEdgeColors -> {Blue}]];**

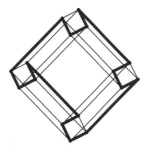

A *vertex coloring* of a graph is an assignment of colors to vertices such that no two adjacent vertices are assigned the same color. The function MinimumVertexColoring colors a given graph using the fewest possible colors.

In[120]:= **c = MinimumVertexColoring[g = RandomTree[8]]**

Out[120]= {1, 1, 2, 1, 1, 2, 1, 1}

For any *n*-vertex graph, `MinimumVertexColoring` returns a size-*n* list in which the *i*th entry is the color assigned to the *i*th vertex. Any tree can be colored with two colors, so we use the coloring to partition the set of vertices.

```
In[121]:= cp = {Flatten[Position[c, 1]], Flatten[Position[c , 2]]}
Out[121]= {{1, 2, 4, 5, 7, 8}, {3, 6}}
```

`Highlight` can then be used to color each subset of vertices. By setting the option `HighlightedVertexColors` appropriately, we get the vertices to be colored red and gray. The option `HighlightedVertexStyle` is set to `Disk[Large]` by default. Here this setting is changed to `Box[Large]`.

```
In[122]:= ShowGraph[Highlight[g, cp, HighlightedVertexStyle -> Box[Large],
          HighlightedVertexColors -> {Red, Gray}]];
```

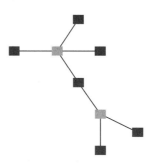

Combinatorica contains a function, `AnimateGraph`, that can used to produce a sequence of graph drawings that can then be converted into an "animation." A nice collection of graph animations is available at `www.combinatorica.com`.

Displays a 5-cycle first with vertex 1 highlighted, then with vertices 1 and 2 highlighted, and finally just vertex 2. The second argument is a list containing vertices and edges. The elements of this list are highlighted in succession. The function accepts an optional third argument that can be `All` or `One`. Previously highlighted elements continue to be highlighted in the default case of `All`. Otherwise, highlighting of earlier elements is not maintained.

```
In[123]:= l = AnimateGraph[Cycle[5], {1, {1, 2}, 2}]
```

```
Out[123]= {-Graphics-, -Graphics-, -Graphics-}
```

Animations can be viewed as cartoons within *Mathematica* or converted to animated gif files using the `Export` function. See the system documentation for details.

```
In[124]:= Export["test.gif", l, "GIF", ConversionOptions -> {"Loop"->True}]
Out[124]= test.gif
```

5.5 Basic Graph Embeddings

Combinatorica provides embeddings that permit attractive drawings of several families of graphs. These embeddings can also be used as building blocks for constructing more complicated drawings. The three types discussed in this section are *circular*, *ranked*, and *radial* embeddings.

■ 5.5.1 Circular Embeddings

A *circular embedding* positions the vertices as evenly spaced points on the unit circle and is often instructive when the graph has a regular structure. Perhaps the most important property of circular embeddings is that no three vertices are collinear, so each edge is unambiguously represented. Computing evenly spaced points on a circle involves simple trigonometry.

```
CircularEmbedding[0] := {}

CircularEmbedding[n_Integer] :=
      Module[{i,x = N[2 Pi / n]},
            Chop[ Table[ N[{{ (Cos[x i]), (Sin[x i]) }}], {i,n} ] ]
      ]

CircularEmbedding[g_Graph] :=
      ChangeVertices[g, CircularEmbedding[ V[g] ] ]
```

Constructing a Circular Embedding

This shows a 20-vertex graph whose vertices are placed on a circle and whose edges connect pairs of vertices *i* and *j*, provided there are 0, 4, or 8 vertices between *i* and *j* on the circle. Such graphs are called *circulant graphs*.

In[125]:= **ShowGraph[CirculantGraph[20, {1, 5, 9}], VertexNumber->True];**

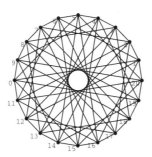

Circular embeddings are natural for circulant graphs, complete graphs, and cycles. Embeddings for various other classes of graphs, such as wheels, stars, and random graphs, are based on circular embeddings.

In[126]:= `ShowGraphArray[{CompleteGraph[10], Wheel[10], Harary[3,13], RandomGraph[10,0.3]}]`

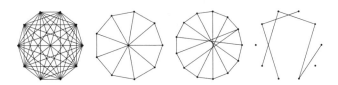

Here, `CircularEmbedding` transforms the standard embedding of a $2 \times 2 \times 2$ grid graph into a circular embedding. Due to the symmetry of the graph, the circular embedding remains fairly attractive.

In[127]:= `ShowGraphArray[{g = GridGraph[2, 2, 2], ChangeVertices[g, CircularEmbedding[8]]}, VertexStyle -> Disk[0.04] ];`

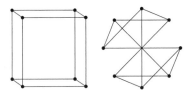

Circular embeddings are the default for random graphs because they clearly show every edge. Here we show four semirandom 3-regular graphs.

In[128]:= `ShowGraphArray[ Table[RegularGraph[3, 12],{4}]];`

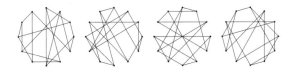

■ 5.5.2 Ranked Embeddings

In a *ranked embedding*, vertices are placed on evenly spaced vertical lines. This embedding can reveal features of the underlying graph when the vertices are partitioned into appropriate subsets.

The *generalized Petersen graph* $P(n,k)$, for $n > 1$ and $k > 0$, contains $2n$ vertices $\{v_0, v_1, \ldots, v_{n-1}, u_0, u_1, \ldots, u_{n-1}\}$ and edges of the form (u_i, u_{i+1}), (u_i, v_i) and (v_i, v_{i+k}). Here $(i + 1)$ and $(i + k)$ are taken modulo n. In the default embedding of $P(n,k)$ shown here, the u_i's are placed on the outer circle and the v_i's are placed in the inner circle.

In[129]:= **ShowGraph[g = GeneralizedPetersenGraph[10, 3]];**

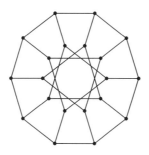

Here, the *Combinatorica* function RankGraph assigns ranks to vertices of $P(10,3)$ based on their distance from the subset of vertices $\{1, 2, 3\}$.

In[130]:= **l = RankGraph[g, {1, 2, 3}]**

Out[130]= {1, 1, 1, 2, 2, 2, 3, 2, 2, 2, 2, 2, 2, 3, 3, 3, 4, 3, 3, 3}

Using the ranking of $P(10,3)$ calculated above, we partition the vertices into appropriate groups.

In[131]:= **Table[Flatten[Position[l, i]], {i, Max[l]}]**

Out[131]= {{1, 2, 3}, {4, 5, 6, 8, 9, 10, 11, 12, 13}, {7, 14, 15, 16, 18, 19, 20}, {17}}

This gives us an embedding in which vertices 1, 2, and 3 appear on the leftmost vertical line and the other vertices in the graph appear on different vertical lines based on how far away they are from the first three vertices.

In[132]:= **ShowGraph[RankedEmbedding[g, %]];**

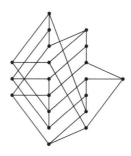

The *chromatic number* of a graph is the fewest number of colors needed to properly color its vertices. The *Mycielski graph* of order *k* is a graph with no triangles (cycles of length 3) whose chromatic number is *k*. The Mycielski graph of order 4 is shown here.

```
In[133]:= ShowGraph[g = MycielskiGraph[4]];
```

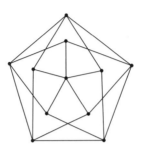

Here a minimum vertex coloring of the Mycielski graph of order 4 is constructed. As expected, four colors are needed.

```
In[134]:= c = MinimumVertexColoring[g]
Out[134]= {1, 2, 2, 1, 3, 3, 1, 2, 4, 1, 2}
```

The vertex set is partitioned into four subsets based on the coloring constructed above.

This partition is used to construct a ranked embedding of the graph. That the partitions correspond to vertices of the same color means that there are no edges between vertices on the same vertical line. Coloring the vertices would be an even better way to show a vertex coloring if this book had colored pages!

```
In[135]:= p = Table[Flatten[Position[c, i]], {i, Max[c]}]
Out[135]= {{1, 4, 7, 10}, {2, 3, 8, 11}, {5, 6}, {9}}
```

```
In[136]:= ShowGraphArray[{RankedEmbedding[g, p], Highlight[g,p]}];
```

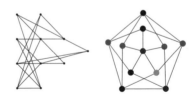

■ 5.5.3 Radial Embeddings

A *radial embedding* is a variation on the idea of a ranked embedding, where we place vertices on concentric circles around the special vertex so vertices of the same rank end up on the same circle. RadialEmbedding is the function that constructs such an embedding. It is clever enough not to distribute all vertices of a particular rank evenly on a circle. Instead, it tries to cluster together vertices of the same rank that have a common neighbor of a smaller rank.

The picture on the right shows a radial embedding of the graph on the left. RadialEmbedding produces attractive drawings if the graph is drawn radiating out of a cut-vertex. Vertices on the outermost circle are not distributed evenly but are clustered based on common neighbors.

In[137]:= **ShowGraphArray[{g = Contract[GraphUnion[Cycle[10], Path[3]], {1, 6, 12}], RadialEmbedding[g, 9]}];**

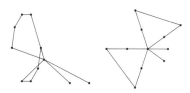

The function RandomTree uses RadialEmbedding from an arbitrary vertex to construct an embedding of a tree. On the left, we have a radial embedding of a 30-vertex tree centered at an arbitrary vertex, while the radial embedding on the right is centered at the tree center. The radial embedding of a tree is guaranteed to be planar, because, for any vertex v, the angle around it is divided among its neighbors so that subtrees rooted at v do not bump into each other.

In[138]:= **ShowGraphArray[{g=RandomTree[30], RadialEmbedding[g,First[GraphCenter[g]]]}];**

■ 5.5.4 Rooted Embeddings

Combinatorica provides *rooted embeddings* as a way to embed graphs that represent hierarchies. Again, one vertex is selected as a special vertex – a root – while the remaining vertices are ranked by distance from the root. Vertices are distributed on parallel lines with vertices of the same rank placed on the same line. Rooted embeddings make an attempt to prevent tree edges from crossing. Specifically, our implementation assigns vertices of equal rank an equal width for drawing their subtrees. Better heuristics, which attempt to minimize total width while maximizing the minimum spacing between vertices of equal rank, have been studied by several researchers [RT81, Vau80, WS79], although under certain aesthetic criteria the problem is NP-complete [SR83].

A rooted embedding of a 100-vertex tree is shown here. This picture makes clear that allocating equal width for each subtree makes large subtrees rather crowded. However, it is simpler and faster than the alternative of assigning a width that is proportional to how wide a subtree is.

In[139]:= `ShowGraph[RootedEmbedding[t = RandomTree[100], 1]];`

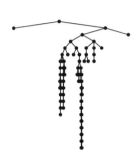

The *eccentricity* of a vertex v in a graph G is the maximum distance of v to any vertex in the graph. The vertices in G with minimum eccentricity are called its *centers*. Intuitively, centers are not too far from any vertices in the graph. Constructing the rooted embedding of a tree with the root at a center makes for a more balanced embedding.

In[140]:= `c = First[GraphCenter[t]];`
`ShowGraph[RootedEmbedding[t,  c]];`

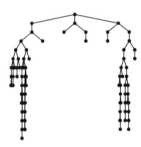

Rooted embeddings can be performed on all graphs. In this example, an unfamiliar drawing of a $3 \times 3 \times 3$ grid graph is constructed by a rooted embedding.

In[142]:= `ShowGraph[RootedEmbedding[GridGraph[3, 3, 3], 1]];`

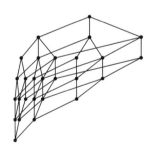

5.6 Improving Embeddings

The embedding strategies discussed thus far have been quite rigid and inflexible. To properly use them to draw arbitrary graphs, we need tools that improve the quality of an embedding by modifying it according to different criteria.

■ 5.6.1 Translating, Dilating, and Rotating Graphs

Performing simple geometric transformations on the set of vertices is useful to change a graph's size, position, or orientation. These transformations are building blocks for other routines for constructing embeddings of graphs.

Here are three embeddings of the Petersen graph. The left embedding is standard, while the middle one is obtained by rotating the interior vertices by $\pi/3$ radians about the origin. The right embedding dilates the interior vertices of the middle embedding.

```
In[143]:= ShowGraphArray[{g = PetersenGraph,
          h = RotateVertices[g, {1, 2, 3, 4, 5}, Pi/3],
          DilateVertices[h, Range[5], 2]}, VertexStyle -> Disk[0.04]];
```

Many embeddings of specific *Combinatorica* graphs are constructed using appropriate translations, dilations, and rotations. Here we show the Meredith graph, the "no perfect matching graph," and the Thomassen graph. Each contains several copies of a small subgraph. Choosing an appropriate position and orientation for each copy of these subgraphs leads to prettier embeddings.

```
In[144]:= ShowGraphArray[{MeredithGraph, NoPerfectMatchingGraph,
          ThomassenGraph}];
```

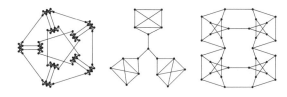

Graphics information associated with the vertices stays invariant under rotation, translation, and dilation of the the graph. This is also true of embedding improvement functions `ShakeGraph` and `SpringEmbedding`.

```
In[145]:= ShowGraphArray[{g = SetGraphOptions[PetersenGraph,
              {1, 2, 3, VertexStyle -> Box[Large], VertexColor -> Gray}],
          TranslateVertices[g, Range[5], {0.5, 0}]}];
```

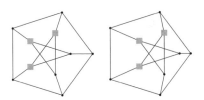

■ 5.6.2 Shaking Graphs

The *Combinatorica* function `ShakeGraph` produces a random perturbation of the embedding of a given graph. Random perturbations of an embedding can place the vertices in *general position*, where no three vertices are collinear and thus all edges are unambiguously displayed. A parameter specifies the maximum magnitude of a perturbation, regulating the extent to which the original embedding is preserved.

In the ranked embedding of the Petersen graph, the rightmost six vertices are connected by some number of edges. These edges are ambiguous because of collinearity, but "shaking" the graph a little bit resolves the ambiguity and distinguishes the real edges from imposters.

```
In[146]:= ShowGraphArray[{g = RankedEmbedding[PetersenGraph, {1}],
          ShakeGraph[g, 0.3]}];
```

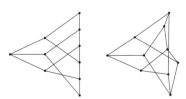

■ 5.6.3 Spring Embeddings

Force-directed algorithms use a physical analogy to draw graphs. The graph is viewed as a system of bodies with forces acting on them. The algorithm seeks a configuration of the bodies with locally minimum energy. Several force-directed algorithms have been proposed and tested [BETT98]. These techniques typically differ in the force or energy model used and in the method used to find an equilibrium or minimal energy configuration. *Combinatorica* contains an implementation of a technique proposed by Eades [Ead84], which models the graph as a system of springs and lets *Hooke's law* space the vertices. Specifically, adjacent vertices attract each other with a force proportional to the logarithm of their separation, and all nonadjacent vertices repel each other with a force proportional to their separation. These provide incentive for all edges to be as short as possible and yet the vertices to be spread apart as far as possible.

```
SpringEmbedding[g_Graph, step_:10, inc_:0.15] := g /; EmptyQ[g]

SpringEmbedding[g_Graph, step_:10, inc_:0.15] :=
    Module[{verts=Vertices[g], new, m=ToAdjacencyMatrix[MakeUndirected[g]]},
        new = UV[step, inc, m, verts];
        ChangeVertices[g, new]
    ]

UV = Compile[{{step, _Real}, {inc, _Real}, {m, _Integer, 2},
        {verts, _Real, 2}},
    Module[{u, i, new = old = verts, n = Length[verts]},
        Do[ Do[new[[u]] = old[[u]] + inc*CF[u, m, old], {u, n}];
            old = new, {i, step}
        ];
        new
    ],
    {{CF[___], _Real, 1}}
    ]

CF = Compile[{{u, _Integer}, {m, _Integer, 2}, {em, _Real, 2}},
    Module[{n = Length[m], stc = 0.25, gr = 10.0, f = {0.0, 0.0}},
        spl = 1.0, v, dsquared},
        Do[dsquared = Max[0.001, Apply[Plus, (em[[u]] - em[[v]])^2]];
            f += (1 - m[[u, v]]) (gr/dsquared) (em[[u]] - em[[v]]) -
                m[[u, v]] stc Log[dsquared/spl] (em[[u]] - em[[v]]),
            {v, n}
        ];
        f
    ]
    ]
```

The Spring Embedding Heuristic

The behavior of such a system can be approximated by determining the force on each vertex at a particular time and then moving the vertex an infinitesimal amount in the appropriate direction. We then repeat until the system stabilizes. The two main tasks: (i) calculating the force on each vertex and (ii) updating vertex positions repeatedly are both computation-intensive. However, both tasks deal with real and integer tensors so the code can be compiled. This leads to a factor 10–15 speedup in the running time of SpringEmbedding over the previous version of *Combinatorica*.

The *connected components* of a graph are maximal subgraphs that are connected. Nonadjacent vertices repel each other, so connected components tend to drift apart from each other. Here the four connected components of the circulant graph drift further apart with each application of SpringEmbedding.

```
In[147]:= ShowGraphArray[NestList[SpringEmbedding,
             CirculantGraph[20, 4], 3]]
```

In Section 2.1.4, we defined the "maximum difference" permutation graph, which later reappeared as the derangement graph. This is a fairly dense graph with 24 vertices and 108 edges.

```
In[148]:= g = MakeGraph[Permutations[{1,2,3,4}], (Count[#1-#2,0]==0)&,
             Type->Undirected]
Out[148]= -Graph:<108, 24, Undirected>-
```

The default circular embedding does not yield any insights into the graph. But after two applications of the spring embedding heuristic the structure becomes clear! The vertices separate out into clusters of size 4 each. If we shrink each cluster to a vertex, we get a 6-vertex graph that contains a Hamiltonian cycle.

```
In[149]:= ShowGraphArray[gt = NestList[SpringEmbedding, g, 2]];
```

One approach to construct a Hamiltonian cycle for the full graph is to take a Hamiltonian cycle in the "shrunk" graph and then expand out each vertex into a path within the cluster it represents. By zooming in on the region around vertex 3, we can see that the cluster of vertices {3, 11, 14, 22} seem to induce a clique.

```
In[150]:= h = gt[[3]];
          ShowGraph[h, PlotRange -> Zoom[{3}], VertexNumber -> True];
```

This clique is easily verified.

In[152]:= **CompleteQ[InduceSubgraph[h, {3, 11, 14, 22}]]**

Out[152]= True

The SpringEmbedding heuristic tends to perform better on sparse graphs. Here it does a good job illustrating the join operation, where each vertex of K_7 is connected to each of two disconnected vertices. In achieving the minimum energy configuration, these two vertices end up on different sides of K_7.

In[153]:= **ShowGraph[SpringEmbedding[GraphJoin[EmptyGraph[2], CompleteGraph[7]]]];**

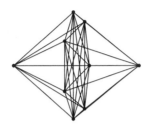

Options controlling the number of iterations and vertex step-size in SpringEmbedding can be more effective than just running it multiple times.

In[154]:= **ShowGraph[SpringEmbedding[CompleteBinaryTree[50],200,0.05]];**

5.7 Storing and Editing Graphs

In order to exchange *Combinatorica* graphs with other programs, or simply to save our work for later, we need the ability to write graphs to files and read them back. In the absence of a truly standard graph format, we rely on the input and output operations in *Mathematica*.

Load in an externally prepared graph written in *Combinatorica* format, in this case the complete pairwise distance graph between 128 U.S. cities taken from [Knu94].

```
In[155]:= g = << "extraCode/usa.graph"
Out[155]= -Graph:<8128, 128, Undirected>-
```

This graph is too dense to show much detail, but its minimum spanning tree clearly reveals the contours of the United States with reasonable driving routes between cities. In this example, the vertex labels that correspond to city names have to be turned off, otherwise the entire graph would be obscured by the labels.

```
In[156]:= h = MinimumSpanningTree[g];
         ShowGraph[SetGraphOptions[h, Table[{i, VertexLabel -> False},
         {i, 128}]]];
```

Combinatorica graphs can be stored in files by writing them to standard output.

```
In[158]:= GraphProduct[Path[6],Wheel[5]] >> "/tmp/product.graph"
```

Reading them back from standard input recovers the graph's topology and its embedding.

In[159]:= **ShowGraph[<< "/tmp/product.graph"];**

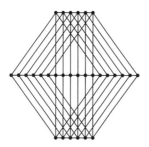

The easiest approach to import graph data into *Combinatorica* from another program or data source is to reduce the data to either ordered/unordered pairs, a matrix, or adjacency lists. Prepare it as a well-formed *Mathematica* list and read it into *Mathematica* using standard input. From here, we can use FromOrderedPairs, FromUnorderedPairs, FromAdjacencyMatrix, or FromAdjacencyLists to turn it into a graph. A nice collection of interestng graph files is available at www.combinatorica.com.

Another way to enter graphs is by using a mouse-driven graph editor, which enables you to point-and-click the positions of vertices and add edges between selected pairs of vertices. Literally dozens of graph editors have been developed over the years, but they tend to be restricted to specific operating systems and graph formats. Unfortunately, the current version of *Mathematica* does not provide the power for us to build a graph editor into *Combinatorica*. However, a portable graph editor that read/writes graphs in *Combinatorica* format is available at our Web site http://www.combinatorica.com. This editor was written in Java by Levon Lloyd.

There are other libraries of combinatorial and graph-theoretic software available on the Web. Particularly notable systems include

- *Leda* [MN99], a C++ library of graph algorithms and data structures;
- *GTL* [LLS01], a graph template library for C++; and
- *Nauty* [McK90], a set of C language procedures for determining the automorphism group of a graph.

Such systems are described in [Ski97] and pointed to from http://www.combinatorica.com.

5.8 Exercises

■ 5.8.1 Thought Exercises

1. How long does it take to test if a particular edge (i,j) appears in an edge list? How long does it take to list all the edges incident on vertex i? Now explain why edge lists are not typically discussed as an important graph representation in standard algorithm texts.

2. When an adjacency matrix representation is used, most graph algorithms require $O(n^2)$ time for an n-vertex graph. Show that determining whether a directed graph contains a *sink* – a vertex with in-degree $n-1$ and out-degree 0 – can be determined in time $O(n)$, even if adjacency matrix representation is used.

3. The *square* of a graph $G = (V,E)$ is a graph $G^2 = (V,E^2)$, where $\{u,v\} \in E^2$ if and only if there is a path of length 2 between u and v in G. Describe an algorithm to compute the square of a given graph using (i) the adjacency list representation and (ii) the adjacency matrix representation.

4. We study *line graphs* in Chapter 6. The line graph $L(G)$ of a graph G consists of a vertex for every edge in G. Two vertices in $L(G)$ are connected by an edge, if the corresponding edges in G share an endpoint. There is a nice relation between the incidence matrix of a graph G and the adjacency matrix of the line graph $L(G)$. Discover this relation and prove that it holds.

■ 5.8.2 Programming Exercises

1. Using the graph representation functions defined within this chapter, plus regular *Mathematica* constructs, implement five different functions for constructing complete graphs. Experiment to determine which one is most efficient.

2. Implement the function `FromIncidenceMatrix` that reconstructs the graph corresponding to a given incidence matrix.

3. Write a function to determine whether the given embedding of a graph is planar, by testing whether any two edges intersect.

4. The current implementation of `DeleteEdges` is relatively slow. Can you devise an implementation that is substantially faster?

5. Given a planar embedding of a G, implement a function that constructs an adjacency list representation of G, in which the list of neighbors of each vertex v is sorted according to the counterclockwise order in which they appear around v. This representation enables algorithms to deal more efficiently with planar graphs. Can you think of any such applications?

6. Suppose we wanted to allow graph drawings in which edges were not merely straight-line segments but were *polylines*. In other words, we would like to allow some number of bends in

the drawing of edges. How would the graph data structure have to be changed to allow this? Implement a function that takes this modified graph data structure and uses ShowGraph to draw the graph with some edges possibly containing bends.

7. Develop and implement an algorithm for drawing rooted embeddings of trees that does a better job than RootedEmbedding of balancing the sizes of the vertical strips associated with each subtree. Thus wide subtrees will not be squashed into a narrow region.

8. The embeddings we have considered all lie in the plane. However, certain embeddings make sense in higher dimensions. Circuit design problems have led to the study of *book embeddings* [CLR87, Mal88], where all vertices are laid out on a line (the spine of the book) and the edges are printed on *pages* such that no two edges on a page cross. Write functions to find and display book embeddings of graphs.

9. Modify SpringEmbedding to stop when the amount of movement per iteration crosses a threshold. Experiment with how many iterations are necessary to obtain a stable drawing.

■ 5.8.3 Experimental Exercises

1. Experiment with heuristics to permute the vertices in a circular embedding so as to minimize the total edge length of the embedding.

2. Experiment with heuristics to permute the vertices in a circular embedding so as to minimize the total number of edge crossings in the embedding.

3. Experiment with repeated contractions of vertex pairs in random graphs, going from n vertices down to one. At what point in the process is the maximum number of edges likely to be deleted in a contraction?

6. Generating Graphs

This chapter is devoted to constructing graphs. Using the functions provided in this chapter, a user can construct a large variety of graphs. Circulant graphs, grid graphs, hypercubes, and butterfly graphs are just a few of the graphs you will encounter. Some of the graph classes we provide are random, and these are especially suited for testing graph algorithms. We also provide a large number of graph operations that build new graphs from old ones. Union, join, product, and contract are some of the operations you will encounter. In addition, we provide an easy way of constructing graphs from binary relations and functions. Many real-life graphs express some underlying binary relation, and being able to easily construct such graphs is one of the highlights of *Combinatorica*.

The properties of the graphs constructed in this chapter will motivate the graph invariants that we compute in later chapters. Many of these graphs are truly beautiful when drawn properly, and they provide a wide range of structures to manipulate and study.

About the illustration overleaf:

Circulant graphs are highly symmetrical and parametrized by subsets of vertices. Here are all the 2^6 circulant graphs on 12 vertices, built from the list of all 6-element subsets with the command:

```
ShowGraphArray[ Partition[Map[(CirculantGraph[12,#])&, Subsets[6]],8]]
```

6.1 Building Graphs from Other Graphs

This section presents operations that build graphs from other graphs. Many of the parametrized graphs in this chapter can be constructed using these operations. Other examples appear in [CM78].

■ 6.1.1 Contracting Vertices

Contracting a pair of vertices, v_1 and v_2, replaces them by one vertex v such that v is adjacent to anything v_1 or v_2 had been. It does not matter whether v_1 and v_2 are connected by an edge; if they are, then the edge disappears when v_1 and v_2 are contracted. The function `Contract` generalizes this and can shrink two or more vertices in a graph into one.

`Contract` runs in linear time by constructing a mapping from the vertices of the original graph to the vertices of the contracted graph. Suppose that we are given an n-vertex graph $G = (V, E)$ and a subset L with k vertices to contract. Contracting G gives a graph H with $n - k + 1$ vertices. Each vertex v in L is mapped to vertex $n - k + 1$ in H. Every other vertex v in G is mapped to vertex $v - i$ in H if there are i vertices in L smaller than v. This mapping is constructed in $\Theta(n)$ time. We then use this mapping to create the edges of H, in time proportional to the number of edges in G.

```
Contract[g_Graph, l_List]  :=
    Module[{v = Vertices[g, All], t = Table[0, {V[g]}],
         cnt = 0, last = V[g] - Length[l] + 1},
        Do[If[MemberQ[l, k], cnt++; t[[k]] = last, t[[k]] = k - cnt], {k, V[g]}];
        Graph[
          DeleteCases[Edges[g, All] /. {{x_Integer, y_Integer}, opts___?OptionQ}
                            :> {Sort[{t[[x]], t[[y]]}], opts}, {{last, last}, opts___?OptionQ}
          ],
          Append[v[[Complement[Range[Length[v]], l]]],
              {Apply[Plus, Map[First, v[[l]]]]/Length[l]}
          ],
          Apply[Sequence, GraphOptions[g]]
        ]
    ]
```

Contracting Vertices in a Graph

This loads the package.   *In[1]:=* **<<DiscreteMath`Combinatorica`**

Contracting edge (1, 2) shrinks the number of vertices and edges by one, because the contracted edge disappears. Note the renumbering of vertices: The new vertex is numbered 9 and all other vertices slide up by 2 in the ordering. Contract maintains the embedding of the old graph: The new vertex is placed at the midpoint of the two contracted vertices, with the locations of all other vertices unchanged.

```
In[2]:= ShowGraphArray[{g = CompleteKaryTree[10, 3], Contract[g, {1, 2}]},
            VertexNumber -> True];
```

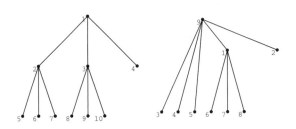

Contracting vertices will create multiple edges whenever contracted vertices have a common neighbor. Thus contract operations can decrease the number of vertices in the graph without decreasing the number of edges.

```
In[3]:= g = Star[10];
        ShowGraphArray[Partition[NestList[Contract[#, {1, 2}] &, g, 9], 3]];
```

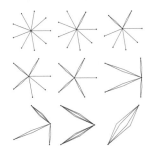

Graph contraction is useful in counting the number of spanning trees of a graph. A *spanning tree* of graph $G = (V, E)$ is a tree whose vertex set equals V and whose edges are all contained in E. The number of spanning trees of G, denoted $\tau(G)$, satisfies the recurrence relation $\tau(G) = \tau(G - e) + \tau(G \cdot e)$. Here $G - e$ and $G \cdot e$ respectively denote the graphs obtained from G by deleting edge e and by contracting the endpoints of edge e.

```
In[5]:= g = RandomGraph[20, .5]; e = First[Edges[g]];
        {NumberOfSpanningTrees[g],
         NumberOfSpanningTrees[DeleteEdges[g, {e}]] +
         NumberOfSpanningTrees[Contract[g, e]]}
Out[6]= {14021885085330334, 14021885085330334}
```

A *minimum cut* of a graph is a smallest set of edges whose removal disconnects the graph. The set of three edges that connect the K_5 on the left to the K_5 on the right is a minimum cut of this graph. Computing a minimum cut of a graph is an important optimization problem.

```
In[7]:= ShowGraph[h1= h2=AddEdges[GraphUnion[g=CompleteGraph[5], g],
            {{1,6}, {1,8}, {2,7}}]];
```

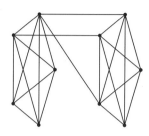

The size of a minimum cut set is the graph's *edge connectivity*.

```
In[8]:= EdgeConnectivity[h1]

Out[8]= 3
```

Repeatedly contracting randomly chosen edges yields a beautiful randomized algorithm for computing a minimum cut [KS96]. Observe that contracting an edge does not decrease the size of a minimum cut, since any cut in G' is also a cut in the original graph G. Here, contracting an edge in one of the K_5's maintains the size of a minimum cut, and contracting an edge between the K_5's increases the minimum cut.

```
In[9]:= ShowGraphArray[Join[{h1}, Table[el=Edges[h1]; h1 = Contract[h1,
            el[[Random[Integer, {1,Length[el]}]]]]], {3}]]];
```

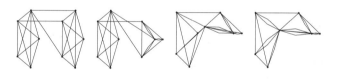

Every edge contraction decreases the number of vertices by one, so after $n-2$ edge contractions we get a 2-vertex graph. The number of edges in this multigraph is an upper bound on the size of a minimum cut in the original graph. This upper bound is not always tight, but the smallest graph encountered after repeating this algorithm polynomially many times is very likely to give a minimum cut.

```
In[10]:= ListPlot[Table[el = Edges[h2]; h2 = Contract[h2,
            el[[Random[Integer, {1, Length[el]}]]]]; M[h2], {8}],
            AxesOrigin->{0,0}];
```

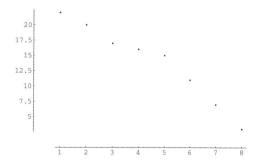

■ 6.1.2 Inducing and Permuting Subgraphs

An *induced subgraph* of a graph G is a subset of the vertices of G together with any edges whose endpoints are both in this subset. Deleting a vertex from a graph is identical to inducing a subgraph of the remaining $n - 1$ vertices. *Combinatorica* provides a function InduceSubgraph that takes a graph G and a subset S of the vertices of G and returns the subgraph of G induced by S. InduceSubgraph calls a more general function PermuteSubgraph, which not only induces a subgraph, but permutes the embedding of the graph according to the given permutation.

Any subset of the vertices in a complete graph defines a clique. This drawing presents an interesting illusion, for although the points seem irregularly spaced, they all are defined as lying on a circle.

In[11]:= ShowGraph[InduceSubgraph[CompleteGraph[20], RandomSubset[20]]];

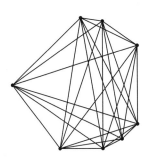

A random induced subgraph of a grid graph looks like a maze. A *connected component* of a graph is a maximal connected subgraph. Random graph theory concerns quantities like the expected number of connected components and the expected size of the largest component in a random graph.

In[12]:= ShowGraph[g = InduceSubgraph[GridGraph[50, 50], RandomSubset[2500]], VertexStyle -> Disk[0]];

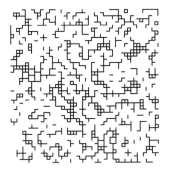

What is the expected number of connected components in a random induced subgraph of an $n \times n$ grid graph?

In[13]:= Length[ConnectedComponents[g]]

Out[13]= 173

This experiment hints at what the average number of connected components in a 20×20 grid graph might be. `ConnectedComponents` is a function to compute the connected components of a graph (see Section 7.2.1).

```
In[14]:= Table[Length[ConnectedComponents[InduceSubgraph[GridGraph[20, 20],
             RandomSubset[400]]]], {5}]
Out[14]= {37, 39, 31, 35, 43}
```

This gives an unfamiliar embedding of the 10-vertex wheel graph. The same locations are used for the ten vertices, but the vertices themselves are moved around according to the provided permutation. `PermuteSubgraph` can be used to generate new embeddings of graphs.

```
In[15]:= ShowGraph[h = PermuteSubgraph[Wheel[10], RandomPermutation[10]],
             VertexNumber -> True, TextStyle -> {FontSize -> 12}];
```

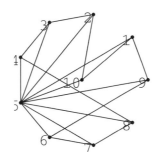

■ 6.1.3 Unions and Intersections

Graphs are sets of vertices and edges, and the most important operations on sets are union and intersection. The *union* operation takes two or more graphs and returns a graph that is formed by taking the union of the vertices and edges of the graphs. `GraphUnion` first normalizes the embeddings of the given graphs, to ensure that their drawings are roughly the same size. It then puts together the edges and vertices of the given graphs, making sure that each successive graph appears to the right of the previous one.

Here is the union of a 5-cycle, $3 \times 3 \times 3$ grid graph and a four-dimensional hypercube. The component graphs of the union are placed in order from left to right. Each component graph is normalized to ensure that the relative sizes of the components are similar.

```
In[16]:= ShowGraph[g=GraphUnion[Cycle[5], GridGraph[3,3,3], Hypercube[4]]];
```

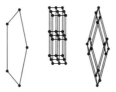

The union of graphs is always disconnected.

```
In[17]:= ConnectedComponents[g]
Out[17]= {{1, 2, 3, 4, 5},
    {6, 7, 8, 9, 10, 11, 12, 13, 14, 15, 16, 17, 18, 19,
     20, 21, 22, 23, 24, 25, 26, 27, 28, 29, 30, 31, 32},
    {33, 34, 35, 36, 37, 38, 39, 40, 41, 42, 43, 44, 45,
     46, 47, 48}}
```

This graph contains 48 vertices, 91 edges, and 3 connected components.

```
In[18]:= {V[g], M[g], Length[ConnectedComponents[g]]}
Out[18]= {48, 91, 3}
```

Here are two graphs with different local and global options set. We will use these graphs as examples to show which graph attributes are preserved by graph operations.

```
In[19]:= g = SetGraphOptions[GridGraph[3, 3], {{2,4,9,
    VertexStyle->Box[Large]}, {{1,2}, EdgeStyle->Thick}},
    VertexStyle->Disk[Large]];
    h = SetGraphOptions[Star[9], {{2,4,9, VertexStyle->Box[Large]},
    {{1,9}, EdgeStyle->Thick}}, VertexColor->Gray];
    ShowGraphArray[{g, h}];
```

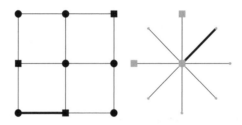

GraphUnion inherits global options from the first graph while preserving all local options. Here all vertices in the union appear Gray because of the global vertex option associated with the first graph. Local options that alter the thickness of edges and size of vertices are preserved for both graphs.

```
In[22]:= ShowGraph[GraphUnion[h, g]];
```

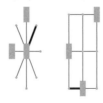

The other form of GraphUnion specifies the number of copies of the graph to union.

In[23]:= **ShowGraph[GraphUnion[5, CompleteGraph[3]]];**

Why does this function call return unevaluated? The first two graphs are directed while the third is undirected. GraphUnion requires all its argument graphs to be uniformly directed or undirected. Mixed input is returned unevaluated.

In[24]:= **GraphUnion[CompleteGraph[6, Type -> Directed],
      CompleteGraph[5, Type -> Directed], CompleteGraph[5]]**

Out[24]= GraphUnion[-Graph:<30, 6, Directed>-,

  -Graph:<20, 5, Directed>-, -Graph:<10, 5, Undirected>-]

The *intersection* of two graphs with the same number of vertices is constructed by taking the intersection of the edges of the graphs.

```
GraphIntersection[g_Graph] := g

GraphIntersection[g_Graph,h_Graph] :=
     Module[{e = Intersection[Edges[g], Edges[h]]},
        ChangeEdges[g, Select[Edges[g, All], (MemberQ[e, First[#]]) &]]
     ] /; (V[g] == V[h]) && (UndirectedQ[g] == UndirectedQ[h])

GraphIntersection[g_Graph,h_Graph, l__Graph] := GraphIntersection[GraphIntersection[g, h], l]
```

The Intersection of Graphs

Intersection with K_n is an identity operation for any graph of order n.

In[25]:= **IdenticalQ[GraphIntersection[Wheel[10], CompleteGraph[10]],
      Wheel[10]]**

Out[25]= True

What is the intersection of a hypercube and grid graph of equal sizes? The SpringEmbedding of the result reveals the original grid graph! Thus the grid graph is a subgraph of the hypercube.

`In[26]:= ShowGraphArray[{gh=GraphIntersection[ Hypercube[4], GridGraph[4,4]], SpringEmbedding[gh,200] }];`

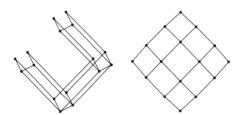

■ 6.1.4 Sums and Differences

Since graphs can be represented by adjacency matrices, they can be added, subtracted, and multiplied in a meaningful way, provided they have the same number of vertices.

The sum of a graph and its complement gives the complete graph.

`In[27]:= CompleteQ[GraphSum[Cycle[10], GraphComplement[Cycle[10]]]]`
`Out[27]= True`

The difference of a graph and itself gives the empty graph.

`In[28]:= EmptyQ[GraphDifference[Cycle[10],Cycle[10]] ]`
`Out[28]= True`

GraphSum's rule of inheritance takes the edges of the second graph and adds them to the first graph. Thus all global options come from the first input graph; each edge in the graph sum belongs to one of the input graphs and preserves its local options; each vertex inherits its local options from the first input graph.

`In[29]:= ShowGraphArray[{GraphSum[g,h], GraphSum[h,g]}];`

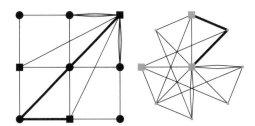

■ 6.1.5 Joins of Graphs

The *join* of two graphs is their union, with the addition of all edges spanning the different graphs. Many of the graphs we have seen as examples and will implement in this chapter can be specified as the join of two graphs, such as complete bipartite graphs, stars, and wheels.

The *Cartesian product* $A \times B$ is the set of element pairs such that one element is from A and one is from B. The edges that get added to the union of the two graphs are exactly the Cartesian product of the two vertex sets.

```
GraphJoin[g_Graph] := g

GraphJoin[g_Graph,h_Graph] :=
      AddEdges[GraphUnion[g, h],
            CartesianProduct[Range[V[g]],Range[V[h]]+V[g]]
      ] /; (UndirectedQ[g] == UndirectedQ[h])

GraphJoin[g_Graph,h_Graph, l__Graph] := GraphJoin[GraphJoin[g, h], l]

CartesianProduct[a_List, b_List] := Flatten[Outer[List, a, b, 1, 1], 1]
```

The Join of Graphs

Complete *k*-partite graphs such as $K_{5,5}$ are naturally described in terms of GraphJoin. Here we show a "spring embedding" of the graph because the default embedding of the join looks somewhat ugly.

```
In[30]:= ShowGraph[SpringEmbedding[
              GraphJoin[EmptyGraph[5], EmptyGraph[5]]]];
```

A wheel is the join of a cycle and a single vertex. A star is the join of an empty graph and a single vertex.

```
In[31]:= IsomorphicQ[Wheel[10], GraphJoin[Cycle[9], EmptyGraph[1]]]

Out[31]= True
```

■ 6.1.6 Products of Graphs

The *product* $G_1 \times G_2$ of two graphs has a vertex set defined by the Cartesian product of the vertex sets of G_1 and G_2. There is an edge between (u_1, v_1) and (u_2, v_2) if $u_1 = u_2$ and v_1 is adjacent to v_2 in G_2 or $v_1 = v_2$ and u_1 is adjacent to u_2 in G_1. The intuition in taking the product is that all the vertices of one graph get replaced by instances of the other graph. Products of graphs have been studied extensively [IK00, Sab60]. *Combinatorica* provides a function GraphProduct that computes the product of a pair of graphs.

Graph products can be very interesting. The embedding of a product has been designed to show off its structure, and is formed by shrinking the first graph and translating it to the position of each vertex in the second graph. Reversing the order of the two arguments thus dramatically changes the appearance of the product, but the resulting graphs are isomorphic.

```
In[32]:= K3=CompleteGraph[3]; K5=CompleteGraph[5];
         ShowGraphArray[{g = GraphProduct[K3, K5],
         h = GraphProduct[K5, K3]}];
```

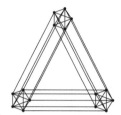

Since both graphs are always isomorphic, the product of two graphs is a commutative operation, even if our embeddings are different when the order of the arguments is changed.

```
In[34]:= IsomorphicQ[g,h]
Out[34]= True
```

Many of the properties of product graphs can be deduced from the corresponding properties of its factor graphs. For example, the product of two Hamiltonian graphs is Hamiltonian, and, similarly, if two graphs have Hamiltonian paths, then their product does too.

```
In[35]:= ShowGraph[g = GraphProduct[Wheel[6], Path[5]]]
```

A wheel and a path have Hamiltonian paths, and so does their product.

```
In[36]:= HamiltonianPath[g]
Out[36]= {1, 2, 3, 4, 5, 6, 12, 8, 9, 10, 11, 17, 16, 15,
         14, 18, 24, 20, 21, 22, 23, 29, 28, 27, 26, 30, 25, 19,
         13, 7}
```

Multiplication by K_1 is an identity operation, although there is no corresponding multiplicative inverse.

```
In[37]:= IdenticalQ[ GraphProduct[CompleteGraph[1], CompleteGraph[5]],
         CompleteGraph[5] ]
Out[37]= True
```

■ 6.1.7 Line Graphs

The *line graph* $L(G)$ of a graph G has a vertex of $L(G)$ associated with each edge of G and an edge of $L(G)$ if and only if the two edges of G share a common vertex. Line graphs are a special type of intersection graph, where each vertex represents a set of size 2 and each edge connects two sets with a nonempty intersection.

The obvious algorithm for constructing the line graph involves iterating through each pair of edges to decide whether they share a vertex between them, but the running time of this algorithm is quadratic in the number of edges of the input graph. However, the number of edges in $L(G)$ may be far smaller than the square of the number of edges in G. A more efficient algorithm is the following. First, lexicographically sort the edges and split them into groups by their first endpoint. Each group of edges shares their first endpoint and therefore form a clique in the line graph. The "helper" function, shown below, `GroupEdgePositions` computes the groupings of edges. Each edge grouping yields a clique, and the union of cliques is the line graph. The running time of this algorithm is proportional to the number of edges in the line graph plus the time to sort the edges in the input graph.

```
GroupEdgePositions[e_List, n_Integer] :=
     Map[Map[Last, #]&,
         Split[Union[Transpose[{e, Range[Length[e]]}], Table[{ {i, 0}, 0}, {i, n}]],
             (#1[[1,1]]=== #2[[1,1]])&
         ]
     ]

LineGraph[g_Graph] :=
     Module[{e = Sort[Edges[g]], ef, eb, c,
            v = Vertices[g]},
         ef = GroupEdgePositions[e, V[g]];
         eb = GroupEdgePositions[ Map[Reverse,e], V[g]];
         c = Table[Rest[Union[ef[[i]], eb[[i]]]], {i, V[g]}];
         Graph[Union[
                Flatten[Map[Table[{{#[[i]], #[[j]]}}, {i, Length[#]-1}, {j, i+1, Length[#]}]&, c], 2]
                ],
                Map[({(v[[ #[[1]] ]] + v[[ #[[2]] ]]) / 2})&, e]
            ]
     ]
```

Constructing Line Graphs

The line graph of a graph with n vertices and m edges contains m vertices and $\frac{1}{2}\sum_{i=1}^{n} d_i^2 - m$ edges. Thus the number of vertices of the line graph of K_n grows quadratically in n. Proofs of this and most of the results we cite on line graphs appear in [Har69]. The coordinates of each vertex in this embedding of $L(G)$ are the averages of the coordinates of the vertices associated with the original edge in G.

In[38]:= **ShowGraph[LineGraph[CompleteGraph[5]]];**

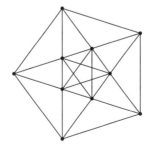

Although some of the edges are ambiguous in the previous embedding, $L(K_5)$ is indeed a 6-regular graph.

The cycle graph is the only connected graph that is isomorphic to its line graph.

No analogous `FromLineGraph` function is given, because not all graphs represent line graphs of other graphs. An example is the claw $K_{1,3}$. A structural characterization of line graphs is given in [vRW65] and refined by Beineke [Bei68], who showed that a graph is a line graph if and only if it does not contain any of these graphs as induced subgraphs.

In introducing line graphs, Whitney [Whi32] showed that, with the exception of K_3 and $K_{1,3}$, any two connected graphs with isomorphic line graphs are isomorphic.

The *degree sequence* of a graph is the sequence of degrees of the vertices sorted in nonincreasing order. `RealizeDegreeSequence` takes a sequence of integers and constructs a random graph with this degree sequence. Here we get a 6-vertex graph of even degree. Such a graph has an Eulerian cycle and is said to be *Eulerian*.

An *Eulerian cycle* is a tour that visits every edge of the graph exactly once.

```
In[39]:= DegreeSequence[ LineGraph[CompleteGraph[5]] ]
Out[39]= {6, 6, 6, 6, 6, 6, 6, 6, 6, 6}
```

```
In[40]:= IsomorphicQ[Cycle[10], LineGraph[Cycle[10]]]
Out[40]= True
```

```
In[41]:= ShowGraph[NonLineGraphs];
```

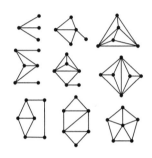

```
In[42]:= IsomorphicQ[LineGraph[CompleteGraph[3]],
             LineGraph[CompleteGraph[1,3]] ]
Out[42]= True
```

```
In[43]:= ShowGraph[g = RealizeDegreeSequence[{4,4,2,2,2,2}],
             VertexNumber->True, TextStyle->{FontSize->12}];
```

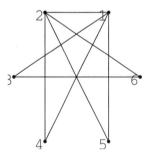

```
In[44]:= EulerianCycle[g]
Out[44]= {2, 4, 1, 3, 6, 2, 5, 1, 2}
```

The line graph of an Eulerian graph is both Eulerian and Hamiltonian, while the line graph of a Hamiltonian graph is always Hamiltonian. Further results on cycles in line graphs appear in [Cha68, HNW65].

```
In[45]:= h = LineGraph[g];
         EulerianQ[h] && HamiltonianQ[h]
Out[46]= True
```

The complement of the line graph of K_5 is the Petersen graph. This is another example of an attractive but potentially misleading embedding. K_5 has 10 edges, so why does this graph have *11* vertices? The centermost "vertex" is just the intersection of five edges. Alternate embeddings of the Peterson graph appear in Section 5.1.4.

```
In[47]:= ShowGraph[ GraphComplement[ LineGraph[CompleteGraph[5]] ] ];
```

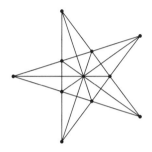

6.2 Regular Structures

Many classes of graphs are defined by very regular structures that often suggests a natural embedding. They are typically parametrized by the number of vertices and occasionally edges.

We have seen that many regular structures can be formulated using such operations as join and product. Here we give more efficient, special-purpose constructions for several classes of graphs.

■ 6.2.1 Complete Graphs

A *complete graph* contains all possible edges. The complete undirected n-vertex graph K_n thus contains $\binom{n}{2}$ undirected edges, while the directed complete graph with n vertices contains $n(n-1)$ edges. Given a positive integer n, the function `CompleteGraph` produces K_n. The function for constructing complete graphs uses a circular embedding for the vertices.

The complete graph on five vertices K_5 is famous as being the smallest nonplanar graph. Rotated appropriately, it becomes a supposed Satanic symbol, the pentagram.

In[48]:= **ShowGraph[RotateVertices[CompleteGraph[5], Pi/10]];**

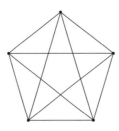

Using the option `Type -> Directed` produces the directed complete graph.

In[49]:= **ShowGraph[CompleteGraph[5, Type -> Directed]];**

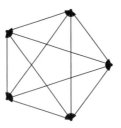

The graph with no vertices and edges is called the *null graph* and has been studied extensively [HR73].

In[50]:= `CompleteGraph[0]`

Out[50]= -Graph:<0, 0, Undirected>-

A generalization of the null graph is the *empty graph* on n vertices, the complement of K_n.

```
In[51]:= EmptyGraph[10]

Out[51]= -Graph:<0, 10, Undirected>-
```

■ 6.2.2 Circulant Graphs

The *circulant* graph $C_n(n_1, n_2, ..., n_k)$ has n vertices with each v_i adjacent to each vertex $v_{i \pm n_j}$ mod n, where $n_1 < n_2 < \cdots < n_k < (n + 1)/2$ [BH90]. Thus circulant graphs include complete graphs and cycles as special cases.

It is useful to think of circulant graphs as those whose adjacency matrix can be constructed by rotating a vector n times. However, to take advantage of their possible sparsity, we do not construct circulant graphs in this way.

```
CirculantGraph[n_Integer?Positive, l_Integer] := CirculantGraph[n, {l}]

CirculantGraph[n_Integer?Positive, l:{_Integer...}] :=
    Graph[Union[
            Flatten[Table[Map[{Sort[{i, Mod[i+#, n]}]+1}&, l], {i,0,n-1}], 1],
            Flatten[Table[Map[{Sort[{i, Mod[i-#, n]}]+1}&, l], {i,0,n-1}], 1]
        ],
        CircularEmbedding[n]
    ]
```

Constructing Circulant Graphs

Here is a circulant graph with 21 vertices, with each vertex connected to a vertex 3 away and a vertex 7 away on each side. The connections to vertices 3 away create three cycles of length 7 each, and the connections to vertices 7 away create seven cycles of length 3 each.

```
In[52]:= ShowGraph[g = CirculantGraph[21, {3, 7}]];
```

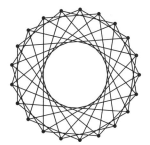

The spring embedding of the above graph makes clear this cycle structure. In fact, this circulant graph can be alternatively viewed as the product of a 3-cycle and a 7-cycle.

```
In[53]:= ShowGraph[SpringEmbedding[g, 30]];
```

Constructing a 21-vertex circulant graph by connecting to vertices 7 away leads to seven connected components, each a 3-cycle.

```
In[54]:= ConnectedComponents[ CirculantGraph[21, {7}] ]
Out[54]= {{1, 8, 15}, {2, 9, 16}, {3, 10, 17}, {4, 11, 18},
          {5, 12, 19}, {6, 13, 20}, {7, 14, 21}}
```

This is an example of an exciting general property.

```
In[55]:= g = CirculantGraph[15, {3, 5}];
         h = GraphProduct[Cycle[3],Cycle[5]];
         Isomorphism[g,h]
Out[57]= {1, 8, 15, 4, 11, 3, 7, 14, 6, 10, 2, 9, 13, 5, 12}
```

■ 6.2.3 Complete *k*-Partite Graphs

A graph is *bipartite* when its vertices can be partitioned into sets *A* and *B* such that every edge connects a vertex in *A* to a vertex in *B*. This notion can be generalized into *k-partite* graphs, whose vertices can be partitioned into *k* subsets such that no two vertices in the same subset are connected by an edge. A *complete k*-partite graph is a *k*-partite graph with every possible edge. Complete *k*-partite graphs are parametrized by the number of vertices in each of the *k* subsets. *Combinatorica* provides a function CompleteKPartiteGraph that takes as input the size of each of the *k* parts and returns the corresponding complete *k*-partite graph.

The standard way to draw a *k*-partite graph is as a leveled embedding in which vertices are partitioned into equally spaced stages, with the vertices of each stage drawn in a vertical line.

The most famous bipartite graph is $K_{3,3}$, the "other" smallest nonplanar graph, although $K_{18,18}$ plays an important role in the novel *Foucault's Pendulum* [Eco89]. A ranked embedding shows the structure of the graph since all edges are between vertices of different ranks.

In[58]:= **ShowGraph[CompleteKPartiteGraph[3,3]];**

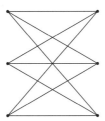

We can construct complete *k*-partite graphs for any *k*. These graphs can get very dense when there are many stages. Whenever three vertices are collinear, there might be edges that overlap. This is unfortunate but costly to prevent.

In[59]:= **ShowGraph[CompleteKPartiteGraph[2,2,2,2]];**

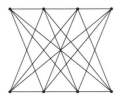

The complete graph K_n can be defined as $K_{1,1,\ldots,1}$.

In[60]:= **IsomorphicQ[CompleteGraph[5],**
 CompleteKPartiteGraph[1,1,1,1,1]]

Out[60]= True

A special case of a complete *k*-partite graph is the *Turán graph*, which provided the answer to the first problem in what is now known as extremal graph theory [Tur41]. An *extremal graph Ex(n, G)* is the largest graph of order *n* that does not contain *G* as a subgraph. Turán was interested in finding the extremal graph that does not contain K_p as a subgraph. Since Turán's paper, extremal graph theory has grown to have a very large literature [Bol78].

```
Turan[n_Integer, 2] := GraphUnion[n, CompleteGraph[1]] /; (n > 0)
Turan[n_Integer,p_Integer] :=
      Module[{k = Floor[ n / (p-1) ], r},
            r = n - k (p-1);
            Apply[CompleteGraph, Join[Table[k,{p-1-r}], Table[k+1,{r}]]]
      ] /; (n >= p) && (p > 2)
Turan[n_Integer, p_Integer] := CompleteGraph[n] /; (n < p) && (p > 2)
```

Constructing the Turán Graph

Since the Turán graph is $(p - 1)$-partite,
it cannot contain K_p as a subgraph.
The idea behind the construction is to
balance the size of each stage as evenly
as possible, maximizing the number of
edges between every pair of stages.

In[61]:= **ShowGraph[Turan[10,4]];**

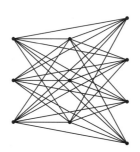

■ 6.2.4 Cycles, Stars, and Wheels

The *cycle C_n* is the connected 2-regular graph of order *n*. Special cases of interest include the *triangle*
K_3 and the *square* C_4. Cycles are a special case of circulant graphs.

Here we show two different
embeddings of C_{20}. Both embeddings
are circular, but there are no edge
crossings in the default embedding.
The minimum number of swaps
between vertices in a random circular
embedding of a cycle to get it into its
proper configuration is an interesting
combinatorial problem. This is related
to the *Bruhat order* of a group
[BW82, Sta86].

In[62]:= **ShowGraphArray[{g = Cycle[20], h = PermuteSubgraph[Cycle[20],**
RandomPermutation[20]]}];

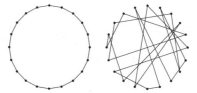

A *star* is a tree with one vertex of degree $n - 1$. Since a star is a tree, it is acyclic. An interesting
property of the star is that the distance between any two vertices is at most two, despite the fact
that it contains the minimum number of edges to be connected. This makes it a good topology for
computer networks because it minimizes communication time between nodes, at least until the center
node goes down.

```
Star[n_Integer?Positive] :=
    Graph[Table[{{i, n}}, {i, n-1}],
        Append[CircularEmbedding[n-1], {{0, 0}}]
    ]
```
Constructing a Star

In this construction, the center of the star is the *n*th vertex.

The complete bipartite graph $K_{1,n-1}$ is a star on n vertices.

```
In[63]:= Isomorphism[ CompleteKPartiteGraph[1,5], Star[6] ]

Out[63]= {6, 1, 2, 3, 4, 5}
```

A *wheel* is the graph obtained by joining a single isolated vertex K_1 to each vertex of a cycle C_{n-1}. The resulting edges that form the star are, logically enough, called the *spokes* of the wheel.

```
Wheel[n_Integer] :=
    Graph[Join[Table[{{i, n}}, {i, n-1}], Table[{{i, i+1}}, {i, n-2}],
            {{{1, n-1}}}
        ],
        Append[CircularEmbedding[n-1], {{0, 0}}]
    ] /; (n >= 3)
```

Constructing a Wheel

The *dual* of a planar embedding of a graph *G* is a graph with a vertex for each region of *G*, with edges if the corresponding regions are adjacent. The dual graph of a wheel is a wheel.

```
In[64]:= ShowGraph[ Wheel[20] ];
```

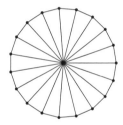

■ 6.2.5 Grid Graphs

Anyone who has used a piece of graph paper is familiar with *grid graphs*. The vertices in an $m \times n$ grid graph correspond to ordered pairs (i, j), where i and j are integers, $1 \le i \le m$, and $1 \le j \le n$. Every edge connects pairs (i, j) and (i', j'), where $|i - i'| + |j - j'| = 1$. Counting the number of distinct paths between two points in a grid graph is a classic application of binomial coefficients, discussed in Section 8.1.4. An $m \times n$ grid graph can be constructed by computing the product of paths of orders m and n. Grid graphs can be generalized to higher dimensions in a natural way. *Combinatorica* provides a function `GridGraph` that takes as input two or three positive integers and returns a two-dimensional or a three-dimensional grid graph that is appropriately embedded.

Combinatorica provides a constructor for three-dimensional grid graphs. A $p \times q \times r$ grid graph can be constructed by computing the product of three paths.

In[65]:= **ShowGraph[g = GridGraph[4,5,3]];**

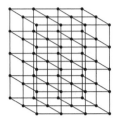

Grid graphs are Hamiltonian if the number of either rows or columns is even. Such a cycle can be constructed by starting in the lower left-hand corner, going all way to the right, and then zig-zagging up and down until reaching the original corner. Other Hamiltonian cycles, like this one, do not follow this pattern.

In[66]:= **ShowGraph[Highlight[g = GridGraph[4, 5],**
      {Partition[HamiltonianCycle[g], 2, 1]}]];

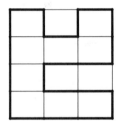

Even this small graph has many Hamiltonian cycles.

In[67]:= **Length[HamiltonianCycle[g, All]]**

Out[67]= 28

Grid graphs are bipartite, for the vertices can be partitioned like the squares on a chessboard.

In[68]:= **TwoColoring[GridGraph[4,5]]**

Out[68]= {1, 2, 1, 2, 2, 1, 2, 1, 1, 2, 1, 2, 2, 1, 2, 1,
      1, 2, 1, 2}

■ 6.2.6 Interconnection Networks

A parallel computer consists of some number of processors connected by an *interconnection network*. Designers of parallel computers typically seek interconnection networks that have few connections but have a small diameter and in which routing of information is easy. The *hypercube* is one of the most versatile and efficient networks for parallel computation [Lei92]. One drawback of the hypercube is that the number of connections to each processor grows logarithmically with the size of the network. Several *hypercubic networks* have been proposed to overcome this problem, including the butterfly, shuffle exchange, and the De Bruijn graphs. In this section, we describe graph-theoretic properties of these networks and provide constructors for them.

Hypercubes

An *n-dimensional hypercube* or an *n-cube* is defined as the product of K_2 and an $(n-1)$-dimensional hypercube. This recursive definition can be used to construct them.

```
Hypercube[n_Integer] := Hypercube1[n]

Hypercube1[0] := CompleteGraph[1]
Hypercube1[1] := Path[2]
Hypercube1[2] := Cycle[4]

Hypercube1[n_Integer] := Hypercube1[n] =
        GraphProduct[
                RotateVertices[Hypercube1[Floor[n/2]], 2Pi/5],
                Hypercube1[Ceiling[n/2]]
        ]
```

Constructing Hypercubes

All hypercubes are Hamiltonian, as proven in Section 2.3.2 when we constructed the binary-reflected Gray code. The vertices of an *n*-dimensional hypercube can be labeled with length *n* binary strings such that adjacent vertices differ in exactly 1 bit. Such labelings can be constructed recursively. Label the two vertices of a one-dimensional hypercube 0 and 1. Partition an *n*-dimensional hypercube into two $(n-1)$-dimensional hypercubes and prepend 0 to the vertex labels of one $(n-1)$-dimensional hypercube and 1 to the vertex labels of the other.

Here is a four-dimensional hypercube. It can be viewed as two three-dimensional cubes connected in a symmetric way. An *n*-dimensional hypercube has 2^n vertices, with each vertex having degree *n*, for an total of $n2^{n-1}$ edges.

In[69]:= **ShowGraph[g = Hypercube[4]];**

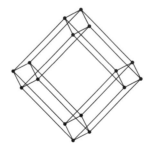

This shows the distribution of vertices according to their distance from a particular vertex in a *d*-dimensional hypercube. Does it look familiar? These numbers are binomial coefficients, reinforcing the connection between subsets, binary strings, and hypercubes.

```
In[70]:= Table[ Distribution[ First[ AllPairsShortestPath[Hypercube[i]] ] ],
            {i,0,6}] // TableForm
Out[70]//TableForm= 1
```

1	1					
1	2	1				
1	3	3	1			
1	4	6	4	1		
1	5	10	10	5	1	
1	6	15	20	15	6	1

All *n*-cubes are bipartite, as can be seen from the recursive construction.

```
In[71]:= c = TwoColoring[g];
         v1 = Flatten[Position[c, 1]]; v2 = Flatten[Position[c, 2]];
         ShowGraph[ Highlight[g, {v1}]]
```

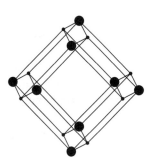

Butterfly Graphs

The *r-dimensional butterfly graph* has $(r+1)2^r$ vertices and $r2^{r+1}$ edges. The vertices correspond to pairs (w, i), where i is the *level* or *dimension* of the vertex $(0 \le i \le r)$ and w is an *r*-bit binary number that denotes the *row* of the vertex. Two vertices (w, i) and $(w', i+1)$ are connected by an edge if and only if either (i) w and w' are identical, or (ii) w and w' differ in precisely the $(i+1)$th bit.

```
Options[ButterflyGraph] = {VertexLabel->False}

ButterflyGraph[n_Integer?Positive, opts___?OptionQ] :=
    Module[{v = Map[Flatten, CartesianProduct[Strings[{0, 1}, n], Range[0, n]]], label},
        label = VertexLabel /. Flatten[{opts, Options[ButterflyGraph]}];
        RankedEmbedding[
            MakeUndirected[
                MakeGraph[v,
                    (#1[[n+1]]+1 == #2[[n+1]]) &&
                    (#1[[Range[#2[[n+1]]-1]]] == #2[[Range[#2[[n+1]]-1]]]) &&
                    (#1[[Range[#2[[n+1]]+1, n]]] == #2[[Range[#2[[n+1]]+1, n]]])&,
```

```
                    VertexLabel -> label
            ]
        ],
        Flatten[Position[v, {__, 0}]]
    ]
]
```

Constructing a Butterfly Graph

To construct a butterfly graph, we use `CartesianProduct` to obtain the set of all pairs (w, i) and then `MakeGraph` to construct the edges from the pairs. `MakeGraph` takes as input the set of vertices (w, i) and a Boolean predicate that indicates which pairs of vertices are to be connected by edges. Finally, a ranked embedding of the graph is constructed, with rows representing vertices that have identical w and columns representing vertices that have identical levels.

This is the two-dimensional butterfly graph. To produce cleaner labels, i is appended to w in the label for vertex (w, i). Edges that connect vertices with the same binary string are called *straight* edges. The remaining edges are called *cross* edges and go between level i and level $i + 1$ vertices that differ in the $(i + 1)$th bit.

```
In[74]:= ShowGraph[g = ButterflyGraph[2, VertexLabel -> True],
             TextStyle->{FontSize->12}, PlotRange->0.2];
```

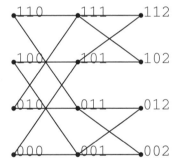

Here we show a series of graphs obtained by contracting rows of vertices in a three-dimensional butterfly. The bottommost row is contracted first, then the row above it, and so on. The contracted vertices end up on a vertical line with multiple edges between pairs of these. At the end we have eight vertices on a vertical line with the multiple edges making a nice pattern.

```
In[75]:= g = Contract[ButterflyGraph[3], {1, 2, 3, 4}];
         ShowGraphArray[Partition[l = NestList[Contract[#,
         {1, 2, 3, 4}] &, g, 7], 4]];
```

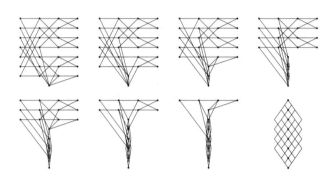

We start with the final 8-vertex graph obtained by repeatedly contracting the butterfly graph, make it simple by getting rid of multiple edges, and finally give it a new embedding to reveal it as a three-dimensional hypercube, which is just a "folded-up" butterfly. If all vertices from the same level in an *r*-dimensional butterfly are contracted to a single vertex, we get an *r*-dimensional hypercube.

```
In[77]:= ShowGraphArray[{g = l[[8]], h = RandomVertices[MakeSimple[g]],
         SpringEmbedding[h,200] }, VertexStyle->Disk[0.06]];
```

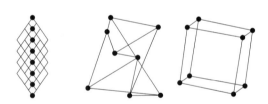

The butterfly graph also has a beautiful recursive structure. Deleting the level 0 vertices of an *r*-dimensional butterfly leaves two (*r* − 1)-dimensional butterflies, as shown in the graph on the left. Deleting the level *r* vertices *also* gives two (*r* − 1)-dimensional butterflies. This is shown on the right, though it is less obvious that this graph has two connected components.

```
In[78]:= ShowGraphArray[{DeleteVertices[g = ButterflyGraph[3],
         Table[i, {i, 1, V[g], 4}]],
         h = DeleteVertices[g, Table[i, {i, 4, V[g], 4}]]}]
```

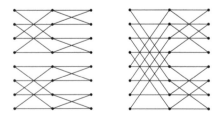

The graph obtained by deleting the level r vertices from an r-dimensional butterfly indeed contains two equal-sized connected components.

```
In[79]:= w = ConnectedComponents[h]

Out[79]= {{1, 2, 3, 7, 8, 9, 13, 14, 15, 19, 20, 21},
         {4, 5, 6, 10, 11, 12, 16, 17, 18, 22, 23, 24}}
```

Further, each of these components is isomorphic to the two-dimensional butterfly.

```
In[80]:= {IsomorphicQ[InduceSubgraph[h, w[[1]]], ButterflyGraph[2]],
          IsomorphicQ[InduceSubgraph[h, w[[2]]], ButterflyGraph[2]]}

Out[80]= {True, True}
```

There is a unique shortest path between each level 0 vertex w and each level r vertex w'. The path traverses each level exactly once, using the cross edge from level i to level $(i + 1)$ if and only if w and w' differ in the $(i + 1)$st bit. A consequence of this is that N-vertex butterflies have diameter $O(\log N)$.

```
In[81]:= ShowGraph[Highlight[g = ButterflyGraph[4],
          {Partition[ShortestPath[g, 1, 70], 2, 1]} ]];
```

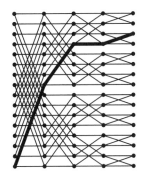

Shuffle-Exchange Graphs

The r-dimensional *shuffle-exchange* graph has $N = 2^r$ vertices and $3 \cdot 2^{r-1}$ edges. Each vertex corresponds to a unique r-bit binary string, and two vertices u and v are connected by an edge if (a) u and v differ precisely in the last bit or (b) u is a left or right cyclic shift of v. If u and v differ in the last bit, the edge is called an *exchange edge*; otherwise the edge is called a *shuffle edge*.

```
Options[ShuffleExchangeGraph] = {VertexLabel -> False}

ShuffleExchangeGraph[n_Integer?Positive, opts___?OptionQ] :=
    Module[{label},
        label = VertexLabel /. Flatten[{opts, Options[MakeGraph]}];
        MakeGraph[Strings[{0, 1}, n],
            (Last[#1] != Last[#2]) && (Take[#1,(n-1)]==Take[#2,(n-1)]) ||
            (RotateRight[#1,1] == #2) || (RotateLeft[#1, 1] == #2)&,
            Type -> Undirected, VertexLabel -> label
        ]
    ]
```

Constructing a Shuffle-Exchange Graph

The three-dimensional shuffle-exchange graph is shown here to reveal its recursive structure. Consider the vertex 011. It is connected by an exchange edge to 010 and by shuffle edges to 101 and 110. A few applications of `SpringEmbedding` produces the drawing that is more often seen in textbooks.

```
In[82]:= ShowGraphArray[{g = ShuffleExchangeGraph[3, VertexLabel -> True],
             SpringEmbedding[g, 100]}, PlotRange -> 0.1];
```

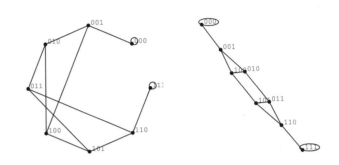

Here we report a shortest path between a pair of randomly chosen vertices in a five-dimensional shuffle-exchange graph. Note that every vertex is obtained from the previous one by either a shuffle operation or an exchange operation.

```
In[83]:= g = ShuffleExchangeGraph[5, VertexLabel -> True];
         s = Random[Integer, {1, 32}]; t = Random[Integer, {1, 32}];
         GetVertexLabels[g][[ShortestPath[g, s, t]]]
Out[85]= {01111, 01110, 00111, 00110, 00011, 10001}
```

Any r-bit binary string u can be converted to any other r-bit binary string v by $r - 1$ shuffles and at most r exchanges. This implies that an r-dimensional shuffle-exchange graph has diameter $2r - 1 = 2\log N - 1$. Going from $00...0$ to $11...1$ requires exactly r exchanges for a total of $2r - 1$ operations.

```
In[86]:= Table[Diameter[ShuffleExchangeGraph[i]], {i, 1, 7}]
Out[86]= {1, 3, 5, 7, 9, 11, 13}
```

De Bruijn Graphs

The *r-dimensional De Bruijn graph* consists of 2^r vertices and 2^{r+1} directed edges. Each vertex corresponds to a unique r-bit binary string. There is a directed edge from each node $u_1 u_2 ... u_r$ to $u_2 u_3 ... u_r 0$ and to $u_2 u_3 ... u_r 1$. Each vertex in a De Bruijn graph has in-degree 2 and out-degree 2. *Combinatorica* provides a function `DeBruijnGraph` that constructs De Bruijn graphs.

This shows the three-dimensional De Bruijn graph. Each vertex has in-degree 2 and out-degree 2, assuming that the self-loops at vertices 000 and 111 each contribute one in-coming and one out-going edge. Applying SpringEmbedding to the De Bruijn graph reveals the symmetry in its structure.

```
In[87]:= ShowGraphArray[{g = DeBruijnGraph[{0, 1}, 4, VertexLabel -> True],
           SpringEmbedding[g, 100]}];
```

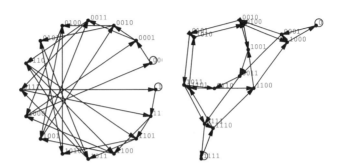

The function DeBruijnGraph also constructs graphs over alphabets with more than two elements. Here the nine vertices correspond to all ternary strings of length 2. For each string x and each symbol α in the alphabet, there is an edge going from x to the string obtained by shifting x to the left one position and inserting α into the last position. In the case of the ternary De Bruijn graph, this means that each vertex has in-degree and out-degree equal to 3.

```
In[88]:= ShowGraph[SpringEmbedding[ DeBruijnGraph[3, 3] ]];
```

The important connection between shuffle-exchange graphs and De Bruijn graphs is as follows. Take an $(r + 1)$-dimensional shuffle-exchange graph and "contract" out all the exchange edges from the graph. In other words, replace every pair of vertices $u_1 u_2 ... u_r 0$ and $u_1 u_2 ... u_r 1$ by $u_1 u_2 ... u_r$. This leaves only the shuffle edges.

```
In[89]:= g = ShuffleExchangeGraph[4]; Do[g = Contract[g, {1, 2}], {8}];
           g = MakeSimple[g]; ShowGraph[Nest[SpringEmbedding, g, 10]];
```

The resulting graph is isomorphic to the undirected version of the De Bruijn graph.

```
In[91]:= IsomorphicQ[g, MakeSimple[DeBruijnGraph[2, 3]]]
Out[91]= True
```

6.3 Trees

A *tree* is a connected graph with no cycles. Trees are the simplest interesting class of graphs, so "Can you prove it for trees?" should be the first question asked after formulating a new graph-theoretic conjecture. In this section we first discuss the problem of enumerating labeled trees. With most enumeration problems, counting the number of unlabeled objects is harder than counting the number of labeled ones, and so it is with trees. Algorithms for the systematic generation of free and rooted trees appear in [NW78, Wil89].

■ 6.3.1 Labeled Trees

One of the first theorems in graphical enumeration was Cayley's proof [Cay89] that there are n^{n-2} distinct labeled trees on n vertices. Prüfer [Pr8] established a bijection between such trees and strings of $n-2$ integers between 1 and n, providing a constructive proof of Cayley's result. This bijection can then be exploited to give algorithms for systematically and randomly generating labeled trees.

The key to Prüfer's bijection is the observation that for any tree there are always at least two *leaves*, that is, vertices of degree 1. Start with an n-vertex tree T, whose vertices are labeled 1 through n. Let u be the leaf with the smallest label and let v be the neighbor of u. Note that u and v are uniquely defined. We now let v be the first symbol in our string, or Prüfer code. After deleting vertex u we have a tree on $n-1$ vertices, and repeating this operation until only one edge is left gives us $n-2$ integers between 1 and n.

```
LabeledTreeToCode[g_Graph] :=
    Module[{e=ToAdjacencyLists[g],i,code},
        Table [
                {i} = First[ Position[ Map[Length,e], 1 ] ];
                code = e[[i,1]];
                e[[code]] = Complement[ e[[code]], {i} ];
                e[[i]] = {};
                code,
                {V[g]-2}
            ]
        ]
    ]
```

Constructing a Prüfer Code from a Labeled Tree

To reconstruct T from its Prüfer code, we observe that a particular vertex appears in the code exactly one time less than its degree in T. Thus we can compute the degree sequence of T and thereby identify the lowest labeled degree-1 vertex in the tree. Since the first symbol in the code is the vertex it is incident upon, we have determined the first edge and, by induction, the entire tree.

```
CodeToLabeledTree[l_List] :=
     Module[{m=Range[Length[l]+2],x,i},
          FromUnorderedPairs[
               Append[
                    Table[
                         x = Min[Complement[m,Drop[l,i-1]]];
                         m = Complement[m,{x}];
                         Sort[{x,l[[i]]}],
                         {i,Length[l]}
                    ],
                    Sort[m]
               ]
          ]
     ] /; (Complement[l, Range[Length[l]+2]] == {})
```

Constructing a Labeled Tree from its Code

A star contains $n - 1$ vertices of degree 1, all incident on one center. Since the degree of a particular vertex is one more than its frequency in the Prüfer code, the ith labeled star is defined by a code of $n - 2$ i's.

In[92]:= **ShowGraph[RadialEmbedding[**
          CodeToLabeledTree[{10,10,10,10,10,10,10,10}]]];

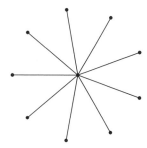

Since there is a bijection between trees and codes, composing the two functions gives an identity operation.

In[93]:= **LabeledTreeToCode[CodeToLabeledTree[{3,3,3,2,3}]]**

Out[93]= {3, 3, 3, 2, 3}

Each labeled path on n vertices is represented by a pair of permutations of length n, for a total of $n!/2$ distinct labeled paths. The Prüfer codes of paths are exactly the sequences of $n - 2$ distinct integers, since the two vertices of degree 1 do not appear in the code.

In[94]:= **LabeledTreeToCode[Path[10]]**

Out[94]= {2, 3, 4, 5, 6, 7, 8, 9}

Enumerating all labeled trees is a matter of enumerating Prüfer codes and applying CodeToLabeledTree. Here we use the function Strings to enumerate Prüfer codes for 5-vertex trees and then convert the first six codes into labeled trees. There are only two distinct unlabeled trees in this list because the last five trees are isomorphic.

```
In[95]:= s = Strings[Range[5], 3];
         ShowGraphArray[Partition[Map[CodeToLabeledTree,
         s[[Range[6]]]], 3], VertexNumber -> True,
         TextStyle -> {FontSize -> 12}];
```

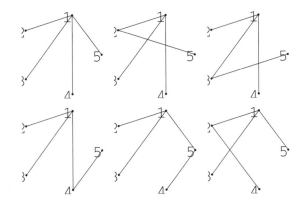

Cayley's result was the first of many in graphical enumeration [HP73], counting how many distinct graphs of a given type exist. An interesting table of the number of a dozen different types of graphs on up to eight vertices appears in [RW97, Wil85].

The bijection between Prüfer codes and labeled trees yields an algorithm for selecting a random labeled tree. Simply generate a random Prüfer code and convert it into the tree.

```
RandomTree[1] := Graph[{}, {{{0, 0}}}]
RandomTree[n_Integer?Positive] :=
       RadialEmbedding[CodeToLabeledTree[Table[Random[Integer,{1,n}], {n-2}] ], 1]
```

Selecting a Random Labeled Tree

Here are four randomly selected 10-vertex trees. RandomTree uses a radial embedding as the default embedding for the constructed tree.

```
In[97]:= ShowGraphArray[Table[RandomTree[10], {2}],
         VertexStyle -> Disk[0.05]];
```

■ 6.3.2 Complete Trees

In a rooted tree, the distance between a vertex v and the root is called the *depth* of v. The maximum depth of any vertex in a rooted tree is the *height* of the tree. A *k-ary tree* is a rooted tree in which each vertex has at most k children. A *complete k-ary tree* is a k-ary tree in which all vertices at depth $h-1$ or less have exactly k children, where h is the height of the tree. With this definition, for fixed n and k, there can be several distinct n-vertex complete k-ary trees, depending on how the leaves of the tree are distributed. The function `CompleteKaryTree` takes as input n and k and produces a complete k-ary tree with n vertices in which leaves in the last level are all on the "left."

These are complete k-ary trees with 20 vertices for $1 \leq k \leq 5$. Notice that the tree gets shorter with increasing k. A special case of a complete k-ary tree is a complete binary tree, where $k = 2$.

In[98]:= **ShowGraphArray[Table[CompleteKaryTree[20, i], {i,5}]];**

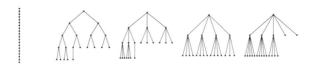

A *complete binary tree* is a special case of complete k-ary trees for $k = 2$. `CompleteBinaryTree` produces complete binary trees.

In[99]:= **ShowGraph[CompleteBinaryTree[31]]**

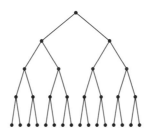

6.4 Random Graphs

The easiest way to generate a graph is by tossing a coin for each edge to decide whether it should be included. The theory of *random graphs* considers questions of the type, "What density of edges in a graph is necessary, on average, to ensure that the graph has monotone graph property X?". A *monotone graph property* is an invariant that is preserved as more edges are added, such as whether the graph is connected or has a cycle. The theory of random graphs was introduced by Erdös and Renyi in a classic paper [ER60].

■ 6.4.1 Constructing Random Graphs

The classical theory of random graphs deals with two primary models. In the first, a parameter p represents the probability that any given edge is in the graph. In other words, each edge is chosen *independently* with probability p to be in the graph. When $p = 1/2$, this model generates all labeled graphs with equal probability, since the edge probabilities are independent.

The simplest way to construct a random graph in this model is to build an adjacency matrix in which each entry is set to 1 with probability p. However, the running time of this algorithm is $\Theta(n^2)$, independent of p. When p is very small, the graph has few edges, so this is rather inefficient. We make the algorithm much faster by noting that the number of edges in the graph has a binomial distribution with $\binom{n}{2}$ trials, each with success of probability p. The *Mathematica* add-on package `Statistics`DiscreteDistributions`` contains a function `BinomialDistribution` that allows us to define a random variable d that has this distribution with the appropriate parameters. Picking a random value for this random variable gives us the number of edges the graph should have. We then use the *Combinatorica* function `RandomKSubset` to generate a random subset of size d of the set $\{1, 2, \ldots, \binom{n}{2}\}$, which gives us the indices of the edges in the graph. Finally, we turn these indices into actual edges by using the *Combinatorica* function `NthPair`.

```
RandomGraph[n_Integer?Positive, p_?NumericQ, opts___?OptionQ] :=
    Module[{type},
        type = Type /. Flatten[{opts, Options[RandomGraph]}];
        If[type === Directed, RDG[n, p], RG[n, p] ]
    ]

RG[n_, p_] :=
    Module[{d = BinomialDistribution[Binomial[n, 2], p]},
        Graph[Map[{NthPair[#]}&, RandomKSubset[Range[Binomial[n,2]], Random[d]]], CircularEmbedding[n]]
    ]
```

Constructing Model 1 Random Graphs

NthPair is a function that unranks all unordered pairs of positive integers.

In[100]:= **NthPair[1000000]**

Out[100]= {1009, 1415}

The ordering that NthPair assumes is shown here as a directed path. From the picture, it is clear that if n is the rank of the unordered pair (i, j), then j is the largest integer such that $(j-1)(j-2)/2 \le n$ and $i = n - (j-1)(j-2)/2$. The code for NthPair solves this quadratic equation for j.

In[101]:= **ShowGraph[ChangeVertices[MakeGraph[v = Map[NthPair, Range[15]],**
        Position[v, #1][[1, 1]] + 1 == Position[v, #2][[1, 1]] &,
        VertexLabel -> True], v], TextStyle->{FontSize->10},
        PlotRange->0.2];

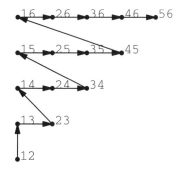

```
NthPair = Compile[{{n, _Integer}},
        Module[{j}, j = Ceiling[(1 + Sqrt[1 + 8n])/2]; {Round[n - (j-1)(j-2)/2], j}]
     ]
```
Unranking Unordered Pairs

This shows 10-vertex random graphs with increasing p, from 0 to 1. We start with an empty graph and end up with a complete graph as p increases.

In[102]:= **ShowGraphArray[Table[RandomGraph[10, p], {p, 0, 1, .25}]];**

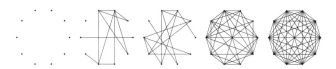

The interesting issue in random graph theory is how many edges are needed before the graph can be expected to have some monotone graph property. Random graph theory is discussed in [Bol79, ES74, Pal85, JLR00]. Through the probabilistic model, it can be proven that almost all graphs are connected and almost all graphs are nonplanar.

Large model 1 random graphs with probability 1/2 seem likely to be connected, while those with probability $1/n$ seem disconnected. At what p does the transition from disconnected to connected take place? These kinds of questions are addressed by random graph theory.

```
In[103]:= {Map[ConnectedQ, Table[RandomGraph[n, .5], {n, 100, 200, 15}]],
           Map[ConnectedQ, Table[RandomGraph[n, 1/n], {n, 100, 200, 15}]]} //
          TableForm
Out[103]//TableForm=
          True    True    True    True    True    True    True
          False   False   False   False   False   False   False
```

There are eight labeled graphs on three vertices. When the edge probability is 1/2, each is equally likely to occur. Larger complete catalogs of graphs appear in [RW97] and on the page maintained by Gordon Royle [Roy02].

```
In[104]:= Distribution[ Table[RandomGraph[3,0.5], {200}] ]
Out[104]= {25, 26, 23, 21, 27, 29, 22, 27}
```

Random directed graphs can be constructed in a similar manner by using the option `Type -> Directed`.

```
In[105]:= ShowGraph[ RandomGraph[10, .3, Type -> Directed]];
```

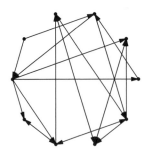

The second model generates random unlabeled graphs with exactly m edges, which is difficult to do both efficiently and correctly, since it implies describing the set of nonisomorphic graphs. Our algorithm produces random *labeled* graphs of the given size, by selecting m integers from 1 to $\binom{n}{2}$ and defining a bijection between such integers and ordered pairs. This does not result in a random unlabeled graph, as shown in the following example.

```
ExactRandomGraph[n_Integer,e_Integer] :=
      Graph[Map[{NthPair[#]}&, Take[ RandomPermutation[n(n-1)/2], e] ], CircularEmbedding[n]]
```

Constructing Random Labeled Graphs on m Edges

This shows the six unlabeled 5-vertex graphs with four edges. Of these, three are trees, one of which is the path of length 5.

In[106]:= **ShowGraphArray[Partition[ListGraphs[5, 4], 3]];**

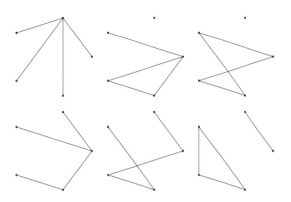

Here we generate 1000 instances of 5-vertex random graphs via `ExactRandomGraph`, each containing four edges. Very few are identical, but...

In[107]:= **Length[Union[l = Table[ExactRandomGraph[5, 4], {1000}]]]**

Out[107]= 910

...many are isomorphic. More than a quarter of the random trees are 5-paths. If `ExactRandomGraph` had generated unlabeled graphs uniformly at random, this number would have been about one-sixth of the total number generated.

In[108]:= **Count[Map[TreeIsomorphismQ[Path[5], #] &, l], True]**

Out[108]= 272

Stars are extremely rare as random labeled trees. Why?

In[109]:= **Count[Map[TreeIsomorphismQ[Star[5], #] &, l], True]**

Out[109]= 37

■ 6.4.2 Realizing Degree Sequences

The *degree sequence* of an undirected graph is the number of edges incident on each vertex. Perhaps the most elementary theorem in graph theory is that the sum of the degree sequence for any graph must be even, or, equivalently, that any simple graph has an even number of odd-degree vertices. By convention, degree sequences are sorted into decreasing order. The degree of a vertex is sometimes called its *valency*, and the minimum and maximum degrees of graph G are denoted $\delta(G)$ and $\Delta(G)$, respectively.

A degree sequence is *graphic* if there exists a simple graph with that degree sequence. Erdös and Gallai [EG60] proved that a degree sequence is graphic if and only if the sequence observes the following condition for each integer $r < n$:

$$\sum_{i=1}^{r} d_i \le r(r-1) + \sum_{i=r+1}^{n} \min(r, d_i).$$

The Erdös-Gallai condition also generalizes to directed graphs [Ful65, Rys57].

Alternatively, [Hak62, Hav55] proved that if a degree sequence is graphic, there exists a graph G where the vertex of highest degree is adjacent to the $\Delta(G)$ next highest degree vertices of G. This gives an inductive definition of a graphic degree sequence, as well as a construction of a graph that realizes it.

```
DegreeSequence[g_Graph] := Reverse[ Sort[ Degrees[g] ] ]
Degrees[g_Graph] := Map[Length, ToAdjacencyLists[g]]

GraphicQ[s_List] := False /; (Min[s] < 0) || (Max[s] >= Length[s])
GraphicQ[s_List] := (First[s] == 0) /; (Length[s] == 1)
GraphicQ[s_List] :=
    Module[{m,sorted = Reverse[Sort[s]]},
        m = First[sorted];
        GraphicQ[ Join[ Take[sorted,{2,m+1}]-1, Drop[sorted,m+1] ] ]
    ]
```

Identifying Graphic Degree Sequences

The degree sequence shows that K_{30} is a 29-regular graph.

```
In[110]:= DegreeSequence[CompleteGraph[30]]
```

```
Out[110]= {29, 29, 29, 29, 29, 29, 29, 29, 29, 29, 29, 29,
           29, 29, 29, 29, 29, 29, 29, 29, 29, 29, 29, 29,
           29, 29, 29, 29}
```

Degrees returns the degrees of vertices in vertex order, whereas DegreeSequence produces these in nonincreasing order.

```
In[111]:= g = RandomGraph[10, .5];
          {Degrees[g], DegreeSequence[g]} // ColumnForm
```

```
Out[112]= {3, 3, 3, 6, 5, 4, 3, 6, 5, 8}
          {8, 6, 6, 5, 5, 4, 3, 3, 3, 3}
```

By definition, the degree sequence of any graph is graphic.

```
In[113]:= GraphicQ[DegreeSequence[RandomGraph[10,1/2]]]
```

```
Out[113]= True
```

The diagonal of the square of the adjacency matrix of a simple graph gives the unsorted degree sequence of the graph. This is because the square of the adjacency matrix counts the number of walks of length 2 between any pair of vertices, and the only walks of length 2 from a vertex to itself are to an adjacent vertex and directly back again.

```
In[114]:= (g = RealizeDegreeSequence[{3, 2, 2, 1}];
          TableForm[ToAdjacencyMatrix[g].ToAdjacencyMatrix[g]])
```

```
Out[114]//TableForm= 3   1   1   0
                     1   2   1   1
                     1   1   2   1
                     0   1   1   1
```

No degree sequence can be graphic if all the degrees occur with multiplicity 1 [BC67]. Any sequence of positive integers summing up to an even number can be realized by a multigraph with self-loops [Hak62].

```
In[115]:= GraphicQ[{7,6,5,4,3,2,1}]
Out[115]= False
```

The direct implementation of the inductive definition of graphic degree sequences gives a deterministic algorithm for realizing any such sequence. However, GraphicQ provides a means to construct semirandom graphs of a particular degree sequence. We attempt to connect the vertex of degree Δ to a random set of Δ other vertices. If, after deleting 1 from the degrees of each of these vertices, the remaining sequence is graphic, then there exists a way to finish off the construction of the graph appropriately. If not, we keep trying other random vertex sets until it does.

This algorithm does not pick a graph that realizes the given degree sequence, uniformly at random. Generating a graph that realizes a given degree sequence, uniformly at random, is a fairly hard problem [Luc92, MR98, MR95] that has drawn some attention lately due to applications in modeling the Web as a graph [ACL00, ACL01]. Our algorithm produces some graphs more often than others, but the function is still useful to produce test graphs satisfying certain degree constraints.

This is a graphic sequence, since it is the degree sequence of a graph.

```
In[116]:= d = DegreeSequence[g = RandomGraph[10, .25]]
Out[116]= {3, 2, 2, 2, 2, 2, 1, 0, 0, 0}
```

We apply RealizeDegreeSequence to produce graphs that realize this degree sequence. Since the function is randomized, its output may differ for different runs. If treated as labeled graphs, these two graphs are likely to be distinct. It is also possible that these are distinct unlabeled graphs.

```
In[117]:= ShowGraphArray[{g, RealizeDegreeSequence[d]}];
```

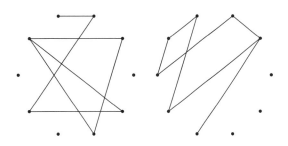

Most of these entries should be false, indicating that the generated graphs are nonisomorphic even if they have the same degree sequence.

```
In[118]:= Map[IsomorphicQ[g, #]&, Table[RealizeDegreeSequence[d], {10}]]
Out[118]= {False, True, False, False, False, False, False,
           False, False, False}
```

Here `RealizeDegreeSequence` is called with a second argument that is an integer seed for the random number generator used in the function. Specifying a seed has the effect of making the function deterministic, so all five graphs generated here are identical.

```
In[119]:= Map[IdenticalQ[#, RealizeDegreeSequence[d,4]] &,
                Table[RealizeDegreeSequence[d,4], {5}]]
Out[119]= {True, True, True, True, True}
```

The construction is powerful enough to produce disconnected graphs when there is no other way to realize the degree sequence.

```
In[120]:= ConnectedComponents[ RealizeDegreeSequence[{2,2,2,1,1,1,1}] ]
Out[120]= {{1, 2, 3, 5, 7}, {4, 6}}
```

An important set of degree sequences are defined by *regular graphs*. A graph is regular if all vertices are of equal degree. An algorithm for constructing regular random graphs appears in [Wor84], although here we construct semirandom regular graphs as a special case of `RealizeDegreeSequence`.

```
RegularQ[g_Graph] := Apply[ Equal, Degrees[g] ]
RegularGraph[k_Integer, n_Integer] := RealizeDegreeSequence[Table[k,{n}]]
```

Constructing and Testing Regular Graphs

Here we construct and test a 4-regular graph on eight vertices. All cycles and complete graphs are regular.

```
In[121]:= RegularQ[ RegularGraph[4,8]]
Out[121]= True
```

Complete bipartite graphs are regular if and only if the two stages contain equal numbers of vertices.

```
In[122]:= RegularQ[CompleteGraph[10,9]]
Out[122]= False
```

The join of two regular graphs is not necessarily regular.

```
In[123]:= DegreeSequence[GraphJoin[Cycle[4], CompleteGraph[2]]]
Out[123]= {5, 5, 4, 4, 4, 4}
```

Constructing regular graphs is a special case of realizing arbitrary degree sequences. Here we build a 3-regular graph of order 12. Such graphs are the adjacency graphs of convex polyhedra.

```
In[124]:= ShowGraph[g = RegularGraph[3, 12]; Nest[SpringEmbedding, g, 5]];
```

6.5 Relations and Functional Graphs

The reason graphs are so important for modeling structures is that they are natural representations of binary relations. Here we provide tools for constructing graphs out of relationships between objects.

■ 6.5.1 Graphs from Relations

As defined in Section 3.3.3, a binary relation R on a set of objects S is a subset of the Cartesian product $S \times S$. Thus each element in R is an ordered pair of elements from S, and therefore R can be represented by a directed graph. `MakeGraph` takes a set of objects and a binary relation defined on the objects, and constructs a graph whose edges are defined by the binary relation. `MakeGraph` has quietly been used to construct many *Combinatorica* graphs, including butterfly, shuffle-exchange, and De Bruijn graphs.

The binary relation "u is not equal to v" defines a complete graph on the given set of objects. The relation is symmetric, and so the direction on edges is ignored by using the `Type` option.

```
In[125]:= CompleteQ[ MakeGraph[Range[5], (#1!=#2)&, Type->Undirected]]
Out[125]= True
```

The *odd graphs* O_k [Big74] have vertices corresponding to the $k-1$ subsets of $\{1, ..., 2k-1\}$ where two vertices are connected by an edge if and only if the associated subsets are disjoint. O_2 gives K_3, and here we prove that O_3 is the Petersen graph.

```
In[126]:= Isomorphism[PetersenGraph, MakeGraph[KSubsets[Range[5],2],
            (SameQ[Intersection[#1,#2], {}])&, Type -> Undirected]]
Out[126]= {1, 2, 8, 10, 7, 9, 6, 4, 5, 3}
```

Permutations differing by one transposition can be ordered by the number of inversions. The *inversion poset* [SW86] relates permutations p and q if there is a sequence of transpositions from p to q such that each transposition increases the number of inversions. Inversion posets and other partial orders are discussed in detail in Section 8.5. We can begin construction of this graph by linking all permutations that differ by one transposition in the direction of increasing disorder.

```
In[127]:= ShowGraph[SpringEmbedding[g=MakeGraph[ Permutations[{1,2,3,4}],
            (Count[#1-#2,0] == 2 && (Inversions[#1]>Inversions[#2]))&]]];
```

Taking the *transitive closure* of the previous graph adds an edge between any two vertices connected by a path, thus completing the construction of the inversion poset. The *Hasse diagram* of a poset eliminates those edges implied by other edges in the graph and ranks the vertices according to their position in the defined order. Here, the lowest ranked vertex corresponds to the identity permutation and the highest ranked vertex to its reverse. Each path from bottom to top through this lattice defines a sequence of transpositions that increase the number of inversions.

`In[128]:= ShowGraphArray[{h = TransitiveClosure[g], HasseDiagram[h]}];`

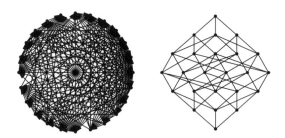

■ 6.5.2 Functional Graphs

A *functional graph* is a directed graph defined by a set of functions. More precisely, given a set S of objects and a set F of functions $f : S \to S$, the graph has vertex set S and for each $v \in S$ and each function $f \in F$ the graph contains a directed edge from v to $f(v)$.

Here, the vertices are 4-permutations with edges joining permutations π and π' if π' can be obtained by swapping either the first two elements or the second and third elements. `SpringEmbedding` reveals that the graph contains four disjoint 6-cycles, corresponding to the six 4-permutations that contain a given last element.

```
In[129]:= ShowGraph[SpringEmbedding[FunctionalGraph[
              {Permute[#, {2, 1, 3, 4}]&, Permute[#, {1, 3, 2, 4}] &},
              Permutations[4], Type -> Undirected]]];
```

Adding one more function to the list of functions changes the structure of the graph dramatically. Now we get the familiar adjacent transposition graph. `MakeGraph` was used to construct this graph in Section 2.1.4.

```
In[130]:= ShowGraph[SpringEmbedding[FunctionalGraph[
            {Permute[#, {2, 1, 3, 4}] &, Permute[#, {1, 3, 2, 4}] &,
            Permute[#, {1, 2, 4, 3}] &}, Permutations[4],
            Type -> Undirected]]];
```

`FunctionalGraph` provides a convenient way of constructing *Cayley graphs*. A Cayley graph is defined by a group G and a set of generators S for G. The vertices of the graph are elements of G, and there is an edge from group element g to group element h if there is a generator s in S such that $g \times s = h$.

Here is a set of generators for the symmetric group of order 4. Each generator is obtained by swapping an element with the first element.

```
In[131]:= s=Table[p=Range[4]; {p[[1]],p[[i]]}={p[[i]],p[[1]]};
            p, {i,2,4}]
Out[131]= {{2, 1, 3, 4}, {3, 2, 1, 4}, {4, 2, 3, 1}}
```

These generators are converted into "functional forms" that can be used as the set of functions in `FunctionalGraph`.

```
In[132]:= l = Map[Function[x, Permute[x, #]] &, s]
Out[132]= {Function[x, Permute[x, {2, 1, 3, 4}]],
            Function[x, Permute[x, {3, 2, 1, 4}]],
            Function[x, Permute[x, {4, 2, 3, 1}]]]}
```

Here is the Cayley graph defined by the above set of generators. It is a cubic graph because there are three generators.

```
In[133]:= g = FunctionalGraph[l, Permutations[4], Type -> Undirected];
            ShowGraph[Nest[SpringEmbedding, g, 10]];
```

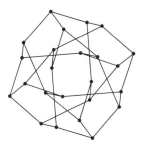

The diameter of this graph is the number of operations needed to sort a permutation, assuming each operation swaps an element with the first element.

```
In[135]:= Map[(UnrankPermutation[#-1,4])&, ShortestPath[g,
              RankPermutation[{1,2,3,4}]+1,
                    RankPermutation[{4,3,2,1}]+1]]
Out[135]= {{1, 2, 3, 4}, {2, 1, 3, 4}, {3, 1, 2, 4},
            {1, 3, 2, 4}, {4, 3, 2, 1}}
```

Both MakeGraph and FunctionalGraph can be used to construct the same graph. Sometimes one is more convenient than the other.

```
In[136]:= n = 300;
          Timing[h = MakeGraph[Range[0, n - 1],
            (Mod[#1 + 1, n] == #2) || (Mod[#1 + 2, n] == #2) &]]
Out[137]= {11.5 Second, -Graph:<600, 300, Directed>-}
```

FunctionalGraph is faster for sparse graphs, since MakeGraph fills the adjacency matrix of the graph and thus takes $O(n^2)$ time independent of the size of the graph.

```
In[138]:= Timing[g = FunctionalGraph[{Mod[# + 1, n] &, Mod[# + 2, n] &},
              Range[0, n - 1]]]
Out[138]= {0.31 Second, -Graph:<600, 300, Directed>-}
```

The two graphs constructed above are indeed identical.

```
In[139]:= IdenticalQ[g, h]
Out[139]= True
```

6.6 Exercises

■ 6.6.1 Thought Exercises

1. Prove that the graph product operation is commutative, that is, $G \times H$ is isomorphic to $H \times G$.

2. Is the graph product of two Hamiltonian graphs Hamiltonian? Is the graph product of two Eulerian graphs Eulerian? Prove your results.

3. Prove that the line graph of an Eulerian graph is both Eulerian and Hamiltonian, while the line graph of a Hamiltonian graph is always Hamiltonian.

4. Under what conditions is `CirculantGraph[m*n,{m,n}]` isomorphic to the graph product of cycles $C_m \times C_n$? Prove your results.

5. Prove that the contraction schemes described on butterfly graphs result in hypercubes.

6. Show that any r-bit binary string u can be converted to any other r-bit binary string v by $r - 1$ shuffles and at most r exchanges.

7. Show that the Prüfer codes of paths are exactly the sequences of $n - 2$ distinct integers.

8. What is the probability that a random labeled tree is a star?

9. Prove that the diagonal of the square of the adjacency matrix of a simple graph gives the unsorted degree sequence of the graph.

10. Prove that no degree sequence can be graphic if all the degrees occur exactly once.

11. Prove that any sequence of positive integers summing up to an even number can be realized by a multigraph with self-loops.

12. Give degree sequences such that any pair of graphs with such a degree sequence is isomorphic.

■ 6.6.2 Programming Exercises

1. Give more direct implementations of `GraphUnion` and `GraphIntersection`. How does their performance compare with the existing versions?

2. Write a function to embed a hypercube in a grid graph, meaning to assign vertices of a hypercube to all the vertices of a grid graph such that the grid graph is contained within an induced subgraph of these hypercube vertices. How many of the $n!$ embeddings work?

3. The *total graph* $T(G)$ of a graph G has a vertex for each edge and each vertex of G, and an edge in $T(G)$ for every edge–edge and vertex–edge adjacency in G [CM78]. Thus total graphs are a generalization of line graphs. Write a function to construct the total graph of a graph.

4. Write functions to construct the following graphs from `GraphIntersection`, `GraphJoin`, `GraphUnion`, and `GraphProduct`: complete graphs, complete bipartite graphs, cycles, stars, and wheels.

5. What special cases of complete k-partite graphs are circulant graphs? Implement them accordingly.

6. Implement the function `RandomBipartiteGraph` that produces a labeled bipartite graph chosen uniformly at random from the set of all labeled bipartite graphs.

7. An alternate nondeterministic `RealizeDegreeSequence` can be based on the result [Egg75, FHM65] that every realization of a given degree sequence can be constructed from any other using a finite number of *edge-interchange* operations, where an edge interchange takes a graph with edges (x, y) and (w, z) and replaces them with edges (x, w) and (y, z). Implement a nondeterministic `RealizeDegreeSequence` function based on a sequence of edge-interchange operations.

8. A *degree set* for a graph G is the set of integers that make up the degree sequence. Any set of positive integers is the degree set for some graph. Design and implement an algorithm for constructing a graph that realizes an arbitrary degree set.

■ 6.6.3 Experimental Exercises

1. Experiment to determine the expected number of edges, vertices, and connected components remaining after deleting a random subset of the vertices of an $n \times m$ grid graph. How does the ratio of n to m effect the results?

2. Experiment with `RealizeDegreeSequence` to determine how many random subsets must be selected, in connecting the ith vertex of an order n graph, before finding one that leaves a graphic degree sequence.

3. Assign the vertices of a cycle C_n to a convex set of n points. A *swap* operation exchanges the points associated with two vertices of the graph. How many swaps are required to disentangle the graph and leave a planar embedding of the cycle?

4. What is the probability that a random unlabeled tree has a center of one vertex versus two vertices? For labeled trees, asymptotically half the trees are central and half bicentral [Sze83].

5. Consider a random graph with n vertices and edge probability p. Keep n fixed and increase p. This results in the graph becoming more dense. Experiment with `RandomGraph` to determine if there is a threshold probability $p(n)$ at which point isolated vertices disappear. Also, experiment to determine if there is a threshold probability at which the graph becomes connected.

7. Properties of Graphs

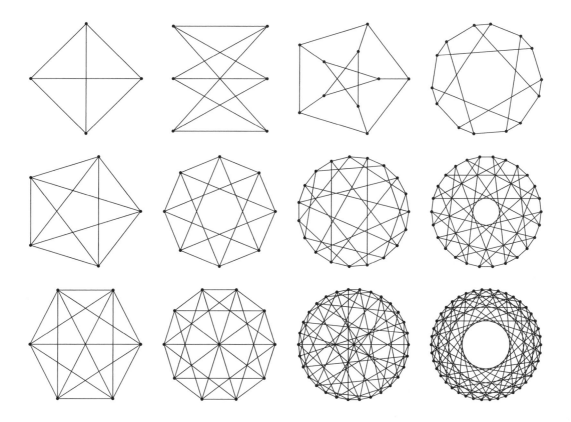

Graph theory is the study of *invariants* of graphs. Among the properties of interest are such things as connectivity, cycle structure, and chromatic number. In this chapter, we discuss invariants of graphs and how to compute them.

We make a somewhat arbitrary distinction between the properties of graphs – discussed in this chapter – and algorithmic graph theory – discussed in the next. Algorithms are necessary to calculate the properties of graphs, and the study of these properties is necessary for the development of efficient algorithms, so clearly there is a lot of room for overlap. Because of this close relationship, some of the algorithms used as subroutines in this chapter, such as NetworkFlow and BipartiteMatching, will be discussed in detail only after they have been used.

About the illustration overleaf:

The *girth* of a graph is the size of a smallest cycle in it. A (g,k)-*cage graph* is a smallest k-regular graph with girth g. Cage graphs are known only for small values of g and k, and researchers are actively searching for these graphs for larger values of g and k. Here is a table of (g,k)-cage graphs for $k = 3, 4, 5$ and $g = 3, 4, 5, 6$. The first three graphs in the top row are familiar 3-regular graphs: K_4, $K_{3,3}$, and the Petersen graph. This table was produced by the command:

```
ShowGraphArray[c=Table[CageGraph[k, g], {k, 3, 5}, {g, 3, 6}]]
```

7.1 Graph Traversals

It is often necessary to explore all the edges and vertices of a graph in some reasonable order to determine whether it has a particular property. Two traversals are particularly important from an algorithmic point of view, namely, *breadth-first* and *depth-first* searches. Breadth-first search will be used for problems such as coloring bipartite graphs and finding the shortest cycle in a graph. Depth-first search will be used to find connected and biconnected components and test if a graph is acyclic.

■ 7.1.1 Breadth-First Search

A *breadth-first* search (BFS) of a graph explores all the vertices adjacent to the current vertex before moving on. A breadth-first search is shallow rather than deep, hence the name. Our implementation of breadth-first traversal uses a queue data structure to keep track of the order in which vertices are to be explored. The next vertex to be explored sits at the front of the queue, while newly discovered vertices get inserted at the back. The search ends when the queue is empty.

`BreadthFirstTraversal` is a "wrapper" function that massages the output of BFS, which does the real work. BFS returns a list of three arrays. The first contains the *BFS numbers* of the vertices; these are assigned to vertices in the order in which they were visited. The second contains *parent* pointers, where the parent of a vertex u is the neighboring vertex v from which u was first visited. The third contains the distance of each vertex from the source of the search. These arrays provide a wealth of information about the structure of the graph and are used by many other *Combinatorica* functions.

```
BFS[g_Graph, start_Integer] :=
    Module[{e, bfi=Table[0,{V[g]}]}, cnt=1, queue={start},
        parent=Table[i, {i, V[g]}],lvl=Table[Infinity,{V[g]}]},
        e = ToAdjacencyLists[g]; bfi[[start]] = cnt++; lvl[[start]]=0;
        While[ queue != {},
            {v,queue} = {First[queue],Rest[queue]};
            Scan[(If[bfi[[#]] == 0,
                bfi[[#]]=cnt++; parent[[#]]=v; lvl[[#]]=lvl[[v]]+1; AppendTo[queue,#]
                ])&,
                e[[v]]
            ];
        ];
        {bfi, parent, lvl}
    ] /; (1 <= start) && (start <= V[g])

BreadthFirstTraversal[g_Graph, s_Integer?Positive] := First[BFS[g,s]] /; (s <= V[g])
```

Breadth-First Traversal

This loads the package.   *In[1]:=* `<<DiscreteMath`Combinatorica``

A breadth-first search of a simple cycle alternates sides as it wraps around the cycle.

In[2]:= **BreadthFirstTraversal[Cycle[10], 1]**

Out[2]= {1, 2, 4, 6, 8, 10, 9, 7, 5, 3}

The vertices are given in discovery order by the inverse of this permutation.

In[3]:= **InversePermutation[%]**

Out[3]= {1, 2, 10, 3, 9, 4, 8, 5, 7, 6}

Using the tag Edge causes the function to produce *tree edges*, which are edges that connect vertices to their parents. All edges in the cycle, except one that is "opposite" the start vertex, are tree edges.

In[4]:= **BreadthFirstTraversal[Cycle[10], 1, Edge]**

Out[4]= {{1, 2}, {1, 10}, {2, 3}, {10, 9}, {3, 4}, {9, 8}, {4, 5}, {8, 7}, {5, 6}}

If we start with a connected graph, perform a breadth-first search and delete all edges from the graph that are not tree edges, we get a *BFS tree*. Using the tag Tree causes the function to produce the BFS tree. Here we show a BFS tree of a three-dimensional butterfly graph.

In[5]:= **ShowGraph[h = BreadthFirstTraversal[g = ButterflyGraph[3], 1, Tree]];**

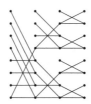

If we take the BFS tree as being rooted at the source of the search, then the distance from root *r* to any vertex *v* along the unique simple path in the tree equals the distance between them in the original graph. Thus the BFS tree provides a convenient representation of all shortest paths from the root. Using the tag Level in BreadthFirstTraversal causes the function to return these distances.

In[6]:= **nh = RootedEmbedding[**
          BreadthFirstTraversal[g = ButterflyGraph[3], 1, Tree]];
       ShowGraph[SetVertexLabels[nh, BreadthFirstTraversal[g,1,Level]]];

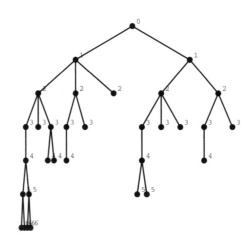

The BFS numbers of the vertices (right) radiate out sequentially from the root, unlike the original vertex labels (left), which are scrambled around the tree.

`In[8]:= ShowGraphArray[{SetVertexLabels[nh,Range[V[nh]]],`
`            SetVertexLabels[nh,BreadthFirstTraversal[g,1]]}];`

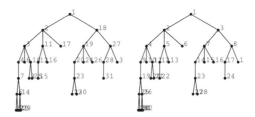

We add the nontree edges of the butterfly graph to its BFS tree to get an unfamiliar embedding of the three-dimensional butterfly graph. Notice that all edges connect a vertex at depth d to a vertex at depth $(d + 1)$ for some d. This implies that the graph has no cycles of odd length, and *that* in turn implies that the graph is bipartite.

`In[9]:= ne = Complement[Edges[g] , Edges[h]];`
`        ShowGraph[SetGraphOptions[AddEdges[nh, ne],`
`        Append[ne, EdgeColor -> Gray]]];`

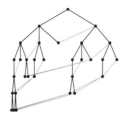

Performing a breadth-first search explores just one connected component of the graph. The 0's in the output correspond to unexplored vertices.

`In[11]:= BreadthFirstTraversal[GraphUnion[2, Cycle[5]], 1]`

`Out[11]= {1, 2, 4, 5, 3, 0, 0, 0, 0, 0}`

Here we construct a directed graph by starting with two directed cycles and adding an edge from the first cycle to the second.

`In[12]:= ShowGraph[g=AddEdge[GraphUnion[2, Cycle[5, Type->Directed]],`
`         {5, 10}]];`

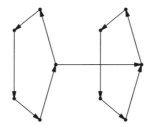

If we start the breadth-first search from a vertex in the left cycle, we traverse the entire graph.

```
In[13]:= BreadthFirstTraversal[g, 1]

Out[13]= {1, 2, 3, 4, 5, 7, 8, 9, 10, 6}
```

But if we start the search in the right cycle, we get trapped and can never reach the vertices on the left.

```
In[14]:= BreadthFirstTraversal[g, 10]

Out[14]= {0, 0, 0, 0, 0, 2, 3, 4, 5, 1}
```

■ 7.1.2 Depth-First Search

In a *depth-first search* (DFS), the children of the first child of a vertex are explored before visiting its siblings. Hopcroft and Tarjan [HT73, Tar72] showed that depth-first search leads to linear-time algorithms for many fundamental graph problems. The *Combinatorica* implementation of depth-first search is fairly standard. A recursive function DFS starts with a vertex and scans its neighbors until it finds the first unexplored neighbor. It then makes a recursive call to start a depth-first search from that neighbor. DepthFirstSearch is a "wrapper" function that calls DFS appropriately and interprets its output for the user.

```
DFS[v_Integer] :=
     ( AppendTo[visit,v];
       Scan[ (If[parent[[#]]==0, AppendTo[edges,{v,#}]; parent[[#]] = v; DFS[#]])&, e[[v]] ])

DepthFirstTraversal[g_Graph, start_Integer, flag_:Vertex] :=
     Block[{visit={},e=ToAdjacencyLists[g],edges={}, parent=Table[0,{V[g]}], cnt=1,
          $RecursionLimit = Infinity},
          parent[[start]] = start;
          DFS[start];
          Switch[flag, Edge, edges,
                  Tree, ChangeEdges[g, edges],
                  Vertex, visit
          ]
     ] /; (1 <= start) && (start <= V[g])
```

Depth-First Traversal of a Graph

This is a *DFS tree* of the three-dimensional butterfly graph. The DFS tree consists of edges that connect vertices to their parents. The DFS tree of a connected graph is indeed a tree. Because of the nature of the traversal, the DFS tree of the three-dimensional butterfly graph is much deeper than the BFS tree.

```
In[15]:= g = ButterflyGraph[3];
ShowGraphArray[{
h=RootedEmbedding[DepthFirstTraversal[g,1,Tree], 1],
RootedEmbedding[BreadthFirstTraversal[g,1,Tree], 1]
}];
```

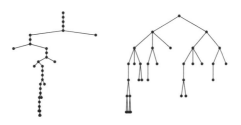

Any nontree edge in the depth-first search of an undirected graph is called a *back edge*, because it connects a vertex to an ancestor. Here back edges are shown in gray. Each back edge (v, u) makes a cycle with the path from u to v in the DFS tree. As a result, DFS is at the heart of algorithms that find cycles, biconnected components, and strongly connected components.

```
In[17]:= ne = Complement[Edges[g] , Edges[h]];
ShowGraph[SetGraphOptions[AddEdges[h, ne],
Append[ne, EdgeColor -> Gray]]];
```

Here is another example that dramatizes the difference between breadth-first and depth-first traversals. The depth-first traversal of a 3×3 grid graph is simply a path – a Hamiltonian path. The breadth-first traversal produces a much shallower tree, one in which every vertex can be reached in at most six hops from the starting vertex.

```
In[19]:= g = GridGraph[3, 3, 3];
ShowGraphArray[{DepthFirstTraversal[g, 1, Tree],
BreadthFirstTraversal[g, 1, Tree]}, VertexStyle -> Disk[0.05]];
```

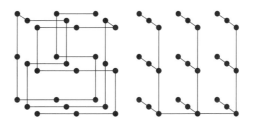

This directed graph is the three-dimensional De Bruijn graph on two symbols. We will use this example to illustrate depth-first search on directed graphs. Directed graph traversal is somewhat more complicated in that DFS partitions the edge set into four classes, as opposed to two.

In[21]:= **ShowGraph[g = DeBruijnGraph[2, 3]];**

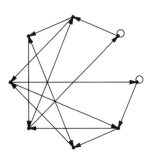

Here we show a rooted embedding of the DFS tree of this De Bruijn graph. Gray edges that connect a vertex to an ancestor are *back edges*. Edges, such as (2,4), that connect a vertex to a descendant are *forward edges*. The remaining edges, such as (8,7) and (7,5), go across the tree and are called *cross edges*.

In[22]:= **h = RootedEmbedding[DepthFirstTraversal[g, 1, Tree] , 1];**
            ne = Select[Complement[Edges[g], Edges[h]], #[[1]] != #[[2]] &];
            ShowGraph[SetGraphOptions[AddEdges[h, ne],
            Append[ne, EdgeColor -> Gray]], VertexNumber -> True];

7.2 Connectivity

The notion of graph connectivity has already shown up in several contexts. Connectivity can be generalized in two distinct ways: (a) to directed graphs and (b) to quantifying the notion of connectivity. In this section, we study graph connectivity from an algorithmic point of view.

■ 7.2.1 Connected Components

We can use traversal to determine whether a graph is connected and hence to find the connected components of a graph. Performing a depth-first or breadth-first search from any vertex eventually visits all vertices in a connected component. The graph is connected if, at the end of the search, all vertices have been explored. This idea is implemented in the function ConnectedQ, which is shown below. Since the vertices in distinct connected components are disjoint, starting a new traversal from any unvisited vertex identifies a new component. This is the idea behind ConnectedComponents.

```
ConnectedQ[g_Graph] := True /; (V[g] == 0)
ConnectedQ[g_Graph, _] := True /; (V[g] == 0)

ConnectedQ[g_Graph] := Length[DepthFirstTraversal[g,1]]==V[g] /; UndirectedQ[g]
ConnectedQ[g_Graph] := Length[DepthFirstTraversal[MakeUndirected[g],1]]==V[g]

ConnectedComponents[g_Graph] :=
     Block[{untraversed=Range[V[g]], visit, comps={}, e=ToAdjacencyLists[g],
          parent=Table[0,{V[g]}], cnt=1, $RecursionLimit = Infinity, start},
          While[untraversed != {},
               visit = {}; edges = {};
               start = First[untraversed];
               parent[[start]] = start;
               DFS[start];
               AppendTo[comps,visit];
               untraversed = Complement[untraversed,visit]
          ];
          ToCanonicalSetPartition[comps]
     ] /; UndirectedQ[g]

ConnectedComponents[g_Graph] := ConnectedComponents[MakeUndirected[g]]
```

Testing for Connectivity in Undirected Graphs

A randomly induced subgraph of a
50 × 50 grid graph is constructed and
displayed. We use the option
`VertexStyle` here to reduce the sizes
of the disks representing the vertices.

```
In[25]:= ShowGraph[g = InduceSubgraph[GridGraph[50, 50],
            RandomSubset[Range[2500]]], VertexStyle->Disk[0]];
```

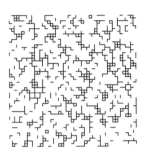

The number of connected components
in this graph and the size of the largest
component are reported here.

```
In[26]:= c = ConnectedComponents[g]; {Length[c], Max[Map[Length, c]]}
Out[26]= {187, 140}
```

`GraphUnion` creates disconnected
graphs.

```
In[27]:= ConnectedComponents[
            g=GraphUnion[CompleteGraph[3], CompleteGraph[4]] ]
Out[27]= {{1, 2, 3}, {4, 5, 6, 7}}
```

Calling `InduceSubgraph` on each of the
connected components provides a
means to extract them as independent
connected graphs.

```
In[28]:= Map[InduceSubgraph[g, #] &, ConnectedComponents[g]]
Out[28]= {-Graph:<3, 3, Undirected>-,
          -Graph:<6, 4, Undirected>-}
```

If a graph is disconnected, its
complement must be connected.

```
In[29]:= ConnectedComponents[GraphComplement[g]]
Out[29]= {{1, 2, 3, 4, 5, 6, 7}}
```

Any graph with minimum degree
$\delta \geq (n-1)/2$ must be connected.

```
In[30]:= ConnectedQ[RealizeDegreeSequence[{4,4,4,4,4,4,4,4}]]
Out[30]= True
```

■ 7.2.2 Strong and Weak Connectivity

There are two distinct notions of connectivity in directed graphs. A directed graph is *weakly connected*
if there is a path between each pair of vertices in the underlying undirected graph. Thus the graph
hangs together in one piece, even though it might not be possible to get from one vertex to another.

However, consider the directed graph representing the Manhattan traffic grid. If it were only
weakly connected, there might exist points a and b such that only people willing to ignore one-way
signs could drive from a to b. A directed graph is *strongly connected* if there is a *directed* path between
every pair of vertices.

The strong connectivity algorithm implemented in *Combinatorica* is based on depth-first search and
due to Tarjan [Tar72]. When a depth-first search is performed, after everything reachable from a vertex

v has been traversed, the search backs up to the parent of v. If there are no back edges to v or an ancestor of v, then there is no directed path from some descendant of v to v. Thus v must be in a strongly connected component that is separate from its children. *Combinatorica* provides functions to compute strongly connected and weakly connected components of a directed graph.

These are the strongly connected components of a random directed graph. This is a partition of the vertices, for if a vertex belonged to two distinct strongly connected components, then the two would collapse into one.

```
In[31]:= g = RandomGraph[20, 0.1, Type -> Directed];
         c = StronglyConnectedComponents[g]
Out[32]= {{1, 2, 4, 6, 8, 9, 10, 11, 12, 15, 16, 17, 19,
         20}, {3}, {5}, {7}, {13}, {14}, {18}}
```

To understand the structure of strongly connected components of a graph, label the components $1, 2, \dots$ and represent each edge (u, v) in the graph by an ordered pair (i, j) if u belongs to component i and v to component j.

```
In[33]:= ne = DeleteCases[Union[Edges[g] /. {x_Integer, y_Integer} :>
         {Position[c, x][[1, 1]], Position[c, y][[1, 1]]}],
         {x_Integer, x_Integer}];
```

If we think of the components themselves as vertices, then the ordered pairs computed above can be viewed as directed edges. This induces a directed graph on the set of strongly connected components.

```
In[34]:= g = Graph[Map[{#} &, ne], CircularEmbedding[Length[c]],
         EdgeDirection -> True];
         ShowGraph[SpringEmbedding[g, 150]];
```

This graph cannot contain a directed cycle, for, if it did, two or more components would collapse into one.

```
In[36]:= AcyclicQ[g]
Out[36]= True
```

Since any strongly connected component is weakly connected, strongly connected components form a finer vertex partition than the weakly connected components.

```
In[37]:= g = RandomGraph[10, 0.1, Type -> Directed];
         {WeaklyConnectedComponents[g], StronglyConnectedComponents[g]} //
         ColumnForm
Out[38]= {{1, 2, 4, 5, 6, 7, 9, 10}, {3}, {8}}
         {{1}, {2}, {3}, {4}, {5}, {6}, {7}, {8}, {9}, {10}}
```

A sparse directed graph is likely to have more strongly connected components than weakly connected ones.

```
In[39]:= g = RandomGraph[20, 0.1, Type->Directed];
         {Length[WeaklyConnectedComponents[g]],
         Length[StronglyConnectedComponents[g]]}
Out[40]= {1, 19}
```

But as the graph becomes dense, it has a single strongly connected component and therefore a single weakly connected component as well.

```
In[41]:= g = RandomGraph[200, 0.1, Type->Directed];
        {Length[WeaklyConnectedComponents[g]],
         Length[StronglyConnectedComponents[g]]}
Out[42]= {1, 1}
```

■ 7.2.3 Orienting Graphs

An *orientation* of an undirected graph G is an assignment of exactly one direction to each of the edges of G. For transportation applications, it is often necessary to find a strongly connected orientation of a graph, if one exists.

A *bridge* is an edge whose deletion disconnects the graph. In the next section we show how to compute bridges in a graph. Only connected, bridgeless graphs can have a strongly connected orientation, since deleting a bridge leaves two disconnected components, and so assigning the bridge an orientation permits travel to proceed in only one direction between them. Robbins [Rob39] showed that this condition is sufficient, by presenting an algorithm to find such an orientation. Extract all the cycles from the graph and orient each as a directed cycle. If two or more directed cycles share a vertex, there exists a directed path between each pair of vertices in the component. If the union of these cycles is disconnected, there are at least two edges connecting them, since the graph is bridgeless. Therefore, orienting them in opposite directions yields a strongly connected graph. The function OrientGraph takes a graph with no bridges and produces a strongly connected orientation of it.

This orientation of a wheel directs each edge in the outer cycle in the same direction and completes it by giving the center an in-degree of $n - 1$ and out-degree of 1.

```
In[43]:= ShowGraph[ OrientGraph[Wheel[10]]];
```

■ 7.2.4 Biconnected Components

An *articulation vertex* (or a *cut-point*) of a graph G is a vertex whose deletion disconnects G. Any graph with no articulation vertices is said to be *biconnected*. Biconnectivity is an important property for a variety of reasons. For example, *Menger's theorem* [Men27, Whi32] implies that any graph with at least three vertices is biconnected if and only if there are at least two vertex disjoint paths between any pair of vertices. From the perspective of communication networks, biconnected networks are more fault-tolerant, since blowing away any single node does not cut off communication for any other node. The *biconnected components* of a graph are maximal induced subgraphs that are biconnected. It is easy to see that any vertex that belongs to more than one biconnected component is an articulation vertex.

An undirected graph can be tested for biconnectivity by using an algorithm similar to that which tested a directed graph for strong connectivity. A depth-first search is performed, with an articulation vertex occurring when there are no back edges, implying no cycles. This implementation finds the biconnected components and articulation vertices during the same traversal and returns both. Special care must be taken to test whether the root of the depth-first search tree is an articulation vertex, since no back edge can originate from it [AHU74]. All of this work is done by a function called `FindBiconnectedComponents`. To make for more user-friendly functionality, *Combinatorica* provides "wrapper" functions for finding bridges, articulation vertices, and biconnected components. These functions call `FindBiconnectedComponents` and extract the appropriate information. For example, finding the bridges of a graph is simply a matter of selecting biconnected components of size 2.

```
ArticulationVertices[g_Graph]  := Union[Last[FindBiconnectedComponents[g]]];

Bridges[g_Graph] := Select[BiconnectedComponents[g],(Length[#] == 2)&]

BiconnectedComponents[g_Graph]:= Map[{#}&, Range[V[g]] ]/; (EmptyQ[g])
BiconnectedComponents[g_Graph] := First[FindBiconnectedComponents[g]] /; UndirectedQ[g]
BiconnectedComponents[g_Graph] := First[FindBiconnectedComponents[MakeUndirected[g]]]

BiconnectedQ[g_Graph] := (Length[ BiconnectedComponents[g] ] == 1)
```

Applications of the Biconnectivity Algorithm

The distribution of the sizes of biconnected components in a random graph is not uniform. Typically, there is one giant component along with several tiny components.

```
In[44]:= g = RandomGraph[20, .15];
         c = BiconnectedComponents[g];
         ShowGraph[ Apply[GraphUnion, Map[InduceSubgraph[g, #] &, c]]];
```

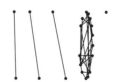

We start with five disjoint 5-cycles and add six randomly chosen edges between them. The results are unpredictable. Maybe all the extra edges would be added within cycles, resulting in five biconnected components. Or maybe the extra edges would connect the 5-cycles into one single biconnected component.

```
In[47]:= ShowGraph[g = AddEdges[GraphUnion[5, Cycle[5]],
           Table[RandomKSubset[Range[25], 2], {6}]], VertexNumber->True];
```

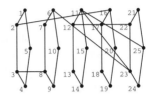

These are the biconnected components of the resulting graph.

```
In[48]:= b = BiconnectedComponents[g]

Out[48]= {{11, 12, 13, 14, 15, 21, 22, 23, 24, 25},
          {6, 23}, {6, 7, 8, 9, 10}, {3, 8},
          {16, 17, 18, 19, 20}, {2, 16}, {1, 2, 3, 4, 5}}
```

These are the articulation vertices.

```
In[49]:= a = ArticulationVertices[g]

Out[49]= {2, 3, 6, 8, 16, 23}
```

The interaction between biconnected components and articulation points is best understood by constructing the *block-cutpoint* graph of G. This is a bipartite graph whose vertices are the biconnected components and articulation points of G, where edges connect each articulation point to the biconnected components that it belongs to. Here we construct and display the block-cutpoint graph of the above graph. Vertices corresponding to blocks are shown by large disks.

```
In[50]:= bcg = FromUnorderedPairs[Flatten[Table[Map[{{i, # + Length[a]}} &,
           Map[First, Position[b, a[[i]]]]], {i, Length[a]}], 2] ];
         bcg = SetGraphOptions[bcg, {Append[Table[i + Length[a],
           {i, Length[b]}], VertexStyle -> Disk[Large]]}];
         ShowGraph[SpringEmbedding[bcg]];
```

The block-cutpoint graph is a forest in general, and if G is connected, it is a tree.

```
In[53]:= {ConnectedQ[g], ConnectedQ[bcg]}

Out[53]= {True, True}
```

This graph may be disconnected if the original graph is, but it will always be acyclic.

```
In[54]:= AcyclicQ[bcg]

Out[54]= True
```

Any graph with a vertex of degree 1 cannot be biconnected, since deleting the neighbor of the vertex with degree 1 disconnects the graph.

```
In[55]:= BiconnectedComponents[ RealizeDegreeSequence[{4,4,3,3,3,2,1}] ]
Out[55]= {{2, 7}, {1, 2, 3, 4, 5, 6}}
```

The only articulation vertex of a star is its center, even though its deletion leaves $n - 1$ connected components. Deleting a leaf leaves a connected tree.

```
In[56]:= ArticulationVertices[ Star[10] ]
Out[56]= {10}
```

All Hamiltonian graphs are biconnected.

```
In[57]:= BiconnectedQ[ Cycle[10] ]
Out[57]= True
```

Every edge in a tree is a bridge.

```
In[58]:= Bridges[ RandomTree[10] ]
Out[58]= {{2, 7}, {2, 10}, {4, 5}, {3, 9}, {6, 9}, {5, 6},
         {5, 10}, {8, 10}, {1, 8}}
```

A *cubic* or 3-regular graph contains a bridge if and only if it contains an articulation vertex. Most such graphs appear to be biconnected.

```
In[59]:= Table[g = RegularGraph[3, i];
             {ArticulationVertices[g], Bridges[g]}, {i, 4, 14, 2}]
Out[59]= {{{}, {}}, {{}, {}}, {{}, {}}, {{}, {}}, {{}, {}},
         {{}, {}}}
```

■ 7.2.5 *k*-**Connectivity**

A graph is said to be *k-connected* if there does not exist a set of $(k - 1)$ vertices whose removal disconnects it. Thus a connected graph is 1-connected and a biconnected graph is 2-connected. A graph is *k-edge-connected* if there does not exist a set of $(k - 1)$ edges whose removal disconnects the graph.

Both edge and vertex connectivity can be found by using network flow techniques. The "edge version" of Menger's theorem [Men27, Whi32], alluded to in the previous section, states that a graph is *k*-edge-connected if and only if between every pair of vertices there are at least *k* edge-disjoint paths. Finding the number of edge-disjoint paths between a pair of vertices is a network flow problem. The *network flow problem*, to be discussed later in Section 8.3, interprets a weighted graph as a network of pipes where the maximum capacity of an edge is its weight and seeks to maximize the flow between two given vertices of the graph. If all edges have unit capacities, then the maximum flow from a vertex *s* to a vertex *t* is the maximum number of edge-disjoint paths from *s* to *t*. Thus the edge connectivity of a graph can be found by computing the maximum flow between a vertex *s* and each of the other $(n - 1)$ vertices and picking the minimum of these $(n - 1)$ maximum flows.

```
EdgeConnectivity[g_Graph] := Module[{i}, Apply[Min, Table[NetworkFlow[g,1,i], {i, 2, V[g]}]]]
```

Finding the Edge Connectivity of a Graph

The edge connectivity of a graph is at most its minimum vertex degree, since deleting all edges incident on a vertex disconnects the graph. Hypercubes realize this bound.

```
In[60]:= EdgeConnectivity[Hypercube[5]]

Out[60]= 5
```

We connect two cubic graphs together using two edges. In the resulting graph every vertex has degree at least 3.

```
In[61]:= g  = RegularGraph[3, 8]; h = RegularGraph[3, 8];
         gh = AddEdges[GraphUnion[g, h], {{1, 10}, {2, 9}}];
         ShowGraph[ gh = SpringEmbedding[gh, 100]];
```

But the edge connectivity is 2.

```
In[64]:= EdgeConnectivity[gh]

Out[64]= 2
```

Using the tag Cut as the second argument to the function EdgeConnectivity produces a set of edges corresponding to the minimum cut. Here we show the graph that results when the cut edges are deleted.

```
In[65]:= ShowGraph[ DeleteEdges[gh, EdgeConnectivity[gh, Cut]] ];
```

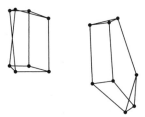

Deleting any edge from a tree disconnects it, so the edge connectivity of a tree is 1.

```
In[66]:= EdgeConnectivity[ RandomTree[10] ]

Out[66]= 1
```

The "vertex version" of Menger's theorem [Men27, Whi32] states that a graph is k-connected if and only if every pair of vertices is joined by at least k vertex-disjoint paths. Network flow techniques cannot be used directly to find vertex-disjoint paths. So we construct a directed graph G' with the property that any set of edge-disjoint paths in G' corresponds to vertex-disjoint paths in G. We can then use network flows to find the edge connectivity of G' and from this the vertex connectivity of G.

The details are as follows. G' is constructed by adding two vertices $v_{i,1}$ and $v_{i,2}$ and edge $(v_{i,1}, v_{i,2})$ to G' for each $v_i \in G$. This edge in G' is the representative of the vertex v_i in G. For every edge $\{v_i, v_j\}$ in G, add directed edges $(v_{i,1}, v_{j,0})$ and $(v_{j,1}, v_{i,0})$ to G'. Thus, we can only enter into the "tail" vertices $v_{i,0}$ and leave from the "head" vertices $v_{i,1}$. Then edge-disjoint paths in G' correspond to vertex-disjoint paths in G, so network flow in G' determines the vertex connectivity of G. This construction is implemented in `VertexConnectivityGraph`.

Here is the directed graph produced by `VertexConnectivityGraph` on a 3×3 grid graph. The embedding emphasizes the structural connections between the two graphs. Vertices in the resulting graph are numbered so that vertex i in the original graph corresponds to the edges $(2i - 1, 2i)$ in the new graph. The number of vertices needed to separate s and t in G equals the maximum flow from vertex $2s$ to vertex $2t - 1$ in G'.

```
In[67]:= g = GridGraph[3, 3];
        ShowGraph[h=VertexConnectivityGraph[g], VertexNumber->True];
```

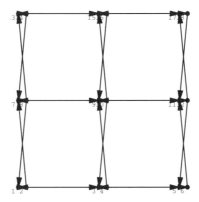

Computing the vertex connectivity of G is then a matter of making repeated calls to `NetworkFlow` with G' as the input. Specifically, for each pair of nonadjacent vertices s and t in G, we compute the maximum flow from $2s$ to $2t - 1$ and then pick the minimum of these flows.

```
VertexConnectivity[g_Graph] := V[g] - 1 /; CompleteQ[g]

VertexConnectivity[g_Graph] :=
     Module[{p=VertexConnectivityGraph[g],k=V[g],i=0,notedges},
          notedges = ToUnorderedPairs[ GraphComplement[g] ];
          While[i++ <= k,
               k=Min[
                    Map[
                         (NetworkFlow[p,2 #[[1]],2 #[[2]]-1])&,
                         Select[notedges,(First[#]==i)&]
                    ],
                    k
               ]
          ];
          k
     ]
```

Computing the Vertex Connectivity of a Graph

The vertex connectivity of a complete bipartite graph is the number of vertices in the smaller stage, since all of them must be deleted to disconnect the graph.

```
In[69]:= VertexConnectivity[CompleteGraph[3,4]]
Out[69]= 3
```

The wheel is the basic triconnected graph [Tut61]. Deleting the central vertex and two other nonadjacent vertices disconnects the graph. This example also demonstrates the use of the tag Cut as an argument, which produces a minimum-sized set of vertices whose deletion disconnects the graph.

```
In[70]:= c = VertexConnectivity[g = Wheel[10], Cut];
         ShowGraphArray[{g, DeleteVertices[g, c]}];
```

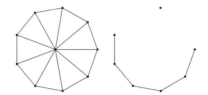

■ 7.2.6 Harary Graphs

In general, the higher the connectivity of a graph, the more edges it must contain. Every vertex in a k-connected graph must have degree at least k, so a k-connected graph on n vertices must have at least $\lceil kn/2 \rceil$ edges. The *Harary graph* $H_{k,n}$ [Har62] realizes this bound, and hence it is the smallest k-connected graph with n vertices.

There are three different cases, depending on the parity of n and k; two are circulant graphs, but when n and k are odd the graph is not symmetrical.

```
Harary[k_?EvenQ, n_Integer] := CirculantGraph[n,Range[k/2]] /; (k > 1) && (n > k)

Harary[k_?OddQ, n_?EvenQ] := CirculantGraph[n,Append[Range[k/2],n/2]] /; (k > 1)&& (n > k)

Harary[k_?OddQ, n_?OddQ] :=
    AddEdges[Harary[k-1, n],
            Join[{{1,(n+1)/2}}, {{1,(n+3)/2}}}, Table[{{i,i+(n+1)/2}}, {i,2,(n-1)/2}]]
    ] /; (k > 1) && (n > k)
```

Constructing the Harary Graph

A cycle is the minimum biconnected graph.

```
In[72]:= IdenticalQ[Cycle[12],Harary[2,12]]
Out[72]= True
```

When *n* or *k* is even, the Harary graph is a circulant graph, which implies that it is regular. In other cases, there must be one distinguished vertex of higher degree. With at least one vertex of degree *k*, the Harary graph $H_{k,n}$ is clearly at most *k*-connected. A proof that it is in fact *k*-connected appears in [BM76].

In[73]:= **ShowGraph[Harary[7,13]];**

Here is a table of 10-vertex Harary graphs. As the connectivity increases, the number of edges in the graph increases.

In[74]:= **ShowGraphArray[Partition[Table[Harary[k,10], {k,2,9}], 4]];**

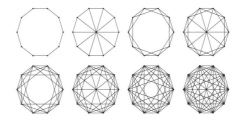

And, as advertised, the vertex connectivity increases for increasing *k*.

In[75]:= **Table[VertexConnectivity[Harary[k,n]], {k,2,4}, {n,5,9}] // TableForm**

Out[75]//TableForm=

2	2	2	2	2
3	3	3	3	3
4	4	4	4	4

7.3 Cycles in Graphs

A *cycle* in a graph is a simple closed path. We will represent a cycle in G as a list of vertices $C = \{v_1, v_2, ..., v_1\}$ such that there is an edge of G from each vertex to the next in C. In this section, we will present algorithms to search for several kinds of cycles in graphs – from small cycles to large cycles to cycles on edges instead of vertices.

■ 7.3.1 Acyclic Graphs

A graph is *acyclic* if it contains no cycles. Finding a cycle is a matter of doing a depth-first search and looking for a back edge; adding this edge to the DFS tree creates a cycle. However, there are two complications. First, DFS must correctly identify back edges in directed graphs as well. Second, the graph may contain several connected components, some of which may be acyclic. Thus all connected components must be examined before we can report acyclicity.

FindCycle performs a depth-first search embellished to find back edges. It works for both directed and undirected graphs by exploiting the vertex ordering induced by a depth-first search. Specifically, each vertex v is marked by a start time and a finish time, indicating the time the vertex was first visited and the time when the traversal finally exited v. An edge (v, u) is a back edge provided u is not v's parent and $s[u] < s[v]$ and $f[u] > f[v]$, where s and f denote start time and finish time, respectively. Once we can find a cycle, we can use this function to perform other useful operations:

Any simple graph with minimum degree δ contains a cycle of length at least $\delta + 1$. This cycle decomposition does not necessarily find it, however.

```
In[76]:= c = ExtractCycles[g = RealizeDegreeSequence[{3,3,3,3,3,3,3,3}]]

Out[76]= {{8, 1, 6, 3, 8}, {5, 2, 4, 5}}
```

We highlight the cycles extracted above. Note that after all cycles have been extracted, there remain edges left over because of the odd-degree vertices.

```
In[77]:= ShowGraph[SpringEmbedding[ Highlight[g, Map[Sort,
            Map[Partition[#, 2, 1] &, c], 2],
            HighlightedEdgeColors -> {Black, Gray}]]];
```

A tree can be identified without explicitly showing that the graph is acyclic, since this is implied if the graph is connected with exactly $n-1$ edges.

```
In[78]:= TreeQ[g = RandomTree[10]]
Out[78]= True
```

A self-loop is a cycle of length 1.

```
In[79]:= FindCycle[AddEdges[g, {{1, 1}}]]
Out[79]= {1, 1}
```

Multiple edges between vertices are responsible for cycles of length 2. Both kinds of cycles are detected by FindCycle.

```
In[80]:= FindCycle[AddEdges[Path[4], {{1, 2}}]]
Out[80]= {1, 2, 1}
```

A directed graph with half the edges is almost certain to contain a cycle. Directed acyclic graphs are often called *DAGs*.

```
In[81]:= AcyclicQ[RandomGraph[20,0.5, Type->Directed]]
Out[81]= False
```

■ 7.3.2 Girth

The *girth* of a graph is the length of its shortest cycle. Simple graphs of minimal girth can be constructed by including a triangle, but achieving large girth in a graph with many edges is a difficult and interesting problem.

Our algorithm for finding the girth searches for the smallest cycle originating from each vertex v_i, since the smallest of these defines the girth of the graph. A breadth-first search starting from v_i finds the shortest distance to all expanded vertices. Any edge connecting two vertices in the tree creates a cycle. We continue the search until it is clear that no shorter cycle can be found. The correctness of our pruning procedure follows from the observation that the shortest cycle through vertex v containing edge (x,y) must consist of the shortest vertex-disjoint paths from v to x and v to y. If the shortest paths are not vertex-disjoint, then there will be a shorter cycle associated with another vertex.

These are the first six 3-regular *cage graphs*. A *g-cage graph* is a smallest 3-regular graph with girth g. The graphs listed here are for $g = 3, 4, 5, 6, 7, 8$. A *(g,k)-cage graph* is a smallest *k*-regular graph with girth g, which is known only for very small values of k and g.

```
In[82]:= ShowGraphArray[c = Table[CageGraph[g], {g, 3, 8}]];
```

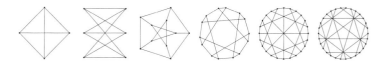

Mapping the function Girth onto each of the six cage graphs shown above correctly identifies their girth.

```
In[83]:= Map[Girth, c]
Out[83]= {3, 4, 5, 6, 7, 8}
```

Every cycle extracted from a girth-8 graph is of length ≥ 8. We subtract one from each cycle to avoid double counting the start/end vertex.

```
In[84]:= Map[Length, ExtractCycles[CageGraph[8]]] - 1
Out[84]= {8, 10, 8}
```

These are (g, k)-cages for $k = 3, 4, 5$ and $g = 3, 4, 5, 6$.

```
In[85]:= ShowGraphArray[c=Table[CageGraph[k, g], {k, 3, 5}, {g, 3, 6}]];
```

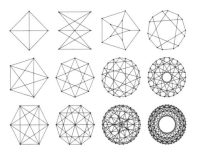

This verifies that the graphs constructed by CageGraph satisfy the regularity property and have the correct degree and girth.

```
In[86]:= Map[{RegularQ[#], Degrees[#][[1]], Girth[#]} &, Flatten[c, 1]]
Out[86]= {{True, 3, 3}, {True, 3, 4}, {True, 3, 5},
    {True, 3, 6}, {True, 4, 3}, {True, 4, 4}, {True, 4, 5},
    {True, 4, 6}, {True, 5, 3}, {True, 5, 4}, {True, 5, 5},
    {True, 5, 6}}
```

The girth of a tree is ∞, since there is no shortest cycle in the graph.

```
In[87]:= Girth[RandomTree[10]]
Out[87]= Infinity
```

Since the search is cut off promptly once the shortest cycle is discovered, Girth is reasonably fast even on this 70-vertex graph of large girth. The time complexity of Girth is $O(mn)$.

```
In[88]:= Timing[ Girth[CageGraph[3,10]] ]
Out[88]= {2.37 Second, 10}
```

It is fairly quickly established that the girth of a 1000-vertex grid graph is 4.

```
In[89]:= Timing[Girth[ GridGraph[10, 10, 10]]]
Out[89]= {28.14 Second, 4}
```

The length of the longest cycle in a graph is its *circumference*. Since testing whether a graph is Hamiltonian is equivalent to asking if its circumference is n, computing the circumference is a computationally expensive operation.

■ 7.3.3 Eulerian Cycles

Euler initiated the study of graph theory in 1736 with the famous Seven Bridges of Königsberg problem. The town of Königsberg straddled the Pregel River with a total of seven bridges connecting the two shores and two islands. The townsfolk were interested in crossing every bridge exactly once and returning to the starting point. Euler proved that this was impossible. More generally, he proved that a tour of all edges without repetition in a connected, undirected graph is possible if and only if each vertex is of even degree. Such graphs are known as *Eulerian graphs*.

An *Eulerian cycle* is a complete tour of all the edges of a graph. The term *circuit* is more appropriate than cycle, because vertices (but not edges) might be visited repeatedly in a simple circuit. Directed graphs have directed Eulerian cycles if and only if they are *weakly* connected and each vertex has the same in-degree as out-degree. The strong connectivity necessary for an Eulerian cycle falls out of the equality between in- and out-degrees.

```
EulerianQ::obsolete = "Usage of Directed as a second argument to EulerianQ is obsolete."
EulerianQ[g_Graph, Directed] := (Message[EulerianQ::obsolete]; EulerianQ[g])
EulerianQ[g_Graph] := ConnectedQ[g] && (InDegree[g] === OutDegree[g]) /; !UndirectedQ[g]
EulerianQ[g_Graph] := ConnectedQ[g] && Apply[And,Map[EvenQ, Degrees[g]]] /; UndirectedQ[g]

OutDegree[g_Graph, n_Integer] := Length[Select[Edges[g], (First[#]==n)&]]
OutDegree[g_Graph] := Map[Length, ToAdjacencyLists[g]]
InDegree[g_Graph, n_Integer] := Length[Select[Edges[g], (Last[#]==n)&]]
InDegree[g_Graph] := OutDegree[ReverseEdges[g]]
```

Identifying Eulerian Graphs

We can display the bridges of Königsberg appropriately as a multigraph using *Combinatorica*. An English translation of Euler's original paper appears in [BLW76].

In[90]:= **ShowGraph[k=FromAdjacencyMatrix[{{0,1,1,1}, {1,0,2,0}, {1,2,0,2}, {1,0,2,0}}]];**

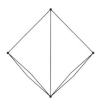

The people of Königsberg never could find a way to tour the bridges, and it became even more difficult after they were destroyed in World War II. They were located in the present-day city of Kaliningrad in Russia [Wil86].

In[91]:= **EulerianQ[k]**

Out[91]= False

It is appropriate that Fleury's algorithm [Luc91], an elegant way to construct an Eulerian cycle, uses bridges for a solution. Start walking from any vertex and erase any edge that has been traversed. The only criterion in picking an edge is that we do not select a bridge unless there are no other alternatives. Of course, no Eulerian graph contains a bridge, but what remains after traversing some edges eventually ceases to be biconnected. Fleury's algorithm is more elegant than efficient, since it is expensive to recompute which edges are bridges after each deletion. Thus we use a different algorithm, attributed to [Hie73], which extracts all the cycles and then concatenates them by finding common vertices.

```
EulerianCycle::obsolete = "Usage of Directed as a second argument to EulerianCycle is obsolete."
EulerianCycle[g_Graph, Directed] := (Message[EulerianCycle::obsolete]; EulerianCycle[g])
EulerianCycle[g_Graph] :=
      Module[{euler,c,cycles,v},
              cycles = Map[(Drop[#,-1])&, ExtractCycles[g]];
              {euler, cycles} = {First[cycles], Rest[cycles]};
              Do [
                      c = First[ Select[cycles, (Intersection[euler,#]=!={})&] ];
                      v = First[Intersection[euler,c]];
                      euler = Join[
                              RotateLeft[c, Position[c,v] [[1,1]] ],
                              RotateLeft[euler, Position[euler,v] [[1,1]] ]
                      ];
                      cycles = Complement[cycles,{c}],
                      {Length[cycles]}
              ];
              Append[euler, First[euler]]
      ] /; EulerianQ[g]
```

Finding an Eulerian Tour

We find an Eulerian cycle in the three-dimensional De Bruijn graph. The cycle is listed as a sequence of vertices in the order in which they are visited.

```
In[92]:= c = EulerianCycle[DeBruijnGraph[2, 3]]

Out[92]= {4, 7, 5, 2, 3, 6, 4, 8, 8, 7, 6, 3, 5, 1, 1, 2, 4}
```

De Bruijn graphs are always Eulerian, because every vertex in every De Bruijn graph has equal in-degree and out-degree.

```
In[93]:= Map[EulerianQ, Table[DeBruijnGraph[2, i], {i, 2, 7}]]

Out[93]= {True, True, True, True, True, True}
```

An Eulerian cycle of a bipartite graph bounces back and forth between the stages.

```
In[94]:= EulerianCycle[ CompleteKPartiteGraph[4,4] ]

Out[94]= {7, 2, 8, 1, 5, 4, 6, 3, 7, 4, 8, 3, 5, 2, 6, 1, 7}
```

Every edge is traversed exactly once in an Eulerian cycle.

```
In[95]:= EmptyQ[ DeleteCycle[CompleteGraph[19],
                  EulerianCycle[CompleteGraph[19]]] ]

Out[95]= True
```

The Chinese postman problem [Kwa62] asks for a shortest tour of a graph that visits each edge at least once. Clearly, if the graph is Eulerian, an Eulerian cycle is an optimal postman tour since each edge is visited exactly once. A Chinese postman tour traverses each edge in a tree twice. In fact, no edge in any graph need ever be traversed more than twice. A polynomial-time algorithm for finding an optimal postman tour appears in [EJ73]. A different generalization of the Eulerian cycle problem for odd vertices seeks the largest subgraph of a graph that is Eulerian. This problem can be shown to be NP-complete by a simple reduction from Hamiltonian cycle on a 3-regular graph.

De Bruijn Sequences

Suppose a safecracker is faced with a combination lock, where the possible combinations consist of strings of n numbers from an alphabet of size σ. Thus there are a total of σ^n combinations. Further, the lock does not have a reset mechanism, so that it opens whenever the last n numbers entered are the combination. By exploiting the overlap between successive combinations, all combinations can be tried while entering fewer numbers. The safecracker's problem is this: What is a shortest string that contains each of the σ^n combinations as contiguous subsequences? An upper bound is $n\sigma^n$, by concatenating all combinations. A lower bound is σ^n, because each of the σ^n combinations must start at different locations in the string.

A *De Bruijn sequence* [dB46] is a circular sequence of length σ^n with the property that each string of length n over an alphabet of size σ occurs as a contiguous part of the sequence. Since the length of a De Bruijn sequence equals the number of strings of this size, and different strings cannot share the same endpoint in a sequence, a De Bruijn sequence gives an optimal solution to the safecracker's problem. De Bruijn sequences are constructed by finding an Eulerian cycle in a De Bruijn graph [Goo46]. The first symbol of each visited string on this cycle describes a De Bruijn sequence.

```
DeBruijnSequence[{}, n_Integer?Positive] := {}
DeBruijnSequence[alph_List, 1] := Union[alph]
DeBruijnSequence[alph_List, n_Integer?Positive] :=
        Rest[Strings[Union[alph], n-1]
           [[ EulerianCycle[DeBruijnGraph[Union[alph], n-1]], 1]]
        ]
```

Constructing De Bruijn Sequences

De Bruijn sequences can also be generated by feedback shift registers [Gol66, Ron84] and have properties that are useful for random number generation. For example, each substring occurs an equal number of times.

```
In[96]:= s = DeBruijnSequence[{0,1}, 3]

Out[96]= {1, 0, 1, 0, 0, 0, 1, 1}
```

Taking every four consecutive symbols of this De Bruijn sequence gives all the strings of length 4. The number of De Bruijn sequences on n symbols of a σ symbol alphabet is determined in [Knu67].

```
In[97]:= Table[Take[RotateLeft[s,q],4], {q,0,15}]

Out[97]= {{1, 0, 1, 0}, {0, 1, 0, 0}, {1, 0, 0, 0},
   {0, 0, 0, 1}, {0, 0, 1, 1}, {0, 1, 1, 1}, {1, 1, 1, 0},
   {1, 1, 0, 1}, {1, 0, 1, 0}, {0, 1, 0, 0}, {1, 0, 0, 0},
   {0, 0, 0, 1}, {0, 0, 1, 1}, {0, 1, 1, 1}, {1, 1, 1, 0},
   {1, 1, 0, 1}}
```

Eulerian tours and postman walks on De Bruijn sequences arise in DNA sequencing by hybridization [CK94, Pev89], where we seek to reconstruct a string *S* from the spectrum of *k*-length substrings of *S*.

```
In[98]:= Apply[StringJoin, Map[ToString, DeBruijnSequence[{A,C,G,T}, 3]]]
Out[98]= TCTGCGCCCATGATCACAGTAGGGTTTGTGGAGCAATTATAAGAAACTAC\
         GACCTCCGTCGGCT
```

■ 7.3.4 Hamiltonian Cycles and Paths

A *Hamiltonian cycle* of a graph *G* visits every *vertex* exactly once, as opposed to an Eulerian cycle, which visits each *edge* exactly once. A *Hamiltonian path* is like a Hamiltonian cycle, except that it is a path. The problem of computing a Hamiltonian cycle or a Hamiltonian path is fundamentally different from the problem of computing an Eulerian cycle, because testing whether a graph is Hamiltonian is NP-complete.

We can use backtracking to find one or all of the Hamiltonian cycles of a graph, advancing when we reach a new vertex and retreating when all edges return to previously visited vertices. By starting all cycles at vertex 1, each Hamiltonian cycle is generated only once. To quickly terminate paths that cannot lead to a Hamiltonian cycle, we use the following test. If the current path that we have is $v_1, v_2, \ldots, v_k$, we check whether the graph obtained by deleting vertices $v_2, \ldots, v_{k-1}$ and adding the edge $\{v_1, v_k\}$ is biconnected. If not, there is no hope that we can complete the current path into a Hamiltonian cycle. We use the Hamiltonian cycle algorithm to compute Hamiltonian paths. *Combinatorica* provides functions HamiltonianCycle and HamiltonianPath that perform these computations.

$K_{n,n}$ for $n > 1$ are the only Hamiltonian complete bipartite graphs.

```
In[99]:= HamiltonianCycle[CompleteKPartiteGraph[3,3],All]
Out[99]= {{1, 4, 2, 5, 3, 6, 1}, {1, 4, 2, 6, 3, 5, 1},
         {1, 4, 3, 5, 2, 6, 1}, {1, 4, 3, 6, 2, 5, 1},
         {1, 5, 2, 4, 3, 6, 1}, {1, 5, 2, 6, 3, 4, 1},
         {1, 5, 3, 4, 2, 6, 1}, {1, 5, 3, 6, 2, 4, 1},
         {1, 6, 2, 4, 3, 5, 1}, {1, 6, 2, 5, 3, 4, 1},
         {1, 6, 3, 4, 2, 5, 1}, {1, 6, 3, 5, 2, 4, 1}}
```

All Hamiltonian graphs are biconnected, but not vice versa. This provides a useful heuristic in quickly identifying non-Hamiltonian graphs.

```
In[100]:= HamiltonianQ[ CompleteKPartiteGraph[3,4] ]
Out[100]= False
```

Ore [Ore60] showed that an *n*-vertex graph is Hamiltonian if the sum of degrees of nonadjacent vertices is always greater than *n*. Here we show a Hamiltonian cycle in such an *Ore graph*. Such cycles in such graphs can be constructed in polynomial time [BC76].

In[101]:= **g = SpringEmbedding[RegularGraph[6, 11]];**
ShowGraph[Highlight[g, {Map[Sort,
Partition[HamiltonianCycle[g], 2, 1]]}]];

Tait [Tai80] "proved" the four-color theorem by using the assumption that all cubic 3-connected graphs are Hamiltonian. Tutte [Tut46, Tut72] gave this non-Hamiltonian graph as a counterexample to Tait's assumption.

In[103]:= **ShowGraph[TutteGraph];**

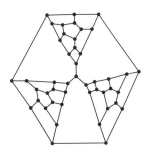

Even though the Tutte graph is fairly large (46 vertices and 69 edges), our function is able to prove that it is not Hamiltonian.

In[104]:= **Timing[HamiltonianCycle[TutteGraph]]**

Out[104]= {137.66 Second, {}}

The dodecahedron holds a special place in the history of graph theory. In 1857 [BC87], Hamilton developed the "around the world game," which challenged the player to find a cycle that visits each of the 20 vertices of the dodecahedron exactly once. Unfortunately, the game did not sell well enough to make a profit.

```
In[105]:= ShowGraph[Highlight[d = DodecahedralGraph,
            {Partition[HamiltonianCycle[d ], 2, 1]}]];
```

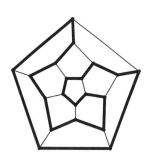

There are 60 possible Hamiltonian cycles in the dodecahedron, and 30 if we take a cycle and its reversal to be identical. The 12 regular faces of the dodecahedron make it of crucial importance to the calendar paperweight industry [Cha85].

```
In[106]:= Length[HamiltonianCycle[d, All]]
Out[106]= 60
```

The *m × n knight's tour graph* represents all possible moves that a knight can make on an *m × n* chessboard. Any Hamiltonian cycle in this graph solves the old puzzle asking whether a knight can visit every every square in a chessboard exactly once and return home. `KnightsTourGraph` produces these graphs for any *m* and *n*. Here we show a successful knight's tour on a 6 × 6 board.

```
In[107]:= ShowGraph[Highlight[k = KnightsTourGraph[6, 6],
            {Partition[HamiltonianCycle[k], 2, 1]}]];
```

The four-dimensional hypercube with one vertex deleted is not Hamiltonian...

```
In[108]:= g = DeleteVertex[Hypercube[4], 1];
          HamiltonianQ[g]
Out[109]= False
```

...but it contains a Hamiltonian path.

```
In[110]:= HamiltonianPath[g]
Out[110]= {1, 2, 6, 5, 4, 7, 11, 8, 9, 10, 14, 13, 12, 15, 3}
```

The *Meredith graph* is a 4-regular 4-connected graph that is not Hamiltonian, providing a counterexample to a conjecture by Nash-Williams [Mer73]. The *Thomassen graph* is an example of a *hypotraceable graph*. A graph *G* is hypotraceable if it has no Hamiltonian path but whose subgraph $G - v$ has a Hamiltonian path for every vertex v.

```
In[111]:= ShowGraphArray[{MeredithGraph, ThomassenGraph}];
```

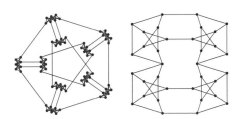

■ 7.3.5 Traveling Salesman Tours

The traveling salesman problem (TSP) is perhaps the most notorious NP-complete problem [LLKS85]. Given a collection of cities connected by roads, find the *shortest* route that visits each city exactly once. Its appealing title and real applications have made TSP the favorite hard problem of the popular press.

A backtracking algorithm similar to that of `HamiltonianCycle` serves to find an optimal tour. The best tour found to date is saved, and the search backtracks unless the partial solution is cheaper than the cost of the best tour. In a graph with positive edge weights, such a partial solution cannot expand into a better tour. *Combinatorica* provides a function `TravelingSalesman` that solves the TSP.

The cost of any Hamiltonian cycle in unweighted graphs equals the number of vertices.

```
In[112]:= CostOfPath[g=CompleteKPartiteGraph[3,3],HamiltonianCycle[g]]
Out[112]= 6
```

Here we construct an edge-weighted complete graph, with edge weights as randomly chosen integers from [1, 10].

```
In[113]:= g = SetEdgeWeights[CompleteGraph[7], WeightingFunction ->
          RandomInteger,
          WeightRange -> {1, 10}];
```

The assigned weights of this complete graph are shown. The nonuniform weights imply that different Hamiltonian cycles will return different cost tours.

```
In[114]:= ToAdjacencyMatrix[g,EdgeWeight] // ColumnForm
Out[114]= {Infinity, 10, 2, 2, 5, 5, 1}
          {10, Infinity, 9, 7, 8, 8, 6}
          {2, 9, Infinity, 6, 7, 2, 5}
          {2, 7, 6, Infinity, 6, 3, 10}
          {5, 8, 7, 6, Infinity, 5, 9}
          {5, 8, 2, 3, 5, Infinity, 8}
          {1, 6, 5, 10, 9, 8, Infinity}
```

Since *g* is a complete graph, it is Hamiltonian and thus contains a noninfinite solution. Here are edges appearing in the optimal solution.

```
In[115]:= Partition[p = TravelingSalesman[g],2,1]
Out[115]= {{1, 3}, {3, 6}, {6, 4}, {4, 5}, {5, 2}, {2, 7},
          {7, 1}}
```

The optimal tour avoids the heaviest edges. Its cost is shown here along with that of visiting all vertices in order.

```
In[116]:= {CostOfPath[g, p], CostOfPath[g, {1, 2, 3, 4, 5, 6, 7, 1}]}
Out[116]= {28, 45}
```

Since the traveling salesman problem is so difficult to solve exactly, it would be nice to be able to find good but nonoptimal tours quickly. However, for *general* weight matrices, no polynomial-time algorithm exists that closely approximates the optimal tour, unless $P = NP$ [CLRS01].

The *metric traveling salesman* problem assumes that the distances in the graph form a metric. A *metric* is a function d that obeys the triangle inequality, is nonnegative, and $d(x, y) = 0$ if and only if $x = y$. A function d obeys the *triangle inequality* if and only if for all x, y, and z, $d(x, y) + d(y, z) \geq d(x, z)$. *Combinatorica* provides a function `TriangleInequalityQ` that tests if a given square matrix specifies a function that satisfies the triangle inequality.

Even if the weights of a particular graph are not metric, the all-pairs shortest-path function of it is. `AllPairsShortestPath` returns an $n \times n$ matrix whose $[i, j]$th entry contains the shortest-path distance from vertex i to vertex j in the graph.

```
In[117]:= TriangleInequalityQ[
            AllPairsShortestPath[RandomGraph[10,1,{1,10}] ] ]
Out[117]= True
```

An approximation algorithm for metric TSP can be obtained by using minimum spanning trees. A *minimum spanning tree* of an edge-weighted graph G is a spanning tree of G with minimum weight. Given a metric graph G, we first compute a minimum spanning tree T of G. We then perform a depth-first traversal of T starting from any vertex, and we order the vertices of the G as they were discovered in this traversal. This ordering gives a tour that is at most twice the optimal tour in metric graphs [RSL77].

This places the vertices of K_{10} at randomly chosen positions in the plane and assigns weights to the edges that equal the Euclidean distance between endpoints.

```
In[118]:= g = SetEdgeWeights[g = RandomVertices[CompleteGraph[10]],
            WeightingFunction -> Euclidean]
Out[118]= -Graph:<45, 10, Undirected>-
```

This is a minimum spanning tree of the above graph. Because it observes the triangle inequality, no two edges in the minimum spanning tree cross.

```
In[119]:= ShowGraph[t = MinimumSpanningTree[g], VertexNumber->True];
```

This lists the vertices of the graph ordered by a depth-first traversal of the minimum spanning tree.

```
In[120]:= d = DepthFirstTraversal[t, 1]
Out[120]= {1, 9, 3, 5, 8, 4, 2, 6, 10, 7}
```

This highlights the corresponding tour. Observe that certain edges on this tour do not appear in the minimum spanning tree. These are shortcuts taken instead of repeatedly visiting the same vertices. The resulting tour is at most twice the weight of the minimum spanning tree.

```
In[121]:= e = Map[Sort, Partition[Append[d, 1], 2, 1]];
          ne = Complement[e, Edges[t]];
          h = AddEdges[t, ne];
          ShowGraph[Highlight[h, {e}], VertexStyle -> Disk[0.05]];
```

Christofides [Chr76] has improved on this algorithm, by using minimum weight matchings instead of minimum spanning trees. His algorithm gives a tour that is within 3/2 of the optimal. A special case of the metric TSP is the *Euclidean traveling salesman* problem, in which the cities to be toured are points in Euclidean space and the distances between cities are Euclidean distances between corresponding points. In a breakthrough result, Arora [Aro98] and Mitchell [Mit99] presented approximation algorithms for the Euclidean TSP that produce a tour whose cost is within ε times the cost of the optimal tour and that run in time polynomial in the number of cities and $1/\varepsilon$.

Another heuristic for the traveling salesman problem that has proven quite effective in practice mutates a Hamiltonian cycle by deleting a small number of edges and then connects them in a different way. The performance of such a heuristic depends on the mutation schedule and selection procedure [Lin65].

7.4 Graph Coloring

A *vertex coloring* is an assignment of labels or colors to each vertex of a graph such that no edge connects two identically colored vertices. It is easy to color an n-vertex graph with n colors by coloring each vertex uniquely, but the problem gets harder when the goal is minimizing the number of colors. The *chromatic number* of a graph $\chi(G)$ is the smallest number of colors with which it is possible to color all vertices of G.

The one-colorable graphs are totally disconnected, and two-colorability is a synonym for bipartiteness. The situation gets more interesting when at least three colors are necessary. Applications of graph coloring include scheduling and compiler optimization [OR81, JL94, VEM93, HLM$^+$90, RP97].

Perhaps the most notorious problem in graph theory was whether all planar graphs are four-colorable. The history of the four-color problem dates back to 1852 [SK86], culminating with the computer-aided proof of Appel and Haken [AH77, AHK77]. The unusual nature of this proof made it the focus of some nasty rumors, which are debunked in [AH86].

■ 7.4.1 Bipartite Graphs

A graph is bipartite if the vertices can be partitioned into two disjoint sets such that no edge spans vertices of different sets. Thus "two-colorable" and "bipartite" are exactly the same property. An alternate characterization of bipartite graphs is that a graph is bipartite if and only if all cycles are of even length. The presence of an odd-length cycle is easy to recognize using breadth-first search, because a graph contains an odd-length cycle if and only if in every BFS tree of the graph there is an edge that connects two vertices at the same distance from the root. TwoColoring, given below, assigns each vertex one of two colors, such that the coloring is valid if the given graph is bipartite.

```
TwoColoring[g_Graph] := {} /; (V[g] == 0)
TwoColoring[g_Graph] := TwoColoring[MakeSimple[g]] /; (!SimpleQ[g]) || (!UndirectedQ[g])
TwoColoring[g_Graph] :=
     Module[{c = ConnectedComponents[g], p, b},
           Mod[Flatten[Map[Cases[#, _Integer]&,
                       Transpose[Map[BreadthFirstTraversal[g, #[[1]], Level]&, c]]
                     ], 1
               ], 2
           ] + 1
     ]
BipartiteQ[g_Graph] :=
     Module[{c = TwoColoring[g]}, Apply[And, Map[c[[ #[[1]] ]] != c[[ #[[2]] ]]&, Edges[g]]]]
```

Finding a Two-Coloring of a Graph

Here is a ranked embedding of a four-dimensional hypercube, with its two-coloring highlighted. Vertices appear in levels depending on their distance from a particular vertex. Since all edges go from one level to the next, the hypercube contains no odd-length cycles and is therefore bipartite.

```
In[125]:= g=RankedEmbedding[Hypercube[4], {1}];
          s={Disk[0.05], Box[0.05]}; c=TwoColoring[g];
          ShowGraphArray[{g, SetGraphOptions[g,Table[{i,
            VertexStyle->s[[Mod[c[[i]], 2]+1]]}, {i, V[g]}]] }];
```

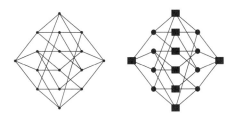

The output of TwoColoring is valid only if the graph is bipartite.

```
In[128]:= If [BipartiteQ[g], TwoColoring[g]]
Out[128]= {1, 2, 1, 2, 2, 1, 2, 1, 1, 2, 1, 2, 2, 1, 2, 1}
```

Trees, grid graphs, and even-length cycles are bipartite, but not odd cycles.

```
In[129]:= {BipartiteQ[RandomTree[10]], BipartiteQ[Cycle[12]],
            BipartiteQ[GridGraph[3, 3, 3]], BipartiteQ[Cycle[11]]}
Out[129]= {True, True, True, False}
```

■ 7.4.2 Chromatic Polynomials

Any labeled graph G can be colored in a certain number of ways with exactly k colors $1,...,k$. Thus G defines a particular chromatic function $\pi_G(z)$ such that $\pi_G(k)$ is the number of ways G can be k-colored. Birkhoff [Bir12, BL46] presented a nice way to compute this *chromatic polynomial* of a graph, for the function is indeed always a polynomial.

Observe that, for an empty graph E on n vertices, $\pi_E(z) = z^n$, since every vertex can be assigned any color. Now consider the chromatic polynomial of an arbitrary graph G. If we delete an edge (x, y) of G, yielding G', we get a graph that can be colored in more ways than G, since x and y in G' can be assigned the same color, which was prevented by (x, y). In fact, G' can be colored in all the ways G can, plus other ways in which x and y have identical colors. Contracting (x, y) in G' gives a graph that can be colored every way G' can, restricted so x and y receive the same color. Thus the chromatic polynomial of G is the chromatic polynomial of $G - (x, y)$ minus the chromatic polynomial of the contraction of (x, y) in G. Since both graphs are smaller than G, this computation eventually ends with an empty graph.

This gives a recursive algorithm to compute the chromatic polynomial of a graph. If we start with a dense graph, it will take many deletions before we get to the base case of an empty graph, so to make the computation more efficient we may rearrange the recurrence relation to add edges and terminate instead on a complete graph. Since no two vertices in a complete graph K_n can have the same color, the chromatic polynomial $\pi_{K_n}(z) = z(z - 1) \cdots (z - n + 1)$. Further, we can exploit the fact that the chromatic polynomial is known for trees. Except for such special cases, the computation is exponential in the minimum of the number of edges in the graph and its complement. Heuristics for fast graph polynomial computation are presented in [HM99].

Our `ChromaticPolynomial` function calls `ChromaticSparse` or `ChromaticDense`, depending on the density of the graph.

```
ChromaticPolynomial[g_Graph,z_]:= ChromaticPolynomial[MakeSimple[g], z]/; !SimpleQ[g]
ChromaticPolynomial[g_Graph,z_]:=0/;IdenticalQ[g,CompleteGraph[0]]
ChromaticPolynomial[g_Graph,z_] := Module[{i}, Product[z-i, {i,0,V[g]-1}] ] /; CompleteQ[g]
ChromaticPolynomial[g_Graph,z_]:=z ( z - 1 ) ^ (V[g]-1) /; TreeQ[g]
ChromaticPolynomial[g_Graph,z_] := If[M[g]>Binomial[V[g],2]/2, ChromaticDense[g,z], ChromaticSparse[g,z]]

ChromaticSparse[g_Graph,z_] := z^V[g] /; EmptyQ[g]
ChromaticSparse[g_Graph,z_] :=
        Block[{e = Edges[g]},
              ChromaticSparse[ DeleteEdges[g,{First[e]}], z] -
              ChromaticSparse[MakeSimple[Contract[g,First[e]]], z]
        ]

ChromaticDense[g_Graph, z_] := ChromaticPolynomial[g,z] /; CompleteQ[g]
ChromaticDense[g_Graph, z_] :=
        Block[{el = Edges[GraphComplement[g]]},
              ChromaticDense[AddEdges[g,{{First[el]}}], z] +
              ChromaticDense[MakeSimple[Contract[g,First[el]]], z]
        ]
```

Computing the Chromatic Polynomial of a Graph

For dense graphs, the computation terminates on complete graphs, which have a chromatic polynomial defined in terms of the falling factorial function.

```
In[130]:= ChromaticPolynomial[ DeleteEdge[CompleteGraph[5],{1,2}], z ]
Out[130]= (-3 + z) (-2 + z) (-1 + z) z +
          (-4 + z) (-3 + z) (-2 + z) (-1 + z) z
```

The computed polynomial is not always in the simplest possible form.

```
In[131]:= Simplify[ % ]
                        2            2
Out[131]= (-3 + z)  z (2 - 3 z + z )
```

Finding the chromatic polynomial of a cycle would proceed more quickly on certain graphs if the special case of the tree were tested in each iteration. However, this will slow down the computation for most graphs.

```
In[132]:= ChromaticPolynomial[Cycle[10], z]
                        2         3         4         5         6
Out[132]= -9 z + 45 z  - 120 z + 210 z  - 252 z  + 210 z  -
                    7        8        9     10
             120 z  + 45 z  - 10 z  + z
```

The chromatic polynomial of a disconnected graph is the product of the chromatic polynomials of its connected components.

```
In[133]:= Factor[ ChromaticPolynomial[ GraphUnion[
              CompleteKPartiteGraph[2,2], Cycle[3] ], z] ]
                             2  2             2
Out[133]= (-2 + z) (-1 + z)  z  (3 - 3 z + z )
```

Some of the terms in the chromatic polynomial of the graph union above are the contributions of the chromatic polynomial of $K_{2,2}$...

...whereas the rest of the terms are contributed by the 3-cycle.

The chromatic polynomial of a graph of order n has degree n. The coefficients alternate in sign and the coefficient of the $(n-1)$st term is $-m$, where m is the number of edges.

To three-color the wheel, one color must be selected for the center and the other two alternate red-black or black-red around the cycle, for a total of six three-colorings. Observe that the chromatic polynomial is still defined when the number of colors exceeds the degree.

```
In[134]:= Factor[ Expand[ ChromaticPolynomial[
              CompleteKPartiteGraph[2, 2], z ]]]

Out[134]= (-1 + z) z (3 - 3 z + z )
                               2

In[135]:= Factor[Expand[ChromaticPolynomial[Cycle[3], z ]]]

Out[135]= (-2 + z) (-1 + z) z

In[136]:= Expand[ wheelpoly[z_] = ChromaticPolynomial[Wheel[7],z] ]

                   2        3        4       5       6
Out[136]= 62 z - 191 z + 240 z - 160 z + 60 z - 12 z +

           7
          z

In[137]:= Table[wheelpoly[z], {z,1, 10}]

Out[137]= {0, 0, 6, 264, 3660, 24600, 109410, 373296,

           1058904, 2621520}
```

■ 7.4.3 Finding a Vertex Coloring

The problem of finding a vertex coloring that uses fewest colors is NP-complete for three or more colors [Kar72]. Our function `MinimumVertexColoring` uses backtracking to compute a vertex coloring of a graph with the fewest colors. Specifically, given a graph G and a positive integer k, the function does a brute-force search to test if G has a k-coloring. To obtain a minimum vertex coloring, we start with a heuristic coloring and then attempt to improve this by a brute-force search.

```
MinimumVertexColoring[g_Graph] := MinimumVertexColoring[MakeSimple[g]] /; !UndirectedQ[g]

MinimumVertexColoring[g_Graph] := Table[1, {V[g]}] /; EmptyQ[g]
MinimumVertexColoring[g_Graph] := TwoColoring[g] /; BipartiteQ[g]
MinimumVertexColoring[g_Graph] := {} /; (V[g] == 0)
MinimumVertexColoring[g_Graph] := {1} /; (V[g] == 1)
MinimumVertexColoring[g_Graph] :=
    Module[{col, oldCol, c},
        c = Max[oldCol = VertexColoring[g, Algorithm->Brelaz]];
        col = oldCol;
        For[i = c-1, i >= 3, i--,
           col = MinimumVertexColoring[g, i];
           If[col == {}, Return[oldCol], oldCol = col]
        ];
        col
    ]
```

```
MinimumVertexColoring[g_Graph, k_Integer, number_Symbol:One] := {} /; (V[g] == 0)
MinimumVertexColoring[g_Graph, k_Integer, number_Symbol:One] := {1} /; ((V[g] == 1) && (k == 1))
MinimumVertexColoring[g_Graph, k_Integer, number_Symbol:One] := {} /; ((V[g] == 1) && (k != 1))
MinimumVertexColoring[g_Graph, k_Integer, number_Symbol:One] :=
    Module[{e},
           e = ToAdjacencyLists[g, Type->Simple];
           Backtrack[
               Join[{{1}}, Table[Range[k], {V[g] - 1}]],
               (!MemberQ[#[[PriorEdges[e[[Length[#]]], Length[#]]]], Last[#]]) &,
               (!MemberQ[#[[PriorEdges[e[[Length[#]]], Length[#]]]], Last[#]]) &,
               number
           ]
    ]

PriorEdges[l_List, k_Integer] := Select[l, (# <= k) &]
```

Computing a Minimum Vertex Coloring

The function `MinimumVertexColoring` calls a general-purpose backtracking function `Backtrack` to do brute-force search. Other *Combinatorica* functions such as `MaximumClique` that do brute-force searches also use `Backtrack`. There is a trade-off between having a small and compact function that simply calls `Backtrack` with appropriate arguments and having a more complicated search function that does everything from scratch and is more fine-tuned to the particular problem.

The implementation of `Backtrack` is based on the principle that when the solution space to a problem consists of ordered configurations of elements, each prefix to a solution represents a *partial solution*. If we can demonstrate that a given prefix does not lead to to any solutions, there is no reason to expand the prefix and look further. *Backtracking* lets us start with the smallest possible configuration and keep on adding elements to it until either we have achieved a final solution or we can prove that there are no solutions with this prefix. In the first case, we return the answer; in the second, we remove the last element from the configuration and then replace it with the next possibility. Backtracking can greatly reduce the amount of work in an exhaustive search or, in this case, an exhaustive construction.

```
Backtrack[space_List,partialQ_,solutionQ_,flag_:One] :=
    Module[{n=Length[space],all={},done,index, v=2, solution},
        index=Prepend[ Table[0,{n-1}],1];
        While[v > 0,
            done = False;
            While[!done && (index[[v]] < Length[space[[v]]]),
                index[[v]]++;
                done = Apply[partialQ,{Solution[space,index,v]}];
            ];
            If [done, v++, index[[v--]]=0 ];
            If [v > n,
                solution = Solution[space,index,n];
                If [Apply[solutionQ,{solution}],
                    If [SameQ[flag,All],
                        AppendTo[all,solution],
                        all = solution; v=0
                    ]
                ];
                v--
            ]
        ];
        all
    ]

Solution[space_List,index_List,count_Integer] :=
    Module[{i}, Table[space[[ i,index[[i]] ]], {i,count}] ]
```

Generalized Backtracking

`Backtrack` takes four arguments. The first describes the *state space*, which are the possible elements that can be in each position. The second is a predicate that is applied in testing whether a partial solution can be extended, while the third argument is a predicate to test whether a configuration is the final solution. Finally, an optional flag specifies whether the search should stop on the first solution or continue the search to find all of them.

The key to `Backtrack` is the index array, which keeps track of the state of the partial solution. Since the index always increases lexicographically, the search will terminate without finding duplicates. The partial solution at any given point can be obtained by copying the indexed elements of space.

For the problem of testing if a graph can be *k*-colored, the state space consists of all *k* colors for each of the vertices, except for the first, which we can color 1 without any loss of generality. The predicate to test the legality of both partial and complete solutions is whether the most recently colored vertex has a color distinct from the colors of neighbors. If so, we go on to the next vertex; otherwise, we are at a dead end and need to backtrack.

The *Mycielski graph* of order k is a triangle-free graph with chromatic number k. Here we color the first four Mycielski graphs optimally, each using the highest numbered color only once.

```
In[138]:= Table[MinimumVertexColoring[ MycielskiGraph[i] ], {i,1,4}]
Out[138]= {{1}, {1, 2}, {1, 2, 1, 2, 3},
           {1, 2, 2, 1, 3, 3, 1, 2, 4, 1, 2}}
```

Every vertex in a complete graph needs a distinct color.

```
In[139]:= MinimumVertexColoring[CompleteGraph[5]]
Out[139]= {1, 2, 3, 4, 5}
```

Using the tag All makes the vertex coloring algorithm return all colorings it can construct with a given number of colors. Any connected bipartite graph has a unique 2-coloring once we fix the color of any vertex.

```
In[140]:= MinimumVertexColoring[Hypercube[4], 2, All]
Out[140]= {{1, 2, 1, 2, 2, 1, 2, 1, 1, 2, 1, 2, 2, 1, 2, 1}}
```

Brook's theorem [Bro41, Lov75] states that the chromatic number of a graph is at most the maximum vertex degree Δ, unless the graph is complete or an odd cycle. RealizeDegreeSequence generates semirandom graphs, so the colorings are not necessarily identical each time.

```
In[141]:= TableForm[ Table[VertexColoring[
             RealizeDegreeSequence[{4,4,4,4,4,4}] ], {5}] ]
Out[141]//TableForm= 1   2   1   3   2   3
                     1   2   3   1   3   2
                     1   2   3   3   1   2
                     1   2   3   2   1   3
                     1   2   2   3   3   1
```

Large cliques (or even short cycles) are not necessary for high chromatic numbers. For any two positive integers g and k there exists a graph of girth at least g with chromatic number at least k [Erd61, Lov68].

```
In[142]:= VertexColoring[CageGraph[7]]
Out[142]= {1, 2, 1, 2, 1, 2, 1, 2, 1, 2, 1, 2, 1, 2, 3, 1,
           3, 1, 3, 2, 3, 2, 4, 3}
```

Computing the chromatic number is easy given a minimum vertex coloring – just count the number of colors used.

```
ChromaticNumber[g_Graph] := 0 /; (V[g] == 0)
ChromaticNumber[g_Graph] := 1 /; EmptyQ[MakeSimple[g]]
ChromaticNumber[g_Graph] := 2 /; BipartiteQ[MakeSimple[g]]
ChromaticNumber[g_Graph] := V[g] /; CompleteQ[MakeSimple[g]]
ChromaticNumber[g_Graph] := Max[MinimumVertexColoring[g]]
```

Computing the Chromatic Number

The brute-force algorithm to find a minimum vertex coloring is hopeless for large graphs. We need heuristics to effectively color them. Brelaz [Bre79] recommends the following algorithm, which defines a total order on the colors by numbering them from 1 to k. First, color the vertex of largest degree with color 1. Then repeatedly select the vertex with the highest *color degree*, where the color degree is the number of adjacent vertices that have already been colored, and color it with the smallest possible color. `BrelazColoring` implements this heuristic.

```
BrelazColoring[g_Graph] := BrelazColoring[MakeSimple[g]] /; !UndirectedQ[g]

BrelazColoring[g_Graph] := {} /; (V[g] == 0)

BrelazColoring[g_Graph] :=
      Module[{cd = color = Table[0, {V[g]}], m = 0, p, nc,
            e = ToAdjacencyLists[g]},
            While[ m >= 0,
                  p = Position[cd, m][[1, 1]];
                  nc = Append[color[[ e[[p]] ]], 0];
                  color[[ p ]] = Min[Complement[ Range[Max[nc] + 1], nc]];
                  cd[[ p ]] = -2 V[g];
                  Scan[(cd[[ # ]]++)&, e[[ p ]] ];
                  m = Max[cd]
            ];
            color
      ]
Options[VertexColoring] = {Algorithm -> Brelaz};

VertexColoring[g_Graph, opts___?OptionQ] :=
      Module[{algo = Algorithm /. Flatten[{opts, Options[VertexColoring]}]},
            If[algo === Brelaz, BrelazColoring[g], MinimumVertexColoring[g] ]
      ]
```

Brelaz's Heuristic Graph-Coloring Algorithm

The Brelaz heuristic appears optimal for Mycielski graphs. The heuristic is fast enough to handle `MycielskiGraph[10]`, which has 767 vertices and 22,196 edges!

```
In[143]:= Table[ Max[ BrelazColoring[MycielskiGraph[i]] ], {i,1,10}]
Out[143]= {1, 2, 3, 4, 5, 6, 7, 8, 9, 10}
```

The Brelaz heuristic is optimal for trees. The algorithm starts with a vertex of highest degree and continues to color vertices that have an already colored neighbor.

```
In[144]:= Table[Max[BrelazColoring[RandomTree[20]]], {40}]
Out[144]= {2, 2, 2, 2, 2, 2, 2, 2, 2, 2, 2, 2, 2, 2, 2, 2,
          2, 2, 2, 2, 2, 2, 2, 2, 2, 2, 2, 2, 2, 2, 2, 2,
          2, 2, 2, 2, 2, 2}
```

A complete *k*-partite graph is *k*-colorable. Further, Brelaz's algorithm colors such graphs with the minimum number of colors.

```
In[145]:= BrelazColoring[ CompleteKPartiteGraph[1,2,3,1] ]
Out[145]= {1, 2, 2, 3, 3, 3, 4}
```

Like any heuristic, Brelaz's can be improved by making it more sophisticated, at a cost of speed and complexity. Other studies of coloring heuristics include [Gou88, Man85b, MMI72].

■ 7.4.4 Edge Colorings

Finding a minimum edge coloring of a graph is equivalent to finding a minimum vertex coloring of its line graph. Thus the chromatic polynomial and vertex coloring functions can be applied to edge colorings. The *edge chromatic number* of a graph must be at least Δ, the largest degree vertex of the graph, but Vizing [Viz64] and Gupta [Gup66] proved that any graph can be edge colored with at most $\Delta + 1$ colors.

```
EdgeColoring[g_Graph] :=
    Module[{c = VertexColoring[LineGraph[g]], e = Edges[g], se},
        se = Sort[ Table[{e[[i]], i}, {i, Length[e]}]];
        Map[Last, Sort[Map[Reverse, Table[Prepend[se[[i]], c[[i]]], {i, Length[se]}]]]]
    ]
EdgeChromaticNumber[g_Graph] := ChromaticNumber[ LineGraph[g] ]
```

Finding an Edge Coloring of a Graph

The edge chromatic number of a complete bipartite graph is Δ ...

```
In[146]:= EdgeColoring[CompleteKPartiteGraph[3,4]]
Out[146]= {1, 2, 3, 4, 2, 1, 4, 3, 3, 4, 1, 2}
```

...and so is the edge chromatic number of a hypercube. König showed in 1916 [Kon16] that the edge chromatic number of any bipartite multigraph equals its maximum vertex degree.

```
In[147]:= EdgeColoring[Hypercube[4]]
Out[147]= {1, 2, 1, 2, 1, 2, 1, 2, 1, 2, 1, 2, 1, 2, 1, 2,
          3, 3, 3, 3, 4, 4, 4, 4, 3, 3, 3, 3, 4, 4, 4, 4}
```

These are 3-edge and 4-edge colorings of 3/4-dimensional hypercubes, respectively. Edges in each dimension get assigned the same color. Every edge coloring of the hypercube has this property.

```
In[148]:= s = {Normal, Thick, NormalDashed, ThickDashed};
          ShowGraphArray[ Table[
              c = EdgeColoring[g = Hypercube[j]]; e = Edges[g];
              SetGraphOptions[g, Table[{e[[i]],
              EdgeStyle -> s[[c[[i]]]]}, {i, M[g]}]], {j,3,4} ];
```

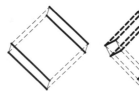

The Petersen graph is a 3-regular graph whose edge chromatic number is 4. Graph theorists have spent considerable effort trying to separate graphs with edge chromatic number Δ from those with edge chromatic number $\Delta + 1$. In a sense, this program is hopeless, because Hoyler showed that determining the exact value is NP-complete [Hol81].

```
In[150]:= EdgeColoring[PetersenGraph]

Out[150]= {1, 2, 1, 2, 3, 1, 4, 1, 4, 2, 3, 3, 2, 3, 1}
```

Edge coloring has applications in a variety of scheduling problems. For example, consider a group of processors each capable of performing a group of jobs. This defines a bipartite graph, and a minimum edge coloring of this graph is the minimum amount of time it will take to complete the job. Edge coloring has also been used to model problems of data migration in a network [HHK+01].

7.5 Cliques, Vertex Covers, and Independent Sets

NP-completeness proofs consist of reductions from known NP-complete problems to the problem in question. Usually these constructions are too baroque to be particularly useful for computation. A notable exception is the relationship between maximum clique, minimum vertex cover, and maximum independent set, which are all different manifestations of the same underlying structure.

■ 7.5.1 Maximum Clique

Every member of a group of people in a social clique knows everybody else. Likewise, a *clique* in a graph G is a subset of the vertices that induce a complete graph. Any vertex or edge defines cliques of size 1 and 2, respectively, but the most interesting cliques are the largest ones. The largest clique can be found by testing all vertex subsets of G to see if they induce a complete graph, but this is frightfully expensive. If we consider the subsets in order of decreasing size, the first clique found must be the largest. Further, we do not have to consider all k-subsets of the vertices in testing for a clique of size k, merely all k-subsets of the vertices that are of degree $k - 1$ or greater, since they cannot be in any clique of that size. These heuristics help somewhat, but finding a largest clique in a graph is a notoriously difficult problem [ALM+92]. *Combinatorica* provides a function `MaximumClique` that computes a largest size clique of a given graph.

We highlight a maximum clique in a random graph. The spring embedding tends to bring vertices in large cliques together.

```
In[151]:= g = SpringEmbedding[RandomGraph[10, .6]];
          ShowGraph[Highlight[g, MaximumClique[g]]];
```

Any subset of the vertices of a complete graph forms a clique.

```
In[153]:= CliqueQ[ CompleteGraph[10], RandomSubset[Range[10]] ]
Out[153]= True
```

No bipartite graph contains a clique larger than 2.

```
In[154]:= MaximumClique[CompleteKPartiteGraph[3,3]]
Out[154]= {1, 4}
```

The Turán graph $T_{n,p}$ is the largest order-n graph that does not contain K_p as a subgraph. Any complete k-partite graph has a maximum clique of size k.

```
In[155]:= MaximumClique[Turan[12,4]]
Out[155]= {1, 5, 9}
```

■ 7.5.2 Minimum Vertex Cover

A *vertex cover* V' of a graph G is a subset of the vertices such that every edge in E is incident on a vertex $v \in V'$. Two vertices not in the cover cannot be connected by an edge, or else V' is not a cover. Thus, in the graph complement of G, the vertices not in a clique define a cover. This observation permits us to use `MaximumClique` to find a minimum vertex cover.

```
VertexCoverQ[g_Graph, vc_List] := CliqueQ[ GraphComplement[g], Complement[Range[V[g]], vc] ]

MinimumVertexCover[g_Graph] := {} /; EmptyQ[g]
MinimumVertexCover[g_Graph] := Flatten[Position[Last[BipartiteMatchingAndCover[g]], 1]]/; BipartiteQ[g]
MinimumVertexCover[g_Graph] := Complement[ Range[V[g]], MaximumClique[ GraphComplement[g] ] ]
```

Finding a Smallest Vertex Cover

Any subset of $n - 1$ vertices is a minimum vertex cover of K_n.

```
In[156]:= MinimumVertexCover[CompleteGraph[20]]
Out[156]= {2, 3, 4, 5, 6, 7, 8, 9, 10, 11, 12, 13, 14, 15,
            16, 17, 18, 19, 20}
```

Every vertex cover in a complete k-partite graph contains vertices from at least $k - 1$ different stages.

```
In[157]:= MinimumVertexCover[CompleteKPartiteGraph[2,10,2]]
Out[157]= {1, 2, 13, 14}
```

The minimum vertex cover problem is NP-complete [Kar72], but it has a very nice approximation algorithm. A *matching* in a graph G is a set of edges, no two of which share an endpoint. If M is a maximal matching of G, then any vertex cover of G must contain at least M vertices. Why? Because every edge in M needs to be covered, and the cover vertices for these matching edges must all be distinct since no two edges in M share a vertex. Taking both endpoints of all edges in M gives us a vertex cover because if any edge not covered could be added to M to give a larger matching. This is ruled out because of the maximality of M. Thus, computing a maximal matching of a graph and taking the endpoints of the edges in the matching gives us a vertex cover whose size is within 2 times the optimal.

The size of this vertex cover can be improved using a greedy heuristic. Suppose V' is a vertex cover of a graph G. Start with a maximum degree vertex v in V' and throw it into the improved vertex cover, deleting all edges incident on v. Repeat this until all edges of G are covered. It is possible that this greedy heuristic might not improve the size of the vertex cover, but it cannot hurt.

Unlike the approximation algorithm, the greedy algorithm provides no performance guarantees. However, it sometimes beats the approximation algorithm.

```
In[158]:= g = MeredithGraph;
          Map[Length, {GreedyVertexCover[g], ApproximateVertexCover[g]}]
Out[159]= {39, 50}
```

This gives a lower bound on the size of any vertex cover of the Meredith graph.

```
In[160]:= Length[MaximalMatching[g]]
Out[160]= 30
```

The greedy vertex cover algorithm can deal with graphs with at least 60 vertices in a reasonable time.

```
In[161]:= Timing[GreedyVertexCover[RandomGraph[60, .5]];]
Out[161]= {7.49 Second, Null}
```

Despite its theoretical pedigree, ApproximateVertexCover fairly consistently loses to GreedyVertexCover on random trees.

```
In[162]:= Map[(Length[GreedyVertexCover[#]] -
             Length[ApproximateVertexCover[#]])&,
               Table[ RandomTree[30], {20}] ]
Out[162]= {0, 0, 1, 0, 0, 1, 1, 0, 1, 0, 1, 1, 0, 0, 0, 0,
       0, 0, 0, 0}
```

The approximation algorithm does better than greedy on dense random graphs, however. The relative performance of heuristics depends greatly on the distribution of inputs.

```
In[163]:= Map[(Length[GreedyVertexCover[#]] -
             Length[ApproximateVertexCover[#]])&,
               Table[ RandomGraph[30,0.5], {20}] ]
Out[163]= {0, -1, 0, -2, 0, -1, 0, 0, -1, 0, 0, -2, 0, 0, 0,
       -1, 0, 0, 0, -1}
```

■ 7.5.3 Maximum Independent Set

An *independent set* of a graph G is a subset of vertices S such that no two vertices in S represent an edge of G. Given any vertex cover of a graph, all vertices not in the cover define an independent set, since all edges are incident on the cover. The *independence number* of a graph is the cardinality of a largest independent set. By definition, the independence number of a graph plus the cover number equals the number of vertices.

```
IndependentSetQ[g_Graph, indep_List] :=
    (Complement[indep, Range[V[g]]] == {}) && VertexCoverQ[ g, Complement[ Range[V[g]], indep] ]

MaximumIndependentSet[g_Graph] := Complement[Range[V[g]], MinimumVertexCover[g]]
```

Finding a Largest Independent Set

A largest independent set in a grid graph consists of the white squares of a chessboard, namely, every other point on every other row.

```
In[164]:= MaximumIndependentSet[GridGraph[5, 5]]
Out[164]= {1, 3, 5, 7, 9, 11, 13, 15, 17, 19, 21, 23, 25}
```

Covers and independent sets can be defined in a similar way for edges. Gallai [Gal59] showed that the size of a minimum edge cover (matching) plus the size of a maximum number of independent edges adds up to the number of vertices n.

7.6 Exercises

■ 7.6.1 Thought Exercises

1. Show that a graph has no cycles of odd length if and only if it is bipartite. Use this to prove that all BFS edges connect pairs of vertices at different levels if and only if the graph is bipartite.

2. Prove that the complement of a disconnected graph must be connected.

3. Prove that any graph with minimum degree $\delta \geq (n-1)/2$ is connected.

4. Prove that any vertex that belongs to more than one biconnected component is an articulation vertex.

5. Prove that an edge (u, v) is a bridge if and only if it defines a biconnected component of two vertices.

6. Prove that a cubic (3-regular) graph contains a bridge if and only if it contains an articulation vertex.

7. Prove that any simple graph with minimum degree δ contains a cycle of length at least $\delta + 1$.

8. Prove that any weakly connected graph whose vertices all have the same in-degree and out-degree must be strongly connected.

9. Interval graphs are defined by sets of intervals on the line, where each interval represents a vertex, and an edge is defined if and only if the corresponding intervals overlap. Which of the following graphs are interval graphs: complete graphs, complete bipartite graphs, cycles, stars, or wheels? For those that are, implement functions that use `IntervalGraph` to construct them.

10. Devise an algorithm that colors a given interval graph using the fewest number of colors.

11. Show that the edges of any bipartite graph G can be properly colored with Δ colors, where Δ is the maximum degree of a vertex in G.

12. Show a graph for which `GreedyVertexCover` produces a vertex cover whose size is more than ten times the size of an optimal vertex cover.

13. Section 7.5.2 mentions two facts: (i) There is a simple algorithm that produces a vertex cover whose size is within twice the optimal, and (ii) a maximum clique in a graph is the complement of a minimum vertex cover in the complement. Together, do these imply a simple algorithm that computes a clique that is fairly close in size to the maximum clique? Explain.

■ 7.6.2 Programming Exercises

1. Improve the efficiency of `EdgeConnectivity` and `VertexConnectivity` by using heuristics to minimize the number of times `NetworkFlow` is called.

2. Implement a version of `MaximumClique` that deletes all vertices of degree less than the desired clique size from the graph, possibly creating more low-degree vertices that can be deleted. How much does this speed up the algorithm?

3. Use the generalized backtrack algorithm `Backtrack` to find the Hamiltonian cycles of a graph.

4. Modify `Girth` to return the shortest cycle in a graph. Also, make `Girth` work correctly for weighted graphs.

5. Modify `TopologicalSort` to return all the topological orderings of a directed acyclic graph.

6. The vertex cover problem is defined, more generally, for vertex-weighted graphs. The problem is to find a vertex cover whose total weight (defined as the sum of the weights of the vertices in it) is minimized. Extend the greedy vertex cover algorithm to the vertex-weighted case.

7. A *dominating set* in a graph $G = (V, E)$ is a set $V' \subseteq V$ of vertices such that for every vertex $v \in V$, either $v \in V'$ or v has a neighbor in V'. Implement a function `DominatingSet` that computes a minimum-sized dominating set in a given graph. Extend this to the case of vertex-weighted graphs, where the goal is to compute a dominating set with minimum weight.

■ 7.6.3 Experimental Exercises

1. Can you find example planar graphs that Brelaz's algorithm colors with at least five colors?

2. Experiment with connectivity in random graphs. Estimate the expected connectivity of a graph on n vertices with m edges, for small n and m. How many edges are usually necessary before the graph is connected?

3. Hunt for or design cage-link graphs with large girth. The basic tools for a computer search exist in `Girth` and `RegularGraph`.

4. The vertex cover problem for vertex-weighted graphs can be formulated as an *integer program* as follows. Let $x_i \in \{0, 1\}$ be an indicator variable telling us if vertex i is in the solution or not. Let w_i be the weight of vertex i. Then we want to minimize $\sum_{i=1}^{n} w_i \cdot x_i$ subject to the constraints that $x_i + x_j \geq 1$ for every edge $\{i, j\}$ in the graph and $x_i \in \{0, 1\}$ for every vertex i. If we relax the last constraint to $0 \leq x_i \leq 1$, we get a linear program that is a "relaxation" of the original integer program. Use *Mathematica*'s `LinearProgramming` function to solve this linear program. Experiment with various graphs. What do you observe about the fractional values that x_i takes on? Use your observation to devise an approximation algorithm that produces a vertex cover whose weight is within twice the weight of an optimal vertex cover.

8. Algorithmic Graph Theory

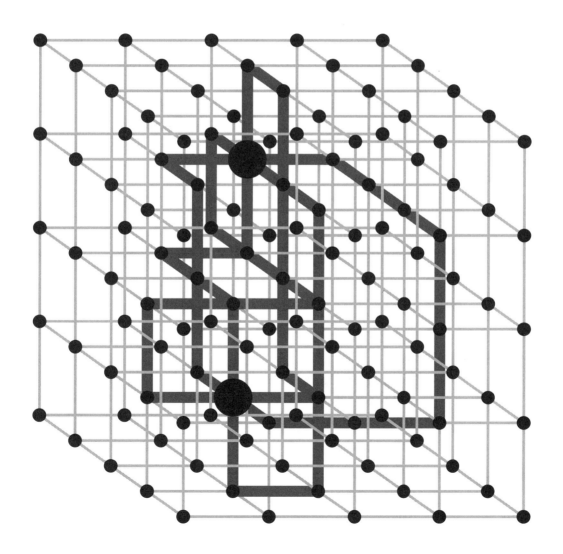

Algorithmic graph theory is one of the best examples of mathematics inspired and nurtured by computer science. As we have seen, there is a natural division between problems that can be solved efficiently and problems that are hard. Most of the problems discussed in this chapter have efficient algorithms, and all are of practical importance.

Several fundamental graph algorithms are fairly complicated, and thus the implementations in the chapter are often longer and uglier than in the previous chapters. That is one reason for hiding them in the back of the book. This chapter is also where we pay most dearly for not having access to a traditional model of computation, since many of these algorithms make frequent modifications to data structures. Still, through clever programming we can compute interesting invariants on reasonably large graphs.

About the illustration overleaf:

One of the most important problems in algorithmic graph theory is computing the maximum amount of flow that can be sent from a source vertex to a target vertex, given capacity constraints on the edges. Many problems can be modeled as flow problems. Here we illustrate the computation of edge-disjoint paths between pairs of vertices using a solution to the maximum flow problem. There are six edge-disjoint paths between vertex 32 and vertex 93, as shown in this $5 \times 5 \times 5$ grid graph.

```
ShowGraph[Highlight[g = GridGraph[5, 5, 5], {{32, 93}, First[Transpose[
NetworkFlow[g, 32, 93, Edge]]]}], EdgeColor -> Gray];
```

8.1 Shortest Paths

The classic example of a real-life graph is a network of roads connecting cities. The most important algorithmic problem on such road networks is finding the shortest path between pairs of vertices.

In unweighted graphs, the length of a path is simply the number of edges in it. The shortest paths in such graphs can be found by using breadth-first search, as discussed in Section 7.1.1. Things get more complicated with weighted graphs, since a shortest path between two vertices might not be the one with the fewest edges.

There are several closely related variants of the shortest path problem. The *s-t shortest-path problem* seeks a shortest path from a source vertex s to a given sink t. The *single-source shortest-path problem* aims to find the shortest paths from s to all other vertices in the graph. The *all-pairs shortest-path problem* seeks the shortest paths from every vertex to every other vertex.

No one knows how to find *s-t* shortest paths without essentially solving the single-source shortest-path problem, so we focus on the latter. The all-pairs problem can, of course, be reduced to solving the single-source problem by using each vertex as the source, but the fastest algorithms work differently. We first focus on finding single-source shortest-paths before turning to the all-pairs problem.

■ 8.1.1 Single-Source Shortest Paths

There are two basic algorithms for finding single-source shortest paths. The simpler and more efficient *Dijkstra's algorithm* works correctly on graphs where no edges have negative weight. Negative-weight edges are rare in practice but not unheard of. The *Bellman-Ford algorithm* finds the shortest paths correctly in general-weighted graphs. Both are discussed below.

Dijkstra's Algorithm

Dijkstra's algorithm [Dij59], independently discovered by Whiting and Hillier [WH60], performs a "best-first search" on the graph G starting from source s. In the context of shortest paths, we will think of all graphs as directed and interpret each edge in an undirected graph as two directed edges going in opposite direction.

The algorithm maintains two distinct arrays to record the structure of the shortest paths in G:

- The distance array – For each vertex i, `dist[i]` maintains the length of the shortest known path from s to i. Clearly `dist[s]` = 0. For all vertices i distinct from s, `dist[i]` is initialized to ∞.

- The parent array – For each vertex i, `parent[i]` maintains the predecessor of i on the shortest known path from s to i. The `parent` array is initialized by the algorithms to `parent[i]` = i for all vertices i.

If `dist` contained the correct distances from s to every other vertex, then for any edge (i, j) with weight $w(i, j)$ we know that $\mathtt{dist}[j] \leq \mathtt{dist}[i] + w(i, j)$. Any edge (i, j) for which this inequality holds is said to be *relaxed*. When Dijkstra's algorithm terminates, all edges are relaxed and `dist` has the correct shortest-path distances.

Dijkstra's algorithm goes through $n - 1$ iterations. In each iteration it finds a shortest path from s to another new vertex. The efficiency of the algorithm depends on the following observation.

> Let S be the set of vertices to which the algorithm has already found shortest paths; that is, `dist` contains the correct values for every vertex $i \in S$. Furthermore, suppose that every edge outgoing from S is relaxed. Then, among all the vertices not in S, the vertex i with the smallest `dist` value has its `dist` value set correctly.

In each iteration, we scan the vertices not in S and pick a vertex i with the smallest `dist` value to include in S. Then we scan each edge (i, j) outgoing from i and if necessary relax it; that is, we check if $\mathtt{dist}[j] > \mathtt{dist}[i] + w(i, j)$ and, if so, reset $\mathtt{dist}[j]$ to $\mathtt{dist}[i] + w(i, j)$. This reset means we have found a shorter path to j, so $\mathtt{parent}[j]$ is set to i.

When Dijkstra's algorithm ends, the edges between parents and their children define a *shortest-path spanning tree* of the graph, rooted at the source s. Our implementation returns both the distance and parent arrays.

```
Dijkstra[al_List, start_Integer] :=
     Module[{dist = Table[Infinity,{i, Length[al]}], parent = Table[i, {i, Length[al]}],
          untraversed = Range[Length[al]], m, v},
          dist[[start]] = 0;
          While[untraversed != {},
               m = Infinity;
               Scan[(If[dist[[#]]<=m, v=#;m=dist[[#]]])&, untraversed];
               untraversed = Complement[untraversed, {v}];
               n = Table[{al[[v, i, 1]], m + al[[v, i, 2]]}, {i, Length[ al[[v]] ]}];
               Scan[If[dist[[ #[[1]] ]] > #[[2]], dist[[ #[[1]] ]] = #[[2]]; parent[[#[[1]]]] = v]&, n];
          ];
          {parent, dist}
     ]

Dijkstra[g_Graph, start_Integer] := Dijkstra[ToAdjacencyLists[g, EdgeWeight], start]

Dijkstra[g_Graph, start_List] :=
     Module[{al = ToAdjacencyLists[g, EdgeWeight]},
          Map[Dijkstra[ToAdjacencyLists[g, EdgeWeight], #]&, start]
     ]
```

Dijkstra's Shortest-Path Algorithm

This loads the package.   *In[1]:=* `<<DiscreteMath`Combinatorica``

The *second* list returned by Dijkstra gives the distances from the source to all other vertices of the graph. The vertex numbers are displayed in the lower left corner, and the distances are displayed in the upper right corner of each vertex. In this unweighted graph, every edge has unit length, and the shortest paths minimize the number of edges. The "Manhattan" distance across an $n \times m$ grid graph is $n + m - 2$ and is computed here.

```
In[2]:= g = GridGraph[5, 5];
        ShowGraph[g, VertexLabel -> Dijkstra[g, 1][[2]],
        VertexNumber -> True, PlotRange -> 0.1,
        TextStyle->{FontSize->11}];
```

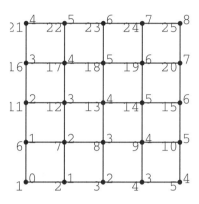

The first list returned by Dijkstra contains the parent relation in the shortest-path spanning tree. We use this information to label each vertex v with its parent on the shortest path from v to the source of the search. Observe that all parents are lower-numbered vertices, because the search originates from 1.

```
In[4]:= ShowGraph[g, VertexLabel -> Dijkstra[g, 1][[1]],
        VertexNumber -> True, PlotRange -> 0.15,
        TextStyle->{FontSize->11}];
```

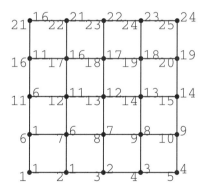

This parent relation is best illustrated by the *shortest-path spanning tree* defined by edges to parents. Since all edges are of equal weight, there are many different possible shortest-path spanning trees, depending on how the algorithm breaks ties.

```
In[5]:= ShowGraph[ShortestPathSpanningTree[g,1],
          VertexNumber->True, PlotRange->0.05];
```

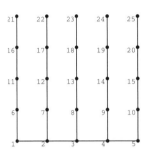

Here we run Dijkstra's algorithm on a 30-vertex graph whose edge weights equal the Euclidean distances between endpoints. The shortest path to every vertex is a direct hop of one edge from the root because the edge weights satisfy the triangle inequality.

```
In[6]:= g = SetEdgeWeights[ChangeVertices[RandomGraph[30,1],
          RandomVertices[30]], WeightingFunction -> Euclidean];
        ShowGraphArray[{g,ShortestPathSpanningTree[g,1]}];
```

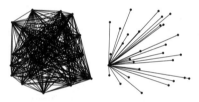

Here we do the same experiment on a sparser random graph. Now there does not necessarily exist a direct route from the root to every vertex, so we see some branching and bending. Still, the tree reflects the geometry of the points. The root is identifiable as the vertex with high degree.

```
In[8]:= g = SetEdgeWeights[ChangeVertices[RandomGraph[30,0.3],
          RandomVertices[30]], WeightingFunction -> Euclidean];
        ShowGraphArray[{g,ShortestPathSpanningTree[g,1]}];
```

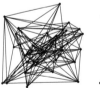

With edge weights that are independent of the vertex position, the embedding of the spanning tree has many crossings. It is unclear which vertex is the root, because fewer neighbors link directly to it.

```
In[10]:= g = SetEdgeWeights[ChangeVertices[RandomGraph[30,0.3],
         RandomVertices[30]], WeightingFunction -> Random ];
         ShowGraphArray[{g,ShortestPathSpanningTree[g,1]}];
```

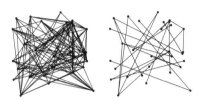

Dijkstra's algorithm works correctly on disconnected graphs as well. The infinities here are distances to vertices that cannot be reached from 1.

```
In[12]:= Dijkstra[GraphUnion[CompleteGraph[3], CompleteGraph[3]], 1]
Out[12]= {{1, 1, 1, 4, 5, 6},
         {0, 1, 1, Infinity, Infinity, Infinity}}
```

Dijkstra's algorithm runs in $\Theta(n^2)$ time on an n-vertex graph. This can be implemented in $O(m \log n)$ time by using binary heaps. By using the more sophisticated Fibonacci heap, it can be made to run in $O(n \log n + m)$ time on the RAM model of computation [FT87].

```
In[13]:= gt = Table[SetEdgeWeights[GridGraph[5, 5 i + 1] ], {i,0,10}];
         ListPlot[ Table[ {i-1, Timing[Dijkstra[gt[[i]], 1];][[1, 1]]},
         {i,0,10}], PlotJoined->True];
```

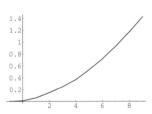

Bellman-Ford Algorithm

The Bellman-Ford algorithm correctly computes shortest paths even in the presence of negative-weight edges, provided the graph contains no negative cycles. A *negative cycle* is a directed cycle, the sum of whose edge weights is negative. This is clear trouble for any shortest-path algorithm, because we can make any path arbitrarily cheap by repeatedly cycling through this negative cost cycle.

Like Dijkstra's algorithm, the Bellman-Ford algorithm makes $(n-1)$ passes over the vertices, and on each pass it relaxes every edge that is not currently relaxed. However, unlike Dijkstra, Bellman-Ford scans all edges m in every pass to overcome negative edges.

To show the correctness of this algorithm, observe that after pass i the first $(i + 1)$ vertices in any path from s have their `dist` values set correctly. If there are no negative cycles in the graph, $n - 1$ is the maximum number of edges possible in any shortest path, so therefore $(n - 1)$ passes suffice.

We implement an improvement of the Bellman-Ford algorithm due to Yen that uses $\lceil n/2 \rceil$ passes instead of $(n - 1)$. This improvement depends on relaxing the edges in the graph in a certain order on each pass. Specifically, partition the set of edges E into "forward edges" $E_f = \{(i, j) \in E \mid i < j\}$ and "backward edges" $E_b = \{(i, j) \in E \mid i > j\}$. In each pass, first visit the vertices in the order $1, 2, ..., n$, relaxing the edges of E_f that leave each vertex. Then visit the vertices in the order $n, n-1, ..., 1$, relaxing the edges of E_b that leave each vertex. If there are no negative cycles, then $\lceil n/2 \rceil$ passes suffice to get all the `dist` values correct. This is implemented in the *Combinatorica* function BellmanFord.

This 5-vertex directed graph has only one negative-weight edge, but that is enough to cause trouble for Dijkstra's algorithm. It does not recognize that vertex 3 is more cheaply reached from vertex 1 via vertex 4 than via vertex 2.

```
In[15]:= g = FromOrderedPairs[{{1,2},{2,3},{1,4},{4,3},{4,5},{3,5}}];
         h = SetEdgeWeights[g, {2, 2, 5, -3, 1, 3}];
         ShowGraph[SetEdgeLabels[h, GetEdgeWeights[h]],
         VertexNumber -> True, VertexNumberPosition -> UpperLeft,
         TextStyle -> {FontSize -> 11}];
```

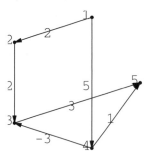

Dijkstra's algorithm tells us that going to vertex 5 via vertex 4 is best and costs us 6 units ...

```
In[18]:= TableForm[ Dijkstra[h, 1] ]
Out[18]//TableForm= 1    1    4    1    4
                    0    2    2    5    6
```

...while BellmanFord tells us that it only costs 5 units via vertex 3. Who do you believe?

```
In[19]:= TableForm[ BellmanFord[h, 1] ]
Out[19]//TableForm= 1    1    4    1    3
                    0    2    2    5    5
```

Adding the edge $(5, 2)$ with weight -7 creates a negative-weight cycle $(2, 3, 5, 2)$, so the shortest paths are no longer well-defined. Bellman-Ford returns an answer, but it is easy to verify that the answer is bogus since edge $(2, 3)$ is not relaxed.

```
In[20]:= h = AddEdges[h, {{{5, 2}, EdgeWeight -> -7}}];
         {par, dist} = BellmanFord[h, 1]
Out[21]= {{1, 5, 2, 1, 3}, {0, -5, -1, 5, 2}}
```

Bellman-Ford can be used to detect the presence of negative cycles. Run the algorithm for $n-1$ iterations and then test if there exists an edge that is not yet relaxed.

```
In[22]:= w = GetEdgeWeights[h]; e = Edges[h];
         Table[dist[[e[[i, 1]]]] + w[[i]] <= dist[[ e[[i, 2]]]], {i,
         Length[e]}]
Out[23]= {False, True, True, False, False, True, True}
```

The Bellman-Ford algorithm runs in $\Theta(mn)$ time on n-vertex, m-edge graphs. Both Dijkstra and Bellman-Ford have the same asymptotic running time on sparse graphs. In our experiments, Bellman-Ford beats Dijkstra, unless...

```
In[24]:= g = SetEdgeWeights[GridGraph[20, 20]];
         {Timing[Dijkstra[g, 1];], Timing[BellmanFord[g, 1];]}
Out[25]= {{4.15 Second, Null}, {1.11 Second, Null}}
```

...the input graph is sufficiently large and dense.

```
In[26]:= g = CompleteGraph[200];
         {Timing[Dijkstra[g, 1];], Timing[BellmanFord[g, 1];]}
Out[27]= {{10.83 Second, Null}, {15.11 Second, Null}}
```

Related Functions

Combinatorica provides a few "wrapper" functions that make it easier to use the shortest-path information. `ShortestPath` produces a sequence of vertices that define a shortest path from a given source to a given destination. `ShortestPathSpanningTree` produces a shortest-path spanning tree, containing the shortest paths from a source to all vertices in the graph. Both functions call `ChooseShortestPathAlgorithm` to determine whether to use Dijkstra's algorithm or Bellman-Ford. It makes its decision based on the presence of negative edge weights and the sparsity of the graph.

This shows the Euclidean shortest paths from vertex 1 to all other vertices in a dodecahedral graph. The dodecahedral graph is the "skeleton" of a dodecahedron, one of the five Platonic solids. The skeleton of any polyhedron is a planar graph. A *planar graph* can be drawn in the plane with no edge crossings. Shortest paths can be computed more quickly in planar graphs than in arbitrary graphs [Fre87, KRRS94].

```
In[28]:= g = DodecahedralGraph;
         t = ShortestPathSpanningTree[SetEdgeWeights[g,
         WeightingFunction -> Euclidean], 1];
         ShowGraphArray[{g, t}, VertexStyle -> Disk[0.05]]
```

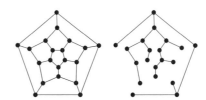

This shows a shortest path from the bottom left to the top right in a grid graph with random edge weights. Since the edge weights are random, there is no guarantee that the path will travel upward or to the right always. Can you determine how likely this is via experiment or analysis?

```
In[31]:= p = ShortestPath[g = SetEdgeWeights[GridGraph[20, 20]], 1, 400];
         ShowGraph[ Highlight[g, {Map[Sort, Partition[p, 2, 1]]}]];
```

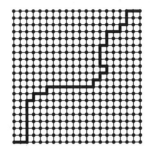

■ 8.1.2 All-Pairs Shortest Paths

Shortest paths between every pair of vertices can be computed in $\Theta(n^3)$ time using Dijkstra's algorithm or in $\Theta(n^2 m)$ time using the Bellman-Ford algorithm repeatedly. We now present the *Floyd-Warshall algorithm* for computing all-pairs shortest paths. Asymptotically, it is as fast as Dijkstra's algorithm, however, it is much faster in practice because the algorithm is so short and simple.

```
AllPairsShortestPath[g_Graph] := {} /; (V[g] == 0)
AllPairsShortestPath[g_Graph] :=
    Module[{p = ToAdjacencyMatrix[g, EdgeWeight, Type->Simple], m},
        m = V[g]*Ceiling[Max[Cases[Flatten[p], _Real | _Integer]]]+1;
        Zap[DP1[p /. {0 -> 0.0, x_Integer -> 1.0 x, Infinity -> m*1.0}, m]] /. m -> Infinity
    ]

DP1 = Compile[{{p, _Real, 2}, {m, _Integer}},
    Module[{np = p, k, n = Length[p]},
        Do[np = Table[If[(np[[i, k]] == 1.0*m) || (np[[k, j]] == 1.0*m),
                    np[[i,j]], Min[np[[i,k]]+ np[[k,j]], np[[i,j]]]
                    ], {i,n},{j,n}
                ], {k, n}];
            np
        ]
    ]
```

The Floyd-Warshall Shortest Path Algorithm

The Floyd-Warshall algorithm [Flo62] is an application of dynamic programming. Single edges in the initial graph provide the shortest way to get between pairs of vertices with no intermediate stops. The algorithm successively computes the shortest paths between all pairs of vertices using the first k vertices as possible intermediaries, as k goes from 1 to n. The best way to get from s to t with $1, ..., k$

as possible intermediaries is the minimum of the best way using the first $k - 1$ vertices and the best way known from s to t that goes through k. This gives an $\Theta(n^3)$-time algorithm that is essentially the same as the transitive closure algorithm to be discussed in Section 8.5.

We start by generating random integer weights in the range $[0, 10]$ for the edges of K_7 and use the Floyd-Warshall algorithm to compute the matrix of shortest-path distances between pairs of vertices.

```
In[33]:= g = SetEdgeWeights[ CompleteGraph[7],
         WeightingFunction -> RandomInteger, WeightRange -> {0, 10}];
         (s = AllPairsShortestPath[g]) // TableForm
```

Out[34]//TableForm= 0	3	4	4	3	5	2
	3	0	6	6	6	5	5
	4	6	0	2	6	6	6
	4	6	2	0	4	6	6
	3	6	6	4	0	2	5
	5	5	6	6	2	0	7
	2	5	6	6	5	7	0

Specifying the Parent tag as the second argument to AllPairsShortestPath produces parent information, in addition to shortest-path distances. The (i, j)th entry in the parent matrix contains the predecessor of j in a shortest path from i to j.

```
In[35]:= First[AllPairsShortestPath[g, Parent]] // TableForm
```

Out[35]//TableForm= 0	3	4	4	3	5	2
	3	0	6	6	6	5	5
	4	6	0	2	6	6	6
	4	6	2	0	4	6	6
	3	6	6	4	0	2	5
	5	5	6	6	2	0	7
	2	5	6	6	5	7	0

How much shorter does travel get if we take shortest paths rather than direct hops between pairs of vertices? The positive entries tell us that, for those pairs of vertices, the edge directly connecting them is not the shortest path.

```
In[36]:= (ToAdjacencyMatrix[g, EdgeWeight] - s) /.
         Infinity -> 0 // TableForm
```

Out[36]//TableForm= 0	0	0	0	0	4	0
	0	0	0	0	0	0	1
	0	0	0	0	0	0	3
	0	0	0	0	0	4	2
	0	0	0	0	0	0	2
	4	0	0	4	0	0	1
	0	1	3	2	2	1	0

Although Floyd-Warshall has the same worst-case time complexity as n calls to Dijkstra, it is much faster in practice.

```
In[37]:= g = RandomGraph[30,0.5];
         {Timing[ Table[ Dijkstra[g,i], {i,1,V[g]}];] [[1,1]],
         Timing[ AllPairsShortestPath[g];] [[1,1]]}
```

Out[38]= {4.08, 0.59}

■ 8.1.3 Applications of All-Pairs Shortest Paths

Several graph invariants depend on the all-pairs shortest-path matrix. The *eccentricity* of a vertex v in a graph is the length of the longest shortest path from v to some other vertex. From the eccentricity come other graph invariants. The *radius* of a graph is the smallest eccentricity of any vertex, while the *center* is the set of vertices whose eccentricity is the radius. The *diameter* of a graph is the maximum eccentricity of any vertex.

In the following we present functions that compute these graph invariants. We try to improve the efficiency of Eccentricity by distinguishing between weighted and unweighted graphs. In the latter case, it is sufficient to call the breadth-first search function to compute distances.

```
Eccentricity[g_Graph, start_Integer, NoEdgeWeights] := Max[ BreadthFirstTraversal[g, start, Level] ]
Eccentricity[g_Graph, start_Integer] := Eccentricity[g, start, NoEdgeWeights] /; UnweightedQ[g]
Eccentricity[g_Graph, start_Integer] := Map[Max, Last[BellmanFord[g, start]]]
Eccentricity[g_Graph] := Table[Eccentricity[g, i, NoEdgeWeights], {i, V[g]}] /; UnweightedQ[g]
Eccentricity[g_Graph] := Map[ Max, AllPairsShortestPath[g] ]

Radius[g_Graph] := Min[ Eccentricity[g] ]
Diameter[g_Graph] := Max[ Eccentricity[g] ]
GraphCenter[g_Graph] :=
     Module[{eccentricity = Eccentricity[g]},
            Flatten[ Position[eccentricity, Min[eccentricity]] ]
     ]
```

Finding the Eccentricity, Diameter, Radius, and Center

In graph theory as in business, high eccentricity is not characteristic of a wheel.

```
In[39]:= Eccentricity[ Wheel[10] ]
Out[39]= {2, 2, 2, 2, 2, 2, 2, 2, 2, 1}
```

A wheel has diameter 2 and radius 1, because a path through the center connects any pair of vertices.

```
In[40]:= {Diameter[Wheel[10]], Radius[Wheel[10]]}
Out[40]= {2, 1}
```

The diameter and the radius of disconnected graphs are infinite.

```
In[41]:= {Diameter[g = GraphUnion[Star[4], Star[4]]], Radius[g]}
Out[41]= {Infinity, Infinity}
```

Here we calculate the diameter of random graphs. The graphs corresponding to row i have an edge probability of $1/i$. So the graphs in the first row are completely connected, and as we go down the rows the graphs become more and more sparse. The corresponding increase in diameter is evident. To make the table more compact, infinities have been replaced by -1's.

```
In[42]:= (Table[Diameter[RandomGraph[20, 1/i]], {i, 10}, {5}]
              /. Infinity -> -1) // TableForm
Out[42]//TableForm= 1    1    1    1    1
                    2    3    3    2    2
                    3    3    3    3    3
                    4    4    4    4    3
                    4    4    5   -1    4
                    5   -1    5    4    4
                    4   -1   -1   -1   -1
                    5   -1   -1   -1   -1
                   -1   -1   -1   -1   -1
                   -1   -1   -1   -1   -1
```

Because the distance function satisfies the triangle inequality, the diameter of a graph is at most twice its radius.

```
In[43]:= g = RandomGraph[30,0.2]; {Diameter[g], Radius[g]}
Out[43]= {4, 3}
```

The cycle does not have a unique center like the wheel does.

```
In[44]:= GraphCenter[ Cycle[10] ]
Out[44]= {1, 2, 3, 4, 5, 6, 7, 8, 9, 10}
```

The center of any tree always consists of either one vertex or two adjacent vertices. Note: The two adjacent vertices in a tree do not necessarily have adjacent labels assigned to them.

```
In[45]:= Table[ GraphCenter[RandomTree[30]], {5}]
Out[45]= {{29}, {16}, {19}, {7, 22}, {14}}
```

■ 8.1.4 Number of Paths

The kth *power* of a graph G is a graph with the same set of vertices as G and an edge between two vertices if and only if there is a path of length at most k between them. Since a path of length 2 between u and v exists for every vertex v' such that $\{u, v'\}$ and $\{v', v\}$ are edges in G, the square of the adjacency matrix of G counts the number of such paths. By induction, the (u, v)th element of the kth power of the adjacency matrix of G gives the number of paths of length k between vertices u and v. Therefore, summing up the first k powers of the adjacency matrix counts all paths of length up to k.

```
GraphPower[g_Graph,1] := g
GraphPower[g_Graph, k_Integer] :=
      Module[{prod = power = p = ToAdjacencyMatrix[g]},
          FromAdjacencyMatrix[Do[prod = prod.p; power=power+prod, {k-1}]; power, Vertices[g, All]]
      ]
```

Computing the Power of a Graph

The diameter of a cycle on seven vertices is 3, so the cube of such a graph is complete. There are four distinct but nonsimple paths of length at most 3 between adjacent vertices in a cycle. These show up as edges connecting adjacent vertices in the cube of the cycle. The two self-loops at each vertex are the two distinct ways of going from a vertex to itself in three or fewer hops.

The number of shortest paths between opposite corners of an $m \times n$ grid graph is $\binom{n+m-2}{m-1}$, as shown in the last entry of the first row. Which entry in the matrix is largest, and why?

```
In[46]:= ShowGraphArray[ Table[GraphPower[Cycle[7], i], {i,1,3}] ];
```

```
In[47]:= ToAdjacencyMatrix[GraphPower[GridGraph[3, 3],4]] // TableForm
```

Out[47]//TableForm=								
12	6	9	6	18	3	9	3	6
6	21	6	18	9	18	3	15	3
9	6	12	3	18	6	6	3	9
6	18	3	21	9	15	6	18	3
18	9	18	9	36	9	18	9	18
3	18	6	15	9	21	3	18	6
9	3	6	6	18	3	12	6	9
3	15	3	18	9	18	6	21	6
6	3	9	3	18	6	9	6	12

Fleischner [Fle74] showed that the square of any biconnected graph is Hamiltonian.

The cube of any connected graph is also Hamiltonian.

```
In[48]:= HamiltonianCycle[GraphPower[CompleteGraph[10,2], 2]]
Out[48]= {1, 2, 3, 4, 5, 6, 7, 8, 9, 10, 11, 12, 1}
```

```
In[49]:= HamiltonianCycle[GraphPower[RandomTree[15], 3]]
Out[49]= {1, 4, 6, 7, 2, 3, 10, 5, 9, 11, 14, 12, 13, 15,
          8, 1}
```

8.2 Minimum Spanning Trees

A *minimum spanning tree* (MST) [GH85] of an edge-weighted graph is a set of $n-1$ edges of minimum total weight that form a spanning tree of the graph. The two classical algorithms for finding such a tree are *Prim's algorithm* [Pri57], which greedily adds edges of minimum weight that extend the existing tree and do not create cycles, and *Kruskal's algorithm* [Kru56], which greedily adds edges that connect components. We implement Kruskal's algorithm.

Students sometimes cast a jaded eye at the minimum spanning tree problem because a simple greedy approach suffices for finding the optimal solution. However, it is quite remarkable that a minimum spanning tree can be computed in polynomial time. Many simple variants of the problem, such as finding a spanning tree with maximum degree k or a spanning tree minimizing the total length between all pairs of vertices, are NP-complete [GJ79]. The minimum spanning tree problem can be formulated as a *matroid* [PS82], a system of independent sets whose largest weighted independent set can be found by using the greedy algorithm.

■ 8.2.1 Union-Find

Kruskal's algorithm repeatedly picks the lowest-weight edge and tests whether it bridges two connected components in the current partial tree. If so, then the two components are merged and the edge is added to the partial tree. Thus components can be maintained as a collection of disjoint sets supporting two operations: FindSet, which returns the name of the set containing a given element, and UnionSet, which, given the names of two sets, merges them into one. When a new candidate edge (i, j) arrives, we find the names of the sets containing i and j by making calls to FindSet. We then check if the two sets are identical – if not, we merge them into one by calling UnionSet.

Our data structure maintains each set in the collection as a tree such that the name of each set is its root. UnionSet merges two sets by assigning the bigger tree to be the root of the shorter one, thus giving the sets the same name while minimizing the height of the tree for efficiency. Because the smaller tree becomes a child of the bigger one on each union, the trees are balanced and FindSet can be shown to take $O(\log n)$ time per operation. The UnionSet operation makes two calls to FindSet and then spends $O(1)$ extra time to connect the two sets together, and so this operation also takes $O(\log n)$ time. Adding *path compression* [Tar75] would make the data structure even more efficient.

```
InitializeUnionFind[n_Integer] := Module[{i}, Table[{i,1},{i,n}] ]

FindSet[n_Integer,s_List] :=
     Block[{$RecursionLimit = Infinity}, If [n == s[[n,1]], n, FindSet[s[[n,1]],s]]]

UnionSet[a_Integer,b_Integer,s_List] :=
     Module[{sa=FindSet[a,s], sb=FindSet[b,s], set=s},
          If[ set[[sa,2]] < set[[sb,2]], {sa,sb} = {sb,sa} ];
```

```
        set[[sa]] = {sa, Max[ set[[sa,2]], set[[sb,2]]+1 ]};
        set[[sb]] = {sa, set[[sb,2]]};
        set
    ]
]
```

The Union-Find Data Structure

Element *i* is represented by an ordered pair in the *i*th position of a list. The first element is a parent pointer, while the second is the height of the subtree rooted at that node. This example contains three sets: a singleton containing 1; a singleton containing 2; and a set containing 3, 4, and 5.

The name of the root is not particularly significant. Here the first set is called 1, the second is called 2, and the third is called 4.

```
In[50]:= UnionSet[3,4, UnionSet[4,5, InitializeUnionFind[5] ] ]
Out[50]= {{1, 1}, {2, 1}, {4, 1}, {4, 2}, {4, 1}}

In[51]:= Table[FindSet[i,%], {i, 5}]
Out[51]= {1, 2, 4, 4, 4}
```

■ 8.2.2 Kruskal's Algorithm

Kruskal's algorithm sorts the edges in order of increasing cost and then repeatedly adds edges that bridge components until the graph is fully connected. The union-find data structure maintains the connected components in the forest. That this algorithm gives a minimum spanning tree follows because in any cycle the most expensive edge is the last one considered, and thus it cannot appear in the minimum spanning tree. The code for MinimumSpanningTree is given below. By negating the weights for each edge, this implementation can also be used to find a maximum-weight spanning tree.

```
MinimumSpanningTree[e_List, g_Graph] :=
    Module[{ne=Sort[e, (#1[[2]] <= #2[[2]])&],
            s=InitializeUnionFind[V[g]]},
        ChangeEdges[g,
            Select[Map[First, ne],
                (If[FindSet[#[[1]],s]!=FindSet[#[[2]], s],
                    s=UnionSet[#[[1]],#[[2]], s]; True, False
                ])&
            ]
        ]
    ]
MinimumSpanningTree[g_Graph] := MinimumSpanningTree[ Edges[g, EdgeWeight], g ] /; UndirectedQ[g]

MaximumSpanningTree[g_Graph] := MinimumSpanningTree[Map[{First[#], -Last[#]}&, Edges[g, EdgeWeight]], g]
```

Finding a Minimum Spanning Tree

Minimum spanning trees are useful in encoding the gross structure of geometric graphs. Here we take the minimum spanning tree of 128 North American cities and can clearly recognize the outline of the United States.

```
In[52]:= usa = SetVertexLabels[<< "extraCode/usa.graph",{" "}]
         ShowGraph[mst = MinimumSpanningTree[usa] ];
```

The shortest-path spanning tree on such a complete graph is a star. This, of course, obscures the outline and the internal structure of the map.

```
In[54]:= ShowGraph[spt = ShortestPathSpanningTree[usa,55] ];
```

This reports the total costs of the minimum spanning tree and the shortest-path spanning tree. By definition, the cost of the shortest-path spanning tree should be at least as large. The difference here is very dramatic because the U.S. graph was complete.

```
In[55]:= {Apply[ Plus, GetEdgeWeights[usa, Edges[mst]]],
          Apply[Plus, GetEdgeWeights[usa, Edges[spt]]]}
Out[55]= {16598, 259641}
```

The maximum spanning tree must be no smaller than the shortest-path spanning tree, and should generally be heavier.

```
In[56]:= Apply[Plus, GetEdgeWeights[usa, Edges[MaximumSpanningTree[usa]]]]
Out[56]= 341365
```

The minimum spanning tree not only minimizes the sum of the costs of the edges, it also minimizes the cost of the maximum edge or the "bottleneck" edge. Thus the minimum spanning tree is also a *minimum bottleneck spanning tree.*

```
In[57]:= {Max[GetEdgeWeights[usa, Edges[mst]]], Max[GetEdgeWeights[usa,
           Edges[spt]]]}
Out[57]= {423, 3408}
```

A *Euclidean minimum spanning tree* is the MST of a complete graph whose vertices are points in Euclidean space and whose edges have Euclidean distances as weights. A Euclidean MST for a set of points evenly distributed on the circumference of a circle is always a path along the circumference, while every shortest-path spanning tree is a star.

```
In[58]:= g = SetEdgeWeights[CompleteGraph[30], WeightingFunction ->
           Euclidean];
         ShowGraphArray[{MinimumSpanningTree[g], ShortestPathSpanningTree[g,
           1]} ];
```

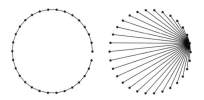

One way to produce random spanning trees is to assign random weights to edges and run the minimum spanning tree algorithm on it. Here we show two runs of this on K_{20}.

```
In[60]:= g = CompleteGraph[20];
         ShowGraphArray[Map[MinimumSpanningTree[SetEdgeWeights[#]] &, {g,
           g}]];
```

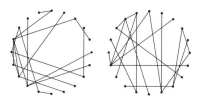

In a large complete graph with random edge weights, it is unlikely that the maximum and minimum spanning trees will have any edges in common.

```
In[62]:= g = SetEdgeWeights[ CompleteGraph[20], WeightingFunction -> Random];
         M[GraphIntersection[ MinimumSpanningTree[g],
           MaximumSpanningTree[g]]]
Out[63]= 0
```

Prim's algorithm consists of $(n-1)$ iterations, each of which takes $O(n)$ time to select a smallest edge connecting a vertex in the connected component to one that is not. This total time complexity of $O(n^2)$ is optimal on dense graphs. The trick is maintaining a shortest edge to each outside vertex in an array, so, after adding the ith edge to the tree, only $n-i-1$ edges must be tested to update this array. More efficient algorithms rely on sophisticated data structures [FT87] or randomization [KKT95].

■ 8.2.3 Counting Spanning Trees

The number of spanning trees of a graph G was determined by Kirchhoff [Kir47] by using certain operations on the adjacency matrix of G.

The (i,j) *minor* of a matrix M is the determinant of M with the ith row and jth column deleted. The (i,j) *cofactor* of a matrix M is $(-1)^{i+j}$ times the (i,j) minor of M.

```
Cofactor[m_?MatrixQ, {i_Integer?Positive , j_Integer?Positive}] :=
     (-1)^(i+j) * Det[ Drop[ Transpose[ Drop[Transpose[m],{j,j}]], {i,i}]] /; (i <= Length[m]) &&
                                                      (j <= Length[m[[1]]])
```

Computing a Cofactor of a Matrix

The number of spanning trees of a graph G is equal to any cofactor of the degree matrix of G minus the adjacency matrix of G, where the degree matrix of a graph is a diagonal matrix with the degree of v_i in the (i,i) position of the matrix. This *matrix-tree theorem* is due to Chaiken [Cha82].

```
NumberOfSpanningTrees[g_Graph] := 0 /; (V[g] == 0)
NumberOfSpanningTrees[g_Graph] := 1 /; (V[g] == 1)
NumberOfSpanningTrees[g_Graph] :=
     Module[{m = ToAdjacencyMatrix[g]},
          Cofactor[ DiagonalMatrix[Map[(Apply[Plus,#])&,m]] - m, {1,1}]
     ]
```

Counting Spanning Trees of a Graph

Any tree contains exactly one spanning tree.

```
In[64]:= NumberOfSpanningTrees[Star[20]]

Out[64]= 1
```

A cycle on n vertices contains exactly n spanning trees, since deleting any edge creates a tree.

```
In[65]:= NumberOfSpanningTrees[Cycle[20]]

Out[65]= 20
```

The number of spanning trees of a complete graph is n^{n-2}, as was shown by the Prüfer bijection between labeled trees and strings of integers discussed in Section 6.3.1.

```
In[66]:= NumberOfSpanningTrees[CompleteGraph[10]]

Out[66]= 100000000
```

The set of spanning trees of a graph can be ranked and unranked and thus can be generated systematically or randomly. See [CDN89] for $O(n^3)$ ranking and unranking algorithms.

8.3 Network Flow

We introduced shortest paths by discussing optimization on networks of roads. When we have a network of pipes and want to push sewage through the graph instead of cars, we have a *network flow* problem. More formally, a network flow problem consists of an edge-weighted graph G and *source* and *sink* vertices s and t. The weight of each edge signifies its capacity, the maximum amount of stuff that can be pumped through it. The *maximum-flow problem* seeks the maximum possible flow from s to t, satisfying the capacity constraint at each edge and satisfying the constraint that at each vertex other than s and t the net flow through the vertex should be 0. Network flow is important because many other problems can be easily reduced to it, including k-connectivity and bipartite matching.

Traditional network flow algorithms use the *augmenting path* idea of Ford and Fulkerson [FF62], which repeatedly finds a path of positive capacity from s to t and adds it to the flow. It can be shown that the flow through a network of rational capacities is optimal if and only if it contains no augmenting path. Since each augmentation adds to the flow, if all capacities are rational, we will eventually find the maximum. However, each augmenting path may add but a little to the total flow, and so the algorithm might take a long time to converge.

Edmonds and Karp [EK72] proved that always selecting a *shortest* geodesic augmenting path guarantees that $O(n^3)$ augmentations suffice for optimization. The Edmonds-Karp algorithm is fairly easy to implement, since a breadth-first search from the source can find a shortest path in linear time.

The key structure is the *residual flow graph*, denoted $R(G,f)$, where G is the input graph and f is the current flow through it. This directed, edge-weighted $R(G,f)$ has the same vertices as G and for each edge (i,j) in G with capacity $c(i,j)$ and flow $f(i,j)$, $R(G,f)$ may contain two edges:

(i) an edge (i,j) with weight $c(i,j) - f(i,j)$, if $c(i,j) - f(i,j) > 0$ and

(ii) an edge (j,i) with weight $f(i,j)$, if $f(i,j) > 0$.

Edge (i,j) in the residual graph indicates that a positive amount of flow can be pushed from i to j. The weight of the edge gives the exact amount that can be pushed. A path in the residual flow graph from s to t implies that more flow can be pushed from s to t and the minimum weight of an edge in this path equals the amount of extra flow that can be pushed.

In the *Combinatorica* function `NetworkFlow`, we repeatedly start with a flow, construct the residual flow graph for it, perform a breadth-first search on this graph to find a path from s to t, and push the flow along that path, thereby ending up with a new and improved flow. The algorithm starts with a flow of 0 through every edge, and the algorithm terminates when the residual flow graph has no path from s to t.

Here we compute the flow across a cube with all edge capacities equal to 1. This flow is returned as an augmented adjacency list, where the flow appears along with each edge. For example, vertex 1 has neighbors 2, 3, and 5, and in the maximum flow a unit flow is pushed from 1 to each of its neighbors.

```
In[67]:= NetworkFlow[g = GridGraph[2, 2, 2], 1, 8, All] // ColumnForm
Out[67]= {{2, 1}, {3, 1}, {5, 1}}
         {{1, 0}, {4, 1}, {6, 0}}
         {{1, 0}, {4, 0}, {7, 1}}
         {{2, 0}, {3, 0}, {8, 1}}
         {{1, 0}, {6, 1}, {7, 0}}
         {{2, 0}, {5, 0}, {8, 1}}
         {{3, 0}, {5, 0}, {8, 1}}
         {{4, 0}, {6, 0}, {7, 0}}
```

The connection between network flows and edge connectivity is illustrated here. In any graph whose edge capacities are all 1, the maximum flow from *s* to *t* corresponds to the number of edge-disjoint paths from *s* to *t*. Specifically, the edges along which positive flow is pushed form paths from *s* to *t*. Here three units of flow can be pushed from vertex 1 to vertex 27 along the edge-disjoint paths shown.

```
In[68]:= ShowGraph[Highlight[g = GridGraph[3, 3, 3],
            {First[Transpose[NetworkFlow[g, 1, 27, Edge]]]}]];
```

Here we construct the directed edge-weighted graph that will be our running network flow example.

```
In[69]:= g = AddEdges[EmptyGraph[6, Type -> Directed],
               {{1, 2}, {2, 3}, {1, 3}, {3, 4}, {1, 5},
                {5, 6}, {5, 4}, {6, 4}, {6, 2}} ];
         h = SetEdgeWeights[g, {10, 4, 3, 14, 6, 4, 12, 10, 7}];
         h = SetEdgeLabels[h,GetEdgeWeights[h]];
```

Calling NetworkFlow tells us that 13 units of flow will be sent from vertex 1 to vertex 4.

```
In[72]:= NetworkFlow[h, 1, 4]
Out[72]= 13
```

These are the original graph (left) and residual flow graph (right) corresponding to the maximum flow from vertex 1 to vertex 4. There is no directed 1-to-4 path in the residual graph, because such a path means that more flow can be pushed from source to sink. Only vertices 1 and 2 remain reachable from the source, yielding a source–sink partition $S = \{1, 2\}$ and $T = \{3, 4, 5, 6\}$. All edges that go from S to T are *saturated*, meaning they carry the maximum possible flow. Similarly, edges from T to S in the residual graph carry no flow.

```
In[73]:= f = NetworkFlow[h, 1, 4, All];
         ShowGraphArray[{h,ResidualFlowGraph[h,f]}, VertexNumber->True];
```

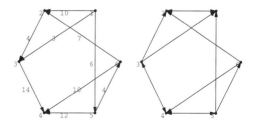

A *minimum s-t cut* in an edge-weighted graph is a set of edges with minimum total weight whose removal separates vertex s from vertex t. The *max-flow min-cut* theorem states that the weight of a minimum s-t cut equals the maximum flow that can be sent from s to t when interpreting the weights as capacities. The minimum s-t cut is defined by the source–sink partition above. Specifically, the edges from S to T give the minimum s-t cut.

```
In[75]:= cut = NetworkFlow[h, 1, 4, Cut];
         ShowGraph[Highlight[h, {cut}], TextStyle->{FontSize->10}];
```

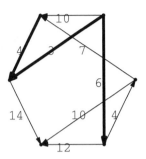

Here the edge connectivity of the graph matches that of the s-t cut, but in general we need to minimize over all possible source–sink cuts.

```
In[77]:= EdgeConnectivity[ MakeUndirected[g] ]
Out[77]= 3
```

A fast algorithm for 0-1 network flow appears in [ET75]. This is useful for problems that use network flow as a subroutine. Such algorithms often require solving flow problems between every pair of vertices in the graph. For undirected graphs, $n-1$ applications of the maximum-flow algorithm suffice to determine all $\binom{n}{2}$ pairwise flows [GH61].

Active research continues in finding better network flow algorithms, with [Tar83] an excellent text and [AMO93] reflective of the state of the art.

8.4 Matching

A *matching* in a graph G is a set of edges of G no two of which have a vertex in common. Clearly, every matching consists of at most $n/2$ edges; matchings with exactly $n/2$ edges are called *perfect*. Not all graphs have perfect matchings, but every graph has a *maximum* or largest matching.

A perfect matching on a graph is a 1-regular subgraph of order n. In general, a *k-factor* of a graph is a k-regular subgraph of order n. k-factors are a generalization of perfect matchings, since perfect matchings are 1-factors. A graph is *k-factorable* if it is the union of disjoint k-factors.

■ 8.4.1 Maximal Matching

The problem of finding matchings is naturally generalized to edge-weighted graphs, where the goal is to find a matching that maximizes the sum of the weights of the edges. An excellent reference on matching theory and algorithms is [LP86].

A *maximal matching* is one that cannot be enlarged by simply adding an edge. Maximal matchings are easy to compute: Repeatedly pick an edge disjoint from those already picked until this is no longer possible. Maximal matchings need not be maximum matchings. Indeed, a graph may have maximal matchings of varying sizes and it is hard to find a maximal matching of smallest size. Fortunately larger matchings are usually more useful.

Here is a maximal matching in a generalized Petersen graph. Clearly, the matching is not perfect. Now walk along the path $5, 3, 1, 7, 8, 9, 10, 11, 12, 6$, changing each matched edge to an unmatched and each unmatched edge to a matched. In the process, four matched edges are replaced by five matched edges, giving a perfect matching.

```
In[78]:= g = GeneralizedPetersenGraph[6, 4];
         ShowGraph[Highlight[g, {MaximalMatching[g]}],
         VertexNumber->True];
```

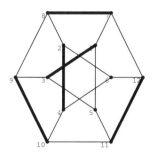

A grid graph is bipartite and so is every induced subgraph. Here we construct a maximal matching in a random induced subgraph of a 20×20 grid graph. Is this a largest possible matching? Look for paths that start and end with unmatched vertices and contain edges that are alternately matched and unmatched. Flipping the status of edges in such a path increases the size of the matching by 1.

```
In[80]:= g = InduceSubgraph[GridGraph[20, 20], RandomSubset[400]];
         ShowGraph[Highlight[g, {mm=MaximalMatching[g]}]];
```

This shows the difference in sizes of a maximum matching and a maximal matching for the above graph.

```
In[82]:= {Length[BipartiteMatching[g]], Length[mm]}
Out[82]= {90, 79}
```

The maximal matching shown here is in fact maximum. Any larger matching would have to be perfect, but none exists. To see this, remove the central vertex. Three odd-sized components result, each of which needs the central vertex to match with a vertex in it. But the central vertex can match with only one vertex, leaving two components stranded.

```
In[83]:= ShowGraph[Highlight[g = NoPerfectMatchingGraph,
         {MaximalMatching[g]}]]
```

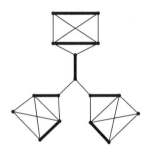

More generally, a graph $G = (V, E)$ has no perfect matching if there is a set $S \subseteq V$ whose removal results in more odd-sized components than $|S|$. Tutte's theorem shows that the converse is true, providing a complete characterization of graphs with perfect matchings.

```
In[84]:= Map[Length, ConnectedComponents[ DeleteVertices[
             NoPerfectMatchingGraph,{6}] ] ]
Out[84]= {5, 5, 5}
```

■ 8.4.2 Bipartite Matching

The study of matchings in graphs arose from the *marriage problem*, where each of b boys knows some subset of g girls. It asks under what conditions the boys can be married so each of them gets a girl that he knows. In graph-theoretic terms, this asks if there is a matching in the bipartite graph $G = (X, Y, E)$ that matches each vertex in X to one in Y. Hall's marriage theorem [Hal35] states that there is a matching in which every boy can be married if and only if every subset S of boys knows a subset of girls at least as large as $|S|$. This criterion provides a way to test whether such a marriage is possible and also to construct one, albeit in exponential time.

A polynomial-time matching algorithm follows from Berge's theorem [Ber57], which states that a matching is maximum if and only if it contains no *augmenting path*. For matching M in a graph G, an *M-alternating path* is a simple path whose edges are alternately matched and unmatched. Any vertex incident on some edge in M is said to be *saturated*. An *M-augmenting path* is an M-alternating path that starts and ends at unsaturated vertices. Berge's theorem suggests the following algorithm: Improve an arbitrary matching M by finding an M-augmenting path P and replacing M with the symmetric difference $(M - P) \cup (P - M)$. This is the matching obtained by flipping the status of the edges in P and is one larger than the old matching. The matching must be maximum when it contains no augmenting path.

The following function implements a breadth-first traversal of G to find M-alternating paths starting from vertices in S.

```
AlternatingPaths[g_Graph, start_List, ME_List] :=
    Module[{MV = Table[0, {V[g]}], e = ToAdjacencyLists[g],
          lvl = Table[Infinity, {V[g]}], cnt = 1,
          queue = start, parent = Table[i, {i, V[g]}]},
          Scan[(MV[[#[[1]]]] = #[[2]]; MV[[#[[2]]]] = #[[1]]) &, ME];
          Scan[(lvl[[#]] = 0) &, start];
          While[queue != {},
                {v, queue} = {First[queue], Rest[queue]};
                If[EvenQ[lvl[[v]]],
                   Scan[(If[lvl[[#]] == Infinity, lvl[[#]] = lvl[[v]] + 1;
                        parent[[#]] = v; AppendTo[queue, #]]) &, e[[v]]]
                   ],
                   If[MV[[v]] != 0,
                     u = MV[[v]];
                     If[lvl[[u]] == Infinity,
                        lvl[[u]] = lvl[[v]] + 1;
                        parent[[u]] = v;
                        AppendTo[queue, u]
                     ]
                   ]
                ]
          ];
          parent
    ]
```

Finding Augmenting Paths

The matching shown in this graph is maximal, but not maximum. The sequence $\{7, 5, 2, 3\}$ is an augmenting path that can improve the matching.

```
In[85]:= g = DeleteVertices[GridGraph[3, 3], {7}];
         m = {{1, 4}, {2, 5}, {6, 8}};
         ShowGraph[Highlight[g, {m}], VertexNumber -> True]
```

Here we compute a tree of alternating paths emanating from 3. The tree is represented by parent pointers – so the parent of vertex 1 is 4, the parent of vertex 2 is 3, and so on. The path $\{7, 5, 2, 3\}$ is represented because 7 points to 5, 5 points to 2, and 2 points to 3. It is an augmenting path because the two endpoints are unsaturated.

```
In[88]:= AlternatingPaths[g, {3}, m]
Out[88]= {4, 3, 3, 5, 2, 3, 5, 6}
```

The *Combinatorica* bipartite matching implementation is based on network flow [HK75]. Take the given bipartite graph G to be an unweighted, directed graph in which every edge goes from the first stage to the second. Add a source s, with edges of unit capacity going from s to each vertex in the first stage, and a sink t, with edges of capacity 1 going from each vertex in the second stage to t. The maximum flow from s to t must correspond to a maximum matching, since it will find a largest set of vertex-disjoint paths, which in this graph consists of disjoint edges from G.

The connection between network flows and augmenting paths works both ways. Finding a path to push flow along in a residual graph is the same problem as finding an M-augmenting path to flip edges on. Thus the Edmonds-Karp network flow algorithm is analogous to the augmenting path algorithm for bipartite matching.

```
BipartiteMatching[g_Graph] :=
     Module[{p,v1,v2,coloring=TwoColoring[g],n=V[g],flow},
          v1 = Flatten[Position[coloring,1]];
          v2 = Flatten[Position[coloring,2]];
          p = BipartiteMatchingFlowGraph[MakeSimple[g],v1,v2];
          Complement[
            Map[Sort[First[#]]&, NetworkFlow[p, n+1, n+2, Edge]],
            Map[{#,n+1}&, v1],
            Map[{#,n+2}&, v2]
          ]
     ]
```

```
        ] /; BipartiteQ[g] && UnweightedQ[g]

BipartiteMatching[g_Graph] := First[BipartiteMatchingAndCover[g]] /; BipartiteQ[g]

BipartiteMatchingFlowGraph[g_Graph, v1_List, v2_List] :=
    Module[{n = V[g], ng},
        ng = ChangeEdges[
                SetGraphOptions[g, EdgeDirection -> True],
                Map[If[MemberQ[v1, #[[1]]], #, Reverse[#]] &, Edges[g]]
            ];
        AddEdges[AddVertices[ng, 2],
                Join[Map[{{n + 1, #}} &, v1], Map[{{#, n + 2}} &, v2]]
        ]
    ]
```

Finding a Maximum Bipartite Matching

Here is a maximum matching in a random induced subgraph of a grid graph. Roughly half the vertices will be removed from the grid. The matching may leave unsaturated vertices, but there are guaranteed not to be any augmenting paths remaining.

```
In[89]:= g = InduceSubgraph[GridGraph[20, 20], RandomSubset[400]];
         m = BipartiteMatching[g];
         ShowGraph[Highlight[g, {m}]];
```

Here is a *maximal matching* of the same graph. It is maximal in the sense that no edges can be added to it without violating the matching property. However, a maximal matching need not be *maximum*. See if you can find an *M*-augmenting path for this matching.

```
In[92]:= mm = MaximalMatching[g]; ShowGraph[Highlight[g, {mm}]];
```

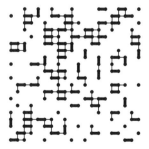

By definition, there cannot be a matching larger than a maximum matching.

```
In[93]:= {Length[mm], Length[m]}

Out[93]= {72, 79}
```

■ 8.4.3 Weighted Bipartite Matching and Vertex Cover

Weighted bipartite matching seeks a matching in an edge-weighted bipartite graph whose total weight is maximum. There is a remarkable duality between the weighted matching problem and the weighted vertex cover problem, which can be exploited to produce polynomial-time solutions to both problems on bipartite graphs. In this setting, a *vertex cover* seeks to find the *costs* u_i, $1 \le i \le n$, and v_j, $1 \le j \le n$, such that for each i, j, $u_i + v_j \ge w_{ij}$ and the sum of the costs is minimum. Letting u and v respectively denote the vectors $(u_1, u_2, \dots, u_n)$ and $(v_1, v_2, \dots, v_n)$, we call the pair (u, v) a *cover*. The *cost* of the cover (u, v), denoted $c(u, v)$, is simply $\sum_i u_i + \sum_j v_j$, and this is what we seek to minimize.

Without loss of generality, we assume that the input graph is the complete weighted bipartite graph $K_{n,n}$. Why complete? Because if it is not we can add vertices to make the two stages of equal size and set all the missing edges to have weight 0 without changing the total weight. We assume the vertices in each of the two stages are labeled 1 through n, and that w_{ij} represents the weight of the edge connecting vertex i to vertex j.

Let M be a perfect matching of $K_{n,n}$ and let $w(M)$ denote its weight. The "duality theorem" expressing the connection between the maximum weight matching problem and the minimum cost vertex cover problem is as follows:

> For any vertex cover (u, v) and any perfect matching M, $c(u, v) \ge w(M)$. Furthermore, $c(u, v) = w(M)$ if and only if every edge $\{i, j\}$ in M satisfies $u_i + v_j = w_{ij}$. In this case, M is a maximum matching and (u, v) is a minimum vertex cover.

Kuhn proposed the *Hungarian algorithm* to exploit this duality, naming it to honor the contributions of Konig and Egervary. The Hungarian algorithm provides a polynomial-time solution to both of these problems. Suppose we have a feasible cover (u, v), that is, a cover (u, v) satisfying $u_i + v_j \ge w_{ij}$ for all edges $\{i, j\}$. By the duality theorem, if this cover is optimal, then we should be able to find a matching whose weight is identical to the cost of the cover. Furthermore, the duality theorem tells us that such a matching can be found among the edges that are "tightly" covered, that is, those edges $\{i, j\}$ for which $u_i + w_j = w_{ij}$. We construct the *equality subgraph* $G_{u,v}$, a spanning subgraph of $K_{n,n}$ whose edges $\{i, j\}$ are all those that satisfy $u_i + w_j = w_{ij}$. Now construct a maximum matching M of $G_{u,v}$. If M is a perfect matching of $K_{n,n}$, we are done, because in this case $c(u, v) = w(M)$.

If not, M can be improved. Here is how. Let X and Y be the vertices in the two stages of $K_{n,n}$. Let U be the unmatched vertices in X, S be the vertices in X reachable by M-alternating paths from U, and T be the vertices in Y reachable by M-alternating paths from U. To increase the size of M, we attempt to bring more edges into $G_{u,v}$ by changing the cover (u, v). First note that edges from S to $Y - T$ are not in $G_{u,v}$. After all, if there is an edge $\{i, j\}$, $i \in S$, $j \in Y - T$ in $G_{u,v}$, what prevents j from being in T? Therefore, for any edge $\{i, j\}$, $i \in S$, and $j \in Y - T$, $u_i + v_j > w_{i,j}$. Now define $\epsilon = \min\{u_i + v_j - w_{i,j} \mid i \in S, j \in Y - T\}$ and reduce u_i by ϵ for all $i \in S$ and increase v_j by ϵ for all

$j \in T$. This implies that the sum $u_i + v_j$ remains unaffected for edges between S and T, increases for edges between $X - S$ and T, remains unaffected for edges between $X - S$ and $Y - T$, and decreases just the right amount for edges between S and $Y - T$. This guarantees that $G_{u,v}$ loses no edges and acquires at least one new edge. Now we find a maximum matching in the new graph $G_{u,v}$. This leads to an iterative improvement in M until it becomes a perfect matching of $K_{n,n}$. This algorithm is implemented in the *Combinatorica* function BipartiteMatchingAndCover.

We give an edge-weighted $K_{6,6}$ as input to BipartiteMatchingAndCover, which returns a maximum matching along with a minimum vertex cover.

```
In[94]:= g = SetEdgeWeights[CompleteGraph[6, 6],
             WeightingFunction->RandomInteger, WeightRange->{1,10}];
         {m, c} = BipartiteMatchingAndCover[g]

Out[95]= {{{1, 8}, {2, 7}, {3, 12}, {4, 11}, {5, 10},
          {6, 9}}, {9, 10, 8, 9, 10, 9, 0, 0, 1, 0, 1, 0}}
```

The equality of these two quantities is proof that the matching and the cover computed above are optimal.

```
In[96]:= {Apply[Plus, GetEdgeWeights[g, m]], Apply[Plus, c]}

Out[96]= {57, 57}
```

The unweighted vertex cover problem can be solved for a bipartite graph G by thinking of edges in G as having weight 1 and edges missing from G as having weight 0. Vertices assigned cost 1 appear in the vertex cover. The duality between matching and vertex cover implies that the size of a maximum matching M equals the size of a minimum vertex cover C, so for every edge in M exactly one of its endpoints is in C.

```
In[97]:= g = InduceSubgraph[GridGraph[10, 10], RandomSubset[100]];
         {m, c} = BipartiteMatchingAndCover[g];
         ShowGraph[Highlight[g, {m, Flatten[Position[c, 1]]}]];
```

The graph h is g plus one edge, but this edge is sufficient to make it nonbipartite. Thus MinimumVertexCover uses a brute-force algorithm on h but uses the fast Hungarian algorithm for g. The difference is clear.

```
In[100]:= g = GridGraph[5, 5]; h = AddEdges[g, {{2, 6}}];
          {Timing[c=MinimumVertexCover[h];],
              Timing[MinimumVertexCover[g];]}

Out[101]= {{217.52 Second, Null}, {0.81 Second, Null}}
```

■ 8.4.4 Stable Marriages

Not all matching problems are most naturally described in terms of graphs. Perhaps the most amusing example is the *stable marriage problem*.

   Given a set of n men and n women, it is desired to marry them off, one man to one woman. As in the real world, each man has an opinion of each woman and ranks them in terms of desirability from

1 to n. The women do the same to the men. Now suppose they are all married off, including couples $\{m_1, w_1\}$ and $\{m_2, w_2\}$. If m_1 prefers w_2 to w_1 and w_2 prefers m_1 to her current spouse m_2, domestic bliss is doomed. Such a marriage is *unstable* because m_1 and w_2 would run off to be with each other. The goal of the stable marriage problem is to find a way to match men and women subject to their preference functions, such that the matching is stable. Obviously, stability is a desirable property, but can it always be achieved?

Gale and Shapely [GS62] proved that, for *any* set of preference functions, a stable marriage exists. Even if one person is so unattractive that everyone ranks that person last, he or she can be assigned a spouse s undesirable enough to all others that no one would be willing to give up their spouse to rescue s. The proof is algorithmic. Starting from his favorite, each unmarried men take turns proposing to the highest rated woman he has not yet proposed to. If a woman gets more than one proposal, she takes the best one, leaving the loser unmarried. Eventually, everyone gets married, since a woman cannot turn down a proposal unless she has a better one, and further, this marriage is stable, since each man always proposes to the highest ranked woman who hasn't rejected him yet. Thus no man can better his lot with further proposals.

The Gale-Shapely algorithm is used in matching hospitals to interns and has led to a well-developed theory of stable marriage [GI89].

```
StableMarriage[mpref_List,fpref_List] :=
    Module[{n=Length[mpref],freemen,cur,i,w,husband},
           freemen = Range[n];
           cur = Table[1,{n}];
           husband = Table[n+1,{n}];
           While[ freemen != {},
                   {i,freemen}={First[freemen],Rest[freemen]};
                   w = mpref[[ i,cur[[i]] ]];
                   If[BeforeQ[ fpref[[w]], i, husband[[w]] ],
                           If[husband[[w]] != n+1,
                                   AppendTo[freemen,husband[[w]] ]
                           ];
                           husband[[w]] = i,
                           cur[[i]]++;
                           AppendTo[freemen,i]
                   ];
           ];
           InversePermutation[ husband ]
    ] /; Length[mpref] == Length[fpref]
```

The Gale-Shapely Algorithm for Stable Marriages

The Gale-Shapely algorithm finds a stable marriage for any set of preference functions. The *i*th element of the returned permutation is the wife of man *i*.

```
In[102]:= TableForm[{ men=Table[RandomPermutation[9],{9}],
          women=Table[RandomPermutation[9],{9}]}]
```

```
Out[102]//TableForm=  7  4  8  7  3  4  6  7  2
                      9  5  7  6  2  8  4  3  7
                      8  1  9  1  5  2  3  8  3
                      1  6  6  9  1  5  2  4  9
                      6  8  1  5  4  1  5  9  8
                      2  3  3  2  6  3  7  2  1
                      3  2  4  3  9  9  8  5  5
                      4  7  5  4  7  6  9  1  4
                      5  9  2  8  8  7  1  6  6

                      3  8  5  9  1  2  4  8  5
                      8  1  4  8  8  7  7  7  4
                      4  3  3  1  9  6  8  5  7
                      9  4  1  3  2  4  6  9  2
                      2  2  2  5  3  1  2  3  1
                      7  6  8  2  4  7  5  2  8
                      1  7  7  7  5  3  9  6  6
                      6  9  9  4  7  5  1  4  3
                      5  5  6  6  6  9  3  1  9
```

Because of the proposal sequence, the Gale-Shapely algorithm yields the *male-optimal* marriage, under which each man gets his best possible match in any stable marriage.

```
In[103]:= StableMarriage[men,women]
```

```
Out[103]= {9, 4, 1, 7, 3, 2, 6, 8, 5}
```

The sexual bias can be reversed by simply exchanging the roles of men and women. The inverse permutation returns who the men are married to. It can be verified that in all couples that differ from the previous matching, the men are less well off and the women happier.

```
In[104]:= InversePermutation[ StableMarriage[women,men] ]
```

```
Out[104]= {2, 4, 1, 7, 3, 6, 9, 8, 5}
```

8.5 Partial Orders

In this section, we consider several important problems on directed acyclic graphs (DAGs) and their close cousins, partial orders. A *partially ordered set* (or *poset*) is a set with a consistent ordering relation over its elements. More formally, a partial order is a binary relation that is reflexive, transitive, and antisymmetric. Interesting binary relations between combinatorial objects often are partial orders.

```
PartialOrderQ[r_?SquareMatrix] := ReflexiveQ[r] && AntiSymmetricQ[r] && TransitiveQ[r]
PartialOrderQ[g_Graph] := ReflexiveQ[g] && AntiSymmetricQ[g] && TransitiveQ[g]
```

Partial Order Predicates

■ 8.5.1 Topological Sorting

A directed acyclic graph defines a precedence relation on the vertices, if arc (i, j) is taken as meaning that vertex i must occur before vertex j. A *topological sort* is a permutation p of the vertices of a graph such that an edge (i, j) implies that i appears before j in p.

Only directed acyclic graphs can be topologically sorted, since no vertex in a directed cycle can take precedence over all the rest. Every acyclic graph contains at least one vertex v of out-degree 0. Clearly, v can appear last in the topological ordering. Deleting v leaves a graph with at least one other vertex of out-degree 0. Repeating this argument gives an algorithm for topologically sorting any directed acyclic graph.

```
TopologicalSort[g_Graph] := Range[V[g]] /; EmptyQ[g]
TopologicalSort[g_Graph] :=
    Module[{g1 = RemoveSelfLoops[g],e,indeg,zeros,v},
        e=ToAdjacencyLists[g1];
        indeg=InDegree[g1];
        zeros = Flatten[ Position[indeg, 0] ];
        Table[{v,zeros}={First[zeros],Rest[zeros]};
            Scan[(indeg[[#]]--; If[indeg[[#]]==0, AppendTo[zeros,#]])&, e[[v]]];
            v,
            {V[g]}
        ]
    ] /; AcyclicQ[RemoveSelfLoops[g]] && !UndirectedQ[g]
```

Topologically Sorting a Graph

The divisibility relation induces a partial order on positive integers. More precisely, $i < j$ if and only if i divides j. The Hasse diagram (see Section 8.5.3) of this poset is shown here. Each relation $i < j$ is represented by an "upward path" from i to j in the diagram. Since there is an upward path from 1 to everything else, every topological sort of this poset starts with 1. Any listing of the integers in nondecreasing order of their ranks is a topological sort.

```
In[105]:= ShowGraph[HasseDiagram[g = MakeGraph[Range[12],
          (Mod[#2, #1] == 0) &]], VertexNumber -> True,
          TextStyle->{FontSize->11}];
```

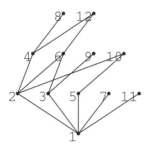

Such a "ranked" topological ordering on the elements is produced here.

```
In[106]:= TopologicalSort[g]
Out[106]= {1, 2, 3, 5, 7, 11, 4, 6, 9, 10, 8, 12}
```

Any permutation of the vertices of an empty graph defines a topological order.

```
In[107]:= TopologicalSort[ EmptyGraph[10] ]
Out[107]= {1, 2, 3, 4, 5, 6, 7, 8, 9, 10}
```

On the other hand, a complete directed acyclic graph defines a total order, so there is only one possible output from TopologicalSort.

```
In[108]:= TopologicalSort[ MakeGraph[Range[10],(#1 > #2)&] ]
Out[108]= {10, 9, 8, 7, 6, 5, 4, 3, 2, 1}
```

■ 8.5.2 Transitive Closure and Reduction

A directed graph is *transitive* if its edges represent a transitive relation. More precisely, $G = (V, E)$ is transitive if, for any three vertices $x, y, z \in V$, the existence of edges $(x, y), (y, z) \in E$ implies that $(x, z) \in E$. We extend this definition to undirected graphs by interpreting each undirected edge as two directed edges headed in opposite directions.

Any graph G can be made transitive by adding enough extra edges. We define the *transitive closure* $C(G)$ of G as the graph that contains an edge $(u, v) \in C(G)$ if and only if there is a directed path from u to v in G. This definition translates into an $O(n^3)$ algorithm, where we start with the adjacency matrix of G and update it repeatedly to ensure that if slot $[i, j]$ and slot $[j, k]$ are nonzero, then so is slot $[i, k]$.

This algorithm is a perfect candidate for compilation. It consists of three simple nested loops that manipulate a square integer matrix, and therefore it contains no *Mathematica* features that are an obstacle to compilation. In the implementation below, function TC is compiled while the wrapper function TransitiveClosure converts the graph into an adjacency matrix and passes it along to TC.

```
TransitiveClosure[g_Graph] := g /; EmptyQ[g]

TransitiveClosure[g_Graph] :=
      Module[{e = ToAdjacencyMatrix[g]},
            If[UndirectedQ[g],
               FromAdjacencyMatrix[TC[e], Vertices[g, All]],
               FromAdjacencyMatrix[TC[e], Vertices[g, All], Type -> Directed]
            ]
      ]

TC = Compile[{{e, _Integer, 2}},
          Module[{ne = e, n = Length[e], i, j, k},
                Do[If[ne[[j, i]] != 0,
                    Do[If[ne[[i, k]] != 0, ne[[j, k]] = 1], {k, n}]
                  ], {i, n}, {j, n}
                ];
                ne
          ]
      ]
```

Finding the Transitive Closure of a Graph

A *transitive reduction* of a graph G is a smallest graph $R(G)$ such that $C(G) = C(R(G))$. Determining a transitive reduction of a binary relation is more difficult, since arcs that were not part of the relation can be in the reduction. Although it is hard to find a smallest subset of the *arcs* determining the relation, Aho, Garey, and Ullman [AGU72] give an efficient algorithm to determine a smallest subset of *vertex pairs* determining the relation. All of these complications go away when the graph is acyclic, as is true with a partial order. In this case, any edge of G that would have been added in finding the transitive closure cannot appear in the transitive reduction. Thus any edge implied by other edges in the graph can simply be deleted. For graphs with directed cycles, this policy might delete every edge in a directed cycle. To get around this problem, we modify the algorithm so that it deletes only edges that are implied by two edges in the current transitive reduction instead of the original graph. This gives *a* reduction, but one that is not necessarily minimal. Like transitive closure, this algorithm is a perfect candidate for compilation.

```
TransitiveReduction[g_Graph] := g /; EmptyQ[g]

TransitiveReduction[g_Graph] :=
      Module[{closure = ToAdjacencyMatrix[g]},
            If[UndirectedQ[g],
               FromAdjacencyMatrix[TR[closure], Vertices[g, All]],
               If[AcyclicQ[RemoveSelfLoops[g]],
                  FromAdjacencyMatrix[TRAcyclic[closure], Vertices[g, All], Type->Directed],
                  FromAdjacencyMatrix[TR[closure], Vertices[g, All], Type->Directed]
               ]
            ]
```

```
          ]

TR = Compile[{{closure, _Integer, 2}},
      Module[{reduction = closure, n = Length[closure], i, j, k},
            Do[
               If[reduction[[i,j]]!=0 && reduction[[j,k]]!=0 &&
                  reduction[[i,k]]!=0 && (i!=j) && (j!=k) && (i!=k),
                  reduction[[i,k]] = 0
               ],
               {i,n},{j,n},{k,n}
            ];
            reduction
      ]
   ]
```

Finding a Transitive Reduction of an Acyclic Graph

This graph shows the divisibility relation between positive integers as a directed graph. This relation is a partial order, and hence this graph is acyclic modulo self-loops. Since 1 divides everyone else, there is an edge from 1 to every other vertex.

```
In[109]:= g = MakeGraph[Range[12], (Mod[#2, #1] == 0) &];
          ShowGraph[g=Nest[SpringEmbedding,g,10], VertexNumber->True];
```

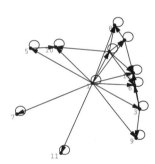

Here we see the TransitiveReduction of the above graph, which eliminates all implied edges in the divisibility relation, such as 4 ⊢ 8, 1 ⊢ 4, 1 ⊢ 6, and 1 ⊢ 8.

```
In[111]:= ShowGraph[RemoveSelfLoops[ h=RankedEmbedding[
          TransitiveReduction[g], {1}]], VertexNumber->True,
          VertexNumberPosition->UpperRight, TextStyle->{FontSize->11},
          PlotRange -> 0.1];
```

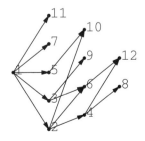

Transitive reduction applied to an already reduced graph makes no change to it.

```
In[112]:= IdenticalQ[h, TransitiveReduction[h]]
Out[112]= True
```

The transitive closure of the transitive reduction of a transitive graph is an identity operation.

```
In[113]:= IdenticalQ[g, TransitiveClosure[TransitiveReduction[g]] ]
Out[113]= True
```

The transitive reduction of a nonacyclic graph is not necessarily minimal under our simple reduction algorithm. The directed 5-cycle implies all edges of a complete directed graph. Therefore, we have an unnecessary edge here.

```
In[114]:= ShowGraph[TransitiveReduction[CompleteGraph[5, Type->Directed]]];
```

■ 8.5.3 Hasse Diagrams

What is the best embedding for a partial order? It should clearly identify the hierarchy imposed by the order while containing as few edges as possible to avoid cluttering up the picture. Such a drawing is called a *Hasse diagram* and is the preferred pictorial representation of a partial order.

More precisely, the Hasse diagram of a poset P is a drawing with the properties that (i) if $i < j$ in P, then i appears below j and (ii) the drawing contains no edge implied by transitivity. Since all edges in such a drawing go upwards, directions are typically omitted in these drawings.

We have seen how ranked embeddings (Section 5.5.2) can be used to represent a hierarchy. At the bottom of the hierarchy are the vertices that have no ancestors or, equivalently, have in-degree 0. The vertices that have out-degree 0 represent maxima of the partial order and are ranked together at the top. Performing a transitive reduction minimizes the number of edges in the graph. The *Combinatorica* function `HasseDiagram` takes a directed acyclic graph as input and outputs a Hasse diagram.

It is impossible to understand the *Boolean algebra*, the partial order on subsets defined by inclusion, from this circular embedding. Beyond the arbitrary position of the vertices, this graph contains too many edges to understand.

```
In[115]:= ShowGraph[s = MakeGraph[Subsets[4],
          ((Intersection[#2,#1]===#1) && (#1 != #2))&]];
```

On the other hand, the Hasse diagram clearly shows the lattice structure, with top and bottom elements. Notice that the vertices of the poset have been placed on horizontal lines or *levels*, with all edges of the Hasse diagram going between vertices in consecutive levels. This makes the Boolean algebra a *ranked poset*, and elements in the same level form a *level set*.

```
In[116]:= l = Map[StringJoin[Map[ToString, #]] &, Subsets[4]];
          ShowGraph[HasseDiagram[s], VertexLabel->l];
```

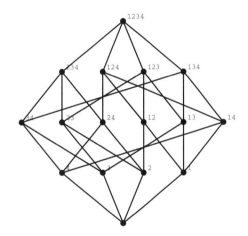

The Boolean algebra and its Hasse diagram are important enough that we provide a function BooleanAlgebra to construct a Hasse diagram of this poset.

In[118]:= **ShowGraph[BooleanAlgebra[6]];**

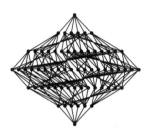

An *antichain* is a set of unrelated elements in a poset. For ranked posets, such as these, it is clear that the level sets are antichains. Can a poset have larger antichains than its largest level set? A finite-ranked poset has the *Sperner property* if the size of a largest antichain equals the size of a largest level set. The Boolean algebra is known to have the Sperner property [SW86].

In[119]:= **ShowGraphArray[Partition[Table[BooleanAlgebra[n], {n, 2, 5}], 2]];**

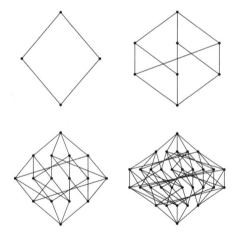

BooleanAlgebra takes an option Type, which if set to Directed produces the underlying directed acyclic graph. While a Hasse diagram is more convenient for visualization, the underlying DAG is more convenient for computations.

In[120]:= **ShowGraphArray[{BooleanAlgebra[3], BooleanAlgebra[3, Type -> Directed]}];**

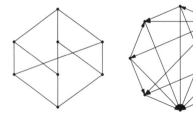

The Boolean algebra is just another
fancy embedding for the hypercube!

In[121]:= **IsomorphicQ[Hypercube[4], BooleanAlgebra[4]]**

Out[121]= True

The *inversion poset* defines a partial order on *n*-permutations. For *n*-permutations π and π', $\pi < \pi'$ if π' can be obtained from π by a sequence of adjacent transpositions, each of which cause a larger element to appear before a smaller one. *Combinatorica* provides a function `InversionPoset` that takes a positive integer *n* and computes an inversion poset on *n*-permutations.

As we go up this poset, we go from
order to disorder. Despite its
seemingly simple structure, no one
knows if inversion posets have the
Sperner property, in general. In this
example, the largest level set is the one
in the middle – with size 6. Showing
that this poset is Sperner requires
showing that it contains no antichain
with seven elements.

In[122]:= **ShowGraph[InversionPoset[4, VertexLabel -> True]];**

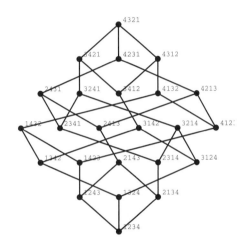

Another important partial order is the *domination lattice* on integer partitions. Consider integer partitions $\lambda = (\lambda_1, \lambda_2, \ldots, \lambda_k)$ and $\mu = (\mu_1, \mu_2, \ldots, \mu_j)$ of some positive integer *n*. We say that λ *dominates* μ if $\lambda_1 + \lambda_2 + \cdots + \lambda_t \geq \mu_1 + \mu_2 + \cdots + \mu_t$ for all $t \geq 1$. We assume that the integer partition with fewer parts is padded with 0's at the end. `DominatingIntegerPartitionQ` tests whether one integer partition dominates another. `DominationLattice` then uses this predicate to construct the partial order on integer partitions and its Hasse diagram.

Since $5 + 1$ is smaller than $4 + 3$, the
first partition does not dominate the
second...

In[123]:= **DominatingIntegerPartitionQ[{5, 1, 1, 1 } , {4, 3, 1}]**

Out[123]= False

...and since 4 is smaller than 5, the two
partitions are incomparable.

In[124]:= **DominatingIntegerPartitionQ[{4, 3, 1}, {5, 1, 1, 1}]**

Out[124]= False

This shows the domination lattice on integer partitions of 8. It can be verified by hand that the largest antichain in this poset is of size 2, and hence this poset has the Sperner property. In general, however, domination lattices do not have the Sperner property [SW86].

```
In[125]:= ShowGraph[ DominationLattice[8, VertexLabel -> True],
            PlotRange->0.25];
```

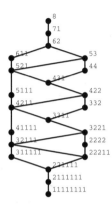

The last poset we discuss here is the *partition lattice*, which is a partial order on set partitions. Given two set partitions p and q of a set S, we say $p \le q$ if p is "coarser" than q. In other words, every block in q is contained in some block in p. *Combinatorica* provides a function `PartitionLattice` that takes a positive integer n and computes a partition lattice on set partitions of $\{1, 2, ..., n\}$.

This shows the partition lattice on 3-element set partitions. The bottom element is the coarsest partition, while the top top element is the finest partition possible. The second level (from the bottom) corresponds to set partitions with two blocks and the level above to those with three blocks. The numbers of elements at each level are, therefore, counted by Stirling numbers of the second kind.

```
In[126]:= ShowGraph[PartitionLattice[3, VertexLabel -> True],
            PlotRange -> 0.1];
```

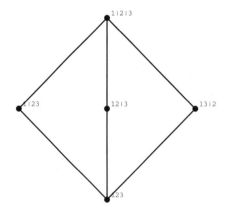

Rota [Rot67] conjectured that partition lattices have the Sperner property. Ten years later, Canfield [Can78a] disproved this conjecture using asymptotic methods. No one yet knows the smallest n for which the partition lattice on set partitions of a size n set does not have the Sperner property.

■ 8.5.4 Dilworth's Theorem

A *chain* in a partially ordered set is a collection of elements $v_1, v_2, ..., v_k$ such that v_i is related to v_{i+1}, $i < k$. An *antichain* is a collection of elements no pair of which are related. Dilworth's theorem [Dil50] states that, for any partial order, the maximum size of an antichain equals the minimum number of chains that partition the elements.

To compute a maximum antichain, observe that there is an edge between any two related elements in any transitive relation, such as a partial order. Thus a largest antichain is described by a maximum independent set in the order. To compute a minimum chain partition of the transitive reduction of a partial order G, of order n, we construct a bipartite graph $D(G)$ with two stages of n vertices each, with each vertex v_i of G now associated with vertices $v_{i'}$ and $v_{i''}$. Now each directed edge $\{x, y\}$ of G defines an undirected edge $\{x', y''\}$ of $D(G)$. Each matching of $D(G)$ defines a chain partition of G, since edges $\{x', y''\}$ and $\{y', z''\}$ in the matching represent the chain $\{x, y, z\}$ in G. Further, the maximum matching describes the minimum chain partition.

```
MinimumChainPartition[g_Graph] :=
      ConnectedComponents[
            FromUnorderedPairs[
                  Map[(#-{0,V[g]})&, BipartiteMatching[DilworthGraph[g]]],
                  Vertices[g, All]
            ]
      ]
MaximumAntichain[g_Graph] := MaximumIndependentSet[MakeUndirected[TransitiveClosure[g]]]

DilworthGraph[g_Graph] :=
      FromUnorderedPairs[
            Map[
                  (#+{0,V[g]})&,
                  ToOrderedPairs[RemoveSelfLoops[TransitiveReduction[g]]]
            ]
      ]
```

Partitioning a Partial Order into a Minimum Number of Chains

The is the minimum chain partition of the domination lattice on integer partitions of 8.

```
In[127]:= MinimumChainPartition[d=DominationLattice[8, Type->Directed]]
Out[127]= {{1, 2, 3, 4, 6, 7, 11, 12, 16, 17, 20, 21, 22},
          {5, 8, 9, 10, 13, 14, 15, 18, 19}}
```

By Dilworth's theorem, the length of the maximum antichain equals the size of the minimum chain partition for any partial order. This is confirmed by this experiment.

The Hasse diagram of the inversion poset on 4-permutations was shown earlier. From the picture it was clear that 6 is the largest level set in the poset. This shows that the Sperner property is satisfied for this poset.

```
In[128]:= antichain = MaximumAntichain[d]
Out[128]= {4, 5}
```

```
In[129]:= MaximumAntichain[InversionPoset[4, Type->Directed]]
Out[129]= {6, 8, 10, 14, 15, 19}
```

8.6 Graph Isomorphism

Two graphs are *isomorphic* if there exists a renaming of the vertices of the graphs such that they are identical. Two graphs are isomorphic when they have identical structures, although they may be represented differently.

Unfortunately, this notion of equality does not come cheap. There exists no known polynomial-time algorithm for isomorphism testing, despite the fact that isomorphism has not been shown to be NP-complete. It seems to fall in the crack somewhere between P and NP-complete (if such a crack exists), although a polynomial-time algorithm is known when the maximum degree vertex is bounded by a constant [Luk80]. Ironically, an original interest of Leonid Levin, one of two independent developers of the notion of NP-completeness [Lev73], in defining this complexity class was proving that graph isomorphism is hard!

■ 8.6.1 Finding Isomorphisms

We now present an algorithm for finding isomorphisms that, although usually efficient in practice, is not guaranteed to take polynomial time.

An isomorphism between two graphs is described by a one-to-one mapping between the two sets of vertices. Two labeled graphs are *identical* if their current labelings represent an isomorphism.

```
IdenticalQ[g_Graph, h_Graph] := True /; (EmptyQ[g]) && (EmptyQ[h]) && (V[g] == V[h])
IdenticalQ[g_Graph, h_Graph] := False /; (UndirectedQ[g] != UndirectedQ[h])
IdenticalQ[g_Graph, h_Graph] := (V[g]==V[h]) && (Sort[Edges[g]]===Sort[Edges[h]])
```

Testing if Two Graphs are Identical

Every permutation of a complete graph represents a complete graph.

```
In[130]:= Isomorphism[CompleteGraph[10],CompleteGraph[10]]

Out[130]= {1, 2, 3, 4, 5, 6, 7, 8, 9, 10}
```

These graphs are clearly isomorphic but are not identical.

```
In[131]:= {IdenticalQ[g=CompleteGraph[3,2],h=CompleteGraph[2,3]],
           IsomorphicQ[g,h]}

Out[131]= {False, True}
```

To test for isomorphisms efficiently, we must examine as few of the $n!$ permutations as possible. Using *graph invariants* allows us to prune the number of permutations we must consider, usually to manageable proportions. Graph invariants are measures of a graph that are invariant under isomorphism. Specifically, given a pair of graphs G and H and a vertex v in G, we ask: What vertices in H can map to G in a valid isomorphism? For example, no two vertices of different degrees can be mapped to each other, and so the set of vertices in H that are candidates for being mapped on to v can be pruned by using degree information. Of course, just using vertex degrees may not help at all, but using vertex degrees in conjunction with a few other easily computed graph invariants can significantly help in distinguishing nonisomorphic graphs quickly. The function `Equivalences`, shown below, provides the basic mechanism for pruning the number of candidate permutations that we need to consider.

```
Equivalences[g_Graph, h_Graph, f___] :=
      Module[{dg = Degrees[g], dh = Degrees[h], eq},
            eq = Table[Flatten[Position[dh, dg[[i]]], 1], {i, Length[dg]}];
            EQ[g, h, eq, f]
      ]

EQ[g_Graph, h_Graph, eq_List] := eq
EQ[g_Graph, h_Graph, eq_List, f1_, f___] :=
            If[Position[eq, {}] == {},
               EQ[g, h, RefineEquivalences[eq, g, h, f1], f],
                eq
            ]

Equivalences[g_Graph, f___] := Equivalences[g, g, f]
```

Pruning Candidate Isomorphisms

Equivalences uses vertex degrees as the default graph invariant. The output here tells us that either of the two endpoints of the path can be mapped on to the four leaves of the star graph. The central vertex in the star graph is a degree-4 vertex, and there is no degree-4 vertex in a path. This is enough to certify these two graphs as being nonisomorphic.

In[132]:= **g = Star[5]; h = Path[5]; Equivalences[g, h]**

Out[132]= {{1, 5}, {1, 5}, {1, 5}, {1, 5}, {}}

Vertex degrees are not useful as an invariant in this case.

In[133]:= **g = RegularGraph[3, 6]; h = RegularGraph[3, 6];**
                      Equivalences[g, h]

Out[134]= {{1, 2, 3, 4, 5, 6}, {1, 2, 3, 4, 5, 6},
                 {1, 2, 3, 4, 5, 6}, {1, 2, 3, 4, 5, 6},
                 {1, 2, 3, 4, 5, 6}, {1, 2, 3, 4, 5, 6}}

Combinatorica provides a few functions to compute some other measures of the local structure of a graph. These measures are invariant under graph isomorphism and hence are useful in pruning the isomorphism search space and in distinguishing nonisomorphic graphs.

```
Neighborhood[g_Graph, v_Integer?Positive, 0] := {v} /; (1 <= v) && (v <= V[g])

Neighborhood[g_Graph, v_Integer?Positive, k_Integer?Positive] :=
    Neighborhood[ToAdjacencyLists[g], v, k] /; (1 <= v) && (v <= V[g])
```

```
Neighborhood[al_List, v_Integer?Positive, 0] := {v} /; (1 <= v)&&(v<=Length[al])
Neighborhood[al_List, v_Integer?Positive, k_Integer?Positive] :=
    Module[{n = {v}},
         Do[n = Union[n, Flatten[al[[ n ]], 1]], {i, k}];
         n
    ] /; (1 <= v) && (v <= Length[al])
DegreesOf2Neighborhood[g_Graph, v_Integer?Positive] :=
    Module[{al = ToAdjacencyLists[g], degrees = Degrees[g]},
         Sort[degrees[[ Neighborhood[al, v, 2] ]]]
    ]

NumberOfKPaths[g_Graph, v_Integer?Positive, 0] := 1 /; (1 <= v) && (v <= V[g])

NumberOfKPaths[g_Graph, v_Integer?Positive, k_Integer?Positive] :=
    NumberOfKPaths[ToAdjacencyLists[g], v, k]

NumberOfKPaths[al_List, v_Integer?Positive, 0] := 1 /; (1<=v)&&(v<=Length[al])
NumberOfKPaths[al_List, v_Integer?Positive, k_Integer?Positive] :=
    Module[{n = {v}},
         Do[n = Flatten[al[[ n ]], 1]  , {i, k}];
         Sort[Map[Length, Split[Sort[n]]]]
    ] /; (1 <= v) && (v <= Length[al])
NumberOf2Paths[g_Graph, v_Integer?Positive] := NumberOfKPaths[g, v, 2]

Distances[g_Graph, v_Integer?Positive] := Sort[BreadthFirstTraversal[g, v, Level]]
```

Some Local Graph Isomorphism Invariants

Here we construct two 3-regular 8-vertex graphs that will form our running example for most of this section. Are these graphs isomorphic? If not, can we distinguish them by using some simple invariants?

```
In[135]:= h = DeleteEdges[CirculantGraph[8, {1, 2}],
             {{2, 8}, {4, 6}, {1, 3}, {5, 7}}];
          g = Hypercube[3]; ShowGraphArray[{g, h}, VertexNumber -> True];
```

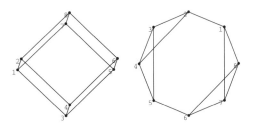

Here we use DegreesOf2Neighborhood to compute a sorted list of degrees of vertices in the graph that are within two hops of each vertex. In a three-dimensional hypercube, seven vertices are within two hops of each vertex.

```
In[137]:= Table[DegreesOf2Neighborhood[g, i], {i, V[g]}] // ColumnForm

Out[137]= {3, 3, 3, 3, 3, 3, 3}
          {3, 3, 3, 3, 3, 3, 3}
          {3, 3, 3, 3, 3, 3, 3}
          {3, 3, 3, 3, 3, 3, 3}
          {3, 3, 3, 3, 3, 3, 3}
          {3, 3, 3, 3, 3, 3, 3}
          {3, 3, 3, 3, 3, 3, 3}
          {3, 3, 3, 3, 3, 3, 3}
```

This graph is not as symmetric as the hypercube. We can get to seven vertices in two hops from some vertices. But we can only get to six vertices in two hops from vertices 3, 4, 7, and 8, and ...

```
In[138]:= Table[DegreesOf2Neighborhood[h, i], {i, V[g]}] // ColumnForm
Out[138]= {3, 3, 3, 3, 3, 3, 3}
          {3, 3, 3, 3, 3, 3, 3}
          {3, 3, 3, 3, 3, 3}
          {3, 3, 3, 3, 3, 3}
          {3, 3, 3, 3, 3, 3, 3}
          {3, 3, 3, 3, 3, 3, 3}
          {3, 3, 3, 3, 3, 3}
          {3, 3, 3, 3, 3, 3}
```

...this means that none of these four vertices can be mapped onto any vertex in the hypercube. This is enough to distinguish the two graphs.

```
In[139]:= Equivalences[g, h, DegreesOf2Neighborhood]
Out[139]= {{1, 2, 5, 6}, {1, 2, 5, 6}, {1, 2, 5, 6},
           {1, 2, 5, 6}, {1, 2, 5, 6}, {1, 2, 5, 6}, {1, 2, 5, 6},
           {1, 2, 5, 6}}
```

Each vertex has a path of length 1 to each of its neighbors. A refinement of this is the number of paths of length 2 from a vertex v to various vertices in the graph. These paths need not be simple; here each vertex has three length-2 paths to itself via each of its neighbors. The output here distinguishes the vertex numbered 1 in the two graphs.

```
In[140]:= {NumberOf2Paths[g, 1], NumberOf2Paths[h, 1]}
Out[140]= {{2, 2, 2, 3}, {1, 1, 1, 1, 2, 3}}
```

In fact, using NumberOf2Paths as the invariant emphatically distinguishes the two graphs by telling us that no vertex in h can map to any vertex in g.

```
In[141]:= Equivalences[g, h, NumberOf2Paths]
Out[141]= {{}, {}, {}, {}, {}, {}, {}, {}}
```

An invariant that is more difficult to fool is the set of shortest distances between one vertex and all the others [SD76]. For most graphs, this is sufficient to eliminate most nonisomorphic vertex pairs, although there exist nonisomorphic graphs that realize the same set of distances [BH90].

For our example, using Distances as an invariant is not as effective as using NumberOf2Paths, even though there is some pruning of the search space.

```
In[142]:= Equivalences[g, h, Distances]
Out[142]= {{1, 2, 5, 6}, {1, 2, 5, 6}, {1, 2, 5, 6},
           {1, 2, 5, 6}, {1, 2, 5, 6}, {1, 2, 5, 6}, {1, 2, 5, 6},
           {1, 2, 5, 6}}
```

As a starting point for isomorphism testing we use the set of candidate permutations computed by Equivalences and refined by applying various invariants. If, at this point, we are already able to distinguish between the graphs, we are done. Otherwise, we may have pruned the search space significantly as preparation for a brute-force backtracking search. We use the general-purpose Backtrack function described in Section 7.4.3. Our partial solution will consist of a list of vertices with the property that the ith element belongs to the ith equivalence class. The predicates for testing partial and complete solutions make certain that the induced subgraphs are identical to this point. Other approaches to finding isomorphisms appear in [CG70].

```
Isomorphism[g_Graph, h_Graph, equiv_List, flag_Symbol:One] :=
      If[!MemberQ[equiv,{}],
         Backtrack[equiv,
                  (IdenticalQ[
                      PermuteSubgraph[g,Range[Length[#]]],
                      PermuteSubgraph[h,#]
                   ] &&
                   !MemberQ[Drop[#,-1],Last[#]]
                  )&,
                  (IsomorphismQ[g,h,#])&,
                  flag
            ],
            {}
         ]
```

Finding Isomorphisms

We already know that graphs *g* and *h*
are nonisomorphic, and this is
confirmed here.

In[143]:= **IsomorphicQ[g, h]**

Out[143]= False

Using our semirandom regular graph
generator, we generate ten 8-vertex
3-regular graphs here. We test pairs of
these for isomorphism and represent
this information in a graph. Vertices of
the displayed graph represent 3-regular
graphs, and pairs of isomorphic graphs
are connected by edges. This graph is
a set of disconnected cliques, with each
clique representing a set of isomorphic
graphs.

In[144]:= **gt = Table[RegularGraph[3, 8], {10}];**
ShowGraph[h=MakeSimple[MakeGraph[gt, IsomorphicQ, Type ->
Undirected]]];

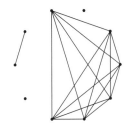

An independent set in this graph
represents a set of mutually
nonisomorphic graphs. Here we find a
maximum independent set and display
the corresponding 3-regular graphs. Do
you spot the three-dimensional
hypercube here?

In[146]:= **ShowGraphArray[Map[SpringEmbedding[#, 30]&,**
gt[[MaximumIndependentSet[h]]]]];

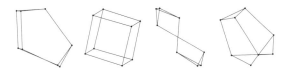

The functions `IsomorphicQ` and `Isomorphism` take an option `Invariants` that can inform the functions about what invariants to use in pruning the search space. By default, these functions use vertex degrees as the first invariant, followed by `DegreesOf2Neighborhood`, `NumberOf2Paths`, and `Distances`. The order in which these invariants are used may affect the efficiency of the function because the functions return as soon as they can distinguish between the graphs, since there is no point in searching any further.

It is likely that two 3-regular 10-vertex graphs generated using `RegularGraph` are nonisomorphic, and this is usually identified by using the default invariants. The difference in the running times of these two tests comes from the fact that not using invariants forces `IsomorphicQ` to search through many permutations before discovering the futility of it all.

```
In[147]:= g = RegularGraph[3, 10]; h = RegularGraph[3, 10];
         {Timing[IsomorphicQ[g, h];], Timing[IsomorphicQ[g, h,
         Invariants->{}];];]}
```

```
Out[148]= {{0.15 Second, Null}, {24.59 Second, Null}}
```

We test pairs of random graphs for isomorphism. Usually, the function zips through any pairs of nonisomorphic graphs but will labor over pairs of isomorphic graphs

```
In[149]:= Table[g = RandomGraph[50, .5]; h = RandomGraph[50, .5];
         Timing[ IsomorphicQ[g, h];][[1,1]], {20}]
```

```
Out[149]= {0.19, 0.19, 0.19, 0.19, 0.19, 0.19, 0.19, 0.19,
          0.19, 0.19, 0.19, 0.18, 0.19, 0.19, 0.19, 0.18, 0.19,
          0.19, 0.19, 0.19}
```

This gives us an isomorphism ...

```
In[150]:= g = Hypercube[3]; Isomorphism[g, g]
```

```
Out[150]= {1, 2, 3, 4, 5, 6, 7, 8}
```

...from among the 48 possible isomorphisms.

```
In[151]:= Length[Isomorphism[g, g, All]]
```

```
Out[151]= 48
```

■ 8.6.2 Tree Isomorphism

In the previous section we tested if pairs of graphs are isomorphic by actually attempting to construct an isomorphism between them. Here we present a somewhat different approach, involving the computation of *certificates*, that results in a polynomial-time isomorphism testing algorithm for trees [Rea72]. In general, the fastest graph isomorphism algorithms use the method of computing certificates [KS99].

We compute the certificate of an n-vertex tree T, which is a binary string of length $2n$, as follows. Start with all vertices in T labeled 01. Repeat the following step until two or fewer vertices are left. For each vertex x of T that is not a leaf, let Y be the set of labels of the leaves adjacent to x and the label of x, with the initial 0 and the trailing 1 deleted from the label of x. Replace the label of x with the concatenation of the labels in Y sorted in increasing lexicographic order, with 0 prepended and a 1 appended. Then remove all leaves adjacent to x. After repeating this sufficiently many times, we have one or two vertices left in T. If there is only one vertex x, then the label of x is reported as the certificate. If there are two vertices x and y left, then order these two labels in increasing lexicographic order and report their concatenation as the certificate. This is implemented in the function `TreeToCertificate` and we use this for tree isomorphism testing in `TreeIsomorphismQ`.

The 20-bit certificate of a random 10-vertex tree.

In[152]:= **TreeToCertificate[RandomTree[10]]**

Out[152]= 00001011110000111011

Using `TreeIsomorphismQ` is much faster than using `IsomorphicQ` for testing the isomorphism of trees.

In[153]:= **g = RandomTree[100];**
          h = PermuteSubgraph[g, RandomPermutation[V[g]]];
          {Timing[TreeIsomorphismQ[g, h];],
          Timing[IsomorphicQ[g, h];]}

Out[155]= {{0.55 Second, Null}, {28.28 Second, Null}}

■ 8.6.3 Self-Complementary Graphs

A graph is *self-complementary* if it is isomorphic to its complement.

```
SelfComplementaryQ[g_Graph] := IsomorphicQ[g, GraphComplement[g]]
```

Testing Self-Complementary Graphs

The smallest nontrivial self-complementary graphs are the path on four vertices and the cycle on five.

In[156]:= **SelfComplementaryQ[Cycle[5]] && SelfComplementaryQ[Path[4]]**

Out[156]= True

A simple parity argument shows that every self-complementary graph contains $4k$ or $4k + 1$ vertices.

In[157]:= **SelfComplementaryQ[CompleteGraph[3,3]]**

Out[157]= False

All self-complementary graphs have diameter 2 or 3 [Sac62].

In[158]:= **Diameter[Cycle[5]]**

Out[158]= 2

8.7 Planar Graphs

Planar graphs can be embedded in the plane with no pair of edges crossing. There is an interesting connection between convex polyhedra in E^3 and planar embeddings. For a given polyhedron, replace one of the vertices with a lightbulb, make the faces of the polyhedron out of glass, and make the edges where the faces meet out of lead. These leaded edges cast lines as shadows, which meet at the shadows of the vertices of the polyhedron or, if incident on the light, extend on to infinity. Since the polyhedron is convex, any ray originating from the light passes through exactly one other point on the polyhedron, so no two lines can cross.

The five *Platonic* solids are the convex polyhedra whose faces are all regular *d*-vertex polygons and whose vertices have the same number of incident edges. They are the *tetrahedron* (four vertices, four triangular faces), the *cube* (eight vertices, six square faces), the *octahedron* (six vertices, eight triangular faces), the *icosahedron* (12 vertices, 20 triangular faces), and the *dodecahedron* (20 vertices, 12 pentagonal faces).

`In[159]:= ShowGraphArray[gl = {{TetrahedralGraph, CubicalGraph, OctahedralGraph}, {IcosahedralGraph, DodecahedralGraph}} ];`

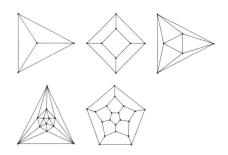

PlanarQ confirms that these graphs are indeed planar.

`In[160]:= Map[PlanarQ, Flatten[gl]]`

`Out[160]= {True, True, True, True, True}`

A polynomial-time algorithm for testing planarity can be obtained from the famous Kuratowski's theorem [Kur30]. Two graphs are *homeomorphic* if they can be obtained from the same graph by replacing edges with paths. Kuratowski's theorem states that a graph is planar if and only if it contains no subgraph homeomorphic to K_5 or $K_{3,3}$. It is easy to verify that K_5 and $K_{3,3}$ have no planar drawings. What is not as easy to see is that these are essentially the only two obstacles to planarity.

Planar graphs have also drawn attention because of the famous *four–color theorem*, which says that the vertices of any planar graph can be colored with at most four colors. It took more than 100 years and many incorrect proofs before this claim was proved by Hakan and Appel [AHK77, AH77]. One of the side effects of this quest was an algorithm by Kempe that produces a 5-coloring of any planar graph. Wagon [Wag98] describes a nice *Mathematica* package built on top of *Combinatorica* that implements Kempe's 5-coloring algorithm and a modification of it that produces 4-colorings on most planar graphs. This package also contains a semirandom algorithm for generating planar graphs and several examples of large planar graphs.

■ 8.7.1 Testing Planarity

Although there are several efficient algorithms [CHT90, Eve79, HT74] for testing planarity, all are difficult to implement. Most of these algorithms are based on ideas from an old $O(n^3)$ algorithm by Auslander and Parter [AP61]. Their algorithm is based on the observation that if a graph is planar, for any cycle there is a way to embed it in the plane so that the vertices of this cycle lie on a circle. This follows because an embedding on a sphere is equivalent to an embedding in the plane, as shown above. If this cycle is then deleted from the graph, the connected components that are left are called *bridges*. Obviously, if any bridge is nonplanar, the graph is nonplanar. Further, the graph is nonplanar if these bridges interlock in the wrong way.

By Kuratowski's theorem, neither $K_{3,3}$ nor K_5 is planar.

```
In[161]:= PlanarQ[CompleteGraph[5]] || PlanarQ[CompleteGraph[3,3]]
Out[161]= False
```

Every planar graph on nine vertices has a nonplanar complement [BHK62].

```
In[162]:= PlanarQ[ GraphComplement[GridGraph[3,3]] ]
Out[162]= False
```

All trees are planar. The current embedding has no effect on whether PlanarQ rules planar or nonplanar.

```
In[163]:= Apply[And, Map[PlanarQ, Table[RandomTree[i], {i,1,20}] ]]
Out[163]= True
```

The Platonic solids can all be constructed using other *Combinatorica* commands. Here we build the tetrahedron, cube, and octahedron. A proof [Mes83] that there exist no other Platonic solids follows from Euler's formula that for any planar graph with V vertices, E edges, and F faces, $V - E + F = 2$.

```
In[164]:= PlanarQ[CompleteGraph[4]] && PlanarQ[CompleteGraph[2,2,2]] &&
          PlanarQ[GraphProduct[CompleteGraph[2], Cycle[4]]]
Out[164]= True
```

Euler's formula implies that every planar graph has at most $3n - 6$ edges for $n \geq 5$.

```
In[165]:= Apply[Or, Map[PlanarQ, Table[ExactRandomGraph[n,3n-5],
          {n,5,15}]]]
Out[165]= False
```

Coming in under this limit gives us a chance at planarity, at least for small enough n.

```
In[166]:= Map[PlanarQ, Table[ExactRandomGraph[n,3n-6], {n,5,15}]]
Out[166]= {True, True, False, False, False, False, False,
          False, False, False, False}
```

8.8 Exercises

■ 8.8.1 Thought Exercises

1. In Section 8.1 we mentioned that the Bellman-Ford algorithm can be used to detect the presence of negative cycles in a graph. Show how the Bellman-Ford algorithm can be extended to return a negative cycle if the given graph contains at least one.

2. Which pair of vertices in the $n \times n$ grid graphs have the largest number of length-k paths between them, as a function of k?

3. Prove that the most expensive edge on any cycle of G will not appear in the minimum spanning tree of G.

4. Prove that the minimum spanning tree also minimizes the cost of the maximum edge (i.e., the "bottleneck" edge) over all such trees.

5. Prove that the center of any tree consists of at most two adjacent vertices.

6. Consider a graph in which each edge has an upper bound and a nonnegative lower bound on the permitted flow through that edge. Show how to determine if such a graph has a *feasible flow*, that is, a flow that satisfies flow conservation at every vertex and flow bounds at each edge. **Hint:** Reduce the problem to the maximum-flow problem.

7. The problem of finding a minimum-size maximal matching is NP-complete, even for planar bipartite graphs [YG80]. Construct a graph that has maximal matchings of many different sizes.

8. Construct a family of graphs such that, for infinitely many positive integers n, there exists a graph in the family with minimum vertex cover size equal to $2n$ and maximum matching size equal to n.

9. The sizes of the level sets of a Boolean algebra are the binomial coefficients. What about the sizes of the level sets of an inversion poset? Have you encountered these combinatorial numbers in an earlier chapter?

10. Determine if the inversion poset on size-4 permutations has the Sperner property.

11. Devise an algorithm that takes a length-$2n$ binary string s and tests if s is a tree certificate and, if so, computes the tree for which s is a certificate.

12. In 1758, Euler proved his famous formula for planar graphs. If a connected graph with n vertices and m edges has a planar embedding with f faces, then $n - m + f = 2$. Use this to derive the fact that every n-vertex planar graph has at most $3n - 6$ edges. Use this upper bound on the number of edges to conclude that every planar graph has a vertex of degree at most 5.

13. Use Euler's formula to show that the cube, tetrahedron, octahedron, dodecahedron, and icosahedron are the only possible Platonic solids.

14. The *dual graph* G^* of a planar graph G is a graph with a vertex for every face in G. For every edge e in G with faces X and Y on either of its sides, there is an edge e^* in G^* connecting the vertices corresponding to faces X and Y. Note that a dual graph is not necessarily simple and may have multiple parallel edges and self-loops. Different planar embeddings of a graph may produce different dual graphs. Show two planar embeddings of a planar graph whose dual graphs are nonisomorphic.

15. An *outerplanar graph* is a planar graph with a planar embedding in which all vertices lie on the single unbounded face. Show that an outerplanar graph has at most $2n - 3$ edges.

16. Show that a graph is outerplanar if and only if it has no subgraph homeomorphic to K_4 or $K_{2,3}$.

■ 8.8.2 Programming Exercises

1. Use the *Mathematica* function `LinearProgramming` to compute the maximum flow through a network by setting up a system of inequalities such that the flow through each edge is bounded by its capacity and the flow into each vertex equals the flow out, while maximizing the flow into the sink. How does the efficiency of this routine compare to `NetworkFlow`?

2. Write a function to find the strongly connected components of a graph using `TransitiveClosure`. How does your function's performance compare to `StronglyConnectedComponents`?

3. Write a function to partition the edges of K_{2n} into n spanning trees.

4. Develop and implement a simple algorithm for finding the maximum matching in a tree, which is special case of bipartite matching. Find a tree for which `MaximalMatching` does not find the maximum matching.

5. Implement Prim's algorithm for finding minimum spanning trees and compare it with `MinimumSpanningTree` for efficiency on a variety of graphs.

6. Write a function to test whether a given matching is stable, for a given pair of male and female preference functions.

7. Rewrite `PlanarQ` so that it positions the vertices of the graph in a way that permits a planar embedding. These positions do not have to permit a straight-line embedding.

8. Implement a function that takes a planar embedding of a graph and returns the faces of the embedding.

9. Use the function in the previous exercise to implement a function that takes the planar embedding of a graph and constructs the dual graph.

■ 8.8.3 Experimental Exercises

1. How does the expected diameter of a complete random graph grow as a function of the number of vertices?

2. Both the domination lattice and the partition lattice do not, in general, have the Sperner property [SW86]. See if you can find what values of n give the smallest non-Sperner lattices for either of them.

3. Experiment with computing shortest-path spanning trees, minimum spanning trees, and traveling salesman tours on random Euclidean graphs. Are these subgraphs always planar embeddings?

4. What is the expected size of the maximum matching in a tree on n vertices?

5. Experiment to determine what graphs are "square roots" [Muk67] of some graph G, meaning a graph whose square is G.

6. The *divorce digraph* [GI89] is a binary relation associated with an instance of the stable marriage problem. The vertices correspond to the $n!$ matchings. There is a directed edge $\{a, b\}$ between matchings a and b if b results from an unstable pair in a leaving their respective spouses and marrying each other, with the rejects getting paired off. Stable marriages are vertices with out-degree 0 in the divorce digraph.

   Write a function to construct the divorce digraph of a stable marriage instance. Verify that the following male $\{\{1, 2, 3\}, \{1, 2, 3\}, \{2, 1, 3\}\}$ and female $\{\{3, 2, 1\}, \{2, 3, 1\}, \{1, 2, 3\}\}$ preference functions result in a divorce digraph that contains a directed cycle. Further, show that whatever permutations represent male 1's and female 3's preference functions, the divorce digraph contains a cycle. Does there always exist a directed path from any unstable marriage to a stable one in the divorce digraph of the previous problem [GI89]?

7. Experiment to find pairs of nonisomorphic graphs for which the graph invariants built into IsomorphicQ are useless. Are there other simple graph invariants that distinguish between these graphs?

Appendix

Reference Guide

■ **AcyclicQ**

AcyclicQ[g] yields True if graph g is acyclic.

See also FindCycle, TreeQ ▪ See page 285

■ **AddEdge**

AddEdge[g, e] returns a graph g with the new edge e added. e can have the form $\{a, b\}$ or the form $\{\{a, b\}, options\}$.

See also AddVertex, DeleteEdge ▪ See page 193

■ **AddEdges**

AddEdges[g, l] gives graph g with the new edges in l added. l can have the form $\{a, b\}$, to add a single edge $\{a, b\}$, or the form $\{\{a, b\}, \{c, d\}, ...\}$, to add edges $\{a, b\}, \{c, d\}, ...$, or the form $\{\{\{a, b\}, x\}, \{\{c, d\}, y\}, ...\}$, where x and y can specify graphics information associated with $\{a, b\}$ and $\{c, d\}$, respectively.

New function ▪ See also AddEdge ▪ See page 193

■ **AddVertex**

AddVertex[g] adds one disconnected vertex to graph g. AddVertex[g, v] adds to g a vertex with coordinates specified by v.

See also AddEdge, DeleteVertex ▪ See page 195

■ **AddVertices**

AddVertices[g, n] adds n disconnected vertices to graph g. AddVertices[g, vList] adds vertices in *vList* to g. *vList* contains embedding and graphics information and can have the form $\{x, y\}$ or $\{\{x_1, y_1\}, \{x_2, y_2\} ...\}$ or the form $\{\{\{x_1, y_1\}, g_1\}, \{\{x_2, y_2\}, g_2\}, ...\}$, where $\{x, y\}$, $\{x_1, y_1\}$, and $\{x_2, y_2\}$ are point coordinates and g_1 and g_2 are graphics information associated with vertices.

New function ▪ See also AddVertex ▪ See page 195

■ **Algorithm**

Algorithm is an option that informs functions such as ShortestPath, VertexColoring, and VertexCover about which algorithm to use.

New function ▪ See also ShortestPath, VertexColoring, VertexCover ▪ See page 313

■ **AllPairsShortestPath**

AllPairsShortestPath[g] gives a matrix, where the (i, j)th entry is the length of a shortest path in g between vertices i and j. AllPairsShortestPath[g, Parent] returns a three-dimensional matrix with dimensions $2 \times V[g] \times V[g]$, in which the $(1, i, j)$th entry is the length of a shortest path from i to j and the $(2, i, j)$th entry is the predecessor of j in a shortest path from i to j.

See also ShortestPath, ShortestPathSpanningTree ▪ See page 330

- ## AlternatingGroup

    `AlternatingGroup[n]` generates the set of even size-*n* permutations, the alternating group on *n* symbols. `AlternatingGroup[l]` generates the set of even permutations of the list *l*.

    New function ▪ See also `SymmetricGroup`, `OrbitInventory` ▪ See page 110

- ## AlternatingGroupIndex

    `AlternatingGroupIndex[n, x]` gives the cycle index of the alternating group of size-*n* permutations as a polynomial in the symbols $x[1], x[2], \ldots, x[n]$.

    New function ▪ See also `SymmetricGroupIndex`, `OrbitInventory` ▪ See page 125

- ## AlternatingPaths

    `AlternatingPaths[g, start, ME]` returns the alternating paths in graph *g* with respect to the matching *ME*, starting at the vertices in the list *start*. The paths are returned in the form of a forest containing trees rooted at vertices in *start*.

    New function ▪ See also `BipartiteMatching`, `BipartiteMatchingAndCover` ▪ See page 345

- ## AnimateGraph

    `AnimateGraph[g, l]` displays graph *g* with each element in the list *l* successively highlighted. Here *l* is a list containing vertices and edges of *g*. An optional flag, which takes on the values `All` and `One`, can be used to inform the function about whether objects highlighted earlier will continue to be highlighted or not. The default value of flag is `All`. All the options allowed by the function `Highlight` are permitted by `AnimateGraph` as well. See the usage message of `Highlight` for more details.

    New function ▪ See also `Highlight`, `ShowGraph` ▪ See page 212

- ## AntiSymmetricQ

    `AntiSymmetricQ[g]` yields `True` if the adjacency matrix of *g* represents an antisymmetric binary relation.

    New function ▪ See also `EquivalenceRelationQ`, `SymmetricQ` ▪ See page 352

- ## Approximate

    `Approximate` is a value that the option `Algorithm` can take in calls to functions such as `VertexCover`, telling it to use an approximation algorithm.

    New function ▪ See also `VertexCover` ▪ See page 318

■ **ApproximateVertexCover**

ApproximateVertexCover[g] produces a vertex cover of graph *g* whose size is guaranteed to be within twice the optimal size.

New function ▪ See also BipartiteMatchingAndCover, VertexCover ▪ See page 318

■ **ArticulationVertices**

ArticulationVertices[g] gives a list of all articulation vertices in graph g. These are vertices whose removal will disconnect the graph.

See also BiconnectedComponents, Bridges ▪ See page 287

■ **Automorphisms**

Automorphisms[g] gives the automorphism group of the graph *g*.

See also Isomorphism, PermutationGroupQ ▪ See page 111

■ **Backtrack**

Backtrack[s, partialQ, solutionQ] performs a backtrack search of the state space *s*, expanding a partial solution so long as *partialQ* is True and returning the first complete solution, as identified by *solutionQ*.

See also DistinctPermutations, Isomorphism, MaximumClique, MinimumVertexColoring ▪ See page 311

■ **BellB**

BellB[n] returns the *n*th Bell number.

New function ▪ See also SetPartitions, StirlingSecond ▪ See page 154

■ **BellmanFord**

BellmanFord[g, v] gives a shortest-path spanning tree and associated distances from vertex *v* of graph *g*. The shortest-path spanning tree is given by a list in which element *i* is the predecessor of vertex *i* in the shortest-path spanning tree. BellmanFord works correctly even when the edge weights are negative, provided there are no negative cycles.

New function ▪ See also AllPairsShortestPath, ShortestPath ▪ See page 328

■ **BiconnectedComponents**

BiconnectedComponents[g] gives a list of the biconnected components of graph *g*. If *g* is directed, the underlying undirected graph is used.

See also ArticulationVertices, BiconnectedQ, Bridges ▪ See page 287

■ **BiconnectedQ**

BiconnectedQ[g] yields True if graph g is biconnected. If g is directed, the underlying undirected graph is used.

See also ArticulationVertices, BiconnectedComponents, Bridges ▪ See page 287

■ **BinarySearch**

BinarySearch[l, k] searches sorted list l for key k and gives the position of l containing k, if k is present in l. Otherwise, if k is absent in l, the function returns $(p + 1/2)$ where k falls between the elements of l in positions p and $p + 1$. BinarySearch[l, k, f] gives the position of k in the list obtained from l by applying f to each element in l.

See also SelectionSort ▪ See page 5

■ **BinarySubsets**

BinarySubsets[l] gives all subsets of l ordered according to the binary string defining each subset. For any positive integer n, BinarySubsets[n] gives all subsets of $\{1, 2, ..., n\}$ ordered according to the binary string defining each subset.

See also Subsets ▪ See page 77

■ **BipartiteMatching**

BipartiteMatching[g] gives the list of edges associated with a maximum matching in bipartite graph g. If the graph is edge-weighted, then the function returns a matching with maximum total weight.

See also BipartiteMatchingAndCover, MinimumChainPartition, StableMarriage ▪ See page 346

■ **BipartiteMatchingAndCover**

BipartiteMatchingAndCover[g] takes a bipartite graph g and returns a matching with maximum weight along with the dual vertex cover. If the graph is not weighted, it is assumed that all edge weights are 1.

New function ▪ See also BipartiteMatching, VertexCover ▪ See page 349

■ **BipartiteQ**

BipartiteQ[g] yields True if graph g is bipartite.

See also CompleteGraph, TwoColoring ▪ See page 306

■ BooleanAlgebra

BooleanAlgebra[n] gives a Hasse diagram for the Boolean algebra on n elements. The function takes two options: Type and VertexLabel, with default values Undirected and False, respectively. When Type is set to Directed, the function produces the underlying directed acyclic graph. When VertexLabel is set to True, labels are produced for the vertices.

New function ■ See also HasseDiagram, Hypercube ■ See page 358

■ Box

Box is a value that the option VertexStyle, used in ShowGraph, can be set to.

New function ■ See also GraphOptions, SetGraphOptions, ShowGraph ■ See page 302

■ BreadthFirstTraversal

BreadthFirstTraversal[g, v] performs a breadth-first traversal of graph g starting from vertex v and gives the breadth-first numbers of the vertices. BreadthFirstTraversal[g, v, Edge] returns the edges of the graph that are traversed by breadth-first traversal. BreadthFirstTraversal[g, v, Tree] returns the breadth-first search tree. BreadthFirstTraversal[g, v, Level] returns the level number of the vertices.

See also DepthFirstTraversal ■ See page 277

■ Brelaz

Brelaz is a value that the option Algorithm can take when used in the function VertexColoring.

New function ■ See also BrelazColoring, VertexColoring ■ See page 313

■ BrelazColoring

BrelazColoring[g] returns a vertex coloring in which vertices are greedily colored with the smallest available color in decreasing order of the vertex degree.

New function ■ See also ChromaticNumber, VertexColoring ■ See page 313

■ Bridges

Bridges[g] gives a list of the bridges of graph g, where each bridge is an edge whose removal disconnects the graph.

See also ArticulationVertices, BiconnectedComponents, BiconnectedQ ■ See page 287

■ ButterflyGraph

ButterflyGraph[n] returns the *n*-dimensional butterfly graph, a directed graph whose vertices are pairs (w, i), where w is a binary string of length n and i is an integer in the range 0 through n and whose edges go from vertex (w, i) to $(w', i + 1)$, if w' is identical to w in all bits with the possible exception of the $(i + 1)$th bit. Here bits are counted left to right. An option VertexLabel, with default setting False, is allowed. When this option is set to True, vertices are labeled with strings (w, i).

New function ■ See also DeBruijnGraph, Hypercube ■ See page 253

■ CageGraph

CageGraph[k, r] gives a smallest *k*-regular graph of girth *r* for certain small values of *k* and *r*. CageGraph[r] gives CageGraph[3, r]. For $k = 3$, *r* can be 3, 4, 5, 6, 7, 8, or 10. For $k = 4$ or 5, *r* can be 3, 4, 5, or 6.

New function ■ See also Girth, RegularGraph ■ See page 295

■ CartesianProduct

CartesianProduct[l1, l2] gives the Cartesian product of lists *l*1 and *l*2.

See also GraphJoin ■ See page 239

■ Center

Center is a value that options VertexNumberPosition, VertexLabelPosition, and EdgeLabelPosition can take on in ShowGraph.

New function ■ See also GraphOptions, SetGraphOptions, ShowGraph ■ See page 202

■ ChangeEdges

ChangeEdges[g, e] replaces the edges of graph *g* with the edges in *e*. *e* can have the form $\{\{s_1, t_1\}, \{s_2, t_2\}, ...\}$ or the form $\{\{\{s_1, t_1\}, gr1\}, \{\{s_2, t_2\}, gr2\}, ...\}$, where $\{s_1, t_1\}, \{s_2, t_2\}, ...$ are endpoints of edges and $gr1, gr2, ...$ are graphics information associated with edges.

See also ChangeVertices ■ See page 192

■ ChangeVertices

ChangeVertices[g, v] replaces the vertices of graph *g* with the vertices in the given list *v*. *v* can have the form $\{\{x_1, y_1\}, \{x_2, y_2\}, ...\}$ or the form $\{\{\{x_1, y_1\}, gr1\}, \{\{x_2, y_2\}, gr2\}, ...\}$, where $\{x_1, y_1\}, \{x_2, y_2\}, ...$ are coordinates of points and $gr1, gr2, ...$ are graphics information associated with vertices.

See also ChangeEdges ■ See page 192

■ **ChromaticNumber**

ChromaticNumber[g] gives the chromatic number of the graph, which is the fewest number of colors necessary to color the graph.

See also ChromaticPolynomial, MinimumVertexColoring ■ See page 312

■ **ChromaticPolynomial**

ChromaticPolynomial[g, z] gives the chromatic polynomial $P(z)$ of graph g, which counts the number of ways to color g with, at most, z colors.

See also ChromaticNumber, MinimumVertexColoring ■ See page 308

■ **ChvatalGraph**

ChvatalGraph returns a smallest triangle-free, 4-regular, 4-chromatic graph.

New function ■ See also FiniteGraphs, MinimumVertexColoring ■ See page 23

■ **CirculantGraph**

CirculantGraph[n, l] constructs a circulant graph on n vertices, meaning that the ith vertex is adjacent to the $(i + j)$th and $(i - j)$th vertices for each j in list l. CirculantGraph[n, l], where l is an integer, returns the graph with n vertices in which each i is adjacent to $(i + l)$ and $(i - l)$.

See also CompleteGraph, Cycle ■ See page 245

■ **CircularEmbedding**

CircularEmbedding[n] constructs a list of n points equally spaced on a circle. CircularEmbedding[g] embeds the vertices of g equally spaced on a circle.

New function ■ See also CircularVertices ■ See page 213

■ **CircularVertices**

CircularVertices[n] constructs a list of n points equally spaced on a circle. CircularVertices[g] embeds the vertices of g equally spaced on a circle. This function is obsolete; use CircularEmbedding instead.

See also ChangeVertices, CompleteGraph, Cycle ■ See page 19

■ **CliqueQ**

CliqueQ[g, c] yields True if the list of vertices c defines a clique in graph g.

See also MaximumClique, Turan ■ See page 316

■ CoarserSetPartitionQ

CoarserSetPartitionQ[a, b] yields True if set partition *b* is coarser than set partition *a*, that is, every block in *a* is contained in some block in *b*.

New function ■ See also SetPartitionQ, ToCanonicalSetPartition ■ See page 360

■ CodeToLabeledTree

CodeToLabeledTree[l] constructs the unique labeled tree on *n* vertices from the Prüfer code *l*, which consists of a list of *n* − 2 integers between 1 and *n*.

See also LabeledTreeToCode, RandomTree ■ See page 259

■ Cofactor

Cofactor[m, i, j] calculates the (i, j)th cofactor of matrix *m*.

See also NumberOfSpanningTrees ■ See page 339

■ CompleteBinaryTree

CompleteBinaryTree[n] returns a complete binary tree on *n* vertices.

New function ■ See also CompleteKaryTree, RandomTree ■ See page 261

■ CompleteGraph

CompleteGraph[n] creates a complete graph on *n* vertices. An option Type that takes on the values Directed or Undirected is allowed. The default setting for this option is Type -> Undirected. CompleteGraph[a, b, c,...] creates a complete *k*-partite graph of the prescribed shape. The use of CompleteGraph to create a complete *k*-partite graph is obsolete; use CompleteKPartiteGraph instead.

New function ■ See also CirculantGraph, CompleteKPartiteGraph ■ See page 244

■ CompleteKaryTree

CompleteKaryTree[n, k] returns a complete *k*-ary tree on *n* vertices.

New function ■ See also CodeToLabeledTree, CompleteBinaryTree ■ See page 261

■ CompleteKPartiteGraph

CompleteKPartiteGraph[a, b, c, ...] creates a complete *k*-partite graph of the prescribed shape, provided the *k* arguments *a, b, c,...* are positive integers. An option Type that takes on the values Directed or Undirected is allowed. The default setting for this option is Type -> Undirected.

New function ■ See also CompleteGraph, GraphJoin, Turan ■ See page 247

■ CompleteQ

CompleteQ[g] yields True if graph *g* is complete. This means that between any pair of vertices there is an undirected edge or two directed edges going in opposite directions.

See also CompleteGraph, EmptyQ ■ See page 198

■ Compositions

Compositions[n, k] gives a list of all compositions of integer *n* into *k* parts.

See also NextComposition, RandomComposition ■ See page 147

■ ConnectedComponents

ConnectedComponents[g] gives the vertices of graph *g* partitioned into connected components.

See also BiconnectedComponents, ConnectedQ, StronglyConnectedComponents, WeaklyConnectedComponents ■ See page 283

■ ConnectedQ

ConnectedQ[g] yields True if undirected graph *g* is connected. If *g* is directed, the function returns True if the underlying undirected graph is connected. ConnectedQ[g, Strong] and ConnectedQ[g, Weak] yield True if the directed graph *g* is strongly or weakly connected, respectively.

See also ConnectedComponents, StronglyConnectedComponents, WeaklyConnectedComponents ■ See page 283

■ ConstructTableau

ConstructTableau[p] performs the bumping algorithm repeatedly on each element of permutation *p*, resulting in a distinct Young tableau.

See also DeleteFromTableau, InsertIntoTableau ■ See page 164

■ Contract

Contract[g, x, y] gives the graph resulting from contracting the pair of vertices {*x, y*} of graph *g*.

See also ChromaticPolynomial, InduceSubgraph ■ See page 231

■ CostOfPath

CostOfPath[g, p] sums up the weights of the edges in graph *g* defined by the path *p*.

See also TravelingSalesman ■ See page 303

■ CoxeterGraph

CoxeterGraph gives a non-Hamiltonian graph with a high degree of symmetry such that there is a graph automorphism taking any path of length 3 to any other.

New function ▪ See also FiniteGraphs ▪ See page 23

■ CubeConnectedCycle

CubeConnectedCycle[d] returns the graph obtained by replacing each vertex in a d-dimensional hypercube by a cycle of length d. Cube-connected cycles share many properties with hypercubes but have the additional desirable property that for $d > 1$ every vertex has degree 3.

New function ▪ See also ButterflyGraph, Hypercube ▪ See page 23

■ CubicalGraph

CubicalGraph returns the graph corresponding to the cube, a Platonic solid.

New function ▪ See also DodecahedralGraph, FiniteGraphs ▪ See page 370

■ Cut

Cut is a tag that can be used in a call to NetworkFlow to tell it to return the minimum cut.

New function ▪ See also EdgeConnectivity, NetworkFlow ▪ See page 292

■ CycleIndex

CycleIndex[pg, x] returns the polynomial in $x[1], x[2], \ldots, x[index[g]]$ that is the cycle index of the permutation group pg. Here, $index[pg]$ refers to the length of each permutation in pg.

New function ▪ See also DistinctPermutations, OrbitInventory ▪ See page 122

■ Cycle

Cycle[n] constructs the cycle on n vertices, the 2-regular connected graph. An option Type that takes on values Directed or Undirected is allowed. The default setting is Type -> Undirected.

See also AcyclicQ, RegularGraph ▪ See page 248

■ Cycles

Cycles is an optional argument for the function Involutions.

New function ▪ See also DistinctPermutations, Involutions ▪ See page 6

■ CycleStructure

CycleStructure[p, x] returns the monomial in $x[1], x[2], \ldots, x[Length[p]]$ that is the cycle structure of the permutation p.

New function ■ See also CycleIndex, Orbits ■ See page 122

■ Cyclic

Cyclic is an argument to the Polya-theoretic functions ListNecklaces, NumberOfNecklace, and NecklacePolynomial, which count or enumerate distinct necklaces. Cyclic refers to the cyclic group acting on necklaces to make equivalent necklaces that can be obtained from each other by rotation.

New function ■ See also ListNecklaces, NecklacePolynomial, NumberOfNecklaces ■ See page 6

■ CyclicGroup

CyclicGroup[n] returns the cyclic group of permutations on n symbols.

New function ■ See also OrbitInventory, SymmetricGroup ■ See page 110

■ CyclicGroupIndex

CyclicGroupIndex[n, x] returns the cycle index of the cyclic group on n symbols, expressed as a polynomial in $x[1], x[2], \ldots, x[n]$.

New function ■ See also OrbitInventory, SymmetricGroupIndex ■ See page 124

■ DeBruijnGraph

DeBruijnGraph[m, n] constructs the n-dimensional De Bruijn graph with m symbols for integers $m > 0$ and $n > 1$. DeBruijnGraph[alph, n] constructs the n-dimensional De Bruijn graph with symbols from *alph*. Here *alph* is nonempty and $n > 1$ is an integer. In the latter form, the function accepts an option VertexLabel, with default value False, which can be set to True if users want to associate strings on *alph* to the vertices as labels.

New function ■ See also DeBruijnSequence, Hypercube ■ See page 257

■ DeBruijnSequence

DeBruijnSequence[a, n] returns a De Bruijn sequence on the alphabet a, a shortest sequence in which every string of length n on alphabet a occurs as a contiguous subsequence.

See also DeBruijnGraph, EulerianCycle, Strings ■ See page 299

■ DegreeSequence

DegreeSequence[g] gives the sorted degree sequence of graph g.

See also Degrees, GraphicQ, RealizeDegreeSequence ■ See page 266

■ Degrees

Degrees[g] returns the degrees of vertex $1, 2, 3,\ldots$ in that order.

New function ■ See also `DegreeSequence`, `Vertices` ■ See page 266

■ DegreesOf2Neighborhood

DegreesOf2Neighborhood[g, v] returns the sorted list of degrees of vertices of graph g within a distance of 2 from v.

New function ■ See also `Isomorphism` ■ See page 365

■ DeleteCycle

DeleteCycle[g, c] deletes a simple cycle c from graph g. c is specified as a sequence of vertices in which the first and last vertices are identical. g can be directed or undirected. If g does not contain c, it is returned unchanged; otherwise, g is returned with c deleted.

See also `ExtractCycles`, `FindCycle` ■ See page 298

■ DeleteEdge

DeleteEdge[g, e] gives graph g minus e. If g is undirected, then e is treated as an undirected edge; otherwise, it is treated as a directed edge. If there are multiple edges between the specified vertices, only one edge is deleted. DeleteEdge[g, e, All] will delete all edges between the specified pair of vertices. Using the tag `Directed` as a third argument in DeleteEdge is now obsolete.

See also `AddEdge`, `DeleteVertex` ■ See page 194

■ DeleteEdges

DeleteEdges[g, l] gives graph g minus the list of edges l. If g is undirected, then the edges in l are treated as undirected edges; otherwise, they are treated as directed edges. If there are multiple edges that qualify, then only one edge is deleted. DeleteEdges[g, l, All] will delete all edges that qualify. If only one edge is to be deleted, then l can have the form $\{s, t\}$; otherwise, it has the form $\{\{s_1, t_1\}, \{s_2, t_2\}, \ldots\}$.

New function ■ See also `AddEdges`, `DeleteVertex` ■ See page 194

■ DeleteFromTableau

DeleteFromTableau[t, r] deletes the last element of row r from Young tableaux t.

See also `ConstructTableau`, `InsertIntoTableau` ■ See page 165

■ DeleteVertex

DeleteVertex[g, v] deletes a single vertex v from graph g. Here v is a vertex number.

See also `AddVertex`, `DeleteEdge` ■ See page 196

■ DeleteVertices

DeleteVertices[g, vList] deletes vertices in *vList* from graph *g*. *vList* has the form $\{i, j, \ldots\}$, where $i, j, \ldots$ are vertex numbers.

New function ■ See also AddVertices, DeleteEdges ■ See page 196

■ DepthFirstTraversal

DepthFirstTraversal[g, v] performs a depth-first traversal of graph *g* starting from vertex *v* and gives a list of vertices in the order in which they were encountered. DepthFirstTraversal[g, v, Edge] returns the edges of the graph that are traversed by the depth-first traversal in the order in which they are traversed. DepthFirstTraversal[g, v, Tree] returns the depth-first tree of the graph.

See also BreadthFirstTraversal ■ See page 280

■ DerangementQ

DerangementQ[p] tests whether permutation *p* is a derangement, that is, a permutation without a fixed point.

See also Derangements, NumberOfDerangements ■ See page 107

■ Derangements

Derangements[p] constructs all derangements of permutation *p*.

See also DerangementQ, NumberOfDerangements ■ See page 107

■ Diameter

Diameter[g] gives the diameter of graph *g*, the maximum length among all pairs of vertices in *g* of a shortest path between each pair.

See also Eccentricity, Radius ■ See page 332

■ Dihedral

Dihedral is an argument to the Polya-theoretic functions ListNecklaces, NumberOfNecklace, and NecklacePolynomial, which count or enumerate distinct necklaces. Dihedral refers to the dihedral group acting on necklaces to make equivalent necklaces that can be obtained from each other by a rotation or a flip.

New function ■ See also ListNecklaces, NecklacePolynomial, NumberOfNecklaces ■ See page 6

■ DihedralGroup

DihedralGroup[n] returns the dihedral group on n symbols. Note that the order of this group is $2n$.

New function ■ See also OrbitInventory, SymmetricGroup ■ See page 110

■ DihedralGroupIndex

DihedralGroupIndex[n, x] returns the cycle index of the dihedral group on n symbols, expressed as a polynomial in $x[1], x[2], ..., x[n]$.

New function ■ See also OrbitInventory, SymmetricGroupIndex ■ See page 125

■ Dijkstra

Dijkstra[g, v] gives a shortest-path spanning tree and associated distances from vertex v of graph g. The shortest-path spanning tree is given by a list in which element i is the predecessor of vertex i in the shortest-path spanning tree. Dijkstra does not work correctly when the edge weights are negative; BellmanFord should be used in this case.

See also ShortestPath, ShortestPathSpanningTree ■ See page 324

■ DilateVertices

DilateVertices[v, d] multiplies each coordinate of each vertex position in list v by d, thus dilating the embedding. DilateVertices[g, d] dilates the embedding of graph g by the factor d.

See also NormalizeVertices, RotateVertices, TranslateVertices ■ See page 219

■ Directed

Directed is an option value for Type.

New function ■ See also MakeGraph, ToOrderedPairs ■ See page 188

■ Disk

Disk is a value taken by the VertexStyle option in ShowGraph.

New function ■ See also ShowGraph, VertexStyle ■ See page 202

■ Distances

Distances[g, v] returns the distances in nondecreasing order from vertex v to all vertices in g, treating g as an unweighted graph."

New function ■ See also BreadthFirstTraversal, ShortestPath ■ See page 365

■ DistinctPermutations

DistinctPermutations[l] gives all permutations of the multiset described by list l.

See also LexicographicPermutations, MinimumChangePermutations ■ See page 5

■ Distribution

Distribution[l, set] lists the frequency of each element of a set in list *l*.

See also RankedEmbedding ■ See page 61

■ DodecahedralGraph

DodecahedralGraph returns the graph corresponding to the dodecahedron, a Platonic solid.

New function ■ See also FiniteGraphs, OctahedralGraph ■ See page 370

■ DominatingIntegerPartitionQ

DominatingIntegerPartitionQ[a, b] yields True if integer partition *a* dominates integer partition *b*; that is, the sum of a size-*t* prefix of *a* is no smaller than the sum of a size-*t* prefix of *b* for every *t*.

New function ■ See also PartitionQ, Partitions ■ See page 359

■ DominationLattice

DominationLattice[n] returns a Hasse diagram of the partially ordered set on integer partitions of *n* in which $p < q$ if q dominates p. The function takes two options: Type and VertexLabel, with default values Undirected and False, respectively. When Type is set to Directed, the function produces the underlying directed acyclic graph. When VertexLabel is set to True, labels are produced for the vertices.

New function ■ See also HasseDiagram, Partitions ■ See page 360

■ DurfeeSquare

DurfeeSquare[p] gives the number of rows involved in the Durfee square of partition *p*, the side of the largest-sized square contained within the Ferrers diagram of *p*.

See also FerrersDiagram, TransposePartition ■ See page 8

■ Eccentricity

Eccentricity[g] gives the eccentricity of each vertex *v* of graph *g*, the maximum length among all shortest paths from *v*.

See also AllPairsShortestPath, Diameter, GraphCenter ■ See page 332

■ Edge

Edge is an optional argument to inform certain functions to work with edges instead of vertices.

New function ■ See also BreadthFirstTraversal, DepthFirstTraversal, NetworkFlow ■ See page 278

■ EdgeChromaticNumber

EdgeChromaticNumber[g] gives the fewest number of colors necessary to color each edge of graph g, so that no two edges incident on the same vertex have the same color.

See also ChromaticNumber, EdgeColoring ▪ See page 314

■ EdgeColor

EdgeColor is an option that allows the user to associate colors with edges. Black is the default color. EdgeColor can be set as part of the graph data structure or in ShowGraph.

New function ▪ See also GraphOptions, SetGraphOptions ▪ See page 204

■ EdgeColoring

EdgeColoring[g] uses Brelaz's heuristic to find a good, but not necessarily minimal, edge coloring of graph g.

See also LineGraph, VertexColoring ▪ See page 314

■ EdgeConnectivity

EdgeConnectivity[g] gives the minimum number of edges whose deletion from graph g disconnects it. EdgeConnectivity[g, Cut] gives a set of edges of minimum size whose deletion disconnects the graph.

See also NetworkFlow, VertexConnectivity ▪ See page 289

■ EdgeDirection

EdgeDirection is an option that takes on values True or False, allowing the user to specify whether the graph is directed or not. EdgeDirection can be set as part of the graph data structure or in ShowGraph.

New function ▪ See also SetGraphOptions, ShowGraph ▪ See page 204

■ EdgeLabel

EdgeLabel is an option that can take on values True or False, allowing the user to associate labels to edges. By default, there are no edge labels. The EdgeLabel option can be set as part of the graph data structure or in ShowGraph.

New function ▪ See also GraphOptions, SetGraphOptions ▪ See page 204

■ EdgeLabelColor

EdgeLabelColor is an option that allows the user to associate different colors to edge labels. Black is the default color. EdgeLabelColor can be set as part of the graph data structure or in ShowGraph.

New function ■ See also GraphOptions, SetGraphOptions ■ See page 204

■ EdgeLabelPosition

EdgeLabelPosition is an option that allows the user to place an edge label in a certain position relative to the midpoint of the edge. LowerLeft is the default value of this option. EdgeLabelPosition can be set as part of the graph data structure or in ShowGraph.

New function ■ See also GraphOptions, SetGraphOptions ■ See page 204

■ Edges

Edges[g] gives the list of edges in *g*. Edges[g, All] gives the edges of *g* along with the graphics options associated with each edge. Edges[g, EdgeWeight] returns the list of edges in *g* along with their edge weights.

See also M, Vertices ■ See page 182

■ EdgeStyle

EdgeStyle is an option that allows the user to associate different sizes and shapes to edges. A line segment is the default edge. EdgeStyle can be set as part of the graph data structure or in ShowGraph.

New function ■ See also GraphOptions, SetGraphOptions ■ See page 204

■ EdgeWeight

EdgeWeight is an option that allows the user to associate weights with edges; 1 is the default weight. EdgeWeight can be set as part of the graph data structure.

New function ■ See also GraphOptions, SetGraphOptions ■ See page 197

■ Element

Element is now obsolete in *Combinatorica*, though the function call Element[a, p] still gives the *p*th element of the nested list *a*, where *p* is a list of indices.

■ EmptyGraph

EmptyGraph[n] generates an empty graph on *n* vertices. An option Type that can take on values Directed or Undirected is provided. The default setting is Type -> Undirected.

See also EmptyQ, CompleteGraph ■ See page 239

■ **EmptyQ**

EmptyQ[g] yields True if graph *g* contains no edges.

See also CompleteQ, EmptyGraph ■ See page 198

■ **EncroachingListSet**

EncroachingListSet[p] constructs the encroaching list set associated with permutation *p*.

See also Tableaux ■ See page 5

■ **EquivalenceClasses**

EquivalenceClasses[r] identifies the equivalence classes among the elements of matrix *r*.

See also EquivalenceRelationQ ■ See page 114

■ **EquivalenceRelationQ**

EquivalenceRelationQ[r] yields True if the matrix *r* defines an equivalence relation. EquivalenceRelationQ[g] tests whether the adjacency matrix of graph *g* defines an equivalence relation.

See also EquivalenceClasses ■ See page 114

■ **Equivalences**

Equivalences[g, h] lists the vertex equivalence classes between graphs *g* and *h* defined by their vertex degrees. Equivalences[g] lists the vertex equivalences for graph *g* defined by the vertex degrees. Equivalences[g, h, f1, f2, ...] and Equivalences[g, f1, f2, ...] can also be used, where $f1, f2, ...$ are functions that compute other vertex invariants. It is expected that for each function *fi*, the call fi[g, v] returns the corresponding invariant at vertex *v* in graph *g*. The functions $f1, f2, ...$ are evaluated in order, and the evaluation stops either when all functions have been evaluated or when an empty equivalence class is found. Three vertex invariants, DegreesOf2Neighborhood, NumberOf2Paths, and Distances, are *Combinatorica* functions and can be used to refine the equivalences.

See also Isomorphism, NumberOf2Paths ■ See page 364

■ **Euclidean**

Euclidean is an option for SetEdgeWeights.

New function ■ See also Distances, GraphOptions, SetEdgeWeights ■ See page 196

■ **Eulerian**

Eulerian[n, k] gives the number of permutations of length *n* with *k* runs.

See also Runs, StirlingFirst ■ See page 75

■ **EulerianCycle**

EulerianCycle[g] finds an Eulerian cycle of *g*, if one exists.

See also DeBruijnSequence, EulerianQ, HamiltonianCycle ■ See page 298

■ **EulerianQ**

EulerianQ[g] yields True if graph *g* is Eulerian, meaning that there exists a tour that includes each edge exactly once.

See also EulerianCycle, HamiltonianQ ■ See page 297

■ **ExactRandomGraph**

ExactRandomGraph[n, e] constructs a random labeled graph with exactly *e* edges and *n* vertices.

See also NthPair, RandomGraph, RealizeDegreeSequence ■ See page 264

■ **ExpandGraph**

ExpandGraph[g, n] expands graph *g* to *n* vertices by adding disconnected vertices. This is obsolete; use AddVertices[g, n] instead.

See also AddVertex, InduceSubgraph ■ See page 38

■ **ExtractCycles**

ExtractCycles[g] gives a maximal list of edge-disjoint cycles in graph *g*.

See also DeleteCycle ■ See page 294

■ **FerrersDiagram**

FerrersDiagram[p] draws a Ferrers diagram of integer partition *p*.

See also Partitions, TransposePartition ■ See page 143

■ **FindCycle**

FindCycle[g] finds a list of vertices that define a cycle in graph *g*.

See also AcyclicQ, DeleteCycle, ExtractCycles ■ See page 294

■ **FindSet**

FindSet[n, s] gives the root of the set containing *n* in the union-find data structure *s*.

See also InitializeUnionFind, MinimumSpanningTree, UnionSet ■ See page 336

■ FiniteGraphs

FiniteGraphs produces a convenient list of all the interesting, finite, parameterless graphs built into *Combinatorica*.

New function ▪ See also CageGraph ▪ See page 2

■ FirstLexicographicTableau

FirstLexicographicTableau[p] constructs the first Young tableau with shape described by partition *p*.

See also Tableaux ▪ See page 167

■ FolkmanGraph

FolkmanGraph returns a smallest graph that is edge-transitive but not vertex-transitive.

New function ▪ See also Automorphisms, FiniteGraphs ▪ See page 116

■ FranklinGraph

FranklinGraph returns a 12-vertex graph that represents a 6-chromatic map on the Klein bottle. It is the sole counterexample to Heawood's map coloring conjecture.

New function ▪ See also ChromaticNumber, FiniteGraphs ▪ See page 23

■ FromAdjacencyLists

FromAdjacencyLists[l] constructs an edge list representation for a graph from the given adjacency lists *l*, using a circular embedding. FromAdjacencyLists[l, v] uses *v* as the embedding for the resulting graph. An option called Type that takes on the values Directed or Undirected can be used to affect the type of graph produced. The default value of Type is Undirected.

See also ToAdjacencyLists, ToOrderedPairs ▪ See page 188

■ FromAdjacencyMatrix

FromAdjacencyMatrix[m] constructs a graph from a given adjacency matrix *m*, using a circular embedding. FromAdjacencyMatrix[m, v] uses *v* as the embedding for the resulting graph. An option Type that takes on the values Directed or Undirected can be used to affect the type of graph produced. The default value of Type is Undirected. FromAdjacencyMatrix[m, EdgeWeight] interprets the entries in *m* as edge weights, with infinity representing missing edges, and from this constructs a weighted graph using a circular embedding. FromAdjacencyMatrix[m, v, EdgeWeight] uses *v* as the embedding for the resulting graph. The option Type can be used along with the EdgeWeight tag.

New function ▪ See also IncidenceMatrix, ToAdjacencyMatrix ▪ See page 190

■ **FromCycles**

FromCycles[c1, c2, ...] gives the permutation that has the given cycle structure.

See also HideCycles, RevealCycles, ToCycles ■ See page 95

■ **FromInversionVector**

FromInversionVector[v] reconstructs the unique permutation with inversion vector v.

See also Inversions, ToInversionVector ■ See page 69

■ **FromOrderedPairs**

FromOrderedPairs[l] constructs an edge list representation from a list of ordered pairs l, using a circular embedding. FromOrderedPairs[l, v] uses v as the embedding for the resulting graph. The option Type that takes on values Undirected or Directed can be used to affect the kind of graph produced. The default value of Type is Directed. Type -> Undirected results in the underlying undirected graph.

See also FromUnorderedPairs, ToOrderedPairs, ToUnorderedPairs ■ See page 185

■ **FromUnorderedPairs**

FromUnorderedPairs[l] constructs an edge list representation from a list of unordered pairs l, using a circular embedding. FromUnorderedPairs[l, v] uses v as the embedding for the resulting graph. The option Type that takes on values Undirected or Directed can be used to affect the kind of graph produced.

See also FromOrderedPairs, ToOrderedPairs, ToUnorderedPairs ■ See page 185

■ **FruchtGraph**

FruchtGraph returns the smallest 3-regular graph whose automorphism group consists of only the identity.

New function ■ See also Automorphisms, FiniteGraphs ■ See page 112

■ **FunctionalGraph**

FunctionalGraph[f, v] takes a set v and a function f from v to v and constructs a directed graph with vertex set v and edges $(x, f(x))$ for each x in v. FunctionalGraph[f, v], where f is a list of functions, constructs a graph with vertex set v and edge set $(x, f_i(x))$ for every f_i in f. An option called Type that takes on the values Directed and Undirected is allowed. Type -> Directed is the default, while Type -> Undirected returns the corresponding underlying undirected graph.

See also IntervalGraph, MakeGraph ■ See page 271

■ GeneralizedPetersenGraph

GeneralizedPetersenGraph[n, k] returns the generalized Petersen graph, for integers $n > 1$ and $k > 0$, which is the graph with vertices $\{u_1, u_2, \ldots, u_n\}$ and $\{v_1, v_2, \ldots, v_n\}$ and edges $\{u_i, u_{i+1}\}, \{v_i, v_{i+k}\}$, and $\{u_i, v_i\}$. The Petersen graph is identical to the generalized Petersen graph with $n = 5$ and $k = 2$.

New function ■ See also FiniteGraphs, PetersenGraph ■ See page 215

■ GetEdgeLabels

GetEdgeLabels[g] returns the list of labels of the edges of g. GetEdgeLabels[g, es] returns the list of labels in graph g of the edges in *es*.

New function ■ See also GraphOptions, SetGraphOptions ■ See page 197

■ GetEdgeWeights

GetEdgeWeights[g] returns the list of weights of the edges of g. GetEdgeWeights[g, es] returns the list of weights in graph g of the edges in *es*.

New function ■ See also GraphOptions, SetGraphOptions ■ See page 197

■ GetVertexLabels

GetVertexLabels[g] returns the list of labels of vertices of g. GetVertexLabels[g, vs] returns the list of labels in graph g of the vertices specified in list *vs*.

New function ■ See also GraphOptions, SetGraphOptions ■ See page 197

■ GetVertexWeights

GetVertexWeights[g] returns the list of weights of vertices of g. GetVertexWeights[g, vs] returns the list of weights in graph g of the vertices in *vs*.

New function ■ See also GraphOptions, SetGraphOptions ■ See page 197

■ Girth

Girth[g] gives the length of the shortest cycle in a simple graph g.

See also FindCycle, ShortestPath ■ See page 296

■ Graph

`Graph[e, v, opts]` represents a graph object where *e* is the list of edges annotated with graphics options, *v* is a list of vertices annotated with graphics options, and *opts* is a set of global graph options. *e* has the form $\{\{\{i1, j1\}, opts1\}, \{\{i2, j2\}, opts2\}, ...\}$, where $\{i1, j1\}, \{i2, j2\}, ...$ are edges of the graph and *opts1, opts2, ...* are options that respectively apply to these edges. *v* has the form $\{\{\{x1, y1\}, opts1\}, \{\{x2, y2\}, opts2\}, ...\}$, where $\{x1, y1\}, \{x2, y2\}, ...$ respectively denote the coordinates in the plane of vertices 1, 2, ... and *opts1, opts2, ...* are options that respectively apply to these vertices. Permitted edge options are `EdgeWeight`, `EdgeColor`, `EdgeStyle`, `EdgeLabel`, `EdgeLabelColor`, and `EdgeLabelPosition`. Permitted vertex options are `VertexWeight`, `VertexColor`, `VertexStyle`, `VertexNumber`, `VertexNumberColor`, `VertexNumberPosition`, `VertexLabel`, `VertexLabelColor`, and `VertexLabelPosition`. The third item in a `Graph` object is *opts*, a sequence of zero or more global options that apply to all vertices or all edges or to the graph as a whole. All of the edge options and vertex options can also be used as global options. If a global option and a local edge option or vertex option differ, then the local edge or vertex option is used for that particular edge or vertex. In addition to these options, the following two options also can be specified as part of the global options: `LoopPosition` and `EdgeDirection`. Furthermore, all the options of the *Mathematica* function `Plot` can be used as global options in a `Graph` object. These can be used to specify how the graph looks when it is drawn. Also, all options of the graphics primitive `Arrow` also can be specified as part of the global graph options. These can be used to affect the look of arrows that represent directed edges. See the usage message of individual options to find out more about values that these options can take on. Whether a graph is undirected or directed is given by the option `EdgeDirection`. This has the default value `False`. For undirected graphs, the edges $\{i1, j1\}, \{i2, j2\}, ...$ have to satisfy $i1 \leq j1, i2 \leq j2, ...$, and for directed graphs, the edges $\{i1, j1\}, \{i2, j2\}, ...$ are treated as ordered pairs, each specifying the direction of the edge as well.

See also `FromAdjacencyLists`, `FromAdjacencyMatrix` ▪ See page 179

■ GraphCenter

`GraphCenter[g]` gives a list of the vertices of graph *g* with minimum eccentricity.

See also `AllPairsShortestPath`, `Eccentricity` ▪ See page 332

■ GraphComplement

`GraphComplement[g]` gives the complement of graph *g*.

See also `SelfComplementaryQ` ▪ See page 238

■ GraphDifference

`GraphDifference[g, h]` constructs the graph resulting from subtracting the edges of graph *h* from the edges of graph *g*.

See also `GraphProduct`, `GraphSum` ▪ See page 238

■ GraphicQ

GraphicQ[s] yields True if the list of integers s is a graphic sequence and thus represents a degree sequence of some graph.

See also DegreeSequence, RealizeDegreeSequence ■ See page 266

■ GraphIntersection

GraphIntersection[g1, g2, ...] constructs the graph defined by the edges that are in all the graphs $g1, g2, ...$

See also GraphJoin, GraphUnion ■ See page 237

■ GraphJoin

GraphJoin[g1, g2, ...] constructs the join of graphs $g1, g2, ...$ This is the graph obtained by adding all possible edges between different graphs to the graph union of $g1, g2, ...$

See also GraphProduct, GraphUnion ■ See page 239

■ GraphOptions

GraphOptions[g] returns the display options associated with g. GraphOptions[g, v] returns the display options associated with vertex v in g. GraphOptions[g, u, v] returns the display options associated with edge $\{u, v\}$ in g.

New function ■ See also SetGraphOptions ■ See page 181

■ GraphPolynomial

GraphPolynomial[n, x] returns a polynomial in x in which the coefficient of x^m is the number of nonisomorphic graphs with n vertices and m edges. GraphPolynomial[n, x, Directed] returns a polynomial in x in which the coefficient of x^m is the number of nonisomorphic directed graphs with n vertices and m edges.

New function ■ See also ListGraphs, NumberOfGraphs ■ See page 129

■ GraphPower

GraphPower[g, k] gives the kth power of graph g. This is the graph whose vertex set is identical to the vertex set of g and that contains an edge between vertices i and j if g contains a path between i and j of length, at most, k.

See also ShortestPath ■ See page 333

■ **GraphProduct**

GraphProduct[g1, g2, ...] constructs the product of graphs $g1, g2, ...$.

See also GraphDifference, GraphSum ■ See page 240

■ **GraphSum**

GraphSum[g1, g2, ...] constructs the graph resulting from joining the edge lists of graphs $g1, g2, ...$

See also GraphDifference, GraphProduct ■ See page 238

■ **GraphUnion**

GraphUnion[g1, g2, ...] constructs the union of graphs $g1, g2, ...$. GraphUnion[n, g] constructs n copies of graph g, for any nonnegative integer n.

See also GraphIntersection, GraphJoin ■ See page 235

■ **GrayCode**

GrayCode[l] constructs a binary reflected Gray code on set l. GrayCode is obsolete, so use GrayCodeSubsets instead.

See also GrayCodeSubsets ■ See page 38

■ **GrayCodeKSubsets**

GrayCodeKSubsets[l, k] generates k-subsets of l in Gray code order.

New function ■ See also GrayCodeSubsets, KSubsets ■ See page 86

■ **GrayCodeSubsets**

GrayCodeSubsets[l] constructs a binary reflected Gray code on set l.

New function ■ See also GrayCodeSubsets, Subsets ■ See page 79

■ **GrayGraph**

GrayGraph returns a 3-regular, 54-vertex graph that is edge-transitive but not vertex-transitive; it is the smallest known such example.

New function ■ See also Automorphisms, FiniteGraphs ■ See page 23

■ Greedy

Greedy is a value that the option Algorithm can take in calls to functions such as VertexCover, telling the function to use a greedy algorithm.

New function ■ See also GreedyVertexCover ■ See page 31

■ GreedyVertexCover

GreedyVertexCover[g] returns a vertex cover of graph *g* constructed using the greedy algorithm. This is a natural heuristic for constructing a vertex cover, but it can produce poor vertex covers.

New function ■ See also BipartiteMatchingAndCover, VertexCover ■ See page 317

■ GridGraph

GridGraph[n, m] constructs an $n \times m$ grid graph, the product of paths on *n* and *m* vertices. GridGraph[p, q, r] constructs a $p \times q \times r$ grid graph, the product of GridGraph[p, q] and a path of length *r*.

See also GraphProduct, Path ■ See page 250

■ GrotztschGraph

GrotztschGraph returns the smallest triangle-free graph with chromatic number 4. This is identical to MycielskiGraph[4].

New function ■ See also MycielskiGraph ■ See page 23

■ HamiltonianCycle

HamiltonianCycle[g] finds a Hamiltonian cycle in graph *g*, if one exists. HamiltonianCycle[g, All] gives all Hamiltonian cycles of graph *g*.

See also EulerianCycle, HamiltonianQ, HamiltonianPath ■ See page 300

■ HamiltonianPath

HamiltonianPath[g] finds a Hamiltonian path in graph *g*, if one exists. HamiltonianPath[g, All] gives all Hamiltonian paths of graph *g*.

See also EulerianCycle, HamiltonianPath, HamiltonianQ ■ See page 302

■ HamiltonianQ

HamiltonianQ[g] yields True if there exists a Hamiltonian cycle in graph *g*, or, in other words, if there exists a cycle that visits each vertex exactly once.

See also EulerianQ, HamiltonianCycle ■ See page 300

■ Harary

Harary[k, n] constructs the minimal *k*-connected graph on *n* vertices.

See also EdgeConnectivity, VertexConnectivity ■ See page 292

■ HasseDiagram

HasseDiagram[g] constructs a Hasse diagram of the relation defined by directed acyclic graph *g*.

See also PartialOrderQ, TransitiveReduction ■ See page 357

■ Heapify

Heapify[p] builds a heap from permutation *p*.

See also HeapSort, RandomHeap ■ See page 5

■ HeapSort

HeapSort[l] performs a heap sort on the items of list *l*.

See also Heapify, SelectionSort ■ See page 5

■ HeawoodGraph

HeawoodGraph returns a smallest (6, 3)-cage, a 3-regular graph with girth 6.

New function ■ See also CageGraph, FiniteGraphs ■ See page 23

■ HerschelGraph

HerschelGraph returns a graph object that represents a Herschel graph.

New function ■ See also FiniteGraphs ■ See page 23

■ HideCycles

HideCycles[c] canonically encodes the cycle structure *c* into a unique permutation.

See also FromCycles, RevealCycles, ToCycles ■ See page 100

■ **Highlight**

Highlight[g, p] displays *g* with elements in *p* highlighted. The second argument *p* has the form {$s_1, s_2, ...$}, where the s_i's are disjoint subsets of vertices and edges of *g*. The options HighlightedVertexStyle, HighlightedEdgeStyle, HighlightedVertexColors, and HighlightedEdgeColors are used to determine the appearance of the highlighted elements of the graph. The default settings of the style options are HighlightedVertexStyle->Disk[Large] and HighlightedEdgeStyle->Thick. The options HighlightedVertexColors and HighlightedEdgeColors are both set to {Black, Red, Blue, Green, Yellow, Purple, Brown, Orange, Olive, Pink, DeepPink, DarkGreen, Maroon, Navy}. The colors are chosen from the palette of colors with color 1 used for s_1, color 2 used for s_2, and so on. If there are more parts than colors, then the colors are used cyclically. The function permits all the options that SetGraphOptions permits, for example, VertexColor, VertexStyle, EdgeColor, and EdgeStyle. These options can be used to control the appearance of the nonhighlighted vertices and edges.

New function ■ See also AnimateGraph, ShowGraph ■ See page 211

■ **HighlightedEdgeColors**

HighlightedEdgeColors is an option to Highlight that determines which colors are used for the highlighted edges.

New function ■ See also GraphOptions, Highlight ■ See page 211

■ **HighlightedEdgeStyle**

HighlightedEdgeStyle is an option to Highlight that determines how the highlighted edges are drawn.

New function ■ See also GraphOptions, Highlight ■ See page 212

■ **HighlightedVertexColors**

HighlightedVertexColors is an option to Highlight that determines which colors are used for the highlighted vertices.

New function ■ See also GraphOptions, Highlight ■ See page 212

■ **HighlightedVertexStyle**

HighlightedVertexStyle is an option to Highlight that determines how the highlighted vertices are drawn.

New function ■ See also GraphOptions, Highlight ■ See page 212

■ **Hypercube**

Hypercube[n] constructs an *n*-dimensional hypercube.

See also GrayCode ■ See page 251

■ **IcosahedralGraph**

IcosahedralGraph returns the graph corresponding to the icosahedron, a Platonic solid.

New function ■ See also DodecahedralGraph, FiniteGraphs ■ See page 370

■ **IdenticalQ**

IdenticalQ[g, h] yields True if graphs g and h have identical edge lists, even though the associated graphics information need not be the same.

See also IsomorphicQ, Isomorphism ■ See page 363

■ **IdentityPermutation**

IdentityPermutation[n] gives the size-n identity permutation.

New function ■ See also DistinctPermutations, LexicographicPermutations ■ See page 56

■ **IncidenceMatrix**

IncidenceMatrix[g] returns the $(0,1)$ matrix of graph g, which has a row for each vertex and a column for each edge and $(v,e) = 1$ if and only if vertex v is incident on edge e. For a directed graph, $(v,e) = 1$ if edge e is outgoing from v.

See also LineGraph, ToAdjacencyMatrix ■ See page 191

■ **InDegree**

InDegree[g, n] returns the in-degree of vertex n in the directed graph g. InDegree[g] returns the sequence of in-degrees of the vertices in the directed graph g.

New function ■ See also Degrees, OutDegree ■ See page 297

■ **IndependentSetQ**

IndependentSetQ[g, i] yields True if the vertices in list i define an independent set in graph g.

See also CliqueQ, MaximumIndependentSet, VertexCoverQ ■ See page 318

■ **Index**

Index[p] gives the index of permutation p, the sum of all subscripts j such that $p[j]$ is greater than $p[j+1]$.

See also Inversions ■ See page 73

■ **InduceSubgraph**

InduceSubgraph[g, s] constructs the subgraph of graph *g* induced by the list of vertices *s*.

See also Contract ▪ See page 234

■ **InitializeUnionFind**

InitializeUnionFind[n] initializes a union-find data structure for *n* elements.

See also FindSet, MinimumSpanningTree, UnionSet ▪ See page 336

■ **InsertIntoTableau**

InsertIntoTableau[e, t] inserts integer *e* into Young tableau *t* using the bumping algorithm. InsertIntoTableau[e, t, All] inserts *e* into Young tableau *t* and returns the new tableau as well as the row whose size is expanded as a result of the insertion.

See also ConstructTableau, DeleteFromTableau ▪ See page 164

■ **IntervalGraph**

IntervalGraph[l] constructs the interval graph defined by the list of intervals *l*.

See also FunctionalGraph, MakeGraph ▪ See page 319

■ **Invariants**

Invariants is an option to the functions Isomorphism and IsomorphicQ that informs these functions about which vertex invariants to use in computing equivalences between vertices.

New function ▪ See also DegreesOf2Neighborhood, NumberOf2Paths ▪ See page 368

■ **InversePermutation**

InversePermutation[p] yields the multiplicative inverse of permutation *p*.

See also Involutions, Permute ▪ See page 56

■ **InversionPoset**

InversionPoset[n] returns a Hasse diagram of the partially ordered set on size-*n* permutations in which $p < q$ if q can be obtained from p by an adjacent transposition that places the larger element before the smaller. The function takes two options: Type and VertexLabel, with default values Undirected and False, respectively. When Type is set to Directed, the function produces the underlying directed acyclic graph. When VertexLabel is set to True, labels are produced for the vertices.

New function ▪ See also DominationLattice, MinimumChangePermutations ▪ See page 359

■ Inversions

Inversions[p] counts the number of inversions in permutation *p*.

See also FromInversionVector, ToInversionVector ■ See page 71

■ InvolutionQ

InvolutionQ[p] yields True if permutation *p* is its own inverse.

See also InversePermutation, NumberOfInvolutions ■ See page 104

■ Involutions

Involutions[l] gives the list of involutions of the elements in the list *l*. Involutions[l, Cycles] gives the involutions in their cycle representation. Involution[n] gives size-*n* involutions. Involutions[n, Cycles] gives size-*n* involutions in their cycle representation.

New function ■ See also DistinctPermutations, InvolutionQ ■ See page 105

■ IsomorphicQ

IsomorphicQ[g, h] yields True if graphs *g* and *h* are isomorphic. This function takes an option Invariants -> {$f_1, f_2, \ldots$}, where $f_1, f_2, \ldots$ are functions that are used to compute vertex invariants. These functions are used in the order in which they are specified. The default value of Invariants is {DegreesOf2Neighborhood, NumberOf2Paths, Distances}.

See also IdenticalQ, Isomorphism ■ See page 367

■ Isomorphism

Isomorphism[g, h] gives an isomorphism between graphs *g* and *h*, if one exists. Isomorphism[g, h, All] gives all isomorphisms between graphs *g* and *h*. Isomorphism[g] gives the automorphism group of *g*. This function takes an option Invariants -> {$f_1, f_2, \ldots$}, where $f_1, f_2, \ldots$ are functions that are used to compute vertex invariants. These functions are used in the order in which they are specified. The default value of Invariants is {DegreesOf2Neighborhood, NumberOf2Paths, Distances}.

See also Automorphisms, IdenticalQ, IsomorphicQ ■ See page 367

■ IsomorphismQ

IsomorphismQ[g, h, p] tests if permutation *p* defines an isomorphism between graphs *g* and *h*.

See also IsomorphicQ ■ See page 367

■ Josephus

Josephus[n, m] generates the inverse of the permutation defined by executing every mth member in a circle of n members.

See also InversePermutation ■ See page 5

■ KnightsTourGraph

KnightsTourGraph[m, n] returns a graph with $m \times n$ vertices in which each vertex represents a square in an $m \times n$ chessboard and each edge corresponds to a legal move by a knight from one square to another.

New function ■ See also GridGraph, HamiltonianCycle ■ See page 302

■ KSetPartitions

KSetPartitions[set, k] returns the list of set partitions of a set with k blocks. KSetPartitions[n, k] returns the list of set partitions of $\{1, 2, ..., n\}$ with k blocks. If all set partitions of a set are needed, use the function SetPartitions.

New function ■ See also RandomKSetPartition, SetPartitions ■ See page 150

■ KSubsetGroup

KSubsetGroup[pg, s] returns the group induced by a permutation group pg on the set s of k-subsets of $\{1, 2, ..., n\}$, where n is the index of pg. The optional argument Type can be Ordered or Unordered, and, depending on the value of Type, s is treated as a set of k-subsets or k-tuples.

New function ■ See also OrbitInventory, SymmetricGroup ■ See page 114

■ KSubsetGroupIndex

KSubsetGroupIndex[g, s, x] returns the cycle index of the k-subset group on s expressed as a polynomial in $x[1], x[2], ...$. This function also takes the optional argument Type that tells the function whether the elements of s should be treated as sets or tuples.

New function ■ See also OrbitInventory, SymmetricGroupIndex ■ See page 6

■ KSubsets

KSubsets[l, k] gives all subsets of set l containing exactly k elements, ordered lexicographically.

See also LexicographicSubsets, NextKSubset, RandomKSubset ■ See page 83

■ K

The use of K to create a complete graph is obsolete. Use CompleteGraph to create a complete graph.

■ LabeledTreeToCode

LabeledTreeToCode[g] reduces the tree *g* to its Prüfer code.

See also CodeToLabeledTree, Strings ■ See page 258

■ Large

Large is a symbol used to denote the size of the object that represents a vertex. The option VertexStyle can be set to Disk[Large] or Box[Large] either inside the graph data structure or in ShowGraph.

New function ■ See also GraphOptions, VertexStyle ■ See page 202

■ LastLexicographicTableau

LastLexicographicTableau[p] constructs the last Young tableau with shape described by partition *p*.

See also Tableaux ■ See page 167

■ Level

Level is an option for the function BreadthFirstTraversal that makes the function return levels of vertices.

See also BreadthFirstTraversal ■ See page 278

■ LeviGraph

LeviGraph returns the unique (8, 3)-cage, a 3-regular graph whose girth is 8.

New function ■ See also CageGraph, FiniteGraphs ■ See page 23

■ LexicographicPermutations

LexicographicPermutations[l] constructs all permutations of list *l* in lexicographic order.

See also NextPermutation, NthPermutation, RankPermutation ■ See page 58

■ LexicographicSubsets

LexicographicSubsets[l] gives all subsets of set *l* in lexicographic order. LexicographicSubsets[n] returns all subsets of $\{1, 2, ..., n\}$ in lexicographic order.

See also NthSubset, Subsets ■ See page 82

■ LineGraph

LineGraph[g] constructs the line graph of graph *g*.

See also IncidenceMatrix ■ See page 241

■ ListGraphs

ListGraphs[n, m] returns all nonisomorphic undirected graphs with *n* vertices and *m* edges. ListGraphs[n, m, Directed] returns all nonisomorphic directed graphs with *n* vertices and *m* edges. ListGraphs[n] returns all nonisomorphic undirected graphs with *n* vertices. ListGraphs[n, Directed] returns all nonisomorphic directed graphs with *n* vertices.

New function ▪ See also NumberOfGraphs, RandomGraph ▪ See page 121

■ ListNecklaces

ListNecklaces[n, c, Cyclic] returns all distinct necklaces whose beads are colored by colors from *c*. Here, *c* is a list of *n*, not necessarily distinct colors, and two colored necklaces are considered equivalent if one can be obtained by rotating the other. ListNecklaces[n, c, Dihedral] is similar except that two necklaces are considered equivalent if one can be obtained from the other by a rotation or a flip.

New function ▪ See also NecklacePolynomial, NumberOfNecklaces ▪ See page 6

■ LNorm

LNorm[p] is a value that the option WeightingFunction, used in the function SetEdgeWeights, can take. Here, *p* can be any integer or Infinity.

New function ▪ See also GetEdgeWeights, SetEdgeWeights ▪ See page 197

■ LongestIncreasingSubsequence

LongestIncreasingSubsequence[p] finds the longest increasing subsequence of permutation *p*.

See also Inversions, TableauClasses, Runs ▪ See page 171

■ LoopPosition

LoopPosition is an option to ShowGraph whose values tell ShowGraph where to position a loop around a vertex. This option can take on values UpperLeft, UpperRight, LowerLeft, and LowerRight.

New function ▪ See also GraphOptions, SetGraphOptions ▪ See page 204

■ LowerLeft

LowerLeft is a value that options VertexNumberPosition, VertexLabelPosition, and EdgeLabelPosition can take on in ShowGraph.

New function ▪ See also GraphOptions, SetGraphOptions ▪ See page 202

■ LowerRight

LowerRight is a value that options VertexNumberPosition, VertexLabelPosition, and EdgeLabelPosition can take on in ShowGraph.

New function ▪ See also GraphOptions, SetGraphOptions ▪ See page 202

■ M

M[g] gives the number of edges in the graph *g*. M[g, Directed] is obsolete because M[g] works for directed as well as undirected graphs.

See also Edges, V ▪ See page 182

■ MakeDirected

MakeDirected[g] constructs a directed graph from a given undirected graph *g* by replacing each undirected edge in *g* by two directed edges pointing in opposite directions. The local options associated with edges are not inherited by the corresponding directed edges. Calling the function with the tag All, as MakeDirected[g, All], ensures that the local options associated with each edge are inherited by both corresponding directed edges.

New function ▪ See also MakeUndirected, OrientGraph ▪ See page 14

■ MakeGraph

MakeGraph[v, f] constructs the graph whose vertices correspond to *v* and edges between pairs of vertices *x* and *y* in *v* for which the binary relation defined by the Boolean function *f* is True. MakeGraph takes two options, Type and VertexLabel. Type can be set to Directed or Undirected, and this tells MakeGraph whether to construct a directed or an undirected graph. The default setting is Directed. VertexLabel can be set to True or False, with False being the default setting. Using VertexLabel -> True assigns labels derived from *v* to the vertices of the graph.

See also FunctionalGraph, IntervalGraph ▪ See page 269

■ MakeSimple

MakeSimple[g] gives the undirected graph, free of multiple edges and self-loops derived from graph *g*.

See also MakeUndirected, SimpleQ ▪ See page 254

■ MakeUndirected

MakeUndirected[g] gives the underlying undirected graph of the given directed graph *g*.

See also MakeSimple, UndirectedQ ▪ See page 199

■ **MaximalMatching**

MaximalMatching[g] gives the list of edges associated with a maximal matching of graph *g*.

See also BipartiteMatching, BipartiteMatchingAndCover ▪ See page 343

■ **MaximumAntichain**

MaximumAntichain[g] gives a largest set of unrelated vertices in partial order *g*.

See also BipartiteMatching, MinimumChainPartition, PartialOrderQ ▪ See page 361

■ **MaximumClique**

MaximumClique[g] finds a largest clique in graph *g*. MaximumClique[g, k] returns a *k*-clique, if such a thing exists in *g*; otherwise, it returns {}.

See also CliqueQ, MaximumIndependentSet, MinimumVertexCover ▪ See page 316

■ **MaximumIndependentSet**

MaximumIndependentSet[g] finds a largest independent set of graph *g*.

See also IndependentSetQ, MaximumClique, MinimumVertexCover ▪ See page 318

■ **MaximumSpanningTree**

MaximumSpanningTree[g] uses Kruskal's algorithm to find a maximum spanning tree of graph *g*.

See also MinimumSpanningTree, NumberOfSpanningTrees ▪ See page 336

■ **McGeeGraph**

McGeeGraph returns the unique (7, 3)-cage, a 3-regular graph with girth 7.

New function ▪ See also CageGraph, FiniteGraphs ▪ See page 23

■ **MeredithGraph**

MeredithGraph returns a 4-regular, 4-connected graph that is not Hamiltonian, providing a counterexample to a conjecture by C. St. J. A. Nash-Williams.

New function ▪ See also FiniteGraphs, HamiltonianCycle ▪ See page 303

■ **MinimumChainPartition**

MinimumChainPartition[g] partitions partial order *g* into a minimum number of chains.

See also BipartiteMatching, MaximumAntichain, PartialOrderQ ▪ See page 361

■ MinimumChangePermutations

MinimumChangePermutations[l] constructs all permutations of list *l* such that adjacent permutations differ by only one transposition.

See also DistinctPermutations, LexicographicPermutations ■ See page 64

■ MinimumSpanningTree

MinimumSpanningTree[g] uses Kruskal's algorithm to find a minimum spanning tree of graph *g*.

See also MaximumSpanningTree, NumberOfSpanningTrees, ShortestPathSpanningTree ■ See page 336

■ MinimumVertexColoring

MinimumVertexColoring[g] returns a minimum vertex coloring of *g*. MinimumVertexColoring[g, k] returns a *k*-coloring of *g*, if one exists.

New function ■ See also ChromaticNumber, VertexColoring ■ See page 310

■ MinimumVertexCover

MinimumVertexCover[g] finds a minimum vertex cover of graph *g*. For bipartite graphs, the function uses the polynomial-time Hungarian algorithm. For everything else, the function uses brute force.

See also MaximumClique, MaximumIndependentSet, VertexCoverQ ■ See page 317

■ MultipleEdgesQ

MultipleEdgesQ[g] yields True if *g* has multiple edges between pairs of vertices. It yields False otherwise.

New function ■ See also MakeSimple, SimpleQ ■ See page 198

■ MultiplicationTable

MultiplicationTable[l, f] constructs the complete transition table defined by the binary relation function *f* on the elements of list *l*.

See also PermutationGroupQ ■ See page 112

■ MycielskiGraph

MycielskiGraph[k] returns a triangle-free graph with chromatic number *k*, for any positive integer *k*.

New function ■ See also ChromaticNumber, Harary ■ See page 312

■ NecklacePolynomial

NecklacePolynomial[n, c, Cyclic] returns a polynomial in the colors in *c* whose coefficients represent numbers of ways of coloring an *n*-bead necklace with colors chosen from *c*, assuming that two colorings are equivalent if one can be obtained from the other by a rotation. NecklacePolynomial[n, c, Dihedral] is different in that it considers two colorings equivalent if one can be obtained from the other by a rotation or a flip or both.

New function ■ See also ListNecklaces, NumberOfNecklaces ■ See page 6

■ Neighborhood

Neighborhood[g, v, k] returns the subset of vertices in *g* that are at a distance of *k* or less from vertex *v*. Neighborhood[al, v, k] behaves identically, except that it takes as input an adjacency list *al*.

New function ■ See also Distances, GraphPower ■ See page 364

■ NetworkFlow

NetworkFlow[g, source, sink] returns the value of a maximum flow through graph *g* from source to sink. NetworkFlow[g, source, sink, Edge] returns the edges in *g* that have positive flow along with their flows in a maximum flow from source to sink. NetworkFlow[g, source, sink, Cut] returns a minimum cut between source and sink. NetworkFlow[g, source, sink, All] returns the adjacency list of *g* along with flows on each edge in a maximum flow from source to sink. *g* can be a directed or an undirected graph.

See also EdgeConnectivity, NetworkFlowEdges, VertexConnectivity ■ See page 341

■ NetworkFlowEdges

NetworkFlowEdges[g, source, sink] returns the edges of the graph with positive flow, showing the distribution of a maximum flow from source to sink in graph *g*. This is obsolete, and NetworkFlow[g, source, sink, Edge] should be used instead.

See also NetworkFlow ■ See page 38

■ NextBinarySubset

NextBinarySubset[l, s] constructs the subset of *l* following subset *s* in the order obtained by interpreting subsets as binary string representations of integers.

New function ■ See also NextKSubset, NextSubset ■ See page 77

■ NextComposition

NextComposition[l] constructs the integer composition that follows *l* in a canonical order.

See also Compositions, RandomComposition ■ See page 148

■ NextGrayCodeSubset

NextGrayCodeSubset[l, s] constructs the successor of *s* in the Gray code of set *l*.

New function ■ See also NextKSubset, NextSubset ■ See page 81

■ NextKSubset

NextKSubset[l, s] gives the *k*-subset of list *l*, following the *k*-subset *s* in lexicographic order.

See also KSubsets, RandomKSubset ■ See page 83

■ NextLexicographicSubset

NextLexicographicSubset[l, s] gives the lexicographic successor of subset *s* of set *l*.

New function ■ See also NextKSubset, NextSubset ■ See page 82

■ NextPartition

NextPartition[p] gives the integer partition following *p* in reverse lexicographic order.

See also Partitions, RandomPartition ■ See page 137

■ NextPermutation

NextPermutation[p] gives the permutation following *p* in lexicographic order.

See also NthPermutation ■ See page 57

■ NextSubset

NextSubset[l, s] constructs the subset of *l* following subset *s* in canonical order.

See also NthSubset, RankSubset ■ See page 6

■ NextTableau

NextTableau[t] gives the tableau of shape *t*, following *t* in lexicographic order.

See also RandomTableau, Tableaux ■ See page 9

■ NoMultipleEdges

NoMultipleEdges is an option value for Type.

New function ■ See also GraphOptions, ShowGraph ■ See page 31

■ NonLineGraphs

NonLineGraphs returns a graph whose connected components are the nine graphs whose presence as a vertex-induced subgraph in a graph g makes g a nonline graph.

New function ▪ See also FiniteGraphs, LineGraph ▪ See page 242

■ NoPerfectMatchingGraph

NoPerfectMatchingGraph returns a connected graph with 16 vertices that contains no perfect matching.

New function ▪ See also BipartiteMatching, FiniteGraphs ▪ See page 344

■ Normal

Normal is a value that options VertexStyle, EdgeStyle, and PlotRange can take on in ShowGraph.

New function ▪ See also GraphOptions, SetGraphOptions ▪ See page 201

■ NormalDashed

NormalDashed is a value that the option EdgeStyle can take on in the graph data structure or in ShowGraph.

New function ▪ See also GraphOptions, SetGraphOptions ▪ See page 204

■ NormalizeVertices

NormalizeVertices[v] gives a list of vertices with a similar embedding as v but with all coordinates of all points scaled to be between 0 and 1.

See also DilateVertices, RotateVertices, TranslateVertices ▪

■ NoSelfLoops

NoSelfLoops is an option value for Type.

New function ▪ See also GraphOptions, ShowGraph ▪ See page 31

■ NthPair

NthPair[n] returns the nth unordered pair of distinct positive integers when sequenced to minimize the size of the larger integer. Pairs that have the same larger integer are sequenced in increasing order of their smaller integer.

See also Contract, ExactRandomGraph ▪ See page 263

■ **NthPermutation**

NthPermutation[n, l] gives the *n*th lexicographic permutation of list *l*. This function is obsolete; use UnrankPermutation instead.

See also LexicographicPermutations, RankPermutation ■ See page 39

■ **NthSubset**

NthSubset[n, l] gives the *n*th subset of list *l* in canonical order.

See also NextSubset, RankSubset ■ See page 6

■ **NumberOf2Paths**

NumberOf2Paths[g, v, k] returns a sorted list that contains the number of paths of length 2 to different vertices of *g* from *v*.

New function ■ See also Invariants ■ See page 365

■ **NumberOfCompositions**

NumberOfCompositions[n, k] counts the number of distinct compositions of integer *n* into *k* parts.

See also Compositions, RandomComposition ■ See page 146

■ **NumberOfDerangements**

NumberOfDerangements[n] counts the derangements on *n* elements, that is, the permutations without any fixed points.

See also DerangementQ, Derangements ■ See page 107

■ **NumberOfDirectedGraphs**

NumberOfDirectedGraphs[n] returns the number of nonisomorphic directed graphs with *n* vertices. NumberOfDirectedGraphs[n, m] returns the number of nonisomorphic directed graphs with *n* vertices and *m* edges.

New function ■ See also ListGraphs, NumberOfGraphs ■ See page 9

■ **NumberOfGraphs**

NumberOfGraphs[n] returns the number of nonisomorphic undirected graphs with *n* vertices. NumberOfGraphs[n, m] returns the number of nonisomorphic undirected graphs with *n* vertices and *m* edges.

New function ■ See also ListGraphs, NumberOfGraphs ■ See page 129

■ **NumberOfInvolutions**

> NumberOfInvolutions[n] counts the number of involutions on n elements.
>
> See also InvolutionQ ■ See page 105

■ **NumberOfKPaths**

> NumberOfKPaths[g, v, k] returns a sorted list that contains the number of paths of length k to different vertices of g from v. NumberOfKPaths[al, v, k] behaves identically, except that it takes an adjacency list *al* as input.
>
> New function ■ See also GraphPower, Invariants ■ See page 365

■ **NumberOfNecklaces**

> NumberOfNecklaces[n, nc, Cyclic] returns the number of distinct ways in which an n-bead necklace can be colored with *nc* colors, assuming that two colorings are equivalent if one can be obtained from the other by a rotation. NumberOfNecklaces[n, nc, Dihedral] returns the number of distinct ways in which an n-bead necklace can be colored with *nc* colors, assuming that two colorings are equivalent if one can be obtained from the other by a rotation or a flip.
>
> New function ■ See also ListNecklaces, NecklacePolynomial ■ See page 9

■ **NumberOfPartitions**

> NumberOfPartitions[n] counts the number of integer partitions of n.
>
> See also Partitions, RandomPartition ■ See page 136

■ **NumberOfPermutationsByCycles**

> NumberOfPermutationsByCycles[n, m] gives the number of permutations of length n with exactly m cycles.
>
> See also Polya ■ See page 103

■ **NumberOfPermutationsByInversions**

> NumberOfPermutationsByInversions[n, k] gives the number of permutations of length n with exactly k inversions. NumberOfPermutationsByInversions[n] gives a table of the number of length-n permutations with k inversions, for all k.
>
> New function ■ See also Inversions, ToInversionVector ■ See page 73

■ **NumberOfPermutationsByType**

> NumberOfPermutationsByTypes[l] gives the number of permutations of type l.
>
> New function ■ See also OrbitRepresentatives, ToCycles ■ See page 99

■ NumberOfSpanningTrees

NumberOfSpanningTrees[g] gives the number of labeled spanning trees of graph *g*.

See also Cofactor, MinimumSpanningTree ■ See page 399

■ NumberOfTableaux

NumberOfTableaux[p] uses the hook length formula to count the number of Young tableaux with shape defined by partition *p*.

See also CatalanNumber, Tableaux ■ See page 168

■ OctahedralGraph

OctahedralGraph returns the graph corresponding to the octahedron, a Platonic solid.

New function ■ See also DodecahedralGraph, FiniteGraphs ■ See page 370

■ OddGraph

OddGraph[n] returns the graph whose vertices are the size-$(n-1)$ subsets of a size-$(2n-1)$ set and whose edges connect pairs of vertices that correspond to disjoint subsets. OddGraph[3] is the Petersen graph.

New function ■ See also GeneralizedPetersenGraph, Harary ■ See page 23

■ One

One is a tag used in several functions to inform the functions that only one object need be considered or only one solution need be produced, as opposed to all objects or all solutions.

New function ■ See also Backtrack ■ See page 212

■ Optimum

Optimum is a value that the option Algorithm can take on when used in the functions VertexColoring and VertexCover.

New function ■ See also VertexColoring, VertexCover ■ See page 31

■ OrbitInventory

OrbitInventory[ci, x, w] returns the value of the cycle index *ci* when each formal variable $x[i]$ is replaced by *w*. OrbitInventory[ci, x, weights] returns the inventory of orbits induced on a set of functions by the action of a group with cycle index *ci*. It is assumed that each element in the range of the functions is assigned a weight in list weights.

New function ■ See also OrbitRepresentatives, Orbits ■ See page 127

■ OrbitRepresentatives

OrbitRepresentatives[pg, x] returns a representative of each orbit of x induced by the action of the group pg on x. pg is assumed to be a set of permutations on the first n natural numbers, and x is a set of functions whose domain is the first n natural numbers. Each function in x is specified as an n-tuple.

New function ■ See also OrbitInventory, Orbits ■ See page 117

■ Orbits

Orbits[pg, x] returns the orbits of x induced by the action of the group pg on x. pg is assumed to be a set of permutations on the first n natural numbers, and x is a set of functions whose domain is the first n natural numbers. Each function in x is specified as an n-tuple.

New function ■ See also OrbitInventory, OrbitRepresentatives ■ See page 117

■ Ordered

Ordered is an option to the functions KSubsetGroup and KSubsetGroupIndex that tells the functions whether they should treat the input as sets or tuples.

New function ■ See also KSubsetGroup ■ See page 114

■ OrientGraph

OrientGraph[g] assigns a direction to each edge of a bridgeless, undirected graph g, so that the graph is strongly connected.

See also ConnectedQ, StronglyConnectedComponents ■ See page 286

■ OutDegree

OutDegree[g, n] returns the out-degree of vertex n in directed graph g. OutDegree[g] returns the sequence of out-degrees of the vertices in directed graph g.

New function ■ See also Degrees, InDegree ■ See page 297

■ PairGroup

PairGroup[g] returns the group induced on 2-sets by the permutation group g.
PairGroup[g, Ordered] returns the group induced on ordered pairs with distinct elements by the permutation group g.

New function ■ See also OrbitInventory, SymmetricGroup ■ See page 6

■ PairGroupIndex

PairGroupIndex[g, x] returns the cycle index of the pair group induced by g as a polynomial in $x[1], x[2], \ldots$ PairGroupIndex[ci, x] takes the cycle index ci of a group g with formal variables $x[1], x[2], \ldots$ and returns the cycle index of the pair group induced by g. PairGroupIndex[g, x, Ordered] returns the cycle index of the ordered pair group induced by g as a polynomial in $x[1], x[2], \ldots$ PairGroupIndex[ci, x, Ordered] takes the cycle index ci of a group g with formal variables $x[1], x[2], \ldots$ and returns the cycle index of the ordered pair group induced by g.

New function ■ See also OrbitInventory, SymmetricGroupIndex ■ See page 129

■ Parent

Parent is a tag used as an argument to the function AllPairsShortestPath in order to inform this function that information about parents in the shortest paths is also wanted.

New function ■ See also AllPairsShortestPath ■ See page 331

■ ParentsToPaths

ParentsToPaths[l, i, j] takes a list of parents l and returns the path from i to j encoded in the parent list. ParentsToPaths[l, i] returns the paths from i to all vertices.

New function ■ See also AllPairsShortestPath, BreadthFirstTraversal ■ See page 31

■ PartialOrderQ

PartialOrderQ[g] yields True if the binary relation defined by edges of the graph g is a partial order, meaning it is transitive, reflexive, and antisymmetric. PartialOrderQ[r] yields True if the binary relation defined by the square matrix r is a partial order.

See also HasseDiagram, TransitiveQ ■ See page 352

■ PartitionLattice

PartitionLattice[n] returns a Hasse diagram of the partially ordered set on set partitions of 1 through n in which $p < q$ if q is finer than p, that is, each block in q is contained in some block in p. The function takes two options: Type and VertexLabel, with default values Undirected and False, respectively. When Type is set to Directed, the function produces the underlying directed acyclic graph. When VertexLabel is set to True, labels are produced for the vertices.

New function ■ See also DominationLattice, HasseDiagram ■ See page 360

■ PartitionQ

PartitionQ[p] yields True if p is an integer partition. PartitionQ[n, p] yields True if p is a partition of n.

See also Partitions ■ See page 136

■ Partitions

Partitions[n] constructs all partitions of integer *n* in reverse lexicographic order. Partitions[n, k] constructs all partitions of the integer *n* with maximum part at most *k*, in reverse lexicographic order.

See also NextPartition, RandomPartition ▪ See page 136

■ Path

Path[n] constructs a tree consisting only of a path on *n* vertices. Path[n] permits an option Type that takes on the values Directed and Undirected. The default setting is Type -> Undirected.

See also GridGraph, ShortestPath ▪ See page 240

■ PathConditionGraph

Usage of PathConditionGraph is obsolete. This functionality is no longer supported in *Combinatorica*.

■ PerfectQ

PerfectQ[g] yields True if *g* is a perfect graph, meaning that for every induced subgraph of *g* the size of the largest clique equals the chromatic number.

See also ChromaticNumber, MaximumClique ▪ See page 26

■ PermutationGraph

PermutationGraph[p] gives the permutation graph for the permutation *p*.

New function ▪ See also DistinctPermutations, MakeGraph ▪ See page 71

■ PermutationGroupQ

PermutationGroupQ[l] yields True if the list of permutations *l* forms a permutation group.

See also Automorphisms, MultiplicationTable ▪ See page 6

■ PermutationQ

PermutationQ[p] yields True if *p* is a list representing a permutation and False otherwise.

See also Permute ▪ See page 55

■ PermutationToTableaux

PermutationToTableaux[p] returns the tableaux pair that can be constructed from *p* using the Robinson-Schensted-Knuth correspondence.

New function ▪ See also Involutions, Tableaux ▪ See page 166

■ **PermutationType**

PermutationType[p] returns the type of permutation *p*.

New function ▪ See also NumberOfPermutationsByType, ToCycles ▪ See page 98

■ **PermutationWithCycle**

PermutationWithCycle[n, i, j, ...] gives a size-n permutation in which $\{i, j, ...\}$ is a cycle and all other elements are fixed points.

New function ▪ See also FromCycles, ToCycles ▪ See page 96

■ **Permute**

Permute[l, p] permutes list *l* according to permutation *p*.

See also InversePermutation, PermutationQ ▪ See page 55

■ **PermuteSubgraph**

PermuteSubgraph[g, p] permutes the vertices of a subgraph of *g* induced by *p* according to *p*.

New function ▪ See also InduceSubgraph, Isomorphism ▪ See page 235

■ **PetersenGraph**

PetersenGraph returns the Petersen graph, a graph whose vertices can be viewed as the size-2 subsets of a size-5 set with edges connecting disjoint subsets.

New function ▪ See also FiniteGraphs, GeneralizedPetersenGraph ▪ See page 190

■ **PlanarQ**

PlanarQ[g] yields True if graph *g* is planar, meaning it can be drawn in the plane so no two edges cross.

See also ShowGraph ▪ See page 370

■ **PointsAndLines**

PointsAndLines is now obsolete.

■ **Polya**

Polya[g, m] returns the polynomial giving the number of colorings, with *m* colors, of a structure defined by the permutation group *g*. Polya is obsolete; use OrbitInventory instead.

See also Automorphisms, PermutationGroupQ ▪ See page 39

■ PseudographQ

PseudographQ[g] yields True if graph *g* is a pseudograph, meaning it contains self-loops.

See also RemoveSelfLoops ■ See page 198

■ RadialEmbedding

RadialEmbedding[g, v] constructs a radial embedding of the graph *g* in which vertices are placed on concentric circles around *v* depending on their distance from *v*. RadialEmbedding[g] constructs a radial embedding of graph *g*, radiating from the center of the graph.

See also RandomTree, RootedEmbedding ■ See page 217

■ Radius

Radius[g] gives the radius of graph *g*, the minimum eccentricity of any vertex of *g*.

See also Diameter, Eccentricity ■ See page 332

■ RandomComposition

RandomComposition[n, k] constructs a random composition of integer *n* into *k* parts.

See also Compositions, NumberOfCompositions ■ See page 146

■ RandomGraph

RandomGraph[n, p] constructs a random labeled graph on n vertices with an edge probability of *p*. An option Type is provided, which can take on values Directed and Undirected and whose default value is Undirected. Type->Directed produces a corresponding random directed graph. The usages Random[n, p, Directed], Random[n, p, range], and Random[n, p, range, Directed] are all obsolete. Use SetEdgeWeights to set random edge weights.

See also ExactRandomGraph, RealizeDegreeSequence ■ See page 262

■ RandomHeap

RandomHeap[n] constructs a random heap on *n* elements.

See also Heapify, HeapSort ■ See page 5

■ RandomInteger

RandomInteger is a value that the WeightingFunction option of the function SetEdgeWeights can take.

New function ■ See also GraphOptions, SetEdgeWeights ■ See page 197

■ **RandomKSetPartition**

RandomKSetPartition[set, k] returns a random set partition of a set with *k* blocks.
RandomKSetPartition[n, k] returns a random set partition of the first *n* natural numbers into *k* blocks.

New function ▪ See also KSetPartitions, RandomSetPartition ▪ See page 158

■ **RandomKSubset**

RandomKSubset[l, k] gives a random subset of set *l* with exactly *k* elements.

See also KSubsets, NextKSubset ▪ See page 87

■ **RandomPartition**

RandomPartition[n] constructs a random partition of integer *n*.

See also NumberOfPartitions, Partitions ▪ See page 144

■ **RandomPermutation**

RandomPermutation[n] generates a random permutation of the first *n* natural numbers.

See also NthPermutation ▪ See page 61

■ **RandomPermutation1**

RandomPermutation1 is now obsolete. Use RandomPermutation instead.

See also RandomPermutation

■ **RandomPermutation2**

RandomPermutation2 is now obsolete. Use RandomPermutation instead.

See also RandomPermutation

■ **RandomRGF**

RandomRGF[n] returns a random restricted growth function (RGF) defined on the first *n* natural numbers. RandomRGF[n, k] returns a random RGF defined on the first *n* natural numbers having a maximum element equal to *k*.

New function ▪ See also RandomSetPartition, RGFs ▪ See page 9

■ RandomSetPartition

RandomSetPartition[set] returns a random set partition of *set*. RandomSetPartition[n] returns a random set partition of the first *n* natural numbers.

New function ▪ See also RandomPartition, RandomRGF ▪ See page 158

■ RandomSubset

RandomSubset[l] creates a random subset of set *l*.

See also NthSubset, Subsets ▪ See page 78

■ RandomTableau

RandomTableau[p] constructs a random Young tableau of shape *p*.

See also NextTableau, Tableaux ▪ See page 170

■ RandomTree

RandomTree[n] constructs a random labeled tree on *n* vertices.

See also CodeToLabeledTree, TreeQ ▪ See page 260

■ RandomVertices

RandomVertices[g] assigns a random embedding to graph *g*.

See also RandomGraph ▪ See page 304

■ RankBinarySubset

RankBinarySubset[l, s] gives the rank of subset *s* of set *l* in the ordering of subsets of *l*, obtained by interpreting these subsets as binary string representations of integers.

New function ▪ See also RankSubset, UnrankSubset ▪ See page 77

■ RankedEmbedding

RankedEmbedding[l] takes a set partition *l* of vertices $\{1, 2, ..., n\}$ and returns an embedding of the vertices in the plane such that the vertices in each block occur on a vertical line with block 1 vertices on the leftmost line, block 2 vertices on the next line, and so on. RankedEmbedding[g, l] takes a graph *g* and a set partition *l* of the vertices of *g* and returns the graph *g* with vertices embedded according to RankedEmbedding[l]. RankedEmbedding[g, s] takes a graph *g* and a set *s* of vertices of *g* and returns a ranked embedding of *g* in which vertices in *s* are in block 1, vertices at distance 1 from any vertex in block 1 are in block 2, and so on.

See also RankGraph ▪ See page 215

■ RankGraph

RankGraph[g, l] partitions the vertices into classes based on the shortest geodesic distance to a member of list *l*.

See also RankedEmbedding ■ See page 215

■ RankGrayCodeSubset

RankGrayCodeSubset[l, s] gives the rank of subset *s* of set *l* in the Gray code ordering of the subsets of *l*.

New function ■ See also GrayCodeSubsets, UnrankGrayCodeSubset ■ See page 80

■ RankKSetPartition

RankKSetPartition[sp, s] ranks *sp* in the list of all *k*-block set partitions of *s*. RankSetPartition[sp] ranks *sp* in the list of all *k*-block set partitions of the set of elements that appear in any subset in *sp*.

New function ■ See also RankSetPartition, UnrankKSetPartition ■ See page 156

■ RankKSubset

RankKSubset[s, l] gives the rank of *k*-subset *s* of set *l* in the lexicographic ordering of *k*-subsets of *l*.

New function ■ See also UnrankGrayCodeSubset, UnrankKSubset ■ See page 84

■ RankPermutation

RankPermutation[p] gives the rank of permutation *p* in lexicographic order.

See also LexicographicPermutations, NthPermutation ■ See page 60

■ RankRGF

RankRGF[f] returns the rank of a restricted growth function (RGF) *f* in the lexicographic order of all RGFs.

New function ■ See also RankSetPartition, UnrankRGF ■ See page 9

■ RankSetPartition

RankSetPartition[sp, s] ranks *sp* in the list of all set partitions of set *s*. RankSetPartition[sp] ranks *sp* in the list of all set partitions of the set of elements that appear in any subset in *sp*.

New function ■ See also RankRGF, UnrankSetPartition ■ See page 156

■ RankSubset

RankSubset[l, s] gives the rank, in canonical order, of subset *s* of set *l*.

See also NextSubset, NthSubset ■ See page 6

■ ReadGraph

ReadGraph[f] reads a graph represented as edge lists from file *f* and returns a graph object.

See also WriteGraph

■ RealizeDegreeSequence

RealizeDegreeSequence[s] constructs a semirandom graph with degree sequence *s*.

See also GraphicQ, DegreeSequence ■ See page 267

■ ReflexiveQ

ReflexiveQ[g] yields True if the adjacency matrix of *g* represents a reflexive binary relation.

New function ■ See also PartialOrderQ, SymmetricQ ■ See page 115

■ RegularGraph

RegularGraph[k, n] constructs a semirandom *k*-regular graph on *n* vertices, if such a graph exists.

See also RealizeDegreeSequence, RegularQ ■ See page 268

■ RegularQ

RegularQ[g] yields True if *g* is a regular graph.

See also DegreeSequence, RegularGraph ■ See page 268

■ RemoveMultipleEdges

RemoveMultipleEdges[g] returns the graph obtained by deleting multiple edges from *g*.

New function ■ See also MakeSimple, MultipleEdgesQ ■ See page 199

■ RemoveSelfLoops

RemoveSelfLoops[g] returns the graph obtained by deleting self-loops in *g*.

See also PseudographQ, SimpleQ ■ See page 199

■ ResidualFlowGraph

ResidualFlowGraph[g, flow] returns the directed residual flow graph for a graph *g* with respect to *flow*.

New function ■ See also NetworkFlow ■ See page 341

■ RevealCycles

RevealCycles[p] unveils the canonical hidden cycle structure of permutation *p*.

See also ToCycles, FromCycles, RevealCycles ■ See page 100

■ ReverseEdges

ReverseEdges[g] flips the directions of all edges in a directed graph.

New function ■ See also MakeUndirected, OrientGraph ■ See page 14

■ RGFQ

RGFQ[l] yields True if *l* is a restricted growth function. It yields False otherwise.

New function ■ See also RGFs, SetPartitionQ ■ See page 9

■ RGFs

RGFs[n] lists all restricted growth functions on the first *n* natural numbers in lexicographic order.

New function ■ See also KSetPartitions, SetPartitions ■ See page 159

■ RGFToSetPartition

RGFToSetPartition[rgf, set] converts the restricted growth function *rgf* into the corresponding set partition of *set*. If the optional second argument, set, is not supplied, then *rgf* is converted into a set partition of $\{1, 2, ..., n\}$, where *n* is the length of *rgf*.

New function ■ See also RandomRGF, SetPartitionToRGF ■ See page 159

■ RobertsonGraph

RobertsonGraph returns a 19-vertex graph that is the unique (4, 5)-cage graph.

New function ■ See also CageGraph, FiniteGraphs ■ See page 23

■ RootedEmbedding

RootedEmbedding[g, v] constructs a rooted embedding of graph *g* with vertex *v* as the root.
RootedEmbedding[g] constructs a rooted embedding with a center of *g* as the root.

See also RadialEmbedding ■ See page 218

■ RotateVertices

RotateVertices[v, theta] rotates each vertex position in list *v* by *theta* radians about the origin (0, 0).
RotateVertices[g, theta] rotates the embedding of the graph *g* by *theta* radians about the origin (0, 0).

See also RotateVertices, TranslateVertices ■ See page 219

■ Runs

Runs[p] partitions *p* into contiguous increasing subsequences.

See also Eulerian ■ See page 74

■ SamenessRelation

SamenessRelation[l] constructs a binary relation from a list *l* of permutations, which is an equivalence relation if *l* is a permutation group.

See also EquivalenceRelationQ, PermutationGroupQ ■ See page 6

■ SelectionSort

SelectionSort[l, f] sorts list *l* using ordering function *f*.

See also BinarySearch, HeapSort ■ See page 5

■ SelfComplementaryQ

SelfComplementaryQ[g] yields True if graph *g* is self-complementary, meaning it is isomorphic to its complement.

See also GraphComplement, Isomorphism ■ See page 369

■ SelfLoopsQ

SelfLoopsQ[g] yields True if graph *g* has self-loops.

New function ■ See also MultipleEdgesQ, SimpleQ ■ See page 26

■ SetEdgeLabels

SetEdgeLabels[g, l] assigns the labels in l to edges of g. If l is shorter than the number of edges in g, then labels get assigned cyclically. If l is longer than the number of edges in g, then the extra labels are ignored.

New function ▪ See also GraphOptions, SetGraphOptions ▪ See page 197

■ SetEdgeWeights

SetEdgeWeights[g] assigns random real weights in the range $[0, 1]$ to edges in g. SetEdgeWeights accepts options WeightingFunction and WeightRange. WeightingFunction can take values Random, RandomInteger, Euclidean, or LNorm[n] for nonnegative n, or any pure function that takes two arguments, each argument having the form {Integer, {Number, Number}}. WeightRange can be an integer range or a real range. The default value for WeightingFunction is Random, and the default value for WeightRange is $[0, 1]$. SetEdgeWeights[g, e] assigns edge weights to the edges in the edge list e. SetEdgeWeights[g, w] assigns the weights in the weight list w to the edges of g. SetEdgeWeights[g, e, w] assigns the weights in the weight list w to the edges in edge list e.

New function ▪ See also GraphOptions, SetGraphOptions ▪ See page 197

■ SetGraphOptions

SetGraphOptions[g, opts] returns g with the options *opts* set.
SetGraphOptions[g, v1, v2, ..., vopts, gopts] returns the graph with the options *vopts* set for vertices $v1, v2,...$ and the options *gopts* set for the graph g.
SetGraphOptions[g, e1, e2,..., eopts, gopts], with edges $e1, e2,...$, works similarly.
SetGraphOptions[g, elements1, opts1, elements2, opts2,..., opts] returns g with the options *opts*1 set for the elements in the sequence *elements*1, the options *opts*2 set for the elements in the sequence *elements*2, and so on. Here, elements can be a sequence of edges or a sequence of vertices. A tag that takes on values One or All can also be passed in as an argument before any options. The default value of the tag is All, and it is useful if the graph has multiple edges. It informs the function about whether all edges that connect a pair of vertices are to be affected or only one edge is affected.

New function ▪ See also GraphOptions ▪ See page 196

■ SetPartitionListViaRGF

SetPartitionListViaRGF[n] lists all set partitions of the first n natural numbers, by first listing all restricted growth functions (RGFs) on these and then mapping the RGFs to corresponding set partitions. SetPartitionListViaRGF[n, k] lists all RGFs on the first n natural numbers whose maximum element is k and then maps these RGFs into the corresponding set partitions, all of which contain exactly k blocks.

New function ▪ See also RGFs, SetPartitions ▪ See page 9

■ SetPartitionQ

SetPartitionQ[sp, s] determines if *sp* is a set partition of set *s*. SetPartitionQ[sp] tests if *sp* is a set of disjoint sets.

New function ■ See also CoarserSetPartitionQ, PartitionQ ■ See page 149

■ SetPartitions

SetPartitions[s] returns the list of set partitions of *s*. SetPartitions[n] returns the list of set partitions of $\{1, 2, ..., n\}$. If all set partitions with a fixed number of subsets are needed, use KSetPartitions.

New function ■ See also KSetPartitions, RandomSetPartition ■ See page 152

■ SetPartitionToRGF

SetPartitionToRGF[sp, s] converts the set partition *sp* of set *s* into the corresponding restricted growth function. If the optional argument *s* is not specified, then it is assumed that *Mathematica* knows the underlying order on the set for which *sp* is a set partition.

New function ■ See also RGFToSetPartition, RGFs ■ See page 159

■ SetVertexLabels

SetVertexLabels[g, l] assigns the labels in *l* to vertices of *g*. If *l* is shorter than the number of vertices in *g*, then labels get assigned cyclically. If *l* is longer than the number of vertices in *g*, then the extra labels are ignored.

New function ■ See also GraphOptions, SetGraphOptions ■ See page 197

■ SetVertexWeights

SetVertexWeights[g] assigns random real weights in the range $[0, 1]$ to vertices in *g*. SetVertexWeights accepts options WeightingFunction and WeightRange. WeightingFunction can take values Random, RandomInteger, or any pure function that takes two arguments, an integer as the first argument and a pair {*number, number*} as the second argument. WeightRange can be an integer range or a real range. The default value for WeightingFunction is Random, and the default value for WeightRange is $[0, 1]$. SetVertexWeights[g, w] assigns the weights in the weight list *w* to the vertices of *g*. SetVertexWeights[g, vs, w] assigns the weights in the weight list *w* to the vertices in the vertex list *vs*.

New function ■ See also GraphOptions, SetGraphOptions ■ See page 197

■ ShakeGraph

ShakeGraph[g, d] performs a random perturbation of the vertices of graph *g*, with each vertex moving, at most, a distance *d* from its original position.

See also ShowGraph, SpringEmbedding ■ See page 220

■ ShortestPath

ShortestPath[g, start, end] finds a shortest path between vertices *start* and *end* in graph *g*. An option Algorithm that takes on the values Automatic, Dijkstra, or BellmanFord is provided. This allows a choice between using Dijkstra's algorithm and the Bellman-Ford algorithm. The default is Algorithm -> Automatic. In this case, depending on whether edges have negative weights and depending on the density of the graph, the algorithm chooses between Bellman-Ford and Dijkstra.

See also AllPairsShortestPath, ShortestPathSpanningTree ■ See page 329

■ ShortestPathSpanningTree

ShortestPathSpanningTree[g, v] constructs a shortest-path spanning tree rooted at *v*, so that a shortest path in graph *g* from *v* to any other vertex is a path in the tree. An option Algorithm that takes on the values Automatic, Dijkstra, or BellmanFord is provided. This allows a choice between Dijkstra's algorithm and the Bellman-Ford algorithm. The default is Algorithm -> Automatic. In this case, depending on whether edges have negative weights and depending on the density of the graph, the algorithm chooses between Bellman-Ford and Dijkstra.

See also AllPairsShortestPath, MinimumSpanningTree, ShortestPath ■ See page 329

■ ShowGraph

ShowGraph[g] displays the graph *g*. ShowGraph[g, options] modifies the display using the given options. ShowGraph[g, Directed] is obsolete and is currently identical to ShowGraph[g]. All options that affect the look of a graph can be specified as options in ShowGraph. The list of options is VertexColor, VertexStyle, VertexNumber, VertexNumberColor, VertexNumberPosition, VertexLabel, VertexLabelColor, VertexLabelPosition, EdgeColor, EdgeStyle, EdgeLabel, EdgeLabelColor, EdgeLabelPosition, LoopPosition, and EdgeDirection. In addition, options of the Mathematica function Plot and options of the graphics primitive Arrow can also be specified here. If an option specified in ShowGraph differs from options explicitly set within a graph object, then options specified inside the graph object are used.

See also AnimateGraph, ShowGraphArray ■ See page 200

■ ShowGraphArray

ShowGraphArray[{g1, g2, ...}] displays a row of graphs.
ShowGraphArray[{ {g1, ...}, {g2, ...}, ...}] displays a two-dimensional table of graphs.
ShowGraphArray accepts all the options accepted by ShowGraph, and the user can also provide the option GraphicsSpacing -> d.

New function ■ See also AnimateGraph, ShowGraph ■ See page 210

■ ShowLabeledGraph

ShowLabeledGraph[g] displays graph g according to its embedding, with each vertex labeled with its vertex number. ShowLabeledGraph[g, l] uses the ith element of list l as the label for vertex i.

See also ShowGraph ▪ See page 19

■ ShuffleExchangeGraph

ShuffleExchangeGraph[n] returns the n-dimensional shuffle-exchange graph whose vertices are length-n binary strings with an edge from w to w' if (i) w' differs from w in its last bit or (ii) w' is obtained from w by a cyclic shift left or a cyclic shift right. An option VertexLabel is provided, with default setting False, which can be set to True if the user wants to associate the binary strings to the vertices as labels.

New function ▪ See also ButterflyGraph, DeBruijnGraph, Hypercube ▪ See page 255

■ SignaturePermutation

SignaturePermutation[p] gives the signature of permutation p.

See also MinimumChangePermutations, ToCycles ▪ See page 97

■ Simple

Simple is an option value for Type.

New function ▪ See also MakeGraph, ToAdjacencyMatrix ▪ See page 185

■ SimpleQ

SimpleQ[g] yields True if g is a simple graph, meaning it has no multiple edges and contains no self-loops.

See also PseudographQ, UnweightedQ ▪ See page 198

■ Small

Small is a symbol used to denote the size of the object that represents a vertex. The option VertexStyle can be set to Disk[Small] or Box[Small] either inside the graph data structure or in ShowGraph.

New function ▪ See also GraphOptions, SetGraphOptions ▪ See page 202

■ SmallestCyclicGroupGraph

SmallestCyclicGroupGraph returns a smallest nontrivial graph whose automorphism group is cyclic.

New function ▪ See also Automorphisms, FiniteGraphs ▪ See page 23

■ Spectrum

Spectrum[g] gives the eigenvalues of graph *g*.

See also Edges ▪ See page 27

■ SpringEmbedding

SpringEmbedding[g] beautifies the embedding of graph *g* by modeling the embedding as a system of springs. SpringEmbedding[g, step, increment] can be used to refine the algorithm. The value of *step* tells the function how many iterations to run the algorithm. The value of *increment* tells the function the distance to move the vertices at each step. The default values are 10 and 0.15 for *step* and *increment*, respectively.

See also ShakeGraph, ShowGraph ▪ See page 221

■ StableMarriage

StableMarriage[mpref, fpref] finds the male optimal stable marriage defined by lists of permutations describing male and female preferences.

See also BipartiteMatching, MaximalMatching ▪ See page 350

■ Star

Star[n] constructs a star on *n* vertices, which is a tree with one vertex of degree $n - 1$.

See also TreeQ, Wheel ▪ See page 248

■ StirlingFirst

StirlingFirst[n, k] returns a Stirling number of the first kind. This is obsolete. Use the built-in *Mathematica* function StirlingS1 instead.

See also NumberOfPermutationsByCycles ▪ See page 103

■ StirlingSecond

StirlingSecond[n, k] returns a Stirling number of the second kind.

See also KSetPartitions and BellB ▪ See page 153

■ Strings

Strings[l, n] constructs all possible strings of length *n* from the elements of list *l*.

See also CodeToLabeledTree, DistinctPermutations ▪ See page 88

■ StronglyConnectedComponents

StronglyConnectedComponents[g] gives the strongly connected components of directed graph g as lists of vertices.

See also ConnectedQ, WeaklyConnectedComponents ▪ See page 285

■ Strong

Strong is an option to ConnectedQ that seeks to determine if a directed graph is strongly connected.

New function ▪ See also ConnectedQ, StronglyConnectedComponents ▪ See page 31

■ Subsets

Subsets[l] gives all subsets of set l.

See also BinarySubsets, GrayCode, LexicographicSubsets ▪ See page 6

■ SymmetricGroup

SymmetricGroup[n] returns the symmetric group on n symbols.

New function ▪ See also AlternatingGroup, OrbitInventory ▪ See page 110

■ SymmetricGroupIndex

SymmetricGroupIndex[n, x] returns the cycle index of the symmetric group on n symbols, expressed as a polynomial in $x[1], x[2], ..., x[n]$.

New function ▪ See also AlternatingGroupIndex, OrbitInventory ▪ See page 123

■ SymmetricQ

SymmetricQ[r] tests if a given square matrix r represents a symmetric relation. SymmetricQ[g] tests if the edges of a given graph represent a symmetric relation.

New function ▪ See also PartialOrderQ, ReflexiveQ ▪ See page 115

■ TableauClasses

TableauClasses[p] partitions the elements of permutation p into classes according to their initial columns during Young tableaux construction.

See also InsertIntoTableau, LongestIncreasingSubsequence ▪ See page 171

■ TableauQ

TableauQ[t] yields True if and only if *t* represents a Young tableau.

See also RandomTableau, Tableaux ■ See page 162

■ Tableaux

Tableaux[p] constructs all tableaux having a shape given by integer partition *p*.

See also NextTableau, RandomTableau ■ See page 163

■ TableauxToPermutation

TableauxToPermutation[t1, t2] constructs the unique permutation associated with Young tableaux *t1* and *t2*, where both tableaux have the same shape.

See also DeleteFromTableau, InsertIntoTableau ■ See page 166

■ TetrahedralGraph

TetrahedralGraph returns the graph corresponding to the tetrahedron, a Platonic solid.

New function ■ See also DodecahedralGraph, FiniteGraphs ■ See page 370

■ Thick

Thick is a value that the option EdgeStyle can take on in the graph data structure or in ShowGraph.

New function ■ See also GraphOptions, SetGraphOptions ■ See page 204

■ ThickDashed

ThickDashed is a value that the option EdgeStyle can take on in the graph data structure or in ShowGraph.

New function ■ See also GraphOptions, SetGraphOptions ■ See page 204

■ Thin

Thin is a value that the option EdgeStyle can take on in the graph data structure or in ShowGraph.

New function ■ See also GraphOptions, SetGraphOptions ■ See page 204

■ ThinDashed

ThinDashed is a value that the option EdgeStyle can take on in the graph data structure or in ShowGraph.

New function ■ See also GraphOptions, SetGraphOptions ■ See page 204

■ ThomassenGraph

ThomassenGraph returns a hypotraceable graph, a graph G that has no Hamiltonian path but whose subgraph $G - v$ for every vertex v has a Hamiltonian path.

New function ■ See also FiniteGraphs, HamiltonianCycle ■ See page 303

■ ToAdjacencyLists

ToAdjacencyLists[g] constructs an adjacency list representation for graph g. It allows an option called Type that takes on values All or Simple. Type -> All is the default setting of the option, and this permits self-loops and multiple edges to be reported in the adjacency lists. Type -> Simple deletes self-loops and multiple edges from the constructed adjacency lists. ToAdjacencyLists[g, EdgeWeight] returns an adjacency list representation along with edge weights.

See also FromAdjacencyLists, ToOrderedPairs ■ See page 186

■ ToAdjacencyMatrix

ToAdjacencyMatrix[g] constructs an adjacency matrix representation for graph g. An option Type that takes on values All or Simple can be used to affect the matrix constructed. Type -> All is the default, and Type -> Simple ignores any self-loops or multiple edges that g may have. ToAdjacencyMatrix[g, EdgeWeight] returns edge weights as entries of the adjacency matrix with Infinity representing missing edges.

New function ■ See also FromAdjacencyMatrix, ToAdjacencyLists ■ See page 189

■ ToCanonicalSetPartition

ToCanonicalSetPartition[sp, s] reorders sp into a canonical order with respect to s. In the canonical order, the elements of each subset of the set partition are ordered as they appear in s, and the subsets themselves are ordered by their first elements. ToCanonicalSetPartition[sp] reorders sp into canonical order, assuming that *Mathematica* knows the underlying order on the set for which sp is a set partition.

New function ■ See also KSetPartitions, SetPartitions ■ See page 149

■ ToCycles

ToCycles[p] gives the cycle structure of permutation p as a list of cyclic permutations.

See also FromCycles, HideCycles, RevealCycles ■ See page 94

■ ToInversionVector

ToInversionVector[p] gives the inversion vector associated with permutation p.

See also FromInversionVector, Inversions ■ See page 69

■ ToOrderedPairs

ToOrderedPairs[g] constructs a list of ordered pairs representing the edges of the graph g. If g is undirected, each edge is interpreted as two ordered pairs. An option called Type that takes on values Simple or All can be used to affect the constructed representation. Type -> Simple forces the removal of multiple edges and self-loops. Type -> All keeps all information and is the default option.

See also FromOrderedPairs, FromUnorderedPairs, ToUnorderedPairs ■ See page 184

■ TopologicalSort

TopologicalSort[g] gives a permutation of the vertices of directed acyclic graph g such that an edge (i, j) implies that vertex i appears before vertex j.

See also AcyclicQ, PartialOrderQ ■ See page 352

■ ToUnorderedPairs

ToUnorderedPairs[g] constructs a list of unordered pairs representing the edges of graph g. Each edge, directed or undirected, results in a pair in which the smaller vertex appears first. An option called Type that takes on values All or Simple can be used, and All is the default value. Type -> Simple ignores multiple edges and self-loops in g.

See also FromOrderedPairs, FromUnorderedPairs, ToOrderedPairs ■ See page 184

■ TransitiveClosure

TransitiveClosure[g] finds the transitive closure of graph g, the supergraph of g that contains edge {x, y} if and only if there is a path from x to y.

See also TransitiveQ, TransitiveReduction ■ See page 354

■ TransitiveQ

TransitiveQ[g] yields True if graph g defines a transitive relation.

See also PartialOrderQ, TransitiveClosure, TransitiveReduction ■ See page 115

■ TransitiveReduction

TransitiveReduction[g] finds a smallest graph that has the same transitive closure as g.

See also HasseDiagram, TransitiveClosure ■ See page 355

■ TranslateVertices

TranslateVertices[v, x, y] adds the vector {x, y} to the vertex embedding location of each vertex in list v. TranslateVertices[g, x, y] translates the embedding of the graph g by the vector {x, y}.

See also NormalizeVertices ■ See page 220

■ TransposePartition

TransposePartition[p] reflects a partition p of k parts along the main diagonal, creating a partition with maximum part k.

See also DurfeeSquare, FerrersDiagram ▪ See page 143

■ TransposeTableau

TransposeTableau[t] reflects a Young tableau t along the main diagonal, creating a different tableau.

See also Tableaux ▪ See page 162

■ TravelingSalesman

TravelingSalesman[g] finds an optimal traveling salesman tour in graph g.

See also HamiltonianCycle, TravelingSalesmanBounds ▪ See page 303

■ TravelingSalesmanBounds

TravelingSalesmanBounds[g] gives upper and lower bounds on a minimum cost traveling salesman tour of graph g.

See also TravelingSalesman, TriangleInequalityQ ▪ See page 31

■ Tree

Tree is an option that informs certain functions for which the user wants the output to be a tree.

New function ▪ See also BreadthFirstTraversal, DepthFirstTraversal ▪ See page 278

■ TreeIsomorphismQ

TreeIsomorphismQ[t1, t2] yields True if the trees $t1$ and $t2$ are isomorphic and False otherwise.

New function ▪ See also Isomorphism, TreeToCertificate ▪ See page 369

■ TreeQ

TreeQ[g] yields True if graph g is a tree.

See also AcyclicQ, RandomTree ▪ See page 295

■ TreeToCertificate

TreeToCertificate[t] returns a binary string that is a certificate for the tree t such that trees have the same certificate if and only if they are isomorphic.

New function ▪ See also Isomorphism, TreeIsomorphismQ ▪ See page 369

■ **TriangleInequalityQ**

TriangleInequalityQ[g] yields True if the weights assigned to the edges of graph *g* satisfy the triangle inequality.

See also AllPairsShortestPath, TravelingSalesmanBounds ▪ See page 304

■ **Turan**

Turan[n, p] constructs the Turan graph, the extremal graph on *n* vertices that does not contain K_p, the complete graph on *p* vertices.

See also CompleteKPartiteGraph, MaximumClique ▪ See page 247

■ **TutteGraph**

TutteGraph returns the Tutte graph, the first known example of a 3-connected, 3-regular, planar graph that is non-Hamiltonian.

New function ▪ See also FiniteGraphs, HamiltonianCycle ▪ See page 301

■ **TwoColoring**

TwoColoring[g] finds a two-coloring of graph *g* if *g* is bipartite. It returns a list of the labels 1 and 2 corresponding to the vertices. This labeling is a valid coloring if and only the graph is bipartite.

See also BipartiteQ, CompleteKPartiteGraph ▪ See page 306

■ **Type**

Type is an option for many functions that transform graphs. Depending on the functions it is being used in, it can take on values such as Directed, Undirected, Simple, etc.

New function ▪ See also GraphOptions, SetGraphOptions ▪ See page 184

■ **Undirected**

Undirected is an option to inform certain functions that the graph is undirected.

New function ▪ See also GraphOptions, SetGraphOptions

■ **UndirectedQ**

UndirectedQ[g] yields True if graph *g* is undirected.

See also MakeUndirected ▪ See page 198

■ UnionSet

UnionSet[a, b, s] merges the sets containing *a* and *b* in union-find data structure *s*.

See also FindSet, InitializeUnionFind, MinimumSpanningTree ■ See page 336

■ Uniquely3ColorableGraph

Uniquely3ColorableGraph returns a 12-vertex, triangle-free graph with chromatic number 3 that is uniquely 3-colorable.

New function ■ See also ChromaticPolynomial, FiniteGraphs ■ See page 23

■ UnitransitiveGraph

UnitransitiveGraph returns a 20-vertex, 3-unitransitive graph discovered by Coxeter that is not isomorphic to a 4-cage or a 5-cage.

New function ■ See also FiniteGraphs, Isomorphism ■ See page 23

■ UnrankBinarySubset

UnrankBinarySubset[n, l] gives the *n*th subset of list *l*, listed in increasing order of integers corresponding to the binary representations of the subsets.

New function ■ See also BinarySubsets, RankBinarySubset ■ See page 77

■ UnrankGrayCodeSubset

UnrankGrayCodeSubset[n, l] gives the *n*th subset of list *l*, listed in Gray code order.

New function ■ See also GrayCodeSubsets, RankGrayCodeSubset ■ See page 80

■ UnrankKSetPartition

UnrankSetPartition[r, s, k] finds a *k*-block set partition of *s* with rank *r*.
UnrankSetPartition[r, n, k] finds a *k*-block set partition of $\{1, 2, ..., n\}$ with rank *r*.

New function ■ See also RankKSetPartition, UnrankSetPartition ■ See page 157

■ UnrankKSubset

UnrankKSubset[m, k, l] gives the *m*th *k*-subset of set *l*, listed in lexicographic order.

New function ■ See also RankKSubset, UnrankSubset ■ See page 85

■ UnrankPermutation

UnrankPermutation[r, l] gives the rth permutation in the lexicographic list of permutations of list l. UnrankPermutation[r, n] gives the rth permutation in the lexicographic list of permutations of $\{1, 2, ..., n\}$.

New function ■ See also DistinctPermutations, RankPermutation ■ See page 60

■ UnrankRGF

UnrankRGF[r, n] returns a restricted growth function defined on the first n natural numbers whose rank is r.

New function ■ See also RankRGF, UnrankSetPartition ■ See page 9

■ UnrankSetPartition

UnrankSetPartition[r, s] finds a set partition of s with rank r. UnrankSetPartition[r, n] finds a set partition of $\{1, 2, ..., n\}$ with rank r.

New function ■ See also RankSetPartition, UnrankKSetPartition ■ See page 158

■ UnrankSubset

UnrankSubset[n, l] gives the nth subset of list l, listed in some canonical order.

New function ■ See also RankSubset, UnrankGrayCodeSubset ■ See page 6

■ UnweightedQ

UnweightedQ[g] yields True if all edge weights are 1 and False otherwise.

See also SimpleQ ■ See page 198

■ UpperLeft

UpperLeft is a value that options VertexNumberPosition, VertexLabelPosition, and EdgeLabelPosition can take on in ShowGraph.

New function ■ See also GraphOptions, SetGraphOptions ■ See page 202

■ UpperRight

UpperRight is a value that options VertexNumberPosition, VertexLabelPosition, and EdgeLabelPosition can take on in ShowGraph.

New function ■ See also GraphOptions, SetGraphOptions ■ See page 202

■ **V**

V[g] gives the order or number of vertices of the graph *g*.

See also M, Vertices ▪ See page 182

■ **Value**

Value is an option for the function NetworkFlow that makes the function return the value of the maximum flow.

New function ▪ See also NetworkFlow

■ **VertexColor**

VertexColor is an option that allows the user to associate colors with vertices. Black is the default color. VertexColor can be set as part of the graph data structure, and it can be used in ShowGraph.

New function ▪ See also GraphOptions, SetGraphOptions ▪ See page 202

■ **VertexColoring**

VertexColoring[g] uses Brelaz's heuristic to find a good, but not necessarily minimal, vertex coloring of graph *g*. An option Algorithm that can take on the values Brelaz or Optimum is allowed. The setting Algorithm -> Brelaz is the default, while the setting Algorithm -> Optimum forces the algorithm to do an exhaustive search to find an optimum vertex coloring.

See also ChromaticNumber, ChromaticPolynomial, EdgeColoring ▪ See page 313

■ **VertexConnectivity**

VertexConnectivity[g] gives the minimum number of vertices whose deletion from graph *g* disconnects it. VertexConnectivity[g, Cut] gives a set of vertices of minimum size, whose removal disconnects the graph.

See also EdgeConnectivity, Harary, NetworkFlow ▪ See page 291

■ **VertexConnectivityGraph**

VertexConnectivityGraph[g] returns a directed graph that contains an edge corresponding to each vertex in *g* and in which edge-disjoint paths correspond to vertex-disjoint paths in *g*.

New function ▪ See also NetworkFlow, VertexConnectivity ▪ See page 291

■ **VertexCover**

VertexCover[g] returns a vertex cover of the graph *g*. An option Algorithm that can take on values Greedy, Approximate, or Optimum is allowed. The default setting is Algorithm -> Approximate. Different algorithms are used to compute a vertex cover depending on the setting of the option Algorithm.

New function ▪ See also BipartiteMatchingAndCover, MinimumVertexCover ▪ See page 317

■ **VertexCoverQ**

VertexCoverQ[g, c] yields True if the vertices in list *c* define a vertex cover of graph *g*.

See also CliqueQ, IndependentSetQ, MinimumVertexCover ■ See page 317

■ **VertexLabel**

VertexLabel is an option that can take on values True or False, allowing the user to set and display vertex labels. By default, there are no vertex labels. VertexLabel can be set as part of the graph data structure or in ShowGraph.

New function ■ See also GraphOptions, SetGraphOptions ■ See page 202

■ **VertexLabelColor**

VertexLabelColor is an option that allows the user to associate different colors to vertex labels. Black is the default color. VertexLabelColor can be set as part of the graph data structure or in ShowGraph.

New function ■ See also GraphOptions, SetGraphOptions ■ See page 202

■ **VertexLabelPosition**

VertexLabelPosition is an option that allows the user to place a vertex label in a certain position relative to the vertex. The default position is upper right. VertexLabelPosition can be set as part of the graph data structure or in ShowGraph.

New function ■ See also GraphOptions, SetGraphOptions ■ See page 202

■ **VertexNumber**

VertexNumber is an option that can take on values True or False. This can be used in ShowGraph to display or suppress vertex numbers. By default, the vertex numbers are hidden. VertexNumber can be set as part of the graph data structure or in ShowGraph.

New function ■ See also GraphOptions, ShowGraph ■ See page 202

■ **VertexNumberColor**

VertexNumberColor is an option that can be used in ShowGraph to associate different colors to vertex numbers. Black is the default color. VertexNumberColor can be set as part of the graph data structure or in ShowGraph.

New function ■ See also GraphOptions, SetGraphOptions ■ See page 202

■ VertexNumberPosition

VertexNumberPosition is an option that can be used in ShowGraph to display a vertex number in a certain position relative to the vertex. By default, vertex numbers are positioned to the lower left of the vertices. VertexNumberPosition can be set as part of the graph data structure or in ShowGraph.

New function ■ See also GraphOptions, SetGraphOptions ■ See page 202

■ VertexStyle

VertexStyle is an option that allows the user to associate different sizes and shapes to vertices. A disk is the default shape. VertexStyle can be set as part of the graph data structure, and it can be used in ShowGraph.

New function ■ See also GraphOptions, SetGraphOptions ■ See page 202

■ VertexWeight

VertexWeight is an option that allows the user to associate weights with vertices. 0 is the default weight. VertexWeight can be set as part of the graph data structure.

New function ■ See also GraphOptions, SetGraphOptions ■ See page 17

■ Vertices

Vertices[g] gives the embedding of graph *g*, that is, the coordinates of each vertex in the plane. Vertices[g, All] gives the embedding of the graph along with graphics options associated with each vertex.

See also Edges, V ■ See page 182

■ WaltherGraph

WaltherGraph returns the Walther graph.

New function ■ See also FiniteGraphs ■ See page 23

■ Weak

Weak is an option to ConnectedQ that seeks to determine if a directed graph is weakly connected.

New function ■ See also ConnectedQ, WeaklyConnectedComponents ■ See page 31

■ WeaklyConnectedComponents

WeaklyConnectedComponents[g] gives the weakly connected components of directed graph *g* as lists of vertices.

See also ConnectedQ, StronglyConnectedComponents ■ See page 285

■ **WeightingFunction**

WeightingFunction is an option to the functions SetEdgeWeights and SetVertexWeights, and it tells the functions how to compute edge-weights and vertex-weights, respectively. The default value for this option is Random.

New function ■ See also Euclidean, LNorm ■ See page 197

■ **WeightRange**

WeightRange is an option to the functions SetEdgeWeights and SetVertexWeights that gives the range for these weights. The default range is [0, 1] for real as well as integer weights.

New function ■ See also GraphOptions, SetGraphOptions ■ See page 197

■ **Wheel**

Wheel[n] constructs a wheel on n vertices, which is the join of a single vertex and the cycle with $n - 1$ vertices.

See also Cycle, Star ■ See page 249

■ **WriteGraph**

WriteGraph[g, f] writes graph g to file f using an edge list representation.

See also ReadGraph

■ **Zoom**

Zoom[{i, j, k, ...}] is a value that the PlotRange option can take on in ShowGraph. Setting PlotRange to this value zooms the display to contain the specified subset of vertices, $i, j, k, \cdots$

New function ■ See also Highlight, ShowGraph ■ See page 208

Bibliography

[ACL00]   W. Aiello, F. R. K. Chung, and L. Lu. A random graph model for massive graphs. In *ACM Symposium on Theory of Computing*, pages 171–180, 2000.

[ACL01]   W. Aiello, F. R. K. Chung, and L. Lu. Random evolution of massive graphs. In *IEEE Foundations of Computer Science*, pages 510–519, 2001.

[AGU72]   A. Aho, M. R. Garey, and J. D. Ullman. The transitive reduction of a directed graph. *SIAM J. Computing*, 1:131–137, 1972.

[AH77]   K. I. Appel and W. Haken. Every planar map is four colorable. II: Reducibility. *Illinois J. Math.*, 21:491–567, 1977.

[AH86]   K. I. Appel and W. Haken. The four color proof suffices. *Mathematical Intelligencer*, 8-1:10–20, 1986.

[AHK77]   K. I. Appel, W. Haken, and J. Koch. Every planar map is four colorable. I: Discharging. *Illinois J. Math.*, 21:429–490, 1977.

[AHU74]   A. Aho, J. Hopcroft, and J. Ullman. *The Design and Analysis of Computer Algorithms*. Addison-Wesley, Reading, MA, 1974.

[Aig79]   M. Aigner. *Combinatorial Theory*. Springer-Verlag, New York, 1979.

[ALM+92]   A. Arora, C. Lund, R. Motwani, M. Sudan, and M. Szegedy. Proof verification and the intractability of approximation problems. In *IEEE Symposium on Foundations of Computer Science*, pages 13–22, 1992.

[AMO93]   R. K. Ahuja, T. L. Magnanti, and J. B. Orlin. *Network Flows: Theory, Algorithms, and Applications*. Prentice-Hall, 1993.

[AMU88]   M. J. Atallah, G. K. Manacher, and J. Urrutia. Finding a minimum independent dominating set in a permutation graph. *Discrete Applied Mathematics*, 21:177–183, 1988.

[And76]   G. Andrews. *The Theory of Partitions*. Addison-Wesley, Reading, MA, 1976.

[AO01]   S. Ahlgren and K. Ono. Addition and counting: The arithmetic of partitions. *Notices of the AMS*, 48(9):978–984, 2001.

[AP61]   L. Auslander and S. Parter. On imbedding graphs in the sphere. *J. Mathematics and Mechanics*, 10:517–523, 1961.

[Aro98]   S. Arora. Polynomial time approximation schemes for the Euclidean traveling salesman and other geometric problems. *J. ACM*, 45(5):753–782, 1998.

[BC67]   M. Behzad and G. Chartrand. No graph is perfect. *Amer. Math. Monthly*, 74:962–963, 1967.

[BC76]   J. A. Bondy and V. Chvátal. A method in graph theory. *Discrete Math.*, 15:111–136, 1976.

[BC87]   W. W. R. Ball and H. S. M. Coxeter. *Mathematical Recreations and Essays*. Dover, New York, 1987.

[BC02]   W. Bosma and J.J. Cannon. The Magma computational algebra system. The Computational Algebra Group, University of Sydney, Australia, http://www.maths.usyd.edu.au:8000/u/magma/index.html, 2002.

[Bei68]   L. W. Beineke. Derived graphs and digraphs. In H. Sachs, H. Voss, and H. Walther, editors, *Beiträge zur Graphentheorie*, pages 17–33. Teubner, Leipzig, 1968.

[Bel86]   E. T. Bell. *Men of Mathematics*. Touchstone Books, reissue edition, 1986.

[Ber57]   C. Berge. Two theorems in graph theory. *Proc. Nat. Acad. Sci. USA*, 43:842–844, 1957.

[BETT98]   G. Di Battista, P. Eades, R. Tamassia, and I. Tollis. *Graph Drawing: Algorithms for Visualization of Graphs*. Prentice-Hall, Englewood Cliffs, NJ, 1998.

[BH90]   F. Buckley and F. Harary. *Distances in Graphs*. Addison-Wesley, Redwood City, CA, 1990.

[BHK62]   J. Battle, F. Harary, and Y. Kodama. Every planar graph with nine points has a nonplanar complement. *Bull. Amer. Math. Soc.*, 68:569–571, 1962.

[Big74]   N. L. Biggs. *Algebraic Graph Theory*. Cambridge University Press, London, 1974.

[Bir12]   G. D. Birkhoff. A determinant formula for the number of ways of coloring a map. *Ann. of Math.*, 14:42–46, 1912.

[BK87]   A. Brandstadt and D. Kratsch. On domination problems for permutation and other graphs. *Theoretical Computer Science*, 54:181–198, 1987.

[BL46]   G. D. Birkhoff and D. C. Lewis. Chromatic polynomials. *Trans. Amer. Math. Soc.*, 60:355–451, 1946.

[BLW76]   N. L. Biggs, E. K. Lloyd, and R. J. Wilson. *Graph Theory 1736–1936*. Clarendon Press, Oxford, 1976.

[BM76]   J. A. Bondy and U. S. R. Murty. *Graph Theory with Applications*. North-Holland, New York, 1976.

[Bol78]   B. Bollobás. *Extremal Graph Theory*. Academic Press, London, 1978.

[Bol79]   B. Bollobás. *Graph Theory*. Springer-Verlag, New York, 1979.

[Bre79]   D. Brelaz. New methods to color the vertices of a graph. *Comm. ACM*, 22:251–256, 1979.

[Bro41]   R. L. Brooks. On coloring the nodes of a network. *Proc. Cambridge Philos. Soc.*, 37:194–197, 1941.

[Bro89]   A. Broder. Generating random spanning trees. In *IEEE Foundations of Computer Science*, pages 442–447, 1989.

[BW82]   A. Björner and M. Wachs. Bruhat order of Coxeter groups and shellability. *Advances in Math.*, 43:87–100, 1982.

[Can78a]   E. R. Canfield. On a problem of Rota. *Advances in Math.*, 29:1–10, 1978.

[Can78b]   E. R. Canfield. On the location of the maximum stirling number(s) of the second kind. *Studies in Appl. Math.*, 59:83–93, 1978.

[Cay89]   A. Cayley. A theorem on trees. *Quart. J. Math.*, 23:376–378, 1889.

[CDN89]   C. J. Colbourn, R. P. J. Day, and L. D. Nel. Unranking and ranking spanning trees of a graph. *J. Algorithms*, 10:271–286, 1989.

[CG70]   D. G. Corneil and C. C. Gottlieb. An efficient algorithm for graph isomorphism. *J. ACM*, 17:51–64, 1970.

[Cha68]   G. Chartrand. On Hamiltonian line graphs. *Trans. Amer. Math. Soc.*, 134:559–566, 1968.

[Cha73]   P. J. Chase. Transposition graphs. *SIAM J. Computing*, 2:128–133, 1973.

[Cha82]   S. Chaiken. A combinatorial proof of the all-minors matrix tree theorem. *SIAM J. Alg. Disc. Methods*, 3:319–329, 1982.

[Cha85]   G. Chartrand. *Introductory Graph Theory*. Dover, New York, 1985.

[Chr76]   N. Christofides. Worst-case analysis of a new heuristic for the traveling salesman problem. In *Symposium on Algorithms and Complexity, Department of Computer Science, Carnegie-Mellon University*, April 1976.

[CHT90]   J. Cai, X. Han, and R. E. Tarjan. New solutions to four planar graph problems. Technical report, New York University, 1990.

[CK94]   A. Chetverin and F. Kramer. Oligonucleotide arrays: New concepts and possibilities. *Bio/Technology*, 12:1093–1099, 1994.

[CLR87]   F. Chung, T. Leighton, and A. Rosenberg. Embedding graphs in books: A layout problem with applications to VLSI design. *SIAM J. Algebraic and Discrete Methods*, 8:33–58, 1987.

[CLRS01] T. Cormen, C. Leiserson, R. Rivest, and C. Stein. *Introduction to Algorithms, second edition*. MIT Press, Cambridge, MA, 2001.

[CM78] M. Capobianco and J. Molluzzo. *Examples and Counterexamples in Graph Theory*. North-Holland, New York, 1978.

[CRS⁺00] K. Cattell, F. Ruskey, J. Sawada, M. Serra, and R. Miers. Fast algorithms to generate necklaces, and irreducible polynomials over GF(2). *J. Algorithms*, 37(2):267–282, 2000.

[dB46] N. G. de Bruijn. A combinatorial problem. *Koninklijke Nederlandse Akademie v. Wetenschappen*, 49:758–764, 1946.

[Dij59] E. W. Dijkstra. A note on two problems in connection with graphs. *Numerische Math.*, 1:269–271, 1959.

[Dil50] R. P. Dilworth. A decomposition theorem for partially ordered sets. *Ann. of Math.*, 51:161–166, 1950.

[DM91] J. D. Dixon and B. Mortimer. *Permutation Groups*. Springer-Verlag, New York, 1991.

[Ead84] P. Eades. A heuristic for graph drawing. *Congressus Numerantium*, 42:149–160, 1984.

[Eco89] U. Eco. *Foucault's Pendulum*. Harcourt Brace Jovanovich, San Diego, 1989.

[EG60] P. Erdös and T. Gallai. Graphs with prescribed degrees of vertices. *Mat. Lapok (Hungarian)*, 11:264–274, 1960.

[Egg75] R. B. Eggleton. Graphic sequences and graphic polynomials. In A. Hajnal, editor, *Infinite and Finite Sets*, volume 1, pages 385–392. North-Holland, Amsterdam, 1975.

[Ehr73] G. Ehrlich. Loopless algorithms for generating permutations, combinations, and other combinatorial configurations. *J. ACM*, 20:500–513, 1973.

[EJ73] J. Edmonds and E. L. Johnson. Matching, Euler tours, and the Chinese postman. *Math. Programming*, 5:88–124, 1973.

[EK72] J. Edmonds and R. M. Karp. Theoretical improvements in algorithmic efficiency for network flow problems. *J. ACM*, 19:248–264, 1972.

[ER60] P. Erdös and A. Renyi. On the evolution of random graphs. *Publ. Math. Inst. Hungar. Acad. Sci.*, 5:17–61, 1960.

[Erd61] P. Erdös. Graph theory and probability II. *Canad. J. Math.*, 13:346–352, 1961.

[ES35] P. Erdös and G. Szekeres. A combinatorial problem in geometry. *Compositio Math.*, 2:464–470, 1935.

[ES74] P. Erdös and J. Spencer. *Probabilistic Methods in Combinatorics*. Academic Press, New York, 1974.

[ET75] S. Even and R. E. Tarjan. Network flow and testing graph connectivity. *SIAM J. Computing*, 4:507–518, 1975.

[Eve79] S. Even. *Graph Algorithms*. Computer Science Press, Rockville, MD, 1979.

[EW85] R. B. Eggleton and W. D. Wallis. Problem 1186: Solution i. *Mathematics Magazine*, 58(2):112–113, 1985.

[FF62] L. R. Ford and D. R. Fulkerson. *Flows in Networks*. Princeton University Press, Princeton, NJ, 1962.

[FHM65] D. R. Fulkerson, A. J. Hoffman, and M. H. McAndrew. Some properties of graphs with multiple edges. *Canad. J. Math.*, 17:166–177, 1965.

[Fle74] H. Fleischner. The square of every two-connected graph is Hamiltonian. *J. Combinatorial Theory B*, 16:29–34, 1974.

[Flo62] R. W. Floyd. Algorithm 97: Shortest path. *Comm. ACM*, 5:345, 1962.

[Fre87]   G. Frederickson. Fast algorithms for shortest paths in planar graphs. *SIAM J. Computing*, 16(6):1004–1022, 1987.

[Fru39]   R. Frucht. Herstellung von Graphen mit vorgegebener abstrakter Gruppe. *Compositio Math.*, 6:239–250, 1939.

[FT87]   M. Fredman and R. E. Tarjan. Fibonacci heaps and their uses in improved network optimization algorithms. *J. ACM*, 34(3):596–615, 1987.

[Ful65]   D. R. Fulkerson. Upsets in round robin tournaments. *Canad. J. Math.*, 17:957–969, 1965.

[FZ82]   D. Franzblau and D. Zeilberger. A bijective proof of the hook-length formula. *J. Algorithms*, 3:317–342, 1982.

[Gal59]   T. Gallai. Über extreme Punkt- und Kantenmengen. *Ann. Univ. Sci. Budapest, Eötvös Sect. Math.*, 2:133–138, 1959.

[GAP99]   The GAP Group, Aachen, St Andrews. *GAP – Groups, Algorithms, and Programming, Version 4.2*, 1999. (http://www-gap.dcs.st-and.ac.uk/~gap).

[Gar78]   M. Gardner. Puzzling over a problem solving matrix, cubes of many colors and three-dimensional dominos. *Scientific American*, 239:22–28, 1978.

[Gas67]   B. J. Gassner. Sorting by replacement selection. *Comm. ACM*, 10:89–93, 1967.

[GGM58]   H. Gupta, A. E. Gwyther, and J. C. P. Miller. *Tables of Partitions*, volume 4. Royal Society Mathematical Tables, London, 1958.

[GH61]   R. E. Gomery and T. C. Hu. Multiterminal network flows. *J. SIAM*, 9:551–570, 1961.

[GH85]   R. L. Graham and P. Hell. On the history of the minimum spanning tree problem. *Ann. History of Computing*, 7:43–57, 1985.

[GI89]   D. Gusfield and R. Irving. *The Stable Marriage Problem*. MIT Press, Cambridge, MA, 1989.

[Gil58]   E. N. Gilbert. Gray codes and paths on the *n*-cube. *Bell System Tech. J.*, 37:815–826, 1958.

[GJ79]   M. Garey and D. Johnson. *Computers and Intractability: a Guide to the Theory of NP-Completeness*. W. H. Freeman, San Francisco, 1979.

[GKP89]   R. Graham, D. Knuth, and O. Patashnik. *Concrete Mathematics*. Addison-Wesley, Reading, MA, 1989.

[Gol66]   S. W. Golomb. *Shift Register Sequences*. Holden-Day, San Francisco, 1966.

[Goo46]   I. J. Good. Normal recurring decimals. *J. London Math. Soc.*, 21:167–172, 1946.

[Gou88]   R. Gould. *Graph Theory*. Benjamin Cummings, Menlo Park, CA, 1988.

[Gra53]   F. Gray. Pulse code communication. United States Patent Number 2,632,058, March 17, 1953.

[GS62]   D. Gale and L. S. Shapley. College admissions and the stability of marriage. *Amer. Math. Monthly*, 69:9–14, 1962.

[Gup66]   R. P. Gupta. The chromatic index and the degree of a graph. *Notices of the Amer. Math. Soc.*, 13:66T–429, 1966.

[Hak62]   S. Hakimi. On the realizability of a set of integers as degrees of the vertices of a graph. *SIAM J. Appl. Math.*, 10:496–506, 1962.

[Hal35]   P. Hall. On representatives of subsets. *J. London Math. Soc.*, 10:26–30, 1935.

[Har62]   F. Harary. The maximum connectivity of a graph. *Proc. Nat. Acad. Sci. USA*, 48:1142–1146, 1962.

[Har69]   F. Harary. *Graph Theory*. Addison-Wesley, Reading, MA, 1969.

[Hav55] V. Havel. A remark on the existence of finite graphs (Czech.). *Časopis Pest. Mat.*, 80:477–480, 1955.

[Hea63] B. R. Heap. Permutations by interchanges. *Computer J.*, 6:293–294, 1963.

[HHK⁺01] J. Hall, J. Hartline, A. Karlin, J. Saia, and J. Wilkes. On algorithms for efficient data migration. In *ACM-SIAM Symposium on Discrete Algorithms*, pages 620–629, 2001.

[Hie73] C. Hierholzer. Ueber die Möglichkeit, einen Linienzug ohne Wiederholung und ohne Unterbrechnung zu umfahren. *Math. Ann.*, 6:30–42, 1873.

[HK75]   J. Hopcroft and R. Karp. An $n^{5/2}$ algorithm for maximum matching in bipartite graphs. *SIAM J. Computing*, pages 225–231, 1975.

[HLM⁺90] S. H. Hosseini, B. Litow, M. Malkawi, J. McPherson, and K. Vairavan. Analysis of a graph coloring based distributed load balancing algorithm. *J. Parallel and Distributed Computing*, 10(2):160–166, 1990.

[HM99]   G. Haggard and T. Mathies. The computation of chromatic polynomials. *Discrete Math.*, 199:227–231, 1999.

[HNW65] F. Harary and C. J. A. Nash-Williams. On Eulerian and Hamiltonian graphs and line graphs. *Canad. Math. Bull.*, 8:701–709, 1965.

[Hoc97] D. Hochbaum, editor. *Approximation Algorithms for NP-Hard Problems*. PWS Publishing Company, Boston, MA, 1997.

[Hol81] I. Holyer. The NP-completeness of edge colorings. *SIAM J. Computing*, 10:718–720, 1981.

[HP73]   F. Harary and E. M. Palmer. *Graphical Enumeration*. Academic Press, New York, 1973.

[HR73]   F. Harary and R. Read. Is the null graph a pointless concept? In *Graphs and Combinatorics Conference*. Springer-Verlag, New York, 1973.

[HS93]   D. Holton and J. Sheehan. *The Petersen Graph*. Cambridge University Press, Cambridge, UK, 1993.

[HT73]   J. Hopcroft and R. E. Tarjan. Algorithm 447: Efficient algorithms for graph manipulation. *Comm. ACM*, 16:372–378, 1973.

[HT74]   J. Hopcroft and R. E. Tarjan. Efficient planarity testing. *J. ACM*, 21:549–568, 1974.

[IK00]   W. Imrich and S. Klavzar. *Product Graphs: Structure and Recognition*. Wiley-Interscience, New York, 2000.

[Jac80] B. Jackson. Hamilton cycles in regular 2-connected graphs. *J. Combinatorial Theory B*, 29:27–46, 1980.

[JL94]   R. Jeurissen and W. Layton. Load balancing via graph coloring: An algorithm. *Computers and Mathematics with Applications*, 27:27–32, 1994.

[JLR00] S. Janson, T. Luczak, and A. Rucinski. *Theory of Random Graphs*. Wiley Interscience, New York, 2000.

[Joh63] S. M. Johnson. Generation of permutations by adjacent transpositions. *Math. Computation*, 17:282–285, 1963.

[JS90]   M. Jerrum and A. Sinclair. Fast uniform generation of regular graphs. *Theoretical Computer Science*, 73:91–100, 1990.

[Kar72] R. M. Karp. Reducibility among combinatorial problems. In R. E. Miller and J. W. Thatcher, editors, *Complexity of Computer Computations*, pages 85–103. Plenum Press, New York, 1972.

[Kir47] G. Kirchhoff. Über die Auflösung der Gleichungen, auf welche man bei der untersuchung der linearen verteilung galvanischer Ströme geführt wird. *Ann. Phys. Chem.*, 72:497–508, 1847.

[KKT95] D. R. Karger, P. N. Klein, and R. E. Tarjan. A randomized linear-time algorithm to find minimum spanning trees. *J. ACM*, 42(2):321–328, 1995.

[Kli82]   P. Klingsberg. A Gray code for compositions. *J. Algorithms*, 3:41–44, 1982.

[Knu67]   D. E. Knuth. Oriented subtrees of an arc digraph. *J. Combinatorial Theory*, 3:309–314, 1967.

[Knu70]   D. E. Knuth. Permutations, matrices, and generalized young tableaux. *Pacific J. Math.*, 34:709–727, 1970.

[Knu73a]   D. E. Knuth. *Fundamental Algorithms*, volume 1 of *The Art of Computer Programming*. Addison-Wesley, Reading, MA, second edition, 1973.

[Knu73b]   D. E. Knuth. *Sorting and Searching*, volume 3 of *The Art of Computer Programming*. Addison-Wesley, Reading, MA, 1973.

[Knu92]   D. E. Knuth. Two notes on notation. *Amer. Math. Monthly*, 99:403–422, 1992.

[Knu94]   D. E. Knuth. *The Stanford GraphBase: A Platform for Combinatorial Computing*. ACM Press, New York, 1994.

[Kon16]   D. Konig. Uber graphen und ihre anwendung auf determinantentheorie und mengenlehre. *Math. Ann.*, 77:453–465, 1916.

[Kri85]   V. Krishnamurthy. *Combinatorics: Theory and Applications*. Affiliated East-West Press Private Limited, New Delhi, India, 1985.

[KRRS94]   P. Klein, S. Rao, M. Rauch, and S. Subramanian. Faster shortest-path algorithms for planar graphs. In *ACM Symposium on the Theory of Computing*, pages 27–37, 1994.

[Kru56]   J. B. Kruskal. On the shortest spanning subtree of a graph and the traveling salesman problem. *Proc. Amer. Math. Soc.*, 7:48–50, 1956.

[KS96]   D. R. Karger and C. Stein. A new approach to the minimum cut problem. *J. ACM*, 43(4):601–640, 1996.

[KS99]   D. L. Kreher and D. R. Stinson. *Combinatorial Algorithms: Generation, Enumeration, and Search*. CRC Press, Boca Raton, FL, 1999.

[Kur30]   K. Kuratowski. Sur le problème des courbes gauches en topologie. *Fund. Math.*, 15:217–283, 1930.

[Kwa62]   M. K. Kwan. Graphic programming using odd or even points. *Chinese Math.*, 1:273–277, 1962.

[Lay76]   R. Laye. A gray code for set partitions. *Information Processing Letters*, 5(6):171–173, 1976.

[Lei92]   F. T. Leighton. *Introduction to Parallel Algorithms and Architecture: Arrays, Trees and Hypercubes*. Morgan-Kauffmann, Boston, 1992.

[Lev73]   L. A. Levin. Universal searching problems. *Problems of Information Transmission*, 9:265–266, 1973.

[Lin65]   S. Lin. Computer solutions of the traveling salesman problem. *Bell System Tech. J.*, 44:2245–2269, 1965.

[LLKS85]   E. Lawler, J. K. Lenstra, A. H. G. Rinnooy Kan, and D. B. Shmoys. *The Traveling Salesman Problem*. John Wiley and Sons, New York, 1985.

[LLS01]   L. Lee, A. Lumsdaine, and J. Siek. *The Boost Graph Library User Guide and Reference Manual*. Addison Wesley Professional, Reading, MA, 2001.

[LNS85]   R. Lipton, S. North, and J. Sandberg. A method for drawing graphs. In *Proc. First ACM Symposium on Computational Geometry*, pages 153–160, 1985.

[Lov68]   L. Lovász. On chromatic number of finite set-systems. *Acta. Math. Acad. Sci. Hungar.*, 19:59–67, 1968.

[Lov75]   L. Lovász. Three short proofs in graph theory. *J. Combinatorial Theory B*, 19:111–113, 1975.

[LP86]   L. Lovász and M. D. Plummer. *Matching Theory*. North-Holland, Amsterdam, 1986.

[Luc91]   E. Lucas. *Récréations Mathématiques*. Cauthier-Villares, Paris, 1891.

[Luc92]   T. Luczak. Sparse random graphs with a given degree sequence. In A.M. Frieze and T. Luczak, editors, *Random Graphs*, volume 2, pages 165–182. Wiley, New York, 1992.

[Luk80]   E. M. Luks. Isomorphism of bounded valence can be tested in polynomial time. In *IEEE Symposium on Foundations of Computer Science*, pages 42–49, 1980.

[Mac60]   P. MacMahon. *Combinatory Analysis*. Chelsea Publishing, New York, 1960.

[Mal88]   S. M. Malitz. Genus g graphs have pagenumber $O(g^{1/2})$. In *IEEE Symposium on Foundations of Computer Science*, pages 458–468, 1988.

[Man85a] H. Mannila. Measures of presortedness and optimal sorting algorithms. *IEEE Trans. Computers*, 34:318–325, 1985.

[Man85b] B. Manvel. Extremely greedy coloring algorithms. In F. Harary and J. Maybee, editors, *Graphs and Applications*, pages 257–270. Wiley, New York, 1985.

[Man89]   U. Manber. *Introduction to Algorithms*. Addison-Wesley, Reading, MA, 1989.

[McK90]   B. McKay. Nauty user's guide. Technical Report TR-CS-90-02, Department of Computer Science, Australian National University, 1990.

[Men27]   K. Menger. Zur allgemeinen Kurventheorie. *Fund. Math.*, 10:95–115, 1927.

[Mer73]   G. H. J. Meredith. Regular n-valent n-connected nonhamiltonian non-n-edge-colorable graphs. *J. Combinatorial Theory, Series B*, 14:55–60, 1973.

[Mes83]   B. E. Meserve. *Fundamental Concepts of Geometry*. Dover, New York, 1983.

[Mit99]   J. Mitchell. Guillotine subdivisions approximate polygonal subdivisions: a simple polynomial-time approximation scheme for geometric TSP, k-MST, and related problems. *SIAM J. Computing*, 28:1298–1309, 1999.

[MMI72]   D. W. Matula, G. Marble, and J. D. Isaacson. Graph coloring algorithms. In R. Read, editor, *Graph Theory and Computing*, pages 109–122. Academic Press, New York, 1972.

[MN99]   K. Mehlhorn and S. Naher. *The LEDA Platform of Combinatorial and Geometric Computing*. Cambridge University Press, Cambridge, UK, 1999.

[MR95]   M. Molloy and B. Reed. A critical point for random graphs with a given degree sequence. *Random Structures and Algorithms*, 6:161–180, 1995.

[MR98]   M. Molloy and B. Reed. The size of the largest component of a random graph on a fixed degree sequence. *Combinatorics, Probability and Computing*, 7:295–306, 1998.

[MS80]   J. I. Munro and H. Suwanda. Implicit data structures for fast search and update. *J. Computer and System Sciences*, 21:236–250, 1980.

[Muk67]   A. Mukhopadhyay. The square root of a graph. *J. Combinatorial Theory*, 2:290–295, 1967.

[NW78]   A. Nijenhuis and H. Wilf. *Combinatorial Algorithms*. Academic Press, New York, second edition, 1978.

[OR81]   R. J. Opsut and F. S. Roberts. On the fleet maintenance, mobile radio frequency, task assignment, and traffic phasing problems. In G. Chartrand, Y. Alavi, D. L. Goldsmith, L. Lesniak-Foster, and D. R. Lick, editors, *The Theory and Applications of Graphs*, pages 479–492. Wiley, New York, 1981.

[Ore60]   O. Ore. A note on Hamiltonian circuits. *Amer. Math. Monthly*, 67:55, 1960.

[Pal85]   E. M. Palmer. *Graphical Evolution: An Introduction to the Theory of Random Graphs*. Wiley-Interscience, New York, 1985.

[Pev89]   P.A. Pevzner. *l*-tuple DNA sequencing: Computer analysis. *J. Biomol. Struct. Dyn.*, 9:399–410, 1989.

[Pr8]   H. Prüfer. Neuer beweis eines Satzes über Permutationen. *Arch. Math. Phys.*, 27:742–744, 1918.

[Pri57]   R. C. Prim. Shortest connection networks and some generalizations. *Bell System Tech. J.*, 36:1389–1401, 1957.

[Pro89]   J. Propp. Some variants of Ferrers diagrams. *J. Combinatorial Theory A*, 52:98–128, 1989.

[PS82]   C. H. Papadimitriou and K. Steiglitz. *Combinatorial Optimization: Algorithms and Complexity*. Prentice-Hall, Englewood Cliffs, NJ, 1982.

[Rea72]   R. C. Read. The coding of various kinds of unlabeled trees. In R. C. Read, editor, *Graph Theory and Computing*, pages 153–182. Academic Press, New York, 1972.

[Rob39]   H. E. Robbins. A theorem on graphs with an application to a problem of traffic control. *Amer. Math. Monthly*, 46:281–283, 1939.

[Ron84]   C. Ronse. *Feedback Shift Registers*, volume 146. Lecture Notes in Computer Science, Springer-Verlag, Berlin, 1984.

[Rot67]   G. Rota. A generalization of Sperner's theorem. *J. of Combinatorial Theory*, 2, 1967.

[Roy02]   G. Royle. Combinatorial catalogues. http://www.cs.uwa.edu.au/~gordon/data.html, 2002.

[RP97]   T. Rus and S. V. Pemmaraju. Using graph coloring in an algebraic compiler. *Acta Informatica*, 34(3), 1997.

[RS87]   D. F. Rall and P. J. Slater. Generating all permutations by graphical derangements. Unpublished manuscript, 1987.

[RS00]   F. Ruskey and J. Sawada. A fast algorithm to generate unlabeled necklaces. In *Proceedings of the ACM-SIAM Symposium on Discrete Algorithms*, pages 256–262, Philadelphia, 2000.

[RSL77]   D. J. Rosenkrantz, R. E. Stearns, and P. M. Lewis. An analysis of several heuristics for the traveling salesman problem. *SIAM J. Computing*, 6:563–581, 1977.

[RT81]   E. Reingold and J. Tilford. Tidier drawings of trees. *IEEE Trans. Software Engineering*, 7:223–228, 1981.

[RW97]   R. Read and R. Wilson. *An Atlas of Graphs*. Oxford University Press, Oxford, UK, 1997.

[Rys57]   H. J. Ryser. Combinatorial properties of matrices of zeros and ones. *Canad. J. Math.*, 9:371–377, 1957.

[Sab60]   G. Sabidussi. Graph multiplication. *Math. Z.*, 72:446–457, 1960.

[Sac62]   H. Sachs. Über selbstkomplementäre Graphen. *Publ. Math. Debrecen*, 9:270–288, 1962.

[Sav89]   C. D. Savage. Gray code sequences of partitions. *J. Algorithms*, 10:577–595, 1989.

[Sav97]   C. D. Savage. A survey of combinatorial gray codes. *SIAM Review*, 39:605–629, 1997.

[Sch61]   C. Schensted. Longest increasing and decreasing subsequences. *Canadian J. Math.*, 13:179–191, 1961.

[SD76]   D. C. Schmidt and L. E. Druffel. A fast backtracking algorithm to test directed graphs for isomorphism using distance matrices. *J. ACM*, 23:433–445, 1976.

[Sed77]   R. Sedgewick. Permutation generation methods. *Computing Surveys*, 9:137–164, 1977.

[SK86]   T. L. Saaty and P. C. Kainen. *The Four-Color Problem*. Dover, New York, 1986.

[Ski88]   S. Skiena. Encroaching lists as a measure of presortedness. *BIT*, 28:775–784, 1988.

[Ski90]   S. Skiena. *Implementing Discrete Mathematics: Combinatorics and Graph Theory with Mathematica*. Addison-Wesley, Redwood City, CA, 1990.

[Ski97]   S. Skiena. *The Algorithm Design Manual*. Springer-Verlag, New York, 1997.

[SR83]   K. Supowit and E. Reingold. The complexity of drawing trees nicely. *Acta Informatica*, 18:377–392, 1983.

[Sta71]   R. Stanley. Theory and application of plane partitions I, II. *Studies in Applied Math.*, 50:167–188, 259–279, 1971.

[Sta86]   R. Stanley. *Enumerative Combinatorics*, volume 1. Wadsworth & Brooks/Cole, Monterey, CA, 1986.

[SW86]   D. Stanton and D. White. *Constructive Combinatorics*. Springer-Verlag, New York, 1986.

[Sze83]   G. Szekeres. *Distribution of Labeled Trees by Diameter*, volume 1036, pages 392–397. Springer-Verlag, New York, 1983.

[Tai80]   P. G. Tait. Remarks on the colouring of maps. *Proc. Royal Soc. Edinburgh*, 10:729, 1880.

[Tar72]   R. E. Tarjan. Depth-first search and linear graph algorithms. *SIAM J. Computing*, 1:146–160, 1972.

[Tar75]   R. E. Tarjan. Efficiency of a good but not linear set union algorithm. *J. ACM*, 22:215–225, 1975.

[Tar83]   R. E. Tarjan. *Data Structures and Network Algorithms*. Society for Industrial and Applied Mathematics, Philadelphia, 1983.

[Tho56]   C. B. Thompkins. Machine attacks on problems whose variables are permutations. In *Proc. Symposium Applied Mathematics*, page 203, Providence, RI, 1956. American Mathematical Society.

[Tro62]   H. F. Trotter. Perm (algorithm 115). *Comm. ACM*, 5:434–435, 1962.

[Tur41]   P. Turán. On an extremal problem in graph theory. *Mat. Fiz. Lapok*, 48:436–452, 1941.

[Tut46]   W. T. Tutte. On Hamilton circuits. *J. London Math. Soc.*, 21:98–101, 1946.

[Tut61]   W. T. Tutte. A theory of 3-connected graphs. *Indag. Math.*, 23:441–455, 1961.

[Tut72]   W. T. Tutte. Non-Hamiltonian planar maps. In R. Read, editor, *Graph Theory and Computing*, pages 295–301. Academic Press, New York, 1972.

[Vau80]   J. Vaucher. Pretty printing of trees. *Software Practice and Experience*, 10:553–561, 1980.

[VEM93]   W. Layton V. Ervin and J. Maubach. Some graph coloring problems in parallel numerical methods. In A. H. M. Levelt, editor, *Algorithms in Algebra*, pages 39–48. 1993.

[Viz64]   V. G. Vizing. On an estimate of the chromatic class of a p-graph (in Russian). *Diskret. Analiz*, 3:23–30, 1964.

[vRW65]   A. van Rooij and H. Wilf. The interchange graph of a finite graph. *Acta Math. Acad. Sci. Hungar.*, 16:263–269, 1965.

[Wag98]   S. Wagon. *Mathematica in Action*. Springer-Verlag, New York, 1998.

[WH60]   P. D. Whiting and J. A. Hillier. A method for finding the shortest route through a road network. *Operational Res. Quart.*, 11:37–40, 1960.

[Whi32]   H. Whitney. Congruent graphs and the connectivity of graphs. *Amer. J. Math.*, 54:150–168, 1932.

[Wil85]   R. J. Wilson. *Introduction to Graph Theory*. Longman, Essex, England, third edition, 1985.

[Wil86]   R. J. Wilson. An Eulerian trail through Königsberg. *J. Graph Theory*, 10:265–275, 1986.

[Wil89]   H. Wilf. *Combinatorial Algorithms: An Update*. Society for Industrial and Applied Mathematics, Philadelphia, 1989.

[Wil90]   H. Wilf. *generatingfunctionology*. Academic Press, New York, second edition, 1990.

[Wil96]   D. B. Wilson. Generating random spanning trees more quickly than the cover time. In *Proc. ACM Symp. on Theory of Computing*, pages 296–303, 1996.

[Wol99]   S. Wolfram. *The Mathematica Book*. Cambridge University Press, New York, fourth edition, 1999.

[Wor84]   N. Wormald. Generating random regular graphs. *J. Algorithms*, 5:247–280, 1984.

[WS79]   C. Wetherell and A. Shannon. Tidy drawing of trees. *IEEE Trans. Software Engineering*, 5:514–520, 1979.

[YG80]   M. Yannakakis and F. Gavril. Edge dominating sets in graphs. *SIAM J. Applied Math.*, 38(3):364–372, 1980.

Index